JOHN WILLIS

SCREEN WORLD

1992

VOLUME 43

Golddiggers of 1933

with Fred Astaire in *Swing Time*

Tom, Dick and Harry

with James Stewart in *Vivacious Lady*

The Barkleys of Broadway

with Fred Astaire in *The Barkleys of Broadw*

1956

1965

1980

2

To

GINGER ROGERS

AN ENGAGING ACTRESS OF CHARM AND WIT,
AND A PEERLESS DANCER OF STYLE AND GRACE.

FILMS: Young Man of Manhattan, Queen High, The Sap From Syracuse, Follow the Leader (1930), Honor Among Lovers, The Tip-Off, Suicide Fleet (1931), Carnival Boat, The Tenderfoot, The Thirteenth Guest, Hat Check Girl, You Said a Mouthful (1932), 42nd Street, Broadway Bad, Golddigers of 1933, Professional Sweetheart, A Shriek in the Night, Don't Bet on Love, Sitting Pretty, Flying Down to Rio, Chance at Heaven (1933), Rafter Romance, Finishing School, Twenty Million Sweethearts, Change of Heart, Upper World, The Gay Divorcee, Romance in Manhattan (1934), Roberta, Star of Midnight, Top Hat, In Person (1935), Follow the Fleet, Swing Time (1936), Shall We Dance, Stage Door (1937), Having Wonderful Time, Vivacious Lady, Carefree (1938), The Story of Vernon and Irene Castle, Bachelor Mother, Fifth Avenue Girl (1939), The Primrose Path, Lucky Partners, Kitty Foyle (Academy Award for Best Actress, 1940), Tom, Dick and Harry (1941), Roxie Hart, Tales of Manhattan, The Major and the Minor, Once Upon a Honeymoon (1942), Tender Comrade (1943), Lady in the Dark, I'll Be Seeing You (1944), Weekend at the Waldorf (1945), Heartbeat, Magnificent Doll (1946), It Had to Be You (1947), The Barkleys of Broadway (1949), Perfect Strangers, Storm Warning (1950), The Groom Wore Spurs (1951), We're Not Married, Monkey Business, Dreamboat (1952), Forever Female (1953), Black Widow, Twist of Fate (a.k.a. Beautiful Stranger, 1954), Tight Spot (1955), The First Traveling Saleslady, Teenage Rebel (1956), Oh Men! Oh Women! (1957), Quick, Let's Get Married (a.k.a. Seven Different Ways, 1964), Harlow (1965).

Anthony Hopkins
in *The Silence of the Lambs*
Academy Award for Best Picture
(Orion Pictures Corp.)

CONTENTS

EDITOR: JOHN WILLIS
ASSOCIATE EDITOR: BARRY MONUSH

Staff: Marco Starr Boyajian, William Camp, Jimmie Hollifield II,
Tom Lynch, Stanley Reeves, John Sala
Designer: Peggy Goddard

Acknowledgments: Ted Albert, Nina Barron, Andrew Chandler, David
Christopher, Willa Clinton, Richard D'Attile, Gerard Dapena, Samantha
Dean, Marcy Engleman, Mary Flanagan, Jamie Geller, Sharon Greytak,
Rich Hauser, Jeff Hill, Doris Hirsch, Lauren Hyman, Terry Kane, Craig
Kelemen, Sabrina Laufer, Steve Lavine, Leo Lawrence, Mary Lugo,
Bruce Lynn, Jonathan Marder, Sam Mattingly, Lisa McEttrick, David
Munro, Sherry Natco, Kevin O'Grady, Lorraine Osmundsen, Elizabeth
Petit, Mark Reina, Vicki Rosen, Greg Rossi, George Scherling, Kimberly
Scherling, Steven Soba, Sheldon Stone, Dave Zeliff, Stephen Zeller

1. Kevin Costner

2. Arnold Schwarzenegger

3. Robin Williams

4. Julia Roberts

5. Macaulay Culkin

6. Jodie Foster

7. Billy Crystal

8. Dustin Hoffman

9. Robert De Niro

10. Mel Gibson

11. Steve Martin

12. Harrison Ford

13. Michael J. Fox

14. Nick Nolte

15. Patrick Swayze

16. Barbra Streisand

6

TOP BOX OFFICE STARS OF 1991
(Tabulated by Quigley Publications)

17. Danny DeVito

18. Cher

19. Demi Moore

20. Anthony Hopkins

1991 RELEASES

January 1 through December 31, 1991

21. Michelle Pfeiffer

22. Bill Murray

23. Sean Connery

24. Anjelica Huston

25. Warren Beatty

Steven Seagal

Goldie Hawn

Kevin Bacon

7

NOT WITHOUT MY DAUGHTER

(MGM) Producers, Harry J. Ufland, Mary Jane Ufland; Director, Brian Gilbert; Screenplay, David W. Rintels; Based on the book by Betty Mahmoody, William Hoffer; Photography, Peter Hannan; Designer, Anthony Pratt; Music, Jerry Goldsmith; Editor, Terry Rawlings; Costumes, Nic Ede; Associate Producer, Anthony Waye; Casting, Mike Fenton, Judy Taylor, Joyce Gallie; Assistant Director, Adi Shoval; a Pathe Entertainment presentation of an Ufland production; Dolby Stereo; Fuji color; Rated PG-13; 117 minutes; January release

CAST

Betty Mahmoody	Sally Field
Moody	Alfred Molina
Mahtob	Sheila Rosenthal
Houssein	Roshan Seth
Nicole	Sarah Badel
Ameh Bozorg	Mony Rey
Mohsen	Georges Corraface
Grandma	Mary Nell Santacroce
Grandpa	Ed Grady
Doctors	Marc Gowan, Bruce Evers
Mammal	Jonathan Cherchi
Nasserine	Soudabeh Farrokhnia
Zia	Michael Morim
Fereshte	Gili Ben-Ozilio
Zoreh	Racheli Chaimian
Reza	Yossi Tabib
Baba Hajji	Amir Shmuel
Aga Hakim	Yacov Banai
Koran Teacher	Defna Armoni
Ellen	Judith Robinson
Hormoz	Avraham Morr
Hamid	Sasson Gabai
Miss Nassimi	Ahuva Keren
Khanun Shaheen	Farzaneh Taidi
Mahtob's Teacher	Yerusha Tirosh
Mohsen's Companion	Yossi Shiloach
Iranian Soldier	Shaul Mizrachi

Top: Sally Field, Sheila Rosenthal
Below: Rosenthal, Alfred Molina
© Pathe Entertainment

Sally Field, Alfred Molina

Sheila Rosenthal, Sally Field

Jean-Claude Van Damme, Deborah Rennard
Left: Van Damme

LIONHEART

(UNIVERSAL) formerly *A.W.O.L.*; Producers, Ash R. Shah, Eric Karson; Executive Producers, Sundip R. Shah, Anders P. Jensen, Sunil R. Shah; Director, Sheldon Lettich; Screenplay, Sheldon Lettich, Jean-Claude Van Damme; Story, Jean-Claude Van Damme; Based on a screenplay by S.N. Warren; Photography, Robert C. New; Designer, Gregory Pickrell; Editor, Mark Conte; Costumes, Joseph Porro; Casting, Triangle Casting, James F. Tarzia, Thomas E. Daniels; a co-presentation of Imperial Entertainment; Dolby Stereo; Consolidated color; Rated R; 105 minutes; January release

CAST

Lyon	Jean-Claude Van Damme
Joshua	Harrison Page
Cynthia	Deborah Rennard
Helene	Lisa Pelikan
Nicole	Ashley Johnson
Russell	Brian Thompson
Sgt. Hartog	Voyo
Moustafa	Michel Qissi
Adjutant	George McDaniel
Doctor	Eric Karson
Francois	Jason Adams
Drug Dealer	William Terry Amos
Nurse	Roz Bosley
Irish Legionnaire	Dennis Wayne Rucker
African Legionnaire	Billy Blanks
Jeep Driver	Stefanos Miltsakakis
Ship's Mate	Lew Hopson
Ship's Engineers	Sebastian Massa
Interpol Inspector	Roger Etienne
N.Y. Security Guard	Douglas Du Val
Garage Fight Heckler	Lawrence Bender
Heckler's Date	Tracy Shakespeare
Bookies	Lenny Gaines, Lonnie Burr
Street Gang Leader	Christopher M. Brown
Landlord	Roger La Page
Sales Person	Loren Freeman
N.Y. Homeless Fighters	Marc D. Williams, Mark Dealessandro
N.Y. Monster Fighter	James Brewster Thompson
Garage Fighter	Tony "Satch" Williams
Cynthia's Fighter	Jeff Langton
Scottish Fighter	Stuart Wilson
Raquetball Fighter	Magic Schwartz
Pool Fighter	Paco Prieto
Attila	Abdel Qissi
Street Gang Members	Lindsey Carlos, Maurice Lamont, Sifu Williams, Thunder Wolf, Carlton Holder
Video Fighters	Michael Foley, A.D. Muyich
BMW Passengers	Donald Pike, Dean Milor Thomas

and Tony Valentino (Hospital Technician), Clement Von Franckenstein (English Investor), Christopher Nixon (German Investor), Eduardo Ricard (Spanish Investor), Julie Rudolph (Homeless Mother), Micheline Lettich (Homeless Child), Galen Yuen (Desk Bookie), Jeff Speakman (Mansion Security Man), Steven R. Purwin (Airplane Pilot), Freeman King (Homeless Man), Scott Spiegel (Pool Fight Bookie

Voyo, Jean-Claude Van Damme, Michel Qissi
Above: Van Damme, Stuart Wilson

© *Universal City Studios*

Ethan Hawke Top Right: Seymour Cassel, Hawke
Top Left: Hawke, Jed Below: Hawke
© *Buena Vista Pictures*

WHITE FANG

(WALT DISNEY PICTURES) Producer, Marykay Powell; Executive Producers, Mike Lobell, Andrew Bergman; Director, Randal Kleiser; Screenplay, Jeanne Rosenberg, Nick Thiel, David Fallon; Based on the novel by Jack London; Photography, Tony Pierce-Roberts; Designer, Michael Bolton; Costumes, Jenny Beavan, John Bright; Music, Basil Poledouris; Editor, Lisa Day; Casting, Michael Fenton, Judy Taylor, Valorie Massalas; Assistant Director, Doug Metzger; White Fang Owner/Trainer, Clint Rowe; Stunts, Rick Barker; Presented in Association with Silver Screen Partners IV; Distributed by Buena Vista Pictures; Dolby Stereo; Technicolor; Rated PG; 104 minutes; January release

CAST

Alex Larson	Klaus Maria Brandauer
Jack Conroy	Ethan Hawke
Skunker	Seymour Cassel
Belinda	Susan Hogan
Beauty Smith	James Remar
Luke	Bill Moseley
Tinker	Clint B. Youngreen
Grey Beaver	Pius Savage
Little Beaver	Aaron Hotch
Older Indian	Charles Jimmie, Sr.
Old Timers	Clifford Fossman, Irvin Sogge
Prospector	Tom Fallon
Sled Dog Prospector	Dick Mackey
Heather	Suzanne Kent
Bar Patron	Robert G. Hoelen
Registrar	George Rogers
Sykes	Michael David Lally
Shopkeeper	Raymond R. Menaker
Lookout	David Fallon
Teenager	Michael A. Hagen
Grey Beaver's Wife	Diane Benson

and Rob Kyker, Tom Yewell (Frozen Prospectors), John Beers (Sykes' Dog Handler), Van Clifton (Piano Player), Jim Moore (Violin Player), Marliese Schneider (Woman of the night), Jed (White Fang), Bart (Bear)

Ethan Hawke, Klaus Maria Brandauer
Above: Hawke, Jed

FLIGHT OF THE INTRUDER

(PARAMOUNT) Producer, Mace Neufeld; Executive Producer, Brian Frankish; Co-Executive Producer, Ralph Winter; Director, John Milius; Screenplay, Robert Dillon, David Shaber; Based on the novel by Stephen Coonts; Photography, Fred J. Koenekamp; Designer, Jack T. Collis; Music, Basil Poledouris; Editors, C. Timothy O'Meara, Steve Mirkovich, Peck Prior; Visual Effects Producer, Mark Vargo; Casting, Mindy Marin; Assistant Director, Steve Danton; Dolby Stereo; Panavision; Technicolor; Rated PG-13; 115 minutes; January release

CAST

Cmdr. Frank Camparelli	Danny Glover
Lt. Cmdr. Virgil Cole	Willem Dafoe
Lt. Jake Grafton	Brad Johnson
Callie	Rosanna Arquette
Boxman	Tom Sizemore
Cowboy Parker	J. Kenneth Campbell
Razor	Jared Chandler
Mad Jack	Dann Florek
"Cag"	Madison Mason
C.P.O. Frank McRae	Ving Rhames
Morg	Christopher Rich
Guffy	Douglas Roberts
Hardesty	Scott Newton Stevens
Lt. Sammy Lundeen	Justin Williams
Captain Copeland	Fred Dalton Thompson
Little Augie	Adam Nelson
Big Augie	John Corbett
Librarian	Adam Biesk
Air Boss	Reb Brown
Clerk	Peter Sherayko
Admirals	J. Patrick McNamara, David Glyn Price
New Guy	James O'Neel
Newsman	Hugo Napier
Duty Officer	David Schwimmer
Intelligence Captain	Richard Fancy
Fighter Pilot Drunk	Rick Dano
Merchant Thugs	Mike Jolly, Tom Kriss, Jeff O'Haco
Bartender-"Skipper"	Grove E. Johnson
Philippino Taxi Driver	Jonnie C. Pangyarihan, Sr.
Jack "Hammer" Johnson	Duane Matthews
Cole's Killer	Eddie Badiang
Pathet Lao Soldier	Minh Huu Do
NVA Officer	Brian Khaw
Sniper	Dr. Akio Matamura
Sallie	Alison Furrevig
Hooker	Connie P. Canales
Thug	Ernie Seliceo
Aide	Ken Wright

Top: Brad Johnson, Douglas Roberts, Willem Dafoe
Below: Johnson, Rosanna Arquette
© *Paramount Pictures Corp.*

Brad Johnson, Danny Glover, Willem Dafoe

Brad Johnson, Danny Glover

11

CADENCE

(NEW LINE CINEMA) Producer, Richard Davis; Executive Producers, Peter E. Strauss, Frank Guistra, Timothy Gamble; Director, Martin Sheen; Screenplay, Dennis Shryack; Based on the novel *Count a Lonely Cadence* by Gordon Weaver; Co-Producer, Glennis Liberty; Photography, Richard Leiterman; Music, Georges Delerue; Editor, Martin Hunter; Song: "Chain Gang" by Sam Cooke; Stockade Shuffle Creator, Russell Clark; Assistant Director, Lee Knippelberg; a presentation of Republic Pictures Corporation in association with The Movie Group and Northern Lights Media; Dolby Stereo; Color; Rated PG-13; 97 minutes; January release

CAST

Pfc. Franklin F. Bean ....Charlie Sheen
Sgt. Otis McKinney ....Martin Sheen
Stokes ....Larry Fishburne
Webb ....Michael Beach
Lawrence ....John Toles-Bey
Spoonman (Bryce)..Blu Mankuma
Harry "Sweetbread" Crane ....Harry Stewart
Pfc. Gerald Gessner..Ramon Estevez
Pfc. Harold Lamar ....James Marshall
Capt. Garcia..F. Murray Abraham
Bean Sr..Matt Clark
Tatooist..Jennifer Griffin
Sager...David Michael O'Neill
Brooks...Roark Chritchlow
Cecil Haig...Joe Lowry
Col. Clark ....Steve Hilton
Mr. Vito...Jay Brazeau
and Tom McBeath (Principal), David Glyn-Jones (Funeral Director), Tony Pantages (G.I. in bar), Deryl Hayes (M.P. in bar), Lochlyn Munro (Bartender), Allan Lysell (Prosecutor), Douglas Judge, Brent Strait (Psychiatric Ward M.P.s), Samantha Langevin (Mrs. Vito)

Top: Martin Sheen, Ramon Estevez, Charlie Sheen
Left: Charlie Sheen
© *Republic Pictures Corp.*

James Marshall, Ramon Estevez, Larry Fishburne, Michael Beach, John Toles-Bey, Blu Mankuma, Harry Stewart, Charlie Sheen

Holly Hunter, Richard Dreyfuss
Top Right: Danny Aiello, Gena Rowlands
Right: Rowlands, Aiello, Dreyfuss
© *Universal City Studios*

ONCE AROUND

(**UNIVERSAL**) Producers, Griffin Dunne, Amy Robinson; Co-Producers, Dreyfuss/James Productions; Director, Lasse Hallstrom; Screenplay, Malia Scotch Marmo; Executive Producer, G. Mac Brown; Photography, Theo Van De Sande; Designer, David Gropman; Costumes, Renee Kalfus; Music, James Horner; Song "Fly Me to the Moon" by Bart Howard; Editor, Andrew Mondshein; Casting, Meg Simon, Fran Kumin; Assistant Director, Louis D'Esposito; a co-presentation from Cinecom Entertainment Group of a Double Play production; Dolby Stereo; Deluxe color; Rated R; 115 minutes; January release

CAST

Sam Sharpe	Richard Dreyfuss
Renata Bella	Holly Hunter
Joe Bella	Danny Aiello
Jan Bella	Laura San Giacomo
Marilyn Bella	Gena Rowlands
Gail Bella	Roxanne Hart
Tony Bella	Danton Stone
Peter Hedges	Tim Guinee
Jim Redstone	Greg Germann
Rob	Griffin Dunne
Sonny	Cullen O. Johnson
Aunt	Joan Gay
Uncle	Lou Criscuolo
Trainers	Myra Taylor, Michael Steve Jones
Belly Dancer	Sabah
Honey Beach	Caroline Parton
Minister	John Bennes
Little Boy	Archie Fallon
Lithuanian Priest	Rev. William Wolkovich
Justice of the Peace	Dorothy Stevenson-Bigby
Roving Violinist	Allen A. Mele
Young Joe Bella	Barry Reed
Young Renata Bella	Heather Reed
Young Jan Bella	Susan Reed
Young Tony Bella	Jonathan A. Cramer
Wedding Guests	Gerald A. Benullo, Sal Ruffino

Holly Hunter, Richard Dreyfuss
Above: Laura San Giacomo, Hunter

13

BOOK OF LOVE

(NEW LINE CINEMA) Producer, Rachel Talalay; Executive Producer, Sara Risher; Director, Robert Shaye; Screenplay, William Kotzwinkle, based on his novel *Jack in the Box*; Photography, Peter Deming; Designer, C.J. Strawn; Music Supervisor, Bonnie Greenberg; Title song written by Warren Davis, George Mallone and Charles Patrick; Music, Stanley Clarke; Casting, Penny Perry, Annette Benson; Costumes, Susan Desanto; Assistant Director, Josh King; Dolby Stereo; CFI color; Rated PG-13; 88 minutes; February release

CAST

Jack Twiller	Chris Young
Crutch Kane	Keith Coogan
Peanut	Aeryk Egan
Lily	Josie Bissett
Gina Gabooch	Tricia Leigh Fisher
Spider Bomboni	Danny Nucci
Floyd	John Cameron Mitchell
Angelo Gabooch	Beau Dremann
Mrs. Twiller	Jill Jaress
Mr. Twiller	John Achorn
Adult Jack Twiller	Michael McKean
Ubaldini	Michael Cavalieri
Drainpipe	Gary Ellenberg
Meatball	Brent Fraser
Mr. Malloy	Lewis Arquette
Wanda	Elizabeth Rainey
Mama Gabooch	Anna Berger
Cleaning Lady Bomboni	Madeleine Berger
Mechanic	Donna Wilson
Moving Van Driver	Ritch Brinkley
Schank	Brian Evans
Sparta	Allison Barron
Dove	Scarlet Bernard
Bunny	Sylvie Spector
Mrs. Flynn	Lin Shaye
Gypsy Girl	Rio Knott
Snake	Clayton Landey
Ticket Taker	Jack McGee
Diner Owner	Dana Craig
Dance Instructor	Jeremy D. Lawrence
Teacher	Delana Michaels
Body Builder	Tom Platz
Honeymoon	Leesa Rowland

and Bob Sweeney (Mr. Snow), Joseph Svezia (Nazareth Pronka), Claudia Bloom (TV Actress), Cameron Perry (TV Actor), "Big Daddy": John Hatton, Marty Kaniger, Don Raymond, Robert Sandman, Billy Block (Prom Band), "The Nickelodeons": Randy Crenshaw, Kevin Dalby, Ken Neufeld, Bill New (Barbershop Quartet)

Top: Beau Dremann, Chris Young, Tricia Leigh Fisher
Right: Young, Aeryk Egan
© New Line Cinema Corp.

Keith Coogan, Chris Young, Tricia Leigh Fisher, Danny Nucci, Josie Bissett, John Cameron Mitchell

Josie Bissett, Elizabeth Rainey, Keith Coogan, Chris Young

Glenn Shadix, Ed Begley Jr., Stockard Channing, Bobby
Jacoby, Cami Cooper Top Right: Dabney Coleman
© *Triton Pictures/Heron Communications Inc.*

MEET THE APPLEGATES

(**TRITON PICTURES**) Producer, Denise Di Novi; Executive
Producers, Christopher Webster, Steve White; Director, Michael
Lehmann; Screenplay, Redbeard Simmons, Michael Lehmann;
Photography, Mitchell Dubin; Music, David
Newman; Costumes, Joseph Porro; Makeup Effects, Kevin Yagher;
Casting, Sally Dennison, Justine Jacoby, Julie Selzer; a New World
Pictures in association with Cinemarque Entertainment presentation in
association with Heron Communications, Inc.; Dolby Stereo; DuArt
color; Rated R; 90 minutes; February release

CAST

Dick Applegate	Ed Begley, Jr.
Jane Applegate	Stockard Channing
Aunt Bea	Dabney Coleman
Johnny Applegate	Bobby Jacoby
Sally Applegate	Cami Cooper
Greg Samson	Glenn Shadix
Opal Withers	Susan Barnes
Vince Samson	Adam Biesk
Dottie	Savannah Smith Boucher
Sheriff Heidegger	Roger Aaron Brown
Nita Samson	Lee Garlington
Kenny	Philip Arthur Ross
Kevin	Steven Robert Ross
Rich Block	Mark Bringelson
Glen Shedd	Chuck LaFont
Peace Corps Volunteers	Alan David Fox, Sherrie Wills
Amazon Native	Jerry Craig
Russell Withers	Joe Van Slyke
Coach Himler	Mindy Bell
Courtney	Meg Weldon
Ingrid	Chelsea Lee
Monica	Jessica Schwartz
Vince's Friend	Mike Rieden
Jr. Cartwright	Bob Fox
Drones	Kathryn Garrison, Margret Mazon, Gustavo Mellado, Michael Raysses
Relative #1 (Hector)	Sherry Narens
Mr. Goodpastor	Les Podewell
Pastor Cooter	Bradley Mott
Bea Bug	Patrick Donahue
Cocktail Waitress	Barbara Lehmann

and Lisa Sutton (Pregnant Woman), Kiki Huygelen (Gail), Adrian
Tafoya (Motorboat Captain), John Escobar (Jorge), Tony Cecere
(Banana Boat Helmsman), Rick Snyder (Bank Officer), Joe Liss
(Customs Official), Ivan H. Migel (Cashier), Dan Bradley, Richard
Barker (Power Plant Worker), Mark Roberts (Screaming Guard in
plant)

Dabney Coleman Above: Cami Cooper,
Ed Begley Jr., Stockard Channing, Bobby Jacoby

15

Joe Mantegna, Kevin Bacon, John Malkovich, Tony
Spiridakis Top Right: Mantegna, Linda Fiorentino
Right: Bacon, Spiridakis
© *Seven Arts*

QUEENS LOGIC

(7 ARTS/NEW LINE CINEMA) Producers, Russ Smith, Stuart
Oken; Executive Producers, Taylor Hackford, Stuart Benjamin;
Director, Steve Rash; Screenplay, Tony Spiridakis; Story, Tony
Spiridakis, Joseph W. Savino; Photography, Amir Mokri; Designer,
Edward Pisoni; Music, Joe Jackson; Music Supervisors, Gary
Goetzman, Sharon Boyle; Editor, Patrick Kennedy; Costumes, Linda
Bass; Associate Producer, Patricia Churchill; a New Visions
presentation of a Seven Arts release; Dolby Stereo; Deluxe color;
Rated R; 116 minutes; February release

CAST

Dennis	Kevin Bacon
Carla	Linda Fiorentino
Eliot	John Malkovich
Al	Joe Mantegna
Ray	Ken Olin
Vinny	Tony Spiridakis
Monte	Tom Waits
Patricia	Chloe Webb
Grace	Jamie Lee Curtis
Marty	Michael Zelniker
Maria	Kelly Bishop
Jeremy	Terry Kinney
Jack	Ed Marinaro
Kate	Wendy Gazelle
Inez	Jodie Markell
Asha	Jenny Wright
Joey Clams' Nephew	Bruce MacVittie
Joey Clams	J.J. Johnston
Madame Rosa	Camille Saviola
Dolores (Drunk Woman)	Megan Mullally
Cecil	Todd Field
Cashier	Liane Curtis
Girl in club bathroom	Brigitta Stenberg
Actor	Rich Kind
Girl with hair	Chase Winton
Mrs. Rondi	Janet Brandt
Bouncer	Russell Curry
Girl in Camaro	Candace Coster
Underage Girl at bar	Emily Perret
Angelica	Summer Donaldson
Roberta	Zoe Jess Levy
Young Al	Marc Fousteris
Young Ray	Robert Fidalgo
Young Vinny	J.D. Daniels
Young Dennis	Darren Higgins
Young Carla	Jaclyn Thornberg
Young Patricia	Amy McDonald

Kevin Bacon, Chloe Webb
Above: Joe Mantegna, Ken Olin

SLEEPING WITH THE ENEMY

(20th CENTURY FOX) Producer, Leonard Goldberg; Executive Producer, Jeffrey Chernov; Director, Joseph Ruben; Screenplay, Ronald Bass; Based on the novel by Nancy Price; Photography, John W. Lindley; Designer, Doug Kraner; Costumes, Richard Hornung; Music, Jerry Goldsmith; Editor, George Bowers; Casting, Karen Rea; Associate Producers, C. Tad Devlin, Michael E. Steele; Assistant Director, Michael E. Steele; Dolby Stereo; Deluxe color; Rated R; 99 minutes; February release

CAST

Laura Burney (Sara Waters)	Julia Roberts
Martin Burney	Patrick Bergin
Ben Woodward	Kevin Anderson
Chloe	Elizabeth Lawrence
Fleishman	Kyle Secor
Dr. Rissner	Claudette Nevins
Locke	Tony Abatemarco
Julie	Marita Geraghty
Garber	Harley Venton
Woman on bus	Nancy Fish
Edna	Sandi Shackelford
Mrs. Nepper	Bonnie Cook
Minister	Graham Harrington
Straw-haired Boy	John David Ward
Sharon the Nurse	Sharon J. Robinson

Right: Julia Roberts
© *Twentieth Century Fox*

Julia Roberts, Kevin Anderson

Patrick Bergin, Julia Roberts
Above: Roberts, Bergin

17

Steve Martin, Victoria Tennant Top Left: Martin,
Sarah Jessica Parker Left: Martin
© *Tri-Star Pictures*

L.A. STORY

(TRI-STAR) Producer, Daniel Melnick, Michael Rachmil; Executive Producers, Mario Kassar, Steve Martin; Director, Mick Jackson; Screenplay, Steve Martin; Photography, Andrew Dunn; Designer, Lawrence Miller; Costumes, Rudy Dillon; Music, Peter Melnick; Editor, Richard A. Harris; Casting, Mindy Marin; Assistant Director, Albert Shapiro; a Daniel Melnick/Indieprod/L.A. Films production from Carolco Pictures; Dolby Stereo; Technicolor; Rated PG-13; 95 minutes; February release

CAST

Harris K. Telemacher	Steve Martin
Sara McDowel	Victoria Tennant
Roland Mackey	Richard E. Grant
Trudi	Marilu Henner
SanDeE*	Sarah Jessica Parker
Ariel	Susan Forristal
Frank Swan	Kevin Pollak
Morris Frost	Sam McMurray
Maitre D' at L'Idiot	Patrick Stewart
News Reporters	Andrew Amador, Gail Grate
Maitre D' at Brunch	Eddie DeHarp
Rap Waiter at L'Idiot	M.C. Shan
June	Frances Fisher
Cynthia	Iman
Ted	Tommy Hinkley
Tom	Larry Miller
Sharon	Anne Crawford
Sheila	Samantha Caulfield
Man	Thornton Simmons
Crook	Dennis Dragon
Bank Executive	Richard Stahl
Boring Speaker	Aaron Lustig
Woman	Juliana McCarthy
Floss Waiter at L'Idiot	Time Winters
Chef	Pierre Epstein
Jesse	Wesley Thompson
Straight Weatherman	George Plimpton
Station Manager	Woody Harrelson
Gravedigger	Rick Moranis
Carlo Christopher	Chevy Chase

and David G. Price (Pilot), Wesley Mann (Gas Station Attendant), Mark Steen, Jaime Gomez, Amy Wallace (Tod PAs), Cheryl Baker (Changing Room Woman), Mary R. Boss (Old Woman), Scott Johnston (Co-pilot), Robert Lind (Chainsaw Juggler), Tony Marsico (Hard Rock Patron), Burt Nacke (Cameraman), Mary Pedersen (Airline Ticket Agent), Matt Stetson (Spokesmodel Teacher)

Steve Martin, Victoria Tennant

Steve Martin Top Left: Sarah Jessica Parker, Martin Below Left: Marilu Henner; Richard E. Grant Top Right: Victoria Tennant, Martin

Pan Qingfu Top Left: Mark Salzman Top Right: Qingfu
Below Right Vivian Wu, Salzman
© *Prestige*

IRON & SILK

(PRESTIGE) Producer/Director, Shirley Sun; Screenplay, Mark Salzman, Shirley Sun; Based on the book by Mark Salzman; Photography, James Hayman; Designer, Calvin Tsao; Music, Michael Gibbs; Editors, Geraldine Peroni, James Y. Kwei; Associate Producer, Mei Kwong Franklin; Distributed by Miramax Films; DuArt color; Not rated; 90 minutes; February release

CAST

Teacher Mark ....Mark Salzman
Teacher Pan...Pan Qingfu
Teacher Hei...Jeanette Lin Tsui
Ming...Vivian Wu
Sinbad..Sun Xudong
Mr. Song ....Zheng Guo
Old Sheep ....To Funglin
Fatty Du ....Hu Yun
Teacher Cai...Dong Hancheng
Teacher Li ....Lu Zhiquan
April...Xiao Ying
Dr. Wang ....Yang Xiru
Teacher Xu ....Zhuang Genyua
Teacher Zhang...Jiang Xihong

Jeanette Lin Tsui, Mark Salzman
Above: Pan Qingfu

John Goodman Top Right: Goodman, Peter O'Toole
Right: Goodman
© *Universal City Studios*

KING RALPH

(**UNIVERSAL**) Producer, Jack Brodsky; Executive Producers, Sydney Pollack, Mark Rosenberg; Director/Screenplay, David S. Ward; Based on the novel *Headlong* by Emlyn Williams; Co-Producers, Julie Bergman, John Comfort; Photography, Kenneth MacMillan; Designer, Simon Holland; Costumes, Catherine Cook; Music, James Newton Howard; Song "Good Golly Miss Molly" by Robert A. Blackwell and John Marascalco, performed by John Goodman; Casting, Mary Selway; Assistant Director, Derek Cracknell; a Mirage/JBRO production; Dolby Stereo; Rank color; Rated PG; 99 minutes; February release

CAST

Ralph Jones	John Goodman
Sir Cedric Willingham	Peter O'Toole
Lord Graves	John Hurt
Miranda Green	Camille Coduri
Duncan Phipps	Richard Griffiths
Gordon	Leslie Phillips
Hale	James Villiers
Princess Anna	Joely Richardson
McGuire	Niall O'Brien
King Gustav	Julian Glover
Queen Katherine	Judy Parfitt
Dysentery	Ed Stobart
Punk Girl	Gedren Heller
King Mulambon	Rudolph Walker
Hamilton	Michael Johnson
Miranda's Father	Jack Smethurst
Miranda's Mother	Ann Beach
Royal Photographer	Roger Ashton Griffiths
Ed Mayes	Brian Greene
MC Strip Club	Dallas Adams
Fanny Oakley	Adele Lakeland
Bouncer	Guy Fithen
Riding Instructor	Ian Geldor
Graves' Photographer	Cameron Blakely
Counter Girl	Caroline Paterson
Onlooker	Sally Nesbitt
Guard (Funeral)	Patrick Cremin
Newscasters	Richard Whitmore, Jennie Stoller
Sax Player	Kirk St. James
King of England	Tim Seely
Duke	Gareth Forwood
Assistant Photographer	Alan McMahon
Gamekeeper	Richard Bebb
Butler	David Stoll
Tailor	Paul Beech
Assistant Tailor	Angus MacKay

and Josanne Haydon-Pearce, Vanessa Lee Hicks, Jazzi Northover, Dawn Spence (Chorus Girls), Chantal-Claire, Topaze Hasfal-School (Dukettes Back-up Singers), Charlotte Pyecroft (Chorus Girl/Dukette)

Camille Coduri, John Goodman
Above: Richard Griffiths; John Hurt

21

SCENES FROM A MALL

(TOUCHSTONE) Producer/Director, Paul Mazursky; Co-Producers, Pato Guzman, Patrick McCormick; Screenplay, Roger L. Simon, Paul Mazursky; Photography, Fred Murphy; Designer, Pato Guzman; Editor/Associate Producer, Stuart Pappé; Costumes, Albert Wolsky; Music and Adaptations, Marc Shaiman; Casting, Joy Todd; Assistant Director, Henry J. Bronchtein; presented in association with Silver Screen Partners IV; Distributed by Buena Vista Pictures; Dolby Stereo; Technicolor; Rated R; 87 minutes; February release

CAST

Deborah Fifer	Bette Midler
Nick Fifer	Woody Allen
Mime	Bill Irwin
Sam Fifer	Daren Firestone
Jennifer Fifer	Rebecca Nickels
Dr. Hans Clava	Paul Mazursky
Barber Shop Quartet	Gregory Moore, Michael Brown, Jonathan Guss, David Frye
Joe Cool & The Coolers (Rap Group)	Joseph Warren, Brian Warren, Darrel Mason
Pianist	Marc Shaiman
El Mariachi Bustamante	Augustin Bustamante, Leonel Cruz, Telmo Hernandez, Steve Ortiz, Ramon Ponce, Fernando Quinones
Interviewer	Joan Delaney
Interviewee	Amanda Bruce
Information Woman	Betsy Mazursky
Pharmacist	Jack Brodsky
Owner - Museum Shop	Glen Alterman
Woman at book store	Marilyn Pasekoff
Santa	Patrick Farrelly
Sushi Chef	Hidehiko Takada
Ticket Seller	Tichina Arnold
Dress Shop Saleswoman	Wanakee Legardy
Waitress - Nuvo Navajo	Carol Harris
Security Guards	Vira Colorado, Billy Graham
Chinese Acrobat	Chun Long Zhang
Magician	Kamarr
Magician's Assistant	Kathy Kamarr
Bartender	Robert Garrett
Handsome Man	Fabio Lanzoni
Sikhs	Steven Dominic Prestianni, Heather Golden
Bus Boy	Jose Rafael Arango
Man in parking garage	Bobby Caravella

and Laura Baler (Chocolate Candy Girl), James Duane Polk (Man on movie line), Penny Gaston, Minna Rose, Stewart Russell, Joe Viviani (Pharmacy Patrons), Larry Sherman, Shiro Oishi, Ron Barry-Barry (Men on carphones), Michael Greene, Stuart Pappé (Motorcyclists), Andrew Phillipe (Taxi Driver), Phillip Nozaki, Donnie Kelber (Kids in van)

Top: Woody Allen, Bette Midler, Bill Irwin
Below: Midler, Allen Right: Allen, Midler
© Touchstone Pictures

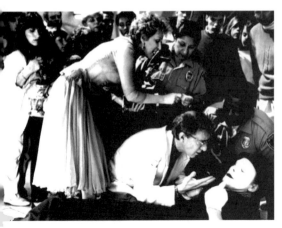

Bette Midler, Vira Colorado, Woody Allen, Billy Graham, Bill Irwin

Woody Allen, Bette Midler

Kevin Bacon, Elizabeth Perkins
Top Left: Nathan Lane, Perkins
© Paramount Pictures

HE SAID, SHE SAID

(PARAMOUNT) Producer, Frank Mancuso, Jr.; Directors, Ken Kwapis ("He Said"), Marisa Silver ("She Said"); Screenplay, Brian Hohlfeld; Photography, Stephen H. Burum; Designer, Michael Corenblith; Editor, Sidney Levin; Casting, Carrie Frazier, Shani Ginsberg; Associate Producer, Vikki Williams; Music, Miles Goodman; Costumes, Deena Appel; Assitant Director, John Hockridge; Dolby Stereo; Panavision; Technicolor; Rated PG-13; 115 minutes; February release

CAST

Dan Hanson	Kevin Bacon
Lorie Bryer	Elizabeth Perkins
Wally Thurman	Nathan Lane
Mark	Anthony LaPaglia
Linda	Sharon Stone
Bill Weller	Stanley Anderson
Cindy	Charlayne Woodard
Eric	Danton Stone
Mr. Spepk	Phil Leeds
Mrs. Spepk	Rita Karin
Al, at the Deli	Paul Butler
Rita, his Daughter	Erika Alexander
Susan	Ashley Gardner
Adam	M.K. Harris
Ray, the Technical Director	Damien Leake
Makeup Girl	Constance Shulman
Harry	Leon Russom
Ed	Steven Gilborn
Janet	Dana Andersen
Sheila	Petie Perkins
Diana	Hope Miles
Lou, the Florist	Bruce MacVittie
Mr. Bryer	George Martin
Mrs. Bryer	Tanya Berezin
Jack Bryer	Maury Efrems
Susan Bryer	Claudia Silver
The Waiter	David Cale
Man at restaurant	Rick Warner
Waitress	Elizabeth Brower
Theatre Dancers	David Storey, Alycea Baylis
Guy (aka Steve)	Mark Tymchyshyn
Uncle Olaf	F. William Parker
Olga, his Bride	Karen K. Kirschenbauer

and Tom McDermott, Bobby B., Dennis Michael, Dave Smith, Bart Lay (Live Band), David Long (Mr. Hanson), Rita Hennessy (Mrs. Hanson), Lucy Brightman (Aunt), Van Dyke Parks (Priest), The Boys from Baltimore (Polka Band), Shelley North, Mark Brutsche (Hanson Family Member), Merri Biechler (Wally's Secretary), Alice O'Connor, Ida Eustis, Cynthia L. Miller (Receptionists), Brian Hohlfeld, Lisa Hohlfeld (Bar Patrons), Alan J. Wendl (Bartender), Pamela Martin ("A.M. Baltimore" Host), Michael Chaban, Val Almendarez, Bernard Lee (Basketball Players), Rebecca Krimski (Woman Walking Dog), Jeff Mandon (Technician), Bill Britt (News Anchor), Helen R. Williams (Grocery Clerk), Leeza Gibbons, John Tesh (Themselves)

Kevin Bacon, Elizabeth Perkins
Above: Sharon Stone, Bacon

THE DOORS

(TRI-STAR) Producers, Bill Graham, Sasha Harari, A. Kitman Ho; Executive Producers, Mario Kassar, Nicholas Clainos, Brian Grazer; Director, Oliver Stone; Screenplay, J. Randal Johnson, Oliver Stone; Associate Producers, Clayton Townsend, Joseph Reidy; Photography, Robert Richardson; Designer, Barbara Ling; Editors, David Brenner, Joe Hutshing; Costumes, Marlene Stewart; Executive Music Producer, Budd Carr; Music Producer, Paul A. Rothchild; Songs written and performed by The Doors, with additional vocals by Val Kilmer; Casting, Risa Bramon, Billy Hopkins; Assistant Director, Joseph Reidy; a Sasha Harari/Bill Graham Films/Imagine Entertainment production from Carolco Pictures; Dolby Stereo; Panavision; Deluxe color; Rated R; 135 minutes; March release

CAST

Jim Morrison	Val Kilmer
Robby Krieger	Frank Whaley
John Densmore	Kevin Dillon
Pamela Courson	Meg Ryan
Ray Manzarek	Kyle MacLachlan
Cat	Billy Idol
Dog	Dennis Burkley
Bill Siddons	Josh Evans
Tom Baker	Michael Madsen
Paul Rothchild	Michael Wincott
Patricia Kennealy	Kathleen Quinlan
Shaman	Floyd Red Crow Westerman
Dorothy	Kelly Ann Hu
Jac Holzman	Mark Moses
Bruce Botnick	Frank Military
Ed Sullivan	Will Jordan
Sullivan's Producer	Sam Whipple
Magazine Photographer	Mimi Rogers
Warhol PR	Paul Williams
Andy Warhol	Crispin Glover

and John Densmore (Engineer - Last Session), Gretchen Becker (Mom), Jerry Sturm (Dad), Sean Stone (Young Jim), Kendall Deichen (Little Sister), Rion Hunter, Wes Studi, Steve Reevis (Indians in desert), Bernie Telsey (Young Man with Pam), Bruce MacVittie, Andrew Lauer (UCLA students), Oliver Stone (Film Teacher), Harmonica Fats (Blues Singer on Venice Boardwalk), John T. Forristal III (Bouncer), Josie Bissett (Robby Krieger's Girlfriend), Fiona (Fog Groupie), Bob Lupone (Music Manager), Paul Rothchild (Music Manager's Sidekick), John Capodice (Jerry), Eric Burden (Backstage Manager), Nellie Red Owl (Old Crone), Victoria Seeger, Debbie Mazar, Jacqui Bell (Whiskey Girls), Sergio Premoli (Patron at the Whiskey), Debbie Falconer (John Densmore's Girlfriend), Michele Bronson (New York Groupie), Charlie Spradling (CBS Girl backstage), Lisa Edelstein (Makeup Artist), Erik Dellems (Hairdresser at the Sullivan Show), Jennifer Rubin (Edie), Kristina Hare (Partygoer), Costas Mandylor (Italian Count), Kristina Fulton (Nico), Bernt Kuhlman, Claire Stansfield (Warhol Eurosnobs), Karina Lombard (Warhol Actress), Christopher Lawford, Dani Klein, Laura Esterman, Deborah Lupard, Ashley Stone, Richard B. Rifkin, Chris Boyle, Adrian Scott (New York Journalists), Bill Graham (New Haven Promoter), Titus Welliver (Macing Cop), Eagle Eye Cherry, David Allen Brooks (Roadies), Danny Sullivan, Stanley White (New Haven Cops), Frank Girardeau (Police Lieutenant), Bonnie Bramlett (Bartender), Rodney Grant (Patron at Barney's), Brad Von Beltz (Hippie at party), Hawthorne James (Chuck Vincent), Csynbidium, Cirsten Weldon (Girls in car), Patricia Kennealy (Wicca Priestess), Davidson Thomson (High Priest), Leonard Crow Dog, Carmella Runnels (Indians at the outdoor concert), Pride in Peril (Miami Warm-up Band), Keith Reddin (Miami Journalist), Billy Vera (Miami Promoter), Allan Graf, Jack McGee (Miami Cops), Alan Manson (Judge), Bill Kunstler (Lawyer), Peter Crombie (Associate Lawyer), Bob Marshall (Prosecutor), Annie McEnroe (Secretary), Tudor Sherrard (Office Publicist), Jad Mager (Office P.A.), Kelly Leach (Birthday Girl), Richard Rutowski.

Top: Meg Ryan, Val Kilmer
Below: Kyle MacLachlan
© *Tri-Star Pictures*

Kyle MacLachlan, Val Kilmer, Frank Whaley, Kevin Dillon Above: Kilmer, Kathleen Quinlan

Kyle MacLachlan, Frank Whaley, Kevin Dillon, Val Kilmer
Top Left & Top Right: Kilmer Below Left: Dillon

Clarence Williams III, Balthazar Getty, Ben Johnson
Top Left: Tess Harper, Scott Glenn
Top Right: Getty, Johnson
© *Home Grown Inc.*

MY HEROES HAVE ALWAYS BEEN COWBOYS

(SAMUEL GOLDWYN CO.) Producers, Martin Poll, E.K. Gaylord II; Director, Stuart Rosenberg; Screenplay, Joel Don Humphreys; Photography, Bernd Heinl; Associate Producer, Anthony Poll; Music, James Horner; Editor, Dennis M. Hill; Costumes, Rudy Dillon; Casting, Hank McCann & Associates; Color; Rated PG; 106 minutes; March release

CAST

H.D. Dalton	Scott Glenn
Jolie Meadows	Kate Capshaw
Jesse Dalton	Ben Johnson
Cheryl Hornby	Tess Harper
Jud Meadows	Balthazar Getty
Clint Hornby	Gary Busey
Junior	Mickey Rooney
Virgil	Clarence Williams III
Gimme Cap	Dub Taylor
Dark Glasses	Clu Gulager
Straw Hat	Dennis Fimple
Becky Meadows	Megan Parlen

Scott Glenn, Balthazar Getty, Megan Parlen, Kate
Capshaw Above: Glenn, Gary Busey

Michael J. Fox Top Right: James Woods, Fox
Right: Woods, Stephen Lang
© *Universal City Studios*

THE HARD WAY

(**UNIVERSAL**) Producers, William Sackheim, Rob Cohen; Co-Producer, Peter R. McIntosh; Director, John Badham; Screenplay, Daniel Pyne, Lem Dobbs; Story, Lem Dobbs, Michael Kozoll; Photogrpahy, Don McAlpine, Robert Primes; Designer, Philip Harrison; Costumes, Mary Vogt; Editors, Frank Morriss, Tony Lombardo; Music, Arthur B. Rubinstein; Casting, Bonnie Timmermann; Associate Producers, Keith Rubinstein, D.J. Caruso; Assistant Director, David Sosna; Stunts, Conrad E. Palmisano; Dolby Stereo; Panavision; Deluxe color; Rated R; 111 minutes; March release

CAST

Nick Lang	Michael J. Fox
John Moss	James Woods
Party Crasher	Stephen Lang
Susan	Annabella Sciorra
Grainy	John Capodice
Pooley	Luis Guzman
Billy	LL Cool J
China	Mary Mara
Captain Brix	Delroy Lindo
Witherspoon	Conrad Roberts
Bonnie	Christina Ricci
Angie	Penny Marshall
Drug Dealer	George Cheung
Newsman	Frank Geraci
Pizza Waitress	Sophie Maletsky
Bankers	Lewis Black, Rand Foerster, Anderson Matthews
Lang's Girl Friday	Kathy Najimy
Asian Gang Leader	Keenan Leung
Raggedy Man	Bill Cobbs
Diner Waitress	Reno
Fake Dead Guy/Cop	John Costelloe
Ticket Taker	Jack Gindi
Head Mugger	Leif Riddell
Muggers	Johnny Sanchez, Joseph Tripi
Woman in subway	Karen Lynn Gorney
Continental Representative	Janet Sarno
TV Reporter	Jan Speck
"Smoking Gun" Girl	Holly Kuespert
Homeboy Cop	John Ring

and Dante Smith, Dwayne McClary, Sharrieff Pugh, Anthony Thomas, Howard "Stick" Baines, Shawn McLean, Curtis L. McClarin (Dead Romeos), Michael Jeffrey Woods (Cop), William Truesdale (Witherspoon's Bodyguard), Mark Woodcock (Clothing Salesman), Ed Setrakian (Chief Villain), David O. Sosna (Frog Dog Vendor), Adore O'Hara (Dead Entertainer), Michael Badalucco (Pizza Man), Jordanna Freedman (Moviegoer), Merrill Witten (Scared Subway Woman), Fracaswell Hyman (Wino), Mario Bosco (Boy in theatre), Bryant Gumbel (Himself)

Annabella Sciorra, James Woods
Above: Penny Marshall, Michael J. Fox

27

NEW JACK CITY

(WARNER BROS.) Producers, Doug McHenry, George Jackson; Co-Producers, Preston L. Holmes; Director, Mario Van Peebles; Screenplay, Thomas Lee Wright, Barry Michael Cooper; Story, Thomas Lee Wright; Photography, Francis Kenny; Designer, Charles C. Bennett; Music, Michel Colombier; Editor, Steven Kemper; Costumes, Bernard Johnson; Casting, Pat Golden, John McCabe; Associate Producers, Fab 5 Freddy, Suzanne Broderick, James Bigwood, Dwight Williams; Stunts, Jery Hewitt; Dolby Stereo; Technicolor; Rated R; 97 minutes; March release

CAST

Nino Brown	Wesley Snipes
Scotty Appleton	Ice T
Gee Money	Allen Payne
Pookie	Chris Rock
Stone	Mario Van Peebles
Selina	Michael Michele
Duh Duh Duh Man	Bill Nunn
Park	Russell Wong
Old Man	Bill Cobbs
Kareem Akbar	Christopher Williams
Nick Peretti	Judd Nelson
Keisha	Vanessa Williams
Uniqua	Tracy Camilla Johns
Frankie Needles	Anthony DeSando
Reverend Oates	Nick Ashford
Prosecuting Attorney Hawkins	Phyllis Yvonne Stickney
Police Commissioner	Thalmus Rasulala
Don Armeteo	John Aprea
Master of Ceremonies	Fab 5 Freddy
D.J.	Flavor Flav
Frazier	Clebert Ford
Prom Queen	Laverne Hart
Fat Smitty	Eek-A-Mouse
Biff	Greg Smrz
Teacher	Erica McFarquhar

and Keith Sweat (Singer at wedding), Max Rabinowitz (Gigantor), Marcella Lowery (Woman in hallway), Manuel E. Santiago (Judge), Ben Gotlieb (Prosecuting Attorney), Thelmas Louise Carter, Linda Froehlich (Reporters), Christopher Michael (Bailiff), Tiger Frederick, Rynel Johnson (Basketball Players), Kelly Jo Minter, Tina Lifford, Paul Raczkowski, Erik Kilpatrick (Recovering Addicts), Harold Baines, Sekou Campbell, David Michael Golson, Garvin Holder, Leo O'Brien, Bobby Stancil (Kids on stoop), Teddy Riley, Aaron Hall, Damien Hall (New Year's Eve Band), Rodney Benford, John Harreld, Allen McNeil, Steve Russell, Reggie Warren (Singers -Spring - Troop), Gerald Levert, Sean Levert, Marc Gordon (Singers -Winter - Levert)

Top: Judd Nelson, Chris Rock, Ice T
Below: Wesley Snipes, Allen Payne
Left: Vanessa Williams; Tracy Camilla Johns
© *Warner Bros. Inc.*

Allen Payne, Wesley Snipes,
Christopher Williams

Russell Wong, Mario Van Peebles, Judd Nelson, Ice T

Mary Elizabeth Mastrantonio, Jonathan Silverman,
Colin Friels, Gene Hackman Top Right: Mastrantonio,
Hackman Right: Hackman, Larry Fishburne
© *Twentieth Century Fox*

CLASS ACTION

(20th CENTURY FOX) Producers, Ted Field, Scott Kroopf, Robert W. Cort; Co-Producers, Carolyn Shelby, Christopher Ames; Director, Michael Apted; Screenplay, Carolyn Shelby, Christopher Ames, Samantha Shad; Photography, Conrad L. Hall; Designer, Todd Hallowell; Music, James Horner; Editor, Ian Crafford; Costumes, Rita Ryack; Casting, Lora Kennedy, Linda Lowy; Assistant Director, Marty Ewing; an Interscope Communications production; Dolby Stereo; Deluxe color; Rated R; 109 minutes; March release

CAST

Jedediah Tucker Ward	Gene Hackman
Maggie Ward	Mary Elizabeth Mastrantonio
Michael Grazier	Colin Friels
Estelle Ward	Joanna Merlin
Nick Holbrook	Larry Fishburne
Quinn	Donald Moffat
Pavel	Jan Rubes
Judge Symes	Matt Clark
Dr. Getchell	Fred Dalton Thompson
Brian	Jonathan Silverman
Ann	Joan McMurtrey
Deborah	Anne Elizabeth Ramsay
Carl	David Byron
Howie	Tim Hopper
Steven Kellen	Robert David Hall
Bartender at Bix	Ren Reynolds
Mr. Minh	Wood Moy
Bernstein	Victor Talmadge
Anthony Patricola	Ken Grantham
Laura Holbrook	Hajna O. Moss
Judge Ormsby	Abigail Van Alyn
Bartender at Rosatti's	Gregory B. Goossen
Party Goer	Gretchen Grant
Prosecutor	Richard Zitrin
Clerk	Elizabeth Monti
Judge	Judge John Dearman
Receptionist	Carolyn Reynolds Najera
Lawyer	Carolyn Shelby
Janitor	James Van Harper

Jonathan Silverman, Mary Elizabeth
Mastrantonio, Gene Hackman Above: Mastrantonio

GUILTY BY SUSPICION

(WARNER BROS.) Producer, Arnon Milchan; Executive Producer, Steven Reuther; Co-Producer, Alan C. Blomquist; Director/Screenplay, Irwin Winkler; Photography, Michael Ballhaus; Designer, Leslie Dilley; Music, James Newton Howard; Editor, Priscilla Nedd; Costumes, Richard Bruno; Associate Producer, Nelson McCormick; Casting, Marion Dougherty; Assistant Director, Rob Cowan; Dolby Stereo; Deluxe/Technicolor; Rated PG-13; 105 minutes; March release

CAST

David Merrill	Robert De Niro
Ruth Merrill	Annette Bening
Bunny Baxter	George Wendt
Dorothy Nolan	Patricia Wettig
Felix Graff	Sam Wanamaker
Paulie Merrill	Luke Edwards
Larry Nolan	Chris Cooper
Darryl Zanuck	Ben Piazza
Joe Lesser	Martin Scorsese
Bert Alan	Barry Primus
Chairman Wood	Gailard Sartain
Congressman Tavenner	Robin Gammell
Congressman Velde	Brad Sullivan
Ray Karlin	Tom Sizemore
Felicia Barron	Roxann Biggs
Abe Barron	Stuart Margolin
Jerry Cooper	Barry Tubb
Gene Woods	Gene Kirkwood
Leta Rosen	Margo Winkler
Leonard Marks	Allan Rich
Nan	Illeana Douglas
Ben Saltman	Al Ruscio
Fox Guard	Bill Bailey
FBI Men	Adam Baldwin, Kevin Page
Matt Nolan	Nicholas Cilic
Claude Rowan	Claude Rauvier

and Stephen Root (RKO Guard), John Horn (Mike Rainey), Jon Tenney, Cecile Callan (Shoppers), Tom Rosqui (Norman), Monica Carrico (Nelly Lesser), Jonathan Ames (Cabbie), Brant Van Hoffman (Stanley), F.J. O'Neil (Ad Agency Exec), Joan Scott (Teacher), Dianne E. Reeves (Singer), Paul Collins (Bernard), James Mathers (Director), Joe Bennett (Choreographer), Robert Chimento (A.D.), Craig Smith (D.P.), Maurice Marciano (Costume Designer), Martin Arsenault (Waiter), Ben Dinsdale (Maurice), Russell Bobbitt (Prop Master), Cindy Carey (Party Guest), Ivor Leslie Dilley (1st A.D.), Natalie Zimmerman (Woman on buckboard)

    **Ben Piazza, Robert De Niro
Above: De Niro, Martin Scorsese**

John Cusack, Imogen Stubbs Top Left: James Spader,
Cusack Left: Mandy Patinkin, Cusack
© *Paramount Pictures*

TRUE COLORS

(PARAMOUNT) Producers, Herbert Ross, Laurence Mark; Executive Producer, Joseph M. Carraciolo; Director, Herbert Ross; Screenplay, Kevin Wade; Photography, Dante Spinotti; Designer, Edward Pisoni; Costumes, Joseph G. Aulisi; Editors, Robert Reitano; Stephen A. Rotter; Music, Trevor Jones; Casting, Hank McCann; Assistant Director, Michael Haley; Dolby Stereo; Technicolor; Rated R; 111 minutes; March release

CAST

Peter Burton	John Cusack
Tim Garrity	James Spader
Diana Stiles	Imogen Stubbs
John Palmeri	Mandy Patinkin
Senator Stiles	Richard Widmark
Joan Stiles	Dina Merrill
Senator Steubens	Philip Bosco
John Lawry	Paul Guilfoyle
Abernathy	Brad Sullivan
Todd	Russell Dennis Baker
Stubblefield	Don McManus
Store Clerk	Karen Jablons-Alexander
Janine	Wendee Pratt
Fanne	Rendé Rae Norman
Senator Lackerby	Frank Hoyt Taylor
Sam Minot	Anthony Fusco
Prof. Houseman	Bev Appleton
Sophia Palmeri	Mary Mara
Anchorman	Julian Bell
David	Larry Joshua
Ken	Tom Sean Foley
Mark	Bruce McCarty
Tux Shop Owner	Joe Mattys
Justice Dept. Aides	Steve Morley, Joshua Billings
Justice Dept. Agent	Ronnie Farer
Campus Radical	Kim Criswell
Tony	Tony Carlin
B.J.	Sam Hoffman
Soledad	Antonia Rey
Dr. Burt Tuck	Peter Hackes

and Stephen M. Aronson, Sally Beckner, Michael Stanton Kennedy, Sam Wells (Miami Reporters), Phillip Coccioletti (Carl), John Battle, Mike Fowler (Burton Campaign Aides), Timothy Chambers, Tom Ellis, R.M. Haley (FBI Agents), Richard G. Adee (Palmeri's First Mate), Donald "Spec" Campen Jr., Ernie Dunn, Anne H. Hill (Campaign Aides), O. Dewayne "Bart" Davis, Mary McMillan (Campaign Reporters), Sue Boyd, Chester Holt (Senior Supporters), Ed Sala (Lackerby Aide), Rhonda Fitzgerald (Justice Secretary), Lisa Cooley (Stiles' Secretary), Thomas Hauff, Scott Wickware (Detectives)

Imogen Stubbs, John Cusack, James Spader
Above: Richard Widmark

DEFENDING YOUR LIFE

(WARNER BROS.) Producer/Assistant Director, Michael Grillo; Executive Producer, Herbert S. Nanas; Director/Screenplay, Albert Brooks; Co-Producer, Robert Grand; Photography, Allen Daviau; Designer, Ida Random; Costumes, Deborah L. Scott; Music, Michael Gore; Editor, David Finfer; Casting, Barbara Claman, Mark Saks; Visual Effects, Dream Quest Images; a Geffen Pictures presentation; Dolby Stereo; Technicolor; Rated PG; 110 minutes; March release

CAST

Daniel Miller	Albert Brooks
Agency Head	Michael Durrell
Jeep Owner	James Eckhouse
Car Salesman	Gary Beach
Tram Guide	Julie Cobb
Stan	Peter Schuck
Porter	Time Winters
Bob Diamond	Rip Torn
Susan	Sharlie Stuart
Soap Opera Actors	Beth Black, Clayton Norcross
Game Show Moderator	James Mackrell
Game Show Contestants	Wil Albert, Sage Allen
Waitress	Mary Pat Gleason
Elderly Woman on tram	Maxine Elliott
Helen	Marilyn Rockafellow
Comedian	Roger Behr
Julia	Meryl Streep
Arthur	Art Frankel
Ernie	Ernie Brown
Lena Foster	Lee Grant
Daniel's Judges	George D. Wallace, Lillian Lehman
Daniel as a boy	Raffi Di Blasio
Bully	Kristopher Kent Hill
Child in schoolyard	Eric Ehasz
Daniel as an infant	Matthew Scharch
Daniel's Parents	S. Scott Bullock, Carol Bivins
Steve	Ethan Randall
Mr. Wadworth	Gary Ballard
Sushi Hostess	Mary Mukogawa
Sushi Chefs	Toshio Shikami, Kagko Shikami, Samee Park, Tommy Inouye
Frank	Ken Thorley
Talk Show Host	Bob Braun
Talk Show Guest	Jennifer Barlow
Dick Stanley	Buck Henry
Casio Tipster	Joey Miyashima
Daniel's Date	Nurit Koppel
Daniel's Wife	Susan Walters
Used Car Salesmen	Sidney Chankin, Greg Finley
Sam	Leonard O. Turner
Julia's Prosecutor	Cliff Einstein
Julia's Judges	Rachel Bard, Newell Alexander
Man in Past Lives Pavilion	Hal Landon
Woman in Past Lives Pavilion	Ida Lee
Herself	Shirley MacLaine
Victorian Girl	Noley Thornton
Sumo Wrestler	Glen Chin
Native	James Ekim
Knight	Clarke Coleman
Majestic Doorman	Ron Colby
Peter	David Purdham
Stage Manager	James Paradise
Banquet Manager	Jerry Prell
Fire Marshall	Arell Blanton
Julia's Children	Shana Ballard, Chris Macris
Maitre d'	Joseph Darrell
Eduardo	James Manis
Martin	Alex Sheafe
Ticket Counter Agent	Cathleen Chin
Tram Port Attendants	Lisa Sears, Mark Dunlap, Vernon Roguen
Tram Driver	Dennis Germain

Top: Meryl Streep, Albert Brooks
Below: Brooks, Rip Torn
© *Geffen Film Company*

Lee Grant, Albert Brooks
Above: Rip Torn, Brooks

Ernie Reyes, Jr. Top Left: Michelan Sisti, Paige Turco
Left: Sisti, Vanilla Ice © *New Line Cinema*

TEENAGE MUTANT NINJA TURTLES II: THE SECRET OF THE OOZE

(NEW LINE CINEMA) Producers, Thomas K. Gray, Kim Dawson, David Chan; Co-Producer, Terry Morse; Executive Producer, Raymond Chow; Director, Michael Pressman; Screenplay, Todd W. Langen; Based on characters created by Kevin Eastman and Peter Laird; Photography, Shelly Johnson; Music, John Du Prez; Editor, John Wright, Steve Mirkovich; Costumes, Dodie Shepard; Casting, Lynn Stalmaster; Assistant Director, Rob Corn; Animatronic Characters, Jim Henson's Creature Shop; Stunts/Martial Arts Choreographer, Pat Johnson; Song "Ninja Rap" by Vanilla Ice, Earthquake, Todd W. Langen/performed by Vanilla Ice & Earthquake; a Golden Harvest Production in association with Gary Propper; Dolby Stereo; Technicolor; Rated PG; 88 minutes; March release

CAST

April O'Neil	Paige Turco
Prof. Jordan Perry	David Warner
Michaelangelo/Soho Man	Michelan Sisti
Donatello/Foot #3	Leif Tilden
Raphael	Kenn Troum
Leonardo	Mark Caso
Splinter	Kevin Clash
Keno	Ernie Reyes Jr.
Shredder	Francois Chau
Tatsu	Toshishiro Obata
Chief Sterns	Raymond Serra
Rahzar	Mark Ginther
Tokka	Kurt Bryant
Supershredder	Kevin Nash
Parlor Owner	Joseph Amodei
Parlor Assistant	Nick DeMarinis
Teenager	Kelli Rabke
Thug #1	Keith Coulouris
Soho Woman	Susan Essman
Foot #1	Lee Spencer
Foot #2	Gianpaolo Bonaca
Freddy	Mark Doerr
Himself	Vanilla Ice
Disc Jockey	Earthquake
Crew Member	Tim Parati

and John Brady, Bill Luhrs (TGRI Assistants), Jon Thompson (TGRI Worker), Michael Pressman (News Manager), Mark Caso (News Room Staff), Rick Colella (Teenage Thug), Dewey Webb (Foot Recruiter), Sasha Pressman (Old Woman), David Pressman (Old Man), Shiek Mahmud-Bey, Lisa Chess (Audience), Mark Grinage, John Henry Huffman IV, Everett Fitzgerald (Dancers), Gregg Salata (Promoter), Mak Wilson (Promoter's Aide); Voice Cast: Robbie Rist (Michaelangelo), Brian Tochi (Leonardo), Laurie Faso (Raphael), Adam Carl (Donatello), David McCharen (Shredder), Michael McConnohie (Tatsu), Frank Welker (Rahzar/Tokka), Kevin Clash (Splinter)

Mark Caso, Kenn Troum, Leif Tilden, Michelan Sisti
Above: David Warner

CAREER OPPORTUNITIES

(UNIVERSAL) Producers, John Hughes, A. Hunt Lowry; Executive Producer, Laura Lee; Director, Bryan Gordon; Screenplay, John Hughes; Photography, Don McAlpine; Designer, Paul Sylbert; Editors, Glenn Farr, Peck Prior; Music, Thomas Newman; Costumes, Betsy Cox; Casting, Pam Dixon; Associate Producers, Andi Capoziello, Cliff T.E. Roseman; Assistant Director, David Sosna; a Hughes Entertainment presentation; Dolby Stereo; Deluxe color; Rated PG-13; 84 minutes; March release

CAST

Jim Dodge	Frank Whaley
Josie McClellan	Jennifer Connelly
Nestor Pyle	Dermot Mulroney
Gil Kinney	Kieran Mulroney
Bud Dodge	John M. Jackson
Dotty Dodge	Jenny O'Hara
Roger Roy McClellan	Noble Willingham
Penny Dodge	Nada Despotovich
Cal Dodge	Reid Binion
Officer Don	Barry Corbin
Lorraine	Denise Galik
Bob Bosenbeck	Wilbur Fitzgerald
Dave Hockner	Dan Albright
Otis	Marc Clement
Boys	Andrew Winton, Andy Greenway, Ronreaco M. Lee
Gas Station Owner	Danny Nelson
Custodian	William Forsythe
Farmer in cafe	Lou Walker
Stock Boy	Benji Wilhoite
Girl in car	Heidi Meyer Gilbert
Boy in car	Troy M. Gilbert
Personnel Manager	John Candy

Top: Frank Whaley, Jennifer Connelly
Right: Connelly, Dermot Mulroney
© *Universal City Studios*

Jennifer Connelly, Frank Whaley

PARIS IS BURNING

(OFF-WHITE PRODUCTIONS) Producer/Director, Jennie Livingston; Co-Producer, Barry Swimar; Photography, Paul Gibson; Executive Producers, Davis Lacy, Nigel Finch; Editor, Jonathan Oppenheim; Associate Producers, Claire Goodman, Meg McLagan; Color; Not rated; 78 minutes; March release

CAST

Carmen and Brooke, Andre Christian, Dorian Corey, Paris Dupree, Pepper Labeija, Junior Labeija, Willi Ninja, Sandy Ninja, Kim Pendavis, Freddie Pendavis, Sol Pendavis, Avis Pendavis, Octavia Saint Laurent, Stevie Saint Laurent, Angie Xtravaganza, Bianca Xtravaganza, Danny Xtravaganza, David Xtravaganza, David Ian Xtravaganza, David The Father Xtravaganza, Venus Xtravaganza, and All of the Legendary Children and Upcoming Legends

Paris Is Burning "House" (also above)
© *Off-White Prods.*

THE FIVE HEARTBEATS

(20th CENTURY FOX) Producer, Loretha C. Jones; Executive Producer/Director, Robert Townsend; Co-Producer, Nancy Israel; Screenplay, Robert Townsend, Keenan Ivory Wayans; Photography, Bill Dill; Designer, Wynn Thomas; Music, Stanley Clarke; Supervising Music Producers, Steve Tyrell, George Duke; Editor, John Carter; Costumes, Ruthe Carter; Casting, Jaki Brown; Choreography, Michael Peters; Assistant Director, Richard A. Wells; Associate Producer, Christina Schmidlin; Dolby Stereo; Deluxe color; Rated R; 121 minutes; March release

CAST

Donald "Duck" Matthews	Robert Townsend
Eddie King, Jr.	Michael Wright
James Thomas "J.T." Matthews	Leon
Terrence "Dresser" Williams	Harry J. Lennix
Anthony "Choirboy" Stone	Tico Wells
Eleanor Potter	Diahann Carroll
Sarge	Harold Nicholas
Duck's Baby Sister	Tressa Thomas
Michael "Flash" Turner	John Canada Terrell
Jimmy Potter	Chuck Patterson
Big Red	Hawthorne James
Bird	Roy Fegan
Baby Doll	Troy Beyer
Tanya Sawyer	Carla Brothers
Rose	Deborah Lacey
Brenda	Theresa Randle
Wild Rudy	John Witherspoon
Sydney Todd	Anne-Marie Johnson
Marcia Sayles	Lisa Mende
Leon	Bobby McGee
Lester	Don Barnes
Monroe	O.L. Duke
Bobby Cassanova	Lamont Johnson
Mr. Matthews	Arnold Johnson
Mrs. Matthews	Veronica Redd
Pastor Stone	David McKnight
Myra Stone	Phyllis Applegate
Mr. King	Paul Benjamin
Mrs. King	Marilyn Coleman
Phil Shumway	Harris Peet
Cookie	Kasi Lemmons
Sandra Tillman	Monique Mannen
The Crystals	Suzanne Suter, Gigi Bolden, Kathleen Mitchell
The Ebony Sparks	Ron Jaxson, Recoe Walker, Wayne "Crescendo" Ward
The Midnight Falcons	Gregory "Popeye" Alexander, Bob Mardis, Jimmy Woodward
The Five Horsemen	Brian Bradley, Mike Conn, Barry Diamond, Carl Edwards, Joey Gaynor, Roger Rose
Big Red's Guys	James Anderson, Freddie Asparagus, Randy "Roughhouse" Harris, Al Simon
Matthew's Kids	Tammy Townsend, Shannon Chambers, Devin C. Huff, Lakisha Luke, Jeannel Phillips White, Kamar Phillips White, Brandon Wright
Theater Security	Christopher Bradley, Aaron J. Galang
Speakeasy Guy	Harry Stanback
Speakeasy Girl	Tiffanique Webb
David Green	Eugene Glazer
Buddy Lewis	Timmie Rogers
Jimmy's Doorman	Craig Eisner

and Tommy Redmond Hicks (Pastor Blake), David Drummond, Griff Ruggles (Policemen), Joel Weiss (St. George Hotel Doorman), Regina McLeod (Jackie), Shanel Cason (J.T.'s Little Girl), Jimmy Jackson (Little Duck), Alexis Johnson (Little Girl #1), John Pittman, Vince Isaac (Hitmen), Ron Smith, Frank Fontaine (Poker Players), Donnie Simpson (Himself)

Top: Michael Wright, Leon, Robert Townsend, Harry J. Lennix, Tico Wells
Below: Diahann Carroll, Chuck Patterson
© *Twentieth Century Fox*

Leon, Robert Townsend, Tico Wells, Harry J. Lennix, Michael Wright
Above: Tressa Thomas, Townsend

35

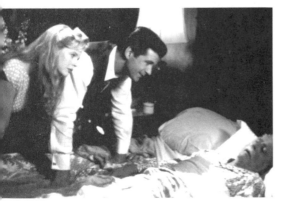

THE MARRYING MAN

(HOLLYWOOD PICTURES) Producer, David Permut; Co-Producer, David Streit; Director, Jerry Rees; Screenplay, Neil Simon; Photography, Donald E. Thorin; Designer, William F. Matthews; Costumes, Ruth Myers; Editor, Michael Jablow; Music, David Newman; Casting, Ronnie Yeskel; Associate Producer, Donald Kreiss; Choreographer, Jeffrey Hornaday; Assistant Director, David Householter; Songs performed by Kim Basinger; Presented in association with Silver Screen Partners IV and Odyssey Entertainment Ltd.; Distributed by Buena Vista Pictures; Dolby Stereo; Technicolor; Rated R; 115 minutes; April release

CAST

Vicki Anderson	Kim Basinger
Charley Pearl	Alec Baldwin
Lew Horner	Robert Loggia
Adele Horner	Elisabeth Shue
Bugsy Siegel	Armand Assante
Phil Golden	Paul Reiser
Sammy Fine	Fisher Stevens
Tony Madden	Peter Dobson
George Bouchet	Steve Hytner
Gus	Jeremy Roberts
Dante	Big John Studd
Sam	Tony Longo
Andy	Tom Milanovich
Woody	Tim Hauser
Cab Driver	Carey Eidel
Sheila	Marla Heasley
Sherry	Karen Medak
Arlene	Rebecca Staab
Dee	Melissa Behr
Butler	Paul Collins
Gas Attendant	Dave Florek
Bartender	Geof Prysirr
Bugsy's Blonde	Teresa Gilmore-Capps
Justice #1	Alan Mandell
Woo Ling	Elly Enriquez
Announcer/Manager	Joe Guzaldo
Nurse	Shanti Khan
Charley's Father	Clarke Gordon
Gwen	Gretchen Wyler
Bobbie	Susan Kellerman
Emma	Kathryn Lang
Liz	Janni Brenn
Waiter	Joe Bellan
Justice #3	Don Keefer
Maitre D'	Jules I. Epstein
Grace	Robin Frates
Louise	Kristen Cloke

**Top: Kim Basinger, Alec Baldwin, Clarke Gordon
Below: Armand Assante, Baldwin, Basinger
Left: Elisabeth Shue, Baldwin**
© *Hollywood Pictures*

Elisabeth Shue, Alec Baldwin, Robert Loggia

Fisher Stevens, Kim Basinger, Alec Baldwin,
Peter Dobson, Paul Reiser

POISON

(ZEITGEIST FILMS) Producer/Assistant Director, Christine Vachon; Director/Screenplay, Todd Haynes; Photography, Maryse Alberti; Black and white Camerawork, Barry Ellsworth; Designer, Sarah Stollman; Costumes, Jessica Haston; Music, James Bennett; Editors, James Lyons, Todd Haynes; Executive Producers, James Schamus, Brian Greenbaum; Casting, Andrew Harpending, Kim Ainouz, Laura Barnett, John Kelly; a Bronze Eye production; Color/Black and white; Not rated; 85 minutes; April release

CAST

Hero

Edith Meeks (Felicia Beacon), Millie White (Millie Sklar), Buck Smith (Gregory Lazar), Anne Giotta (Evelyn McAlpert), Lydia Lafleur (Sylvia Manning), Ian Nemser (Sean White), Rob LaBelle (Jay Wete), Evan Dunsky (Dr. MacArthur), Marina Lutz (Hazel Lamprecht), Barry Cassidy (Officer Rilt), Richard Anthony (Edward Comacho), Angela M. Schreiber (Florence Giddens), Justin Silverstein (Jake), Chris Singh (Chris), Edward Allen (Fred Beacon), Carlos Jiminez (Jose)

Horror

Larry Maxwell (Dr. Graves), Susan Norman (Nancy Olsen), Al Quagliata (Deputy Hansen), Michelle Sullivan (Prostitute), Parlan McGaw (Newscaster), Frank O'Donnell (Old Doctor), Joe Dietl (Man in the alley), Melissa Brown (Woman in the alley), Don Damico (Doctor 1, Cop 2), Charles Cavalier (Cop 1), Kyle de Camp, Aimee Scheff (Neighbors), Jessica, Lorraine Traverson (Nurses), Phil W. Petrie, John Nadeau (Doctors), Jim Cagnard (Bartender), Lauren Zalaznick (Waitress), Chris Henricks (Sleazy Man), Leah Mullen, Elyse Steinberg (Little Girls), Bruce Cook (Dr. Stick), Andrew Bishop (Child's Hands), Tom McCullough, Chava Tiger (Townspeople), Richard Hansen (Narrator)

Homo

Scott Renderer (John Broom), James Lyons (Jack Bolton), John R. Lombardi (Rass), Tony Pemberton (Young Broom), Andrew Harpending (Young Bolton), Tony Gigante (Inspector), Douglas F. Gibson (Van Roven), Damien Garcia (Chanci), Les Simpson (Miss Tim), Joey Grant (Jamoke), Gary Ray (Canon), David Danford (Basco), Jason Bauer (Doran), Ken Schatz (Preacher), Maurice Clapisson, Matthew Ebert (Guards), Marie-Francoise Vachon (Foster Mother), Michael Silverman (Foster Father), Shawn Wilson (Broom, age 6), Nino Bau, Wayne Compton, Raymond Dragen, John Duffy, John McGhee, Michael Miranda, Anthony Rubustillo, Jonathan Smit, Oscar Trevez (Fontenal Inmates), Gideon Joslyn Brown, John Connolly, Tom Cross, Eric Cubano, Dani Michaeli (Baton Inmates)

Joe Dietl, Melissa Brown
Above: James Lyons, Scott Renderer
© *Zeitgeist Films*

CHAMELEON STREET

(NORTHERN ARTS ENTERTAINMENT) Producer, Dan Lawton; Executive Producers, Helen B. Harris, Hobart W. Harris; Director/Screenplay, Wendell B. Harris, Jr.; Photography, Daniel S. Noga; Art Director, Tim Alvaro; Music, Peter S. Moore; Editor, Matthew Mallinson; Assistant Director, Michael Sowie; a Prismatic One, Inc. in association with Filmworld International Productions, Inc. presentation; Color; Rated R; 98 minutes; April release

CAST

William Douglas Street	Wendell B Harris, Jr.
Gabrielle	Angela Leslie
Tatiana	Amina Fakir
Herself	Paula McGee
Dr. Hand	Richard David Kiley, Jr.
Smooth	Alfred Bruce Bradley
Dr. Hardy	Gary Irwin
Melissa	Colette Haywood
Curtis	Anthony Ennis
Eugene Raymond	Henry Watkins
Darlene Street	Anita Gordon
Aldo Jerry Lewis Falco	Dan Lawton
Dimitri Muganias	Robespiere
Themselves	Mayor Coleman Young, Dave Barber

THE *Dave Barber* SHOW

Dave Barber, Wendell B. Harris, Jr. 37
© *Northern Arts*

IMPROMPTU

(HEMDALE) Producers, Stuart Oken, Daniel A. Sherkow; Executive Producer, Jean Nachbaur; Director, James Lapine; Screenplay, Sarah Kernochan; Photography, Bruno De Keyzer; Costumes, Jenny Beavan;Editor, Michael Ellis; Art Director, Gerard Daoudal; Music Supervisor, John Strauss; Assistant Director, Bernard Seitz; a Sovereign Pictures presentation, in association with Governor Prods. and Les Films Ariane; Dolby Stereo; Eclair color; Rated PG-13; 109 minutes; April release

CAST

George Sand	Judy Davis
Frederic Chopin	Hugh Grant
Alfred de Musset	Mandy Patinkin
Marie d'Agoult	Bernadette Peters
Franz Liszt	Julian Sands
Eugene Delacroix	Ralph Brown
Felicien Mallefille	Georges Corraface
Duke d'Antan	Anton Rodgers
Duchess d'Antan	Emma Thompson
George Sand's Mother	Anna Massey
Inn Keeper's Wife	Jezabelle Amato
Chopin's Valet	Claude Berthy
Maurice	David Birkin
Doctor	Georges Bruce
Priest	Andre Chaumeau
Inn Keeper	Jean-Michel Dagory
Philosopher	Nicholas Hawtrey
Princess	Isabelle Guiard
Butler	Fernand Guiot
Sophie	Sylvie Herbert
Local Doctor	Francois Lalande
Editor	Ian Marshall De Garnier
Ursule	Annette Milsom
Didiar	Nimer Rashed
Buloz	John Savident
Clerk	Stuart Seide
Aurore	Lucy Speed
Baroness Laginsky	Elizabeth Spriggs
Solange	Fiona Vincente

Top: Emma Thompson; Anton Rodgers Below: Judy Davis, Hugh Grant Right: Anna Massey; Ralph Brown
© *Hemdale Film Corp.*

Mandy Patinkin, Judy Davis, Julian Sands
Hugh Grant, Bernadette Peters

Hugh Grant, Bernadette Peters

OUT FOR JUSTICE

(WARNER BROS.) Producers, Steven Seagal, Arnold Kopelson; Co-Producer, Peter MacGregor-Scott; Director, John Flynn; Screenplay, David Lee Henry; Executive Producer, Julius R. Nasso; Photography, Ric Waite; Designer, Gene Rudolf; Music, David Michael Frank; Editors, Robert A. Ferretti, Donald Brochu; Costumes, Richard Bruno; Associate Producer, Jacqueline George; Casting, Pamela Basker, Csa & Sue Swan; Assistant Director, Jerry Ziesmer; Stunts, Conrad Palmisano; Dolby Stereo; Panavision; Technicolor; Rated R; 91 minutes; April release

CAST

Gino Felino	Steven Seagal
Richie Madano	William Forsythe
Ronny Donziger	Jerry Orbach
Vicky Felino	Jo Champa
Laurie Lupo	Shareen Mitchell
Frankie	Sal Richards
Patti Madano	Gina Gershon
Bobby Arms	Jay Acovone
Joey Dogs	Nicky Corello
Buchi	Robert Lasardo
King	John Toles-Bey
Bobby Lupo	Joe Spataro
Cops	Ron Brumbelow, Jack Cipolla, Charles Daniel, John Senger, Steve Taylor
Tony Felino	Julius Nasso, Jr.
Woman in car	Diane Peterson
Uniform Cops	Edward Deacy, Vincent Nasso
Frankie's Bodyguard	Jerry Strivelli
Frankie's Guys	Jerome Alvarado, David Basulto, Danny Eglowitz, Frank Faggella, Jr.
Umbrella Man	Serafino Tomasetti
Sammy	Gianni Russo
Don Vittorio	Ron Maccone
Vittorio's Bodyguard	Alan Bialor
Del Gulfo Patron	Frank Faggella, Sr.
Hooker	Willie Anne Gissendanner
Picalino	George Vallejo
Paulie	Carl Ciarfalio
Butcher	Edward Korn
Store Owner	Benedetto Bongiorno
Sales Clerk	Larry Romano
Vinnie Madano	Anthony De Sando
Bennie the Book	Jerry Ciauri
Mr. Madano	Dominic Chianese
Mrs. Madano	Vera Lockwood
Rica	Julianna Margulies
Elena	Christina Solis
Tattoos	Sonny Hurst
Sticks	Daniel Inosanto
Phone Booth Man	Michael Pecina
Sammy's Girlfriend	Marie Todd
Bartender	Nick Dimitri
Go-Go Dancers	Afifi, Cameron
Hookers	Erin Weidner Ashley, Sandy Hernandez, Meadow Spadafino
Boy in alley	John Leguizamo
Chas the Chair	Jorge L. Gil
Chop Shop Foreman	Craig Pinkard
Bouncer	Perry Wayne
Club Bodyguard	Jack Vecchio
Waiter	Charles Guardino
Terry Malloy	Shannon Whirry
Hector	Raymond Cruz
Transvestite	Sandy Allison
Vittorio's Men	Salvatore Bonanno, Vincent Cucci, Jr., Philip Rusty Mignano, Salvatore Sonnie Mignano
Vermeer	Joe Lala
Roxanne Ford	Julie Strain
O'Kelly	Thomas Duffy
Station Wagon Tough Guy	Sonny Zito

Top: Steven Seagal
Below: Seagal, Julius Nasso Jr., Jo Champa
© *Warner Bros. Inc.*

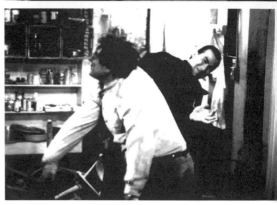

William Forsythe, Steven Seagal   39

MORTAL THOUGHTS

(COLUMBIA) Producers, John Fiedler, Mark Tarlov; Executive Producers, Taylor Hackford, Stuart Benjamin; Director, Alan Rudolph; Screenplay, William Reilly, Claude Kerven; Co-Producer, Demi Moore; Photography, Elliot Davis; Editor, Tom Walls; Line Producer, Joe Caracciolo, Jr.; Music, Mark Isham; Designer, Howard Cummings; Costumes, Hope Hanafin; Casting, Donna Isaacson, John Lyons; Assistant Director, Robert Girolami; a New Visions Entertainment Production/a Polar Entertainment Corporation Production in association with Rufglen Films; Dolby Stereo; Deluxe color; Rated R; 104 minutes; April release

CAST

Cynthia Kellogg	Demi Moore
Joyce Urbanski	Glenne Headly
James Urbanski	Bruce Willis
Arthur Kellogg	John Pankow
Det. John Woods	Harvey Keitel
Linda Nealon	Billie Neal
Dominic Marino	Frank Vincent
Gloria Urbanski	Karen Shallo
Jeanette Marino	Crystal Field
Aunt Rita	Maryanne Leone
Usher	Marc Tantillo
Pat (Cynthia's Mom)	Doris McCarthy
Joey Urbanski	Christopher Scotellaro
Band Leader	Ron J. Amodea
Yuri	Leonid Merzon
Cookie	Kelly Cinnante
Irish Kids	Christopher Peacock, Bruce Smolanoff
Police Sgt.	Elain Graham
Det. Seltzer	Thomas Quinn
Cynthia's Baby	Brandon & Richard Messemer
Sydney Levitt	Larry Attile
Krishna Kolhatkar	Roger Shamas
Lauren (Cynthia's Sister)	Star Jasper
Jennifer Kellogg (3 yrs.)	Lindsay Rodio
Maria Urbanski	Julie Garfield
Detective	Edward Chip Rogers
Mr. Urbanski	David A. Willis
Cop	James Pecora
Customer in salon	Elaine Eldridge
Tina	Kimberly Comprix
Candy	Anna Marie Wieder

Top: Glenne Headly, Demi Moore Below: Bruce Willis, Headly Left: Harvey Keitel, Moore, Billie Neal
© *Columbia Pictures Industries*

Glenne Headly, Demi Moore

Demi Moore, Bruce Willis, Glenne Headly

TALENT FOR THE GAME

(PARAMOUNT) Producer, Martin Elfand; Executive Producer, David Wisnievitz; Director, Robert M. Young; Screenplay, David Himmelstein, Tom Donnelly, Larry Ferguson; Photography, Curtis Clark; Designer, Jeffrey Howard; Editor, Arthur Coburn; Music, David Newman; Costumes, Erica Edell Phillips; Dolby Stereo; Technicolor; Rated PG; 91 minutes; April release

CAST

Virgil Sweet	Edward James Olmos
Bobbie Henderson	Lorraine Bracco
Sammy Bodeen	Jeff Corbett
Tim Weaver	Jamey Sheridan
Gil Lawrence	Terry Kinney
Rev. Bodeen	Tom Bower
Rachel Bodeen	Janet Carroll
Fred	Felton Perry
Paul	Thomas Ryan
Burns	Daniel A. Haro
Dick Bortner	Murphy Sua
Toby Curry	David Riley
Ray Coffey	James Keane
Rudy Coffey	Zachary I. Young
Greg Rossi	Dennis Boutsikaris

and Philip M. Pote (Gil Murphy), Ken Medlock (Scooter Eaton), Tom La Grua (Frank Carbo), Alan J. Krick, Henry Ford Robinson (Umpires), Bill Higham (Bob Morgan), Todd Cantamessa (Lester), Kent Wellborn, Mark David Budaska (Coaches), Karl Grey (Dwayne Seybolt), Tamara Lynne Thompson (Martha Jo Seybolt), Harold Gower (Grandpa Seybolt), Adam Stellmon (Boy), Kathy Gecas (Girl), John Yajko (Riggs), Caroline Barclay (Blonde Secretary), Jeff Barnett Howard (William), Candy Trabucco (Bobbie's Assistant), Leslie Bevis (Marla), Bobby Tolan, Derrel Thomas, Lenny Randle, Barry Moss, Frank Mendoza, John E. Coleman, Danny Davidsmeier ("Angel" Baseball Players)

Lorraine Bracco, Edward James Olmos
Above: Jeff Corbett, Olmos
© *Paramount Pictures*

THOUSAND PIECES OF GOLD

(GREYCAT FILMS) Producers, Nancy Kelly, Kenji Yamamoto; Co-Producer, Sarah Green; Director, Nancy Kelly; Executive Producers, Lindsay Law, Sidney Kantor, John Sham; Associate Producer, Rachel Lyon; Screenplay, Anne Makepeace; Photography, Bobby Bukowski; Designer, Dan Bishop; Music, Gary Remal Malkin; Assistant Director, Eric Heffron; Costumes, Lydia Tanji; an American Playhouse Theatrical Films and Maverick Films International, Ltd. presentation of a Kelly/Yamamoto production in association with Film Four International; Color; Not rated; 105 minutes; April release

CAST

Lalu/Polly	Rosalind Chao
Charlie	Chris Cooper
Hong King	Michael Paul Chan
Jim	Dennis Dun
Jonas	Jimmie F. Skaggs
Miles	Will Oldham
Ohio	David Hayward
Berthe	Beth Broderick
Li Ping	Kim Chan
Shun Lee	Evan Kim
Ah Ling	Freda Foh Shen
Francoise	Mary Matvy
Parker	Albert J. Kalanick
Li Yuan	Mary Lee
Chen	Jianli Zhang
John Span	Ron Dorn
Lung On	George Kee Cheung

Dennis Dun, Rosalind Chao
Above: Chao, Chris Cooper
© *Filmcat Inc.*

41

Sylvester Stallone, Tim Curry
Top Right: Peter Riegert, Stallone, Chazz Palminteri
Right: Stallone, Don Ameche, Ornella Muti
© *Touchstone Pictures*

OSCAR

(TOUCHSTONE) Producer, Leslie Belzberg; Director, John Landis; Screenplay, Michael Barrie, Jim Mulholland; Based on the play by Claude Magnier; Executive Producers, Alex Ponti, Joseph C. Vecchio; Photography, Mac Ahlberg; Designer, Bill Kenney; Editor, Dale Beldin; Costumes, Deborah Nadoolman; Music, Elmer Bernstein; "Largo Al Factotum (from *Il Barbiere di Siviglia*)" by Gioacchino Rossini/performed by Earle Patriarco; Casting, Jackie Burch; Assistant Director, Frank Capra III; Associate Producer, Tony Munafo; Main Title Animator, David Allen Productions; Presented in association with Silver Screen Partners IV; Distributed by Buena Vista Pictures; Dolby Stereo; Technicolor; Rated PG; 109 minutes; April release

CAST

Aldo	Peter Riegert
Connie	Chazz Palminteri
Ace	Joey Travolta
Schemer	Paul Greco
Angelo "Snaps" Provolone	Sylvester Stallone
Knucky	Richard Foronjy
Aunt Rosa	Yvonne DeCarlo
Father Clemente	Don Ameche
Papa Eduardo	Kirk Douglas
Vendetti	Richard Romanus
Manicurist	Arleen Sorkin
Five Spot Charlie	Eddie Bracken
Frankie the Roach	Tony Munafo
Officer Keough	Robert Lesser
Officer Quinn	Art LaFleur
Lieutenant Toomey	Kurtwood Smith
Little Anthony Rossano, C.P.A.	Vincent Spano
Nora	Joycelyn O'Brien
Lisa Provolone	Marisa Tomei
Luigi Finucci	Martin Ferrero
Guido Finucci	Harry Shearer
Overton	William Atherton
Milhous	Mark Metcalf
Whitney Kirkwood	Ken Howard
Van Leland	Sam Chew, Jr.
Theresa	Elizabeth Barondes
Sofia Provolone	Ornella Muti
Vendetti Hood	Sal Vecchio
Dr. Thornton Poole	Tim Curry
Cab Driver	Danny Goldstine
Underwood Chauffeur	Kai Wulff
Roxanne	Linda Gray
Reporters	Marshall Bell, Tom Grant, Louis D'Alto
Vendetti's Driver	Rick Avery
Oscar	Jim Mullholland

Martin Ferrero, Sylvester Stallone, Harry Shearer
Above: Tim Curry, Marisa Tomei

TOY SOLDIERS

(TRI-STAR) Producers, Jack E. Freedman, Wayne S. Williams, Patricia Herskovic; Executive Producers, Mark Burg, Chris Zarpas; Director, Daniel Petrie, Jr.; Screenplay, Daniel Petrie, Jr., David Koepp; Based on the novel by William P. Kennedy; Photography, Thomas Burstyn; Designer, Chester Kaczenski; Editor, Michael Kahn; Costumes, Betsy Cox; Music, Robert Folk; Casting, Caro Jones; Co-Producers, Donald C. Klune, Nicholas Hassitt; Assistant Directors, Doug Metzger, Jerry L. Ballew; Presented in association with Island World; Dolby Stereo; Technicolor; Rated R; 112 minutes; April release

CAST

Billy Tepper	Sean Astin
Joey Trotta	Wil Wheaton
Snuffy Bradberry	Keith Coogan
Luis Cali	Andrew Divoff
General Kramer	R. Lee Ermey
Deputy Director Brown	Mason Adams
Headmaster Dr. Gould	Denholm Elliott
Dean Edward Parker	Louis Gossett, Jr.
Ricardo Montoya	George Perez
Hank Giles	T.E. Russell
Derek	Shawn Phelan
Jack Thorpe	Michael Champion
Jennifer	Tracy Brooks Swope
HRT Commander	Max Maxwell
Agent Grimes	Joe Inscoe
Ben	Jerry Lyden
Colombian Judge	Rene Gatica
Ted	Jeremiah McLerran
Enrique Cali	Jesse Doran
Joey's Father	Jerry Orbach
Sheriff	Stan Kelly
Press Secretary	Carol Shoemaker
Nicholas Josephson	D. Adam Bonifant
Guber	Mark Retz
Brave Student	Paul Sincoff
Frank the Guard	Richard Travis
Woman in pink	Janet Orcutt
"Phil" Donoghue	Knowl Johnson
Carlos	Rafael Robledo
Ruiz	Thomas R. Trigo
Jorge	Jerry Valdez

and Russell C. Gagnon (Guard), Richard Warner (Deputy Marshall), Christopher Northup (Camouflaged Soldier), Joe Banks (Brown's Aide), Rick Warner (FBI SAC), Sarah Stavrou (Agent at console), David Norris (Concerned Student), Tod Bonifant, Mike Rogerson, Grady Weatherford (Students), Darrell Elmore, Dennis Hunsinger (Snipers), Cliff McLaughlin, Brian Williams (Commandos), Jeff Ramsey, Nick Dimitri (Border Patrol Officers), Mark Brutsche, Cynthia Hayden, Denise Gordy, Michael Costello, Mimi Eisman, Lenny Steinline (Angry Parents), Lloyd Williams (Major), Jeremy Caplan, Roy Borden (Deputy Sheriffs), John Shaw (Cali's Lawyer)

Top: Wil Wheaton, Sean Astin
Below: Mason Adams, Louis Gossett Jr., R. Lee Ermey
Left: Andrew Divoff, Wheaton
© *Tri-Star Pictures*

Jeremiah McLerran, Shawn Phelan,
George Perez, T.E. Russell

Sean Astin, George Perez, Keith Coogan,
Wil Wheaton, T.E. Russell

43

A KISS BEFORE DYING

(**UNIVERSAL**) Producer, Robert Lawrence; Director/Screenplay, James Dearden; Based on the novel by Ira Levin; Executive Producer, Eric Fellner; Photography, Mike Southon; Designer, Jim Clay; Music, Howard Shore; Editor, Michael Bradsell; Costumes, Marit Allen; Casting, Billy Hopkins; Associate Producer, Chris Thompson; Assistant Director, Patrick Clayton; an Initial Film/Robert Lawrence production; Dolby Stereo; Technicolor; Rated R; 95 minutes; April release

CAST

Jonathan Corliss	Matt Dillon
Ellen/Dorothy Carlsson	Sean Young
Thor Carlsson	Max von Sydow
Mrs. Corliss	Diane Ladd
Dan Corelli	James Russo
Patricia Farren	Martha Gehman
Cathy	Joy Lee
Tommy Roussell	Ben Browder
Detective Michaelson	Sam Coppola
Landlady	Elzbieta Czyzewska
Terry Dieter	Jim Fyfe
Jay Faraday	Adam Horovitz
Mickey	Freddy Koehler
Mrs. Roussell	Leslie Lyles
Commissioner Mallet	Shane Rimmer
Young Jonathan	James Bonfanti
Lecturer	Sarah Keller
Shoe Saleslady	Lia Chang
Screaming Lady	Yvette Edelhart
Reporter	Lachelle Carl
Waitress	Briony Glassco
Dave	Brett Barth
Susie	Galaxy Craze
Chico	Rory Cochrane
Rose	Kristy Graves
Nurse	Billie Neal
Bellman	P. Jay Sidney
Elderly Woman	Lynn Frazen-Cohen
Mr. Roussell	Mark Potter
Receptionist	Nancy Herman

Top: Matt Dillon, Sean Young Right: Young, Dillon
© *Universal City Studios*

THE BALLAD OF THE SAD CAFE

(**ANGELIKA FILMS**) Producer, Ismail Merchant; Director, Simon Callow; Screenplay, Michael Hirst; Photography, Walter Lassally; Executive Producer, Paul Bradley; Designer, Bruno Santini; Music, Richard Robbins; Editor, Andrew Marcus; Costumes, Marianna Elliott; Casting, Shirley Rich; Associate Producer, Donald Rosenfeld; a Merchant Ivory production; Dolby Stereo; Color; Not rated; 100 minutes; April release

CAST

Miss Amelia	Vanessa Redgrave
Marvin Macy	Keith Carradine
Cousin Lymon	Cork Hubbert
Reverend Willin	Rod Steiger
Lawrence Taylor	Austin Pendleton
Mrs. Hale	Beth Dixon
Merlie Ryan	Lanny Flaherty
Stumpy MacPhail	Mert Hatfield
Henry Macy	Earl Hindman
Mrs. MacPhail	Anne Pitoniak

Keith Carradine, Vanessa Redgrave
© *Angelika Films*

A RAGE IN HARLEM

(MIRAMAX) Producers, Stephen Woolley, Kerry Boyle; Co-Producers, Forest Whitaker, John Nicolella; Executive Producers, Nik Powell, William Horberg, Terry Glinwood, Harvey Weinstein, Bob Weinstein; Director, Bill Duke; Screenplay, John Toles-Bey, Bobby Crawford; Based upon the novel by Chester Himes; Photography, Toyomichi Kurita; Designer, Steven Legler; Editor, Curtiss Clayton; Costumes, Nile Samples; Music, Elmer Bernstein; Casting, Aleta Chappelle; Assistant Director, Warren D. Gray; a Palace Presentation in association with Miramax Films of a Palace Woolley/Boyle production; Dolby Stereo; Deluxe color; Rated R; 115 minutes; May release

CAST

Jackson	Forest Whitaker
Goldy	Gregory Hines
Imabelle	Robin Givens
Big Kathy	Zakes Mokae
Easy Money	Danny Glover
Slim	Badja Djola
Jodie	John Toles-Bey
Hank	Ron Taylor
Coffin Ed	Stack Pierce
Grave Digger	George Wallace
Blind Man	Reynaldo Rey
Smitty	T.K. Carter
Louis	Wendell Pierce
Mr. Clay	Leonard Jackson
Mrs. Canfield	Helen Martin
Teena	Tyler Collins
Minna	Tasha O'Bryant
Claude X	Willard E. Pugh
Gus Parsons	Samm-Art Williams
Porter	Clebert Ford
Lester Bunton	John Seitz
Goon	William L. Schwarber
Sheriff	Jack Beatty
Bo	Arthur Burghardt
Domestics	Birdie M. Hale, Olivette Miller-Briggs
Clerk	Beatrice Winde
Rev. Gaines	John W. Hardy
Mourner	Anthonia Dotson
Junkie	Ernest Perry, Jr.
Bartender	James Spinks
Weasel	Cornelius Stafford
Skanky Whore	Tracy A. Taylor
Pug	Eugene Robinson, Jr.
Cop #1	Kipp Cochran
Jailer	James Copeland
Doorman	Jonathan Booker, Ph.D.
Henchman	Robert Woods, Jr.
Bus Driver	Kevin Ruthven
Himself	"Screamin'" Jay Hawkins

Top: Gregory Hines, Robin Givens Below: Forest Whitaker, Hines Left: Givens, Danny Glover
© *Miramax Films*

Badja Djola, John Toles-Bey, Robin Givens, Ron Taylor

Forest Whitaker, Robin Givens

ONE GOOD COP

(HOLLYWOOD PICTURES) Producer, Laurence Mark; Director/Screenplay, Heywood Gould; Executive Producer, Harry Colomby; Photography, Ralf Bode; Designer, Sandy Veneziano; Editor, Richard Marks; Costumes, Betsy Heimann; Music, David Foster, William Ross; Casting, Risa Bramon, Billy Hopkins, Heidi Levitt; Associate Producer/Unit Production Manager, Joan Bradshaw; Assistant Director, Marty Ewing; Presented in association with Silver Screen Partners IV; Distributed by Buena Vista Pictures; Dolby Stereo; Technicolor; Rated R; 107 minutes; May release

CAST

Artie Lewis	Michael Keaton
Rita Lewis	Rene Russo
Stevie Diroma	Anthony LaPaglia
Lt. Danny Quinn	Kevin Conway
Grace	Rachel Ticotin
Beniamino	Tony Plana
Felix	Benjamin Bratt
Cheryl Clark	Charlayne Woodard
Marian Diroma	Grace Johnston
Barbara Diroma	Rhea Silver-Smith
Carol Diroma	Blair Swanson
Oreste	Victor Rivers
Mickey Garrett	David Barry Gray
Raisa	Lisa Arrindell
Knudson	Rick Aiello
Walsh	Michael G. Hagerty
Capt. Schreiber	J.E. Freeman
Clifford	Kevin Corrigan
Mrs. Cristofaro	Penny Santon
Dr. Gelb	Doug Barron
Father Wills	Vondie Curtis-Hall
Mrs. Frazier	Vivien Straus
Mrs. Garrett	Brigitte Bako
Arthur Garrett	Danny Kramer
Henry Garrett	Tommy Kramer
Farrell	Thomas A. Carlin
Nun	Barbara Townsend
Technician	Frank DiElsi
Captain with megaphone	Ed Deacy
Robin	Alicia Brandt
Bride-To-Be	Maria Tirabassi
Older Shopper	Irene Brafstein
Mother at carnival	Patricia Gould
Martha	Benita André
Irene	Kristina Loggia
Eddie the Bartender	Marco DeLuca

and Keri Johnson (Teen in projects), Ross Leon (Young Man in elevator), DeForest Covan (Older Man), Cora Lee Day (Older Woman), George Kee Cheung (Waiter), Frank Ferrara (Burly Prisoner), Ralph Nieves (Beniamino Scout), Gary C. Smith (Robbery Victim), Joey Banks, Justin DeRosa, Thomas Rosales, Jr. (Beniamino Associates), Chad Randall, Myke Schwartz (Clifford Associates), Tierre Turner, Robby Robinson, Henry Kingi, Jr. (Hoods)

Top: Michael Keaton, Anthony LaPaglia Below: Rachel
Ticotin, Keaton Left: Keaton, Rene Russo
© *Hollywood Pictures Co.*

Michael Keaton, Victor Rivers,
Tony Plana, Rachel Ticotin

Grace Johnston, Michael Keaton, Blair Swanson

**Niki Harris, Madonna, Donna Delroy Top: Madonna
and Her Dancers** © *Miramax Films*

TRUTH OR DARE

(MIRAMAX) Producers, Jay Roewe, Tim Clawson; Director, Alek
Keshishian; Executive Producer, Madonna; Supervising Producers,
Sigurjon Sighvatsson, Steve Golin; Musical Sequences Editor, John
Murray; Editor, Barry Alexander Brown; Photography, Robert
Leacock, Doug Nichol, Christophe Lanzenberg, Marc Reshovsky,
Daniel Pearl, Toby Phillips; Choreographer/Co-Director, Vincent
Paterson; Propaganda Films/Boy Toy, Inc. productions; Dolby Stereo;
Black and white/Color; Rated R; 118 minutes; May release

WITH

Madonna; Donna Delroy, Niki Harris (Vocals/Dancers); Luis
Camacho, Oliver Crumes, Salim Gauwloos, Jose Guiterez, Kevin
Stea, Gabriel Trupin, Carlton Wilborn (Dancers); Sharon Gault
(Mama Make-Up); Joanne Gaire (Hair Stylist); and Warren Beatty,
Sandra Bernhard, Antonio Banderas, Pedro Almodovar, Christopher
Ciccione, Marty Ciccone, others

Madonna   47

Jimmy Smits, Ellen Barkin, Tony Roberts
Top Right: Barkin Right: Smits, Barkin
© *Cinema Plus L.P.*

SWITCH

(WARNER BROS.) Producer, Tony Adams; Director/Screenplay, Blake Edwards; Photography, Dick Bush; Designer, Rodger Maus; Costumes, Ellen Mirojnick; Music, Henry Mancini; Song: "Both Sides Now" by Joni Mitchell/performed by Paul Young & Clannad; Editor, Robert Pergament; Casting, Gail Levin, Lauren Lloyd; Associate Producer, Trish Caroselli Rintels; Presented by HBO in association with Cinema Plus, L.P.; Dolby Stereo; Panavision; Technicolor; Rated R; 102 minutes; May release

CAST

Amanda Brooks	Ellen Barkin
Walter Stone	Jimmy Smits
Margo Brofman	JoBeth Williams
Sheila Faxton	Lorraine Bracco
Arnold Friedkin	Tony Roberts
Steve Brooks	Perry King
The Devil	Bruce Martyn Payne
Liz	Lysette Anthony
Felicia	Victoria Mahoney
Higgins	Basil Hoffman
Steve's Secretary	Catherine Keener
Dan Jones	Kevin Kilner
Attorney Caldwell	David Wohl
Lt. Laster	James Harper
Sgt. Phillips	John Lafayette
The Psychic	Jim J. Bullock
Mrs. Wetherspoon	Diana Chesney
Mac the Guard	Joe Flood
Fur Protester	Emma Walton
Al the Guard	Louis Eppolito
Mae the Maid	Yvette Freeman
Duke	Dennis Paladino
Dream Girl	Tea Leoni
Wiseguy at Duke's	Rick Aiello
Barber	F. William Parker
Minister	Ben Hartigan
Doctor	David Gale
Arnold's Secretary	Jessie Jones
Judge Harcrow	Savant Tanney

and Virginia Morris (Asst. D.A.), Robert Clotworthy (Bailiff), Patricia Clipper (Girl in elevator), Robert Elias (Photographer), Michelle Wong (Photo Assistant), Marti Muller (Woman Client), Mindy Lawson, Kimberly Oja, Teri Gold (F & B Models), Lily Mariye (Nurse), William Shockley, Jennie Nauman, Annette Quinn, Dena Burton, Michelle Reese (Party Guests), Alana Silvani, Jacqulyn Moen (Girls at City Grille), Karen Medak (Saleswoman), Tracy Lambert, Taunie Vrenon (Store Models), Michael Badalucco (Hard Hat), Gregory Barnett, Fred Lerner (Thugs at Duke's), Jay R. Goldenberg (Sardi's Maitre d'), Faith Minton (Nancy the Bouncer), Rebecca Wood, Linda Doná (Gay Club Patrons), Helena Apothaker (Gay Club Waitress), Elena Statheros (Girl at Aiko's), Jim Lovelett (Jogger), Barbara Schillaci, Robert Towers, Tony Genaro (Mental Patients), Ross Brittain (Morning D.J.), Richard Provost (Voice of God), Linda Gary (Voice of God), Molly Okuneff (Little Girl)

Lysette Anthony, JoBeth Williams, Victoria Mahoney
Above: Lorraine Bracco

STONE COLD

(COLUMBIA) Producer, Yoram Ben Ami; Executive Producers, Walter Doniger, Gary Wichard; Director, Craig R. Baxley; Screenplay, Walter Doniger; Co-Producers, Andrew D.T. Pfeffer, Nick Grillo; Photography, Alexander Gruszynski; Designers, John Mansbridge, Richard Johnson; Editor, Mark Helfrich; Music, Sylvester Levay; Stunts, Paul Baxley; Associate Producer, Udi Nedivi; Assistant Director, Benjamin Rosenberg; a Stone Group Pictures presentation of a Mace Neufeld/Yoram Ben Ami/Walter Doniger production; Dolby Stereo; Deluxe color; Rated R; 90 minutes; May release

CAST

Joe Huff (John Stone)	Brian Bosworth
Chains	Lance Henriksen
Ice	William Forsythe
Nancy	Arabella Holzbog
Lance	Sam McMurray
Cunningham	Richard Gant
Bolivian	Paulo Tocha
Brent Whipperton	David Tress
Gut	Evan James
Tool	Tony Pierce
Trouble	Billy Million
Mudfish	Robert Winley
A.W.O.L.	Gregory Scott Cummins
Greek	Demetre Phillips
Poker	Magic Schwartz
Marie	Brenda Klemme
Vitamin	Paul M. Lane
Leroy	Gene Hartline
Hooter	John Hateley
Pool Playing Chick	Tracy Hutchinson
Ice's Girl	Jennifer Synnott
One Eye	Rick L. Birchfield
Big John	John R. Grantham
Smokey	Alfred Stepputat
Six Pack	Thomas F. Ibarra
Martinez	Michael Wren
Judge Townsend	Bill Gratton

and Jerry Colker (Market Psycho), Michael James (Larry), David Eisley (Charlie), Ron Recasner (Police Officer), Charles Stranski (Police Lieutenant), Rene O'Connor (Tinselteeth), Maggie Egan (Mother), Benjamin Rosenberg (Domicci), Frank Ferrara, Troy Brown (Henchmen), Robert Prentiss, Kevin Page (Mobsters), Folkert Schmidt, Matt D. Johnston (Guardsmen), Josie Dapar (Madame Lu), Boyce Holleman (County Judge), Nick Demitri, Dave Efron (Truckers), Tom Magee (Mountain), Janis Flax (Nurse), John Terrence (Minister), Laura Albert (Joe's Girlfriend), Karen Abernathy (News Anchor), Illana Shoshan (Sharon)

Top: Brian Bosworth Below: Bosworth, Arabella Holzbog
© *Columbia Pictures Industries*

Brian Bosworth

Lance Henriksen, Brian Bosworth

Bill Murray, Richard Dreyfuss, Charlie Korsmo,
Julie Hagerty, Kathryn Erbe
Top Left: Dreyfuss, Murray (also left)
© *Touchstone Pictures*

WHAT ABOUT BOB?

(TOUCHSTONE) Producer, Laura Ziskin; Co-Producer, Bernard Williams; Director, Frank Oz; Screenplay, Tom Schulman; Story, Alvin Sargent, Laura Ziskin; Photography, Michael Ballhaus; Designer, Les Dilley; Editor, Anne V. Coates; Costumes, Bernie Pollack; Music, Miles Goodman; Casting, Glenn Daniels; Assistant Director, James W. Skotchdopole; Presented in association with Touchwood Pacific Partners I; Distributed by Buena Vista Pictures; Dolby Stereo; Technicolor; Rated PG; 97 minutes; May release

CAST

Bob Wiley	Bill Murray
Dr. Leo Marvin	Richard Dreyfuss
Fay Marvin	Julie Hagerty
Siggy Marvin	Charlie Korsmo
Anna Marvin	Kathryn Erbe
Mr. Guttman	Tom Aldredge
Mrs. Guttman	Susan Willis
Phil	Roger Bowen
Lily	Fran Brill
Carswell Fensterwald	Brian Reddy
Dr. Tomsky	Doris Belack
Marie Grady	Melinda Mullins
Betty (Switchboard Operator)	Marcella Lowery
Gwen (Switchboard Operator)	Margot Welch
Claire (Dr. Marvin's Secretary)	Barbara Andres
Prostitute	Aida Torturro
Crazy Man in New York street	Stuart Rudin
Lobby Doorman	Cortez Nance, Jr.
Bus Driver	Lori Tan Chinn
Motorcycle Cop	Dennis R. Scott
Nursing Home Guard	Charles Thomas Baxter
Nursing Home Attendant	Donald J. Lee, Jr.
Howie (Director)	Reg E. Cathey
Lennie (Producer)	Tom Stechschulte
TV Crew Member	Russell Bobbitt
Minister	Richard Fancy
Herself	Joan Lunden

STRAIGHT OUT OF BROOKLYN

(SAMUEL GOLDWYN CO.) Producer/Director/Screenplay, Matty Rich; Executive Producers, Lindsay Law, Ira Deutchman; Associate Producer, Allen Black; Photography, John Rosnell; Editor, Jack Haigis; Music, Harold Wheeler; Casting, Dorise Black, Shirley Matthews; produced in association with American Playhouse ; TVC Precision color; Rated R; 91 minutes; May release

CAST

Ray Brown	George T. Odom
Frankie Brown	Ann D. Sanders
Dennis Brown	Lawrence Gilliard, Jr.
Carolyn Brown	Barbara Sanon
Shirley	Reana E. Drummond
Larry	Matty Rich
Kevin	Mark Malone
Luther	Ali Shahid Abdul Wahha
Saledene	Joseph A. Thomas
James	James McFadden
Ms. Walker	Dorise Black
Skeet	Robert N. Nash
Sarah	Fran Sperling
Gas Station Customer	Billy R.
Gas Station Manager	Joseph Pillonia
Uncle Scotty	Booker T. Matthews
Bartender	J.R. Hill
Man in grocery store	Walter Meade
Woman in grocery store	Soraya Hyppolite
Luther's Girlfriend	Krystal Davis
Grocery Clerk	David Belgrave
Secretary in employment office	Albertha Moody
Men in bar	William Erskine, James Mayes
Voice-over	Ulysses Rivers

© Samuel Goldwyn Co.

Lawrence Gilliard Jr., Mark Malone, Matty Rich

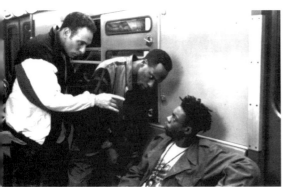

HANGIN' WITH THE HOMEBOYS

(NEW LINE CINEMA) Producer, Richard Brick; Executive Producer, Janet Grillo; Director/Screenplay, Joseph B. Vasquez; Photography, Anghel Decca; Editor, Michael Schweitzer; Executive Music Producers, Joel Sill, David Chackler; Costumes, Mary Jane Fort; Casting, Deborah Aquila; Assistant Director, Howard McMaster; Dolby Stereo; Metrocolor; Rated R; 89 minutes; May release

CAST

Willie	Doug E. Doug
Tom	Mario Joyner
Johnny	John Leguizamo
Vinny	Nestor Serrano
Vanessa	Kimberly Russell
Luna	Mary B. Ward
Rasta	Reggie Montgomery
Daria	Christine Claravall
Lila	Rosemary Jackson
Pedro	Steven Randazzo
Sara	Marisol R. Reyes
Louie-Louie	Victor L. Cook
Caseworker	LaTanya Richardson
Frederick	Clayton Prince
Bobby	Ellis Williams
Angry Father	Anthony Ruiz
Transit Policemen	Gene Canfield, Billy Strong
Beggar	Rony Clanton

and Victor Mack, Cheryl Freeman, Michelle D. Thomas (Telemarketing Operators), Arnold Molina, Rafael Baez, Tony Vasquez (Party Tough Guys), Jonathan Solomon (Bartender), Natalia Lazarus, Paula Garces (Harassed Sisters), Marie Barrientos, Sandra Berrios (Party Women), David E. Weinberg (Tow Truck Driver), Chic Street Man, Danitra Vance (Pool Hall Couple), Tony Cucci (Bouncer), Samantha Carroll, Kira Arne, Ali Thomas (Disco Women), Antone Págan (Waiter)

Doug E. Doug, John Leguizamo, Nestor Serrano, Mario Joyner Above: Serrano, Joyner, Doug
© New Line Cinema

BACKDRAFT

(UNIVERSAL) Producers, Richard B. Lewis, Pen Densham, John Watson; Executive Producers, Brian Grazer, Raffaella DeLaurentiis; Director, Ron Howard; Screenplay, Gregory Widen; Co-Producer, Larry DeWaay; Associate Producer, Todd Hallowell; Photography, Mikael Salomon; Designer, Albert Brenner; Editors, Daniel Hanley, Michael Hill; Costumes, Jodie Tillen; Casting, Jane Jenkins, Janet Hirshenson; Music, Hans Zimmer; Assistant Director, Aldric La'Auli Porter; Special Effects and Pyrotechnics Creator, Allen Hall; Special Visual Effects, Industrial Light & Magic; Stunts, Walter Scott; an Imagine Films Entertainment presentation of a Trilogy Entertainment Group-Brian Grazer production; Dolby Stereo; Panavision; Deluxe color; Rated PG-13; 135 minutes; May release

CAST

Stephen McCaffrey/Father	Kurt Russell
Brian McCaffrey	William Baldwin
Donald Rimgale	Robert De Niro
Ronald Bartel	Donald Sutherland
Jennifer Vaitkus	Jennifer Jason Leigh
John Adcox	Scott Glenn
Helen McCaffrey	Rebecca DeMornay
Tim Krizminksi	Jason Gedrick
Martin Swayzak	J.T. Walsh
Chief John Fitzgerald	Tony Mockus, Sr.
Grindle	Cedric Young
Ray Santos	Juan Ramirez
Nightengale	Kevin M. Casey
Schmidt	Jack McGee
Pengelly	Mark Wheeler
Washington	Richard Lexsee
Sean McCaffrey	Beep Iams
Brian (age 7)	Ryan Todd
Stephen (age 12)	John Duda
Willy (Bartender)	Robert Swan
Ricco	Clint Howard
Alan Seagrave	Ron West
Candidates	Kevin Crowley, Carlos Sanz, Harry Hutchinson, David A.C. Saunders
Psychiatrist	J.J. Chaback
Man at parole board	Tim Grimm
70's Hippie	David Crosby
Firetruck Driver	Mike Mangano
Paramedics	Rick Reardon, Leslie A. Ford, W. Earl Brown, Robert F. Byrnes, Jr.
Mannequin Fire Reporters	Kathryn Jaeck, David Westgor, James Ritz
Donald Cosgrove	Joe Gustaferro

and Don Herion (Repairman), Tony Mockus, Jr. (Jackson), Gregory Widen (Engine Lieutenant), Andrew Lipschultz (Man on party boat), Walter Williams (Security Guard), Bob Krzeminksi (Captain), F. Pat Burns (Battalion Chief at tenement fire), Wandachristine (Mother at tenement fire), Anthony C. Ellis, Jr. (Gasping Child at tenement fire), Peter C. Hobert, Jr. (Probie), Zita Visockis (Grandma Vaitkus), Razz Jenkins (Photographer on boat party), Irma P. Hall, Nydia Rodriguez Terracina (Nurses), Hollis Resnick (Sally), Don Rimgale (Party Crony), Dennis Liddiard (Party Brawler), David Luckenbach (Security Officer), Neil J. Francis, Jr., Andre Melchor (Cops), Karel King, Scott Baity (Swayzak Aides), Gretchen Erickson (Bar Patron), Joan Esposito (Television Reporter), Bob Rice (Detective #1), Marcella DeTineo (Nurse), Tom Clark, Jane MacIver, Burton Stencel (Retirement Party Schmoozers), Robert Martell (Retirement Party Roaster), Tony G. Chrisos, Cay DeVos (Politicos), Gregory Lundsgaard (High Rise Fireman), Charles Burns, Jr. (Battalion Chief at mannequin fire), Louise Woolf (Falling Chair Lady), Ian A. Nevers (Nervous Probie), Kelsey E. McMahon (Child Rescued at 70's fire), Fidel Moreno (70's Onlooker), Zan Heber, Ilene Kwitny, Jane Alderman (Reporters), Kevin Petersen (Doctor), Thomas A. Senderak, Michael Allen Mark (Firemen), The Pipe and Drums of the Emerald Society (Bagpipe Group at funeral), The Drovers (Retirement Party Band)

Top: Kurt Russell, William Baldwin
Below: Anthony C. Ellis Jr., Russell
© *Universal City Studios*

William Baldwin, Cedric Young, Kurt Russell, Kevin M. Casey, Scott Glenn
Top Left: Donald Sutherland, Robert De Niro Below Left: Rebecca DeMornay; Jennifer Jason Leigh

Bruce Willis, Danny Aiello Top Right: James Coburn
Right: Andie MacDowell, Willis
© *Tri-Star Pictures*

HUDSON HAWK

(TRI-STAR) Producer, Joel Silver; Executive Producer, Robert Kraft; Director, Michael Lehmann; Screenplay, Steven E. deSouza, Daniel Waters; Story, Bruce Willis, Robert Kraft; Co-Producer, Michael Dryhurst; Photography, Dante Spinotti; Designer, Jack DeGovia; Editors, Chris Lebenzon, Michael Tronick; Costumes, Marilyn Vance-Straker; Music, Michael Kamen, Robert Kraft; Songs performed by Bruce Willis and Danny Aiello: "Swinging on a Star" by Johnny Burke & James Van Heusen, and "Side by Side" by Harry Woods; Associate Producers, David Willis, Suzanne Todd; Casting, Jackie Burch; Assistant Directors, Michael Alan Kahn, Bob Girolami; Stunts, Charles Picerni; Special Effects, Industrial Light & Magic; Supervisor of Visual Effects and Miniatures, Derek Meddings; a Silver Pictures/Ace Bone production; Dolby Stereo; Technicolor; Widescreen; Rated R; 95 minutes; May release

CAST

Eddie "Hudson Hawk" Hawkins	Bruce Willis
Tommy Five-Tone	Danny Aiello
Anna Baragli	Andie MacDowell
George Kaplan	James Coburn
Darwin Mayflower	Richard E. Grant
Minerva Mayflower	Sandra Bernhard
Alfred	Donald Burton
Snickers	Don Harvey
Kit Kat	David Caruso
Butterfinger	Andrew Bryniarski
Almond Joy	Lorraine Toussaint
Gates	Burtt Harris
Cesar Mario	Frank Stallone
Antony Mario	Carmine Zozorra
Leonardo da Vinci	Stephano Molinari
Apprentice	Enrico Lo Verso
Guy on donkey	Remo Remotti
Mona Lisa	Giselda Volodi
Prison Clerk	P. Randall Bowers
Prison Security Guard	Arthur M. Wolpinsky
Mario's Driver	Frank Page
Big Stan	Bob Vazquez
Dean	Michael Klastorin
Jerry	Scott H. Eddo
Auctioneer	John Savident
Girl in car	Lisa Reich
Vatican Guards	John Lucantonio, Antonio Iurio
Bratty Kid	Courtenay Semel
The Pope	Massimo Ciprari
Igg	Doug Martin
Ook	Steve Martin
Cardinal	Leonard Cimino
Waiter	Giangiacomo Colli
Bunny the Dog	Frank Welker
Narrator	William Conrad

James Coburn, Andrew Bryniarski, Bruce Willis,
David Caruso, Don Harvey
Above: Richard E. Grant, Sandra Bernhard

ONLY THE LONELY

(20th CENTURY FOX) Producers, John Hughes, Hunt Lowry; Executive Producer, Tarquin Gotch; Director/Screenplay, Chris Columbus; Photography, Julio Macat; Editor, John Muto; Designer, Raja Gosnell; Costumes, Mary E. Vogt; Co-Producer/Assistant Director, Mark Radcliffe; Casting, Jane Jenkins; Janet Hirshenson; Music, Maurice Jarre; Title song written by Roy Orbison, Joe Melson/performed by Roy Orbison; a Hughes Entertainment production; Dolby Stereo; Deluxe color; Rated PG-13; 108 minutes; May release

CAST

Danny Muldoon	John Candy
Rose Muldoon	Maureen O'Hara
Theresa Luna	Ally Sheedy
Patrick Muldoon	Kevin Dunn
Doyle Ryan	Milo O'Shea
Spats Shannon	Bert Remsen
Nick Acropolis	Anthony Quinn
Sal Buonarte	James Belushi
Johnny Luna	Joe V. Greco
Father Strapovic	Marvin J. McIntyre
Billy	Macaulay Culkin
O'Neal	Allen Hamilton
Susan	Teri McEvoy
Larry	Bernie Landis
News Vendor	Clarke Devereux
Jack	Les Podewell
Tyrone	John Chandler
Chess Player	Martin Fisher
Cops	Timothy O'Meara, James "Ike" Eichling
Waiter	James Deuter
Leo	John M. Watson, Sr.
Suit Salesman	Dick Sollenberger
Tuxedo Salesmen	Doyle Devereux, Clarke P. Devereux
Carriage Driver	Ed Meekin
Crazed Prisoner	Michael W. Nash
Bum	Porscha Radcliffe
Witch	Brittany Radcliffe
Cop Friend	Marlon A. Morris
Policeman	Jesse J. Donnelly
Stewardess	Sandra Macat
Hoodlum	Rick LeFevour
Tommy Bones	Mahlon Sharp

Top: John Candy, Maureen O'Hara Below: Candy, Ally Sheedy Right: O'Hara, Anthony Quinn
© Twentieth Century Fox

Ally Sheedy, John Candy, Maureen O'Hara

James Belushi, John Candy

Susan Sarandon
**Top Right: Sarandon, Geena Davis
Top Left: Davis**
© *Pathe Entertainment*

THELMA & LOUISE

(MGM) Producers, Ridley Scott, Mimi Polk; Co-Producers, Dean O'Brien, Callie Khouri; Director, Ridley Scott; Screenplay, Callie Khouri; Photography, Adrian Biddle; Designer, Norris Spencer; Editor, Thom Noble; Music, Hans Zimmer; Costumes, Elizabeth McBride; Assistant Director, Steve Danton; Stunts, Bobby Bass; a Pathe Entertainment presentation of a Percy Main production; Dolby Stereo; Panavision; Deluxe color; Rated R; 128 minutes; May release

CAST

Louise Sawyer	Susan Sarandon
Thelma Dickinson	Geena Davis
Hal Slocumbe	Harvey Keitel
Jimmy	Michael Madsen
Darryl Dickinson	Christopher McDonald
Max	Stephen Tobolowsky
J.D.	Brad Pitt
Harlan	Timothy Carhart
Lena, the Waitress	Lucinda Jenny
State Trooper	Jason Beghe
Albert	Sonny Carl Davis
Major	Ken Swofford
East Indian Motel Clerk	Shelly De Sai
Waitress	Carol Mansell
Surveillance Man	Stephen Polk
Plainclothes Cop	Rob Roy Fitzgerald
I.D. Tech	Jack Lindine
Silver Bullet Dancer	Michael Delman
Girl Smoker	Kristel L. Rose
Mountain Bike Rider	Noel Walcott

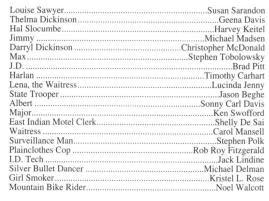

**Susan Sarandon, Geena Davis
Above: Brad Pitt, Davis**

1991 Academy Award for Best Original Screenplay

Brad Pitt Top: Susan Sarandon, Geena Davis Susan Sarandon, Michael Madsen **57**
Above: Harvey Keitel

WILD HEARTS CAN'T BE BROKEN

(WALT DISNEY PICTURES) Producer, Matt Williams; Executive Producer, Oley Sassone; Co-Producer, Robin S. Clark; Director, Steve Miner; Screenplay, Matt Williams, Oley Sassone; Photography, Daryn Okada; Designer, Randy Ser; Editor, Jon Poll; Music, Mason Daring; Costumes, Malissa Daniel; Casting, Mary Gail Artz, Barbara Cohen; Assistant Director, Matt Earl Beesley; Associate Producer, Sarah Brock; Head Animal Trainer, Corky Randall; Presented in association with Silver Screen Partners IV; Distributed by Buena Vista Pictures; Dolby Stereo; Technicolor; Rated G; 89 minutes; May release

CAST

Sonora Webster	Gabrielle Anwar
Al Carver	Michael Schoeffling
Dr. W.F. Carver	Cliff Robertson
Clifford	Dylan Kussman
Marie	Kathleen York
Mr. Slater	Frank Renzulli
Arnette	Nancy Moore Atchison
Aunt Helen	Lisa Norman
Clarabelle	Lorianne Collins
Miss Simpson	Elizabeth Hayes
Mrs. Ellis	Laura Lee Norton
Photographer	Michael J. Matusiak
Reporters	Jeff Woodward, David Massry
Attractive Girl	Cheri Brown
Stagehand	David Dwyer
Little Girl	Haley Aull
Preacher	Ed L. Grady
Kids	Katy Matson, Wendy Ball, Sam Aull, Carson Aull
Farmers	Boyd Peterson, Gene Walker
Wrangler	Lowell D. Smith
Doctor	Rick Warner
Candy Man	Mark Jeffrey Miller

Cliff Robertson

Dylan Kussman, Gabrielle Anwar, Michael Schoeffling
Above: Schoeffling, Anwar

Elisabeth Shue, Kevin Kline Top Left: Sally Field, Kline
Left: Robert Downey Jr., Cathy Moriarty
© *Paramount Pictures*

SOAPDISH

(PARAMOUNT) Producers, Aaron Spelling, Alan Greisman; Executive Producer, Herbert Ross; Co-Producers, Victoria White, Joel Freeman; Director, Michael Hoffman; Screenplay, Robert Harling, Andrew Bergman; Story, Robert Harling; Photography, Ueli Steiger; Designer, Eugenio Zanetti; Editor, Garth Craven; Costumes, Nolan Miller; Music, Alan Silvestri; Casting, Lora Kennedy; Assistant Director, John E. Hockridge; Dolby Stereo; Technicolor; Rated PG-13; 95 minutes; May release

CAST

Celeste Talbert	Sally Field
Jeffrey Anderson	Kevin Kline
David Barnes	Robert Downey, Jr.
Rose Schwartz	Whoopi Goldberg
Montana Moorehead	Cathy Moriarty
Lori Craven	Elisabeth Shue
Betsy Faye Sharon	Carrie Fisher
Edmund Edwards	Garry Marshall
Ariel Maloney	Teri Hatcher
Burton White	Arne Nannestad
Tawny Miller	Kathy Najimy
Bolt Brennan	Paul Johansson
Mark	Costas Mandylor
Fran	Sheila Kelley
A.D.	Tim Choate
Old Man	Phil Leeds
Old Women	Herta Ware, Dorothy Patterson
Receptionist	Cornelia Kiss
Actor	Robert Camiletti
Housewives	Marianne Muellerleile, Mary Pat Gleason
Young Autograph Seeker	Michael Berkowitz
Woman Shopper	Amy Nabi
Bartender	Ivory Ocean
Nitwits	Benjamin Stein, Barry Kivel, David Byron, Willie Garson
P.A.	Vince Melocchi
Homeless Extra	Brick Karnes
Fans	Penny Gumeny, Wai Ching Ho, Mary Thompson Hunt
Bus Boys	Nico DeSilva, Armando Molina
Bus Driver	Gino Lucci
Doorman	Clive Rosengren
Themselves	Leeza Gibbons, John Tesh, Stephen Nichols

Cathy Moriarty, Sally Field, Whoopi Goldberg
Above: Field, Goldberg

CITY SLICKERS

(COLUMBIA) Producer, Irby Smith; Executive Producer, Billy Crystal; Director, Ron Underwood; Screenplay, Lowell Ganz, Babaloo Mandel; Photography, Dean Semler; Designer, Lawrence G. Paull; Music, Marc Shaiman; Costumes, Judy Ruskin; Editor, O. Nicholas Brown; Casting, Pam Dixon; Assistant Director, Jim Chory; Stunts/2nd Unit Director, Mickey Gilbert; a Castle Rock Entertainment in association with Nelson Entertainment presentation; Dolby Stereo; Color; Rated PG-13; 110 minutes; June release

CAST

Mitch Robbins	Billy Crystal
Phil Berquist	Daniel Stern
Ed Furillo	Bruno Kirby
Barbara Robbins	Patricia Wettig
Bonnie Rayburn	Helen Slater
Curly	Jack Palance
Clay Stone	Noble Willingham
Cookie	Tracey Walter
Barry Shalowitz	Josh Mostel
Ira Shalowitz	David Paymer
Ben Jessup	Bill Henderson
Lou	Jeffrey Tambor
Steve Jessup	Phill Lewis
Jeff	Kyle Secor
T.R.	Dean Hallo
Arlene Berquist	Karla Tamburrelli
Nancy	Yeardley Smith
Sal	Robert Costanzo
Kim	Walker Brandt
Millie Stone	Molly McClure
Holly Robbins	Lindsay Crystal
Mrs. Green	Jane Alden
Daniel Robbins	Jake Gyllenhaal
Kids	Danielle Harris, Eddie Palmer
Skycap	Howard Honig
Doctor	Fred Maio
Mitch's Mom (Voice)	Jayne Meadows
Mitch's Dad (Voice)	Alan Charof

Bruno Kirby, Daniel Stern, Billy Crystal
Above: Helen Slater

*Jack Palance received the Academy Award
for Best Supporting Actor of 1991*

Phill Lewis, Bill Henderson Above: Bruno Kirby   **Patricia Wettig Above: Josh Mostel, David Paymer**

Billy Crystal, Bruno Kirby, Daniel Stern

JUNGLE FEVER

(UNIVERSAL) Producer/Director/Screenplay, Spike Lee; Co-Producer, Monty Ross; Line Producer, Jon Kilik; Photography, Ernest Dickerson; Editor, Sam Pollard; Songs by Stevie Wonder; Music Score, Terence Blanchard; Designer, Wynn Thomas; Casting, Robi Reed; Costumes, Ruth E. Carter; Assistant Director, Randy Fletcher; a 40 Acres and a Mule Filmworks production; Dolby Stereo; Deluxe color; Rated R; 132 minutes; June release

CAST

Flipper Purify	Wesley Snipes
Angie Tucci	Annabella Sciorra
Cyrus	Spike Lee
The Good Reverend Doctor Purify	Ossie Davis
Lucinda Purify	Ruby Dee
Gator Purify	Samuel L. Jackson
Drew Purify	Lonette McKee
Paulie Carbone	John Turturro
Mike Tucci	Frank Vincent
Lou Carbone	Anthony Quinn
Vivian	Halle Berry
Orin Goode	Tyra Ferrell
Vera	Veronica Webb
Ming	Veronica Timbers
Charlie Tucci	David Dundara
James Tucci	Michael Imperioli
Vinny	Nicholas Turturro
Sonny	Steven Randazzo
Patty	Joe D'Onofrio
Frankie Botz	Michael Badalucco
Veeshay	Anthony Nocerrino
Denise	Debi Mazar
Louise	Gina Mastrogiacomo
Jerry	Tim Robbins
Leslie	Brad Dourif
Nilda	Phyllis Yvonne Stickney
Inez	Theresa Randle
Angela	Pamala Tyson
Officer Long	Rick Aiello
Officer Ponte	Miguel Sandoval
Livin' Large	Charles Q. Murphy
Iris	Talese Harris

and Averell Curtle (Young Panhandler), Melvin Bethea, Ewart Lauder (Drug Dealers), Randolph May (Man in crack den), El-Shah Muhammad (Gentleman in wheelchair), Suzanna White (Church Lady), Danielle Coleman (Panhandler), Marilyn Nelson (Crack Lady), Bob Adrian (Man on the street), Doug E. Doug, Scot Anthony Robinson (Friends of Livin' Large), Frank Esposito (Frankie, Denise's Brother), Joseph Giammarino, Shawn Lowenthal (Boys in candy store), Queen Latifah (Lashawn), Curtis Atkins (Paperboy), Yvette Brooks, Mamie Louise Anderson (Mouths)

Top: Annabella Sciorra, Wesley Snipes
Left: Snipes, Veronica Timbers
© *Universal City Studios*

Ruby Dee, Samuel L. Jackson

David Dundara, Frank Vincent,
Annabella Sciorra, Michael Imperioli

Wesley Snipes, Spike Lee Top Left: Lonette McKee, Snipes

John Turturro, Anthony Quinn Top Right: Annabella Sciorra, Wesley Snipes

Ossie Davis, Wesley Snipes, Annabella Sciorra, Ruby Dee

ROBIN HOOD: PRINCE OF THIEVES

(WARNER BROS.) Producers, John Watson, Pen Densham, Richard B. Lewis; Co-Producer, Michael J. Kagan; Executive Producers, James G. Robinson, David Nicksay, Gary Barber; Director, Kevin Reynolds; Screenplay, Pen Densham, John Watson; Story, Pen Densham; Photography, Doug Milsome; Designer, John Graysmark; Music, Michael Kamen; Editor, Peter Boyle; Costumes, John Bloomfield; Casting, Ilene Starger (U.S.), Davis and Zimmerman (England); Stunts, Paul Weston; Assistant Director, David Tringham; Special Effects, John Evans; a Morgan Creek production; Dolby Stereo; Technicolor; Rated PG-13; 141 minutes; June release

CAST

Robin of Locksley	Kevin Costner
Azeem	Morgan Freeman
Marian	Mary Elizabeth Mastrantonio
Will Scarlett	Christian Slater
Sheriff of Nottingham	Alan Rickman
Mortianna	Geraldine McEwan
Friar Tuck	Michael McShane
Lord Locksley	Brian Blessed
Guy of Gisborne	Michael Wincott
Little John	Nick Brimble
Fanny	Soo Drouet
Wulf	Daniel Newman
Bull	Daniel Peacock
Duncan	Walter Sparrow
Bishop	Harold Innocent
Much	Jack Wild
Kenneth	Michael Goldie
Peter Dubois	Liam Halligan
Turk Interrogator	Marc Zuber
Old Woman	Merelina Kendall
Sarah	Imogen Bain
Farmer	Jimmy Gardner
Villager	Bobby Parr
Courier	John Francis
Red Headed Baron	John Hallam
Grey Bearded Baron	Douglas Blackwell
Celtic Chieftain	Pat Roach
Ox	Andy Hockley
Broth	John Dallimore
Kneelock	Derek Deadman
Hal	Howard Lew Lewis
Scribe	John Tordoff
Sergeant	Andrew Lawden
Lady in coach	Susannah Corbett
Small Girl	Sarah Alexandra
Soldier	Christopher Adamson
Executioner	Richard Strange
King Richard	Sean Connery

Top: Kevin Costner, Mary Elizabeth Mastrantonio
Left: Costner
© *Warner Bros. Inc.*

64   Kevin Costner, Nick Brimble   Kevin Costner, Christian Slater

Alan Rickman, Mary Elizabeth Mastrantonio
Top Left: Kevin Costner

Morgan Freeman

Christian Slater

Kevin Costner, Walter Sparrow, Morgan
Freeman Above: Freeman, Costner

THE ROCKETEER

(**WALT DISNEY PICTURES**) Producers, Lawrence Gordon, Charles Gordon, Lloyd Levin; Director, Joe Johnston; Screenplay, Danny Bilson, Paul De Meo; Story, Danny Bilson, Paul De Meo, William Dear; Based on the graphic novel created by Dave Stevens; Executive Producer, Larry Franco; Photography, Hiro Narita; Designer, Jim Bissell; Editor, Arthur Schmidt; Co-Producer, Dave Stevens; Music, James Horner; Costumes, Marilyn Vance-Straker; Casting, Nancy Foy; Assistant Director, Betsy Magruder; Associate Producer, Lisa Bailey; Special Visual Effects, Industrial Light & Magic; Visual Effects Supervisor, Ken Ralston; a Gordon Company production, produced in association with Silver Screen Partners IV; Distributed by Buena Vista Pictures; Dolby Stereo; Panavision; Technicolor; Rated PG; 108 minutes; June release

CAST

Cliff Secord	Bill Campbell
Jenny Blake	Jennifer Connelly
Peevy	Alan Arkin
Neville Sinclair	Timothy Dalton
Eddie Valentine	Paul Sorvino
Howard Hughes	Terry O'Quinn
Fitch	Ed Lauter
Wooly	James Handy
Lothar	Tiny Ron
Spanish Johnny	Robert Guy Miranda
Rusty	John Lavachielli
Bigelow	Jon Polito
Malcolm	Eddie Jones
Skeets	William Sanderson
Goose	Don Pugsley
Irma	Nada Despotovich
Millie	Margo Martindale
Patsy	America Martin
Wilmer	Max Grodenchik
Jeff	Michael Milhoan
Mike	Daniel O'Shea
Stevie	Joseph D'Angerio
Monk	Clint Howard
Lenny	Thomas J. Huff
Pauly	Paul De Souza
Mrs. Pye	Pat Crawford Brown

and Julian Barnes (Charlie - Filmstage Actor), Sam Vincent (Filmstage Director), Lisa Pedersen (Noblewoman), Tom Kindle (Clapperboy), Charlie Stavola (Assistant Director), William Boyett, William Frankfather (Government Liaisons), Heinrich James (Nazi Agent), Herman Poppe (Zeppelin Captain), Norbert Weisser (Zeppelin Pilot), Michael Francis Clarke, Darryl Henriques (G-Men), Scanlon Gail (G-Man at Chaplin Field), Melora Hardin (South Seas Singer), Bob Leeman (W.C. Fields), Rick Overton (South Seas Patron), Gene Daily (Clark Gable), Richard Warlock (FBI Agent), Thomas Lee Tully, Mike Finneran, Doug McGrath, Dave Adams (Reporters), Arlee Reed (Cameraman), Kim Sebastian (Nurse), David Pressman (Hospital Guard), Lila Finn (Clothesline Lady), Perry Cook, Tiny Ron (Good Old Boys), Taylor Gilbert (Stewardess), Ele Keats, Danielle Bedau (Girls at newsstand), Chance Michael Corbitt (Newspaper Kid), Bob Sandman (South Seas Bandleader), Lori Lynn Ross (South Seas Mermaid), Kathleen Michaels (South Seas Camera Girl), Merritt Yohnka (Nazi Crewman) Peter Frankland, Kristopher Logan, Paul Forsyth (Nazi Commandos), Peter Bromilow (Nobleman)

Top: Jennifer Connelly, Bill Campbell Below: Campbell Right: Campbell, Alan Arkin © *The Walt Disney Co.*

Bill Campbell, Alan Arkin

Timothy Dalton, Paul Sorvino

Campbell Scott Top Left: Julia Roberts, Scott (also right) © *Twentieth Century Fox*

DYING YOUNG

(20th CENTURY FOX) Producers, Sally Field, Kevin McCormick; Co-Producer, Duncan Henderson; Director, Joel Schumacher; Screenplay, Richard Friedenberg; Based on the novel by Marti Leimbach; Photography, Juan Ruiz Anchia; Art Director, Guy J. Comtois; Editor, Robert Brown; Costumes, Susan Becker; Music, James Newton Howard; Casting, Mary Goldberg; Associate Producer, Mauri Gayton; Assistant Director, Stephen Dunn; a Fogwood Films production; Dolby Stereo; Deluxe color; Rated R; 106 minutes; June release

CAST

Hilary O'Neil	Julia Roberts
Victor Geddes	Campbell Scott
Gordon	Vincent D'Onofrio
Estelle Whittier	Colleen Dewhurst
Richard Geddes	David Selby
Mrs. O'Neil	Ellen Burstyn
Cappy	Dion Anderson
Malachi	George Martin
Shauna	A.J. Johnson
Danny	Daniel Beer
Moamar	Behrooz Afrakhan
Gordon's Friend	Michael Halton
Assistant	Larry Nash
Host of Jeopardy	Alex Trebek
Jeopardy Contestants	Richard Friedenberg, Duncan Henderson, Bettina Rose
Annabel	Fran Lucci
Bandleader	John M. Rosenberg
Shauna's Boyfriend	Patrick Cage
Guest	Tim Bohn
Children in hospital	Holly Del Rosso, Trevor Fant, Kevin O'Connor, Lauren Oymainan, Erin Vallely
Voice on Jetsons	Howard Morris

Julia Roberts

THE NAKED GUN 2 1/2:
The Smell of Fear

(PARAMOUNT) Producer, Robert K. Weiss; Executive Producers, Jerry Zucker, Jim Abrahams, Gil Netter; Director, David Zucker; Screenplay, David Zucker, Pat Proft; Based on the television series *Police Squad!* created by Jim Abrahams, David Zucker, Jerry Zucker; Photography, Robert Stevens; Designer, John J. Lloyd; Editors, James Symons, Chris Greenbury; Co-Producer, John D. Schofield; Associate Producers, Robert Lo Cash, Michael Ewing; Assistant Director, John T. Kretchmer; Dolby Stereo; Technicolor; Rated PG-13; 85 minutes; June release

PEOPLE WHO ACTED IN THE MOVIE

Lt. Frank Drebin ....Leslie Nielsen
Jane Spencer ....Priscilla Presley
Ed Hocken ....George Kennedy
Nordberg ....O.J. Simpson
Quentin Hapsburg ....Robert Goulet
Dr. Meinheimer/Earl Hacker......................................Richard Griffiths
Commissioner Brumford..Jacqueline Brookes
Hector Savage ....Anthony James
Baggett...Lloyd Bochner
Fenzwick..Tim O'Connor
Dunwell ....Peter Mark Richman
Ted Olsen ....Ed Williams
George Bush ....John Roarke
Barbara Bush..Margery Ross
John Sununu ....Peter Van Norden
Winnie Mandela ....Gail Neely
Blues Singer ....Colleen Fitzpatrick
Mrs. Redmond...Sally Rosenblatt
Crackhouse Cop..Alexander Folk
Mariachi...Jose Gonzales-Gonzales
TV Reporter...Larry McCormick
Barbecue Dad...Cliff Bemis
Barbecue Mom...D.D. Howard
TV Commercial Announcer....................................William Woodson
Himself ....Mel Tormé
Herself ....Zsa Zsa Gabor
and Bill Chemerka ("Ladies and Gentlemen, the President of the United States and Mrs. Bush"), Christopher J. Keene ("Hey, Ken, Al! Look what I found."), Ken Kerman ("Hey, that's a pretty nice clock."), Al Fann ("It's four minutes too slow."), Tom McGreevey ("Very well, sir. It's from the lady."), James Gilstrap ("Always nice to see nice people."), "Weird Al" Yankovic ("You pigs...say your prayers."), Gina Mastrogiacomo ("Is this some kind of bust?"), Jeff Wright ("Frank, we got that Sure-Grip suck machine."), C. Lindsay Workman ("Your coat, sir?"), John Stevens ("Phone call, Commissioner."), Datta V. Gokhale ("Hey, what the hell happened to the water pressure?"), Charlotte Zucker ("For a man in a wheelchair, he gets around marvelously."), Don Pugsley ("He's wired!"), Carlos Betancourt ("Ojala que se mejoré pronto!"), Bernardo Marquez ("Recuerdos a todos."), Margarito Mendoza ("Puede decirme donde esta la casa de musica?"), Lee Terri ("Hey, look what he's doing to that man in the wheelchair!"), Claude Jay McLin ("Yeah!"), Manny Perry ("Let's get him!"), Alex Zimmerman ("Yeah!"), Raynor Scheine ("You're on my groin!"), John Fleck ("If that's your attitude, forget it."); People who didn't have lines, but we like 'em: Susan Breslau, Leslie Maier (Party Guests), Ron Rosenblatt, D.D.S. (Mr. Redmond), Jennifer Kretchmer (Barbecue Girl), Ryan Harrison (Barbecue Boy), Robert Weil (George Russell), Robert K. Weiss (Obstetrician), Robert LoCash (FBI Agent), Burton Zucker, Lewis Friedman, Bob Reitman, Gene Mueller, Gino Salomone (Lab Technicians), Robert J. Elisberg (McTigue), David Zucker (Davy Crockett)

Top: Leslie Nielsen Below: George Kennedy,
Nielsen, Ed Williams
© *Paramount Pictures*

Richard Griffiths, Leslie Nielsen, Priscilla
Presley, Robert Goulet Above: Nielsen

TERMINATOR 2: JUDGMENT DAY

(TRI-STAR) Producer/Director, James Cameron; Executive Producers, Gale Anne Hurd, Mario Kassar; Co-Producers, B.J. Rack, Stephanie Austin; Screenplay, James Cameron, William Wisher; Photography, Adam Greenberg; Designer, Joseph Nemec III; Editors, Conrad Buff, Mark Goldblatt, Richard A. Harris; Special Makeup and Terminator Effects Producer, Stan Winston; Industrial Light & Magic Visual Effects Supervisor, Dennis Muren; Music, Brad Fiedel; Costumes, Marlene Stewart; Casting, Mali Finn; Assistant Directors, J. Michael Haynie, Terry Miller; a Pacific Western Production in association with Lightstorm Entertainment, from Carolco Pictures; Dolby Stereo; Widescreen; CFI color; Rated R; 135 minutes; July release

CAST

The Terminator	Arnold Schwarzenegger
Sarah Connor	Linda Hamilton
John Connor	Edward Furlong
T-1000	Robert Patrick
Dr. Silberman	Earl Boen
Miles Dyson	Joe Morton
Tarissa Dyson	S. Epatha Merkerson
Enrique Salceda	Castulo Guerra
Tim	Danny Cooksey
Janelle Voight	Jenette Goldstein
Todd Voight	Xander Berkeley
Twin Sarah	Leslie Hamilton Gearren
Douglas	Ken Gibbel
Cigar Biker	Robert Winley
Lloyd	Pete Schrum
Trucker	Shane Wilder
Old John Connor	Michael Edwards
Kids	Jared Lounsbery, Casey Chavez
Bryant	Ennalls Berl
Mossberg	Don Lake
Weatherby	Richard Vidan
Cop	Tom McDonald
Jocks	Jim Palmer, Gerard G. Williams
Night Nurse	Gwenda Deacon
Lewis, the Guard	Don Stanton
Lewis as T-1000	Dan Stanton
Attendant	Colin Patrick Lynch
Hospital Guard	Noel Evangelisti
Girls	Nikki Cox, Lisa Brinegar
Danny Dyson	De Vaughn Nixon
Vault Guard	Tony Simotes
Jolanda Salceda	Dianne Rodriguez
Infant John Connor	Dalton Abbott

and Ron Young (Pool Cue Biker), Charles Robert Brown (Tattoo Biker), Abdul Salaam El Razzac (Gibbons), Mike Muscat (Moshier), Dean Norris (SWAT Team Leader), Charles Tamburro (Police Chopper Pilot), J. Rob Jordan (Pickup Truck Driver), Terrence Evans (Tanker Truck Driver), Denney Pierce, Mark Christopher Lawrence (Burly Attendants), Pat Kouri (SWAT Leader), Van Ling (Cyberdyne Tech)

**Top: Edward Furlong, Arnold Schwarzenegger
Below: Furlong, Linda Hamilton**
© *Tri-Star Pictures*

1991 Academy Awards for Best Sound, Sound Effects Editing, Makeup and Visual Effects

**Arnold Schwarzenegger, Joe Morton, Linda Hamilton
Above: Robert Patrick**

Harrison Ford, Annette Bening
Top Right: Mikki Allen, Ford Right: Ford
© *Paramount Pictures*

REGARDING HENRY

(PARAMOUNT) Producers, Scott Rudin, Mike Nichols; Executive Producer, Robert Greenhut; Director, Mike Nichols; Screenplay/Co-Producer, Jeffrey Abrams; Photography, Giuseppe Rotunno; Designer, Tony Walton; Editor, Sam O'Steen; Costumes, Ann Roth; Music, Hans Zimmer; Casting, Juliet Taylor, Ellen Lewis; Assistant Director, Michael Haley; Associate Producer, Susan MacNair; Dolby Stereo; Technicolor; Rated PG-13; 107 minutes; July release

CAST

Henry Turner	Harrison Ford
Sarah Turner	Annette Bening
Bradley	Bill Nunn
Rachel Turner	Mikki Allen
Charlie	Donald Moffat
Mrs. O'Brien	Nancy Marchand
Rosella	Aida Linares
Jessica	Elizabeth Wilson
Phyllis	Robin Bartlett
Bruce	Bruce Altman
Linda Palmer	Rebecca Miller
Mr. Matthews	Stanley H. Swerdlow
Mrs. Matthews	Julie Follansbee
George	John MacKay
Julia	Mary Gilbert
Doorman	Peter Appel
Store Owner	Harsh Nayyar
Gunman	John Leguizamo
Dr. Sultan	James Rebhorn
Dr. Marx	Brian Smiar
Hillary	May Quigley
Julie	Marjorie Monaghan
Gloria	Emily Wachtel
Loretta	Kai Soremekun
Rudy	Kirby Mitchell
Jennifer	Kia Graves
Daniel	Benjamin Hendrickson
Brenda	Susan Forristal
Gerald	Ralph Byers
Court Clerk	R.M. Haley
Policeman	Harold House
ICU Nurse	Cynthia Martells
Real Estate Broker	Suzann O'Neill
Elevator Man	Glen Trotiner
Delivery Boy	Jeffrey Abrams
Taxi Driver	Jack McLaughlin
Hot Dog Vendor	Louis Cantarini

and Henry Stram (Waiter), Joan Kindred (Party Guest), Hollis Granville (Butler), Anne Stone (Charlie's Secretary), William Severs, Mark Irish, Bernadette Penotti, Jim Gardner, Fred Fehrmann, Alva Chinn (Lawyers), Harold House (Policeman)

Aida Linares, Annette Bening, Harrison Ford, Mikki
Allen Above: Ford, Bill Nunn

POINT BREAK

(20th CENTURY FOX) Producers, Peter Abrams, Robert L. Levy; Executive Producer, James Cameron; Director, Kathryn Bigelow; Screenplay, W. Peter Iliff; Story, Rick King, W. Peter Iliff; Photography, Donald Peterman; Designer, Peter Jamison; Editor, Howard Smith; Music, Mark Isham; Assistant Director, Herb Gains; Stunts, Glenn Wilder; a Largo Entertainment presentation; Dolby Stereo; Widescreen, Color; Rated R; 122 minutes; July release

CAST

Bodhi	Patrick Swayze
Johnny Utah	Keanu Reeves
Pappas	Gary Busey
Tyler	Lori Petty
Ben Harp	John McGinley
Roach	James Le Gros
Nathanial	John Philbin
Grommet	Bojesse Christopher
Alvarez	Julian Reyes
Babbit	Daniel Beer
Bunker	Chris Pedersen
Warchild	Vincent Klyn
Tone	Anthony Kiedis
Archbold	Dave Olson
Rosie	Lee Tergesen
Miss Deer	Sydney Walsh
"15"	Christopher Pettiet
Psycho-Stick	Dino Andino
Passion for Slashin	Michael Kopelow
Surf Rat	Matt Archbold
Freight Train	Julie Michaels
Fiberglass	Kimberly Martin
Corey	Mike Genovese
Halsey	Jack Kehler
Margarita	Galyn Gorg
Cab Driver	Paulo Tocha
Macrame Girl	Elizabeth Berkely
Neighbor	Raymond Forchion
Girl at party	Betsy Lynn George
Fast Food Girl	Shannon Brook
Fierce Woman	Gloria Mann
Dispatcher	Ping Wu
Pilot	Jared Chandler
Security Guard	John Apicella

and Richard Grove (Cullen), Anthony Mangano (Off Duty Cop), Deborah Lemen (Miss Jennings), Mick Regan (Mr. Duggan), Randy Walker (Combat Alley Supervisor), Marcha L. Carter (FBI Reception), Sedrick J. Azurdia (Fruit Vendor)

Top: Keanu Reeves, Patrick Swayze Below: "The Ex-Presidents" Right: Reeves, Lori Petty
© Largo Entertainment

Keanu Reeves, Patrick Swayze

Gary Busey, Keanu Reeves, John McGinley 71

BOYZ N THE HOOD

(COLUMBIA) Producer, Steve Nicolaides; Director/Screenplay, John Singleton; Photography, Charles Mills; Art Director, Bruce Bellamy; Music, Stanley Clarke; Editor, Bruce Cannon; Casting, Jaki Brown; Assistant Director, Don Wilkerson; Dolby Stereo; Technicolor; Rated R; 107 minutes; July release

CAST

Doughboy	Ice Cube
Tre Styles	Cuba Gooding, Jr.
Ricky Baker	Morris Chestnut
Furious Styles	Larry Fishburne
Brandi	Nia Long
Mrs. Baker	Tyra Ferrell
Reva Styles	Angela Bassett
Chris	Redge Green
Tre (age 10)	Desi Arnez Hines, II
Doughboy (age 10)	Baha Jackson
Ricky (age 10)	Donovan McCrary
Little Chris	Kenneth A. Brown
S.A.T. Man	Hudhail Al-Amir
Club Member	Mia Bell
Mad Dog	Lexie Bigham
Brandi (age 10)	Nicole Brown
Sheryl	Ceal
Keisha	Darneicea Corley
Lewis Crump	John Cothran, Jr.
Trina	Na'Blonka Durden
Mrs. Olaf	Susan Falcon
Officer Coffey	Jesse Ferguson
Dooky	Dedrick D. Gobert
Ice Cream Truck Kid	Kareem J. Grimes
Rosa	Tammy Hanson
Bobby (age 10)	Valentino Harrison
Renee	Dee Dee Jacobs
Officer Graham	Kirk Kinder
Brandi's Mom	Meta King
Shalika	Regina King
The Old Man	Whitman Mayo
Kid	Jimmy Lee Newman
Shanice	Alysia M. Rogers
Tisha's Grandmother	Esther Scott
Tisha	Leonette Scott
Ric Rock	Vonté Sweet
Monster	Baldwin C. Sykes
Ferris	Raymond D. Turner
Yo Yo	Yolanda Whittaker
Knuckleheads	Lloyd Avery II, Malcolm Norrington
Gangsters	Don Nelson, Leanear Lane

Tyra Ferrell, Cuba Gooding Jr. Left: Nia Long, Gooding
© Columbia Pictures Industries

Larry Fishburne   **Desi Arnez Hines II (left)**

Nia Long, Cuba Gooding Jr.   **Tyra Ferrell Above: Morris Chestnut, Cuba Gooding Jr.**

Cuba Gooding Jr., Larry Fishburne, Ice Cube

BILL & TED'S BOGUS JOURNEY

(ORION) Producer, Scott Kroopf; Executive Producers, Ted Field, Robert W. Cort, Barry Spikings, Rick Finkelstein; Screenplay, Chris Matheson, Ed Solomon; Photography, Oliver Wood; Designer, David L. Snyder; Editor, David Finfer; Supervising Producer, Neil Machlis; Music, David Newman; Creature and Makeup Effects, Kevin Yagher; Costumes, Marie France; Visual Effects, Richard Yuricich, Gregory L. McMurry; Co-Producers, Ed Solomon, Chris Matheson, Erwin Stoff, Paul Aaron; Co-Executive Producers, Connie Tavel, Stephen Deutsch; Casting, Karen Rea; a Nelson Entertainment presentation of an Interscope Communications production; Dolby Stereo; Panavision; Deluxe color; Rated PG; 95 minutes; July release

THE STELLAR CAST

Ted Logan	Keanu Reeves
Bill Preston/Granny Preston	Alex Winter
Grim Reaper	William Sadler
De Nomolos	Joss Ackland
Ms. Wardrobe	Pam Grier
Rufus	George Carlin
Missy	Amy Stock-Poynton
Sir James Martin	Jim Martin
Captain Logan/Thomas Edison	Hal Landon, Jr.
Elizabeth	Annette Azcuy
Joanna	Sarah Trigger
Colonel Oats	Chelcie Ross
Gatekeeper	Taj Mahal
Bach	Robert Noble
Ria Paschelle	Eleni Kelakos
Deputy James	Roy Brocksmith
Mr. Preston	J. Patrick McNamara
Seance Members	Dana Stevens, Valerie Spencer, Katharyn Miller, Carol Rosenthal
"Ugly" Seance Member	Chris Matheson
"Stupid" Seance Member	Ed Solomon
Dark Figure	Anthony Schmidt
Young Ted	Brendan Ryan
Young Bill	William Thorne
Stations	Ed Gale, Arturo Gil
Big Station	Tom Allard
Heavenly Greeter	Terry Finn
Albert Einstein	John Ehrin
Benjamin Franklin	Don Forney
Good Robot Bill	Michael "Shrimp" Chambers
Good Robot Ted	Bruno "Taco" Falcon
George Washington Carver	Ed Cambridge
Confucius	Tad Horino
Capt. James Tiberios Kirk	William Shatner
The Smoker	Max Magenta
Primus	Les Claypool, Tim "Herb" Alexander, Larry Lalonde
Kate Axelrod	Tanya Newbould

Alex Winter, William Sadler, Keanu Reeves
© *Orion Pictures*

TRUST

(FINE LINE FEATURES) Producer, Bruce Weiss; Executive Producer, Jerome Brownstein; Director/Screenplay, Hal Hartley; Photography, Mike Spiller; Designer, Daniel Ouellette; Costumes, Claudia Brown; Editor, Nick Gomez; Music, Phil Reed; Assistant Director, Ted Hope; a Zenith in association with True Fiction Pictures presentation from Republic Pictures; Color; Rated R; 103 minutes; July release

CAST

Maria Coughlin	Adrienne Shelly
Matthew Slaughter	Martin Donovan
Jean Coughlin	Merritt Nelson
Jim Slaughter	John MacKay
Peg Coughlin	Edie Falco
John Coughlin	Marko Hunt
Anthony	Gary Sauer
Ed	Matt Malloy
Rachel	Suzanne Castallas
Robert	Jeff Howard
Deli Man	Tom Thon
Biker Mom	Julie Sukman
Nurse Paine	Karen Sillas
Mrs. Blech	Pamela Stewart
Joey Blech	Robby Anderson
Grace Blech	Elizabeth Gouse
Nurse #2	Mildred Jones
Bruce	M.C. Baily
Mr. Santiago	John St. James
Phil (Bartender)	Scott Robinson

and Bill Sage (Bill), Christopher Cooke (Cook), Tamu Favorite (Sales Girl), Jean K. Sifford (Lori), Kathryn Mederos (Factory Woman), Nena Segal (Grandma Coughlin), Bea Delizio (Woman on couch), Leo Gosse (Uncle Leo), Patricia Sullivan (Ruark Boss)

Adrienne Shelly, Martin Donovan
© *Fine Line Features*

THE DOCTOR

(TOUCHSTONE) Producer, Laura Ziskin; Director, Randa Haines; Executive Producer, Edward S. Feldman; Screenplay, Robert Caswell; Based upon the book *A Taste of My Own Medicine* by Ed Rosenbaum, M.D.; Photography, John Seale; Designer, Ken Adam; Editors, Bruce Green, Lisa Fruchtman; Costumes, Joe I. Tompkins; Music, Michael Convertino; Co-Producer, Michael S. Glick; Casting, Lynn Stalmaster; Assistant Director, Dennis Maguire; Presented in association with Silver Screen Partners IV; Distributed by Buena Vista Pictures; Dolby Stereo; Technicolor; Rated PG-13; 123 minutes; July release

CAST

Dr. Jack MacKee	William Hurt
Anne MacKee	Christine Lahti
June Ellis	Elizabeth Perkins
Dr. Murray Caplan	Mandy Patinkin
Dr. Eli Blumfield	Adam Arkin
Nicky MacKee	Charlie Korsmo
Leslie Abbott	Wendy Crewson
Al Cade	Bill Macy
Ralph	J.E. Freeman
Mr. Maris	William Marquez
Alan	Kyle Secor
Sarah	Nicole Orth-Pallavicini
Jay-Jay	Ping Wu
Roger	Tony Fields
Michael	Brian Markinson
Lonnie	Maria Tirabassi
Pete	Ken Lerner
Tim	Bruce Jarchow
Joe	Keith Polk, M.D.
Nancy	Nellye Leonard, O.R.T.
Mr. Richards	Richard McKenzie
Young Patient	Denis Heames
Shirley	Sue Rihr
Nurse Jane	Brandyn Artis
Carrie	Millie Slavin
Laurie	Nancy Parsons
Anthony	John Marshall Jones
Kristin	Laurie Lathem
Joey	Adam Wylie
Dominic	Stephen Moore
Barbara	Cynthia Mason
Joey's Mother	Breon Gorman
Lucy	Renee Victor
Max	Gregor Hesse

and Fran Bennett (Admissions Secretary), Zoaunne LeRoy (Ward Nurse), Jonathan Kohl, M.D. (Anesthesiologist), Ross Eto, M.D. (M.R.I. Tech #1), Michael O'Dwyer (Builder), Karen S. Gregan (Dr. Abbott's Receptionist), Lillian Hurst (Mrs. Maris), Rosa Maria Briz (Mr. Maris' Mother), Steven Gundry, M.D. (Heart Transplant Surgeon), Akuyoe (June's Nurse), Jusak Bernhard (Record Clerk), Nicholas Frangakis (Priest), Matthew T. Clancy, M.D., Jeris Poindexter (Doctors in hallway), Derek Van Longshore (Orderly), Gail Neely, Lily Mariye, Woodryan Alexander, R.N., Susan Schelling Long (O.R. Nurses), Zakes Mokae (Dr. Charles Reed)

Elizabeth Perkins, William Hurt
Above: Hurt, Adam Arkin

Charles Durning, Kathleen Turner
Top Right: Charles McCaughan, Turner
© *Hollywood Pictures*

V. I. WARSHAWSKI

(**HOLLYWOOD PICTURES**) Producer, Jeffrey Lurie; Executive Producers, Penney Finkelman Cox, John P. Marsh; Co-Executive Producers, John Bard Manulis, Lauren C. Weissman; Co-Producer, Doug Claybourne; Director, Jeff Kanew; Screenplay, Edward Taylor, David Aaron Cohen, Nick Thiel; Screen Story, Edward Taylor; Based on the V.I. Warshawski novels by Sara Peretsky; Photography, Jan Kiesser; Designer, Barbara Ling; Editor, C. Timothy O'Meara; Music, Randy Edelman; Costumes, Gloria Gresham; Casting, Glenn Daniels; Assistant Director, Jack F. Sanders; Stunts, Michael Runyard; a Chestnut Hill production; Presented in association with Silver Screen Partners IV; Distributed by Buena Vista Pictures; Dolby Stereo; Technicolor; Rated R; 89 minutes; July release

CAST

V.I. "Vic" Warshawski	Kathleen Turner
Murray	Jay O. Sanders
Lt. Mallory	Charles Durning
Kat Grafalk	Angela Goethals
Paige Grafalk	Nancy Paul
Horton Grafalk	Frederick Coffin
Trumble Grafalk	Charles McCaughan
Bernard "Boom-Boom" Grafalk	Stephen Meadows
Smeissen	Wayne Knight
Sal	Lynnie Godfrey
Lotty	Annie Pitoniak
Mickey	Stephen Root
Phillip Pugh	Robert Clotworthy
Big Eddie	Tom Allard
Babe	Michael G. Hagerty
Flesh	Lee Arenberg
Cabbie	Michael Bacarella
Ernie	John Beasley
McGraw	Everett Smith
Contreras	Herb Muller
Stacy	Theresa Bell
Ron Whortley	Geof Prysirr
Bank Teller	Sandra Foster
Bank Manager	Gregg Almquist
Thugs	Gene Hartline, Gary Epper
Striker	John P. Marsh
Singer	Shirley Johnson
Bassist	Victor Herold
Drummer	Casey Jones
Keyboardist	Professor Eddie Lusk
Guitarist	Maurice Vaughn
Paramedic	Aaron Seville
Maid	Doris Le Gras
Sumitora	John Fujioka
Bodyguards	Roger T. Ito, Robert Wong

Tom Allard, Kathleen Turner Above: Turner

LIFE STINKS

(MGM) Producer/Director, Mel Brooks; Executive Producer, Ezra Swerdlow; Screenplay, Mel Brooks, Rudy De Luca, Steve Haberman; Story, Mel Brooks, Ron Clark, Rudy De Luca, Steve Haberman; Photography, Steven Poster; Designer, Peter Larkin; Costumes, Mary Malin; Editor, David Rawlins; Music, John Morris; Casting, Bill Shepard, Todd Thaler; Associate Producer, Kim Kurumada; Assistant Director, Mitchell Block; a Brooksfilm production from MGM-Pathe Communications Co.; Dolby Stereo; Deluxe color; Rated PG-13; 95 minutes; July release

CAST

Goddard Bolt	Mel Brooks
Molly	Lesley Ann Warren
Vance Crasswell	Jeffrey Tambor
Pritchard	Stuart Pankin
Sailor	Howard Morris
J. Paul Getty	Rudy De Luca
Fumes	Teddy Wilson
Knowles	Michael Ensign
Stevens	Matthew Faison
Willy	Billy Barty
Mean Victor	Brian Thompson
Yo	Raymond O'Connor
Flophouse Owner	Carmine Caridi
Reverend at wedding	Sammy Shore
Spanish Interpreter	Frank Roman
Dr. Kahahn	Marvin Braverman
Fergueson	Robert Ridgley
Dodd	John Welsh
Store Owner	Stanley Brock
Wheelchair Attendant	James Van Patten
Male Nurse	Michael Pniewski
Head Nurse	Marianne Muellerleile
Capacity Nurse	Angela Gordon
Mercedes Driver	Danny Wells
Paramedics	Larry Cedar, Christopher Birt
Burrito-Eating Bum	Johnny Cocktails
Taco Stand Owner	Clifton Wells
Derelict outside flophouse	George Berkeley
Policemen	Anthony Messina, David Correia
Society Patron	Helene Winston
Boy dancing in doorway	Terrence Williams

and Anne Betancourt, Kathryn Skatula, Robin Shepard (Nurses), Mary Watson, Saida Pagan, Tamara Taylor, Henry Kaiser (Newscasters), Joan Crosby (Woman at fire), Ira Miller (Man at fire), James Mapp (Blind Man), Sam Menning (Old Wino), Ralph Ahn (Chinese Cook), Stu Gilliam (Desmond), Darrow Igus (Maynard), James Martinez (Dancing Vagrant at Party), Rose DuCaine (Dancing Dowager at party), Ralph Mauro (Hors d'oeuvres Vagrant at party), Martin Charles Warner (Dirty-Faced Vagrant at party), Anthony Thomas Mitchell (Nibbler Driver), Patrick Valenzuela (Street Person at fight), Carmen Filpi (Pops - elevens-up), Casey King (Shopping Cart Chauffeur), Ronny Graham (Priest's Voice), Jere Laird (Stock Market Reporter)

Gene Wilder, Richard Pryor
© *Tri-Star Pictures*

ANOTHER YOU

(TRI-STAR) Producer/Screenplay, Ziggy Steinberg; Executive Producer, Ted Zachary; Director, Maurice Phillips; Photography, Victor J. Kemper; Designer, Dennis Washington; Editor, Dennis M. Hill; Costumes, Ruth Myers; Music, Charles Gross; Casting, Mike Fenton, Allison Cowitt; Associate Producers, Robert Anderson, Louis D'Esposito, Allan Wertheim; Assistant Director, Louis D'Esposito; Dolby Stereo; Technicolor; Rated R; 98 minutes; July release

CAST

George (Abe Fielding)	Gene Wilder
Eddie Dash	Richard Pryor
Elaine	Mercedes Ruehl
Rupert Dibbs	Stephen Lang
Gloria	Vanessa Williams
Al	Phil Rubenstein
Therapist	Peter Michael Goetz
Harry	Billy Beck
Tim	Jerry Houser
Phil	Kevin Pollak
Walt	Craig Richard Nelson
Gail	Kandis Chappell
Volunteer	Elsa Raven
Nurse	Catherine E. Coulson
Male Patient	Norman Glasser
Maitre 'D	Gil Mandelik
Hatcheck Girl	Tammy Hanson
Headwaiter	Giancarlo Scandiuzzi
Waiter	Maurice Phillips
Dentist	Vincent Schiavelli
Dental Assistant	Romy Rosemont
Dental Patients	Tabi Cooper, Annie O'Donnell
Band Leader	Andy Summers
Masseur	Seppo Viljanen
Benziger	Biff Yeager
Foster	Peter Schuck
Hayes	Gail Cameron
Blumenthal	Bill Washington
Employee	Sheila M. Howard
Carlos	Gianni Russo
Frankenstein	Dennis Washington
Traffic Cop	Dennis O'Sullivan
Fan	Sheryl Bernstein
Bavarian Trio	Willi Vollerthun, Lothar Beer, Peter Vogel
The Bear	Lucky
Patient	Michael J. Pollard

Lesley Ann Warren, Mel Brooks, Teddy Wilson, Howard Morris © *MGM-Pathe Communications*

Leslie Bega, Patrick Dempsey Top Left: Christian Slater, Dempsey, Michael Gambon Left: Slater, Lara Flynn Boyle © *Universal City Studios*

MOBSTERS

(UNIVERSAL) Producer, Steve Roth; Executive Producer, C.O. Erickson; Director, Michael Karbelnikoff; Screenplay, Michael Mahern, Nicholas Kazan; Story, Michael Mahern; Photography, Lajos Koltai; Designer, Richard Sylbert; Editors, Scott Smith, Joe D'Augustine; Costumes, Ellen Mirojnick; Music, Michael Small; Casting, Bonnie Timmerman, Nancy Naylor; Assistant Director, Albert Shapiro; Stunts, Victor Paul; Dolby Stereo; Deluxe color; Rated R; 104 minutes; July release

CAST

Charlie "Lucky" Luciano ....Christian Slater
Meyer Lansky ....Patrick Dempsey
Benny "Bugsy" Siegel ....Richard Grieco
Frank Costello ....Costas Mandylor
Mara Motes ....Lara Flynn Boyle
Don Masseria ....Anthony Quinn
Arnold Rothstein ....F. Murray Abraham
Don Faranzano..Michael Gambon
Tommy Reina ....Christopher Penn
Mad Dog Coll ....Nicholas Sadler
Anna Lansky...Leslie Bega
Short Stick ....Billy Bastiani
Sonny Catania...Frank Collison
Rocco ....Robert Z'Dar
Joey..Rodney Eastman
Antonio Luciano ....Andy Romano
Rosalie Luciano...Bianca Rossini
Mike Shane ....Clark Heathcliffe Brolly
Joe Palermo ....Leonard Termo
Father Bonotto ....Seymour Cassel
Joe Profaci..Joe Viterelli
Tony No Nose..James Michael
Nathan Citron ....Russ Fega
Joe Bonnano ....John Chappoulis
Al Capone ....Titus Welliver
Black Gangster ....Russell Curry
Blues Singer ....Carmen Twillie
Cute Debutante ....Lynette Walden
Luciano's Driver ....Steve Picerni
Crapshooters ....Jeremy Schoenberg, Miles Perlich
Rabbi..Alan Charof
Irish Cop ....Anto Nolan
Little Brother ....Stevie Restivo
Little Sister...Caroline Gillette
Joey's Mother ....Traci Swensen
and Sean Blackmam (Another Italian), Bryan Law (Irish Thug), Trish Steele (Costello's Mother), Emile Nicolaou (Kid), Fyvush Finkel (Tailor), Don Brockett (Irish Politician), Anya Longwell, Monique Noel Lovelace, Karen Russell (Showgirls), Jennifer Gatti (Secretary), Jim Wilkey (Coll's Driver), Ron Marquette (Maitre d'), Linda Fontanette (Maid), Anna Berger (Mrs. Greene), Jan Solomita, Sharmagne Leland-St. John (Wedding Guests), Elizabeth Graham, Ava Fabian (Cute Girls), Stan Berry (Card Player), J.P. Romano, Erik Degn (Goons), Richard Garneau (Room Service Waiter), Willy Garson (Telephone Operator), Charles Picerni, Jr., Nick Dimitri (Bodyguards)

Christian Slater, Patrick Dempsey, Costas Mandylor, Richard Grieco Above: Anthony Quinn; F. Murray Abraham

HOT SHOTS!

Cary Elwes

(20th CENTURY FOX) Producer, Bill Badalato; Executive Producer, Pat Proft; Director, Jim Abrahams; Screenplay, Jim Abrahams, Pat Proft; Photography, Bill Butler; Designer, William A. Elliott; Editors, Jane Kurson, Eric Sears; Music, Sylvester Levay; Costumes, Mary Malin; Casting, Mali Finn; Flying Sequences Director, Richard T. Stevens; Unit Production Manager/Associate Producer, Stephen McEveety; Assistant Director, Tom Davies; Dolby Stereo; CFI color; Rated PG-13; 85 minutes; July release

CAST

Sean "Topper" Harley	Charlie Sheen
Kent Gregory	Cary Elwes
Ramada Thompson	Valeria Golino
Admiral "Tug" Benson	Lloyd Bridges
Lt. Commander James Block	Kevin Dunn
Jim "Wash Out" Pfaffenbach	Jon Cryer
Pete "Dead Meat" Thompson	William O'Leary
Dawn Kowalski	Kristy Swanson
Wilson	Efrem Zimbalist, Jr.
Buzz Harley	Bill Irwin
Mrs. "Dead Meat" Thompson	Heidi Swedberg
"Red" Herring	Bruce A. Young
"Mailman" Farnham	Ryan Stiles
Owatonna, "The Old One"	Rino Thunder
Rosener	Mark Arnott
Captain Margolis	Ryan Cutrona
Doctor	Don Lake
Air Controller	Kelly Connell
Ambulance Driver	Tony Simotes
Paramedic	Don Luce
Nurse	Judith Kahan
Communications Officer	Jeff Bright
Ring Announcer	Jimmy Lennon, Jr.
Francine, the Secretary	Marie Thomas
Piano Player	Marc Shaiman
Drill Sergeants	Cylk Cozart, Christopher J. Keene
Scooter	Ryan Fitzgerald
Rabbi	Ed Herschlar
Amish Man	Jimmie Ray Weeks
Amish Woman	Annie O'Donnell
Eskimo	Mack Yamaguchi
Themselves	Charles Barkley, Bill Laimbeer
Pope John Paul II	Gene Greytak
Humphrey "Bogie" Bogart	Tony Lorea
Saddam Hussein	Jerry Halera
Elvis "The King" Presley	Bob Lenz
Liberace	Willie Collins
Precocious Paper Boy	Robert Puro
Handsome Milkman	Richard Lasting
Boxers	Elston Ridge, Max Jones
Conspiratorial Crewman	Chris Doyle
Parking Valets	Pablo Prietto, John Bankson

and Gary Brayboy, Al Clegg, Kevin Eads, Richard Emanuel, Brent Freeman, Craig McIntosh, Tony Moreno, David Oliver, Kip Pierce, Sean Wright (Sleepy Weasel Squadron)

Top: Charlie Sheen Below: Lloyd Bridges Left: Valeria Golino, Sheen © *Twentieth Century Fox*

Jon Cryer, Charlie Sheen,
William O'Leary, Cary Elwes

DOC HOLLYWOOD

(WARNER BROS.) Producers, Susan Solt, Deborah D. Johnson; Executive Producer, Marc Merson; Director, Michael Caton-Jones; Screenplay, Jeffrey Price, Peter S. Seaman, Daniel Pyne; Based on the book *What...Dead Again?* by Neil B. Shulman, M.D.; Adaptation, Laurian Leggett; Photography, Michael Chapman; Designer, Lawrence Miller; Editor, Priscilla Nedd-Friendly; Music, Carter Burwell; Song: "The One and Only" by Nik Kershaw/performed by Chesney Hawkes; Costumes, Richard Hornung; Casting, Marion Dougherty, Owens Hill; Associate Producer, Neil B. Shulman, M.D.; Dolby Stereo; Technicolor; Rated PG-13; 103 minutes; August release

CAST

Dr. Ben Stone	Michael J. Fox
Lou	Julie Warner
Dr. Hogue	Barnard Hughes
Hank	Woody Harrelson
Nick Nicholson	David Ogden Stiers
Lillian	Frances Sternhagen
Dr. Halberstrom	George Hamilton
Nancy Lee	Bridget Fonda
Melvin	Mel Winkler
Maddie	Helen Martin
Judge Evans	Roberts Blossom
Cotton	Tom Lacy
Aubrey Draper	Macon McCalman
Simon Tidwell	Raye Birk
Nurse Packer	Eyde Byrde
Lane	William Cowart
Violet	Amzie Strickland
Kyle	Time Winters
Mary	K.T. Vogt
John Crawford	Jordon Lund
Mortimer	Robert Munns
McClary	Douglas Brush
Shulman	Barry Sobel
Emma	Amanda Junette Donatelli
Zeb's Father	Billy Gillespie
Zeb's Mother	Kathy Poling
Zeb	Eric Bechtel
Receptionist	Cristi Conaway
Mulready	Kelly Jo Minter

and Michael Caton-Jones (Maitre D'), Michael Chapman (Shooting Gallery Operator), Ted Davis (Taxi Driver), Melanie MacQueen (Woman with spider), Adele Malis-Morey (Woman with glasses), Darrell Jay Cook (Huge Man), Dan Charles (Boy at shooting gallery), Kirsche Smith (Nurse), David Thompkins (Medic), Dan Bell (Patient), Karen Hartman-Golden, Vince Burnes (Loonies), Roxanne Benseman (Farm Lady), Kelly Roland (Squash Queen), Janis Bjorkland (Girl with spider), Daniel Cerny (Boy with spider), Emily Lester (Housewife), David M. Dutch Van Dalsen (Man with rash), David Dupre (Distressed Man), Martin Alan Johnson (Orderly), Ken Josefsberg (Doctor)

Top: Michael J. Fox, Julie Warner
Below: Tom Lacy, Fox Left: Fox, Woody Harrelson
© *Warner Bros. Inc.*

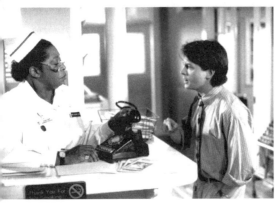

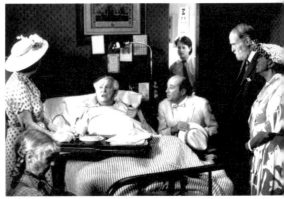

Eyde Byrde, Michael J. Fox

Amzie Strickland, Frances Sternhagen, Barnard
Hughes, Macon McCalman, Michael J. Fox,
Roberts Blossom, Helen Martin

Bolo Yeung, Jean-Claude Van Damme
Top Left: Van Damme Left: Van Damme, Van Damme
© *Columbia Pictures*

DOUBLE IMPACT

(COLUMBIA) Producers, Ashok Amritraj, Jean-Claude Van Damme; Executive Producers, Moshe Diamant, Charles Layton; Director, Sheldon Lettich; Screenplay, Sheldon Lettich, Jean-Claude Van Damme; Story, Sheldon Lettich, Jean-Claude Van Damme, Steve Meerson, Peter Krikes; Co-Producers, Sheldon Lettich, Terry Martin Carr; Line Producer, Evzen Kolar; Supervising Producer, Rick Nathanson; Photography, Richard Kline; Designer, John Jay Moore; Music, Arthur Kempel; Editor, Mark Conte; Costumes, Joseph Porro; Casting, James Tarzia; Fight Choreographer, Jean-Claude Van Damme; a Stone Group Pictures presentation; Dolby Stereo; Technicolor; Rated R; 118 minutes; August release

CAST

Chad/Alex...Jean-Claude Van Damme
Frank Avery..Geoffrey Lewis
Nigel Griffith ....Alan Scarfe
Danielle Wilde...Alonna Shaw
Kara ....Cory Everson
Raymond Zhang...................................Philip Chan Yan Kin
Moon..Bolo Yeung
Katherine Wagner ....Sarah-Jane Varley
Chinese Nurse ....Wu Fong Lung
Baby Chad ....Alicia Stevenson
Baby Alex..Paul Aylett
Paul Wagner ....Andy Armstrong
Mr. Chen..Eugene Choy
Karate Instructor ....Donn Berdahl
Nun at orphanage...Sarah Yuen
Student...Julie Strain
Karate Students..........................Jack Gilardi, Jr., Dave Lea
Dockworkers ....Chan Siu Sing, Leo Lee
Mah Jong Manager...Kamel Krifa
Smuggler ....Galen Yuen
Crewman on Alex's Boat ....Christopher Leung
Chinese Smugglers ....Ng Kwok Kai, Chow Kwok Po,
                                                                              Yu Wai Keung
Hong Kong Marine Police..................Simon Cheung, Shum Kin Sang
Triad Thugs ....Lee Tat Chiu, Lee Bing Chiu, Wong Chi Kin
Gateman for Triad ....John Cheung
2nd Gateman..Tsang Sing Kwok
Card-Playing Guard....................................Ching Wai Chung
Big Thug outside lab...David Ho
Body Guard with spurs ....Peter Malota
Klimax Klub Gangsters...........Tam Chum To, Eric Ng, Chan Siu Wah and Evan Lurie (Klimax Klub Bouncer), Ng Kwok Kai (Mr. Ngyuen), Roland Lor (Klimax Klub Manager), Jennifer Stone (Klimax Klub Hostess), Rita Lau (Hostess with Frank), Wong Chung Ching (Walkie Talkie Thug), Johnny Cheung (Thug on container), Georges Bejue (Thug who mauls Danielle)

Geoffrey Lewis, Jean-Claude Van Damme

PURE LUCK

(UNIVERSAL) Producers, Lance Hool, Sean Daniel; Executive Producer, Francis Veber; Director, Nadia Tass; Screenplay, Herschel Weingrod, Timothy Harris; Photography, David Parker; Designer, Peter Wooley; Editor, Billy Weber; Music, Jonathan Sheffer, Danny Elfman; Casting, Nancy Nayor; Associate Producer, Conrad Hool; Assistant Director, Matt Beesley; a Sean Daniel Company production; Dolby Stereo; Deluxe color; Rated PG; 96 Minutes; August release

CAST

Eugene Proctor	Martin Short
Raymond Campanella	Danny Glover
Valerie Highsmith	Sheila Kelley
George Highsmith	Sam Wanamaker
Frank Grimes	Scott Wilson
Dr. Monosoff	Harry Shearer
Inspector Segura	Jorge Russek
Fernando	Rodrigo Puebla
Tyler	John H. Brennan
Pilot	Jorge Luke
Prisoner	Abel Woolrich
Secretary	Patricia Gage
Girl at club	Ariane Pellicer
Nurses	Alexandra Vicencio, Sharlene Martin
Hotel Porter	Ruben Cristiany
Doorman	Flavio Castillero
Girlfriend at hotel bar	Maria Rosa Manzini
Bouncer	Carlos Gonzalez
Hoods	Gerardo Moreno, Rene Escandon, Alfredo Gutierrez, Nicolas Jasso
Reception Manager	Andaluz Russell
Gambling Club Bartender	Raul Martinez
Indian	Rodolfo De Alejandre
Bandaged Indian	Marco Antonio Arzate
Room Service Waiter	Pepe Olivares
Doorman	Fernando Elizondo
Big Boyfriend	Gonzalo Sanchez
Night Club Bartender	Sergio Calderon
Taxi Driver	Michael Puttonen
Airport Waiter	Carlos Romano

and Josefina Echanove, Malena Doria (Nuns), Magda Rodriguez (Girl's Girlfriend), Julian Bucio, Arminius Arzate, Hector Tavares, Ignacio Gomez (Policia), Gabriella Moreno (Gambler's Girlfriend), Lionel Douglass (Man at airport restaurant), Sammy Ortiz (Gambler), Willebaldo Bucio, Jorge Luis Corzo (Purse Thieves), Gabriel Pingarron, Pedro Altamirano (Prison Guards), Alan C. Peterson (Large Man), David Lisle (Highsmith's Employee), Jorge Zepeda (Airport Guard), Walter Marsh (Airport Security Guard), Deryl Hayes, William MacDonald (Airport Employees), Rolando Pimentel, Jesus Moreno (Hotel Porters), Mario Arreola (Concierge), Juan Manuel (Hotel Bar Waiter), Ana Patricia (Woman at restaurant)

Below: Danny Glover, Martin Short
© *Universal City Studios*

Charles Rocket, Dylan Baker, David Rasche, Raymond Burr, Mariel Hemingway, John Candy, Emma Samms
© *Metro-Goldwyn-Mayer*

DELIRIOUS

(MGM) Producers, Lawrence J. Cohen, Fred Freeman, Doug Claybourne; Executive Producer, Richard Donner; Director, Tom Mankiewicz; Screenplay, Lawrence J. Cohen, Fred Freeman; Photography, Robert Stevens; Designer, Angelo Graham; Music, Cliff Eidelman; Editors, William Gordean, Tina Hirsch; Costumes, Molly Maginnis; Casting, David Rubin; Associate Producers, Ann Ford Stevens, Jill Simpson; Assistant Director, John Kretchmer; Title song written and performed by Prince; from MGM-Pathe Communications; Dolby Stereo; Deluxe color; Rated PG; 95 minutes; August release

CAST

Jack Gable	John Candy
Janet DuBois/Louise	Mariel Hemingway
Rachel Hedison/Laura	Emma Samms
Carter Hedison	Raymond Burr
Blake Hedison	Dylan Baker
Ty Hedison	Charles Rocket
Dr. Paul Kirkland/Dennis	David Rasche
Nurse Helen Caldwell	Andrea Thompson
Mickey	Zach Grenier
Lou Sherwood	Jerry Orbach
Arlene Sherwood	Renee Taylor
Fetterman	Milt Oberman
Cable Man	Mark Boone Junior
Edward the Butler	Tony Steedman
Len	John Michael Bolger
Marge	Rita Gomez
TV Reporter	Stephanie Segal
Chauffeur	Mark Zuelke
Riley	Dick Durock
Mason	Anthony G. Schmidt
Manny	Murray Rubin
Auctioneer	Peter Bromilow
Bellboy	Patrick Bristow
Manu	Jason Ross-Azikiwe
Himself	Robert Wagner

and Brooke Ashley (Cheerleader), Glenn Dixon (Elderly Man), Paul Tuerpe (Waiter), Fred Morsell (Choking Man), Zach Phifer (Attendant), Susan Isaacs (Marie), Marvin Kaplan (Typewriter Repairman), Elaine Swayneson (Secretary), Jay Della (Ashford Falls Cable Man), Michael Caldwell (Busboy), Bill Wittman (Soap Announcer), The Kretchmers (Themselves)

MYSTERY DATE

(ORION) Producer, Cathleen Summers; Director, Jonathan Wacks; Screenplay, Parker Bennett, Terry Runté; Photography, Oliver Wood; Designer, John Willett; Editor, Tina Hirsch; Music, John DuPrez; Casting, Amanda Mackey, Cathy Sandrich, Stuart Aikins; Associate Producer, Susan Moore; Costumes, Jori Woodman; Dolby Stereo; Deluxe color; Rated PG-13; 98 minutes; August release

CAST

Tom McHugh	Ethan Hawke
Geena Matthews	Teri Polo
Craig McHugh	Brian McNamara
Dwight	Fisher Stevens
James Lew	B.D. Wong
Sharpie	Tony Rosato
Doheny	Don Davis
Fortune Teller	James Hong
Janitor	Victor Wong
Vince	Ping Wu
Crully	Duncan Fraser
Detective Condon	Jerry Wasserman
Mr. McHugh	Terry David Mulligan
Mrs. McHugh	Merrilyn Gann
Ben	Stephen Chang
Jerry	Russell Jung
Stella	Michelle Little
Mr. Lusky	Allan Lysell
Mrs. Lusky	Donna Lysell
Mr. Culp	Keith Beardwood
Suzette	Sharlene Martin
Sandy	Celia Martin
Limo Driver	Ian Black
Suzy	Karen Campbell
Aldo	Sean Orr
Earl	David "Squatch" Ward
Bartender	Peter Williams
Bonna	Constance Barnes
Motorcycle Cop	Todd Duckworth
Cops	Peter Lacroix, James Zachery
May Wong	May Wong
Wine Steward	Tom Wong
Waiters	C.K. Tan, Alan To
Lew Mansion Gate Guard	Derek Lowe
Katz	Morris Panych
Bernard	Garrick Jang
Band at Kory's	Tabou Combo
Band at Club Voltaire	Gwar
Combo at McHugh House	Stephen Drake, Craig Northey

Top: Teri Polo, Ethan Hawke Below: Hawke, B.D. Wong
Left: Fisher Stevens
© Orion Pictures

Ethan Hawke, Brian McNamara

Ethan Hawke

BARTON FINK

(20th CENTURY FOX) Producer, Ethan Coen; Director, Joel Coen; Screenplay, Ethan Coen, Joel Coen; Co-Producer, Graham Place; Executive Producers, Ben Barenholtz, Ted Pedas, Jim Pedas, Bill Durkin; Photography, Roger Deakins; Designer, Dennis Gassner; Costumes, Richard Hornung; Music, Carter Burwell; Editor, Roderick Jaynes; Casting, Donna Isaacson, John Lyons; Assistant Director, Joe Camp III; a Circle Films presentation; Dolby Stereo; DuArt color; Rated R; 117 minutes; August release

CAST

Barton Fink	John Turturro
Charlie Meadows	John Goodman
Audrey Taylor	Judy Davis
Jack Lipnick	Michael Lerner
W.P. Mayhew	John Mahoney
Ben Geisler	Tony Shalhoub
Lou Breeze	Jon Polito
Chet	Steve Buscemi
Garland Stanford	David Warrilow
Detective Mastrionotti	Richard Portnow
Detective Deutsch	Christopher Murney
Derek	I.M. Hobson
Poppy Carnahan	Megan Faye
Richard St. Claire	Lance Davis
Pete	Harry Bugin
Maitre D'	Anthony Gordon
Stagehand	Jack Denbo
Clapper Boy	Max Grodenchik
Referee	Robert Beecher
Wrestler	Darwyn Swalve
Geisler's Secretary	Gayle Vance
Sailor	Johnny Judkins
USO Girl	Jana Marie Hupp
Beauty	Isabelle Townsend

Top: John Goodman, John Turturro Left: Turturro, Michael Lerner © *Circle Films Inc.*

John Turturro

John Mahoney, Judy Davis
Above: John Turturro, Jon Polito

William Russ, Glenn Plummer
Top Right: Plummer, Russ Right: Russ
© *Miramax Films*

PASTIME

(MIRAMAX) formerly *One Cup of Coffee*; Producers, Eric Tynan Young, Robin B. Armstrong; Co-Producer, Gerald R. Molen; Director, Robin B. Armstrong; Screenplay, D.M. Eyre, Jr.; Photography, Tom Richmond; Designer, David W. Ford; Associate Producer, Jonathan G. Chambers; Music, Lee Holdridge; Editor, Mark S. Westmore; Casting, Deborah Barylski, Camille Patton; Costumes, Kristine Brown; Assistant Director, Roberto Quezada; a Bullpen Ltd./Open Road production; Color; Rated PG; 94 minutes; August release

CAST

Roy Dean Bream	William Russ
Randy Keever	Scott Plank
Spicer	Reed Rudy
Hahn	Ricky Paull Goldin
Simmons	Peter Murnik
Colbeck	John Jones
Tyrone Debray	Glenn Plummer
Walsh	Pat O'Bryan
Clyde Bigby	Noble Willingham
Arnold	Charles Tyner
Peter Laporte	Jeffrey Tambor
Ethel	Kathryn Kates
Art	Troy Evans
Sliding Base Runner	Joey Banks
1st Base Umpires	Chuck Fick, Sy Mogel
Frank	John Homa
Pool Player	Michael Chieffo
Inez Brice	Dierdre O'Connell
Drunk Old-Timer	Don Perry
Bomber Pitcher	Brogan Roche
Bomber Catcher	Craig Stark
Cal	John Achorn
Bomber Manager	Mark Benedetto
Beaned Bomber	Tom Davidson
Woman at bar	Mary Pat Gleason
Elton	Charles Stranski
Mrs. Laporte	Susan Cash
Catty Women at party	Meghan Geary, Sarah Zinsser
Funeral Director	Tom Pletts
Streamer Fans	Ernie Banks, Duke Snider
VFW Men	Bob Feller, Harmon Killebrew, Bill Mazeroski
Flag Raiser	Don Newcombe

and Aaron Albert, Chris Allen, Darin Burton, Greg Chizek, Tony Jaramillo, John Martin, Rick Slagle, Tony Solis, Darryl Allen, Richard Cavazos, Glen Gillespie, Lonnie Kalapp, David Lyons, Mike Main, Mike Neil, Vince McAllister, Larry Stalhaufer, Joe Szczepanksi, Paul Visone, Mike Wood (Baseball Players)

Ricky Paull Goldin, Scott Plank, William Russ, Peter Murnik Above: Deirdre O'Connell

Kenneth Branagh Top Left: Branagh, Emma Thompson
Top Right: Thompson Below Left: Thompson,
Andy Garcia © *Paramount Pictures*

DEAD AGAIN

(PARAMOUNT) Producers, Lindsay Doran, Charles H. Maguire; Executive Producer, Sydney Pollack; Director, Kenneth Branagh; Screenplay, Scott Frank; Photography, Matthew F. Leonetti; Designer, Tim Harvey; Editor, Peter E. Berger; Costumes, Phyllis Dalton; Music, Patrick Doyle; Casting, Gail Levin; Assistant Director, Steve Danton; Co-Producer, Dennis Feldman; a Mirage Production; Dolby Stereo; Technicolor; Rated R; 108 minutes; August release

CAST

Roman Strauss/Mike Church	Kenneth Branagh
Gray Baker	Andy Garcia
Grace/Margaret Strauss	Emma Thompson
Sister Constance	Lois Hall
Father Timothy	Richard Easton
Sister Madeleine/Starlet	Jo Anderson
Pickup Driver	Patrick Montes
Clerk	Raymond Cruz
Dr. Cozy Carlisle	Robin Williams
"Piccolo" Pete	Wayne Knight
Cop #1/Party Guest #2	Patrick Doyle
Cop #2	Erik Kilpatrick
Handcuffed Woman	Gordana Rashovich
Franklyn Madson	Derek Jacobi
Syd	Obba Babatunde
Lydia Larson	Christine Ebersole
Otto	Vasek C. Simek
Inga	Hanna Schygulla
Frankie	Gregor Hesse
Cafe Owner	John Gould Rubin
Doug	Campbell Scott
Party Guest #1	Steven Culp
Nurse	Yvette Freeman

Kenneth Branagh, Derek Jacobi, Emma Thompson
Above: Thompson, Branagh, Jacobi

HARLEY DAVIDSON AND THE MARLBORO MAN

(MGM) Producer, Jere Henshaw; Director, Simon Wincer; Screenplay/Co-Producer, Don Michael Paul; Photography, David Eggby; Designer, Paul Peters; Music, Basil Poledouris; Editor, Corky Ehlers; Costumes, Richard Shissler; Line Producer, Donald West; Casting, Mike Fenton, Judy Taylor, Valorie Massalas; Associate Producer, Missy Alpern; Assistant Director, Robert Rooy; Stunts, Billy Burton; a Krisjair/Laredo production from MGM-Pathe Communications; Dolby Stereo; Deluxe color; Rated R; 95 minutes; August release

CAST

Harley Davidson	Mickey Rourke
Marlboro	Don Johnson
Virginia Slim	Chelsea Field
Alexander	Daniel Baldwin
Jimmy Jiles	Giancarlo Esposito
Lulu Daniels	Vanessa Williams
Thom	Robert Ginty
Kimiko	Tia Carrere
Old Man	Julius Harris
Jose	Eloy Casados
Jack Daniels	Big John Studd
Chance Wilder	Tom Sizemore
The Woman	Mitzi Martin
Suzie	Kelly Hu
Punk with gun	James Nardini
Punk with knife	Brenan T. Baird
Big Indian	Branscombe Richmond
Indian's Girlfriend	Stacey Elliott
Bartender	Hans Howe
Stripper	Bobbie Tyler
Arm Wrestler	Marlin Darton
Guards	Jordan Lund, Steve Tannen
John	Billy D. Lucas
David	Sven-Ole Thorsen
Peter	Dennis Scott
Michael	Cody Glenn
Honey	Michele Laybourn
Luggage Jockeys	Debbie Lynn Ross, Michael Valverde
Jake McAllister	Stan Ivar
Henchmen	Stan Chambers, R.J. Chambers
Hitchhiker	Theresa San-Nicholas
Disc Jockey	Sean "Hollywood" Hamilton

Top: Mickey Rourke, Don Johnson
Below: Johnson, Rourke Right: Rourke, Johnson
© MGM-Pathe Communications

Vanessa Williams, Mickey Rourke, Don Johnson

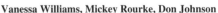

Tom Sizemore, Don Johnson

87

DEFENSELESS

(SEVEN ARTS/NEW LINE CINEMA) Producers, Renee Missel, David Bombyk; Executive Producers, Taylor Hackford, Stuart Benjamin; Director, Martin Campbell; Screenplay, James Hicks; Story, James Hicks, Jeff Burkhart; Photography, Phil Meheux; Designer, Curtis A. Schnell; Editors, Lou Lombardo, Chris Wimble; Music, Curt Sobel; Associate Producer, Whitney Green; Casting, Deborah Lucchesi, Elisabeth Leustig; Costumes, Mary Rose; Assistant Directors, Matia Karrell, Rip Murray; a New Visions Pictures presentation; Dolby Stereo; Deluxe color; Rated R; 104 minutes; August release

CAST

T.K. Katwuller	Barbara Hershey
Det. George Beutel	Sam Shepard
Ellie Seldes	Mary Beth Hurt
Steven Seldes	J.T. Walsh
Janna Seldes	Kellie Overbey
Bull Dozer	Jay O. Sanders
Jack Hammer	John Kapelos
Mrs. Bodeck	Sheree North
Monroe	Randy Brooks
Dubbing Theatre Employee	Christopher M. Brown
Policeman	Michael Collins
Bodeck	George P. Wilbur
T.K.'s Receptionist	Marabina Jaimes
Board Members in law firm	John Achorn, Lisa Darr, William Hayes, Glenn Wilson
Client #1	Anne Alexander
Receptionist at dubbing studio	Mercedes Shirley
Projectionist	Walt Woodson
Cashier at fast food restaurant	Meritta Veilleux
Russell	Steve Zettler
Doctor in morgue	Sandy Ignon
Autopsy Technician	Jeanne Mori
Cindy Bodeck	Christine Elise
Reporter at fundraiser	Michael D. Leinert
Singer at fundraiser	Carrie Jachnuk
Bandleader at fundraiser	Trevor A. Felix
Monroe's Campaign Manager	Caine Richards
Campaign Workers	Paul Collins, Kirk Thornton
Doctor	Time Winters
Nurse	Marilyn Raye Bradfield
Elevator Repairmen	Jonathan Gordon, Vince Melocchi
Judge	Sandy Martin
Costas	Peter Allas
Lab Technician	Mark Bringelson
Jury Foreman	Harold Braun
Court Clerk	Ed Hooks

Top: Mary Beth Hurt, Barbara Hershey Below: J.T. Walsh; Sheree North Right: Sam Shepard, Hershey
© *New Visions Pictures*

Barbara Hershey, Sam Shepard

Mary Beth Hurt, Barbara Hershey

TRUE IDENTITY

(TOUCHSTONE) Producers, Carol Baum, Teri Schwartz; Executive Producers, Sandy Gallin, Howard Rosenman; Director, Charles Lane; Screenplay, Andy Breckman; Photography, Tom Ackerman; Designer, John DeCuir, Jr.; Costumes, Abigail Murray; Editor, Kent Beyda; Music, Marc Marder; Casting, Pat Golden; Associate Producer, Howard M. Brickner; Assistant Director, Ellen H. Schwartz; "Miles Pope" Makeup Designers, John Caglione, Jr., Doug Drexler; Presented in association with Silver Screen Partners IV; Distributed by Buena Vista Pictures; Dolby Stereo; Technicolor; Rated R; 92 minutes

CAST

Miles Pope	Lenny Henry
Frank Luchino/Leland Carver	Frank Langella
Duane	Charles Lane
Craig Houston	J.T. Walsh
Kristi Reeves	Anne-Marie Johnson
Anthony	Andreas Katsulas
Harvey Cooper	Michael McKean
Rita Carver	Peggy Lipton
Grunfeld	Bill Raymond
Himself	James Earl Jones
Tyler	Darnell Williams
Frank LaMotta	Christopher Collins
Taxi Driver	Melvin Van Peebles
Martha	Ruth Brown
Ruth	Fantasia Owens
Janitor	Joe Bellan
FBI Driver	James Landi
FBI Agent	Beth Robbins
Helicopter Pilot	Jim Gavin
Acting Students	Cynthia Blackledge, Eric Briant Wells
Red-Haired Acting Student	Valerie Holvick
Miles' Neighbors	Hazelle Goodman, Maria C. Hurtado
Ticket Agent	Katie Graves
Orlando Ticket Agent	Greg Travis
Man on line	James Bilbrey
Stewardess	Laura Schaefer
Pilot	James Mathers
Flight Engineer	Jonathan Frechette
Airplane Husband	Michael Baskin
Airplane Wife	Tracy Brooks Swope
Cab Men	Robert Black, Joseph A. Jackson
Police Sergeant	Mik Scriba
Cop #1	Ken Miles
Police Lineup Guy	Clifford Shegog
Police Station Woman	Lilyan Chauvin
Burly Cop	Raymond Forchion
Karen	Karen Willins
Lola	Ilona Wilson
FBI Secretary	Roselyn D. Schwartz
Horror Movie Actor	Peter Fitzgerald
Fifth Avenue Pedestrian	George Riddick
Brother	Damon Pooser
Cab Woman	Olivia Sklar
Senator	Grant Owens
FBI Receptionist	Joyce Meadows
Alley Guys	Michael White, Victor Colicchio, Bobby Johnson
Country Club Receptionist	Fred Springer
Distinguished Man	Glenn David Calloway
Audition Actor	Anthony Johnson
Director	Austin Pendleton
Director's Assistant	Jane Marla Robbins
Waitress	Bettiann Fishman
Desdemona	Shannon Holt
Emilia	Lynne Griffin
Iago	Judson Scott
Roderigo	Richard Ganoung
Clown	David Martel Bryant

and Robert Haufrecht (FBI Lobby Agent), Sarah Baley, Ann Schulman, Christina Wright (Audience Members), Shane Dixon (FBI Agent on catwalk), Doug Carfrae (JFK Ticket Agent)

**Top: Anne-Marie Johnson, Lenny Henry
Below: Frank Langella, Henry**
© *Touchstone Pictures*

**Charles Lane, Lenny Henry
Above: Henry**

COMPANY BUSINESS

(MGM) formerly *Russian Roulette*; Producer, Steven-Charles Jaffe; Director/Screenplay, Nicholas Meyer; Photography, Gerry Fisher; Designer, Ken Adam; Editor, Ronald Roose; Music, Michael Kamen; Costumes, Yvonne Blake; Associate Producer, Dirk Petersmann; Casting, Jeremy Zimmerman, Howard Feuer; from Pathe Entertainment; Dolby Stereo; Technicolor; Rated PG-13; 98 minutes; September release

CAST

Sam Boyd	Gene Hackman
Pyiotr Grushenko	Mikhail Baryshnikov
Elliot Jaffe	Kurtwood Smith
Colonel Grissom	Terry O'Quinn
Mike Flinn	Daniel Von Bargen
Grigori Golitsin	Oleg Rudnick
Natasha Grimaud	Geraldine Danon
Faisal	Nadim Sawalha
Dick Maxfield	Michael Tomlinson
Bruce Wilson	Howard McGillin
Gonzalez	Louis Eppolito
Nerdy Young Man	Toby Eckholt
Receptionist	Elsa O'Toole
Secretary	Kate Harper
Chairman	Shane Rimmer
Sobel	Bob Sherman
"Marlene"	Adele Anderson
Klaus	Andreas Grothusen
Subway Driver	Hans Eckhardt
Berlin Policeman	Christof Piesk
Russian Aide	Boris Isarov
Horst	Joachim Bliese

and Francis Le Maire (Maitre D'), Ali Cilasun (Bedouin), Michel Zurek (French Aide), Gerard Lartigau (Salesman)

Mikhail Baryshnikov, Gene Hackman
© *Pathe Entertainment*

LIEBESTRAUM

(MGM) Producer, Eric Fellner; Director/Screenplay/Music, Mike Figgis; "Liebestraum" by Franz Liszt/performed by Earl Bostic and His Orchestra; Co-Producer, Michael Flynn; Photography, Juan Ruiz Anchia; Designer, Waldemar Kalinowski; Editor, Martin Hunter; Costumes, Sharon Simonaire; Casting, Carrie Frazier, Shani Ginsberg, Deborah Brown; Assistant Director, Stephen Buck; an Initial Production; from Pathe Entertainment Inc.; Dolby Stereo; Rank color; Rated R; 106 minutes; September release

CAST

Nick Kaminsky	Kevin Anderson
Jane Kessler	Pamela Gidley
Paul Kessler	Bill Pullman
Mrs. Anderssen	Kim Novak
Sheriff Ricker	Graham Beckel
Barnett Ralston IV	Zach Grenier
Dr. Parker	Thomas Kopache
Nurse #1	Anne Lange
Mike	Jack Wallace
Orderlies	Max Perlich, Hugh Hurd
Mary Parker	Catherine Hicks
Old Mother Ralston	Taina Elg
Night Porter	Tom McDermott
Day Clerk	Joseph McKenna
Buddy	Joe Aufiery
Nurses	Harper Harris, Karen Sillas, Tracy Thorne
Matt	Bill Raymond
Maria	Nola Mae Sanders
Barmaid	Lorie Blanding
Young Mrs. Munnsen	Sarah Fearon
Barnett Ralston III	Bernie Sheredy

and Ian Rob Witt (Boy in dream), Alicia Roanne Witt (Girl in dream), Alberto Sanchez (Waiter at party), Roger Howarth (Boy in rain), Penny Jo White (Girl in rain), Waldemar Kalinowski (Butler), Lydia Radziul (Waitress), Joe Taylor (Ex-Boxer), Ele Keats (Actress on soap opera), Scott Garrison (Actor on soap opera)

Kim Novak Above: Pamela Gidley, Kevin Anderson © *MGM-Pathe Communications*

DOGFIGHT

(WARNER BROS.) Producers, Peter Newman, Richard Guay; Executive Producer, Cathleen Summers; Director, Nancy Savoca; Screenplay, Bob Comfort; Photography, Bobby Bukowski; Designer, Lester W. Cohen; Editor, John Tintori; Associate Producer, Llewellyn Wells; Costumes, Eugenie Bafaloukos; Casting, Marion Dougherty; Dolby Stereo; Technicolor; Rated R; 94 minutes; September release

CAST

Eddie Birdlace	River Phoenix
Rose Fenney	Lili Taylor
Berzin	Richard Panebianco
Okie	Anthony Clark
Benjamin	Mitchell Whitfield
Rose Sr.	Holly Near
Marcie	E.G. Daily
Ruth Two Bears	Sue Morales
Linda	Christina Mastin
Donavin	Christopher Shaw
Fector	John Lacy
Dogfight Buddy	Chris San Nicholas
Dogfight Marine	Brian Gotta
Older Cafe Customer	Peg Phillips
Sergeant Judge	Neal Allen
Lance Corporal Judge	Ron Lynch
Restaurant Maitre D'	Dale Carman
Waiter	Burke Pearson
Thrift Shop Woman	Angie Utt
Thrift Shop Man	Kenny Utt
Navy Bill	Julian Schembri
Alice	Barb Benedetti
Bob	Ivars Mikelson
Sailors	Brendan Fraser, Matt Skerritt
Older Brother on bus	Dion Williams
Younger Brother on bus	Jason Moore
Mother on bus	Denise Williams
Pretty Girl	Kristie Gamer
Bartender	Dave MacIntyre
Bar Owner	Art Cahn
50's Drinker	Bob Munns
Arcade Girl	Jessica Wallenfells
Arcade Hooker	Bonnie Fox
Crying Woman	Sandra Ellis Lafferty
Crying Customer	Joseph Franklin

and Frank Walters (Newscaster), Jacob Luft (Neighborhood Boy), Constance McCord (Dogfight Waitress), Laura Vetter (Truckstop Waitress), Krisha Fairchild (Truckstop Cook), George Evans (Bus Driver), Jillian Armenante (Girl on street), Anne Elizabeth Washburn (Friend of Girl on street), John Fry (Marine on bus), Albert Farrar (Corpsman), Raf Orozco (Hippie)

Top: Lili Taylor, River Phoenix (also left)
Below: Phoenix, Taylor
© *Warner Bros. Inc.*

Dale Carman, River Phoenix, Lili Taylor

Richard Panebianco, River Phoenix, Anthony Clark, Mitchell Whitfield

91

Melanie Griffith, Elijah Wood Top Right: Griffith,
Wood, Don Johnson Top Left: Thora Birch, Wood Below
Left: Johnson, Wood © *Buena Vista Pictures*

PARADISE

(TOUCHSTONE) Producers, Scott Kroopf, Patrick Palmer;
Executive Producers, Jean Francois Lepetit, Ted Field, Robert W.
Cort; Director/Screenplay, Mary Agnes Donoghue; Based on the film
Le Grand Chemin written by Jean Loup Hubert; Photography, Jerzy
Zielinski; Designers, Evelyn Sakash, Marcia Hinds; Costumes, Linda
Palermo Donahue; Music, David Newman; Casting, Johanna Ray;
Assistant Directors, Fredric B. Blankfein, Paul Fonteyn; a co-
production of Interscope Communications, presented in association
with Touchwood Pacific Partners I; Distributed by Buena Vista
Pictures; Dolby Stereo; Technicolor; Rated PG-13; 109 minutes;
September release

CAST

Lily Reed	Melanie Griffith
Ben Reed	Don Johnson
Willard Young	Elijah Wood
Billie Pike	Thora Birch
Sally Pike	Sheila McCarthy
Rosemary	Eve Gordon
Catherine Reston Lee	Louise Latham
Earl McCoy	Greg Travis
Darlene	Sarah Trigger
Minister	Richard K. Olsen
Ernest Parkett	Rick Andosca
Popular Boy (Clay)	Anthony Romano
Darlene's Boyfriend	Timothy Erskine
Bus Driver	Chestley Price
Bartender	Dave Hager
Other Fisherman	John R. Copeman
Eddie (The Attendant)	Jeff Jeffcoat
Greyhound Bus Driver	Scott Hubacek
Marliss	Melanie van Betten
Neighborhood Tough	Jason Robert Somrak
Lou	William Thomas Crumby
Willard's Father	Carl McIntyre
Old Ladies	Lucy Alpaugh, Kay Shroka
DJ	Eric Vest

Melanie Griffith, Don Johnson
Above: Johnson, Elijah Wood, Griffith

THE INDIAN RUNNER

(MGM) Producer, Don Phillips; Executive Producers, Thom Mount, Stephen K. Bannon, Mark Bisgeier; Co-Producer, Patricia Morrison; Director/Screenplay, Sean Penn, inspired by the song "Highway Patrolman" by Bruce Springsteen; Photography, Anthony B. Richmond; Designer, Michael Haller; Editor, Jay Cassidy; Line Producer, David S. Hamberger; Music, Jack Nitzsche; Assistant Director, Artist Robinson; Costumes, Jill Ohanneson; a Mount Film Group in association with MICO/NHK Enterprises presentation from MGM/UA Distribution; Dolby Stereo; Deluxe color; Rated R; 124 minutes; September release

CAST

Joe	David Morse
Frank	Viggo Mortensen
Maria	Valeria Golino
Dorothy	Patricia Arquette
Father	Charles Bronson
Mother	Sandy Dennis
Caesar	Dennis Hopper
Randall	Jordan Rhodes
Raffael	Enzo Rossi
Mr. Baker	Harry Crews
Mrs. Baker	Eileen Ryan
Joe (12)	Trevor Endicott
Frank (7)	Brandon Fleck
Lady at carwash	Kathy Jensen
Deputy #1	Jim Devney
Doctor	Dr. Leland J Olsen
Fat Woman	Annie Pearson
Clyde	Thomas Blair Levin
Lucy	V. Stacy Klein
Miguel	Benicio Del Toro
Randall's Partner	James J. Luxa
Cellmate	Adam Nelson
Guy on commode	Eddie Katz
Indian Runner	Kenny Stabler
Young Indian Runner	Don Shanks
Circus Midget	Neal Stark
Bearded Lady	Elaine Schoonover
Larry	Larry Hoefling
Man at Del Mar	Phil Gould
Frank's Boss	Chuck Ulmer
Dorothy's Father	Joe Martin
Dorothy's Mother	Helen Halmes
Kid on highway	Jimmy Intveld

Top: Viggo Mortensen, David Morse
Below: Dennis Hopper; Charles Bronson
© Westmount Communications

Valeria Golino, Patricia Arquette

David Morse, Viggo Mortensen

SEX, DRUGS, ROCK & ROLL

(AVENUE PICTURES) Producer, Frederick Zollo; Co-Producers, Steven A. Jones, Llewellyn Wells; Executive Producer, Cary Brokaw; Director, John McNaughton; Screenplay, Eric Bogosian; Photography, Ernest Dickerson; Designer, John Arnone; Lighting, Jan Kroeze; Editor, Elena Maganini; Associate Producer, Paul Kurta; Assistant Director, Randy Fletcher; Crest color; Rated R; 96 minutes; September release

CAST

Eric Bogosian

Right: Eric Bogosian
© *Avenue Pictures*

Lily Tomlin (also above left; left and bottom)
© *Orion Classics*

THE SEARCH FOR SIGNS OF INTELLIGENT LIFE IN THE UNIVERSE

(ORION CLASSICS) Producer, Paula Mazur; Executive Producers, Lily Tomlin, Jane Wagner; Director/Photography, John Bailey; Screenplay, Jane Wagner, from her play; Editors, Carol Littleton, Sally Menke; Associate Producer, Janet Beroza; Costumes, Daniel Paredes; Music, Jerry Goodman; Song: "We're the Ones" by Jane Wagner/performed by Toni Childs; Art Director, Ed Richardson; a Tomlin and Wagner Theatricalz presentation in association with Showtime; Dolby Stereo; Color; Rated PG-13; 109 minutes; September release

CAST

Trudy/Chrissy/Kate/Agnus Angst/
Lud/Marie/Paul/Brandy/
Tina/Lyn/Edie/Marge..Lily Tomlin

RAMBLING ROSE

(7 ARTS/NEW LINE CINEMA) Producer, Renny Harlin; Executive Producers, Mario Kassar, Edgar J. Scherick; Director, Martha Coolidge; Screenplay, Calder Willingham, based on his book; Photography, Johnny E. Jensen; Designer, John Vallone; Editor, Steven Cohen; Music, Elmer Bernstein; Costumes, Jane Robinson; Casting, Aleta Chappelle; Assistant Director, Randall Badger; from Carolco Pictures; Dolby Stereo; Technicolor/Eastmancolor; Rated R; 112 minutes; September release

CAST

Rose	Laura Dern
Daddy Hillyer	Robert Duvall
Mother Hillyer	Diane Ladd
Buddy Hillyer	Lukas Haas
Willcox Hillyer	John Heard
Dr. Martinson	Kevin Conway
Dave Wilkie	Robert Burke
Doll Hillyer	Lisa Jakub
Waski Hillyer	Evan Lockwood
Billy	Matt Sutherland
Foster	D. Anthony Pender
Horton	David E. Scarborough
Young Salesman	Robin Dale Robertson
Shadrack	General Fermon Judd, Jr.
Chief of Police	Richard K. Olsen
Man in store	Michael Mott
Minister	James Binns

Top: Laura Dern, Lukas Haas Right: Haas
© *Carolco*

Diane Ladd, Laura Dern
Above: Lukas Haas, Robert Duvall

Diane Ladd, Laura Dern, Robert Duvall
Above: Ladd, Duvall

Robin Williams, Jeff Bridges (also left)
Top Left: Williams, Plummer
© *Tri-Star Pictures*

THE FISHER KING

(TRI-STAR) Producers, Debra Hill, Lynda Obst; Director, Terry Gilliam; Screenplay, Richard LaGravenese; Photography, Roger Pratt; Designer, Mel Bourne; Editor, Lesley Walker; Music, George Fenton; Costumes, Beatrix Pasztor; Casting, Howard Feuer; Associate Producer, Stacey Sher; Assistant Directors, David McGiffert, Joe Napolitano; Red Knight Costume Designers, Keith Greco, Vincent Jefferds; Dolby Stereo; Technicolor; Rated R; 137 minutes; September release

CAST

Jack Lucas	Jeff Bridges
Radio Engineers	Adam Bryant, Paul Lombardi
Lou Rosen	David Pierce
Limo Bum	Ted Ross
Sondra	Lara Harris
TV Anchorman	Warren Olney
News Reporter	Frazer Smith
Anne Napolitano	Mercedes Ruehl
Crazed Video Customer	Kathy Najimy
Sitcom Actor Ben Starr	Harry Shearer
Sitcom Wife	Melinda Culea
Bum at hotel	James Remini
Doorman	Mark Bowden
Father at hotel	John Ottavino
Little Boy	Brian Michaels
Punks	Jayce Bartok, Dan Futterman
Parry	Robin Williams
Hippie Bum	Bradley Gregg
Jamaican Bum	William Jay Marshall
John the Bum	William Preston
Superintendent	Al Fann
Porno Customer	Stephen Bridgewater
Lydia	Amanda Plummer
Stockbroker Bum	John Heffernan
Red Knight	Chris Howell
Homeless Cabaret Singer	Michael Jeter
Strait Jacket Yuppie	Richard LaGravenese
Bag Lady	Anita Dangler
Drooler	Mark Bringelson
Sid (Vietnam Vet)	Tom Waits
Pizza Boy	Johnny Paganelli
Receptionist	Diane Robin
Motorcyclist	John Benjamin Red
Parry's Wife	Lisa Blades
Edwin	Christian Clemenson
Doctor	Carlos Carrasco
Guard	Joe Jamrog
TV Executive	John de Lancie
Nurse	Lou Hancock
Radio Show Call-Ins	Caroline Cromelin, Kathleen Bridget Kelly, Patrick Fraley

Mercedes Ruehl, Jeff Bridges,
Robin Williams, Amanda Plummer

Mercedes Ruehl received the Academy Award for Best Supporting Actress of 1991

Robin Williams

Robin Williams, Jeff Bridges
Top Right: Mercedes Ruehl, Amanda Plummer

Robin Williams, Mercedes Ruehl, Jeff Bridges, Amanda Plummer

LATE FOR DINNER

(COLUMBIA) Producers, Dan Lupovitz, W.D. Richter; Director, W.D. Richter; Screenplay, Mark Andrus; Photography, Peter Sova; Designer, Lilly Kilvert; Editors, Richard Chew, Robert Leighton; Music, David Mansfield; Casting, Terry Liebling; Costumes, Aggie Guerard Rodgers; Co-Producer/Unit Production Manager, Gary Daigler; Assistant Director, Katterli Frauenfelder; a Castle Rock Entertainment in association with New Line Cinema presentation; Dolby Stereo; CFI color; Rated PG; 90 minutes; September release

CAST

Willie Husband	Brian Wimmer
Frank Lovegren	Peter Berg
Joy Husband	Marcia Gay Harden
Jessica Husband	Colleen Flynn
Leland Shakes	Kyle Secor
Dr. David Arrington	Michael Beach
Bob Freeman	Peter Gallagher
Little Jessica Husband	Cassy Friel
Little Donald Freeman	Ross Malinger
Dwane Gardener	Steven Schwartz-Hartley
Officer Tom Bostich	John Prosky
Dr. Dan Chilblains	Bo Brundin
Dr. Chris Underwood	Donald Hotton
Male Radio D.J.	Billy Vera
Truckdriver	Jeremy Roberts
Waving Man	Silent Bit Sam
Counter Girl	Janeane Garofolo
Man in bathroom	Steve Hornyak
Lady with fone in dress	Susan Bugg
Crazy Man in hospital	Tom Noga
Nurse Lilly	Maria Rubell
Nurse Ruth	Emily Kuroda
Man at catering truck	Tim Kelleher
Kissing Couple	Collett Lawson, Ron Byron
Man at money machine	Robert Howe
Susan	Patricia Finn-Lee
Albert	Drew Snyder
Amy	Aimee Aro
Little Frank	Jon Paul Steuer
Harry's Voice	Hudson B. Marquez
Donald Freeman	Richard Steinmetz
Antique Shoppers	Deborah Swanson, David Shinney
Bear	Bunker
Bunker	Bear

Top: Brian Wimmer, Peter Berg
Below: Colleen Flynn, Berg, Wimmer
© *Castle Rock Entertainment*

Marcia Gay Harden, Brian Wimmer   **Marcia Gay Harden, Peter Berg, Brian Wimmer**

John Heard, Goldie Hawn Top Right: Hawn
Right: Ashley Peldon, Hawn
© *Buena Vista Pictures*

DECEIVED

(**TOUCHSTONE**) Producers, Michael Finnell, Wendy Dozoretz, Ellen Collett; Executive Producers, Teri Schwartz, Anthea Sylbert; Director, Damian Harris; Screenplay/Co-Producer, Mary Agnes Donoghue, Derek Saunders; Story, Mary Agnes Donoghue; Photography, Jack N. Green; Designer, Andrew McAlpine; Costumes, Linda Matheson; Editor, Neil Travis; Music, Thomas Newman; Casting, Deborah Aquila; Assistant Director, Tony Lucibello; Presented in association with Silver Screen Partners IV; Distributed by Buena Vista Pictures; Dolby Stereo; Technicolor; Rated PG-13; 102 minutes; September release

CAST

Adrienne	Goldie Hawn
Maitre d'	Damon Redfern
Jack	John Heard
Waiter	Charles Kassatly
Charlotte	Robin Bartlett
Mary	Ashley Peldon
Adrienne's Mother	Beatrice Straight
Adrienne's Father	George R. Robertson
Carol Gingold	Maia Filar
Harvey	Tom Irwin
Tomasz	Jan Rubes
Ellen	Anaïs Granofsky
Mrs. Peabody	Heidi Von Palleske
Detective Kinsella	Stanley Anderson
Ron	Peter Stevens
Jean	Eve Crawford
Museum Employee	Io Perry
Tony	Stephen Hunter
Harvey's Girlfriend	Nancy Cser
Lilian	Francesca Buller
Policemen	Vince Metcalfe, Conrad Coates
Assistant Coroner	Michael Copeman
Mrs. Dagota	Brenda Kamino
Mr. Dagota	Lawrence Nakamura
Social Security Man	Bruce MacVittie
Carol's Nanny	Gemma Barry
Board of Education Woman	Kim Staunton
Evelyn	Amy Wright
Evelyn's Mother	Laura Hawn
Rosalie	Kate Reid
Cab Driver	Jay Bowen
Cathy	Mary Kane
Mrs. Gingold	Ann McDonough
Mr. Gingold	Michael Countryman

Goldie Hawn, Mary Kane   **99**

Scott Bakula, Sinbad Right: Bakula, Kathy Ireland
© Paramount Pictures

NECESSARY ROUGHNESS

(**PARAMOUNT**) Producers, Mace Neufeld, Robert Rehme; Executive Producer, Howard W. Koch, Jr.; Director, Stan Dragoti; Screenplay, Rick Natkin, David Fuller; Photography, Peter Stein; Designer, Paul Peters; Editors, John Wright, Steve Mirkovich; Music, Bill Conti; Costumes, Dan Moore; Casting, Mindy Marin; Assistant Director, John Hockridge; Stunts, Allan Graf; Associate Producer, Lis Kern; Dolby Stereo; Technicolor; Rated PG-13; 108 minutes; September release

CAST

Paul Blake	Scott Bakula
Coach Gennero	Hector Elizondo
Coach Rig	Robert Loggia
Suzanne Carter	Harley Jane Kozak
Dean Phillips Elias	Larry Miller
Andre Krimm	Sinbad
Carver Purcell	Fred Dalton Thompson
Chuck Neiderman	Rob Schneider
Jarvis Edison	Jason Bateman
Wyatt Beaudry	Andrew Bryniarski
Featherstone	Duane Davis
Eric "Samurai" Hansen	Michael Dolan
Sargie	Marcus Giamatti
Lucy Draper	Kathy Ireland
Charlie Banks	Andrew Lauer
McKenzie	Louis Mandylor
Manumana	Peter Navy Tuiasosopo
Popke	Drew Kahn
Olaf Knudson	Spencer Snow
Ingmar Knudson	Scott Snow
Chris Berman	Chris Berman
Flat-Top	Tom Whitenight
Jayhawk Linebacker	Raul Flores
Sidney "Doberman" Harris	Sidney Karlos Bradford
Bessie	Coquina Dunn
Dawne	Debra Carroll
Grant Edison	Garrett Schenck
Sheriff Woods	Rodger Boyce
Manuel	Geoff Garza
Ranch Hand	Agustin Solis
Prison Guard	Dennis Parker
Doctor Sayre	Randy Tallman
Nurse	Desi Doyen
Referee	Darryl Cox
Aerobics Instructor	Kimberly Figge

and Dick Butkus, Earl Campbell, Roger Craig, Ben Davidson, Tony Dorsett, Evander Holyfield, Ed "Too Tall" Jones, Jim Kelly, Jerry Rice, Herschel Walker, Randy White (Convict Football Players), Ken Locker (Athletic Trainer), H. Bud Otto (ESPN Production Manager), Tommy Baker (Football Dropout), Dave Tanner (Pianist), Spencer Prokop (Waiter), Scott Thompson, Michael Petty (Space Cadets), Allan Graf (Billy Bob's Bartender), Lee Gideon, James Edward Savage, Bobby Griffin, Phil M. Sewell (Boosters), Donald R. Collins II, Scott Davis, John L. McGill, Dan D. Brook (Football Players)

Scott Bakula, Harley Jane Kozak
Above: Robert Loggia, Hector Elizondo

MY OWN PRIVATE IDAHO

(FINE LINE FEATURES) Producer, Laurie Parker; Director/Screenplay, Gus Van Sant; Photography, Eric Alan Edwards, John Campbell; Designer, David Brisbin; Editor, Curtiss Clayton; Executive Producers, Gus Van Sant, Allan Mindel; Costumes, Beatrix Aruna Pasztor; Line Producer, Tony Brand; Assistant Director, Kris Krengel; from New Line Cinema; Ultra-Stereo; Color; Rated R; 105 minutes; September release

CAST

Mike Waters	River Phoenix
Scott Favor	Keanu Reeves
Richard Waters	James Russo
Bob Pigeon	William Richert
Gary	Rodney Harvey
Carmella	Chiara Caselli
Digger	Michael Parker
Denise	Jessie Thomas
Budd	Flea
Alena	Grace Zabriskie
Jack Favor	Tom Troupe
Hans	Udo Kier
Jane Lightwork	Sally Curtice
Walt	Robert Lee Pitchlynn
Daddy Carroll	Mickey Cottrell
Wade	Wade Evans
Coverboys	Matt Ebert, Tom Cramer
Sharon Waters	Vana O'Brien
Cafe Kids	Shaun Jordan, Shawn Jones
Coverboy/Cafe Kid	Scott Patrick Green
Bad George	George Conner
Indian Cop	Oliver Kirk
Dirtman	Stanley Hainesworth
Baby Mike	Joshua Halladay
Little Richard	Douglas Tollenen
Hotel Manager	Stephen Clark Pachosa
Disco Manager	Lannie Swerdlow
Rock Promoters	Wally Gaarsland, Bryan Wilson, Mark Weaver, Conrad "Bud" Montgomery
Cops	Pat Patterson, Steve Vernelson, Mike Cascadden
Mayor's Aide	Eric Hull
Minister	James A. Arling
Airline Clerk	James Caviezel

and Ana Cavinato (Stewardess), Melanie Mosely (Lounge Hostess), Greg Murphy (Carl), David Reppinhagen (Yuppie at Jake's), Tiger Warren (Himself), Massimo De Cataldo, Pao Pei Andreoli, Robert Egon, Paolo Baiocco (Italian Street Boys), Mario Stracciarolo (Mike's Italian Client)

Top: Keanu Reeves, River Phoenix Below: Udo Kier
Left: Phoenix, Grace Zabriskie
© *New Line Cinema*

River Phoenix, William Richert

River Phoenix

STEPPING OUT

(PARAMOUNT) Producer/Director, Lewis Gilbert; Co-Producer, John Dark; Executive Producer, Bill Kenwright; Screenplay, Richard Harris, based on his play; Photography, Alan Hume; Designer, Peter Mullins; Editor, Humphrey Dixon; Music, Peter Matz; Title song by John Kander (music) and Fred Ebb (lyrics)/performed by Liza Minnelli; Choreographer, Danny Daniels; Costumes, Candice Paterson; Casting, Ross Clydesdale; Assistant Director, Michel Cheyko; Dolby Stereo; Technicolor; Rated PG; 108 minutes; October release

CAST

Mavis Turner	Liza Minnelli
Mrs. Fraser	Shelley Winters
Geoffrey	Bill Irwin
Maxine	Ellen Greene
Vera	Julie Walters
Sylvia	Robyn Stevan
Lynne	Jane Krakowski
Andy	Sheila McCarthy
Dorothy	Andrea Martin
Rose	Carol Woods
Patrick	Luke Reilly
Pam Leichner	Nora Dunn
Frank	Eugene Robert Glazer
Jerry	Geza Kovacs
Alan	Raymond Rickman
Michael	Michael De Sadeleer
Electrician	Angelo Colavecchia
Patients	Stella Sprowell, Gladys O'Connor
Young Man at bar	Dean McDermott
Priest	Charles Hayter
Stage Door Keeper	Dave Harvey

and Peter Howard (Master of Ceremonies), Brian Leonard (Bongo Player), Vanessa Harwood (Ballerina), Tara Young, Lili Francks, Bonnie Monaghan, Candace Jennings, Janet Kloeble, Kristi Breen, Madeline Paul, Steve Girardi, Lynda Champagne, Lesley Ballantyne, William Orlowski, Anne Hodgkinson (Dancers)

Top: Shelley Winters, Liza Minnelli
Below: Jane Krakowski, Minnelli, Julie Walters
Left: Walters, Minnelli
© *Paramount Pictures*

Jane Krakowski, Bill Irwin, Liza Minnelli, Julie Walters, Carol Woods, Sheila McCarthy, Ellen Greene

Mimi Rogers (also left)
Top Left: Kimberly Cullum, Rogers
© *New Line Cinema*

THE RAPTURE

(FINE LINE FEATURES) Producers, Nick Wechsler, Nancy Tenenbaum, Karen Koch; Executive Producer, Laurie Parker; Director/Screenplay, Michael Tolkin; Photography, Bojan Bazelli; Designer, Robin Standefer; Editor, Suzanne Fenn; Music, Thomas Newman; Casting, Deborah Aquilla; Costumes, Michael A. Jackson; Assistant Director, Josh King; from New Line Cinema; Dolby Stereo; Metrocolor; Rated R; 102 minutes; October release

CAST

Sharon...Mimi Rogers
Randy ....David Duchovny
Vic ....Patrick Bauchau
Mary ....Kimberly Cullum
Sheriff Foster..Will Patton
Paula...Terri Hanauer
Henry ....Dick Anthony Williams
Tommy...James Le Gros
Angie ....Carole Davis
The First Boy...De Vaughn Nixon
The Older Boy ....Christian Belnavis
Louis ....Douglas Roberts
Evangelists............................Scott Burkholder, Vince Grant
Diana..Stephanie Menuez
Maggie...Darwin Carson
Executive ....Patrick Dollaghan
Bartender ....Marvin Elkins
Wayne ....Sam Vlahos
Conrad..Rustam Branaman
Faithful...Victoria Williams
Rock Climber ....Denney Pierce
Cashier ....Joshua Farrell
Manager..Andrew Pressman
Guard ....Kerry Leigh Michaels
Angels ....Henry Kingi, Linda Albertano
Man on television ....Michael David Lally

Patrick Bauchau, Mimi Rogers
Above: Rogers, Kimberly Cullum

RICOCHET

(**WARNER BROS.**) Producers, Joel Silver, Michael Levy; Executive Producer, Barry Josephson; Co-Producers, James Herbert, Suzanne Todd; Director, Russell Mulcahy; Screenplay, Steven E. de Souza; Story, Fred Dekker, Menno Meyjes; Photography, Peter Levy; Music, Alan Silvestri; Editor, Peter Honess; Costumes, Marilyn Vance-Straker; Designer, Jaymes Hinkle; Casting, Robin Lippin, Fern Cassel; 2nd Unit Director/Stunts, Charles Picerni; an HBO in association with Cinema Plus, L.P. presentation of a Silver Pictures production; Dolby Stereo; Panavision; Deluxe color; Rated R; 105 minutes; October release

CAST

Nick Styles	Denzel Washington
Earl Talbot Blake	John Lithgow
Odessa	Ice T
Larry Doyle	Kevin Pollak
Priscilla Brimleigh	Lindsay Wagner
Gail Wallens	Mary Ellen Trainor
Kim	Josh Evans
Alice	Victoria Dillard
Reverend Styles	John Amos
Farris	John Cothran, Jr.
Wanda	Linda Dona
Chief Floyd	Matt Landers
R.C.	Lydell Cheshier
Mrs. Styles	Starletta Dupois
Kiley	Sherman Howard
Babysitter	Viveka Davis
Lisa Styles	Kimberly Natasha Ali
Monica Styles	Aileaha Jones
Chewalski	Jesse Ventura
Jesse	Rick Cramer
Vaca	Miguel Sandoval
Luis	Carlos Lacamara
Book Man	Don Perry
Desk Sergeant	Tom Finnegan
Locker Room Cop	Christopher A. Young
Prison Doctor	Mark Phelan
Prison Guard	Hugh Dane
Blake's Lawyer	Albie Selznick
Parole Board Chairman	Frank Miller

and Betty Carvalho (Board Member), Susan Campos (Channel 6 Reporter), Leonard O. Turner (Committee Chairman), Anita Barone (Waitress), Joe Crummey (Disc Jockey), Irene Forrest (Cleaning Woman), Holly Kaplan (Connie), Michele Landry (Telethon Worker), Heidi Thomas, Robert M. Steinberg, Susan Lentini, Cylk Cozart, James Ishida, Lisa Jo Hunter, Lisa Nelson (Reporters), Ivan E. Roth (City Hall Worker), John Rubinow (ER Doctor), Tim De Zarn (Skinhead), Charles Neville, Quincy Adams, Jr., Andre Dukes (Odessa's Men), George Christy (Talk Show Host), K. Todd Freeman (Talk Show Guest), Marjorie Bransfield (Secretary)

Top: John Lithgow, Denzel Washington
Below: Lindsay Wagner Right: Washington, Ice T
© Cinema Plus

Jesse Ventura, John Lithgow   **Denzel Washington**

Sam Waterston, Reese Witherspoon Top Right:
Witherspoon, Emily Warfield Top Left: Witherspoon,
Jason London Below Left: London
© MGM-Pathe Communications

Emily Warfield, Jason London
Above: Sam Waterston; Tess Harper

THE MAN IN THE MOON

(MGM) Producer, Mark Rydell; Executive Producers, William S. Gilmore, Shari Rhodes; Director, Robert Mulligan; Screenplay, Jenny Wingfield; Photography, Freddie Francis; Designer, Gene Callahan; Editor, Trudy Ship; Music, James Newton Howard; Casting, Shari Rhodes; Associate Producers, Bill Borden, Jerry Grandey; Assistant Director, Jerry Grandey; from Pathe Entertainment; Dolby Stereo; DuArt color; Rated PG; 99 minutes; October release

CAST

Matthew Trant...Sam Waterston
Abigail Trant ....Tess Harper
Marie Foster ....Gail Strickland
Dani Trant ....Reese Witherspoon
Court Foster..Jason London
Maureen Trant ....Emily Warfield
Billy Sanders ....Bentley Mitchum
Will Sanders ....Ernie Lively
Doc White ....Dennis Letts
Mrs. Sanders ....Earleen Bergeron
Mrs. Taylor ....Anna Chappell
Missy Trant..Brandi Smith, Sandi Smith
Foster Twins ....Derek Ball, Spencer Ball

WHORE

(TRIMARK PICTURES) Producers, Dan Ireland, Ronaldo Vasconcellos; Executive Producer, Mark Amin; Director, Ken Russell; Screenplay, Ken Russell, Deborah Dalton; Based on the play *Bondage* by David Hines; Photography, Amir Mokri; Designer, Richard Lewis; Music, Michael Gibbs; Editor, Brian Tagg; Casting, Linda Francis; Line Producer, Michael D. Pariser; Costumes, Leonard Pollack; Dolby Stereo; CFI color; Rated NC-17; 85 minutes; October release

CAST

Liz	Theresa Russell
Blake	Benjamin Mouton
Rasta	Antonio Fargas
Indian	Sanjay
Katie	Elizabeth Morehead
First Man	Michael Crabtree
Derelict	John Diehl
Young Man in Camero	Robert O'Reilly
Old Man in Camero	Charles MaCaulay
Shy Kid	Jason Kristofer
Middle-Aged Man	Jack Nance
Charlie	Frank Smith
Bill	Jason Saucier
Brutal Man	Daniel Quinn
Professional Man	John Carlyle
Chris	Scott Harte
Hippie	Tom Villard
Violent Man	Lee Arenberg

and Ginger-Lynn Allen (Wounded Girl), Scott David-King, Sean Fitzpatrick (Cops), Jered Barclay (Chrysler Man), Doug McHugh (Nice-Looking Man), Amanda Goodwin (Liz's Friend), Barbara Mallory (Rachel), Joy Baggish (Flo), Daniel Beer (Bill's Friend), BJ Ward (Manageress), Stephanie Blake, Barbara Eaton (Strippers), Danny Trejo (Tattoo Man), Bobby Bruce (Strolling Violinist), Bob Prupas (Maitre D'), Ken Russell (Waiter)

Top Right: Antonio Fargas, Theresa Russell
Below Right: Russell © *Vidmark Inc.*

SHOUT

(UNIVERSAL) Producer, Robert Simonds; Executive Producer, Lindsley Parsons, Jr.; Director, Jeffrey Hornaday; Screenplay, Joe Gayton; Photography, Robert Brinkmann; Designer, William F. Matthews; Editor, Seth Flaum; Music, Randy Edelman; Music Supervisor, Karyn Rachtman; Casting, Nancy Nayor; Assistant Director, Patrick H. Kehoe; Costumes, Eduardo Castro; Dolby Stereo; Deluxe color; Rated PG-13; 89 minutes; October release

CAST

Jack Cabe	John Travolta
Jesse Tucker	James Walters
Sara Benedict	Heather Graham
Eugene Benedict	Richard Jordan
Molly	Linda Fiorentino
Bradley Croft	Scott Coffey
Alan Thomas	Glenn Quinn
Toby Blaine	Frank von Zerneck
Big Boy	Michael Bacall
Travis Parker	Sam Hennings
Rebecca	Gwyneth Paltrow
Rachel	Kristina Simonds
Deputy	Charles Taylor
Orphanage Cook	Paula Bellamy-Franklin
Bandstand M.C.	Jerry Tullos
Girls Home Director	Julie Ariola
Eyes	Charles Fowlkes
Mr. Hawkins	Patrik Baldauff
Minister	Redmond M. Gleeson
Girl in bar	Renee Tenison
Orphan	Chris Blasman
Loretta	Michelle Johnston
Singer	Linda M. Womack
Lead Singer	Cecil D. Womack
Young Bell Ringer	Jeremy Jackson
Voice of Midnight Rider	James Avery

James Walters, John Travolta
Above: Walters

© *Universal City Studios*

Joe Pesci, Madolyn Smith Osborne, Vincent Gardenia
Top Left: Pesci, Osborne Left: Pesci
© *Twentieth Century Fox*

THE SUPER

(20th CENTURY FOX) Producer, Charles Gordon; Executive Producer, Ron Frazier; Director, Rod Daniel; Screenplay, Sam Simon; Photography, Bruce Surtees; Designer, Kristi Zea; Costumes, Aude Bronson-Howard; Editor, Jack Hofstra; Music, Miles Goodman; Casting, Avy Kaufman; Unit Production Manager/Associate Producer, Steven Felder; Assistant Director, Henry Bronchtein; a Largo Entertainment presentation; Dolby Stereo; Deluxe color; Rated R; 85 minutes; October release

CAST

Louie Kritski	Joe Pesci
Big Lou Kritski	Vincent Gardenia
Naomi Bensinger	Madolyn Smith Osborne
Marlon	Ruben Blades
Heather	Stacey Travis
Irene Kritski	Carole Shelley
Tito	Kenny Blank
Gilliam	Paul Benjamin
Leotha	Beatrice Winde
Goode	Bhubhesi Bodibe
Stubbs	Abdoulaye N'Gom
Eleanor	Carol Jean Lewis
Ron Nessim	Anthony Heald
Young Louie	Daniel Saltzman
Young Big Lou	Jack Hallett
Pedro Diaz	Steven Rodriguez
Linda Diaz	Eileen Galindo
Judge Smith	Latanya Richardson
Gang Members	Darryl Robinson, Rynel Johnson
Storekeeper	Paul Bates
Pool Shooters	Daniel Margotta, John Ray Barnes
Eddie	Lee Simon, Jr.
Roger	Tyrone Wilson
Men on stoop	Henry Judd Baker, Juan Manual Aguero
Monty Players	Chris Herrera, Billy Marshall Thompson
Females	Marina Durrell, Olga Merediz
Tenant	Leland Gantt
Hooters	Pepe Douglas, Horace Bailey, Gregory Cook, Billy Graham
Electrician	Boris Sichkin
Milkman	Todd Monteiro
D.C.	Drafton Davis
Stanford	Anthony Hargraves
Rudy	Stanley Mills
Construction Worker	Daniel Hagan
Exterminator	Ron Roth
Arsonist	Anthony Caso
Big Man	William Roberts

Carol Jean Lewis, Joe Pesci, Stacey Travis
Above: Ruben Blades, Pesci

HOMICIDE

(TRIUMPH) Producers, Michael Hausman, Edward R. Pressman; Executive Producer, Ron Rotholz; Director/Screenplay, David Mamet; Photography, Roger Deakins; Editor, Barbara Tulliver; Music, Aleric Jans; Designer, Michael Merritt; Costumes, Nan Cibula; an Edward R. Pressman/Cinehaus production; Dolby Stereo; Color; Rated R; 102 minutes; October release

CAST

Bobby Gold	Joe Mantegna
Tim Sullivan	William H. Macy
Chava	Natalija Nogulich
Randolph	Ving Rhames
Miss Klein	Rebecca Pidgeon
Senna	Vincent Guastaferro
Olcott	Lionel Mark Smith
Frank	Jack Wallace
Curren	J.J. Johnston
Deputy Mayor Walker	Paul Butler
Grounder	Colin Stinton
Benjamin	Adolph Mall

and Louis Murray (Patterson), Roberta Custer (Cathy Bates), Charles Stransky (Doug Brown), Bernard Gray (James), Linda Kimbrough (Sgt. Green), Darrel Taylor (Willie Sims), Erica Gimpel (Woman with Randolph), Tony Mamet (Officer Ferro), J.S. Block (Dr. Klein), Mary Jefferson (Randolph's Mother), Marge Kotilsky (Mrs. Klein), Steven Goldstein (Librarian), Alan Polonsky (Scholar), Bernard Mamet (Marv)

Top: Joe Mantegna, William H. Macy
Right: Mantegna, Alan Polonsky
© *Triumph Releasing*

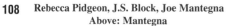

108 Rebecca Pidgeon, J.S. Block, Joe Mantegna
Above: Mantegna

Joe Mantegna, William H. Macy, Louis Murray
Above: Mantegna, Natalija Nogulich

Adam Hann-Byrd, Dianne Wiest Top Right: Hann-Byrd,
Jodie Foster Right: P.J. Ochlan, Hann-Byrd
© *Orion Pictures*

LITTLE MAN TATE

(ORION) Poducers, Scott Rudin, Peggy Rajski; Executive Producer,
Randy Stone; Director, Jodie Foster; Screenplay, Scott Frank;
Photography, Mike Southon; Designer, Jon Hutman; Editor, Lynzee
Klingman; Music, Mark Isham; Costumes, Susan Lyall; Casting, Avy
Kaufman, Lina Todd; Assistant Director, Mike Tapoozian; THX
sound; DuArt color; Rated PG-13; 99 minutes; October release

CAST

Dede Tate	Jodie Foster
Jane Grierson	Dianne Wiest
Fred Tate	Adam Hann-Byrd
Eddie	Harry Connick, Jr.
Garth	David Pierce
Gina	Debi Mazar
Damon Wells	P.J. Ochlan
Winston F. Buckner	George Plimpton
Fred Tate at 2	Alex Lee
Matt Montini	Michael Shulman
Matt's Teammate	Nathan Lee
Miss Nimvel	Celia Weston
Clinic Doctor	Danitra Vance
Bartender	Richard Fredette
Grierson Institute Teacher	Jennifer Trier
Joey X	John Bell
Cherry Reynolds	Ishe Costa
Bob Yee	Chucky Ocampo
Odyssey of the Mind Leaders	Richard Hanson, Mar Ya Zuke
Fenton	Mark Lienhart
Valerie	Lauren Ashley Stacey
Physics Professor	Josh Mostel
Coral Bay Owner	Michael Mantell
Girl outside classroom	Erica Staton
Auctioneer	Michael Keavey
Sorority Girl	Carolyn Lawrence
Eddie's Friend	George Kaufman
Fred's Doctor	Gordon Greene
Preppy Guy in cafeteria	Barry J. Williams
Eddie's Girlfriend	Alexandra Auder
Eddie's Roommate	Sam Womelsdorf
Makeup Woman	Ellen McElduff
Evan	Adam Midkiff
"LIVEWIRE" Boy Guest	Sheadrick Richards
"LIVEWIRE" Girl Guest	Elizabeth Frietsch
Moderator	Bob Balaban

Adam Hann-Byrd, Jodie Foster
Above: Harry Connick Jr., Hann-Byrd

Tom Berenger, Bob Hoskins Top Left: Berenger, Greta Scacchi Top Right: Hoskins, Berenger Below Right: Joanne Whalley-Kilmer, Berenger
© *MGM-Pathe Communications*

SHATTERED

(MGM) Producers, Wolfgang Petersen, John Davis, David Korda; Co-Producers, Ortwin Freyermuth, Gail Katz; Executive Producers, Larry Sugar, Michel Roy; Director/Screenplay, Wolfgang Petersen; Based on the novel *The Plastic Nightmare* by Richard Neely; Photography, Laszlo Kovacs; Designer, Gregg Fonseca; Costumes, Erica Edell Phillips; Line Producer, Neal Nordlinger; Music, Alan Silvestri; Casting, Jane Jenkins, Janet Hirshenson; Assistant Director, Peter Kohn; Special Effects Makeup, Lance Anderson; a Bodo Scriba/Willi Baer/Capella Films production in association with Davis Entertainment Company, from MGM-Pathe Communications; Dolby Stereo; Panavision; Technicolor; Rated R; 98 minutes; October release

CAST

Dan Merrick	Tom Berenger
Gus Klein	Bob Hoskins
Judith Merrick	Greta Scacchi
Jenny Scott	Joanne Whalley-Kilmer
Jeb Scott	Corbin Bernsen
Dr. Berkus	Theodore Bikel
Nancy Mercer	Debi A. Monahan
Rudy Costa	Bert Rosario
Sadie	Jedda Jones
Jack Stanton	Scott Getlin
Lydia	Kellye Nakahara
Pet Shop Woman	Dona Hardy
Cop	Frank Cavestani
Jeb's Secretary	Jasmin Gabler
Receptionist	Charlene Hall
Dr. Benton	Dierk Torsek
Plastic Surgeon	George Herbert Semel, M.D.

Tom Berenger, Greta Scacchi
Above: Berenger, Corbin Bernsen

FRANKIE & JOHNNY

(PARAMOUNT) Producer/Director, Garry Marshall; Executive Producers, Alexandra Rose, Charles Mulvehill; Co-Producer, Nick Abdo; Screenplay, Terrence McNally, based on his stageplay *Frankie and Johnny in the Clair De Lune*; Photography, Dante Spinotti; Designer, Albert Brenner; Editors, Battle Davis, Jacqueline Cambas; Costumes, Rosanna Norton; Music, Marvin Hamlisch; "Claire De Lune" by Claude Debussy; Casting, Lynn Stalmaster; Assistant Director, Ellen H. Schwartz; Dolby Stereo; Technicolor; Rated R; 118 minutes; October release

CAST

Johnny	Al Pacino
Frankie	Michelle Pfeiffer
Nick	Hector Elizondo
Tim	Nathan Lane
Cora	Kate Nelligan
Nedda	Jane Morris
Tino	Greg Lewis
Luther	Al Fann
Artemis	Ele Keats
Jorge	Fernando Lopez
Peter	Glenn Plummer
Lester	Tim Hopper
Mr. Rosen	Harvey Miller
Bobby	Sean O'Bryan

The Diner:
Goldie McLaughlin (Waitress Helen), Phil Leeds (Mr. DeLeon), Marvin Braverman (Officer Joe), Calvin Jung (Officer Lee), Frank Campanella (Retired Customer), Julie Paris (Pregnant Customer), Allan Kent (Racetrack Customer), Bud Markowitz (Juggler Customer), Elizabeth Kerr (Senior Citizen Customer), Marty Nadler (Rude Customer), Jeff Michalski (Seizure Customer), Diane Frazen (Whispering Customer Marge), Hyman Fishman (Cora's Customer), Ronny Hallin (Biker Customer), Harvey Keenan (Salesman Customer), Pricilla Phillips, Joy Rosenthal (Snooty Customers), Robert Brunner (Accident Driver), Mark Scarola (Garment Worker), Karin Calabro (Dental Technician), Flora Berniker (Flora), Steve Restivo (Night Cook), Nick Gambella (Night Busboy), Hope Alexander-Willis, Barbara Mealy, Barbara London (Night Waitresses)
The Party:
Al Sapienza (Peter's Roommate), Diana Kent (Nick's Wife), Tracy Reiner (Attorney at party), Eugenia Bravos (Grandma), Gena Bravos, Shirley Kirks (Greek Dancers), Joli Lallo (Jorge's Girlfriend), Ira Glick (Mutzie Calish)

New York People:
Shannon Wilcox (Christine the Hooker), Dey Young (Johnny's Ex-Wife), Paul Tinder (New Husband), Barbara Marshall (Helen's Nurse), Scott A. Marshall (Sidewalk Preacher), Karen Case Cook (Megaphone Lady), Shawn Frank McLean (Penny Pitcher), John Goldman (Parking Lot Owner), Ashley Baynes, Valery Baynes (Johnny's Daughter), Paul Allison, Richard Allison (Johnny's Son), Blanche Bronte, Lorna Thayer (Flower Vendors), Mychael Bates (Flower Driver), Terri Sigrist, Lori Sigrist (Bowling Twins), Zachary Weintraub (Handsome Bowler), Laurie Quinn (Pretty Girl Bowler), Gordon Belson (Marlon the Disc Jockey)
Frankie's Neighbors:
Lucinda Crosby (The Abused Neighbor), Shane Ross, Richard Gillis (Sexy Neighbors), Robert Ball (Haircombing Neighbor), Lou Evans, Barbara Nabozny (Eating Couple)
Altoona, Pennsylvania:
K Callan (Frankie's Mother), Frank Buxton (Minister), De Dee Pfeiffer (Frankie's Cousin), Marc Raducci (Cousin's Husband), Bill Applebaum (Baby's Godfather), Keith Martell, Sophie Von Haselberg (Party Children), Bettiann Fishman (Aunt Bette), Lori Marshall (Party Guest), Krista H. Davis, Kelly McCray, Blair Richwood (Bus Riders)

Top: Michelle Pfeiffer, Al Pacino
Below: Pfeiffer, Nathan Lane
© *Paramount Pictures*

Hector Elizondo, Ele Keats, Al Pacino Above: 111
Michelle Pfeiffer, Kate Nelligan, Jane Morris

CITY OF HOPE

(SAMUEL GOLDWYN CO.) Producers, Sarah Green, Maggie Renzi; Executive Producers, John Sloss, Harold Welb; Director/Screenplay/Editor, John Sayles; Photography, Robert Richardson; Designers, Dan Bishop, Dianna Freas; Costumes, John Dunn; Music, Mason Daring; Casting, Barbara Hewson Shapiro, Eve Battaglia; Assistant Director, Steve Apicella; an Esperanza production; Dolby Stereo; Pananvision; Color; Rated R; 134 minutes; October release

CAST

Nick	Vincent Spano
Wynn	Joe Morton
Joe	Tony Lo Bianco
Rizzo	Anthony John Denison
Angela	Barbara Williams
Zip	Todd Graff
Reesha	Angela Bassett
Mayor Baci	Louis Zorich
Asteroid	David Strathairn
Les	Bill Raymond
Levonne	Frankie Faison
Bobby	Jace Alexander
Laurie	Gina Gershon
Pauly	Joe Grifasi
Riggs	Chris Cooper
Mad Anthony	Josh Mostel
Pina	Rose Gregorio
O'Brien	Kevin Tighe
Zimmer	Michael Mantell
Carl	John Sayles
Kerrigan	Lawrence Tierney
Yoyo	Stephen Mendillo
Stavros	Charlie Yanko
Vinnie	Scott Tiler
Jeanette	Gloria Foster
Malik	Tom Wright
Connie	Maggie Renzi
Joann	Marianne Leone
Bauer	S.J. Lang
Dawn	Eileen Lynch
District Attorney	Bob North

and Randle Mell (Simms), JoJo Smollett (Desmond), Edward Jay Townsend, Jr. (Tito), Steven Randazzo (Gus), Miriam Colon (Mrs. Ramirez), Daryl Edwards (Franklin), Jude Ciccolella (Paddy), Jaime Tirelli (Fuentes), Serafin Jovet (Ramirez), Mason Daring (Peter), Olga Merediz (Nidia), Bill Raymond (Les), John Griesemer (Thomas), Bernard Canepari (Stroczyk), Blair Shannon (Security Guard), Tony Davis (Kyle), Jon De Vries (Dean Milford), Ginny Yang (Suzanne), Maeve Kinkead (Christine), Dale Carman (Roger), Ray Aranha (Errol), Jon Farris (Kevin)

Top: Jace Alexander, Todd Graff, Vincent Spano
Below: Tony Lo Bianco, Joe Morton
Left: Spano, Anthony John Denison
© *Esperanza Inc.*

Angela Bassett, Joe Morton

Joe Grifasi, Louis Zorich

Gregory Peck, Danny DeVito Top Left: DeVito
Left: DeVito, Penelope Ann Miller
© *Warner Bros. Inc.*

OTHER PEOPLE'S MONEY

(WARNER BROS.) Producers, Norman Jewison, Ric Kidney; Executive Producers, Ellen Krass, Davina Belling; Director, Norman Jewison; Screenplay, Alvin Sargent; Based on the play by Jerry Sterner; Photography, Haskell Wexler; Designer, Philip Rosenberg; Casting, Howard Feuer; Music, David Newman; Costumes, Theoni V. Aldredge; Editors, Lou Lombardo, Michael Pacek, Hubert De La Bouillerie; Associate Producers, Kelley Baker, Sarah Miller Hayward; Assistant Directors, Ned Dowd, Marty Ewing; a Yorktown Production; Dolby Stereo; Technicolor; Rated R; 101 minutes; October release

CAST

Lawrence Garfield	Danny DeVito
Andrew "Jorgy" Jorgenson	Gregory Peck
Kate Sullivan	Penelope Ann Miller
Bea Sullivan	Piper Laurie
Bill Coles	Dean Jones
Arthur	R.D. Call
Harriet	Mo Gaffney
Emma	Bette Henritze
Ozzie	Tom Aldredge
Marcia	Leila Kenzle
Gus	Cullen O. Johnson
Pfeiffer	William De Acutis
Granger	David Wells
Angeli	Stephanie White
Klein	Jeffrey Hayenga
Richardson	Ric Kidney
Woody	Wallace G. Lane, Jr.
Richard	Steve White
Elton	Brian Evers
Ed	Max Robinson
Helicopter Pilot	Al Cerullo, Jr.
Concierge	Michael Laskin
Kate's Neighbor	Barney Brown
Samuels	Sandy Moore
Security Guard	Paul Coyne
Receptionists	Dale Kasman, Kathleen Piche
Garfield's Office Valet	Peter Brocco
Japanese Waitress	Nancy Omi
Bart	Mark Pinter

and Mark Hedahl (TV Reporter), Leslie Devlin (FNN Reporter), William "Skip" Church, Glenn K. Pearson (Reporters), Cam McCormack (Camerawoman), Patrick James Grosswendt (Factory Worker), Raul Korbinsky (Proxy Monitor), Woodrow W. Asai, Ken Kensei, Shiro Oishi (Japanese Businessmen), Philip Perlman (Garfield Supporter), Denise Lynne Roberts (Garfield Employee), Janet M. Smith, Kevin Christy Hayes, Richard Arlen Chapman, Dennis J. Malone (Lawyer), Kevin Lord (Account Executive), Marianne Lewis (Executive Secretary), Tessa Gaynor (Secretary)

Danny DeVito, Gregory Peck, Piper Laurie

CURLY SUE

(WARNER BROS.) Producer/Director/Screenplay, John Hughes; Executive Producer, Tarquin Gotch; Photography, Jeffrey L. Kimball; Designer, Doug Kraner; Music, Georges Delerue; Editors, Peck Prior, Harvey Rosenstock; Costumes, Michael Kaplan; Casting, Janet Hirshenson, Jane Jenkins; Assistant Director, James Giovannetti, Jr.; Song: "You Never Know" by Steve Dorff and John Bettis/performed by Ringo Starr; Dolby Stereo; Technicolor; Rated PG; 102 minutes; October release

CAST

Bill Dancer	James Belushi
Grey Ellison	Kelly Lynch
Curly Sue	Alisan Porter
Walker McCormick	John Getz
Bernard Oxbar	Fred Dalton Thompson
Maitre D'	Cameron Thor
Albert	Branscombe Richmond
Tesio	Steven Carell
Anise Hall	Gail Boggs
Dr. Maxwell	Burke Byrnes
Trina	Viveka Davis
Mrs. Arnold	Barbara Tarbuck
Secretary	Edie McClurg
Prison Guard	Charles Adams
Pawnbroker	James W. Bolinski
Theater Patron	Lyle Brown
Social Worker	Nadine Burke
DCGS Caseworker	Adele Robbins
Soprano	Carol Chickering
Foster Mother	Grace Collette
Drifter	Ralph Foody
Cooks	Cedrick Pipes, Alonzo Hall
Store Clerks	Luke Reichle, Joel Levin,
	Tammy Karabas-Brody, Patricia Hooker
Ticket Taker	Joe Liss
Father of the Bride	Rocco Pecirno
Dinah Tompkins	Ely Pouget
Woman with champagne glass	Susan Mayer
Frank Arnold	John Ashton

Top: Alisan Porter, James Belushi
Right: Kelly Lynch, Porter
© *Warner Bros. Inc.*

MINDWALK

(TRITON PICTURES) Producer, Adrianna A.J. Cohen; Executive Producer, Klaus Lintschinger; Director, Bernt Capra; Screenplay, Floyd Byars, Fritjof Capra; Based on the book *The Turning Point* by Fritjof Capra; Photography, Karl Kases; Music, Philip Glass; Editor, Jean Claude Piroue; Costumes, Bambi Breakstone; Casting, Rick Montgomery, Dan Parada; a Mindwalk Productions, Inc. and The Atlas Company presentation; Color; Rated PG; 112 minutes; October release

CAST

Sonia Hoffman	Liv Ullmann
Jack Edwards	Sam Waterston
Thomas Harriman	John Heard
Kit Hoffman	Ione Skye
Romain	Emmanuel Montes

114 **Liv Ullmann, John Heard, Sam Waterston**
© *Triton Pictures*

THE BUTCHER'S WIFE

(PARAMOUNT) Producers, Wallis Nicita, Lauren Lloyd; Executive Producer, Arne Schmidt; Director, Terry Hughes; Screenplay, Ezra Litwak, Marjorie Schwartz; Photography, Frank Tidy; Designer, Charles Rosen; Editor, Don Cambern; Costumes, Theadora Van Runkle; Music, Michael Gore; Song: "(Love Moves in) Mysterious Ways" by Tom Snow and Dean Pitchford/performed by Julia Fordham; Casting, Gail Levin; Assistant Director, Kenneth D. Collins; Dolby Stereo; Technicolor; Rated PG-13; 104 minutes; October release

CAST

Marina Lemke	Demi Moore
Dr. Alex Tremor	Jeff Daniels
Leo Lemke	George Dzundza
Stella Kefauver	Mary Steenburgen
Grace	Frances McDormand
Robyn Graves	Margaret Colin
Eugene	Max Perlich
Gina	Miriam Margolyes
Molly	Helen Hanft
Mr. Liddle	Christopher Durang
Luis	Luis Avalos
Beau	Charles Pierce
Grammy D'Arbo	Elizabeth Lawrence
Choir Student	Stephanie Laurence
Church Choir	The Carol Lombard Kids
Bicyclist	Barry Neikrug
Uncle Chauncy	Ed Kenney
Trendoid	Diane Salinger
Customer	Cameron Milzer
Transvestite	Thomas Mikal Ford
Fire Eater	Scott Baker
Doorman	Sam Menning
Skater in the park	Steve Love
Young Marina	Sara Noel Herring
Street Sweeper	Ken Fritz

Top: Jeff Daniels, Demi Moore
Left: Max Perlich, Daniels
© *Paramount Pictures*

Mary Steenburgen

George Dzundza, Demi Moore

BILLY BATHGATE

(TOUCHSTONE) Producers, Arlene Donovan, Robert F. Colesberry; Director, Robert Benton; Screenplay, Tom Stoppard; Based upon the book by E.L. Doctorow; Photography, Nestor Almendros; Music, Mark Isham; Editors, Alan Heim, Robert Reitano; Designer, Patrizia Von Brandenstein; Costumes, Joseph G. Aulisi; Casting, Howard Feuer; Assistant Director, Brian Cook; Presented in association with Touchwood Pacific Partners I; Distributed by Buena Vista Pictures; Dolby Stereo; Technicolor; Rated R; 106 minutes; November release

CAST

Dutch Schultz	Dustin Hoffman
Drew Preston	Nicole Kidman
Billy Bathgate	Loren Dean
Bo Weinberg	Bruce Willis
Otto Berman	Steven Hill
Irving	Steve Buscemi
Mickey	Billy Jaye
Lulu	John Costelloe
Dixie Davis	Tim Jerome
Lucky Luciano	Stanley Tucci
Julie Martin	Mike Starr
Jack Kelly	Robert F. Colesberry
Mr. Hines	Stephen Joyce
Mary Behan	Frances Conroy
Rebecca	Moira Kelly
Arnold	Kevin Corrigan
Billy's Gang	Noel Derecki, Josh Weinstein, Danny Zorn, Rob Kramer
Hotel Manager	Simon Jutras
Dutch's Thugs	Kenny Vance, Paul Herman
Supervisor	Teddy Cleanthes
George	William Jay Marshall
Fire Inspector	Harry O'Reilly
Harvey Preston	Xander Berkeley
Father McInerny	Barry McGovern
Banker	Barton Heyman
Harvey's Friend	Christopher Rubin
Carter	Richard Bekins
Charlotte	Katharine Houghton

and Todd Louiso (Bell Boy), Robert D. Raiford (Judge), Terry Loughlin (Mr. Chambers), Stephen M. Aronson, Tom Ambrose, Rick Warner, Chuck Kinlaw, Martin Thompson, Todd Brenner, Charles Ress Lyons (The Reporters), Rachel York (Embassy Club Singer), Kip Newton (Bartender), Karen L. Thorson (Woman at table), Nick Pernice (Tote Man), John Clohessy (Racetrack Program Seller), Darryl Caron, Nicholas E. Tishler (Bell Hops), Joseph Dolphin (News Vendor), Judy Allison (Bingo Winner), John J. Hladik (Auctioneer), Lewis W. Lake (Farmer), Kas Self (Woman at bake sale), James Raitt (Chophouse Bartender), Rick Washburn, John A. Moio, Max Maxwell, Jerry Guarino (Hitmen), Vincent Pantone, Tony Cucci, Anthony Catanese, Paulie DiCocco (Luciano Thugs), William G. Kane (Man in window), Frank McLean (Newsboy)

Top: Dustin Hoffman, Steven Hill, Loren Dean Below: Bruce Willis, Hoffman Left: Nicole Kidman, Dean
© Touchstone Pictures

Barton Heyman, Steven Hill, Dustin Hoffman, Nicole Kidman, Loren Dean

John Costelloe, Nicole Kidman, Steven Hill, Dustin Hoffman, Loren Dean, Billy Jaye, Steve Buscemi

Donna Magnani, Danny Aiello, Lainie Kazan Top Left:
Anthony LaPaglia, Aiello, Frank Pesce Left: Rick Aiello,
LaPaglia © *Twentieth Century Fox*

29TH STREET

(20th CENTURY FOX) Producer, David Permut; Executive
Producer, Jerry A. Baerwitz; Co-Producer, Ellen Erwin;
Director/Screenplay, George Gallo; Associate Producers/Story,
Frank Pesce, James Franciscus; Photography, Steven Fierberg;
Designer, Robert Ziembicki; Editor, Kaja Fehr; Costumes, Peggy
Farrell; Music, William Olvis; Casting, Louis Di Giaimo;
Assistant Director, Carol Bonnefil; Dolby Stereo; Deluxe color;
Rated R; 101 minutes; November release

CAST

Frank Pesce, Sr.	Danny Aiello
Frank Pesce, Jr.	Anthony LaPaglia
Mrs. Pesce	Lainie Kazan
Vito Pesce	Frank Pesce
Sgt. Tartaglia	Robert Forster
Philly the Nap	Ron Karabatsos
Jimmy Vitello	Rick Aiello
Louie Tucci	Vic Manni
Needle Nose Nipton	Paul Lazar
Tony	Pete Antico
Madeline Pesce	Donna Magnani
Sal Las Benas	Darren Bates
Chink Fortunado	Tony Sirico
Father Lowery	Richard Olsen
Dom the Bomb	Richard Cerenzio
Rocky Sav	Philip Ciccone
Carmine Tucci	Joey Gironda
Auggie Falcone	Vic Noto
Angelo	Sal Ruffino
Irv the Pawnbroker	Sam Shamshack
Frankie (Age 8)	Adam LaVorgna
Jimmy (Age 8)	Frank Acciarto
Sgt. Jones	Don Blakely
Lucy Sills	Hope Alexander-Willis
Dr. Puccini	Leonard Termo
Ticket Buyer	Lou Criscuolo
Maria Rios	Karen Duffy
Julie the Usherette	Julie Lott
Cousin Leo	David Ferraro
Pit Boss	Ted Cleanthes
Army Eye Doctor	Vincent Chase
Nun	Shirley Swanger
Newscaster	Tom Ellis

and Tony Lipp (Nicky Bad Lungs), Vinnie Curto (Zippers Bad
Lungs), Mario Todisco (Zippers' Bodyguard), Richard Tacchino
(Social Club Waiter), Rocco Savastano (Social Club Bartender), Jerry
Guarino (Chickens), Bill Ricci (Mickey the Dwarf), Nicky "Pop"
Anest (Tommy the Geep), George "Aggie" Anest (Joe Numbers),
Vito "Baldie" Boccanfuso (Johnny Cake), Anne Sterling (Maternity
Nurse), William Phillips (Lottery Finalist), Joe Roberto (Patrolman
Tollen), Jim Ondatje (2nd Patrolman), Tony Monte (Jesus Rios),
Jessen Noviello (Needle Nose - Age 8), Charles Haugk (Tucci's
Driver), Alexander Fehr Blue (Baby on train), Ingrid Van Dorn
(Nurse), Giovanni Gianoni (Italian Band Singer), Lee Boyd, Cecil
McKiethen, Jerome Alfano, Eugene Kobisky (Italian Wedding Band),
Joe Franklin (Himself), Onyx (Vinnie the Cat)

Rick Aiello, Philip Jordan Giordano, Darren Bates,
Paul Lazar, Richard Cerenzio

THE PEOPLE UNDER THE STAIRS

(UNIVERSAL) Producers, Marianne Maddalena, Stuart M. Besser; Executive Producers, Shep Gordon, Wes Craven; Director/Screenplay, Wes Craven; Photography, Sandi Sissel; Editor, James Coblentz; Designer, Bryan Jones; Music, Don Peake; Co-Producer, Dixie J. Capp; Costumes, Ileane Meltzer; Casting, Eileen Knight; an Alive Films presentation; Dolby Stereo; Deluxe color; Rated R; 102 minutes; November release

CAST

Fool	Brandon Adams
Man	Everett McGill
Woman	Wendy Robie
Alice	A.J. Langer
LeRoy	Ving Rhames
Roach	Sean Whalen
Grandpa Booker	Bill Cobbs
Ruby	Kelly Jo Minter
Spenser	Jeremy Roberts
Mary	Conni Marie Brazelton
Young Cop	Joshua Cox
Veteran Cop	John Hostetter
Police Sergeant	John Mahon
Social Worker	Theresa Velarde
Attic Cop	George R. Parker
Stairmaster	Yan Birch
Stairpersons	Wayne Daniels, Michael Kopelow
Prince	Brutus, Bubba, Schultz & Zeke

© *Universal City Studios*

Sean Whalen Above: Brandon Adams, Everett McGill

YEAR OF THE GUN

(TRIUMPH) Producer, Edward R. Pressman; Executive Producer, Eric Fellner; Director, John Frankenheimer; Screenplay, David Ambrose; Based on the book by Michael Mewshaw; Line Producer, Robert L. Rosen; Photography, Blasco Giuarto; Designer, Aurelio Crugnola; Music, Bill Conti; Costumes, Ray Summers; Casting, Lou Digiamo; Produced in association with Initial Films; Dolby Stereo; Color; Rated R; 111 minutes; November release

CAST

David Raybourne	Andrew McCarthy
Lia Spinelli	Valeria Golino
Alison King	Sharon Stone
Italo Bianchi	John Pankow
Giovanni	Mattia Sbragia
Pierre Bernier	George Murcell
Round-Faced Man	Lou Castel
Woman Terrorist	Francesca Prandi
Lena	Carla Cassola
2nd Man	Pietro Bontempo
1st Terrorist	Luigi Di Fiore
Lucio Spinelli	Roberto Posse
Marco Spinelli	Thomas Elliot
Interviewer	Dick Cavett

118 Andrew McCarthy, Lou Castel, Mattia Sbragia, Sharon Stone Above: Valeria Golino, McCarthy

© *Triumph Releasing*

Joseph C. Phillips, Halle Berry, Tommy Davidson
Top Left: Davidson, Phillips Left: Phillips, Berry
© *Warner Bros. Inc.*

STRICTLY BUSINESS

(WARNER BROS.) formerly *Go, Natalie*; Producers, Andre Harrell, Pam Gibson; Executive Producers, Mark Burg, Chris Zarpas; Co-Producer, David Kappes; Director, Kevin Hooks; Screenplay, Pam Gibson, Nelson George; Photography, Zoltan David; Editor, Richard Nord; Music, Michel Colombier; Designer, Ruth Ammon; Casting, Julie Mossberg, Brian Chavanne; Assistant Director, Gary Marcus; Presented in association with Island World; Dolby Stereo; DuArt color; Rated PG-13; 83 minutes; November release

CAST

Bobby Johnson	Tommy Davidson
Waymon Tinsdale III	Joseph C. Phillips
Diedre LaSalle	Anne Marie Johnson
David	David Marshall Grant
Drake	Jon Cypher
Monroe	Samuel Jackson
Natalie	Halle Berry
Millicent	Kim Coles
Leroy Halloran	Paul Butler
Roland Halloran	James McDaniel
Larry	Paul Provenza
Sheila	Annie Golden
Gary	Sam Rockwell
Mr. Atwell	Ira Wheeler
Karen	Sarah Stavrou
Teddy Halloran	Ellis Williams
Darryl	Joe Torry
Donna	Susan Haskell
Woman at subway	Marita Stavrou
Sondra	Ivelka Reyes
Mr. Kagawa	Glenn Kubota
Mr. Utamaro	Edmund Ikeda
Olivia	Novella Nelson
Young Mother	Trula Hoosier Marcus
Maitre D'	Victor Slezak
Homeless Man	Mansoor Najeeullah
Kyle	Greg Mays "Nice"
Tyrone	Darryl Barnes "Smooth"
Donavan	David "Redhead" Guppy
Uptown Girls	Lyndah McCaskill, Michele Morgan
Jake	Denis Leary
Kilimanjaro Doorman	Angelo DiMascio
Married Man	Kevin Hooks
Hustler	Isaiah Washington
Young Girl at bar	Margaret Crosby
Cocktail Waitress	G. Ellen Cleghorne
Security Guard	Jerome Preston Bates

and Geraldo Alverio (Man at cocktail party), Eugene Key (Waiter), Robin Hamon (Flower Lady), Jodeci (Band at Lola's)

Tommy Davidson, Joseph C. Phillips, Halle Berry

CAPE FEAR

(UNIVERSAL) Producer, Barbara De Fina; Executive Producers, Kathleen Kennedy, Frank Marshall; Director, Martin Scorsese; Screenplay, Wesley Strick; Based on a screenplay by James R. Webb and the novel *The Executioners* by James D. MacDonald; Photography, Freddie Francis; Designer, Henry Bumstead; Costumes, Rita Ryack; Editor, Thelma Schoonmaker; Bernard Herrmann's Original Score Adapted, Arranged, and Conducted by Elmer Bernstein; Casting, Ellen Lewis; Assistant Director, Joseph Reidy; an Amblin Entertainment in association with Cappa Films and Tribeca Productions presentation; Dolby Stereo; Panavision; Technicolor; Rated R; 130 minutes; November release

CAST

Max Cady	Robert De Niro
Sam Bowden	Nick Nolte
Leigh Bowden	Jessica Lange
Danielle Bowden	Juliette Lewis
Claude Kersek	Joe Don Baker
Lieutenant Elgart	Robert Mitchum
Lee Heller	Gregory Peck
Judge	Martin Balsam
Lori Davis	Illeana Douglas
Tom Broadbent	Fred Dalton Thompson
Graciella	Zully Montero
Prisoners	Craig Henne, Forest Burton, Edgar Allan Poe IV, Rod Ball, W. Paul Bodie
Corrections Officers	Joel Kolker, Antoni Corone
Ice Cream Cashier	Tamara Jones
Racquetball Colleagues	Roger Pretto, Parris Buckner
Secretary	Margot Moreland
Detective	Will Knickerbocker
Arresting Officers	Robert L. Gerlach, Bruce E. Holdstein
Parade Watchers	Richard Wasserman, Paul Nagle Jr., Paul Froehler, Mary Ellen O'Brien, Jody Wilson
Waitress	Kate Colburn
Danny's Girlfriend	Domenica Scorsese
Big Men	Garr Stevens, Billy Lucas, Ken Collins
Ticket Agents	Linda Perri, Elizabeth Moyer
Fruit Stand Customers	Catherine Scorsese, Charles Scorsese
Jimmy the Dockmaster	Jackie Davis

Top: Nick Nolte, Jessica Lange
Left: Robert De Niro, Nolte
© *Universal City Studios/Amblin Ent.*

Joe Don Baker; Illeana Douglas   **Robert De Niro**

Juliette Lewis, Jessica Lange, Nick Nolte Top Left: Robert De Niro, Nolte
Below Left: Gregory Peck; Robert Mitchum Top Right: Lewis, Lange

Lumiere, Mrs. Potts, Cogsworth Top Right: Belle
Top Left: Beast, Belle Below Left: Belle

BEAUTY AND THE BEAST

(WALT DISNEY PICTURES) Producer, Don Hahn; Directors, Gary Trousdale, Kirk Wise; Executive Producer, Howard Ashman; Animation Screenplay, Linda Woolverton; Songs, Howard Ashman, Alan Menken; Music Score, Alan Menken; Associate Producer, Sarah McArthur; Art Director, Brian McEntee; Editor, John Carnochan; Story Supervisor, Roger Allers; Layout, Ed Ghertner; Background, Lisa Keene; Cleanup, Vera Lanpher; Visual Effects, Randy Fullmer; Computer Graphics Images, Jim Hillin; Casting, Albert Tavares; Produced in association with Silver Screen Partners IV; Distributed by Buena Vista Pictures; Dolby Stereo; Technicolor; Rated G; 84 minutes; November release

VOICE CAST

Beast..Robby Benson
LeFou ....Jesse Corti
Maurice...Rex Everhart
Mrs. Potts...Angela Lansbury
Belle..Paige O'Hara
Lumiere..Jerry Orbach
Chip...Bradley Michael Pierce
Cogsworth/Narrator ....David Ogden Stiers
Gaston ....Richard White
Wardrobe ....Jo Anne Worley
Bimbette ....Mary Kay Bergman
Stove...Brian Cummins
Bookseller...Alvin Epstein
Monsieur D'Arque...Tony Jay
Baker..Alec Murphy
Featherduster...Kimmy Robertson
Philippe ....Hal Smith
Bimbette ....Kath Soucie
Footstool/Special Vocal Effects ....Frank Welker

Gaston, Le Fou Above: Beast

Belle, Beast (also top) Above Left: Lumiere

Lumiere, Mrs. Potts, Cogsworth
Above Right: Gaston

Leslie Nielsen, Thora Birch Top Right: Birch, Amy
Oberer, Ethan Randall Right: Birch, Randall, Phil Leeds
© *Paramount Pictures*

ALL I WANT FOR CHRISTMAS

(PARAMOUNT) Producer, Marykay Powell; Executive Producer, Stan Rogow; Co-Producer, Vicky Herman; Director, Robert Lieberman; Screenplay, Thom Eberhardt, Richard Kramer; Photography, Robbie Greenberg; Designer, Herman Zimmerman; Editors, Peter E. Berger, Dean Goodhill; Costumes, Nolan Miller; Music, Bruce Broughton; Casting, Judith Holstra; Assistant Director, J. Michael Haynie; Associate Producer, Robert P. Cohen; Song: "All I Want" by David Foster (music) and Linda Thompson (lyric)/performed by Stephen Bishop; Dolby Stereo; Technicolor; Rated G; 96 minutes; November release

CAST

Catherine O'Fallon	Harley Jane Kozak
Michael O'Fallon	Jamey Sheridan
Ethan O'Fallon	Ethan Randall
Tony Boer	Kevin Nealon
Hallie O'Fallon	Thora Birch
Santa	Leslie Nielsen
Lillian Brooks	Lauren Bacall
Stephanie	Amy Oberer
Olivia Hatch	Andrea Martin
Marshall	Patrick LaBrecque
Frankie	Michael Alaimo
Mr. Chase	Alan Brooks
Paige	Elizabeth Cherney
Bruiser	Otto Coelho
Burly #2	Joe Costanza
Santa's Helper	J. Teddy Davis
Girl in line	Tracy Diane
Shep	Joey Gaynor
Burly #1	Frank Girardeau
Susan	Felicity La Fortune
Mr. Feld	Phil Leeds
Caterer	Neal Lerner
Mrs. Graff	Harriet Medin
Kevin Mars	Devin Oatway
Cabbie #2	Kavi Raz
Paramedic #1	Bernardo Rosa, Jr.
Sonya	Camille Saviola
Lollipop Kid	J.D. Stone
Sylvia	Renee Taylor
Stella	Edith Varon
Brad	Joshua Wiener
Salesdervishes	Joanne Baron, Darrell Kunitomi

Ethan Randall, Thora Birch, Lauren Bacall
Above: Jamey Sheridan, Harley Jane Kozak

FOR THE BOYS

(20th CENTURY FOX) Producers, Bette Midler, Bonnie Bruckheimer, Margaret South; Executive Producer/Director, Mark Rydell; Co-Producer, Ray Hartwick; Screenplay, Marshall Brickman, Neal Jiminez, Lindy Laub; Story, Neal Jimenez, Lindy Laub; Photography, Stephen Goldblatt; Designer, Assheton Gorton; Editors, Jerry Greenberg, Jere Huggins; Music, Dave Grusin; Executive Music Producer, Joel Sill; Musical Sequences Devised by Joe Layton; Costumes, Wayne Finkelman; Casting, Lynn Stalmaster; an All Girl production; Dolby Stereo; Deluxe color; Rated R; 145 minutes; November release

CAST

Dixie Leonard	Bette Midler
Eddie Sparks	James Caan
Art Silver	George Segal
Shephard	Patrick O'Neal
Danny	Christopher Rydell
Jeff Brooks	Arye Gross
Sam Schiff	Norman Fell
Luanna Trott	Rosemary Murphy
Phil	Bud Yorkin
Loretta	Dori Brenner
Wally Fields	Jack Sheldon
Vicki	Karen Martin
Margaret Sparks	Shannon Wilcox
General Scott	Michael Green
Corrine	Melissa Manchester
Stan	Steven Kampmann
Dixie's Husband	Arliss Howard

Recording Studio: Richard Portnow (Milt), Pattie Darcy (Myra), Beau Dremann (Army Messenger), Jameson Rodgers (Danny at 4); England: Gary Gershaw (Stage Manager), Jim Raposa (Dancing Airman), Patrick White (Audience Airman), Christopher Kaufman (Band Person), James Patrick (Chris Wilkinson (Niles LaGuardia), Andrew Bilgore (Nervous Production Asst.), Brandon Call (Danny at 12), Hayley Carr (Ann Sparks), Kimberly Ann Evans (Kate Sparks), Kelly Noonan (Merry Sparks), John O'Leary (TV Censor), Stewart J. Zully (TV Stage Manager), Deborah Stern, Heidi Sorenson (Showgirls), Bruce Gay, Richardson Morse, Matthew Faison (Sponsors), Carey Eidel (Green Room Page), Richard Hochberg (Merrill), Andy Milder (Dressing Room Page); Korea: Thom Adcox (Wounded Marine), Andy Lauer (Corpsman on battlefield), Billy Bob Thornton (Marine Sergeant), John Doolittle (Capt. Donelson), Sal Landi (Marine Driver), John Ruskin (Marine who stops trucks), Marc Poppel (Corpsman at MASH), Gabe Bologna (Marine at MASH); Japan: Tamaki Kawakubo (Violinist), Mark Roberts (Vice Admiral), Robert Clotworthy (Navy Commander); Vietnam: Tony Pierce (Major at firebase), Xander Berkeley (Roberts), Maia Winters (Janie), D. David Morin (Cameraman); Awards TV Show: Walter C. Miller (TV Director), David Selberg (Asst. Director), Alan Haufrect (Technical Director), Annie Prager (Assoc. Producer), Barry Michlin (Exec. Producer), Sherlynn Hicks (Teleprompter Operator), Maggie Wagner (Stan's Asst.), Leonard Gaines (Lou Presti), David Bowe (Photographer), Morgan Ames (Awards Conductor); and William Marquez (Caretaker), Fred Parnes (Jeep Driver), Esther Jacobs (Ida Silver), Garrison Singer (Commander at Citadel)

James Caan, Bette Midler (also top)

Christopher Rydell, Bette Midler **125**
Above: Midler

THE ADDAMS FAMILY

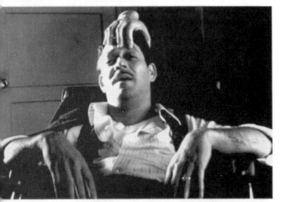

(PARAMOUNT) Producer, Scott Rudin; Executive Producer, Graham Place; Co-Producer, Jack Cummins; Director, Barry Sonnenfeld; Screenplay, Caroline Thompson, Larry Wilson; Based on the characters created by Charles Addams; Photography, Owen Roizman; Designer, Richard MacDonald; Editors, Dede Allen, Jim Miller; Music, Marc Shaiman; Song: "Mamushka" music by Marc Shaiman, lyric by Betty Comden & Adolph Green; Choreographer, Peter Anastos; Casting, David Rubin; Costumes, Ruth Myers; Visual Effects Supervisor, Alan Munro; "Thing" Prosthetics and Puppets, David Miller Studio; Makeup, Fern Buchner; Dolby Stereo; Technicolor; Rated PG-13; 100 minutes; November release

CAST

Morticia Addams	Anjelica Huston
Gomez Addams	Raul Julia
Uncle Fester Addams	Christopher Lloyd
Tully Alford	Dan Hedaya
Abigail Craven	Elizabeth Wilson
Granny	Judith Malina
Lurch	Carel Struycken
Margaret Alford	Dana Ivey
Judge Womack	Paul Benedict
Wednesday Addams	Christina Ricci
Pugsley Addams	Jimmy Workman
Thing	Christopher Hart
Cousin It	John Franklin
Digit Addams	Tony Azito
Dexter Addams	Douglas Brian Martin
Donald Addams	Steven M. Martin
Cousin Ophelia Addams	Allegra Kent
Slosh Addams	Richard Korthaze
Lumpy Addams	Ryan Holihan
Flora Amor	Maureen Sue Levin
Fauna Amor	Darlene Levin
Employment Agent	Kate McGregor-Stewart
Susan Firkins	Lela Ivey
Little Tully	Whitby Hertford
Lois Addams	Patty Maloney
Swedish Blonde	Victoria Hall
Pre-Teen Gomez	Jimmy Ross
Pre-Teen Fester	Ryan Anderson
Teenage Gomez	Daniel Pikus
Teenage Fester	Michael Hittesdorf
Teenage Flora	Lauren Walker
Teenage Fauna	Valeri Walker
Girl Scout	Mercedes McNab

and Joe Zimmerman (Long Arm Addams), Steve Welles (Fingers Addams), Eugene Jackson (One-Armed Bass Player), Richard Tanner (Snake Charmer), Marc Shaiman (Conductor), Sally Jessy Raphael (Herself)

Top: Raul Julia, Anjelica Huston Below: Christina Ricci, Huston, Jimmy Workman Left: Julia, Thing
© *Paramount Pictures*

Christina Ricci, Christopher Lloyd, Jimmy Workman

Raul Julia, Dan Hedaya

Dana Ivey, John Franklin
Top Left: Jimmy Workman, Christina Ricci

Carel Struycken, Jimmy Workman, Judith Malina, Raul
Julia, Anjelica Huston, Christopher Lloyd, Christina Ricci

Raul Julia Above Left: Carel Struycken

Judith Malina Above Right: Anjelica Huston, 127
Raul Julia

AN AMERICAN TAIL: FIEVEL GOES WEST

(UNIVERSAL) Producers, Steven Spielberg, Robert Watts; Executive Producers, Frank Marshall, Kathleen Kennedy, David Kirschner; Directors, Phil Nibbelink, Simon Wells; Screenplay, Flint Dille; Story, Charles Swenson; Created by David Kirschner; Songs by James Horner, Will Jennings; Music, James Horner; Casting, Nancy Nayor, Valerie McCaffrey; Supervising Editor, Nick Fletcher; Layout Supervisor, Mark Marren; Supervising Animators, Nancy Beiman, Kristof Serrand, Rob Stevenhagen; from Amblin Entertainment; Dolby Stereo; Rank color; Rated G; 80 minutes; November release

VOICE CAST

Fievel	Phillip Glaser
Wylie Burp	James Stewart
Mama	Erica Yohn
Tanya	Cathy Cavadini
Papa	Nehemiah Persoff
Tiger	Dom DeLuise
Miss Kitty	Amy Irving
Cat R. Waul	John Cleese
Chula	Jon Lovitz

Additional Voices: Jack Angel, Fausto Bara, Vanna Bonta, Philip Clarke, Jennifer Darling, Annie Holiday, Sherry Lynn, Lev Mailer, Mickie McGowan, Larry Moss, Nigel Pegram, Patrick Pinney, Lisa Raggio, Lawrence Steffan, David Tate, Robert Watts

Top Right: Fievel, Cat R. Waul
Right: Tiger, Fievel, Wylie Burp
© *Universal City Studios/Amblin Entertainment*

Francis Ford Coppola, Dennis Hopper
© *Triton Pictures*

HEARTS OF DARKNESS: A Filmmaker's Apocalypse

(TRITON PICTURES) Producers, George Zaloom, Les Mayfield; Executive Producers, Doug Claybourne, Fred Roos; Directors/ Screenplay, Fax Bahr, George Hickenlooper; Documentary footage directed by Eleanor Coppola; Editors, Michael Greer, Jay Miracle; Music, Todd Boekelheide; a Showtime presentation of a ZM production in association with Zoetrope Studios; Color; Rated R; 96 minutes; November release. A documentary on the making of the 1979 United Artists release *Apocalypse Now*

WITH

Eleanor Coppola, Francis Ford Coppola, Robert Duvall, Dennis Hopper, George Lucas, John Milius, Martin Sheen, Frederic Forrest, Sam Bottoms, Larry Fishburne, Albert Hall

Francis Ford Coppola, Martin Sheen
Above: Coppola

Jamie Lee Curtis, Anna Chlumsky, Dan Aykroyd
Top Left: Macaulay Culkin, Chlumsky
Left: Chlumsky, Curtis
© *Columbia Pictures Industries*

MY GIRL

(COLUMBIA) Producer, Brian Grazer; Executive Producers, Joseph M. Caracciolo, David T. Friendly; Director, Howard Zieff; Screenplay, Laurice Elehwany; Photography, Paul Elliott; Designer, Joseph T. Garrity; Editor, Wendy Greene Bricmont; Music, James Newton Howard; Costumes, Karen Patch; Casting, Mary Colquhoun; Assistant Director, Robert V. Girolami; Associate Producer, Hannah Gold; a Brian Grazer/Imagine Films Entertainment production; Dolby Stereo; Technicolor; Rated PG; 102 minutes; November release

CAST

Harry Sultenfuss	Dan Aykroyd
Shelly DeVoto	Jamie Lee Curtis
Thomas J. Sennett	Macaulay Culkin
Vada Sultenfuss	Anna Chlumsky
Phil Sultenfuss	Richard Masur
Mr. Bixler	Griffin Dunne
Gramoo Sultenfuss	Ann Nelson
Dr. Welty	Peter Michael Goetz
Nurse Randall	Jane Hallaren
Arthur	Anthony Jones
Justin	Tom Villard
Ronda	Lara Steinick
Charles	Kristian Truelsen
Ray	Dave Caprita
Mrs. Hunsaker	Jody Wilson
Betty	Linda Perri
Jackie	Nancy L. Chlumsky
Thomas J.'s Mother	Glenda Chism
Thomas J.'s Father	Bill Cordell
Danny	Ray Buktenica
Ralph	George Colangelo
Howie	Anthony Finazzo
Billy	Shane Obedzinski
Zack	Zachary McLemore
Boy	T.J. Collazo
Judy	Cassi Abel
Girls	Amanda Cole, Bree Butler
Bingo Announcer	Harvey Bellman
Vernon	John De Russy
Carl	Henry Kohn
Margie	Florence Mistrot
Carnival Barkers	Anthony Giaimo, Edgar Allan Poe IV
George	Robert Girolami
Policeman	Kurt Smildsin
Minister	Paul Nagel, Jr.
Suzanne	Lynn Sellers

Dan Aykroyd, Richard Masur, Jamie Lee Curtis,
Anna Chlumsky, Ann Nelson
Above: Macaulay Culkin, Chlumsky

Jeremy Irons Top Right: Joel Grey, Irons Right: Irons
© *Miramax Films*

KAFKA

(**MIRAMAX**) Producers, Stuart Cornfeld, Harry Benn; Executive Producers, Paul Rassam, Mark Johnson; Director/Editor, Steven Soderbergh; Screenplay, Lem Dobbs; Photography, Walt Lloyd; Designer, Gavin Bocquet; Music, Cliff Martinez; Costumes, Michael Jeffery; Casting, Susie Figgis; Assistant Directors, Guy Travers, Jiri Ostry; a Baltimore Pictures, Renn/Pricel S.A. production; Dolby Stereo; Black and white/DuArt color; Rated PG-13; 98 minutes; December release

CAST

Kafka	Jeremy Irons
Gabriela	Theresa Russell
Burgel	Joel Grey
Dr. Murnau	Ian Holm
Bizzlebek	Jeroen Krabbé
Inspector Grubach	Armin Mueller-Stahl
The Chief Clerk	Alec Guinness
Castle Henchman	Brian Glover
Assistant Ludwig	Keith Allen
Assistant Oscar	Simon McBurney
The Keeper of the Files	Robert Flemyng
Concierge	Matyelok Gibbs
Solemn Anarchist	Ion Caramitru
Female Anarchist	Hilde Van Meighem
Mustachioed Anarchist	Jan Nemejovsky
Youthful Anarchist	Toon Agterberg
Anna	Maria Miles
Eduard	Vladimir Gut
Man under microscope	Emil Wolk
Friends of Kafka	Josef Abrham, Guy Fithen, Zuzana Halustokova, Ondrej Havelka, Lenka Korinkova, Petr Lepsa, Leon Silver, Debora Weston
Man at bar	Jan Slovak
Interrogating Attendant	David Shaw Parker
Castle Attendants	Jerome Flynn, Ewan Stewart, James McPhee
Kidnapped Vagrant	Lubos Rychvalsky
Vagrants	Pavel Myslik, Frantisek Stufka
Quarry Laborer	Petr Jakl
Inspector's Assistants	Karel Belohradsky, Josef Sebek
Evil Wagon Driver	Robert Krejcik
Lens Cleaner	Vitezslav Bouchner
The Laughing Man	David Jensen

Jeremy Irons (left) Above: Irons, Theresa Russell

AT PLAY IN THE FIELDS OF THE LORD

(**UNIVERSAL**) Producer, Saul Zaentz; Executive Producers, Francisco Ramalho, Jr., David Nichols; Director, Hector Babenco; Based on the novel by Peter Matthiessen; Photography, Lauro Escorel; Costumes, Rita Murtinho; Designer, Clovis Bueno; Makeup/Hair Design, Jaque Monteiro; Music, Zbigniew Preisner; Editor, William Anderson; Associate Producer, Paul Zaentz; Assistant Director, Steve Andrews; Presented by The Saul Zaentz Company; Dolby Stereo; Technicolor; Rated R; 187 minutes; December release

CAST

Lewis Moon	Tom Berenger
Leslie Huben	John Lithgow
Andy Huben	Daryl Hannah
Martin Quarrier	Aidan Quinn
Wolf	Tom Waits
Hazel Quarrier	Kathy Bates
Boronai	Stenio Garcia
Father Xantes	Nelson Xavier
Commandante Guzman	Jose Dumont
Billy Quarrier	Niilo Kivirinta
Aeore	S. Yriwana Karaja
Uyuyu	Jose Renato Lana
Kori	Rui Polanah
Tukanu	Carlos Xavante
Pindi	Ione Machado
Taweeda	Edwirges Ribeiro
Mutu	Mutahi Pataxo

Top: Tom Berenger Right: John Lithgow, Aidan Quinn
© *The Saul Zaentz Company*

Tom Berenger Above: Kathy Bates, Aidan Quinn

John Lithgow, Daryl Hannah
Above: S. Yriwana Karaja

(I.R.S. MEDIA) Producers, Richard C. Berman, Donald Paul Pemrick; Executive Producers, Miles A. Copeland III, Paul Colichman, Harold Welb; Associate Producers, Melissa Cobb, Toni Phillips, Steven Reich; Director/Screenplay, Gabe Torres; Photography, James Glennon; Designer, Garreth Stover; Editors, Carole Kravetz, Rick Hinson; Music, Deborah Holland; Costumes, Ron Leamon; Dolby Stereo; Color; Rated PG; 91 minutes; December release

CAST

Kipp Gibbs	Wil Wheaton
Stuart Brayton	Chris Young
Russell Littlejohn	Jason London
Allister Gibbs	Balthazar Getty
Tim Mitchell	Brian Krause
Headmaster Thurston	Robert Miller
Mrs. Langley	Ann Hartfield
Billy Wade	Soren Bailey

Below: Balthazar Getty, Brian Krause,
Chris Young, Wil Wheaton

Wil Wheaton Top: Chris Young, Jason London,
Wheaton, Balthazar Getty, Brian Krause
© *I.R.S. Media*

CONVICTS

(M.C.E.G.) Producers, Jonathan D. Krane, Sterling Vanwagenen; Director, Peter Masterson; Screenplay, Horton Foote, based on his play; Line Producer, Elliot Rosenblatt; Music, Peter Melnick; Associate Producers, David Anderson, Leah A. Palco; Photography, Toyomichi Kurita; Editor, Jill Savitt; Designer, Dan Bishop; Color; Not rated; 95 minutes; December release

CAST

Soll Gautier	Robert Duvall
Horace Robedaux	Lukas Haas
Ben Johnson	James Earl Jones
Martha Johnson	Starletta DuPois
Asa	Carlin Glynn
Leroy	Calvin Levels
Billy	Gary Swanson
Jackson	Mel Winkler
Sherman Edwards	Lance E. Nichols
Overseer	Robert Edmundson
Guards	John McConnell, Jerry Biggs, Martin F. Schacker
Singing Convict	Walter Breaux, Jr.
Sheriff	Tony Frank
Lana	Carol Sutton
Convicts	Duriel Harris, Otis Jenkins
Cobb	Joe Cool Davis

132   © *M.C.E.G. Productions*

Robert Duvall, Lukas Haas, James Earl Jones
Above: Duvall

STAR TREK VI: THE UNDISCOVERED COUNTRY

(PARAMOUNT) Producers, Ralph Winter, Steven-Charles Jaffe; Executive Producer, Leonard Nimoy; Director, Nicholas Meyer; Screenplay, Nicholas Meyer, Denny Martin Flinn; Story, Leonard Nimoy, Lawrence Konner, Mark Rosenthal; Based upon *Star Trek* created by Gene Roddenberry; Photography, Hiro Narita; Designer, Herman Zimmerman; Editor, Ronald Roose; Associate Producer, Brooke Breton; Co-Producer, Marty Hornstein; Casting, Mary Jo Slater; Music, Cliff Eidelman; Assistant Director, Douglas E. Wise; Costumes, Dodie Shepard; Visual Effects Supervisor, Scott Farrar; Special Alien Makeup, Edward French; Special Effects, Industrial Light & Magic; Dolby Stereo; Panavision; Technicolor; Rated PG; 110 minutes; December release

CAST

Capt. James T. Kirk	William Shatner
Mr. Spock	Leonard Nimoy
Dr. Leonard "Bones" McCoy	DeForest Kelley
Montgomery Scott	James Doohan
Commander Pavel Chekov	Walter Koenig
Commander Uhura	Nichelle Nichols
Capt. Hikaru Sulu	George Takei
Lieutenant Valeris	Kim Cattrall
Ambassador Sarek	Mark Lenard
"Excelsior" Communications Officer	Grace Lee Whitney
Admiral Cartwright	Brock Peters
Chief in Command	Leon Russom
Federation President	Kurtwood Smith
General Chang	Christopher Plummer
Azetbur	Rosana DeSoto
Chancellor Gorkon	David Warner
Klingon Ambassador	John Schuck
Klingon Defense Attorney	Michael Dorn
Brigadier Kerla	Paul Rossilli
Klingon Judge	Robert Easton
Klingon Officer	Clifford Shegog
Klingon Commander	W. Morgan Sheppard
General Stex	Brett Porter
"Excelsior" Officer	Jeremy Roberts
"Excelsior" Engineer	Michael Bofshever
"Excelsior" Navigator	Angelo Tiffe
"Excelsior" Ensign	Christian Slater
Helmsman Lojur	Boris Lee Krutonog
Martia	Iman
The Brute	Tom Morga
Klingon Translator	Todd Bryant
Behemoth Alien	John Bloom
Klingon Generals	Jim Boeke, Matthias Hues
Munitions Man	Carlos Cestero
Young Crewman	Edward Clements
Martia as a Child	Katie Jane Johnston
Prisoner at Rura Penthe	Douglas Engalla
Nanclus	Darryl Henriques
Sleepy Klingon	David Orange
Military Alien	Judy Levitt
ADC	Shakti
Crewman Dax	Michael Snyder
Col. West	Rene Auberjonois

Top: Walter Koenig, George Takei, DeForest Kelley, Nichelle Nichols, William Shatner, James Doohan, Leonard Nimoy Below: Nimoy, Kim Cattrall
© Paramount Pictures

Bob Hoskins, Dustin Hoffman Top Left: Hoffman Left:
Robin Williams © *TriStar Pictures*

HOOK

(TRISTAR) Producers, Kathleen Kennedy, Frank Marshall, Gerald R. Molen; Co-Producers, Gary Adelson, Craig Baumgarten; Director, Steven Spielberg; Screenplay, Jim V. Hart, Malia Scotch Marmo; Story, Jim V. Hart, Nick Castle; Based upon the original stageplay and books by J.M. Barrie; Photography, Dean Cundey; Designer, Norman Garwood; Editor, Michael Kahn; Music, John Williams; Songs by John Williams (music), Leslie Bricusse (lyrics); Executive Producers, Dodi Fayed, Jim V. Hart; Casting, Janet Hirshenson, Jane Jenkins, Michael Hirshenson; Assistant Director, Bruce Cohen; Visual Effects Supervisor, Eric Brevig; Special Visual Effects, Industrial Light & Magic; Special Makeup Creator, Greg Cannom; an Amblin Entertainment production; Dolby Stereo; Panavision; Deluxe/Technicolor; Rated PG; 143 minutes; December release

CAST

Captain James Hook	Dustin Hoffman
Peter Banning/Peter Pan	Robin Williams
Tinkerbell	Julia Roberts
Smee	Bob Hoskins
Granny Wendy	Maggie Smith
Moira Bannning	Caroline Goodall
Jack Banning	Charlie Korsmo
Maggie Bannning	Amber Scott
Liza	Laurel Cronin
Inspector Good	Phil Collins
Tootles	Arthur Malet
Pockets	Isaiah Robinson
Ace	Jasen Fisher
Rufio	Dante Basco
Thud Butt	Raushan Hammond
Don't Ask	James Madio
Too Small	Thomas Tulak
Latchboy	Alex Zuckerman
No Nap	Ahmad Stoner
Lost Boys	Bogdan Georghe, Adam McNatt, René Gonzalez Jr., Brian Willis, Brett Willis
Young Peter	Ryan Francis
5 year old Peter	Maxwell Hoffman
Peter's Mother	Kelly Rowan

and Stephanie Furst, Shannon Marie Kies, Regina Russell (Mermaids), Jewel Newlander Hubbard (Peter Pan in play), Jeannine Renshaw (Drama Teacher), Rebecca Hoffman (Jane in play), Jeannine Wagner (Pianist), Francesca Serrano, Andre Bollinger, Bryce Armstrong, Alyson Healing, Kevin Gasca, Lauren Friedler-Gow, Margie Takeda, Zoe Koehler (Lost Boys in play), Scott Williamson (Coach), Wayne Aten, Michael Hirshenson (Umpires), Jacob Hoffman (Little League Player), Geoff Lower (Brad), Don S. Davis (Dr. Fields), Cameron Thor (Ron), Brad Blumenthal (Jim), Brenda Isaacs, Jane Cobler, Ruth De Sosa (Secretaries), Stuart White (Chauffeur), Gwyneth Paltrow (Young Wendy), Don McLeod (Mime/Shadow), Kim O'Kelley, Randi Pareira, Beverly Polcyn, Mary Bond Davis (Prostitutes), David Crosby (Tickles), Nick Tate (Noodler), Tony Burton (Bill Jukes), Glenn Close (Gutless), Nick Ullett (Pirate Jailer), Matthew Van Ginkel (Baby Peter), Ray Tveden (Man in stands), Kim Robillard (Toothless Cripple), Mike Runyard (Screaming Pirate), Gary Epper (Growling Pirate), Rick Lazzarini, Mark Bryan Wilson (Puppeteers)

**Dustin Hoffman, Charlie Korsmo,
Bob Hoskins Above: Robin Williams (c)**

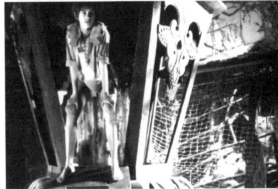

Robin Williams, Charlie Korsmo   **Julia Roberts Top: Glenn Close, Robin Williams**

Robin Williams, Dustin Hoffman

BUGSY

(TRI-STAR) Producers, Mark Johnson, Barry Levinson, Warren Beatty; Director, Barry Levinson; Screenplay, James Toback; Photography, Allen Daviau; Designer, Dennis Gassner; Editor, Stu Linder; Music, Ennio Morricone; Costumes, Albert Wolsky; Casting, Ellen Chenoweth; Co-Producer, Charles Newirth; Assistant Director, Peter Giuliano; a Mulholland Productions/Baltimore Pictures production; Dolby Stereo; Technicolor; Rated R; 135 minutes; December release

CAST

Benjamin "Bugsy" Siegel	Warren Beatty
Virginia Hill	Annette Bening
Mickey Cohen	Harvey Keitel
Meyer Lansky	Ben Kingsley
Harry Greenberg	Elliott Gould
George Raft	Joe Mantegna
Jack Dragna	Richard Sarafian
Countess di Frasso	Bebe Neuwirth
Count di Frasso	Gian-Carlo Scandiuzzi
Esta Siegel	Wendy Phillips
Millicent Siegel	Stefanie Mason
Barbara Siegel	Kimberly McCullough
Del Webb	Andy Romano
Alejandro	Robert Beltran
Charlie Luciano	Bill Graham
Joey Adonis	Lewis Van Bergen
Moe Sedway	Joseph Roman
Gus Greenbaum	James Toback
Vito Genovese	Don Carrara
Frank Costello	Carmine Caridi
Louie Dragna	Don Calfa
Dominic	Robert Glaudini
Chick Hill	Bryan Smith
David Hinton	Ray McKinnon
Ronald the Butler	Eric Christmas
Lawrence Tibbett	Joe Baker
Sulka's Salesman	John C. Moskoff
Elevator Operator	Ralph Tabakin
Girl in elevator	Debrah Farentino
Jerry the Bookie	Anthony Russell
Woman on train	Wendie Malick
Fan at train station	DeVera Marcus
Marlene Dietrich	Ksenia Prohaska
Natalie St. Clair	Traci Lind
D.A. McWilde	Bruce E. Morrow

and Peter Giuliano ("Manpower" Asst. Director), Austin Kelly ("Manpower" Maitre D'), Michael Kenner ("Manpower" Clapper Boy), Clive Rosengren (Deputy D.A. Hartman), Gary McGurk (Tony the Waiter), Gerard Joseph McKenna (Ciro's Photographer), Paul Roache (Taxi Driver), Tommy Townsend, Steven D. Maines (Federal Marshalls), David H. Hebble (Cadillac Driver), Michael Sollenberger (Bond Rally Speaker), Jamie Angell (Courthouse Guard), Julie Christensen, Susan Rumor, Lloyd Baskin, Hal Melia, Fred Lehto, Kal David, Albina Bocchicchio, Cathleen Crone (Ciros Singers)

Top: Warren Beatty Below: Annette Bening
© *TriStar Pictures*
1991 Academy Awards for Best Art Direction
and Costume Design

Ben Kingsley, Annette Bening
Above: Joe Mantegna; Harvey Keitel

Warren Beatty

Warren Beatty Joe Baker, Warren Beatty Top Right: Annette Bening, Beatty

Elliott Gould, Warren Beatty (standing center)
Ben Kingsley, Bill Graham (seated center)

THE LAST BOY SCOUT

(WARNER BROS.) Producers, Joel Silver, Michael Levy; Executive Producers, Shane Black, Barry Josephson; Director, Tony Scott; Screenplay, Shane Black; Story, Shane Black, Greg Hicks; Photography, Ward Russell; Designer, Brian Morris; Editors, Mark Goldblatt, Mark Helfrich; Music, Michael Kamen; Song: "Friday Night's a Great Night for Football" by Steve Dorff, John Bettis/performed by Bill Medley; Co-Producer, Steve Perry; Costumes, Marilyn Vance-Straker; Casting, Marion Dougherty; Stunts, Charles Picerni; a Geffen Pictures presentation of a Silver Pictures production; Dolby Stereo; Panavision; Technicolor; Rated R; 105 minutes; December release

CAST

Joe Hallenbeck	Bruce Willis
Jimmy Dix	Damon Wayans
Sarah Hallenbeck	Chelsea Field
Sheldon Marcone	Noble Willingham
Milo	Taylor Negron
Darian Hallenbeck	Danielle Harris
Cory	Halle Berry
Mike Matthews	Bruce McGill
Alley Thug	Badja Djola
Chet	Kim Coates
Senator Baynard	Chelcie Ross
Bessalo	Joe Santos
McCaskey	Clarence Felder
Big Ray Walton	Tony Longo
Pablo	Frank Collison
Themselves	Bill Medley, Vern Lundquist, Dick Butkus, Lynn Swan
Billy Cole	Billy Blanks
Head Coach	Ken Kells
Locker Room Kid	Morris Chestnut
Wounded Players	Mike Fisher, Doug Simpson
Kids	Joe El Rady, David L. McMillan, Benjamin Agee
Sleeping Party Girl	Donna Wilson
Jacuzzi Party Girl	Denise Ames
Neighbor	Frank Kopyc
Dancers	Teal Roberts, Sara Suzanne Brown
Harp	Ryan Cutrona
M.C.	Eddie Griffin
Main Hitman	John Cenatiempo
Hitman	Mike Papajohn
Ponytail Hitman	Matt Johnston

and Ed Villa (Property Cop), James Keane (Garage Patrolman), Jack Kehler (Scrabble Man), Duke Valenti (Jake), Dennis Garber (Detective), Manny Perry (Cigar Thug), Vic Manni (Granddad Thug), Frank Ferrara (Milo's Goon), Erik Onate (TV Crew Member), Bob Apisa, Shane Dixon (Baynard's Bodyguards), Rick Ducommun (Pool Owner), E. Brian Dean (Stadium Guard), Dick Ziker, Fred Lerner, John Meier, Don Pulford (Marcone's Goons), Dennis Packer (Field Announcer), Gene Borkan, Kevin Bourland (Stadium Cops), Jeff Hochendoner (Henry), Steven Picerni (Helicopter Cop), Craig Pinckes (Presidential Assassin), Carmine Zozzora (Secret Service Man), Theresa St. Clair (Shower Girl), Ed Beheler (The President), Colby Kline (Young Darian)

Top: Bruce Willis, Damon Wayans Below: Willis, Taylor Negron © *Geffen Film Company*

Bruce Willis, Badja Djola
Above: Halle Berry, Damon Wayans

Damon Wayans, Danielle Harris, Bruce Willis

Diane Keaton, Steve Martin Top Right: Kimberly
Williams, George Newbern Right: Williams,
Newbern, Martin, Keaton
© *Touchstone Pictures*

FATHER OF THE BRIDE

(TOUCHSTONE) Producers, Nancy Meyers, Carol Baum, Howard
Rosenman; Executive Producers, Sandy Gallin, James Orr, Jim
Cruickshank; Co-Producer, Cindy Williams; Director, Charles Shyer;
Screenplay, Frances Goodrich, Albert Hackett, Nancy Meyers,
Charles Shyer; Photography, John Lindley; Designer, Sandy
Veneziano; Costumes, Susan Becker; Editor, Richard Marks; Music,
Alan Silvestri; Casting, Donna Isaacson; Associate Producer, Bruce
A. Block; Assistant Director, K.C. Colwell; Presented in association
with Touchwood Pacific Partners I; Distributed by Buena Vista
Pictures; Dolby Stereo; Technicolor; Rated PG; 105 minutes;
December release

CAST

George Banks	Steve Martin
Nina Banks	Diane Keaton
Annie Banks	Kimberly Williams
Matty Banks	Kieran Culkin
Bryan MacKenzie	George Newbern
Franck Eggelhoffer	Martin Short
Howard Weinstein	B.D. Wong
John MacKenzie	Peter Michael Goetz
Joanna MacKenzie	Kate McGregor Stewart
Grace	Carmen Hayward
Olivia	April Ortiz
Marta	Mina Vasquez
David	Gibby Brand
Al, the Tux Salesman	Richard Portnow
Factory Worker	Barbara Perry
Andrea, the Florist	Martha Gehman
Dan, the Field Engineer	Frank Kopyc
Hanck, the Caterer	David Pasquesi
Stock Boy	Ira Heiden
Police Officer	Thomas Wagner
Annie at three	Marissa Lefton
Annie at seven	Sarah Rose Karr
Annie at twelve	Amy Young
Flower Girls	Hallie Meyers-Shyer, Annie Meyers-Shyer
Bridesmaids	Morgan Dox, Elsa Mandell, Christine Beliveau, Natasha Wieland
Ushers	Eric Kay, Scott Hogan, Peter Cooper, David Day
Reverend	Ed Williams
Guests at reception	Patricia Meyers, Irving Meyers
Photographer	Bruce Block
Patrolman	Peter Murnik
Cameron	Chauncey Leopardi

and Mark Steen, Robert Bauer, Kevin Shaw (Waiters), Steve Tyrell
(Bandleader), Eugene Levy (Auditioning Singer), Tom Irish (Ben
Banks)

Diane Keaton, Steve Martin, Martin Short,
Kimberly Williams Above: Williams, Martin

JFK

(WARNER BROS.) Producers, A. Kitman Ho, Oliver Stone; Co-Producer, Clayton Townsend; Executive Producer, Arnon Milchan; Director, Oliver Stone; Screenplay, Oliver Stone, Zachary Sklar; Based on the books *On the Trail of the Assassins* by Jim Garrison, and *Crossfire: The Plot That Killed Kennedy* by Jim Marrs; Photography, Robert Richardson; Designer, Victor Kempster; Music, John Williams; Editors, Joe Hutshing, Pietro Scalia; Costumes, Marlene Stewart; Casting, Risa Bramon Garcia, Billy Hopkins, Heidi Levitt; Associate Producer/Assistant Director, Joseph Reidy; Presented in association with Le Studio Canal + Regency Enterprises and Alcor Films; an Ixtlan Corporation and an A. Kitman Ho production; Dolby Stereo; Panavision; Technicolor/Black and white; Rated R; 189 minutes; December release

CAST

(in order of appearance)

Martin Sheen (Opening Narrator), Sally Kirkland (Rose Cheramie), Anthony Ramirez (Epileptic), Ray LePere (Zapruder), Steve Reed (John F. Kennedy), Jodi Farber (Jackie Kennedy), Columbia Dubose (Nellie Connally), Randy Means (Gov. Connally), Kevin Costner (Jim Garrison), Jay O. Sanders (Lou Ivon), E.J. Morris, Cheryl Penland, Jim Gough (Plaza Witnesses), Perry R. Russo (Angry Bar Patron), Mike Longman (TV Newsman #1), Edward Asner (Guy Banister), Jack Lemmon (Jack Martin), Vincent D'Onofrio (Bill Newman), Gary Oldman (Lee Harvey Oswald), Sissy Spacek (Liz Garrison), Pat Perkins (Mattie), Brian Doyle-Murray (Jack Ruby), Wayne Knight (Numa Bertel), Michael Rooker (Bill Broussard), Laurie Metcalf (Susie Cox), Gary Grubbs (Al Oser), Beata Pozniak (Marina Oswald), Tom Howard (L.B.J.), John William Galt (L.B.J. Voice), Joe Pesci (David Ferrie), Ron Jackson (FBI Spokesman), Walter Matthau (Sen. Russell Long), Sean Stone (Jasper Garrison), Amy Long (Virginia Garrison), Scott Krueger (Snapper Garrison), Allison Pratt Davis (Elizabeth Garrison), Pruitt Taylor Vince (Lee Bowers), Red Mitchell (Sgt. Harkness), Ronald von Klaussen, John S. Davies, Michael Ozag (Hobos), Tony Plana (Carlos Bringuier), Tommy Lee Jones (Clay Shaw), Tomas Milian (Leopoldo), Raul Aranas (Angelo), John Candy (Dean Andrews), John C. Martin (Prison Guard), Kevin Bacon (Willie O'Keefe), Henri Alciatore (Maitre d'), Willem Oltmans (George DeMohrenschildt), Gail Cronauer (Janet Williams), Gary Carter (Bill Williams), Roxie M. Frnka (Earlene Roberts), Zeke Mills (J.C. Price), James N. Harrell (Sam Holland), Ray Redd (Dodd), Ellen McElduff (Jean Hill), Sally Nystuen (Mary Moorman), Jo Anderson (Julia Ann Mercer), Marco Perella, Edwin Neal (Mercer Interrogators), Spain Logue, Darryl Cox (FBI Agents with Hill), T.J. Kennedy (Hill Interrogator), Lolita Davidovich (Beverly), Carolina McCullough (Stripper), Jim Garrison (Earl Warren), J.J. Johnston (Mobster with Broussard), R. Bruce Elliott (Bolton Ford Dealer), Frank Whaley (Oswald Impostor), Barry Chambers (Man at firing range), Linda Flores Wade (Sylvia Odio), William Larsen (Will Fritz), Alec Gifford (TV Newsman #2), Eric A. Vicini (French Reporter), Michael Gurievsky (Russian Reporter), Caroline Crosthwaite-Eyre (British Reporter), Helen Miller (Garrison Receptionist), Harold Herthum (Coroner), Wayne Tippit (FBI Agent - Frank), Donald Sutherland (X), Dale Dye (General Y), Norman Davis (Colonel Reich), Errol McLendon (Man with umbrella), John Seitz (General Lemnitzer), Bruce Gelb, Jerry Douglas, Ryan MacDonald, Duane Grey (Board Room Men), George Robertson, Baxter Harris, Alex Rodzi Rodine, Sam Stoneburner (White House Men), Odin K. Langford (Officer Habighorst), Bob Gunton (TV Newsman #3), Nathan Scott (John Chancler), Jorge Fernandez (Miguel Torres), Roy Barnitt (Irvin F. Dymond), Alvin Spicuzza (Bailiff), John Finnegan (Judge Haggerty), Walter Breaux (Vernon Bundy), Michael Skipper (James Teague), Melodee Bowman (FBI Receptionist), I.D. Brickman (Dr. Peters), Joseph Nadell (Dr.McClelland), Chris Robinson (Dr. Humes), Peter Maloney (Col. Finck), Chris Renna (Bethesda Doctor), Dalton Dearborn (Army General), Merlyn Sexton (Adm. Kennedy), Steve F. Price, Jr., Tom Bullock, Ruary O'Connell (Pathologists), Christopher Kosiciuka (FBI Agent at autopsy), John Reneau (A Team Shooter), Stanley White (B Team Shooter), Richard Rutowski (Fence Shooter), Bill Bolender (Prisoner Powell), Larry Melton (Patrolman Joe Smith), Carol Farabee (Carolyn Arnold), Willie Minor (Bonnie Ray Williams), Ted Pennebaker (Arnold Rowland), Bill Pickle (Marion Baker), Mykel Chaves (Sandra Styles), Price Carson (Tippit), Gil Glasgow (Tippit Shooter), Bob Orwig (Officer Poe), Loys Bergeron (Jury Foreman), Kristina Hare (Reporter)

Top: Sissy Spacek, Kevin Costner
Below: Gary Oldman, Edward Asner
© *Warner Bros. Inc.*
1991 Academy Awards for Best Cinematography
and Film Editing

140   Gary Oldman, Joe Pesci,
Brian Doyle-Murray

Kevin Costner, Jay O. Sanders

Kevin Costner, Jack Lemmon, Michael Rooker
Top Right: Tommy Lee Jones, Rooker, Costner

 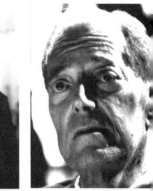

Kevin Costner, Walter Matthau Above Left: Costner,
Kevin Bacon, Michael Rooker

Wayne Knight, Kevin Costner
Above Right: Donald Sutherland; Jim Garrison

141

RUSH

(MGM) Producer, Richard D. Zanuck; Director, Lili Fini Zanuck; Screenplay, Pete Dexter; Based on the book by Kim Wozencraft; Photography, Kenneth MacMillan; Designer, Paul Sylbert; Editor, Mark Warner; Music, Eric Clapton; Costumes, Colleen Atwood; Casting, Shari Rhodes; Unit Production Manager/Associate Producer, Gary Daigler; Assistant Director, Katterli Frauenfelder; a Zanuck Company production; Dolby Stereo; Deluxe color; Rated R; 120 minutes; December release

CAST

Jim Raynor	Jason Patric
Kristen Cates	Jennifer Jason Leigh
Larry Dodd	Sam Elliott
Walker	Max Perlich
Will Gaines	Gregg Allman
Nettle	Tony Frank
Monroe	William Sadler
Willie Red	Special K McCray
Senior District Attorney	Dennis Letts
Motorcycle Guys	Dennis Burkley, Glenn Wilson
Man in disco	Jimmy Pickens
Yellow Rose Bartender	Barbara Lasater
Driller's Waitress	Toni Pilgreen
Defense Attorney	Merrill Connally
Judge	Connie Cooper
Yellow Rose Waitress	Cynthia Scott
Mayor	John Ray Harrison
Grand Jury District Attorney	Michael Kirkland
Police Instructor	Willie Ellison
Domino Player	Ron Kern
Wino	Tom Rosales
Dodd's Wife	Suzanne Savoy
Police Lieutenant	Ken Stadler
Scooter Trash	Gene Nash, Freddy Joe Odiorne, Niles Caldwell
Cop	Brandon Smith
Man in hearse	Jerry King
Medical Examiner	Blue Deckert
Reporter	Dell Gibson
Club Band	"Terrell": C.A. Terrell, Hawke Dixon, Jim Phillips, Morad, Doug Pryzbocki

Top: Jason Patric, Jennifer Jason Leigh
© *MGM-Pathe Communications*

Jason Patric, Jennifer Jason Leigh, Gregg Allman
Above Right: Sam Elliott; Max Perlich

Tom Hulce, Alexandre Zbruev Top Right: Hulce
Right: Hulce, Feodor Chaliapin Jr.
© *Columbia Pictures Industries*

THE INNER CIRCLE

(COLUMBIA) Producer, Claudio Bonivento; Director, Andrei Konchalovsky; Screenplay, Andrei Konchalovsky, Anatoli Usov; Photography, Ennio Guarnieri; Music, Eduard Artemyev; Editor, Henry Richardson; Casting, Robert MacDonald, Perry Bullington; Designer, Ezio Frigerio; Associate Producer, Laura Balbi; Assistant Director, Felix Kleiman; Costumes, Nelli Fomina; Dolby Stereo; Technicolor; Rated PG-13; 137 minutes; December release

CAST

Ivan Sanshin	Tom Hulce
Anastasia Sanshin	Lolita Davidovich
Beria	Bob Hoskins
Stalin	Alexandre Zbruev
Professor Bartnev	Feodor Chaliapin, Jr.
Kathy (16 years)	Bess Myer
Kathy (10 years)	Marla Baranova
Directress	Irina Kuptchenko
Colonel Schelkasov	Vladimir Khulishov
General Rumiantsev	Vsevolod Larionov
Major Khitrov	Aleksandr Filippenko
Governess	Evdokia Germanova
Sonia Gubelman	Liubov Matiushina
Vasily Morda	Aleksandr Garin
Fedosia	Maria Vinogradova
Aaron Gubelman	Aleksandr Lipkov
Claudia Morda	Antonia Anokhina
Voronkin	Aleksandr Sirin
Vlasik	Oleg Tabakov
Voroshilov	Michail Kononov
Bolshakov	Aleksandr Feiklistov
Chrustalev	Vladimir Steklov
Popova (Officer)	Elena Borzunova
Barbara (Waitress)	Irina Lazareva
Kathy (3 years)	Vira Ekroimova
Kaganovich	Ilja Chanbudanov
Molotov	Viktor Balabanov
Kilanin	Viktor Uralsky
Malenkov	Valentin Cherviakov
Mikoyan	Victor Tardian
Projectionist	Ivan Teplov
Tanya	Ivanova Petrova
Commandant of the train	Aleksandr Pashutin
Beria's Officer	Sergei Arzibashev

Bob Hoskins, Lolita Davidovich
Above: Tom Hulce

143

Mary McDonnell, Kevin Kline
Top Left: Kline, Danny Glover
© *Twentieth Century Fox*

GRAND CANYON

(20th CENTURY FOX) Producers, Lawrence Kasdan, Charles Okun, Michael Grillo; Director, Lawrence Kasdan; Screenplay, Lawrence Kasdan, Meg Kasdan; Photography, Owen Roizman; Designer, Bo Welch; Editor, Carol Littleton; Costumes, Aggie Guerard Rodgers; Associate Producer, Meg Kasdan; Music, James Newton Howard; Casting, Jennifer Shull; Assistant Director, Michael Grillo; Dolby Stereo; Panavision; Deluxe color; Rated R; 134 minutes; December release

CAST

Simon	Danny Glover
Mack	Kevin Kline
Davis	Steve Martin
Claire	Mary McDonnell
Dee	Mary-Louise Parker
Jane	Alfre Woodard
Roberto	Jeremy Sisto
Deborah	Tina Lifford
Otis	Patrick Malone
The Alley Baron	Randle Mell
Vanessa	Sarah Trigger
Kelley	Destinee DeWalt
Claire's Baby	Candace Mead, Loren Mead
Rocstar	Shaun Baker
Wipe	K. Todd Freeman
Jimmy	Deon Sams
Rotor	Christopher M. Brown
Eddie	Gregg Dandridge
Ace Cop	Branscombe Richmond
Deuce Cop	Walt Jordan
Myers	Todd Allen
Morning Nurse	Carole Ita White
Insurance Salesman	Basil Wallace
Cathy Fox	Georgina Lindsey
Steve Fox	Jack Kehler
Amanda	Marlee Shelton
Woman in baseball cap	Lynn Salvatori
Bus Driver	Jim Morange
Skin	Henry Kingi
Scar	Steven Keith Davis
Studio Girl	Sharon Lee Jones
Ms. Green	Mary Ellen Trainor
Young Roberto	Ben Chaney
Watch Robber	Gary Cervantes

and Ben McCreary (Jackson), Jeanne Bates (Mrs. Menken), Sam H. Ginsburg (Mr. Menken), Brett A. Jones (Window-Breaking Thug), Paul Short (Myer's Partner), Willie C. Carpenter (Simon's Friend), Antonio Royuela (Carlos), Edward G. Perez, Clifton Gonzalez Gonzalez (Carlos' Friends), Hugh R. Ross, Anne Ward, Roxanne Kasdan (Davis' Assistants), Cora Lee Day (Woman in car), John Ashby (Woman's Driver), Jacqueline Alexandra, Kristen Amber (Forum Twins)

Steve Martin, Kevin Kline
Above: Jeremy Sisto, Kline, Mary McDonnell

Mary-Louise Parker, Mary McDonnell, Kevin Kline, Steve Martin, Danny Glover, Alfre Woodard

Mary McDonnell
Above Left: Alfre Woodard, Danny Glover

Danny Glover
Above Right: Mary-Louise Parker

145

THE PRINCE OF TIDES

(COLUMBIA) Producers, Barbra Streisand, Andrew Karsch; Executive Producers, Cis Corman, James Roe; Director, Barbra Streisand; Screenplay, Pat Conroy, Becky Johnston; Based on the novel by Pat Conroy; Photography, Stephen Goldblatt; Designer, Paul Sylbert; Editor, Don Zimmerman; Music, James Newton Howard; Co-Producer, Sheldon Schrager; Costumes, Ruth Morley; Assistant Director, Thomas A. Reilly; a Barwood/Longfellow production; Dolby Stereo; Technicolor; Rated R; 132 minutes; December release

CAST

Tom Wingo	Nick Nolte
Susan Lowenstein	Barbra Streisand
Sallie Wingo	Blythe Danner
Lila Wingo Newbury	Kate Nelligan
Herbert Woodruff	Jeroen Krabbé
Savannah Wingo	Melinda Dillon
Eddie Detreville	George Carlin
Bernard Woodruff	Jason Gould
Henry Wingo	Brad Sullivan
Lucy Wingo	Maggie Collier
Jennifer Wingo	Lindsay Wray
Chandler Wingo	Brandlyn Whitaker
Tom Wingo (age 6)	Justen Woods
Tom Wingo (age 10)	Bobby Fain
Tom Wingo (age 13)	Trey Yearwood
Savannah Wingo (age 6)	Tiffany Jean Davis
Savannah Wingo (age 10)	Nancy Atchison
Savannah Wingo (age 13)	Kiki Runyan
Luke Wingo (age 9)	Grayson Fricke
Luke Wingo (age 13)	Ryan Newman
Luke Wingo (age 16)	Chris Stacy
Doctor	Milton Clark, Jr.
Nurses	Bonnie Cook, Dottie Soracco
Reese Newbury	Bob Hannah
Rapists	Max Maxwell, R.D. Oprea
Megan Daniels	Rebecca Fleming
Monique	Sandy Rowe
Spencer Richardson	Alan Sader
Madison Kingsley	Frederick Neumann
Man at party	Nick Searcy
Saxophonist	Kirk Whalum
Anna Richardson	Marilyn Carter
Christine Kingsley	Yvonne Brisendine
Ed Rosenberg	Lee Lively
Riva Rosenberg	Ann Pierce
Waiter	Francis Dumaurier
Vendor	John Arceri
Fisherman	Warren Kremin

Top: Nick Nolte, Barbra Streisand (also left)
Below: Jeroen Krabbé, Nolte
© *Columbia Pictures Industries*

146   Blythe Danner, Brandlyn Whitaker,
Nick Nolte, Maggie Collier, Lindsay Wray

Bobby Fain, Kate Nelligan

Nick Nolte, Blythe Danner Top Left: Jason Gould, Nolte

Grayson Fricke, Tiffany Jean Davis,
Kate Nelligan, Justen Woods

Nick Nolte, Barbra Streisand

Mary-Louise Parker, Mary Stuart Masterson
Top Right: Jessica Tandy, Kathy Bates Right:
Masterson, Nick Searcy © *Universal City Studios*

FRIED GREEN TOMATOES

(UNIVERSAL) Producers, Jon Avnet, Jordan Kerner; Executive Producers, Andrew Meyer, Anne Marie Gillen, Tom Taylor, Norman Lear; Co-Producers, Martin Huberty, Lisa Lindstrom, Ric Rondell; Director, Jon Avnet; Screenplay, Fannie Flagg, Jon Avnet; Based on the novel *Fried Green Tomatoes at the Whistle Stop Cafe* by Fannie Flagg; Photography, Geoffrey Simpson; Designer, Barbara Ling; Costumes, Elizabeth McBride; Editor, Debra Neil; Music, Thomas Newman; Casting, David Rubin; Assistant Director, Deborah Love; a co-presentation of Act III Communications in association with Electric Shadow Prods.; Dolby Stereo; Deluxe color; Rated PG-13; 135 minutes; December release

CAST

Evelyn Couch	Kathy Bates
Idgie Threadgoode	Mary Stuart Masterson
Ruth Jamison	Mary-Louise Parker
Ninny Threadgoode	Jessica Tandy
Sipsey	Cicely Tyson
Buddy Threadgoode	Chris O'Donnell
Big George	Stan Shaw
Ed Couch	Gailard Sartain
Smokey Lonesome	Tim Scott
Grady Kilgore	Gary Basaraba
Mama Threadgoode	Lois Smith
Teacher with mirror	Jo Harvey Allen
Prosecutor	Macon McCalman
Reverend Scroggins	Richard Riehle
Curtis Smoote	Raynor Scheine
Eva Bates	Grace Zabriskie
Young Julian	Reid Binion
Leona Threadgoode	Afton Smith
Papa Threadgoode	Danny Nelson
Little Idgie	Nancy Atchison
Missy	Constance Shulman
Frank Bennett	Nick Searcy
Older Julian	Haynes Brooke
Ruth's Mother	Ginny Parker
Boy at supermarket	Tres Holton
Ocie	Ronald McCall
KKK Man	Wallace Merck
Hooded Man	David Dwyer
Young Naughty Bird	Lashondra Phillips
Girls	Catherine Larson, Missy Wolff
Janeen	Latanya Richardson
Buddy Jr.	Grayson Fricke
Older Naughty Bird	Enjolik Oree
Peggy Hadley	Genevieve Fisher
Judge	Tom Even
Defense Attorney	Bob Hannah
Bailiff	Ted Manson
Sue Otis	Carole Mitchell-Leon
Tim	Evan Lockwood
Nurse	Suzi Bass
Instructor	Fannie Flagg

Mary Stuart Masterson, Stan Shaw
Above: Cicely Tyson, Mary-Louise Parker

Cliff DeYoung in *Crackdown*
© Concorde

David Carradine in *Dune Warrior*
© Concorde

CRACKDOWN (Concorde) Producer, Luis Llosa; Executive Producer, Kevin Reidy; Director, Louis Morneau; Screenplay, Ross Bell, Daryl Haney; Photography, Pili Flores Guerra; Music, Terry Plumeri; Editor, Eric L. Beason; Color; Ultra-Stereo; Rated R; 87 minutes; January release. CAST: Cliff De Young (Shaun Broderick), Robert Beltran (Juan Delgado), Jamie Rose (Constance Bigelow), Gerald Anthony (Thurmond), Orlando Sacha (Don Castillo), Kevin Reidy (Cowley), Ramon Garcia (Menendez), Rafael Cabrera (Cruz), Monica Dominquez (Luisa), Ramsy Ross (Teller), Gerald Powell (Gas Station Attendant), Oscar Bravo (Drunk), Baldomero Caceres (Narco Driver), Juan Carlos Alarcon (Young Man), Jorge Rodriguez Paz (Chief of Police), Brayton Lewis (Hotel Manager), Ximena Ruiz Rosas (Carmen), Jorge Falle, Juan Omar Lopez (Bodyguards), Piero Stucchi (Man with mustache), Gilberto Torres, Carlos Victoria (Police), Susan Leon, Rocio Tovar (Castillo Girls)

DEAD SPACE (Concorde) Producer, Mike Elliot; Director, Fred Gallo; Screenplay, Catherine Cyran; Photography, Mark Perry; Music, Daniel May; Designer, Gary Randall; Editor, Lawrence Jordan; Associate Producer, Jonathan Winfrey; Ultra-Stereo; Foto-Kem color; Rated R; 80 minutes; January release. CAST: Marc Singer (Krieger), Laura Tate (Marissa), Bryan Cranston (Darden), Judith Chapman (Stote), Randy Reinholz (Tim), Frank Roman (Sal), Lori Lively (Jill), Greg Blanchard (Joe), Rodger Hall (Tinpan), Liz Rogers (Devon)

DUNE WARRIORS (Concorde) Producer/Director, Cirio H. Santiago; Associate Producers, Kevin Reidy, Steve Rabiner; Screenplay, T.C.McKelvey; Music, The Score Warriors; Photography, Joe Batac; Editors, Joseph Zucchero, Bass Santos; Designer, Jose Mari Avellana; Color; Rated R; 80 minutes; January release. CAST: David Carradine (Michael), Rick Hill (John), Luke Askew (William), Jillian McWhirter (Val), Blake Boyd (Dorian), Val Garay (Jason), Joe Zucchero (Reynaldo), Bon Vibar (Emilio), Henry Strzalkowski (Luis), Dante Varona (Ricardo), Isabel Lopez (Miranda), Nick Nicholson (Tomas), Ned Hourani (Randall), Daniel Nicholson (Village Boy), Joanne Griffin (Mother)

EVE OF DESTRUCTION (Orion) Producer, David Madden; Executive Producers, Robert W. Cort, Melinda Jason, Rick

Finkelstein; Co-Executive Producer, Graham Henderson; Director, Duncan Gibbins; Screenplay, Duncan Gibbins, Yale Udoff; Photography, Alan Hume; Designer, Peter Lamont; Editor, Caroline Biggerstaff; Costumes, Deborah L. Scott; Music, Philippe Sarde; Casting, Marci Liroff; Stunts, John Moio; a Nelson Entertainment presentation of an Interscope Communications production; Dolby Stereo; Deluxe color; Rated R; 99 minutes; January release. CAST: Gregory Hines (Jim McQuade), Renee Soutendijk (Eve Simmons/Eve VIII), Michael Greene (Gen. Curtis), Kurt Fuller (Schneider), John M. Jackson (Peter Arnold), Loren Haynes (Steve, the Robot), Nelson Mashita (Scientist/Waiter), Alan Haufrect (Dr. Heller), Maryedith Burrell (Dawn Perlin), Kevin McCarthy (Old Bill Simmons), Norman Merrill, Jr. (1st Scientist), Craig Oldfather (Young Man on train), Greg Collins (Skaaren), Ed Matthews, Tom Morga (Bank Robbers), Tim Russ (Carter), Mike Jolly (Stevenson), Ross Malinger (Timmy Arnold), Marga Chavez (Elvira), Sharon Sebastian (News Anchor), Daryk Christian (Lt. Griffin), Coleen Maloney (Bartender), David Hayward (Cal), Daniel O'Haco, Eugene Robert Glazer (Buddies), Carl Ciarfalio (Trooper Sgt.), Thomas Lupo, George P. Wilbur (Troopers), Bill Gratton (Capt. Ned Summers),Thomas Knickerbocker (Patrolman in bar), Jeff McCarthy (Young Bill Simmons), Nancy Locke (Catherine Simmons), Bethany Richards (Young Eve), Larry Anderson (BMW Businessman), Jay Pickett (Man in jeep), Jim Antonio (Bill Kleinow), Paul Tuerpe (1st Cop), Richard Cummings, Jr. (Lt. Frankel), Joe Kane (1st Marine), Dakin Matthews (Singleton), Christopher Kriesa (Korman), Ronald William Lawrence (Granton), Randy Hall (Unit 1), Dan Barringer (Unit 2), Derek Barton (Unit 3), John Moio (Man in subway), Sue Burke (Woman in subway), Richard Collier (Transcript in subway)

FIREHEAD (Pyramid Distribution) Producer/Director, Peter Yuval; Executive Producers, David Winters, Marc Winters; Screenplay, Jeff Mandel, Peter Yuval; Photography, Paul Maibaum; Music, Vladimir Horunzhy; Editor, Steve Nielson; an AIP Studios presentation of a Winters Group production, in association with Sovereign Investment; Image Transform color; Rated R; 88 minutes; January release. CAST: Christopher Plummer (Col. Vaughn), Chris Lemmon (Warren Hart), Martin Landau (Adm. Pendleton), Brett Porter (Ivan), Gretchen Becker (Melia Buchanan), George Elliott, Ed Kearney, Douglas Simms, Lauren Levy

Marc Singer in *Dead Space*
© Concorde

Gregory Hines, Renee Soutendijk in
Eve of Destruction © Orion Pictures Corp.

149

Maria Ford, William Katt in *Naked Obsession*
© *Concorde*

Clare Hoak, Andrew Stevens in *The Terror Within II*
© *Concorde*

NAKED OBSESSION (Concorde) Producer, Ron Zwang; Executive Producer, Rodman Flender; Director, Dan Golden; Screenplay, Robert Dodson; Story, Dan Golden, Robert Dodson; Photography, Dick Buckley; Editor, Gabrielle Gilbert-Reeves; Music, Scott Singer; Designer, Johan Le Tenoux; Ultra-Stereo; Foto-kem color; Rated R; 80 minutes; January release. CAST: William Katt (Franklyn Carlyle), Rick Dean (Sam Silver), Maria Ford (Lynne Hauser), Wendy MacDonald (Saundra Carlyle), Elena Sahagun (Becky), Tommy Hinkley (Mitch), Roger Craig (Detective Ludlow), Ria Coyne (Cynthia), Fred Olen Ray (Announcer), Mac Ward (Man), Harriet Harris (Elderly Lady), Madison Stone (Jezebel), Suzy Evans (Table Dancer), Sherri Graham, Melinda Wesley (Waitresses)

THE PISTOL: THE BIRTH OF A LEGEND (Premier Pictures) Producer/Screenplay, Darrel Campbell; Executive Producer/ Director/Editor, Frank C. Schroeder; Story, Darrel Campbell, Peter Maravich, Frank C. Schroeder; Photography, Randy Walsh; Music, Brent Havens; Designer, John Sperry Wade; Costumes, Deanna Doran; Songs, Mirage; an LA Prod. Group presentation, in association with LA Film Partners; Ultra-Stereo; Allied/WBS color; Rated G; 100 minutes; January release. CAST: Millie Perkins (Helen Maravich), Nick Benedict (Press Maravich), Adam Guier (Pete Maravich), Boots Garland (Coach Pendleton), Tom Lester (Pete as an adult), Buddy Petrie, Darrel Campbell, Wendy Le Blanc, John Richardson, Rodney Stone, Eddie Hailey

PRIVILEGE (Zeitgeist) Director/Screenplay/Editor, Yvonne Rainer; Photography, Mark Daniels; Costumes, Alexandra Welker; Color/black and white; Not rated; 103 minutes; January release. CAST: Alice Spivak (Jenny), Novella Nelson (Yvonne Washington), Blaire Baron (Brenda), Rico Elias (Carlos), Gabriella Farrar (Digna), Tyrone Wilson (Stew), Dan Berkey (Robert) , Claudia Gregory (Signer), Yvonne Rainer ("Helen Caldicott"), Mark Niebuhr (White Man in Brenda's apartment), Faith Ringgold, Shirley Triest, Helene Moglen, Minnette Lehmann, Catherine English Robinson, Evelyn Cunningham, Gloria Sparrow, Audrey Goodfriend, Vivian Bonnano (Interviewees)

THE TERROR WITHIN II (Concorde) Producer, Mike Elliott; Director/Screenplay, Andrew Stevens; Based on characters created by Thomas M. Cleaver; Executive Producer, Roger Corman; Photography, Janusz Kaminski; Designer, Johan Le Teneux; Editor, Brent Schoenfeld; Music, Terry Plumieri; Ultra-Stereo; Foto-kem color; Rated R; 83 minutes; January release. CAST: Andrew Stevens (David), Stella Stevens (Kara), Chick Vennera (Kyle), R. Lee Ermey (Von Demming), Burton Gilliam (Dewitt), Clare Hoak (Ariel), Larry Gilman (Jamie), Barbara A. Woods (Sharon), Rene Jones (Robin), Lou Beatty, Jr. (Ernie), Phillip Irven (Phil), Gordon Currie (Aaron), Brad Blaisdell (Bo), Dean Jones (Rafe), Cindi Gossett (Elaba), Brewster Gould (Lusus), Pete Koch (Mutant), Scott Allen, The German Giant (Elaba Henchmen), Butch Stevens (Butch)

TOO MUCH SUN (New Line Cinema) Producer, Lisa M. Hansen; Executive Producers, Seymour Morgenstern, Paul Hertzberg, Al Schwartz; Director, Robert Downey; Screenplay, Robert Downey, Laura Ernst, Al Schwartz; Story, Al Schwartz; Photography, Robert Yeoman; Designer, Shawn Hausman; Music, David Robbins; Editor, Joe D'Augustine; a CineTel Films, Inc. presentation; Ultra-Stereo; Foto-Kem color; Rated R; 100 minutes; January release. CAST: Robert Downey, Jr. (Reed Richmond), Howard Duff (Old Man Rivers), Laura Ernst (Susan Connor), Jim Haynie (Father Seamus Kelly), Eric Idle (Sonny Rivers), Ralph Macchio (Frank Della Rocca, Jr.), Andrea Martin (Bitsy Rivers), Leo Rossi (George Bianco), Jennifer Rubin (Gracia), Allan Arbus (Vincent), Francis R. Hall (Delivery Boy), Lara Harris (Sister Ursula), James Hong (Frank Della Rocca, Sr.), Melissa Jenkins (Nurse), Marin Kanter (Tiny Nun), Jon Korkes (Fuzby Robinson), Christopher Mankiewicz (Mailman), Grace Nuyten (Hispanic Woman), Kyle Rae (Bartender), Michael Ben Rubenstein (Boat Captain), Carla Sherman (Waitress), John Stuckmeyer (Poodle Boy), Heidi Swedberg (Sister Agnes)

UP AGAINST THE WALL (African American Image Prod.) Producers, Chuck Colbert, Zuindi Colbert; Executive Producer, Dr. Jawanza Kunjufu; Director, Ron O'Neal; Screenplay, Emma Young, Songodina Ifatunji, Chuck Colbert, Zuindi Colbert; Story, Dr. Jawanza Kunjufu; Photography, LeRoy Patton; Editor, Thomas Miller; Music, Theodis Rodgers; Color; Rated PG-13; 100 minutes; January release. CAST: Marla Gibbs (Louise Bradley), Ron O'Neal (George Wilkes), Stoney Jackson (Jesse Bradley), Catero Alain Colbert (Sean Bradley)

Blaire Baron, Rico Elias in *Privilege*
© *Zeitgeist*

Andrea Martin, Laura Ernst in *Too Much Sun*
© *New Line Cinema*

Rod Steiger, John Turturro, in
Men of Respect
© Columbia Pictures

At the Crossroads
© Arthur Cantor Films

HANGFIRE (Motion Picture Corp. of America) Producers, Brad Krevoy, Steve Stabler; Director, Peter Maris; Screenplay, Brian D. Jeffries; Photography, Mark Norris; Music, Jim Price; Designer, Stephen Greenberg; Ultra-Stereo; Foto-kem color; Rated R; 89 minutes; January release. CAST: Brad Davis (Sheriff Ike Slayton), Kim Delaney (Maria), Jan-Michael Vincent (Johnson), Ken Foree (Billy), Lee de Broux (Kuttner), George Kennedy (Warden), James Tolkan (Patch), Yaphet Kotto (Lieutenant), Blake Conway, Lyle Alzado, Lou Ferrigno, Robert Miano, Collin Bernsen, Peter Lupus, Nancy Schuster, Lawrence Rothschild, Myron Dubow

KILLER OF SHEEP (Third World Newsreel) Producer/ Director/Screenplay/Editor, Charles Burnett; Color; Not rated; 87 minutes; January release. CAST: Henry Gayle Sanders (Stan), Kaycee Moore (Stan's Wife)

MEN OF RESPECT (Columbia) Producer, Ephraim Horowitz; Director/ Screenplay,William Reilly; Adapted from *The Tragedy of Macbeth* by William Shakespeare; Executive Producers, Arthur Goldblatt, Éric Kitain; Line Producer, Gary Mehlman; Photography, Bobby Bukowski; Music, Misha Segal; Designer, William Barclay; Costumes, Susan Lyall; Editor, Elizabeth Kling; Casting, Pat McCorkle; a Central City Films and Arthur Goldblatt Production presentation; DuArt color; Rated R; 113 minutes; January release. CAST: John Turturro (Mike Battaglia), Katherine Borowitz (Ruthie Battaglia), Dennis Farina (Bankie Como), Peter Boyle (Duffy), Lilia Skala (Lucia), Steven Wright (Sterling), Rod Steiger (Charlie D'Amico), Stanley Tucci (Mal), Carl Capotorto (Don), Michael Badalucco (Sal), Robert Modica (Rossi), David Thornton (Philly), Michael Sergio (Jamesy), Tony Gigante (Ray), Dan Grimaldi (Carmine), Joseph Carberry (Leonetti), John Gallagher (Shea), Richard Petrocelli (Artie), Jeff M. Mazzola (Pete), Joe Paparone (Ralphie), Vinny Pastore (Sammy), Steven Randazzo (Felix), Robert Moresco (Benny), Ron Maccone (The Greek), Richard Spore (Carmella), Andrei Belgrader (Aldo), Olek Krupa (Beda), Edward Gallardo (Manuel), Joseph Ragno (Padrino Ricci), Nicholas Turturro (Bingo), J.R. Nutt (Doug), Julie Garfield (Irene), Beatrice Alda (Susan), Richard Grund (Paulie), Harlan Cary Poe (Bob), Rick Washburn (Louie), Matthew Sussman (Gunman), Ed Setrakian (Dr. Edwards)

WARLOCK (Trimark Pictures) Producer/Director, Steve Miner; Executive Producer, Arnold Kopelson; Screenplay, D.T. Twohy; Photography, David Eggby; Designer, Roy Forge Smith; Editor, David Finfer; Costumes, Louise Frogley; Music, Jerry Goldsmith; Casting, Melissa Skoff; Visual Makeup Effects, Carl Fullerton, Neal Martz; a New World Pictures presentation; Dolby Stereo; Deluxe color; Rated R; 102 minutes; January release. CAST: Julian Sands (Warlock), Richard E. Grant (Giles Redferne), Lori Singer (Kassandra), Mary Woronov (Channel), Kevin O'Brien (Chas), Richard Kuss (Mennonite), Allan Miller (Detective), Anna Levine (Pastor's Wife), David Carpenter (Pastor), Kay E. Kuter (Proctor), Ian Abercrombie, Kenneth Danziger (Magistrates), Art Smith (Scribe), Robert Breeze (Jailor), Frank Renzulli (Cabbie), Brandon Call (Little Boy), Nancy Fox (Boy's Mother), Harry Johnson (Farmer), Juli Burkhart (Daughter-in-law), Rob Paulsen (Gas Station Attendant), Peter Sherayko (Cop), Gyl Roland (Ticket Agent), Meta King (Flight Attendant), Bill Dunnam (Railroad Employee), Wendy Feiner (Passenger)

AT THE CROSSROADS: JEWS IN EASTERN EUROPE TODAY (Arthur Cantor Films) Producers/Directors/Screenplay, Oren Rudavsky, Yale Strom; Co-Producer, Elinor Schull; Photography, Oren Rudavsky; Editors, Richard Smigielski, Mia DeBethune; Narrator, Peter MacNicol; Color; Not rated; 60 minutes; February release. Documentary

BRIDE OF RE-ANIMATOR (50th St. Films) Producer/Director, Brian Yuzna; Co-Producer, Michael Muscal; Executive Producers, Paul White, Keith Walley, Hidetaka Konno; Screenplay, Woody Keith, Rick Fry; Story, Brian Yuzna, Woody Keith, Rick Fry; Based on *Herbert West - Re-Animator* by H.P. Lovecraft; Photography, Rick Fichter; Designer, Philip Duffin; Music, Richard Band; Editor, Peter Teschner; Special Makeup and Visual Effects, Screaming Mad George, Anthony Doublin; a Wildstreet Pictures presentation; Ultra-Stereo; Foto-Kem color; Rated R; 97 minutes; February release. CAST: Jeffrey Combs (Herbert West), Bruce Abbott (Dan Cain), Claude Earl Jones (Lt. Chapman), Fabiana Udenio (Francesca), David Gale (Dr. Hill), Kathleen Kinmont (Gloria/The Bride), Mel Stewart (Dr. Wilbur Graves), Irene Forrest (Nurse), Michael Strasser, Johnny Legend

Julian Sands, Lori Singer, Richard E. Grant in *Warlock*
© Trimark Pictures

Jeffrey Combs, Kathleen Kinmont in
Bride of Re-Animator
© 50th St. Films

151

Brad Pitt, Rick Schroder in *Across the Tracks*
© Desert Prods.

Andy Warhol, Ivan Karp in *Superstar*
© Aries Films

BLOOD IN THE FACE (First Run Features) Producers/Directors, Anne Bohlen, Kevin Rafferty, James Ridgeway; Conceived by James Ridgeway; Editor, Kevin Rafferty; Photography, Kevin Rafferty, Sandi Sissel; Color; Not rated; 76 minutes; February release. Documentary

ACROSS THE TRACKS (Academy Entertainment - Desert Productions) Producer, Dale Rosenbloom; Director/Screenplay, Sandy Tung; Photography, Michael Delahoussaye; Designer, Thomas Meleck; Music, Joel Goldsmith; Editor, Farrel Levy; Line Producer, Nancy Paloian; Casting, Marcia Shulman; Associate Producers, Robert Schacht, Francesca Bill; Ultra-Stereo; CFI color; Rated R; 100 minutes; February release. CAST: Rick Schroder (Billy Maloney), Brad Pitt (Joe Maloney), Carrie Snodgress (Rosemary Maloney), David Anthony Marshall (Louie), Thomas Mikal Ford (Coach Welsh), John Linton (Brad), Cyril O'Reilly (Coach Ryder), Jack McGee (Frank), Annie Dylan (Linda), Bebe Drake-Massey (Mrs. Fisher), Kent Lipham (Big Ed), Jamie P. Gomez (Bobby), Larron D. Tate (Leron), Ron Marquette (Paulie), Andrew Zeller (Tiny), Dorit Sauer (Jessica), Jami Richards (Melanie), Garon Grigsby (Thompson), Mike Marikian (Andy - manager), William Garson (Salesman), Marisa Desimone (Salesgirl), David Belafonte (Stanford Scout), Hoover Stevens (Starter), Lahmard J. Tate (Teen Drug Buyer), Valerie Washington (Store Helper), Brad Peterson (Stolen Car Owner), Chuck Lyons (Officer), Michael Stoyanov (Mike)

RUN (Hollywood Pictures) Producer, Raymond Wagner; Co-Producer, Fitch Cady; Director, Geoff Burrowes; Screenplay, Dennis Shryack, Michael Blodgett; Photography, Bruce Surtees; Designer, John Willett; Music, Phil Marshall; Editor, Jack Hofstra; Casting, Stuart Aikins; Assistant Director, Lee Knippelberg; Stunts, Mic Rodgers, Brent Woolsey; Presented in association with Silver Screen Partners IV; Distributed by Buena Vista Pictures; Dolby Stereo; Technicolor; Rated R; 89 minutes; February release. CAST: Patrick Dempsey (Charlie Farrow), Kelly Preston (Karen Landers), Ken Pogue (Matthew Halloran), Alan C. Peterson (Denny Halloran), James Kidnie (Sammy), Sean McCann (Marv), Michael MacRae (O'Rourke), Tom McBeath (Smithy), Marc Strange (Chief Travers), Christopher Lawford (Martins), William Taylor (Halsey), Jerry Wasserman (Halloran's Lieutenant), Peter Williams (Cab Driver), Mina Mina (Garage Owner), Locklyn Munro, David Cubitt (College

Buddies), Michael Rogers (Electrocuted Gunman), Gerry Bean (Cop at Karen's), Marc Baur (Casino Captain), Alex Daikun (Casino Maitre D'), Babs Chula, Keith Beardwood, Richard Newman (Poker Players), Weston McMillan (Impatient Man at phone), Norman Browning (Porsche Mechanic), Hilary Strang (Nurse), Garry Davey (Sergeant at Karen's), Terry King (Video Manager), Pamela Martin, Kevin Hayes (News Anchors), Sue Mathews (Casino Cashier), Tom Pidgeon (Bowling Alley Cashier), Jonathan Bruce (Bill the Security Guard), Doug Abrahams (Cop outside garage), Curtis Blayne (Mall Roadblock Cop), Steve Adams (Frank), Vincent Gale (Bowler), Doug Greenall (Command Post Patrolman), David Cameron (2nd Security Guard)

SOMETHING TO DO WITH THE WALL (First Run Features) Producers/Directors/Editors/Screenplay/Photography, Marilyn Levine, Ross McElwee; Color; Not rated; 88 minutes; February release. Documentary

SUPERSTAR: THE LIFE AND TIMES OF ANDY WARHOL (Aries Films) Producer/Director/Editor/Screenplay, Chuck Workman; Executive Producer, Marilyn Lewis; Co-Executive Producer, Peter English Nelson; Photography, Burleigh Wartes; Associate Producer, Larry Green; Color; Not rated; 87 minutes; February release. Documentary featuring Holly Woodlawn, Dennis Hopper, Gerard Malanga, Fran Lebowitz, Grace Jones, Ultra Violet, Viva, Henry Geldzahler, David Hockney, Roy Lichtenstein, Taylor Mead, Shelley Winters, Sally Kirkland, Bobby Short, Bob Colacello, Sylvia Miles

NOTHING BUT TROUBLE (Warner Bros.) formerly *Valkenvania*; Producer, Robert K. Weiss; Director/Screenplay, Dan Aykroyd; Story, Peter Aykroyd; Photography, Dean Cundey; Designer, William Sandell; Costumes, Deborah Nadoolman; Editors, Malcolm Campbell, James Symons; Associate Producer, John D. Schofield; Music, Michael Kamen; Casting, Marion Dougherty, Sharon Howard-Field; Special Makeup, David B. Miller; Assistant Director, Jim Van Wyck; an Applied Action production; Dolby Stereo; Technicolor; Rated PG-13; 94 minutes; February release. CAST: Chevy Chase (Chris Thorne), Dan Aykroyd (Judge Valkenheiser/Bobo), John Candy (Dennis/Eldona), Demi Moore (Diane Lightson), Valri Bromfield (Miss Purdah), Taylor Negron (Fausto), Bertila Damas (Renalda), Raymond J. Barry (Mark), Brian

Patrick Dempsey in *Run*
© Hollywood Pictures

Dan Aykroyd, John Candy, Chevy Chase in
Nothing But Trouble
© Warner Bros. Inc.

Jill Schoelen, Tom Villard in *Popcorn*
© *Studio 3 Film Corp.*

David Duchovny, Daphna Kastner in
Julia Has Two Lovers
© *South Gate Entertainment*

Doyle-Murray (Brian), John Wesley (Sam), Peter Aykroyd (Mike the Doorman), Daniel Baldwin, James Staskel (Dealers), Deborah Lee Johnson, Karla Tamburrelli (Dealers' Girlfriends), John Daveikis (Li'l Debbull), Earl Dixon, Danielle Aykroyd, P.H. Aykroyd, Richard Kruk, Robert K. Weiss (Porch People), Laurence Bilzerian, Isaac Tigrett (Town Bikers), Catherine Quinn, Ron Ulstad, Paul LeClair (Party Goers), Stan Garner (Train Master), James Clark (Train Engineer), Jeffrey P. Baggett, Kristina Kochoff, Gary Velasco (State Troopers), Roger Grimsby (TV Anchor), Susan Campos (TV Reporter), Humpty Hump, Shock-G, Money-B, Fuze, Chopmaster-J, 2 Pac Shakur, Kent Racker, Nzazi Muhammed, Schmoovy-Schmoov (Digital Underground - Rap Group), Karen Croney, D'Andrea Bryant, Jennifer Van Buskirk, Gianna Amore (Party Girls)

POPCORN (Studio Three Film Corp.) Producers, Torben Johnke, Gary Goch, Ashok Amritraj; Co-Producer, Sophie Hurst; Director, Mark Herrier; Screenplay, Tod Hackett; Story, Mitchell Smith; Photography, Ronnie Taylor; Executive Producers, Howard Hurst, Karl Hendrickson, Howard Baldwin; Designer, Peter Murton; Music, Paul J. Zaza; Editor, Stan Cole; Special Effects, Georgio Ferrari; Makeup, Bob Clark; a Movie Partners and Century Films production; Dolby Stereo; Film House color; Rated R; 93 minutes; February release. CAST: Jill Schoelen (Maggie), Tom Villard (Toby), Dee Wallace Stone (Suzanne), Derek Rydall (Mark), Malcolm Danare (Bud), Elliott Hurst (Leon), Ivette Soler (Joanie), Freddie Marie Simpson (Tina), Kelly Jo Minter (Cheryl), Karen Witter (Joy), Tony Roberts (Mr. Davis), Ray Walston (Dr. Mnesyne), Scott Thompson (Bearded Guy), Will Knickerbocker (Landlord), Ethan Ormsby (Two Headed Guy), Ben Stotes (Hatchethead), Ken Ryan (Radio Announcer), Adam Ormsby, April Harris, Mike Stephens, Von Von Lindenberg, Ray Garaza, Wayne Farnes, Guy Christopher (Students in theatre); "The Possessor": Mat Falls (Lanyard Gates), Cindy Tavarese-Finson (Gloria Gates), Giana Hanly (Sarah Gates); "Mosquito": Barry Jenner (Lt. Bradley), Suzanne Hunt (Dr. Latimer), Robert Dickman (Skeeter), Thom Adcox (Corky); "Electrified Man": Bruce Glover (Vernon), Munair Zaza (Doctor), Will Knickerbocker (Warden), Bobby Ghisays (Judge), Lori Creevay (Marge), Ed Amatrudo (Boy Friend), George O, Nico Bernuth, Rohan Henry (Hoods); "The Stench": Maki Fame (Lab Technician), Kimio Satoh (Scientist), Fumito Naozaki, Hikonori Washino (Miners)

JULIA HAS TWO LOVERS (South Gate Entertainment) Producer/Director, Bashar Shbib; Executive Producers, C.H. Lehenof, Randall Davis; Screenplay, Daphna Kastner, Bashar Shbib; Story, Daphna Kastner; Photography, Stephen Reizes; Editors, Bashar Shbib, Dan Foegelle; Music, Emilio Kauderer; Original Songs, Tim Ray; an Oneira Pictures International presentation; Ultra-Stereo; Color; Rated R; 91 minutes; March release. CAST: Daphna Kastner (Julia), David Duchovny (Daniel), David Charles (Jack), Tim Ray (Leo), Clare Bancroft (Jackie), Martin Donovan (Freddy), Anita Olanick (Ursulla), Al Samuels (Landlord), Julie Roswal (Landlady), C.H. Lehenhof (Repairman), Lauren Fitch (Passing Girl)

CLOSET LAND (Universal) Producer, Janet Meyers; Executive Producers, Brian Grazer, Ron Howard; Director/Screenplay, Radha Bharadwaj; Photography, Bill Pope; Designer/Costumes, Eiko Ishioka; Editor, Lisa Churgin; Music, Richard Einhorn; Creative Musical Supervisor, Philip Glass; Line Producer/Assistant Director/Unit Production Manager, Karen Koch; Animation Sequences, Sheila M. Sofian, David Fain; an Imagine Entertainment presentation; Dolby Stereo; Deluxe color; Rated R; 90 minutes; March release. CAST: Madeleine Stowe (Woman), Alan Rickman (Man)

THE GIANT OF THUNDER MOUNTAIN (Castle Hill/New Generation) Producer, Joseph Raffill; Executive Producers, John Herklotz, Richard Kiel; Director, James Roberson; Screenplay, Richard Kiel, Tony Lozito; Photography, Stephen G. Shank; Editor, Richard E. Rabjohn; Music, Al Kasha, Joel Hirschhorn; Designer, Phillip Thomas; Ultra-Stereo; Widescreen, Foto-Kem color; Rated PG; 101 minutes; March release. CAST: Richard Kiel (Eli Weaver), Jack Elam (Hezekiah Crow), Marianne Rogers (Alicia Wilson), Bart the Bear (Bear), Chance Michael Corbitt (Tommy), Ryan Todd (Ben), Ellen Crawford (Agnes), William Sanderson (Purcey Crow), Noley Thornton (Amy), Foster Brooks (Doc), James Hampton (Jesse), John Quade (Carl), George "Buck" Flower (Oliver Crow)

SCISSORS (DDM Film Corp.) Producers, Mel Real, Don Levin, Hal Polaire; Director/Screenplay, Frank De Felitta; Story, Joyce Selznick; Photography, Tony Richmond; Designer, Craig Stearns; Editor, John Schreyer; Color; Not rated; 105 minutes; March release. CAST: Sharon Stone (Angie), Steve Railsback (Alex/Cole), Ronny Cox (Dr. Carter), Michelle Phillips (Ann), Leonard Rogel (Red-Beard/Movie), Carl Ciarfalio (Attacker), Vicki Frederick (Nancy), Howie Guma (Clerk/Cutlery), Larry Moss (Kramer), Austin Kelly (Folger), Albert Popwell (Officer), Jim Shankman (Bob the Clerk), Jesse Garcia (Counterman), Ivy Bethune, Hal Riddle (Dog Walkers), Laura Ann Caulfield (Soap Opera Actress), Kelly Noonan (Young Angie), Will Leskin (Billy), Ivy Jones (Mother), Ted Noose (Cabbie #2), Ed Crick (Red-Beard/Party), Mary Reynard (Server at party)

STREET SOLDIERS (Academy Entertainment) Producer/Story, Jun Chong; Director/Editor, Lee Harry; Screenplay, Spencer Grendahl, Lee Harry; Photography, Dennis Peters; Executive Producers, Maria Lim, D.S. Kim; Designer, Matthew Jacobs; Music, David Bergeaud; a Curb/Esquire Films presentation of an Action Bros. production; Ultra-Stereo; Foto-Kem color; Rated R; 98 minutes; March release. CAST: Jun Chong (Master Han), Jeff Rector (Priest), David Homb (Troy), Johnathan Gorman (Max), Joon Kim (Charles), Katherine Armstrong (Julie), Jason Hwang (Tok), Jude Gerard (Spider), Deborah Newmark (Marie), Jay Richardson (Wheelchair Willie), Joel Weiss, Frank Nova

Madeleine Stowe, Alan Rickman   **153**
in *Closet Land*
© *Imagine Films/Universal*

Jeff Speakman (R) in *The Perfect Weapon*
© *Paramount Pictures*

Hana Azulay-Hasfari, Eric Douglas in
Young Commandos
© *Global Pictures*

THE PERFECT WEAPON (Paramount) Producers, Mark DiSalle, Pierre David; Executive Producer, Ralph Winter; Director, Mark DiSalle; Screenplay, David Campbell Wilson; Photography, Russell Carpenter; Designer, Curtis Schnell; Music, Gary Chang; Editor, Wayne Wahrman; Costumes, Joseph Porro; Stunts, Rick Avery; Dolby Stereo; Color; Rated R; 88 minutes; March release. CAST: Jeff Speakman (Jeff Sanders), John Dye (Adam Sanders), Mako (Kim), James Hong (Yung), Mariska Hargitay (Jennifer), Dante Basco (Jimmy Ho), Beau Starr (Carl Sanders), Seth Sakai (Master Lo), Professor Toru Tanaka (Tanaka), Clyde Kusatsu (Detective Wong), Tom Hermann (Jeff - age 17), Micah Roberts (Jeff as a boy)

IF LOOKS COULD KILL (Warner Bros.) Producers, Craig Zadan, Neil Meron; Executive Producer, Elliot Schick; Director, William Dear; Screenplay, Darren Star; Story, Fred Dekker; Photography, Doug Milsome; Designer, Guy J. Comtois; Music, David Foster; Editor, John F. Link; Casting, Marion Dougherty, Sharon Howard-Field; Assistant Director, Tony Lucibello; Title Song by Antonina Armato, Danny Sembello/performed by Glenn Medeiros; Special Effects, Introvision International Inc.; Dolby Stereo; Technicolor; Rated PG-13; 88 minutes; March release. CAST: Richard Grieco (Michael Corben), Linda Hunt (Ilsa Grunt), Roger Rees (Augustus Steranko), Robin Bartlett (Mrs. Grober), Gabrielle Anwar (Mariska), Geraldine James (Vendetta Galante), Michael Siberry (Richardson), Carole Davis (Areola Canasta), Frederick Coffin (Lt. Col. Larabee), Tom Rack (Zigesfeld), Roger Daltrey (Blade), Oliver Dear (Kent), Cyndy Preston (Melissa Tyler), Michael Sinelnikoff (Haywood), Travis Swords (Kelly), Gerry Mendecino (Herb), Fiona Reid (Marge), Michael Vinokur (Brad), Gene Mack (Agent Kramer), Jacques Tourangeau (Lefevre), Dominique Petin, Macha Grenon (Clerks), Claude Gasse (Imperious Stewardess), Isabelle Truchon, Pascale Devigne (1st Class Stewardesses), Marie-Josee Gauthier (Coach Stewardess), Philip Spensley (Principal), Gordon Masten (Ludwig Krupp), Susan Dear (1st Class Hostess), Armand Laroche (Doorman), Chip Chuipka (Gunman #1), Laurent Imbault (Croupier), David Francis (Englishman), Tedd Dillon (Imposter Driver), John Tench (Cell Guard), Bonfield Marcoux (Bus Driver), Jon Baggaley (Ian), William Dear (Bomb Tester), Paul Babeau, Rob Bazos, Michele DeMeo, Iris Gressy, Maxine Guess, Donny Lucas, Nancy McGiffert, Carolyn Raymond, Peter Shinkada (French Club)

YOUNG COMMANDOS (Cannon) Producers, Christopher Pearce, Boaz Davidson; Executive Producer, Harry Alan Towers; Director, Sam Firstenberg; Screenplay, Greg Latter, Boaz Davidson; Music, Robert Thomas Mein; Photography, Avi Karpick; Editor, Michael Duthie; a Global Pictures production; Color; Rated R; 97 minutes; March release. CAST: Nick Cassavetes (Maj. Charles Stewart), Eric Douglas (Sam), Mike Norris (Greg), Matthew Penn (Richard), John Ryan (Sergei), Hana Azulay-Hasfari (Irenia), Sandy Ward

AMERICAN NINJA 4: THE ANNIHILATION (Cannon) Producer, Christopher Pearce; Director, Cedric Sundstrom; Screenplay, James Booth; Photography, Joseph Wein; Editor, Claudio Ytruc; Music, Nicolas Tenbroek; Color; Rated R; 95 minutes; March release. CAST: Michael Dudikoff (Joe Armstrong), James Booth (Mulgrew), David Bradley (Sean Davidson), Dwayne Alexandre (Carl Brackston), Robin Stille (Sarah), Ken Gampu (Dr. Tamba)

GIRLFRIEND FROM HELL (August Entertainment) Producers, Robert S. Lecky, Alberto Lensi; Director/Screenplay, Daniel M. Peterson; Photography, Gerry Lively; Editor, Beth Conwell; Music, Michael Rapp; Designer, Regina Argentine; Costumes, Libby Jacobs; Ultra-Stereo; Foto-Kem color; Rated R; 92 minutes; April release. CAST: Liane Curtis (Maggie), Dana Ashbrook (Chaser), Lezlie Deane (Diane), James Daughton (David), Anthony Barrile (Carl), Ken Abraham (Rocco), Hilary Morse (Alice), Sarah Kaite Coughlin (Freda), Brad Zutaut, James Karen, Alba Francesca, Dawn Jacobs, Christina Veronique

KISS ME A KILLER (Concorde) Producer, Catherine Cyran; Executive Producer, Mike Elliott; Director, Marcus De Leon; Screenplay, Christopher Wooden, Marcus De Leon; Photography, Nancy Schreiber; Editor, Glen Garland; Music, Nigel Holton; Designer, James R. Shumaker; Costumes, Meta Jardine; a Califilm release; Ultra-Stereo; Foto-Kem color; Rated R; 92 minutes; April release. CAST: Julie Carmen (Teresa), Robert Beltran (Tony), Guy Boyd (Jake Bozman), Ramon Franco (Ramon), Charles Boswell (Dennehy), Sam Vlahos (Father Dominquez), Brad Blaisdell (Tom), A.C. Santos (Pedro), Ray Victor (Carlos), Tony Rael (Ruben), Addison Cook (Painter), Pancho Sanchez (Himself), Marita De Leon, Monica Sanchez (Girls entering club)

154   **Richard Grieco, Gabrielle Anwar in**
If Looks Could Kill
© *Warner Bros. Inc.*

Robin Stille, Michael Dudikoff, David Bradley in
American Ninja 4
© *Cannon Pictures, Inc.*

Lianne Curtis in *Girlfriend from Hell*
© *August Entertainment*

Brooke Adams in *The Unborn*
© *Concorde*

MY BROTHER'S WEDDING (AFI USA) Producers, Charles Burnett, Gaye Shannon-Burnett; Director/Screenplay/Photography, Charles Burnett; Editor, Tom Pennick; Color; Not rated; 116 minutes; April release. CAST: Everett Silas (Pierce Monday), Jessie Holmes (Mrs. Monday), Gaye Shannon-Burnett (Sonia), Ronnie Bell (Soldier Richards), Dennis Kemper (Wendell Monday), Sy Richardson (Sonia's Father), Frances Nealy (Sonia's Mother)

NEVER LEAVE NEVADA (Cabriolet) Producer, Diane Campbell; Director/Screenplay, Steve Swartz; Photography, Lee Daniel; Music, Ray Benson; Editor, Gordon A. Thomas; Black and white; Not rated; 88 minutes; April release. CAST: Steve Swartz (Sean Kaplan), Rodney Rincon (Luis Ramirez), Janelle Buchanan (Betty Gurling), Katherine Catmull (Lou Ann Pearlstein), Col. Tom Parker (Duane Pearlstein), De Lewellen (Vela Pearlstein), Barbara Chisholm (Anne), D. Hargrave (Hypathia), John Hawkes (Christo), Loren Loganbill (Carlo Pfeffer), Ken Webster (Russian Gambler), Gordon Thomas (Casino Manager), Mike Dodd (Father Vince)

ODDBALL HALL (Cannon) Producer, Alan Munro; Director/Screenplay, Jackson Hunsicker; Color; Rated PG; 87 minutes; April release. CAST: Don Ameche (Siebriese), Burgess Meredith (Ingersol), Bill Maynard (Copperthwaite), Tiny Skefile (Meetoo-U), Tullio Moneta (Linguine), Graham Armitage (Grand Noble Master), Patrick Mynhardt (Otto)

THE UNBORN (Concorde) Producer/Director, Rodman Flender; Executive Producer, Mike Elliott; Screenplay, Henry Dominic; Photography, Wally Pfister; Designer, Gary Randall; Music, Gary Numan, Mike Smith; Costumes, Greg LaVoi; Special Makeup Effects and Baby Design, Joe Podnar; a Califilm release; Ultra-Stereo; Foto-Kem color; Rated R; 83 minutes; April release. CAST: Brooke Adams (Virginia Marshall), Jeff Hayenga (Brad Marshall), James Karen (Dr. Richard Meyerling), K. Callan (Martha Wellington), Jane Cameron (Beth), Wendy Kamenoff (Gloria), Rick Dean (Abortionist), Jonathan Emerson (Mark Robinson), Angelina Estrada (Isabel), Kathy Griffin (Connie), Daryl Haney (Policeman), Elizabeth Harrett (Clinic Nurse), Janice Kent (Cindy), Lisa Kudrow (Louisa), Matt Roe (Jeff), Rick Podell (Chuck Martinez), Laura Stockton (Janet), Brad Blaisdell (Co-Worker), Elizabeth Burrelle (Sally St. Clair), Michael Castagnola (Man)

CLASS OF NUKE 'EM HIGH PART 2: SUBHUMANOID MELTDOWN (Troma) Producers, Michael Herz, Lloyd Kaufman; Director, Eric Louzil; Executive Producers, Masahiro Ebisawa, Sammy O. Masada, Tetsu Fujimura; Screenplay, Lloyd Kaufman, Eric Louzil, Carl Morano, Marcus Roling, Jeffrey W. Sass, Matt Unger; Additional Material, Andrew Osborne; Photography, Ron Chapman; Editor, Gordon Grinberg; Music, Bob Mithoff; Special Creature Construction and Animation, Brett Piper, Alex Pirnie; Color; Rated R; 95 minutes; April release. CAST: Brick Bronsky (Roger Smith), Lisa Gaye (Prof. Holt), Leesa Rowland (Victoria), Michael Kurtz (Yoke), Scott Resnick (Dean Okra), Shelby Shepard (Prof. Jones), Jacquelyn Rene Moen (Diane), M. Davis (Murray), Phil Rivo (Harvey), Erica Frank (Tour Guide), Sharon Gardner (Mother with baby), Bea Lindgren (Grandmother), Lorraine Parchment (Yoke's Girlfriend), Troy Fromin, Tyler Bowe (Yoke's Sidekicks), Julian Paul Borghese (Basketball Coach), Amy Hilbrich (Basketball Player), Brad Roth (Chainsmoking Student), Nello Scaduto (Nurse Chave), Jean Stewart (Nurse Pony), Greer Course (Doctor), Phil Rivo (Malathion Man), Lyndsay Dawkins, Darla Slavens (Plain White Rappers), Lily Hayes Kaufman (Pre-Pubescent Prof. Holt), Jason Vance Taylor (Green Man), Alex Pirnie (Mutant Squirrel), William J. Kulzer (Chief Brundt), Kaption (Decomposed Green Guy), Madison Monk (Toxic Avenger Director), Greta Rubens (French Teacher), Jon Albert (Fungus Mungus), Julian Paul Borghese (Toxic Avenger Assist. Director), Patricia Kaufman (Nurse at birthday party), Jerri Greene, Patti Woodhull (Screaming Tromatized Housewives)

DIPLOMATIC IMMUNITY (Fries Entertainment) Producer/Director, Peter Maris; Executive Producer, Harry Shuster; Screenplay, Randall Frakes, Jim Trombetta, Richard Donn; Based on the novel *The Stalker* by Theodore Taylor; Photography, Gerald B. Wolfe; Music, John Massari; Editor, Jack Tucker; Designer, Leigh Nicolai Moon; Costumes, Virginia "Gini" Kramer; Foto-Kem color; Rated R; 95 minutes; April release. CAST: Bruce Boxleitner (Cole Hickel), Billy Drago (Cowboy), Tom Breznahan (Klaus Hermann), Christopher Neame (Stefan Noll), Fabiana Udenio (Teresa Escobal), Matthias Hues (Gephardt), Meg Foster (Gerta Hermann), Sharon Kase (Ellen Hickel), Jay Marvin Campbell, Robert DoQui, Ken Foree, Kenneth Kimmons, Robert Forster, Lee DeBroux, Rozlyn Sorrell, Robert Miano

Don Ameche, Tiny Skefile, Burgess Meredith in
Oddball Hall
© *Ravenhill Prods. Inc.*

Bruce Boxleitner in *Diplomatic Immunity*   **155**
© *Fries Entertainment*

Spike Lee, Ranjit Chowdry in *Lonely in America*
© Apple Productions Inc.

Phoebe Cates, Rik Mayall in *Drop Dead Fred*
© New Line Cinema

LONELY IN AMERICA (Arista Films) Producers, Tirlok Malik, Phil Katzman; Line Producer, Chandler B. Malik; Director, Barry Alexander Brown; Screenplay, Barry Alexander Brown, Satyajit Joy Palit; Story, Tirlok Malik; Photography, Phil Katzman; Art Director, Eduardo Capilla; Editor, Tula Goenka; Costumes, Mary Marsicano; Music, Gregory Arnold; Casting, Sue Crystal; DuArt color; Not rated; 95 minutes; April release. CAST: Ranjit Chowdry (Arun), Adelaide Miller (Faye), Tirlok Malik (Max), Robert Kessler (Jim), Melissa Christopher (Becky), David Toney (Duncan), Franke Hughes (Carlos), R. Ganesh (Hari Singh), Anila Singh (Sita), Richard Raphael (Broadway Bum), Ken Forman (Chip), Matt Midler (Leslie), Louis Farber (Old Man), Cee-Cee Rider (Teacher), Christopher Cooke (Airport Cop), Barry Alexander Brown (Bible Salesman), Spike Lee (Man at news stand), Amy Harlib (Chinese Sword Dancer), Chander B. Malik (Computer Store Clerk), Ajay Mehta (Confectioner), Debbie Rochon (Jennie), Puja Malik, Arun Malik (Max's Children), P.K. Sharma (Max's Friend at wedding), Shri Deva (Photographer at wedding), Hettle Pastakia (Poonam), Tanya Soler (Prostitute), Fia Cappello, Gabriella Dahl, Vala Shanti Delsarte (Punk Hairdressers), Fran Capo (Receptionist at LMC), Arun Lahiri (Roommate Anil), Gary Singh (Roommate Giani), Patric Rosario (Roommate Sharma), Horace Bailey (Rupert), Mukesh Patel (Shafiq), Jill Brandsen (Sherri), Murli Lahiri (Mina Singh), Alexander Stephano (Street Vendor), Anwar Ali Mavani (Sundar), Debra Phillips (Tavern Waitress), James Graseck (Violinist), Pamela Berk (Woman in car), Adrienne Shelly (Woman in laundromat), Robin Rich (Woman on bus), Sue Crustal (Woman on park bench), Margi Goldsmith (Woman with dog)

CROOKED HEARTS (MGM) Producers, Rick Stevenson, Dale Pollock, Gil Friesen; Director/Screenplay, Michael Bortman; Based on the novel by Robert Boswell; Photography, Tak Fujimoto; Designer, David Brisbin; Costumes, Susan deLaval; Editor, Richard Francis-Bruce; Music, Mark Isham; Casting, Lora Kennedy, Linda Lowy; Associate Producers, Lianne Halfon, Mark Bentley; an A&M Films production; Dolby Stereo; Color; Rated R; 112 minutes; May release. CAST: Vincent D'Onofrio (Charley Warren), Jennifer Jason Leigh (Marriet), Peter Berg (Tom Warren), Peter Coyote (Edward Warren), Noah Wyle (Ask Warren), Cindy Pickett (Jill Warren), Juliette Lewis (Cassie Warren), Marg Helgenberger (Jenetta)

Jennifer Jason Leigh, Peter Berg
in *Crooked Hearts*
© MGM-Pathe Communications

DROP DEAD FRED (New Line Cinema) Producer, Paul Webster; Executive Producers, Tim Bevan, Carlos Davis, Anthony Fingleton; Director, Ate DeJong; Screenplay, Carlos Davis, Anthony Fingleton; Story, Elizabeth Livingston; Photography, Peter Deming; Designer, Joseph T. Garrity; Editor, Marshall Harvey; Costumes, Carol Wood; Music, Randy Edelman; Casting, Linn Kressel; Assistant Director, Michael Waxman; Special Makeup Effects, Christopher Johnson; a Polygram and Working Title Film; Dolby Stereo; CFI color; Rated PG-13; 98 minutes; May release. CAST: Phoebe Cates (Elizabeth Cronin), Rik Mayall (Drop Dead Fred), Marsha Mason (Polly), Tim Matheson (Charles Gretterson), Carrie Fisher (Janie Shagrue), Keith Charles (Murray), Ashley Peldon (Young Elizabeth), Daniel Gerroll (Nigel), Ron Eldard (Mickey Bunce), Eleanor Mondale (Attractive Customer), Bob Reid (Judge Dubben), Peter Thoemke (Arsonist), Sjoukje De Jong Douma (Grandma Bunce), Paul Holmes (Man in speedboat), Steve Cochran, Robert Meyzen (Waiters), Daniel Buchen (Dr. Ryland), Marie Mathay (Concerned Mom), Peter Breitmayer (Go to Hell Herman), Clark Niederjohn (Velcro Head), Tom Bethke (Graggy), Elizabeth Gray (Namby Pamby), Cheryl Hawker (Nurse), Michael Welker (Waiter at wine gala), Kelly Benson (Natalie), Cathy Lind Hayes (Ms. Fuzzcock)

EDGE OF HONOR (Wind River) Producers, Jay R. Davis, Peter Garrity, David O'Malley; Director, Michael Spence; Screenplay, Mark Rosenbaum, Michael Spence, David O'Malley; Story, Michael Spence, Mark Rosenbaum; Photography, Billy Dickson; Music, William Stromberg; Editor, Ellen Keneshea; Designer, Charles Armstrong; a Merit Badge production, in association with the Guerrilla Film Unit; Ultra-Stereo; Western Cine color; Rated R; 92 minutes; May release. CAST: Corey Feldman (Butler), Meredith Salenger (Alex), Scott Reeves (Luke), Ken Jenkins (Bo Dubs), Don Swayze (Ritchie), Christopher Neame (Blade), Alex "Sasha" Walkup (Eric), Daniel Wartman (Eddie), Benjamin Troy (Jason)

FAST GETAWAY (New Line Cinema) Producers, Paul Hertzberg, Lisa M. Hansen; Executive Producer, Harold Welb; Director, Spiro Razatos; Screenplay, James Dixon; Photography, James Haitkin; Music, Bruce Rowland; Editor, David Kern; a CineTel Films production; Dolby Stereo; Foto-Kem color; Rated PG-13; 85 minutes; May release. CAST: Corey Haim (Nelson), Cynthia Rothrock (Lily), Leo Rossi (Sam), Ken Lerner (Tony), Marcia Strassman (Lorraine), Shelli Lether (Honey)

BORN TO RIDE (Warner Bros.) formerly *The Recruit*; Producers, Fred & Sandra Weintraub; Director, Graham Baker; Screenplay, Michael Pardridge, Janice Hickey; Photography, Frank Gell; Designer, Francis J. Pezza; Music, Shirley Walker; Editor, Alan Balsam; a Fred Weintraub/Incovent production; Dolby Stereo; Technicolor; Rated PG; 90 minutes; May release. CAST: John Stamos (Grady Westfall), John Stockwell (Capt. Jack Hassler), Teri Polo (Beryl Ann Devers), Sandy McPeak (Col. Devers), Kris Kamm (Novak), Keith Cooke (Broadwater), Dean Yacalis (Cartucci), Salvator Xuereb (Levon), Justin Lazard (Brooks), Thom Mathews (Willis), Garrick Hagon (Bridges), Matko Raguz (Estaban), Ed Bishop (Dr. Tate), Lisa Orgolini (Claire Tate), Slavko Juraga (Capt. Rosario), Damir Saban (Lt. Heims), Charles Kahlenberg (Gen. Chaffee), Bob Sweeney (Gus), Dale Swann (Sheriff Greaves), Slobodan Dimitrijevic (Col. Muhl), Kieron Jecchinis, Lee Surdo (MPs), Bill Stamos (DC-3 Pilot), Darko Janes (Devers' Aide), Eliza Gerner (Mrs. Devers), Leslie Eve Herman (Charlene), Aleksandar Cvjetkovic (German Soldier), Semka Sokolovic Bertok (Spanish Woman), Damir Mejovsek (Sam the Bartender), Pedja Petrovic, Zeljko Sestic (Soldiers)

Kris Kamm, Keith Cooke, John Stamos, John Stockwell
in *Born to Ride*
© Warner Bros. Inc.

Jan-Michael Vincent in *Raw Nerve*
© Pyramid Distribution Inc.

F/X 2 (Orion) Producers, Jack Wiener, Dodi Fayed; Executive Producers, Lee R. Mayes, Bryan Brown; Director, Richard Franklin; Screenplay, Bill Condon; Based on characters created by Robert T. Megginson, Gregory Fleeman; Photography, Victor J. Kemper; Designer, John Jay Moore; Costumes, Linda Matheson; Editor, Andrew London; Music, Lalo Schifrin; Casting, Lauren Lloyd, Gail Levin; Special Effects Producer, Eric Allard; Assistant Director, Brian Cook; Dolby Stereo; Deluxe color; Rated PG-13; 107 minutes; May release. CAST: Bryan Brown (Rollie Tyler), Brian Dennehy (Leo McCarthy), Rachel Ticotin (Kim Brandon), Joanna Gleason (Liz Kennedy), Philip Bosco (Ray Silak), Kevin J. O'Connor (Matt Neely), Tom Mason (Mike Brandon), Dominic Zamprogna (Chris Brandon), Josie DeGuzman (Velez), John Walsh (Rado), Peter Boretski (Becker), Lisa Fallon (Kylie), Lee Broker (DeMarco), Philip Akin (Det. McQuay), Tony de Santis (Det. Santoni), Ross Petty (Consigliere), Dee McCafferty (Chambliss), Jeri Craden (Aunt Kate), Karie Stone (Beth), Phil Jarrett, Richard Sali (I.A.D. Cops), James Stacy (Cyborg), Neil Elliot (Movie F/X Man), Leland Crooke (Movie Director), Biff Yeager (Police Sgt.), Foster Fell (Policeman), Jack Orend (Wino), Jenifer Chatfield (Movie Scriptgirl), Kurt Reis (Judge), Damir Andrei (Defense Attorney), Charles Ivey (Defendant), Caroline Yeager (Desk Sgt.), Arlene Duncan (Hooker), Robert Kennedy (Computer Store Clerk), Dwayne McLean (Mall Guard), Gerry Quigley (Supermarket Manager), Harvey Chao (Vendor), Harry Booker (Prison Priest), Bob Clout (Confessional Priest), Jack Newman (Art Expert), Walker Boone, Michael Rhoades, Gene Mack (Mansion Guards), Shane Cardwell, Michael Woods, Matt Birman (Mobsters), Tony Katsaros (Policeman), Dennis Scott (Cop #1), Cynthia Quinn, Karl Bauman (Bluey)

THE PIT AND THE PENDULUM (JGM/Full Moon Entertainment) Producer, Albert Band; Executive Producer, Charles Band; Director, Stuart Gordon; Screenplay, Dennis Paoli; Adapted from the story by Edgar Allan Poe; Photography, Adolfo Bartoli; Art Director; Giovanni Natalucci; Costumes, Michela Gisotti; Music, Richard Band; Editor, Andy Horvitch; Color; Rated R; 97 minutes; May release. CAST: Lance Henriksen (Torquemada), Rona De Ricci (Maria), Jonathan Fuller (Antonio), Frances Bay (Esmeralda), Stephen Lee (Gomez), Oliver Reed (Cardinal), William J. Norris (Dr. Heusos), Mark Margolis (Mandoza)

RAW NERVE (Pyramid Distribution/A.I.P. Studios) Producer, Ruta K. Aras; Executive Producers, David Winters, Marc Winters; Director, David A. Prior; Screenplay, David A. Prior, Lawrence L. Simeone; Photography, Andrew Parke; Music, Greg Turner; Editor, Tony Malanowski; a Winters Group production in association with Sovereign Investment; Image Transform color; Rated R; 93 minutes; May release. CAST: Glenn Ford (Capt. Gavin), Sandahl Bergman (Gloria), Randall "Tex" Cobb (Blake Garrett), Ted Prior (Jimmy Clayton), Traci Lords (Gina Clayton), Jan-Michael Vincent (Lt. Bruce Ellis), Red West (Dave), Yvonne Stancil (Lori Cline), Graham Timbes (Sgt. Mancina), Jerry Douglas Simms (Doc), Doris Hearn (Mrs. Needlemyer), Trevor Hale (Brad), Brian J. Scott (Ken), Jim Aycock (Kincade), Ken Kennedy (Wino), Donna Willard (Brenda), Mary Willard (Marsha), John Graham Jr. (Officer #1), Robert Willoughby (Racetrack Boss), Karen Johnson (Paramedic), Andrea Henry (Kathy), Tracy Britton (Betty-Jo), LaDonna Sue Eggemeyer (Waitress)

AMBITION (Miramax) Producer, Richard E. Johnson; Co-Producer, Gwen Field; Director/Editor, Scott D. Goldstein; Screenplay, Lou Diamond Phillips; Photography, Jeff Jur; Music, Leonard Rosenman; Costumes, Diah Wymont; Designer, Marek Dobrowolski; Casting, Amanda Mackey; Assistant Director, Ian McVey; a Spirit presentation; Dolby Stereo; Deluxe color; Rated R; 100 minutes; May release. CAST: Lou Diamond Phillips (Mitchell Osgood), Clancy Brown (Albert Merrick), Cecilia Peck (Julie), Richard Bradford (Jordan), Willard Pugh (Freddie), Grace Zabriskie (Mrs. Merrick), Katherine Armstrong (Roseanne), J.D. Cullum (Jack), Haing S. Ngor (Tatay), Mik Scriba (Prison Guard #1), Randy Hall, Maria Rangel (Dancers), Robert Harvey (Merrick's Attorney), Teresa Bowman, Rick Scarry, Aaron Seville, Steve Whiteford (Media Reporters), Maggie Egan (Anchor), Anita Ortega (Hispanic Woman), David Burton Morris (Man in Corvette), Celeste Yarnall (Beverly Hills Shopper), Bert Conway (Gruff Man), Kevin Shaw (Co-Worker), Ken Kerman (Prison Guard #2), Karen Landry (Woman in bookstore), Chris Mulkey (Man in bookstore), Michelle Milantoni (Middle-aged Woman), Jake Jacobs (Suit and tie Man), David Allyn (Nondescript Man), Wayne Federman (Wiseass), Daniel Robbins (Waiter), Diana Michelle (Long-haired Hooker)

Bryan Brown, Dominic Zamprogna, Rachel Ticotin in
F/X 2
© Orion Pictures

Clancy Brown, Lou Diamond Phillips in
Ambition
© Miramax Films

Don Michael Paul, Jill Schoelen in *Rich Girl*
© *Studio 3 Film Corp.*

Brian Austin Green, Michael Landes in
An American Summer
© *Castle Hill Prods.*

RICH GIRL (Studio Three Film Corp.) Producer, Michael B. London; Executive Producers, Mark Hoffman, Steven H. Parker; Director, Joel Bender; Photography, Levie Isaacks; Screenplay, Robert Elliot; Music, Jay Chattaway; Music Supervisors, Richard Mann, Arlene Matza; Editors, Mark Helfrich, Richard Candib; a co-presentation of Film West; Foto-Kem color; Rated R; 96 minutes; May release. CAST: Jill Schoelen (Courtney Wells), Don Michael Paul (Rick), Sean Kanan (Jeffrey), Ron Karabatsos (Rocco), Paul Gleason (Marvin Wells), Cherie Currie (Michelle), Bentley Mitchum (Scott), Melanie Tomlin (Diana), Trudi Forristal (Tracy), Ann Gillespie (Cindy), Gail Neely (Cook), Dennis Holahan (Lawyer), Walter Lang (Dennis), Kirk Scott (Investment Banker), Isabelle Cooley (Counselor), Ingrid Berg (Receptionist), Frederick Flynn (Landlord), Linda Galloway (Businesswoman), Anthony Markes, Paul Michael Schell (Bar Patrons), Alicia Lassiter (Blonde Temptress), Daphne Cheung (Oriental Temptress), Maureen Flaherty, Dorrie Krum (Girls in restroom), Mark Riccardi, Lincoln Simonds (Bar Toughs), Cynthia Geary, Linda West (Sorority Girls), B.J. Davis (Motorcycle Cop), Irving W. Mosley, Jr. (Minister), Larry Gelman (Pawnbroker), Chuck Courtney, Christopher Doyle (Policemen), Peter Cohl (Chopin), Steven "Lance" Carter (Drummer), Doyle McCurley (Prison Guard), Eddy Griffith (Rick's Father), Hans Howes (Police Sergeant), Ann McFadden (Waitress), Rick Herman (A & R Man), Kristine Seeley (Groupie), Willie Dixon (Himself), Greg Pope (Miranda Rap Judge), Onita Watson, Lee Harrington, Demesa Bell (Miranda Rap Dancers)

NO SECRETS (I.R.S. Releasing) Producers, Morgan Mason, John Hardy, Shauna Shapiro; Executive Producers, David Jackson, Carol Curb; Director, Dezso Magyar; Screenplay, William Scheuer, Dezso Magyar; Photography, Sandi Sissel; Designer, Clare Scarpulla; Editor, Suzanne Fenn; Costumes, Jan Roton; Music, Vinny Golia; Color; Rated R; 92 minutes; May release. CAST: Adam Coleman Howard (Manny), Amy Locane (Jennifer), Heather Fairfield (Claire), Traci Lind (Sam)

DICE RULES (7 Arts Film Distributors) Producer, Fred Silverstein; Director, Jay Dubin; Concert Material, Andrew Dice Clay; "A Day in the Life" Screenplay, Lenny Shulman, Andrew Dice Clay; Executive Producers, J.R. Guterman, Jana Sue Memel;

Photography (Concert), Michael Negrin; Photography ("A Day in the Life"), Charlie Lieberman; Editors, Mitchell Sinoway, John K. Currin; Co-Producer, Tim Clawson; a Fleebin Dabble production; Dolby Stereo; Foto-Kem color; Rated NC-17; 87 minutes; May release. CAST: Andrew Dice Clay (Dice), Eddie Griffin (Gas Station Attendant), Sylvia Harman (Homeless Woman), Lee Lawrence (Lee), "Noodles" Levenstein (Bank Teller), Maria Parkinson (Berneece), Michael "Wheels" Parise (Dr. Slaughter), Sumont (Convenience Store Clerk), "Hot Tub" Johnny West (Deli Clerk), Fred Silverstein (Man in Love), Carmine Diorio, Frank Diorio, Sal Iuvara, Steve Jankowski, Richard Santa, Robert Santa, Tom Timko (Band)

HEARING VOICES (AFI USA) Director/Screenplay, Sharon Greytak; Photography, Doron Schlair; Music, Wes York; Color; Not rated; 87 minutes; May release. CAST: Erika Nagy (Erika), Stephen Gatta (Lee), Tim Ahearn (Michael Krieger), Michael Davenport (Carl)

KILL LINE (American Pictures/Rocky Group Inc.) Producer, Robert W. Kim; Director/Screenplay, Richard Kim; Color; Rated R; 80 minutes; May release. CAST: Bobby Kim, Michael Parker, Marlene Zimmerman, H. Wayne Lowery, C.R. Valdez, Mark Williams

MANNEQUIN TWO: ON THE MOVE (20th Century Fox) Producer, Edward Rugoff; Co-Producer, Malcolm R. Harding; Director, Stewart Raffill; Screenplay, Edward Rugoff, David Isaacs, Ken Levine, Betsy Israel; Based on characters created by Edward Rugoff and Michael Gottlieb; Photography, Larry Pizer; Designer, William J. Creber; Music, David McHugh; Editor, John Rosenberg, Joan Chapman; Casting, Penny Perry, Annette Benson; Executive Producer, John Foreman; a Gladden Entertainment presentation; Dolby Stereo; DuArt color; Rated PG; 95 minutes; May release. CAST: Kristy Swanson (Jessie), William Ragsdale (Jason Williamson/Prince William), Meshach Taylor (Hollywood/Doorman), Terry Kiser (Count Spretzle/Sorcerer), Stuart Pankin (Mr. James), Cynthia Harris (Mom/Queen), Andrew Hill Newman (Andy Ackerman), Julie Foreman (Gail), John Edmondson (Rolf/Soldier #1), Phil Latella (Egon/Soldier #2), Mark Gray (Arnold/Soldier #3), Erick Weiss, Jackye Roberts (Mr. James' Assistants), John Casino (Horned Soldier), Laurie Wing (Old Queen), Julie Warder (Beauty Technician), G. James Reed (Furniture Salesman), Joanne Bradley, Christine Baur (Garbage Women), Allelon Ruggiero (Employee #1), Heather Henderson (Lipstick Girl), Sherry Wallen (Dress Saleslady), Thom Christopher Warren (Albert), Wendy Worthington (Tour Guide), Jim Mital (Grip), Ilene Morris (Young Female Guest), Hazel Pierce (Customer), Robert N. Hines (Hauptmann-Koenig Pilot), Daphne Lynn Stacey (Cafe Waitress), Eva Andell (Jessie's Sister), Michael J. Anderson (Jewel Box Bearer), Suzanne DeLaurentis (Nightclub Waitress), Dana Dewes, Celeste Russi (Southside Girls), Chris Giannini (Cool Guy), Coco (Lead Dancer), Ellen Sabino (Girl outside club), Christine Vanacore (Happy Girl), Michael Stermel, Jerry Lyden, John Richman, Rocky Cathcart (Cops), Joe Milazzo (Cop on bridge), Matt Myers (Officer Al), Bud Seese (Duty Sergeant), Cliff McMullen (Mannequin Cop #1), Nancy Nicholson (Girl on video), Dana Edward Schmidt (Go Cart Flagman)

AN AMERICAN SUMMER (Castle Hill) Co-Producer, Charles Faithorn; Executive Producer, Jane Hamsher; Producer/Director/Screenplay, James Slocum; Photography, Bruce

158   Meshach Taylor, Kristy Swanson,
William Ragsdale in *Mannequin Two*
© *Gladden Entertainment Corp.*

Lili Taylor, Dermot Mulroney in *Bright Angel*
© *Hemdale Film Corp.*

Pat Morita, Dona Speir in *Do or Die*
© *Andy Sidaris*

Dorfman; Designer, Damon Fortier; Associate Producer, Wade Danielson; Editor, Ron Rosen; Costumes, Linda Susan Howell; Music, Roger Neill; a Boss Entertainment Group presentation; Dolby Stereo; Color; Rated PG-13; 99 minutes; June release. CAST: Michael Landes (Tom Travis), Brian Austin Green (Charles "Fin" Finley), Amber Susa (Traci), Sherrie Krenn (Cari), Brian Krause (Joey), Joanna Kerns (Aunt Sunny), Wayne Pere (Rockman), Tony Crane (Bo Riley).

BRIGHT ANGEL (Hemdale) Producers, Paige Simpson, Robert MacLean; Executive Producers, John Daly, Derek Gibson; Supervising Producer, Sue Baden-Powell; Director, Michael Fields; Screenplay, Richard Ford; Photography, Elliot Davis; Designer, Marcia Hinds-Johnson; Costumes, Karen Patch; Music, Christopher Young; Editors, Melody London, Clement Barclay; Casting, Risa Bramon, Billy Hopkins, Heidi Levitt; Assistant Director, John King; a Northwood/Bright Angel production; Ultra-Stereo; CFI color; Rated R; 94 minutes; June release. CAST: Dermot Mulroney (George Russell), Lili Taylor (Lucy), Sam Shepard (Jack), Valerie Perrine (Aileen), Burt Young (Art), Bill Pullman (Bob), Benjamin Bratt (Claude), Mary Kay Place (Judy), Alex Bulltail (Sherman), Delroy Lindo (Harley), Kevin Tighe (The Man), Will Patton (Woody), Sheila McCarthy (Nina), Tom Dixon (Meat Locker Owner), Lyle N. Cusson (Drunk), Myrna Wilken, Julia Omvig (Barmaids), Tom Connelley, Ed Kraft (Switchmen), Joyce Rogers (Proprietress), Irving Jefferson (Boxing Indian), Jacqueline R. Ziegler (Jail Deputy), Dan Old Elk (Reservation Policeman), Tyde Kierney (Detective), Fred Oakland (Greyhound Ticket Agent)

DELUSION (I.R.S. Releasing) formerly *Mirage* ; Producer, Daniel Hassid; Executive Producers, Seth M. Willenson, Christoph Henkel; Co-Producers, William Ewart, Cevin Cathell; Director, Carl Colpaert; Screenplay, Carl Colpaert, Kurt Voss; Photography, Geza Sinkovics; Editor, Mark Allan Kaplan; Designer, Ildiko Toth; Music, Barry Adamson; Costumes, Kimberly Tillman; Casting, Elisa Goodman; a Cineville Inc. and Seth M. Willenson Productions presentation; Deluxe color; Rated R; 100 minutes; June release. CAST: Jim Metzler (George O'Brien), Jennifer Rubin (Patti), Kyle Secor (Chevy), Jerry

Orbach (Larry), Robert Costanzo (Myron Sales), Tracey Walter (Bus Ticket Cashier), Barbara Alyn Woods (Julie), Barbara Horan (Carly), Angelina Fiordelissi (Biker Girl), Raymond Singer (Jim), Tommy Redmond Hicks (Cop), Kevin West, Darryl Cox, Bob McCracken, Pat Reilly (Thugs), Frankie Maiolo (Gas Station Attendant), Tamara Landey (Arabella), Rudolph Willrich, Brendan McKane (Executives), James Magowan, Marc James (Executives in hallway), Charles Ayers, Jeffrey Madison (Christmas Tree Movers), Maria Gulezian, Roxanne Thompson (Secretaries), Anthony Markes (Man on beach), John W. Hart, Rachel Gebler, Chitra Mojtabai, Robert Moore, Carol Lang, Laura Lang, Craig Sexton, Richard Jordan, Seth M. Willenson, Kristin Stuart, Albert Abala (Conference Room Executives)

DO OR DIE (Malibu Bay Films) Producer, Arlene Sidaris; Director/Screenplay, Andy Sidaris; Photography, Mark Morris; Designer, Cherie Day Ledwith; Music, Richard Lyons; Editor, Michael Haight; Assistant Director, Mike Freedman; Costumes, Merrie Lawson; Special Effects, Eddie Surkin; Ultra-Stereo; Filmservice color; Rated R; 97 minutes; June release. CAST: Pat Morita (Kaneshiro), Erik Estrada (Richard Esteban), Dona Speir (Donna Hamilton), Roberta Vasquez (Nicole Justin), Bruce Penhall (Bruce Christian), Cynthia Brimhall (Edy Stark), William Bumiller (Lucas), Michael Jay Shane (Shane), Stephanie Schick (Atlanta Lee), Richard Cansino (Hebert), Chu Chu Malave (Bodreux), Ava Cadell (Ava), Skip Ward (Skip), James Lew (Lew), Eric Chen (Chen), Paul Hospodar (Duke), H.D. Wood (Woody), Drew Sidaris (Spencer), Rodd Saunders (Dudley), Bill Allen (Fiddle Player), Louis Ballis (Washboard), Tony Bucci (Accordianist), Bonnie McFarland (Big Pines Waitress), Betty Williams, George Williams (Big Pine Diners)

FOREVER ACTVISTS: STORIES FROM THE VETERANS OF THE ABRAHAM LINCOLN BRIGADE (Tara Releasing) Producer/Director, Judith Montell; Photography, T. Robin Hirsh; Narration Written by Yasha Aginsky, Phil Cousineau, Judith Montell; Music, Bruce Barthol, Randy Craig; Narrator, Ronnie Gilbert; Color; Not rated; 60 minutes; June release. Documentary featuring Milt Wolff, Maury Colow, Herman "Gabby" Rosenstein, Sam Gonshak, Steve Nelson, Ruth Davidow, Hilda Roberts

Jerry Orbach, Kyle Secor in *Delusion*
© *I.R.S. Media*

Forever Activists
© *Tara Releasing*

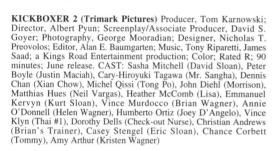

Peter Boyle, Sasha Mitchell in *Kickboxer 2*
© Trimark Pictures

David Hewlett, Deborah Raffin in *Scanners II*
© Triton Pictures

KICKBOXER 2 (Trimark Pictures) Producer, Tom Karnowski; Director, Albert Pyun; Screenplay/Associate Producer, David S. Goyer; Photography, George Mooradian; Designer, Nicholas T. Preovolos; Editor, Alan E. Baumgarten; Music, Tony Riparetti, James Saad; a Kings Road Entertainment production; Color; Rated R; 90 minutes; June release. CAST: Sasha Mitchell (David Sloan), Peter Boyle (Justin Maciah), Cary-Hiroyuki Tagawa (Mr. Sangha), Dennis Chan (Xian Chow), Michel Qissi (Tong Po), John Diehl (Morrison), Matthias Hues (Neil Vargas), Heather McComb (Lisa), Emmanuel Kervyn (Kurt Sloan), Vince Murdocco (Brian Wagner), Annie O'Donnell (Helen Wagner), Humberto Ortiz (Joey D'Angelo), Vince Klyn (Thai #1), Dorothy Dells (Check-out Nurse), Christian Andrews (Brian's Trainer), Casey Stengel (Eric Sloan), Chance Corbett (Tommy), Amy Arthur (Kristen Wagner)

NIGHT OF THE WARRIOR (Trimark) Producers, Mike Erwin, Thomas Ian Griffith; Director, Rafal Zielinski; Screenplay, Thomas Ian Griffith; Photography, Edward Pei; Music, Ed Tomney; Editor, Jonas Thaler; Designer, Michael Helmy; Fight Choreographer, Rick Avery; a Little Bear Films presentation of a Blueline/Ian Page production; Ultra-Stereo; Color; Rated R; 100 minutes; June release. CAST: Lorenzo Lamas (Miles Keane), Anthony Geary (Lynch), Kathleen Kinmont (Katherine Pierce), Ken Foree (Oliver), Felicity Waterman (Joy), Arlene Dahl (Edie Keane), Daniel Kamekona (Chang), Bill Erwin (Coco), Mary Ann Oedy (Ronnie), Richard Redlin (Chance), Willie Dixon, Wilhelm von Hamburg, Sarah Elgart, Tita Omzee, Robin Antin, Naomi Newton

NIGHTSONGS (AFI USA) Producer, Thomas A. Fucci; Director/Screenplay, Marva Nabili; Photography, Ben Davis; Editor, Fritz Liepe; Music, R.I.P. Hayman; an FN Films production; Color; Not rated; 116 minutes; June release. CAST: Mabel Kwong (Chinese/Viet Woman), David Lee (Fung Tak Men), Victor Wong (Fung Leung), Ida F.O. Chung (Fung Lai Ping), Rose Lee (Fung Mei Fun), Roger Chang (Fung Tak Sing), Geoff Lee (Gang Recruiter)

THE PHANTOM OF THE OPERA (Hirschfeld Prods.) Executive Producers, Karen Poindexter, Samantha Klein; Producers, Darwin Knight, Linda Bryant; Stage Director/Choreographer, Darwin Knight; Director, Angel Hernandez; Book/Adaptation, Bruce Falstein; Based

on the novel by Gaston Leroux; Music/Lyrics, Lawrence Rosen, Paul Schierhorn; Color; Not rated; 93 minutes; June release. CAST: David Staller (The Phantom), Elizabeth Walsh (Christine Daae), Beth McVey (Carlotta), Christopher Rath (Raoul De Chagny), Darin De Paul (Moncharmin), Richard Kinter (Richard), Harsh Nayyar (The Persian), Kim Ostrenko (Madame Giry), James Baldwin (Joseph Buquet), Erick Walck (Old Man Daae), Alexandra Kinter (Young Christine), Joey Leone (Young Raoul)

RAMBLIN' GAL (Aquarius) Producer, Carl E. Person; Directors, Roberto Monticello, Lu Ann Horstman Person; Screenplay, Lu Ann Horstman Person; Photography, Mik Cribben; Music, Augie Meyer, Tom Cerrone; Editors, Jack Haigis, Jay Kessel, Richard Dama, Shu Lea; a Ramblin' Gal production; Color; Not rated; 106 minutes; June release. CAST: Deborah Strang (Ruby), Andrew Krawetz (Cyril Hammond), Kirk Condyles (Will), Douglas Cole (Willy)

SCANNERS II: THE NEW ORDER (Triton Pictures) Producer, Rene Malo; Co-Producer, Franco Battista; Executive Producers, Pierre David, Renald Pare, Tom Berry; Director, Christian Duguay; Screenplay, B.J. Nelson; Photography, Rodney Gibbons; Designer, Richard Tasse; Music, Marty Simon; Special Effects, Michael Smithsom; a Malofilm Group presentation; Color; Rated R; 105 minutes; June release. CAST: David Hewlett (David Kellum), Deborah Raffin (Julie Vale), Yvan Ponton (Cmdr. John Forrester), Isabelle Mejias (Alice Leonardo), Tom Butler (Dr. Morse), Raoul Trujillo (Drak), Vlasta Vrana (Lt. Gelson), Murray Westgate (George Kellum), Doris Petrie (Susan Kellum), Dorothee Berryman (Mayor), Michael Rudder (Feck), David Francis (Gruner), Stephan Zarou (Walter), Tom Harvey (Chief Stokes), Jason Cavalier, Russell Yuen (Convenience Store Thugs), Dawn Tyler Watson (Cashier), Tyrone Benskin (Store Owner), Perry Schneiderman (Karmen Lucret), John Walsh (Lucret's Bodyguard), Barbara Jones, Mark Hellman, Al Vandercruys (Reporters), Michael McGill (Milk Murderer), Dorian Joe Clark (Yancy), Carl Alacchi, Kevin Fenlon, Simon Elise Girard, Ais Snyder (Degenerate Scanners), Paul Stewart (Scanner Cell Orderly), Victoris Barkoff (Nurse), Mark Camacho (Paramedic), Philip Spensley (Mayor's Butler), Victor Knight (Vet School Prof.), Claire Rodger (Press Agent), Minor Mustain (Video Arcade Guard)

DON'T TELL MOM THE BABYSITTER'S DEAD (Warner Bros.) Producers, Robert Newmyer, Brian Reilly, Jeffrey Silver; Executive Producer, Michael Phillips; Director, Stephen Herek; Screenplay, Neil Landau, Tara Ison; Photography, Tim Suhrstedt; Designer, Stephen Marsh; Music, David Newman; Associate Producer, Caroline Baron; Editor, Larry Bock; Casting, Richard Pagano, Sharon Bialy; Assistant Director, Bradley M. Gross; an HBO in association with Cinema Plus L.P. and Mercury/Douglas Films presentation of an Outlaw Production; Dolby Stereo; Deluxe color; Rated PG-13; 105 minutes; June release. CAST: Christina Applegate (Sue Ellen "Swell" Crandell), Joanna Cassidy (Rose Lindsey), John Getz (Gus Brandon), Josh Charles (Bryan), Keith Coogan (Kenny Crandell), Concetta Tomei (Mom), David Duchovny (Bruce), Kimmy Robertson (Cathy), Jayne Brook (Carolyn), Eda Reiss Merin (Mrs. Sturak), Robert Hy Gorman (Walter Crandell), Danielle Harris (Melissa Crandell), Christopher Pettiet (Zach Crandell), Chris Claridge (Lizard), Jeff Bollow (Mole), Michael Kopelow (Hellhound), Alejandro Quezada (Skull), Wendy Brainard (Jill),

David Staller, Elizabeth Walsh in
Phantom of the Opera
© Hirschfeld Prods.

Keith Coogan, Christina Applegate in
Don't Tell Mom the Babysitter's Dead
© *Warner Bros. Inc.*

Vincent D'Onofrio, Greta Scacchi, Jimmy Smits in
Fires Within
© *Pathe Entertainment*

Sarah Buxton (Tess), Kawena Charlot (Becky), Laurie Morrison (Katrina), Deborah Tucker (Nicole), Sydney Lassick (Franklin), Michelle Mais (Temp), Oscar Jordan (Mailroom Clerk), Marc Epstein (Lunch Waiter), Jim Holmes (Dinner Waiter), Cathy Ladman (Pam), Frank Dent (Mr. Egg), Bryan Clark (Dr. Permutter), Steve Ruggles (Officious Clerk), Randy Pelish (Delivery Man), E.E. Bell (Umpire), Kristen Corbett (Pretty Little Leaguer), Christopher Plummer ("Howard), Carl Tramon, Ethan Wilson (Musicians), Logan Duncan ("Liza"), David Shawn Michaels ("Dolly"), Christopher Morley ("Marilyn"), Robert F. Newmyer, Brian M. Reilly (Mortuary Workers)

FIRES WITHIN (MGM) Producers, Wallis Nicita, Lauren Lloyd; Executive Producer, Jim Bloom; Director, Gillian Armstrong; Screenplay, Cynthia Cidre; Photography, David Gribble; Designer, Robert Ziembicki; Music, Maurice Jarre; Editor, John Scott; from MGM-Pathe Entertainment; Panavision; Color; Rated R; 87 minutes; June release. CAST: Jimmy Smits (Nestor), Greta Scacchi (Isabel), Vincent D'Onofrio (Sam), Bertila Damas (Estela), Bri Hathaway (Maribi)

BEGOTTEN (Theatre of Material) Producer/Director/Screenplay/Film Effects/Photography, E. Elias Merhige; Sound, Evan Albam; Costumes, Celia Bryant, Harry Duggins; Art Director/Special Effects, Harry Duggins; Black and white; Not rated; 78 minutes; June release. CAST: Brian Salzberg (God Killing Himself), Donna Dempsey (Mother Earth), Stephen Charles Barry (Son of Earth - Flesh of Bone), James Gandia, Garfield White, Arthur Streeter, Daniel Harkins, Michael Phillips, Adolpho Vargas, Erik Slavin, Terry Anderson

THE GOLDEN BOAT (Strand Releasing) Producers, James Schamus, Jordi Torrent; Director/Screenplay, Raul Ruiz; Photography, Maryse Alberti; Designer, Sermin Kardestuncer; Editor, Sylvia Waliga; Music, John Zorn; a Duende Pictures/Symbolic Exchange Production in association with The Kitchen, Nomad Films (Luxembourg), and A.A.L.B. Partners; Color/Black and white; Not rated; 84 minutes; June release. CAST: Federico Muchnik (Israel Williams), Michael Kirby (Austin), Barbet Schroeder (Mean Passerby), Anna Kohler (Bartender), Mary Hestand (Alina), Angelo Orlando (Olaf), Brett Alexander (Doc), Marie Vachon (Antonia), Vernice Miller (Neighbor), Kate Valk (Amelia Lopes), Papo Colo (Juan Jose), Kathy Acker (Professor), David Savage, Peter Bowen, Adam Bresnick, Casey Finch (Graduate Student Voyeurs), Jim Jarmusch (Violent Stranger), Michael Stumm (Tony Luna), Annie Sprinkle (Waitress), Billy Ballantine (Driver), Burton Greenhouse (Cop), Tom Jarmusch (Nice Passerby), Stephan Balint, Karl Soderstrom, Steven Max Grenyo (Hit Men), Javier Maldonado, Trixie the Beast (Themselves), Dale Hoyt (Mike), Barbara Tsumagari (Drawing Neighbor), Kelley Forsyth, Mya Myint (Women on beach), Elizabeth Jenyon (Woman on boardwalk), Vito Acconci (Swiss Killer)

JOEY TAKES A CAB (Bandwagon Prods.) Producer/Director: Albert Band; Screenplay, Frank Ray Perilli; Photography, Jim Stewart; Music, Fritz Heede; Color; Not rated; 82 minutes; June release. CAST: Lionel Stander (Joey Raye), Kathleen Freeman (Lola), Jackie Gayle (Jackie), Michael J. Pollard (Alan), Eileen Brennan, Royal Dano

TEREZIN DIARY (First Run Features) Producer/Director, Dan Weissman; Executive Producer/Screenplay, Zuzana Justman; Photography, Ervin Sanders; Editor, Mark Simon; Narrator, Eli Wallach; a Terezin Foundation Inc. presentation in association with Visible Pictures Ltd.; DuArt color; Not rated; 88 minutes; June release. Documentary

PROBLEM CHILD 2 (Universal) Producer, Robert Simonds; Director, Brian Levant; Screenplay, Scott Alexander, Larry Karaszewski; Photography, Peter Smokler; Designer, Maria Caso; Editor, Lois Freeman-Fox; Music, David Kitay; Associate Producer, Kim Kurumada; an Imagine Film Entertainment production; Dolby Stereo; Deluxe color; Rated PG-13; 91 minutes; July release. CAST: John Ritter (Ben Healy), Michael Oliver (Junior Healy), Jack Warden ("Big" Ben Healy), Laraine Newman (LaWanda Dumore), Amy Yasbeck (Annie Young), Ivyann Schwan (Trixie Young), Gilbert Gottfried (Mr. Peabody), Paul Willson (Smith), Alan Blumenfeld (Aron Burger), Charlene Tilton (Debbie Claukinski), James Tolkan (Mr. Thorn), Martha Quinn (Emily), Zach Grenier (Voytek), Eric Edwards (Murph), Krystal Mataras (Dolly), Tiffany Mataras (Madison), Dennis Redfield, Bill Warren (Animal Control Guys), Kristina Simonds (Rhoda), Aaron Vaughn (Scuzzy Boyfriend), Denise Lecce, Nancy Duerr (Bridal Shower Ladies), Tom Nowicki, Ric Reitz (Health Officials), Bill Cordell (Lab Technician), Hillary Matthews (Upset Wife), Bob Small (Pathetic Defiant Man), Danny Gura (Freckled Boy on ride), Carla Kneeland (Peabody's Date), Tabetha Thomas (Polly), Paul Sutera (Richard), Buddy Stoccardo (Crazy Dance D.J.), Jillian Amburgey ("Hubba Hubba" Lady), Adam Brock (Neighbor Boy), Christopher Oyen (Goofy Waiter), Danny Haneman (Scummy Ride Operator), Brett Rice (Maitre d'), Shaun Padgett (Mother), Aimee Deshayes (Precious Young Girl), Tammy Boalo (6th Grade Mother), Danielle Meierhenry (6th Grade Student), Elaine Klimaszewski, Diane Klimaszewski (Hot Tub Girls), June Foray (Voice of Puppet), Carol French (Horse Rider), Carrell Myers, Angie Harper, Katie Prestwood (Parents), Laura O'Connell (Girl with bikini top), Tim Powell (Guy with toupee), Barclay (Nippy), "Buffalo" Bob Smith (Father Flanagan)

Jack Warden, John Ritter, Amy Yasbeck in **161**
Problem Child 2
© *Universal City Studios*

Ed O'Neill, Ethan Randal in *Dutch*
© *Twentieth Century Fox*

Jimi Hendrix at the Isle of Wight
© *Original Cinema*

DEAD RINGER (Ogden Ave. Prods.) Producers, Alfred Dellentash, David Sonenberg; Director/Screenplay, Allan Nicholls; Story, Allan Nicholls, David Sonenberg, Alfred Dellentash; Photography, Don Lenzer; Editor, Norman Smith; Designer, Franne Lee; DuArt color; Not rated; 101 minutes; July release. CAST: Meat Loaf, Josh Mostel, Fred Coffin, Alan Braunstein, Leah Ayres, MacIntyre Dixon, Davey Johnstone, Terry Williams, Paul Ross Jacobs, Steve Buslowe, George Meyer, Mark Doyle, Ted Neeley, Eric Troyer, Pamela Moore

DUTCH (20th Century Fox) Producers, John Hughes, Richard Vane; Director, Peter Faiman; Screenplay, John Hughes; Executive Producer, Tarquin Gotch; Designer, Stan Jolley; Photography, Charles Minsky; Editors, Paul Hirsch, Adam Bernardi; Music, Alan Silvestri; Costumes, Jennifer Parsons; Casting, Jane Jenkins, Janet Hirshenson; Assistant Director, Josh McLaglen; Dolby Stereo; Deluxe color; Rated PG-13; 107 minutes; July release. CAST: Ed O'Neill (Dutch Dooley), Ethan Randall (Doyle Standish), JoBeth Williams (Natalie), Christopher McDonald (Reed), Ari Meyers (Brock), E.G. Daily (Halley), L. Scott Caldwell (Homeless Woman), Kathleen Freeman (Gritzi), Lisa Figus, Cedering Fox, Shelby Leverington (Party Women), Kyle Fredericks (Maid), David James Alexander, Ross Borden (Men), Joe Baker (Party Butler), Laura Brumage (Party Guest), Will Nipper (Teddy), Robert Sutherland Telfer (Schoolboy), Patrika Darbo (Greasy Spoon Waitress), Ron Payne (Greasy Spoon Cook), Tom Chatlos (Customer at counter), Ina Edell (Woman at counter), Warren Rice (Man at booth), Mickey Jones (Truck Driver), Brenda Pickleman (Motel Waitress), Billy "Sly" Waitress (Man with blaster), Jerry Darr (White Man on bus), Vincent Craig Dupree (Black Man on bus), Sam Menning (Elderly Man), Tracy J. Connor (Gas Station Waitress), Theresa Bell (Grace), Pat Asanti, Barry Doe (Watchmen), Phyllis Franklin (Yuppie Waitress), J.C. MacKenzie (Mike Malloy), Ann Hearn (Riva Malloy), Gene Whittington (Homeless Father), Jesshaye Callier (Homeless Child), Jack Murdock (Homeless Man), Jackie Lee Sander (2nd Truck Driver)

THE HORSEPLAYER (Greycat Films) Producer, Larry J. Rattner; Executive Producers, Robert M. Nau, Daryl Jamison; Director, Kurt Voss; Screenplay, Kurt Voss, Larry J. Rattner, David Birke; Line Producer, Tamar E. Glaser; Photography, Dean Lent; Music, Garry Schyman, The Pixies; Art Director, Steve Karman; Associate

Producer, Lee Anne Kaplan; Costumes, Elisabeth A. Scott; Dolby Stereo; CFI color; Not rated; 87 minutes; July release. CAST: Brad Dourif (Bud Cowan), Sammi Davis (Randi), M.K. Harris (Matthew), Vic Tayback (George Samsa), Max Perlich (Kid), Rocky Giordani (Biker), Debby Steele (Gallery Receptionist), Stephen Saban, Garret Greenwood (Critics), Pino Giordani (Girl in gallery), Bill Barminski (Shopper in liquor store)

JIMI HENDRIX AT THE ISLE OF WIGHT (Original Cinema) Producer, Alan Douglas; Director, Murray Lerner; Editor, Greg Sheldon; Color; Not rated; 60 minutes; July release. Documentary featuring Jimi Hendrix, Billy Cox, Mitch Mitchell

SLACKER (Orion Classics) Producer/Director/Screenplay, Richard Linklater; Photography, Lee Daniel; Casting, Anne Walker; Editor, Scott Rhodes; Art Director, Debbie Pastor; a Detour Filmproduction presentation; Ultra-Stereo; DuArt color; Rated R; 97 minutes; July release. CAST (in order of appearance): Richard Linklater, Rudy Basquez, Jean Caffeine, Jan Hockey, Stephan Hockey, Mark James, Samuel Dietert, Bob Boyd, Terrence Kirk, Keith McCormack, Jennifer Schaudies, Dan Kratochvil, Maris Strautmanis, Brecht Andersch, Tom Pallotta, Jerry Deloney, Heather West, John Spath, Ron Marks, Daniel Dugan, Brian Crokett, Scott Marcus, Stella Weir, Teresa Taylor, Mark Harris, Greg Wilson, Debbie Pastor, Gina Lalli, Sharon Roos, Frank Orrall, Skip Fulton Jr., Abra Moore, Lori Capp, Gus Vayas, Louis Black, Don Stroud, Janelle Coolich, Aleister Barron, Zara Barron, Albans Benchoff, Nigel Benchoff, Kevin Whitley, Steve Anderson, Robert Pierson, Sarah Harmon, David Haymond, John Slate, Scott Van Horn, Lee Daniel, Charles Gunning, Tamsy Ringler, Luke Savisky, Meg Brennan, Phillip Hostak, D Angus MacDonald, Shelly Kristaponis, Louis Mackey, Kathy McCarty, Michael Laird, Jack Meredith, Clark Lee Walker, Kalman Spellitich, Siggouri Wilkovich, Scott Rhodes, D. Montgomery, Mimi Vitetta, Susannah Simone, Bruce Hughes, Keith Fletcher, Eric Buehlman, R. Malice, Mark Quirk, Kim Krizan, Annick Souhami, Regina Garza, Stephen Jacobson, Eric Lord, Kelly Linn, Rachael Reinhardt, Stewart Bennet, Kevin Thompson, Nick Maffei, Nolan Morrison, Dan Kratochvil, Kyle Rosenblad, Ed Hall, Lucinda Scott, Wammo, Marianne Hyatt, Gary Price, Joseph Jones, Kendal Smith, Sean Coffey, Patrice Sullivan, Jennifer Carroll, Charlotte Norris, Greg Ward

Brad Dourif, Vic Tayback in
The Horseplayer
© *Greycat Films*

Slacker
© *Orion Classics*

White Dog
© *Paramount Pictures*

Marc Singer, Kari Wuhrer in *Beastmaster 2*
© *Republic Pictures Corp.*

WHITE DOG (Paramount) Producer, Jon Davison; Executive Producers, Edgar J. Scherick, Nick Vanoff; Director, Samuel Fuller; Screenplay, Samuel Fuller, Curtis Hanson; Based on the story by Romain Gary; Photography, Bruce Surtees; Music, Ennio Morricone; Designer, Brian Eatwell; Editor, Bernard Gribble; 1982; Metrocolor; Rated PG; 90 minutes; July release. CAST: Kristy McNichol (Julie Sawyer), Paul Winfield (Keys), Burl Ives (Carruthers), Jameson Parker (Roland Gray), Lynne Moody (Molly), Marshall Thompson (Director), Bob Minor (Joe), Vernon Weddle (Vet), Christa Lang (Nurse), Tony Brubaker (Sweeper Driver), Samuel Fuller (Charlie Felton), Paul Bartel (Cameraman), Martine Dawson (Martine), Alex A. Brown (Man in church), Parley Baer (Wilber Hull)

BIKINI ISLAND (Curb/Esquire Films) Producers, Anthony Markes, Zachary Matz; Executive Producers, Jim Jeknavorian, Richard Ardi; Director, Anthony Markes; Screenplay, Emerson Bixby; Story, Anthony Markes; Diana Levitt; Photography, Howard Wexler; Designer, Keith Downey; Editor, Ron Resnick; a Rocky Point production in association with Wildcat Prods.; Color; Rated R; 85 minutes; July release. CAST: Holly Floria, Alicia Anne, Jackson Robinson, Sherry Johnson, Gaston LeGaf, Shannon Stiles, Kathleen McOsker, Terry Miller, Cyndi Pass

THE DARK BACKWARD (Greycat Films) Producers, Brad Wyman, Cassian Elwes; Executive Producers, Randolf Turrow, William Talmadge; Director/Screenplay, Adam Rifkin; Photography, Joey Forsyte; Music, Marc David Decker; Editor, Peter Schink; Designer, Sherman Williams; Costumes, Alexandria Forster; Special Makeup Effects, Tony Gardner, Alterion Studios; Casting, Tony Markes; Dolby Stereo; Color; Rated R; 101 minutes; July release. CAST: Judd Nelson (Marty Malt), Bill Paxton (Gus), Wayne Newton (Jackie Chrome), Lara Flynn Boyle (Rosarita), James Caan (Dr. Scurvy), Rob Lowe (Dirk Delta), King Moody (Twinkee Doodle), Claudia Christian (Kitty), Danny Dayton (Syd), Carrie Lynn (Nicolette), Anna Berger (Mrs. Malt), Lydell Cheshier (Dexter), Tom Hodges (Marjorie Zipp), Theodocia Goodrich (Mrs. Bielfuss), Laurianne Jameson (Shirley), Debra Perkins (Pickles), Charles Knapp (Sloppy), Clifford Streit (Raoul), Richard Morrison (Elvis), Charles Winkler (Dirk Delta's Asst.), Landon Godfrey (Unfamiliar Waitress), Gary Vonderlinden (Joey), Robert Gannaway (Denny Ginkle), Marc

David Decker (Barber), Scott Goldman (Mouseman), Adam Rifkin (Rufus Bing), Michele Rifkin (Seamstress), Harold Sokol (Apples Yonahan), Ingrid Rifkin (Cigarette Girl), Elizabeth Sokol (Lady wrapped in gauze), Steve Bing (Basketball Player), Jason Logan (Man behind counter), Tony Markes (Muscle Man), Milica Kastner, Libby White-Cooper (Dirk's Babes), Tony Cox, Tanya Banks, Cindy Sorenson, Arturo Gill, John Hayden (Human Xylophone)

BEASTMASTER 2: THROUGH THE PORTAL OF TIME (New Line Cinema) Producer/Director, Sylvio Tabet; Executive Producer, Stephan Strick; Screenplay, R.J. Robertson, Jim Wynorski, Sylvio Tabet, Ken Hauser, Doug Miles; Photography, Ronn Schmidt; Designer, Allen Jones; Costumes, Betty Madden; Music, Robert Folk; Editor, Adam Bernardi; Casting, Cathy Henderson; Special Effects, Frank Isaacs and Mel; Stunts, Brian McMillan; a Films 21 production from Republic Pictures; Dolby Stereo; Color; Rated PG-13; 107 minutes; August release. CAST: Marc Singer (Dar), Kari Wuhrer (Jackie), Wings Hauser (Arklon), Sarah Douglas (Lyranna), Charles Young (Lead), Charles Hyman (Inquisitor), Eric Waterhouse (Exeter), Robert Zdar (Zavik), John Fifer (Creature), Dan Woren, Carl Ciarfalio (Policemen), David Carrera, Wayne Pere (Punkers), James Avery (Cobberly), Robert Fieldsteel (Bendowski), Doug Franklin (Melwyn), Jeanne Pfleiger (Saleslady), Arthur Malet (Wendell), Paul Goodman (Troy Saunders), Steve Donmeyer (Police Officer), Larry Dobkin (Admiral Binns), Mark Roberts (Herbert Trent)

BODY PARTS (Paramount) Producer, Frank Mancuso, Jr.; Executive Producer, Michael MacDonald; Co-Producers, Jack E. Freedman, Patricia Herskovic; Director, Eric Red; Screenplay, Eric Red, Norman Snider; Screen Story, Patricia Herskovic, Joyce Taylor; Based on the novel *Choice Cuts* by Boileau-Narcejac; Photography, Theo Van de Sande; Designer, Bill Brodie; Editor, Anthony Redman; Music, Loek Dikker; Special Makeup Effects, Gordon J. Smith; Dolby Stereo; Panavision; Technicolor; Rated R; 88 minutes; August release. CAST: Jeff Fahey (Bill Crushank), Lindsay Duncan (Dr. Alice Webb), Kim Delaney (Karen Crushank), Brad Dourif (Remo Lacey), Zakes Mokae (Det. Sawchuk), Peter Murnik (Mark Draper), Paul Benvictor (Ray Kolberg), John Walsh (Charlie Fletcher), Nathaniel Moreau (Billy Crushank), Sarah Campbell (Samantha Crushank

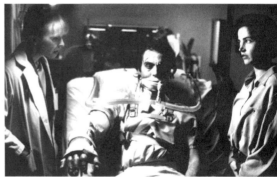

Judd Nelson in *The Dark Backward*
© *Greycat Films*

Lindsay Duncan, Jeff Fahey, Kim Delaney **163**
in *Body Parts*
© *Paramount Pictures*

Antonio Fargas, Tom Towles in *The Borrower*
© Cannon Pictures

Robert J. Steinmiller, Jr., Bingo in *Bingo*
© Tri-Star Pictures

THE BORROWER (Cannon) Producers, R.P. Sekon, Steven A. Jones; Executive Producer, William H. Coleman; Director, John McNaughton; Screenplay, Mason Nage, Richard Fire; Story, Mason Nage; Photography, Julio Mercat, Robert New; Designer, Robert Henderson; Costumes, Theda Deramus; Editor, Elena Maganini; Music, Robert McNaughton, Ken Hale Jones; Makeup, Kevin Yagher; Casting, Jaki Brown; a Vision Pictures production; Ultra-Stereo; Color; Rated R; 90 minutes; August release. CAST: Rae Dawn Chong (Diana Pierce), Don Gordon (Charles Krieger), Antonio Fargas (Julius), Tom Towles (Bob Laney), Neil Giuntoli (Scully), Pam Gordon (Connie), Bentley Mitchum

CHILD'S PLAY 3 (Universal) Producer, Robert Latham Brown; Executive Producer/Chucky Doll Creator, David Kirschner; Co-Producer, Laura Moskowitz; Director, Jack Bender; Screenplay, Don Mancini; Photography, John R. Leonetti; Designer, Richard Sawyer; Editors, Edward A. Warschilka, Jr., Scott Wallace, Edward Warschilka; Music, Cory Lerios, John D'Andrea; Chucky Designed and Engineered by Kevin Yagher; Costumes, Colby Bart; Casting, Glenn Daniels; Assistant Director, Richard Peter Schroer; Dolby Stereo; Deluxe color; Rated R; 90 minutes; August release. CAST: Justin Whalin (Andy Barclay), Perrey Reeves (De Silva), Jeremy Sylvers (Tyler), Travis Fine (Shelton), Dean Jacobson (Whitehurst), Brad Dourif (Voice of Chucky), Peter Haskell (Sullivan), Dakin Matthews (Col. Cochrane), Andrew Robinson (Sgt. Botnick), Burke Byrnes (Sgt. Clark), Matthew Walker (Ellis), Donna Eskra (Ivers), Edan Gross (Voice of Good Guy Doll), Terry Wills (Garbage Man), Richard Marion (Patterson), Laura Owens (Executive), Ron Fassler (Petzold), Michael Chieffo (Security Guard), Henry G. Sanders (Major), Lois Foraker (Sgt. Frazier), David Ellzey (Ghoul), Mark Christopher Lawrence (Cop), Ltc. Richard A. Pack, USA Ret. (Nelson), Michael Renna, Ryan Austine, Kent Winfry, Matt Daniels (Cadets), Aimee Joy Slutske (Carnival Teenager), Alexis Kirschner, Jessica Kirschner, Sophie Owens-Bender, Hannah Owens-Bender (Carnival Kids), Kim Stockdale (Mother)

BINGO (TriStar) Producer, Thomas Baer; Executive Producer, Warren Carr; Co-Producer, John L. Jacobs; Director, Matthew Robbins; Screenplay, Jim Strain; Photography, John McPherson; Designer, Mark Freeborn; Costumes, Larry S. Wells; Editor,

Maryann Brandon; Music, Richard Gibbs; Casting, Robin Lippin, Lynne Carrow; Bingo's Trainer, Boone Narr; Dolby Stereo; Technicolor; Rated PG; 87 minutes; August release. CAST: Bingo (Bingo), Cindy Williams (Natalie Devlin), David Rasche (Hal Devlin), Robert J. Steinmiller, Jr. (Chuckie Devlin), David French (Chickie Devlin), Kurt Fuller (Lennie), Joe Guzaldo (Eli), Glenn Shadix (Duke), Janet Wright (Waitress), Wayne Robson (Four Eyes), Suzie Plakson (Ginger), Simon Webb (Steve), Tamsin Kelsey (Bunny), Norman Browning (Prosecutor), James Kidnie (Defense Attorney), Blu Mankuma (Motorcycle Cop), Jackson Davies (Vet), Stephen E. Miller (Sheriff), Robert Thurston (Mr. Thompson), Sheelah Megill (Mrs. Thompson), Chelan Simmons (Cindy Thompson), Kimberly Warnat (Sandy Thompson), Howard Storey (Coach), Bill Meilen (Vic), Drum Garrett (Dishwasher), Antony Holland (Circus Vet), Sylvia Mitchell (Court Reporter), Denalda Williams (Doctor's Assistant), Gloria Macarenko (Reporter), Betty Linde (Mrs. Wallaby), Ken Kramer (Subpoena Server), Lossen Chambers (911 Operator), Stephen Dimopoulos (911 Supervisor), Chris Rosati (Prison Sentry), Gary Jones (Prison Laundry Guard), Frank C. Turner (Prison Guard), Walter Marsh (Judge), Dana Still (Bailiff), Roman Podhora (Fireman), Rob Roy (Firefighter), Gordon White (Billy the Clown), Nathen Vanering (Swami), Micki Maunsell (Mrs. Grimbleby), Brad Godin, Brad Briggs, Clayton Blanchard (Bicycle Buddies), Kevin McNulty (Network Boss), Bruce Harwood, Richard Side, Ron Chartier (Network Executives)

GOIN' TO CHICAGO (AFI USA) Producer/Director/Screenplay/Editor, Paul Leder; Photography, Francis Grumman; Music, Bob Summers; a Poor Robert Prods. production; Foto-Kem color; Not rated; 105 minutes; August release. CAST: Cleavon Little (Edward Sr.), Viveca Lindfors (Helen), Gary Kroeger (Aaron), Eileen Seely (Elinor), Guy Killum (Edward Jr.), Penny Johnson (Darlene), Lydie Donier (Aline)

GOING UNDER (Warner Bros.) formerly *Dive!*; Producer, Fred T. Gallo; Executive Producer, Darryl Zarubica; Co-Producer, Randolph Davis; Director, Mark W. Travis; Screenplay, Randolph Davis, Darryl Zarubica; Photography, Victor Hammer; Editor, Paul Seydor; Music, David Michael Frank; Color; Rated PG; 81 minutes; August release. CAST: Bill Pullman (Biff Banner), Wendy Schaal (Jan Michaels), Ned Beatty (Admiral Malice), Robert Vaughn (Wedgewood), Roddy McDowall (Secretary Neighbor), Bud Cort (Randy McNally), Chris Demetral (Apple), Tyrone Granderson Jones (Quizby), Dennis Redfield (Turbo), Lou Richards (Skiff), Ernie Sabella (The Mole), Elmarie Wendel (Sonar), Michael Winslow (Reporter), Richard Masur, John Moschitta (Defense Contractors), Frank Bonner, Andrea Stein (Soviet Generals), Rif Hutton (Dr. I.M. Friendly), Joe Namath (Himself), Dianne Turley Travis (Secretary to Wedgewood), Shawne Zarubica (Tour Guide), Artur Cybulski (Soviet Captain), Ivan G'Vera (Soviet Sonar Man), Darryl Zarubica (Soviet Sub Technician), Tad Horino (Japanese Captain), Dayton Callie (General Confusion), Richard Caryle (General Air Quality), Bill Deland (General Alert), Hal England (General Telephone), Tom Fuccello (General Lee Good), William A. Porter (General Electric), Tom Dahlgren (U.S. Admiral), Alan Toy (U.S. Tracking Technician), Haskell V. Anderson III (Bongo Crewman), Clayton Landey (O'Neill), G. Smokey Campbell, Andrew Parks (Shore Patrol), Dean Cain, Eddie Frierson, Richard Kuhlman, Joseph Hardin (Guys in bar), Richard Evans, Mark Haining (Shipyard Workers), Ken Fording (Bartender), Robert Clotworthy (Voice of Submarine)

164 **Justin Whalin, Chucky in**
Child's Play 3
© *Universal City Studios*

Daisy, Rover in *Rover Dangerfield*
© Warner Bros. Inc.

Nana Coburn, Brian Blain, Milla Jovovich, Brian Krause
in *Return to the Blue Lagoon*
© Columbia Pictures

ROVER DANGERFIELD (Warner Bros.) Producers, Willard Carroll, Thomas L. Wilhite; Executive Producer/Screenplay, Rodney Dangerfield; Directors, Jim George, Bob Seeley; Story, Rodney Dangerfield, Harold Ramis; Music, David Newman; Songs, Rodney Dangerfield, Billy Tragesser; Editor, Tony Mizgalski; Designer, Fred Cline; Sequence Directors, Steve Moore, Matthew O'Callaghan, Bruce Smith, Dick Sebast, Frans Vischer, Skip Jones; Produced in association with Hyperion Pictures; Color; Rated G; 74 minutes; August release. VOICE CAST: Rodney Dangerfield (Rover), Susan Boyd (Daisy), Ronnie Schell (Eddie), Ned Luke (Raffles), Shawn Southwick (Connie), Dana Hill (Danny), Sal Landi (Rocky), Tom Williams, Chris Collins, Robert Bergen, Paxton Whitehead, Ron Taylor, Bert Kramer, Eddie Barth, Ralph Monaco, Tress MacNeille, Michael Sheehan, Lara Cody (Additional Voices)

SHOWDOWN IN LITTLE TOKYO (Warner Bros.) Producers, Mark L. Lester, Martin E. Caan; Co-Producer, John Broderick; Director, Mark L. Lester; Screenplay, Stephen Glantz, Caliope Brattlestreet; Photography, Mark Irwin; Designer, Craig Stearns; Music, David Michael Frank; Editors, Steven Kemper, Robert A. Ferretti; Casting, Michelle Guillerman; 2nd Unit Director/Stunts, Terry J. Leonard; Dolby Stereo; Technicolor; Rated R; 77 minutes; August release. CAST: Dolph Lundgren (Detective Chris Kenner), Brandon Lee (Johnny Murata), Carey-Hiroyuki Tagawa (Yoshida), Tia Carrere (Minako), Toshiro Obata (Sato), Philip Tan (Tanaka), Rodney Kageyama (Eddie), Ernie Lively (Det. Nelson), Renee Griffin (Angel), Reid Asato (Muto), Takayo Fischer (Mama Yamaguchi), Simon Rhee (Ito), Vernee Watson-Johnson (Nonnie Russell - Coroner), Lenny Imamura, Roger Yuan (Kickboxers), Susan E. Cox (Mrs. Kenner), Rick Cramer (Mr. Kenner), Keith Boldroff (Kenner as a young boy), Gerald Okamura (Hagata, the Torturer), R. David Smith, Tony Maccario (Hell's Angels), Rome Viharo (Hispanic Gang Leader), Keenan Thomas (Crip Gang Leader), Steve Park, Jim Ishida (Asian Cops), Rachen Assapiomonwait (Bath House Attendant), Ryan Ryusaki (Son at parade with Mama Yamaguchi), Jeff Ramsey, Phil Chong (Samurai Horsemen)

RETURN TO THE BLUE LAGOON (Columbia) Producer/Director, William A. Graham; Executive Producer, Randal Kleiser; Co-Producer, Peter Bogart; Screenplay, Leslie Stevens; Based on the novel *The Garden of God*; by Henry De Vere Stacpoole; Photography, Robert Steadman; Editor, Ronald J. Fagan; Designer, Jon Dowding; Music, Basil Poledouris; Casting, Pennie duPont; a Price Entertainment/Randal Kleiser production; Dolby Stereo; Technicolor; Rated PG-13; 98 minutes; August release. CAST: Milla Jovovich (Lilli), Brian Krause (Richard), Lisa Pelikan (Sarah), Courtney Phillips (Young Lilli), Garette Patrick Ratliff (Young Richard), Emma James (Lilli -infant), Jackson Barton (Richard - infant), Nana Coburn (Sylvia), Brian Blain (Capt. Hilliard), Peter Hehir (Quinlan), Alexander Petersons (Giddens), John Mann (1st Captain), Wayne Pygram (Kearney), John Dicks (Penfield), Gus Mercurio (1st Mate), John Turnbull (Dawes), Todd Rippon (Gullion), John Keightley (LeStrange), Pita Degei (Chief), Mikaele Nasau (Lone Cannibal), Annabel E. Graham (Baby)

MAGDALENA VIRAGA (AFI USA) Producer/Director/Screenplay/ Editor/Photography, Nina Menkes; Music, Grupo Travieso; a Menkes Film production; Color; Not rated; 90 minutes; August release. CAST: Trinka Menkes (Ida), Claire Aguilar (Claire), Victor Flores, Paul Shuler, Nora Bendrich

PRAYER OF THE ROLLER BOYS (Castle Hill) Producer, Robert Mickelson; Executive Producers, Tetsu Fujimura, Martin F. Gold, Richard Lorber, Robert Baruc; Director, Rick King; Screenplay, W. Peter Iliff; Photography, Phedon Papamichael; Designer, Thomas A. Walsh; Music, Stacey Widelitz; Editor, Daniel Loewenthal; Executive in Charge of Production, Trisha Robinson; Stunts, Dan Bradley; Costumes, Merrily Murray-Walsh; Skating Coordinator, Ken Schneider; a Gaga Communications, Fox/Lorber and Academy Entertainment in association with JVC and TV Tokyo presentation; Ultra-Stereo; Foto-Kem color; Rated R; 94 minutes; August release. CAST: Corey Haim (Griffin), Patricia Arquette (Casey), Christopher Collet (Gary Lee), J.C. Quinn (Jaworski), Julius Harris (Speedbagger), Devin Clark (Miltie), Mark Pellegrino (Bango), Morgan Weisser (Bullwinkle), G. Smokey Campbell (Watt), Jake Dengel (Tyler), John P. Connolly (Pinky), Stanley Yale (Grizzled Man), Loren Lester (Anchorman), Tim Eyster (Little Boy), James Patrick (Rollerboy Guard), Cynthia Gatees (Prostitute), Dal Trader (Sargeant), Aron Eisenberg (Teen Boy), Chad Taylor (Partygoer), Bob Wills, Jr. (Old Fisherman), Rodney Kageyama (Mr. Naboru)

Brandon Lee, Dolph Lundgren in
Showdown in Little Tokyo
© Warner Bros. Inc.

Christopher Collet (c) in
Prayer of the Rollerboys
© Castle Hill

165

Martin Lawrence, Jedda Jones in
Talkin' Dirty After Dark
© *New Line Cinema*

Calypso Rose in *One Hand Don't Clap*
© *Riverfilms Prods.*

TALKIN' DIRTY AFTER DARK (New Line Cinema) Producer, Patricia Stallone; Director/Screenplay, Topper Carew; Photography, Misha Suslov; Designer, Dan Whifler; Editor, Julie Franklin; Costumes, Vincent Zarlengo; Casting, Daniel Edwardo Espinosa; Color; Rated R; 86 minutes; August release. CAST: Martin Lawrence (Terry), John Witherspoon (Dukie), Jedda Jones (Rubie Lin), "Tiny" Lister, Jr. (Bigg), Phyllis Stickney (Aretha), Darryl Sivad (Percy), Yolanda King (Mother), Lewis Jackson III, Gregory Le Flore (Boys), Betty Carvalho (Old Woman), Ken Davitian (Seat Mate), Marvin Wright-Bey (Jackie), Cici Lau (Chinese Waitress), Myra J. (Woman #1), Homeselle Joy (Dorothy), Rasheryl McCreary, Inez Edwards (Fans), Dwayne Kennedy (Roach), Mark Curry (Antonio), Vanessa Hampton, Robin Montague (Bad Girls), Renee Jones (Kimmie), Toukie A. Smith (Josephine), Simply Marvelous (Waitress), Nacho (Cabbie), Lance Crouther (Kwame), Rodney Winfield (Rudy Rae, the Cook), Rory Flynn (Busby), Nhan D. Doung (Korean), Barry Diamond (White Man), Charles Cozart, Rocco Turso (Guys), Fats Williams (Barry White Type), Joe Torry (Person #1), James Stevens III (Person #2), Carlos Lacamara (Hispanic Worker), La Wanda Page (Black Angel/Black Devil), Def Jef (Announcer)

BLOWBACK (Northern Arts Entertainment) Producer/Director/Screenplay, Marc Levin; Co-Producer, Paul Marcus; Editor, Tim Squyres; Photography, Mark Benjamin; Designer, Kosmo Vinyl; Music, Wendy Blackstone; from Blowback productions; Color; Not rated; 94 minutes; August release. CAST: Bruce McCarty (Owen Monroe), Jane Hamper (Nancy Jones), Eddie Figueroa (Emilio De Leon), Craig Smith (Dr. Krack), Matt Mitler (Paul), Don Cairns (Dick Jones), Leslie Levinson (Counselor), Richard Raphael (General Blanco), Theodora Castellanos (Marita), Bob Holman (Dr. Hoover), Carlos Lauchu (Pao), James Worthington (Kevin), Erika Bogren (Cin), Pam Haylock (Dancer Lisa), Sandra Hanbury (Dancer Tina), Ericka Peterson (Dancer Eva), Robert Fontaine (Carlos), Joshua Nelson (Jorge), Charles Bludsworth (Terrorist), Edward Daly (Dulles), Joseph Ambrose (Hughes), Henry Alan Mason (Anslinger), Michael Rubenstein (Bartender), Frankie Waters (Lics Dealer), Renee Lerner (Computer Voice), Allison Daniels (Programming Voice), William Ingersoll (Radio Announcer), Gergory Zilborg (The Director)

FEMME FATALE (AFI USA/Republic Pictures) Producers, Andrew Lane, Nancy Rae Stone; Executive Producer, Joel Levine; Director, André Guttfreund; Screenplay, Michael Ferris, John D. Brancato; Photography, Joey Forsyte; Music, Parmer Fuller; Editor, Richard Candib; Designer, Pam Warner; a Gibraltar Entertainment production; Foto-Kem color; Rated R; 96 minutes; August release. CAST: Colin Firth (Joe Prince), Lisa Zane (Elizabeth/Cynthia/Maura), Billy Zane (Elijah), Scott Wilson (Dr. Beaumont), Lisa Blount (Jenny), Suzanne Snyder (Andrea), Pat Skipper (Ted), John Laviachielli (Ed), Carmine Caridi (Dino)

ONE HAND DON'T CLAP (Rhapsody Films) Producers, Kavery Dutta, Bhupender Kaul; Director/Editor, Kavery Dutta; Photography, Don Lenzer, Alicia Weber; a Riverfilms production; DuArt color; Not rated; 92 minutes; August release. CAST: Lord Kitchener, Calypso Rose, Black Stalin, David Rudder, Mighty Duke, Natasha Wilson, Lord Pretender, Growling Tiger

BLOOD MASSACRE (Applause Productions, Inc.) Producers, Barry Gold, Dan Buehl, Don Dohler; Associate Producer, Dann Linck; Director, Don Dohler; Screenplay, Barry Gold, Dan Buehl, Don Dohler; Photography, Chris Chrysler, Jeff Herberger; Additional Photography, Don Dohler; Editor, Don Dohler; Music, Dann Linck, Jon Christopher; Assistant Directors, Dan Buehl, Barry Gold; Makeup Effects, John Cosentino, Larry Schlechter; Pyrotechnic Effects, Philip E. Lister; a Gateway Entertainment Production in association with Pacific Horizon Entertainment; Color; Not rated; 85 minutes; August release. CAST: George Stover (Rizzo), Robin London (Liz Parker), James DiAngelo (Jimmy), Thomas Humes (Pauly), Lisa Defuso (Monica), Richard Ruxton (Howard Parker), Grace Stahl (Chrissy), Anne Frith (Frances), Lucille Jolle (Bonnie), Herb Otter, Jr. (Detective McGuire), Lucie Poirier (Bar dancer), Ted Hakim (Vinnie), Barry Gold (Truck driver), Karl Otter (2nd Cop), Gerard Vanik (Mr. Winston), Mary Ann Pence (Waitress), Theresa Crain (2nd Renter), Mary McFaul, Don Leifert (Video Clerks)

BLOOD & CONCRETE (I.R.S. Releasing) Producer, Richard LaBrie; Executive Producers, Miles A. Copeland III, Paul Colichman, Harold Welb; Director, Jeffrey Reiner; Screenplay/Editors, Richard LaBrie, Jeffrey Reiner; Photography, Declan Quinn; Designer, Pamela Woodbridge; Music, Vinny Golia; Line Producer, Michael Bennett; Costumes, Jan Rowton; Casting, Don Pemrick; Color; Rated R; 98 minutes; September release. CAST: Billy Zane (Joey Turks), Jennifer Beals (Mona), Darren McGavin (Hank Dick), James Le Gros (Lance), Mark Pellegrino (Bart), Nicholas Worth (Spuntz), Harry Shearer (Sammy Rhodes), Steve Freedman (Lounge Lizard), William Bastiani (Mort), Pat Cupo (Stone), Pat O'Bryan (Barton), Tracy Coley (Ack), Ellen Albertini Dow (Old Lady), Lyvingston Holmes (Thelma)

DEAD MEN DON'T DIE (Trans Atlantic Pictures) Producer, Wayne Marmorstein; Director/Screenplay, Malcolm Marmorstein; Associate Producers, Hubie Kerns, Stan Forster; Photography, Tom Fraser; Designers, Phillip Vasels, Diane Hughes; Editor, Michael Ornstein; Music, David Williams; Costumes, Darragh Marmorstein; Casting, Joe Reich & Friends; from Waymar Productions; Color; Rated PG-13; 84 minutes; September release. CAST: Elliott Gould (Barry Barron), Melissa Anderson (Dulcie Niles), Mark Moses (Jordan Penrose), Mabel King (Chafuka), Philip Bruns (Nolan), Jack Betts (Cavanaugh), Robert Dryer (Mungo), Robert Covarrubias

Bruce McCarty, Jane Hamper in
Blowback
© *Northern Arts*

Billy Zane, Jennifer Beals in *Blood & Concrete*
© I.R.S. Media

Michael Biehn, Patsy Kensit in *Timebomb*
© MGM-Pathe

(Carlos), Phil Shipko (Frank), Jerome Guardino (Neal Taggart), Stanley Kamel (Archie), Andee Gray (Isadora), Eric Lawrence (Floor Manager), Judy Kain (Margo), Charlie Brill (Director), John Mengatti (Officer Ramirez), Walt Jordan, Richard Johnson (Policemen), George "Buck" Flower (Wino), Phillip Vasels (Broadcast Engineer), Patrick Phinney (Announcer)

THE DREAM MACHINE (Intl. Creative Exchange) Producer/Director, Lyman Dayton; Executive Producers, James L. Sorenson, Eric Epperson; Screenplay, Eric Hendershot; Photography, T.C. Christenson; Designer, Michael C. Ayers; Music, Lex de Azevedo; Editor, Steve Johnson; Stunts - 2nd Unit Director, Doug Coleman; Co-Producers, Michael Wuergler, Fenton Terry, Michael C. Ayers; a DM Ltd. Partnership presentation; Ultra-Stereo; Hawk color; Rated PG; 86 minutes; September release. CAST: Corey Haim (Barry Davis), Evan Richards (Brent Meese), Jeremy Slate (Jack Chamberlain), Randall England (Lance), Tracy Fraim (Royal Clayton III), Brittney Lewis (Robin), Susan Seaforth Hayes (Margo), James MacKrell, Suzanne Kent, Brynja McGrady

PRIME TARGET (Borde/Hero Films) Producer/Director/ Screenplay, David Heavener; Executive Producer, Gerald Milton; Photography, Peter Wolf; Editors, Christopher Roth, Charles Coleman; Music, Robert Garrett; Designer, Peter Gum; Color; Rated R; 84 minutes; September release. CAST: David Heavener (John Bloodstone), Tony Curtis (Marrietta Coppella), Isaac Hayes (Capt. Thompkins), Robert Reed (Agent Harrington), Andrew Robinson (Commissioner), Jenilee Harrison (Kathy Bloodstone), Michael Gregory (Agent Robbins), Don Stroud (Manny)

TIMEBOMB (MGM) Producer, Raffaella De Laurentiis; Co-Producer, Mike Petzold; Director/Screenplay, Avi Nesher; Photography, Anthony B. Richmond; Music, Patrick Leonard; Costumes, Jill Ohanneson; Editor, Isaac Sehayek; Casting, Craig Campobasso; a Raffaella production; Dolby Stereo; Color; Rated R; 96 minutes; September release. CAST: Michael Biehn (Eddy Kay), Patsy Kensit (Dr. Nolmar), Robert Culp (Mr. Phillips), Tracy Scoggins (Ms. Blue), Richard Jordan (Col. Taylor), Raymond St. Jacques (Detective Sanchez), Billy Blanks (Mr. Brown), Ray "Boom Boom" Mancini (Mr. Black), Carlos Palomino (Mr. Green)

FREDDY'S DEAD: THE FINAL NIGHTMARE (New Line Cinema) Producers, Robert Shaye, Aron Warner; Executive Producer/Screenplay, Michael DeLuca; Director/Story, Rachel Talalay; Based on characters created by Wes Craven; Photography, Declan Quinn; Designer, C.J. Strawn; Editor, Janice Hampton; Associate Producer, Michael Knue; Music, Brian May; Casting, Jane Jenkins, Janet Hirshenson, Roger Mussenden; Costumes, Nanrose Buchman; Freddy Krueger's Makeup Designer, David B. Miller; Special Makeup Effects, Magical Media Industries, Inc.; 3-D Supervision/Special Visual Effects, The Chandler Group; Special Visual Effects, Dream Quest Images; Dolby Stereo; Color; Rated R; 96 minutes; September release. CAST: Robert Englund (Freddy Krueger), Lisa Zane (Maggie), Shon Greenblatt (John), Lezlie Deane (Tracy), Ricky Dean Logan (Carlos), Breckin Meyer (Spencer), Yaphet Kotto (Doc), Tom Arnold, Roseanne Arnold (Childless Couple), Elinor Donahue (Orphanage Woman), Oprah Noodlemantra (Teen on TV), Cassandra Rachel Friel (Little Maggie), David Dunard (Kelly), Marilyn Rockafellow (Maggie's Mother), Virginia Peters (Woman on plane), Stella Hall (Stewardess), Lyndsey Fields (Loretta Krueger), Angelina Estrada (Carlos' Mother), Peter Spellos (Tracy's Father), Tobe Sexton (Teen Freddy), Chason Schirmer (Young Freddy), Michael McNab (Spencer's Father), Matthew Faison (Springwood Teacher), Vic Watterson, Carlease Burke (Officers), L.E. Moko (Ticket Seller), Warren Harrington (Cop in shelter), Mel Scott-Thomas (Security Guard), Jonathan Mazer (Angry Boy), Alice Cooper (Freddy's Father), Johnny Depp (Public Service Announcer)

A MATTER OF DEGREES (Fox/Lorber) Producers, Randall Poster, Roy Kissin; Co-Producer, Lynn Goldner; Director, W.T. Morgan; Screenplay, Randall Poster, Jack Mason, W.T. Morgan; Photography, Paul Ryan; Designer, Mark Friedberg; Music, Jim Dunbar; Editors, Curtiss Clayton, Charlie Mullin; a Backbeat production produced in association with New Front Films and Fujisankei Communications; Color; Not rated; 88 minutes; September release. CAST: Arye Gross (Maxwell Glass), Judith Hoag (Kate Blum), Tom Sizemore (Zeno), Christina Haag (Isabella Allen), Wendell Pierce (Wells), John Doe (Peter Downs), Fred Schneider, Kate Pierson, John Kennedy Jr.

Elliott Gould, Melissa Anderson in *Dead Men Don't Die*
© Waymar Prods.

Lisa Zane, Robert Englund in
Freddy's Dead
© New Line Cinema

Lisa Arrindell, T.C. Carson, Nathaniel "Afrika" Hall in
Livin' Large
© *Samuel Goldwyn Co.*

Christopher Dienstag in *The Money Tree*
© *Hollywood Furb*

KING JAMES VERSION (First Run Features) Producers, Robert Gardner, Joseph E. Taylor; Director, Robert Gardner; Screenplay, Judy Simmons, Renee Roper, Robert Gardner; Photography, Judy Irola; Editor, Jonathan Weld; Music, Wendy Blackstone; a co-presentation of Vitascope, Inc.; Color; Not rated; 91 minutes; September release. CAST: Christina Braggs (Rachel), Joan Pryor (Esther Pearl), Ellwoodson Williams (Jesse), Louise Mike (Grandmother), Lee Roy Giles (Rev. Swan), Neal Harris, Eddie Owens

LIVIN' LARGE (Samuel Golwyn Co.) formerly *The Tapes of Dexter Jackson*; Producer, David V. Picker; Director, Michael Schultz; Screenplay, William M. Payne; Photography, Peter Collister; Editor, Christopher Holmes; Music, Herbie Hancock; Costumes, John Dunn; Art Director, Angie Riserbato; Assistant Director, Victoria E. Rhodes; a David V. Picker/WMG Pictures production; Dolby Stereo; Crest color; Rated R; 96 minutes; September release. CAST: Terrence "T.C." Carson (Dexter Jackson), Lisa Arrindell (Toynelle Davis), Blanche Baker (Kate Penndragin), Nathaniel "Afrika" Hall (Baker Moon), Julia Campbell (Missy Carnes), Bernie McInerney (Clifford Worthy), Loretta Devine (Nadine Biggs), Dan Albright (Martin), Ronald J. Knight (Roger), Randal Patrick (Jimmy), David De Vries (Stage Manager), Dan Chandler (Control Room Director), Joe Washington (Charles Hempstead), Wallace Wilkinson (Rev. Carnes), Suzanne Stewart (Mrs. Carnes), Tonea Stewart (Mrs. Davis), Eloise Whitman (Anna Mae), David Dwyer (Police Sergeant), Ted Henning (Fabian Marks), Jeff Folger (Station Announcer), Gerald Brown (Bubba Knuckles), Harrison Avery (Otis), Tony Franciscus (Four Fingers Felix), George Allen (Old Man), Arlena Starr (Blind Lady), Shilla Benning (Dancing Lady), Lonnie R. Smith, Jr., John Burton, Jr. (Policemen), Eddie Billups (Patient), Ray McKinnon (Harmon)

McBAIN (Shapiro Glickenhaus) Producer, J. Boyce Harman, Jr.; Director/Screenplay, James Glickenhaus; Executive Producers, Leonard Shapiro, Alan Solomon; Associate Producer, Gerrit Van Der Meer; Photography, Robert M. Baldwin, Jr.; Designer, Charles C. Bennett; Music, Christopher Franke; Casting, Donna DeSeta; Visual Effects Supervisor, Joel Hynek; Dolby Stereo; TVC Precision color; Rated R; 102 minutes; September release. CAST: Christopher Walken (Bobby McBain), Maria Conchita Alonso (Christina Santos), Michael Ironside (Frank Bruce), Steve James (Eastland), Jay Patterson (Dr. Dalton), T.G. Waites (Gill), Victor Argo (El Presidente), Hechter Ubarry (Simon Escobar), Russell Dennis Baker (Pilot Daly), Chick Vennera (Santos), Michael Joseph De Sare (Major Tenny), Cristito "Kris" Aquilar (Sing Lau), Protacio "Tony" Dee (General Ho), Craig Walter Judd (Screaming P.O.W.), David Tamayo Pegram (Armodo), Jedd Magalaso, Dinah Dominguez (Rebel Hookers), Joel Torre (Chauffeur), Luv Adele Gaerlan (Wounded Girl), Zenaida Amador (Teresa), John Derek Gaerlan (Hugo), Tony Tacorda (Palace Guard), "Big Boy" Gomez (Fat Soldier), Mary Walter (Old Woman), Maggie De La Riva (Presidente's Secretary), Andy Gill (Secret Service Agent), James Glickenhaus (Cigarette Boat Driver), Forrest Compton (President Flynn), Mark Hammer (Wilbur James), Robert Halberg (General Epper), Richard M. Royer (Marshall Smith), Raoul Aragon (Vargas), Susan Africa (Young Mother), Dominic Marcus (Construction Worker), Helen McNeely, Glenn Kubota (Angry Shareholders), Mel Davidson (Moderator), Joe Basso (Mr. Barton), Constance Shulman (Dr. Blazier), Fern Dorsey (Dr. Elliott), Juanita Fleming (Nurse Simpson), Greg Gault (Crazed Shareholder), Sylvia O'Brien (Bruce's Assist.), Luis Guzman (Papo), Karen Duffy (Crack Den Girl), Dick Boccelli (John Gambotti), Jerry Bailey (Conception), Tom Taus (King), J. Marsh Thomson (Mr. Rich), Bobbie Greenwood (Ms. Bates), Nigel Redding (Hans), Roy Alvarez (Head Federale), Mervyn Samson (Old Man at cantina), Tito Tesoro (Security Guard), Scott Williams (Television Technician)

THE MONEY TREE (Black Sheep Films) Producer, Christopher Dienstag; Director, Alan Dienstag; Dialogue improvised from a story by Alan and Christopher Dienstag; Photography, Don Bonato; Music, Lorin Rowan; Editor, Susan Crutcher; Color; Not rated; 94 minutes; September release. CAST: Christopher Dienstag (David), Monica T. Caldwell (Erica), Nik Martin (Chad), Kathrine Schutzman (Girlfriend), Malcolm Cohen (Vincent), Richard Roughgarden (Charly), Carlos Deloche (Pasquel), Gregory Wilker (Rusty)

PRESENT MEMORY (AFI USA) Producer, Richard Adelman; Director/Editor, Richard Broadman; Photography, John Bishop; Music, Bruno Destrez, Jimmy Giuffre; a Cine Research presentation of a Full Moon production; Color/Black and white; Not rated; 88 minutes; October release. Documentary

Maria Conchita Alonso, Christopher Walken, Michael Ironside in *McBain*
© *SGE Entertainment*

Burtt Harris, Peter Dobson in *Undertow*
© *Capstone*

The Rolling Stones in *At the Max*
© *Imax Corp.*

Harley Cross in *The Boy Who Cried Bitch*
© *Pilgrims 3 Corp.*

TO DIE FOR II: SON OF DARKNESS (Trimark) Producer, Richard Weinman; Executive Producers, Lee Caplin, Greg H. Sims; Director, David F. Price; Screenplay, Leslie King; Photography, Gerry Lively; Music, Mark McKenzie; Editor, Barry Zetlin; an Arrowhead-Lee Caplin production; Ultra-Stereo; Color; Rated R; 96 minutes; September release. CAST: Rosalind Allen (Nina), Steve Bond (Tom), Scott Jacoby (Martin), Michael Praed (Max Schreck/Vlad Tepish), Jay Underwood (Danny), Amanda Wyss (Celia), Remy O'Neill (Jane)

UNDERTOW (Capstone Films) Producers, Burtt Harris, Thomas Mazziotti; Director/Screenplay, Thomas Mazziotti; Based on the play *Raw Youth* by Neal Beal; Photography, Kevin Lombard; Editor, John Carter; Designer, Michael Moran; Costumes, Ticia Blackburn; Technicolor; Not rated; 95 minutes; September release. CAST: Peter Dobson (Sam), Burtt Harris (Mel), Erica Gimpel (Nina), Anita Gillette (Marlene), Greg Mullavey (William Gary), Tom Mazziotti (Hustler)

AT THE MAX (BLC Group/Imax Corp.) Executive Producers, Michael Cohl, Andre Picard; Creative Consultant/Location Director, Julien Temple; Video Director, Christine Strand; Concept, Michael Cohl; Photography, David Douglas, Andrew Kitzanuk; Camera Consultant, Haskell Wexler; Editor, Daniel W. Blevins; Presented in association with Promotour U.S. Inc.; Color; Not rated; 89 minutes; October release. CAST: Mick Jagger, Keith Richards, Charlie Watts, Ron Wood, Bill Wyman (The Rolling Stones), and Chuck Leavell, Matt Clifford (Keyboards), Bobby Keys (Saxophone), Crispin Cioe, Arno Hecht, Hollywood Paul Litteral, Bob Funk (The Uptown Horns), Bernard Fowler, Lorelei McBroom, Sophia Jones (Vocals)

BORN TO SKI (Warren Miller Entertainment) Producers, Kurt Miller, Peter Speek; Director, Don Brolin; Screenplay/Narrator, Warren Miller; Photography, Bill Heath, Gary Nate, Brian Sisselman; Music, Ronnie Montrose; Editors, Katie Hedrick, Kim Schneider; Color; Not rated; 101 minutes; October release. Documentary

THE BOY WHO CRIED BITCH (Pilgrims 3 Corp.) Producer, Louis Tancredi; Executive Producer/Screenplay, Catherine May Levin; Director, Juan Jose Campanella; Photography, Daniel Shulman; Editor, Darren Kloomok; Music, Wendy Blackstone; Designer, Nancy Deren; Costumes, Claudia Brown; Casting, Deborah Aquila, Alison Zimet; DuArt color; Not rated; 105 minutes; October release. CAST: Harley Cross (Dan Love), Karen Young (Candice Love), Jesse Bradford (Mike Love), J.D. Daniels (Nick Love), Gene Canfield (Jim Cutler), Moira Kelly (Jessica), Adrien Brody (Eddie), Dennis Boutsikaris (Orin Fell), Reathel Bean (Dr. Goldstein), John Rothman (Stokes), Samuel Wright (Richard), Perry Moore (William), Sean Ashby (Gene), Edwina Lewis (Ann Marie, R.N.), Ken Eaton (Teacher), Christopher L. McKenna (Ross), Michael Miceli (Chet), Judd Trichter (Jay), Sally Kaye Kaufman (Fern), Les Shenkel (Eddie's Father), Ru Flynn (Ruth Nussbaum), Jody O'Neil (Croissant Kid), Jason Biggs (Robert), Bruce McCarty (Gary), Ron Lee Savin, Cam McGinnis (Homeless Men), Kario Salem (Dr. Habib)

SUBURBAN COMMANDO (New Line Cinema) Producer, Howard Gottfried; Director, Burt Kennedy; Screenplay, Frank Cappello; Executive Producers, Hulk Hogan, Kevin Moreton, Deborah Moore; Photography, Bernd Heinl; Designer, Ivo Cristante; Costumes, Ha Nguyen; Editor, Terry Stokes; Music, David Michael Frank; Visual Effects, Jeff Okun; Casting, Fern Champion, Dori Zuckerman; Dolby Stereo; Deluxe color; Rated PG; 85 minutes; October release. CAST: Hulk Hogan (Shep Ramsey), Christopher Lloyd (Charlie Wilcox), Shelley Duvall (Jenny Wilcox), Larry Miller (Adrian Beltz), William Ball (General Suitor), JoAnn Dearing (Margie Tanen), Jack Elam (Col. Dustin "Dusty" McHowell), Roy Dotrice (Zanuck), Michael Faustino (Mark Wilcox), Tony Longo (Knuckles), Mark Calaway (Hutch), Laura Mooney (Theresa Wilcox), Dennis Burkley (Deak), Luis Contreras (Ringo), Nick Eldredge (President Hashina), Vincent Hammond (Mutant Suitor), Denice Kumagai (Kim), Duane Taniguchi (Yamakawa), Richard Narita (Zukaki), Christopher Neame (Commander), Tony Epper (Teeth), John Furlong (Official), Marcy Goldman (Lady), Jennifer DeLoria (Girl), Ellis Edwards, Keith Campbell (Punks), Michael Ballew, Dave Efron (Car Fanatics), Marc Miles (Mailman), Will Miles (Paperboy), Elisabeth Moss (Little Girl), Malachi Pearson (Eric), Joey Simmrin (Kid), Skip Stellrecht (Soldier), Sumant (Store Owner), Tom Morga (Mime), Louan Gideon (Woman at vending machine), Sparkle (Woman at fruit stand), Billy "Sly" Williams (Bystander), Pat Millicano (Man with dog)

Tom Bowers in *Born to Ski*
© *Grafton Smith*

Christopher Lloyd, Hulk Hogan in
Suburban Commando
© *New Line Cinema*

D.B. Sweeney , Bo Kimble in *Heaven is a Playground*
© New Line Cinema

Matt Frewer, Ken Wahl in *The Taking of Beverly Hills*
© Columbia Pictures

HEAVEN IS A PLAYGROUND (New Line Cinema) Producers, Keith Bank, Billy Higgins; Co-Producers, John Banta, Tony Kamin; Executive Producers, William Stuart, Doug Cook, Larry Edwards; Co-Executive Producers, William Eichengreen, Leonard Pomerantz; Director/Screenplay, Randall Fried; Based upon the book by Rick Telander; Photography, Tom Richmond; Designer, Gregory Wm. Bolton; Editor, Lou Angelo; Music, Patrick O'Hearn; Casting, Jane Alderman, Susan Weider; Story Development/Narration, Rick Telander; a Heaven Corp. presentation in association with Aurora Prods.; Color; Rated R; 111 minutes; October release. CAST: D.B. Sweeney (Zach Telander), Michael Warren (Byron Harper), Richard Jordan (David Racine), Victor Love (Truth Harrison), Janet Julian (Dalton Ellis), Bo Kimble (Matthew Lockhart), Nigel Miguel (Casey Caldwell), Cylk Cozart (Andre), Terry Bradley (Herc), Don James (Cecil), Stavon Lovell Davis (Gus), Hakeem Olajuwon (Luther Hakim), Tom Abbott, Gerald Bogni, Maurice Culpepper, Walter Dejean, Kendall Gill, Ed Hall, Anthony Hall, Montel Hatcher, Curtis Jackson, Derrick Jones, Gerald Jones, Wayne King Jr., John McQueen, Anthony Patty, Keith Sanders, Burtrell Selph, Keith Smith, Kevin Stewart, Kirk Wilson (The Breds), Adrian Byrd (Jesse James), David Pasquesi (Hospital Clerk), Razz Jenkins (Doctor), Juretha Lawson (Janet Harper), Joshuette Gardner (Lawanda), Lataunya Bounds (Adoring Girl), Mike Skewes (Sgt. O'Braun), Magic Slim & The Teardrops, Paul Petraitis, Marty Salzman (Blues Band), Rick Telander (Bartender), Larry Levy (Maitre D'), Tim Hopper (Coach Beverly), Marvin Bank (Coach #1), Ed Wheeler (Otis Winston)

THE HITMAN (Cannon) Producer, Don Carmody; Director, Aaron Norris; Screenplay, Robert Geoffrion, Don Carmody; Photography, Joao Fernandes; Designer, Douglas Higgins; Editor, Jacqueline Carmody; Casting, Stuart Aikens; Music, Joel Derouin; Dolby Stereo; Color; Rated R; 95 minutes; October release. CAST: Chuck Norris (Cliff Garret/Danny Grogan), Michael Parks (Ronny "Del" Delaney), Al Waxman (Marco Luganni), Alberta Watson (Christine De Vera), Salim Grant (Tim Murphy), Ken Pogue (Chambers), Marcel Sabourin (Andre Lacombe), Bruno Gerussi (Nino), Frank Ferrucci (Shabad), James Purcell (Sal), Candus Churchill (Kate), Alan Peterson (Lemke), Paris Mileos (Scolari), Alex Bruhanski (Scarlini), Stephen Dimopoulos (Galione), Anthony Stambouliem (Rigoletti), Michael B.

Enyaer (Hassan), Gerry Bean (Fierro), Nathan Vanering (Nantel), Alex Diakun (Armone), Michelle Goodger (Corrine), Michael Rogers (Sully), Jon Cuthbert (Joe), Rebecca Norris (Waitress), William Davis (Dr. Atkins), Henry Holmes (Chief Surgeon), Fred Henderson (E.R. Doctor), Sylvian Demers, Sue Mathew (Attendants), Beau Heaton (Bo Lemke), Amanda Norris, Meagan Norris (Lacombe Children)

THE TAKING OF BEVERLY HILLS (Columbia) Producer, Graham Henderson; Executive Producers, Barry Spikings, Rick Finkelstein; Director, Sidney J. Furie; Screenplay, Rick Natkin, David Fuller, David J. Burke; Story, Sidney J. Furie, Rick Natkin, David Fuller; Photography, Frank Johnson; Designer, Peter Lamont; Editor, Antony Gibbs; Costumes, Betsy Cox; Music, Jan Hammer; Casting, Nina Axelrod; Special Effects, Thomas L. Fisher, George Erschbamer; a Nelson Entertainment presentation; Dolby Stereo; Panavision; Deluxe color; Rated R; 96 minutes; October release. CAST: Ken Wahl (Terry "Boomer" Hayes), Matt Frewer (Ed Kelvin), Harley Jane Kozak (Laura Sage), Robert Davi (Robert "Bat" Masterson), Lee Ving James (Oliver Varney), Branscombe Richmond (Benitez), Lyman Ward (Chief Healy), Michael Bowen (L.A. Cop at roadblock), William Prince (Mitchell Sage), Michael Kehoe, Mark Haining, Jason Blicker (Cops/Thieves), Tony Ganios (EPA Man), Ken Swofford (Coach), Raymond Singer (Mr. Tobeason), Richard Brestoff, Artur Cybulski (Executives), Michael Alldredge (Dispatch Sergeant), Jeff Benson, Bob Golic, Pete Koch (Football Players), Pamela Anderson, Debra Goodman (Cheerleaders), William John Murphy (Bellman), Henry Watson (B.H. Cop at roadblock), George Wyner (Mayor of Beverly Hills), Tess Foltyn, Stefan Karlsson, Jack Ritschel, Tina Skeisvoll, Robyn Suzanne Scott, Lonnie Shaw-Foxworth, Matt Stetson, Robyn Summers, Scott Wells (Party Guests)

RESIDENT ALIEN (Greycat Films) Producer/Director/Screenplay/Editor, Jonathan Nossiter; Co-Producer, Dean Silvers; Photography, John R. Foster; Line Producer, Stephen J. Ross; a Crisp City Productions presentation; DuArt color; Not rated; 85 minutes; October release. Documentary with Quentin Crisp (Himself), Peter Walker (The Bum), Gilbert Stafford (Man on street), Gus Rogerson (Man), Michaela Murphy (Street Performers), Felicity Mason (Dinner Hostess and Writer), Fran Lebowitz (Writer), Guy Kettelhack (Writer, Former Crisp Agent), John Hurt (Actor), Richard Seiburth

Chuck Norris, Salim Grant in
The Hitman
© Cannon

John Hurt, Quentin Crisp in *Resident Alien*
© Filmcat Inc.

Kristin Minter, Vanilla Ice in *Cool as Ice*
© *Universal City Studios*

Jim Varney, Eartha Kitt in *Ernest Scared Stupid*
© *Buena Vista Pictures*

(Professor), Hunter Madsen (Writer), Sting (Singer), Michael Musto (Gossip Columnist), Sally Jessy Raphael (Talk Show Host), Shi Ringer (Gay Activist), Tom Steele (Publisher), Al Goldstein (Pornographer), Inga (Transvestite Prostitute), Lenny Dean (Cabaret Performer), Robert Patrick (Playwright), Penny Arcade (Performance Artist), Patrick Angus, David McDermott, Peter McGough, Franco the Great (Painters), Paul Bridgewater (Gallery Owner), Orshi Drozdick (Sculptor), Emile de Antonio (Filmmaker), Trey Spiegel (Painters' Friend), Holly Woodlawn (Performer/Actor)

COOL AS ICE (Universal) Producers, Carolyn Pfeiffer, Lionel Wigram; Executive Producers, Charles Koppelman, Martin Bandier, Shep Gordon; Director, David Kellogg; Screenplay, David Stenn; Line Producer, Ted Adams Swanson; Photography, Janusz Kaminski; Designer, Nina Ruscio; Editors, Debra Goldfield, Caroline Biggerstaff; Costumes, Ingrid Ferrin; Music, Stanley Clarke; Casting, Johanna Ray, Donna Jacobson; Music Supervisor, Pete Ganbarg; Choreographer, John "Hi Teck" Huffman IV; a Koppelman/Bandier - Carnegie Pictures production in association with Alive Films; Dolby Stereo; Deluxe color; Rated PG; 93 minutes; October release. CAST: Vanilla Ice (Johnny Van Owen), Kristin Minter (Kathy Winslow), Michael Gross (Gordon Winslow), Sydney Lassick (Roscoe McCallister), Dody Goodman (Mae McCallister), Naomi Campbell (Singer at 1st Club), Candy Clark (Grace Winslow), S.A. Griffin (Morrisey), Jack McGee (Clarke), John Haymes Newton (Nick), Victor DiMattia (Tommy Winslow), Allison Dean (Princess), Kevin Hicks (Sir D), D. Thompson (Jazz), Bobby Brown (Monique), Kathy Morris (Jen), Amy Tenowich (Lisa), Portia Dawson (Tracy), Ted Swanson (Bartender), Louie Bonanno (Bandleader), Crawford Binion (Officer), Brooke Alexander (Reporter), Tracey Bass (Singer at final club), John "Hi Teck" Huffman IV, Marc "Juice" Grinage, Adam "Twist" Pretty, Steven "Boom" Williams (VIP Posse)

ERNEST SCARED STUPID (Touchstone) Producer, Stacy Williams; Co-Producer, Coke Sams; Executive Producer, Martin Erlichman; Director, John Cherry; Screenplay, Charlie Gale, Coke Sams; Story, John Cherry, Coke Sams; Photography, Hanania Baer; Designer, Chris August; Editor, Craig Bassett; Costumes, Shawn Barry; Music, Bruce Arntson, Kirby Shelstad; Casting, Ruth Lambert; Creature Effects, Chiodo Brothers Prods. Inc.; Assistant Director, Patrice Leung; Presented in association with Touchwood Pacific Partners I; Distributed by Buena Vista Pictures; Dolby Stereo; Technicolor; Rated PG; 91 minutes; October release. CAST: Jim Varney (Ernest P. Worrell), Eartha Kitt (Old Lady Hackmore), Austin Nagler (Kenny), Shay Astar (Elizabeth), Jonas Moscartolo (Trantor), John Cadenhead (Tom Tulip), Bill Byrge (Bobby Tulip), Richard Woolf (Matt), Nick Victory (Mike), Alec Klapper (Joey), Steven Moriyon (Gregg), Daniel Butler (Cliff), Esther Huston (Amanda), Larry Black (Mayor Murdock), Denice Hicks (Elizabeth's Mother), Melanie Wheeler (Crying Woman), Jackie Welch (Teacher), Mark Delabarre (Jimmy), Michael Montgomery (Joey's Dad), Mary Jane Harvill (Mother), Lauren Frankenbach (Daughter), Roberta Madison (Parent), Barry Scott (Another Parent), Cathy Susan Pyles, Myke Mueller (Parents), Jessa Fahey (Little Girl), Mike Hutchinson (Steve Swindell), Adora Dupree (Francis's Mother), Joey Anderson (Ernest's Teacher), Dennis Harrison, Jr., Danielle Harrison (Children), Barkley (Rimshot), Ernst Fosselius (Voice of Trantor the Troll), Nellie Batson, Angela Chao, Renee Clary, Deidre Clower, Rhonda Clower, Ann Dresen, Misty Eaker, Ralph Green, Jr., Tammy Harrison, Dana Kennedy, Pamela Kippes, Renee Leblanc, Glenn Seer, Tawanya Smith, Todd Suttles, Douglas Zagorski (Trolls), Jody

Austin, Sabrina Birdine, Jodie Evans, Phyllis Fuller, Mellissa Gerach, Reginald Glimps, Jeanette Green, Marc Gullen, Will Hammond, Vicki Jacobs, John Phillips, Richard Sadler, Dan Sarenana, Gwendolyn Smith, Vanessa Smith, Bobby Storm, Ann Young (Parents), Daniel Higgs, Gregg Higgs, Karson Kanitz, Marin Miller, Luke Roberts (Kids Army)

SMALL TIME (Panorama) Director/Screenplay, Norman Loftis; Photography, Michael C. Miller; Music, Arnold Bieber; Editor, Marc Cohen; Black and white; Not rated; 88 minutes; November release. CAST: Richard Barboza (Vince Williams), Carolyn Kinebrew (Vicki), Scott Ferguson, Keith Allen, Jane Williams

HOUSE PARTY 2 (New Line Cinema) Producers/Directors, Doug McHenry, George Jackson; Executive Producer, Janet Grillo; Co-Producer, Suzanne Broderick; Screenplay, Rusty Cundieff, Daryl G. Nickens; Photography, Francis Kenny; Designer, Michelle Minch; Editor, Joel Goodman; Music, Vassal Benford; Costumes, Ruth E. Carter; Casting, Pat Golden, John McCabe; Executive Music Supervisor, Louil Silas, Jr.; Ultra-Stereo; Deluxe color; Rated R; 94 minutes; October release. CAST: Christopher Reid (Kid), Christopher Martin (Play), Martin Lawrence (Bilal), Tisha Campbell (Sidney), Brian George (Zilla), Lucien George (Pee-wee), Paul Anthony George (Stab), Queen Latifah (Zora), Iman (Sheila), Kamron (Jamal), Georg Stanford Brown (Prof. Sinclair), Helen Martin (Mrs. Deevers), D. Christopher Judge (Miles), Tony Burton (Mr. Lee), Louie Louie (Rick), William Schallert (Dean Kramer), Eugene Allen (Groove), George Anthony Bell (Rev. Simms), Alice Carter (Patty), Barry Diamond (Policeman), Mark "Wiz" Eastmond (Hoodly Brother), George Fisher (Janitor), Randy Harris (Hubert the Humping Man), Hazel Todd Lane (Buppie), Chance Langton (Prof. Vonault), Guy Margo (Brother #1), Amber McIntyre (Cutie), Christopher Michael (Cop #1), Daryl M. Mitchell (Chill), William S. Murray (Yuppie), Angela Nicholson (Salena), Anjul Nigam (Singih), Tony! Tony! Tone!, Ralph Tresvant, Whoopi Goldberg

LIFE IS NICE (AFI USA) Producer/Director/Screenplay, Forest Wise; Photography, Eric J. Swanson; Editor, Macieck Malish; Music, Jesse Loya; a Freakie Pig production; Black and white; Not rated; 96 minutes; October release. CAST: Forest Wise (Josh), Mike Dytry (Silo), Kia Collins (Clara)

Kamron, Christopher Reid in *House Party 2* **171**
© *New Line Cinema*

Sean Connery, Christopher Lambert in
Highlander 2
© *InterStar Releasing*

Louis Zorich, David Patrick Kelly in *Cheap Shots*
© *Twin Swan Film Assocs.*

DRIVING ME CRAZY (Motion Picture Corp. of America) a.k.a. *Trabbi Goes to Hollywood*; Producers, Brad Krevoy, Steven Stabler; Director, Jon Turtletaub; Screenplay, Jon Turtletaub, David Tausik, John London; Photography, Phedon Papamichael; Designer, Gary Randall; Stunts, Jeff Cadiente; Editor, Nancy Richardson; Color; Rated PG; 89 minutes; November release. CAST: Thomas Gottschalk (Gunter Schmidt), Billy Dee Williams (Max), Michelle Johnson (Ricki), James Tolkan (Vince), Steve Kanaly (Goodwyn), Milton Berle (Hotel Clerk), Dom DeLuise (Mr. B), George Kennedy (McCready), Celeste Yarnell (Volvo Boss), Aaron Heyman (Peugot Boss), Ken Shinkai (Honda Boss), Michael Adler (Ford Boss), Roger Siegal (Lee Iacocca)

HEARING VOICES (Phoenix International) Producer/Director/Screenplay, Sharon Greytak; Photography, Doron Schlair; Art Director, Chere Ledwith; Music, Wes York; Color; Not rated; 87 minutes; November release. CAST: Erika Nagy (Erika), Stephen Gatta (Lee), Tim Ahern (Michael Krieger), Michael Davenport (Carl)

HIGHLANDER 2: THE QUICKENING (InterStar) Producers, Peter S. Davis, William Panzer; Executive Producers, Guy Collins, Mario Sotela; Co-Producers, Alejandro Sessa, Robin Clark; Director, Russell Mulcahy; Screenplay, Peter Bellwood; Story, Brian Clemens, William Panzer; Based on characters created by Gregory Widen; Photography, Phil Meheux; Designer, Roger Hall; Editors, Hubert de la Bouillerie, Anthony Redman; Costumes, Deborah Everton; Music, Stewart Copeland; Casting, Fern Champion, Pamela Basker, Sue Swan; Line Producers, Jack Cummins, Chris Chrisafis; Special Effects, John Richardson; a Ziad El Khoury & Jean Luc Defait in association with Lamb Bear Entertainment presentation; Dolby Stereo; Cinemascope; Color; Rated R; 91 minutes; November release. CAST: Christopher Lambert (Connor MacLeod), Sean Connery (Juan Villa-Lobos Ramirez), Virginia Madsen (Louise Marcus), Michael Ironside (General Katana), John C. McGinley (Blake), Allan Rich (Alan Neyman), Eddie Trucco (Bartender), Peter Buccossi (Reno), Peter Antico (Trout), Phil Brock (Cabbie), Rusty Schwimmer (Drunk in cafe), Max Berlinger (Usher), Edwardo Sapag (Holt), Jeff Altman (Doctor)

IN MACARTHUR PARK (AFI USA) Producer/Director/Screenplay/Editor, Bruce R. Schwartz; Photography, John Sharaf; Music, Rocky Davis; Western World prods.; 1977; Black and white; Not rated; 75 minutes; November release. CAST: Adam Silver (Triam Lee), James Espinoza (Ricky), Peter Homer, Sr. (Triam's Uncle), Anna Shorter (Girl in bus station), Marcy Eudal (Ginny), Doug Laffoon (Triam's Son), Anita Noble (Triam's Wife)

REVOLUTION! (Northern Arts) Producer, Travis Preston; Director/Screenplay, Jeff Kahn; Photography, Mike Spiller; Music, Tom Judson; Editor, Chris Tellefsen; Art Director, Kristen Ames; a Dream Bird Prods. presentation; Precision color/black and white; Not rated; 84 minutes; November release. CAST: Christopher Renstrom (Ollie), Kimberly Flynn (Suzy), Georg Osterman (Billy), Johnny Kabalah (Steve), Helen Schumaker (Aunt Kasha), Matthew Courtney (Club M.C.), Frank Conversano (Lead Dancer), Travis Preston (Prunievsky)

AND YOU THOUGHT YOUR PARENTS WERE WEIRD (Trimark) Producer, Just Betzer; Executive Producer, Pernille Siesbye; Co-Producers, Mark Slater, Benni Korzen; Director/Screenplay, Tony Cookson; Photography, Paul Elliott; Editor, Michael Ornstein; Costumes, Sanja M. Hays; a Panorama Film International Production; Ultra-Stereo; Color; Rated PG; 92 minutes; November release. CAST: Marcia Strassman (Sarah Carson), Joshua Miller (Josh Carson), Edan Gross (Max Carson), John Quade (Walter Kotzwinkle), Sam Behrens (Steve Franklin), Alan Thicke (Voice of Matthew Carson), Susan Gibney (Alice Woods), A.J. Langer (Beth Allen), Gustav Vintas (Jaeger), Eric Walker (Dwayne Kotzwinkle), Bill Smillie (Henry Killbrandt), Robert Clotworthy (Mike Abbott), Armin Shimmerman (Contest Announcer), Allan Wasserman (Mel), Susan Brecht (Computer Teacher), Michael Strasser (Policeman), Rowena Balos, Synnove Sofsrud (Gawkers), Jevon P. Lewis, Kelly Packard, Billie Joe Wright (Halloween Kids), Kenneth Learner (Matthew Carson - Home Movies)

CHEAP SHOTS (Hemdale/Select) Producers, William Coppard, Jerry Stoeffhaas, Jeff Ureles; Executive Producer, William Coppard; Directors/Screenplay, Jeff Ureles, Jerry Stoeffhaas; Photography, Thom Marini; Designer, Carl Zollo; Music, Jeff Beal; Editor, Ken McIlwaine; Color; Rated PG-13; 92 minutes; November release. CAST: Louis Zorich (Louie), David Patrick Kelly (Arnold), Mary Louise Wilson (Dotty), Michael Twaine (Jack), Clarke Gordon (Franklin), Patience Moore (Blonde), John Galateo (Paul), Judson Camp (Biker), Brad Fullagar (Pete), John Groth, Robert De Looze (Killers), Sally Kay Cohen (Waitress), Anne La Lopa (Beautician), Rollin Schlicker (Detective)

DEAD WOMEN IN LINGERIE (AFI USA) Producer/Director, Erica Fox; Screenplay, Erica Fox, John Romo; Photography, John C. Newby; Editors, Mark Stratton, Stacia Thompson; Music, Ciro Hurtado; Designer, Adam Leventhal; a Seagate Films production; Ultra-Stereo; Foto-Kem color; Rated R; 89 minutes; November release. CAST: John Romo (Nick), Maura Tierney (Molly Field), Jerry Orbach (Bartoli), Dennis Christopher (Lapin), June Lockhart (Ma), Lyle Waggoner (Daddy), Maria Strova (Carmen), Teresa Gonzalez (Silvia), Jeanne Sal (Bing), Laura Herring (Marcia), Ken Osmond (David), Frazer Smith (Neighbor)

Joshua Miller, Edan Gross in
And You Thought Your Parents Were Weird
© *Vidmark*

James B. Sikking, Hector Elizondo in *Final Approach*
© *Vidmark*

John Cage, Merce Cunningham in *Cage/Cunningham*
© *Cunningham Dance Foundation*

DEEP BLUES (AFI USA/Radio Active Films) Producers, Eileen Gregory, John Stewart; Executive Producer, David A. Stewart; Director/Editor, Robert Mugge; Screenplay/Interviewer/Music Director, Robert Palmer; Photography, Erich Roland; from Oil Factory Ltd.; Color; Not rated; 91 minutes; November release. CAST: Junior Kimbrough, Jessie Mae Hemphill, Roosevelt "Bubba" Barnes, Big Jack Johnson, Lonnie Pitchford

FINAL APPROACH (Trimark) Producer/Director, Eric Steven Stahl; Screenplay, Eric Steven Stahl, Gerald Laurence; Photography, Eric Goldstein; Designer, Ralph E. Stevic; Editor, Stefan Küt; Music, Kirk Hunter; Costumes, Ruth A. Brown; Casting, Tina Gordon, Carrie Deysher; a Filmquest Pictures production; Dolby Stereo; Panavision; Deluxe color; Rated R; 100 minutes; December release. CAST: James B. Sikking (Col. Jason Halsey), Hector Elizondo (Dr. Dio Gottlieb), Madolyn Smith (Casey Halsey), Kevin McCarthy (Gen. Geller), Cameo Kneuer (Brooke Halsey), Wayne Duvall (Doug Slessinger), Karen Person (Ms. Peters), David Bonaiuto (Jason's Father), Duffy Rutledge (Jason's Mother), Colin Vogel (Country Doctor), Robert Jay Stahl (Emergency Room Doctor), Hank Garret (RSO), Maarten Goslins (Younger Jason), Ellen Hilton (Woman in waiting room), James Flynn (Man in waiting room)

PIZZA MAN (Megalomania Prod.) Producer, Gary Goldstein; Director/Screenplay/Editor, J.D. Athens (Jonathan Lawton); Photography, Fred Samia; Music, Daniel May; Designer, Theodore Smudde; Costumes, Debra Goold; Color; Not rated; 90 minutes; December release. CAST: Bill Maher (Elmo Bunn), Annabelle Gurwitch (The Dame), David McKnight (Vince), Bob Delegall (Mayor Bradley), Bryan Clark (Ronald Reagan)

TALKING TO STRANGERS (Baltimore Film Factory) Producer, J.K. Eareckson; Director/Screenplay/Photography, Rob Tregenza; Color; Not rated; 92 minutes; December release. CAST: Ken Gruz (Jesse), Marvin Hunter (General), Dennis Jordan (Red Coat), Caron Tate (Ms. Taylor), Brian Constantini (Angry Man), Bill Sanders (Manager), Henry Strozier (Priest), Joanne Bauer, Lois Evans, Sharrie Valero, Laurie Nettles (Water Taxi People), Richard Foster (Slick), Linda Chambers (Trigger), Sara Rush (Potter)

CAGE/CUNNINGHAM (Cunningham Dance Foundation) Director/ Photography/Editor, Elliot Caplan; Screenplay, David Vaughan; Music, John Cage; Presented in association with La Sept; Color; Not rated; 95 minutes; December release. Documentary with Merce Cunningham, John Cage, Nam June Paik, Robert Rauschenberg, Carolyn Brown, Viola Farber, Alvin Lucier, Christian Wolff, La Monte Young, Gordon Mumma, Rudolf Nureyev, M.C. Richards, Michel Guy, Doris Dennison, David Tudor, Jean Rigg, Jasper Johns, Frank Stella, Edwin Denby, Irwin Kremen, Bonnie Bird, Virgil Thomson, Marianne Preger-Simon, Remy Charlip

TED AND VENUS (Double Helix) Producers, Randolf Turrow, William Talmadge; Executive Producer, Randall Kubota; Director, Bud Cort; Screenplay, Paul Ciotti, Bud Cort; Story, Paul Ciotti; Photography, Dietrich Lohmann; Editor, Katina Zinner; Designer, Lynn Christopher; Music, David Robbins; a Krishna Shah presentation of an L.A. Dreams Production; CFI color; Rated R; 100 minutes; December release. CAST: Bud Cort (Ted Whitley), Jim Brolin (Max Waters), Kim Adams (Linda Turner), Carol Kane (Colette), Pamella D'Pella (Gloria), Brian Thompson (Herb), Rhea Perlman (Grace), Woody Harrelson (Homeless Viet Nam Veteran), Martin Mull (Ted's Attorney), Roberta Wallach (District Attorney), Dr. Timothy Leary (Judge H. Converse), Tricia O'Neil (Judge Katherine Netek), Tony Genaro (Bailiff), Vincent Schiavelli (Publisher), Andrea Martin (Bag Lady), Cassandra Peterson (Lisa), Tracy Reiner (Shelly), Arleen Sorkin (Marcia), Patrick McCormick (Marcia's Elderly Boyfriend), Gena Rowlands (Mrs. Turner), Lady Rowlands (Linda's Grandmother), Lily Mariye (Rose), Bettye Ackerman (Poetry Award Presenter), Jack Eastland (Club Emcee), Jerome Coleman (Skate Boarder/Park Bench Lover), Shelley Werk (Nurse), Victor Talmadge (Orderly), John Barrymore, Rob Moran, Clint Allen (Patients), Zoe Cassavetes (Waitress), Barbara Leary (Guest), Jacqueline Chauvin, Bridget Flaherty, Pat Ast, Grif Griffis (Woman's Group), Philip K. Irven (Ted's Cellmate), Stefanos Miltsakakis, Craig Ryan Ng, Jim Maniaci (Prisoners), Mik Scriba (Prison Guard), Chad Taylor (Chainsaw Juggler), Christopher McMullen (Horseback Rider), Joe Paul (Wino), Tamara DeTereaux (Park Bench Lover), Pete Koch, Karl Rumburg, Chris Paul Davis, Lawrence McNeal III, Norman Maldonado (Cops)

Caron Tate, Ken Gruz in *Talking to Strangers*
© *Baltimore Film Factory*

Bud Cort in *Ted and Venus*
© *Double Helix*

1991 ACADEMY AWARDS

(presented Monday, March 30, 1992)

THE SILENCE OF THE LAMBS

(ORION) Producers, Edward Saxon, Kenneth Utt, Ron Bozman; Executive Producer, Gary Goetzman; Director, Jonathan Demme; Screenplay, Ted Tally; Based on the novel by Thomas Harris; Photography, Tak Fujimoto; Designer, Kristi Zea; Costumes, Colleen Atwood; Music, Howard Shore; Editor, Craig McKay; Casting, Howard Feuer; Associate Producer, Grace Blake; Assistant Director, Ron Bozman; a Strong Heart/Demme Production; Dolby Stereo; Technicolor/Deluxe color; Rated R; 118 minutes; February release

CAST

Clarice Starling	Jodie Foster
Dr. Hannibal Lecter	Anthony Hopkins
Jack Crawford	Scott Glenn
Jame Gumb	Ted Levine
Dr. Frederick Chilton	Anthony Heald
Senator Ruth Martin	Diane Baker
Ardelia Mapp	Kasi Lemmons
Catherine Martin	Brooke Smith
Roden	Dan Butler
Pilcher	Paul Lazar
Sgt. Tate	Danny Darst
Lt. Boyle	Charles Napier
Lamar	Tracey Walter
Officer Jacobs	Cynthia Ettinger
Officer Murray	Brent Hinkley
Paul Krendler	Ron Vawter
Agent Burroughs	Lawrence T. Wrentz
FBI Director Hayden Burke	Roger Corman
Barney	Frankie Faison
Miggs	Stuart Rudin
Young Clarice	Masha Skorobogatov
Clarice's Father	Jeffrie Lane
Mr. Lang	Leib Lensky
Mr. Brigham	Bill Miller
Agent Terry	Chuck Aber
Oscar	Gene Borkan
Sheriff Perkins	Pat McNamara
Dr. Akin	Kenneth Utt
Sgt. Pembry	Alex Coleman
SWAT Commander	Chris Isaak
EMS Attendant	Josh Broder
Stacy Hubka	Lauren Roselli

and Lawrence A. Bonney (FBI Instructor), Don Brockett (Friendly Psychopath), Frank Seals, Jr. (Brooding Psychopath), Red Schwartz (Mr. Lang's Driver), Jim Roche (TV Evangelist), James B. Howard (Boxing Instructor), Adelle Lutz, Obba Babatunde (TV Anchors), George Michael (TV Sportscaster), Jim Dratfield (Sen. Martin's Aide), Stanton-Miranda, Rebecca Saxon (Reporters), Steve Wyatt (Airport Flirt), David Early (Spooked Memphis Cop), Andre Blake (Tall Memphis Cop), Bill Dalzell III (Distraught Memphis Cop), Daniel von Bargen (SWAT Communicator), Tommy LaFitte (SWAT Shooter), Buzz Kilman (EMS Driver), Harry Northup (Mr. Bimmel), Lamont Arnold (Flower Delivery Man)

Top: Jodie Foster Below: Anthony Hopkins
Left: Scott Glenn, Foster
© Orion Pictures

1991 Academy Awards for Best Picture, Director, Actor (Anthony Hopkins), Actress (Jodie Foster), and Screenplay Adaptation

Anthony Heald, Anthony Hopkins
Above Left: Jodie Foster Top Left: Hopkins

Scott Glenn, Anthony Hopkins, Jodie Foster 175
Above Right: Ted Levine
Top Right: Foster, Kasi Lemmons

ANTHONY HOPKINS
in *The Silence of the Lambs*
© *Orion Pictures*
ACADEMY AWARD FOR BEST ACTOR OF 1991

JODIE FOSTER
in *The Silence of the Lambs*
© *Orion Pictures*
ACADEMY AWARD FOR BEST ACTRESS OF 1991

JACK PALANCE
in *City Slickers*
© *Castle Rock Entertainment*
ACADEMY AWARD FOR BEST SUPPORTING ACTOR OF 1991

MERCEDES RUEHL
in *The Fisher King*
© *Tri-Star Pictures*

ACADEMY AWARD FOR BEST SUPPORTING ACTRESS OF 1991

MEDITERRANEO

(MIRAMAX) Producers, Gianni Minervini, Mario Cecchi Gori, Vittorio Cecchi Gori; Director, Gabriele Salvatores; Screenplay, Vincenzo Monteleone; Photography, Italo Pettriccione; Music, Giancarlo Bigazzi; Art Director, Thalia Istikopoulos; Editor, Nino Baragali; Costumes, Francesco Panni; Italian; Technicolor; Not rated; 93 minutes; March 1992 release

CAST

Sgt. Lo Russo	Diego Abatantuono
Lt. Montini	Claudio Bigagli
Farina	Giuseppe Cederna
Noventa	Claudio Bisio
Strazzabosco	Gigio Alberti
Colosanti	Ugo Conti
Felice Munaron	Memo Dini
Libero Munaron	Vasco Mirandolo
Vasilissa	Vanna Barba
Pope	Luigi Montini
Shepherdess	Irene Grazioli
Pilot	Antonio Catalina

Top Right: Diego Abatantuono, Vanna Barba
Right: Barba, Giuseppe Cederna Below: Abatantuono,
Ugo Conti, Claudio Bisio, Gigio Alberti, Cederna,
Vasco Mirandolo, Memo Dini
© *Miramax Films*

Academy Award for
Best Foreign-Language Film of 1991

IN THE SHADOW OF THE STARS

(FIRST RUN FEATURES) Producers/Directors/Editors, Irving Saraf, Allie Light; Photography, Michael Chin; Associate Producer, Lynn O'Donnell; Color; Not rated; 93 minutes; August release. Documentary on the San Francisco Opera

© *First Run Features*

Academy Award for
Best Feature Documentary of 1991

The Chorus of the San Francisco Opera

| Marlon Brando | Claudette Colbert | George Burns | Patty Duke |

PREVIOUS ACADEMY AWARD WINNERS

(1) Best Picture, (2) Actor, (3) Actress, (4) Supporting Actor, (5) Supporting Actress, (6) Director, (7) Special Award, (8) Best Foreign Language Film, (9) Best Feature Documentary

1927-28: (1) "Wings," (2) Emil Jannings in "The Way of All Flesh," (3) Janet Gaynor in "Seventh Heaven," (6) Frank Borzage for "Seventh Heaven", (7) Charles Chaplin.
1928-29: (1) "Broadway Melody," (2) Warner Baxter in "In Old Arizona," (3) Mary Pickford in "Coquette," (6) Frank Lloyd for "The Divine Lady."
1929-1930: (1) "All Quiet on the Western Front," (2) George Arliss in "Disraeli," (3) Norma Shearer in "The Divorcee," (6) Lewis Milestone for "All Quiet on the Western Front."
1930-31: (1) "Cimarron," (2) Lionel Barrymore in "A Free Soul," (3) Marie Dressler in "Min and Bill," (6) Norman Taurog for "Skippy."
1931-32: (1) "Grand Hotel," (2) Fredric March in "Dr. Jekyll and Mr. Hyde" tied with Wallace Beery in "The Champ," (3) Helen Hayes in "The Sin of Madelon Claudet," (6) Frank Borzage for "Bad Girl."
1932-33: (1) "Cavalcade," (2) Charles Laughton in "The Private Life of Henry VIII," (3) Katharine Hepburn in "Morning Glory," (6) Frank Lloyd for "Cavalcade."
1934: (1) "It Happened One Night," (2) Clark Gable in "It Happened One Night," (3) Claudette Colbert in "It Happened One Night," (6) Frank Capra for "It Happened One Night," (7) Shirley Temple.
1935: (1) "Mutiny on the Bounty," (2) Victor McLaglen in "The Informer," (3) Bette Davis in "Dangerous," (6) John Ford for "The Informer," (7) D.W. Griffith.
1936: (1) "The Great Ziegfeld," (2) Paul Muni in "The Story of Louis Pasteur," (3) Luise Rainer in "The Great Ziegfeld," (4) Walter Brennan in "Come and Get It," (5) Gale Sondergaard in "Anthony Adverse," (6) Frank Capra for "Mr. Deeds Goes to Town."
1937: (1) "The Life of Emile Zola," (2) Spencer Tracy in "Captains Courageous," (3) Luise Rainer in "The Good Earth," (4) Joseph Schildkraut in "The Life of Emile Zola," (5) Alice Brady in "In Old Chicago," (6) Leo McCarey for "The Awful Truth," (7) Mack Sennett, Edgar Bergen.
1938: (1) "You Can't Take It with You," (2) Spencer Tracy in "Boys Town," (3) Bette Davis in "Jezebel," (4) Walter Brennan in "Kentucky," (5) Fay Bainter in "Jezebel," (6) Frank Capra for "You Can't Take It with You," (7) Deanna Durbin, Mickey Rooney, Harry M. Warner, Walt Disney.
1939: (1) "Gone with the Wind," (2) Robert Donat in "Goodbye, Mr. Chips," (3) Vivien Leigh in "Gone with the Wind," (4) Thomas Mitchell in "Stagecoach," (5) Hattie McDaniel in "Gone with the Wind," (6) Victor Fleming for "Gone with the Wind," (7) Douglas Fairbanks, Judy Garland.

1940: (1) "Rebecca," (2) James Stewart in "The Philadelphia Story," (3) Ginger Rogers in "Kitty Foyle," (4) Walter Brennan in "The Westerner," (5) Jane Darwell in "The Grapes of Wrath," (6) John Ford for "The Grapes of Wrath," (7) Bob Hope
1941: (1) "How Green Was My Valley," (2) Gary Cooper in "Sergeant York," (3) Joan Fontaine in "Suspicion," (4) Donald Crisp in "How Green Was My Valley," (5) Mary Astor in "The Great Lie," (6) John Ford for "How Green Was My Valley," (7) Leopold Stokowski, Walt Disney.
1942: (1) "Mrs. Miniver," (2) James Cagney in "Yankee Doodle Dandy," (3) Greer Garson in "Mrs. Miniver," (4) Van Heflin in "Johnny Eager," (5) Teresa Wright in "Mrs. Miniver," (6) William Wyler for "Mrs. Miniver," (7) Charles Boyer, Noel Coward.
1943: (1) "Casablanca," (2) Paul Lukas in "Watch on the Rhine," (3) Jennifer Jones in "The Song of Bernadette," (4) Charles Coburn in "The More the Merrier," (5) Katina Paxinou in "For Whom the Bell Tolls," (6) Michael Curtiz for "Casablanca."
1944: (1) "Going My Way," (2) Bing Crosby in "Going My Way," (3) Ingrid Bergman in "Gaslight," (4) Barry Fitzgerald in "Going My Way," (5) Ethel Barrymore in "None but the Lonely Heart," (6) Leo McCarey for "Going My Way," (7) Margaret O'Brien, Bob Hope
1945: (1) "The Lost Weekend," (2) Ray Milland in "The Lost Weekend," (3) Joan Crawford in "Mildred Pierce," (4) James Dunn in "A Tree Grows in Brooklyn," (5) Anne Revere in "National Velvet," (6) Billy Wilder for "The Lost Weekend," (7) Walter Wanger, Peggy Ann Garner.
1946: (1) "The Best Years of Our Lives," (2) Fredric March in "The Best Years of Our Lives," (3) Olivia de Havilland in "To Each His Own," (4) Harold Russell in "The Best Years of Our Lives," (5) Anne Baxter in "The Razor's Edge," (6) William Wyler for "The Best Years of Our Lives," (7) Laurence Olivier, Harold Russell, Ernst Lubitsch, Claude Jarman, Jr.
1947: (1) "Gentleman's Agreement," (2) Ronald Colman in "A Double Life," (3) Loretta Young in "The Farmer's Daughter," (4) Edmund Gwenn in "Miracle on 34th Street," (5) Celeste Holm in "Gentleman's Agreement," (7) James Baskette, (8) "Shoeshine," (Italy).
1948: (1) "Hamlet," (2) Laurence Olivier in "Hamlet," (3) Jane Wyman in "Johnny Belinda," (4) Walter Huston in "The Treasure of the Sierra Madre," (5) Claire Trevor in "Key Largo," (6) John Huston for "The Treasure of the Sierra Madre," (7) Ivan Jandl, Sid Grauman, Adolph Zukor, Walter Wanger, (8) "Monsieur Vincent," (France).
1949: (1) "All the King's Men," (2) Broderick Crawford in "All the

| Michael Caine | Faye Dunaway | Jack Nicholson | Shirley MacLaine |

King's Men," (3) Olivia de Havilland in "The Heiress," (4) Dean Jagger in "Twelve O'Clock High," (5) Mercedes McCambridge in "All the King's Men," (6) Joseph L. Mankiewicz for "A Letter to Three Wives," (7) Bobby Driscoll, Fred Astaire, Cecil B. DeMille, Jean Hersholt, (8) "The Bicycle Thief," (Italy).

1950: (1) "All about Eve," (2) Jose Ferrer in "Cyrano de Bergerac," (3) Judy Holliday in "Born Yesterday," (4) George Sanders in "All about Eve," (5) Josephine Hull in "Harvey," (6) Joseph L. Mankiewicz for "All about Eve," (7) George Murphy, Louis B. Mayer, (8) "The Walls of Malapaga," (France/Italy).

1951: (1) "An American in Paris," (2) Humphrey Bogart in "The African Queen," (3) Vivien Leigh in "A Streetcar Named Desire," (4) Karl Malden in "A Streetcar Named Desire," (5) Kim Hunter in "A Streetcar Named Desire," (6) George Stevens for "A Place in the Sun," (7) Gene Kelly, (8) "Rashomon," (Japan).

1952: (1) "The Greatest Show on Earth," (2) Gary Cooper in "High Noon," (3) Shirley Booth in "Come Back, Little Sheba," (4) Anthony Quinn in "Viva Zapata," (5) Gloria Grahame in "The Bad and the Beautiful," (6) John Ford for "The Quiet Man," (7) Joseph M. Schenck, Merian C. Cooper, Harold Lloyd, Bob Hope, George Alfred Mitchell, (8) "Forbidden Games," (France).

1953: (1) "From Here to Eternity," (2) William Holden in "Stalag 17," (3) Audrey Hepburn in "Roman Holiday," (4) Frank Sinatra in "From Here to Eternity," (5) Donna Reed in "From Here to Eternity," (6) Fred Zinnemann for "From Here to Eternity," (7) Pete Smith, Joseph Breen, (8) no award.

1954: (1) "On the Waterfront," (2) Marlon Brando in "On the Waterfront," (3) Grace Kelly in "The Country Girl," (4) Edmond O'Brien in "The Barefoot Contessa," (5) Eva Marie Saint in "On the Waterfront," (6) Elia Kazan for "On the Waterfront," (7) Greta Garbo, Danny Kaye, Jon Whitley, Vincent Winter, (8) "Gate of Hell," (Japan).

1955: (1) "Marty," (2) Ernest Borgnine in "Marty," (3) Anna Magnani in "The Rose Tattoo," (4) Jack Lemmon in "Mister Roberts," (5) Jo Van Fleet in "East of Eden," (6) Delbert Mann for "Marty," (8) "Samurai," (Japan).

1956: (1) "Around the World in 80 Days," (2) Yul Brynner in "The King and I," (3) Ingrid Bergman in "Anastasia," (4) Anthony Quinn in "Lust for Life," (5) Dorothy Malone in "Written on the Wind," (6) George Stevens for "Giant," (7) Eddie Cantor, (8) "La Strada," (Italy).

1957: (1) "The Bridge on the River Kwai," (2) Alec Guinness in "The Bridge on the River Kwai," (3) Joanne Woodward in "The Three Faces of Eve," (4) Red Buttons in "Sayonara," (5) Miyoshi Umeki in "Sayonara," (6) David Lean for "The Bridge on the River Kwai," (7) Charles Brackett, B.B. Kahane, Gilbert M. (Bronco Billy) Anderson, (8) "Nights of Cabiria," (Italy).

1958: (1) "Gigi," (2) David Niven in "Separate Tables," (3) Susan Hayward in "I Want to Live," (4) Burl Ives in "The Big Country," (5) Wendy Hiller in "Separate Tables," (6) Vincente Minnelli for "Gigi," (7) Maurice Chevalier, (8) "My Uncle," (France).

1959: (1) "Ben-Hur," (2) Charlton Heston in "Ben-Hur," (3) Simone Signoret in "Room at the Top," (4) Hugh Griffith in "Ben-Hur," (5)

Shelley Winters in "The Diary of Anne Frank," (6) William Wyler for "Ben-Hur," (7) Lee de Forest, Buster Keaton, (8) "Black Orpheus," (Brazil).

1960: (1) "The Apartment," (2) Burt Lancaster in "Elmer Gantry," (3) Elizabeth Taylor in "Butterfield 8," (4) Peter Ustinov in "Spartacus," (5) Shirley Jones in "Elmer Gantry," (6) Billy Wilder for "The Apartment," (7) Gary Cooper, Stan Laurel, Hayley Mills, (8) "The Virgin Spring," (Sweden).

1961: (1) "West Side Story," (2) Maximilian Schell in "Judgment at Nuremberg," (3) Sophia Loren in "Two Women," (4) George Chakiris in "West Side Story," (5) Rita Moreno in "West Side Story," (6) Robert Wise for "West Side Story," (7) Jerome Robbins, Fred L. Metzler, (8) "Through a Glass Darkly," (Sweden).

1962: (1) "Lawrence of Arabia," (2) Gregory Peck in "To Kill a Mockingbird," (3) Anne Bancroft in "The Miracle Worker," (4) Ed Begley in "Sweet Bird of Youth," (5) Patty Duke in "The Miracle Worker," (6) David Lean for "Lawrence of Arabia," (8) "Sundays and Cybele," (France).

1963: (1) "Tom Jones," (2) Sidney Poitier in "Lilies of the Field," (3) Patricia Neal in "Hud," (4) Melvyn Douglas in "Hud," (5) Margaret Rutherford in "The V.I.P.'s," (6) Tony Richardson for "Tom Jones," (8) "8 1/2," (Italy).

1964: (1) "My Fair Lady," (2) Rex Harrison in "My Fair Lady," (3) Julie Andrews in "Mary Poppins," (4) Peter Ustinov in "Topkapi," (5) Lila Kedrova in "Zorba the Greek," (6) George Cukor for "My Fair Lady," (7) William Tuttle, (8) "Yesterday, Today, and Tomorrow," (Italy).

1965: (1) "The Sound of Music," (2) Lee Marvin in "Cat Ballou," (3) Julie Christie in "Darling," (4) Martin Balsam in "A Thousand Clowns," (5) Shelley Winters in "A Patch of Blue," (6) Robert Wise for "The Sound of Music," (7) Bob Hope, (8) "The Shop on Main Street," (Czech).

1966: (1) "A Man for All Seasons," (2) Paul Scofield in "A Man for All Seasons," (3) Elizabeth Taylor in "Who's Afraid of Virginia Woolf?," (4) Walter Matthau in "The Fortune Cookie," (5) Sandy Dennis in "Who's Afraid of Virginia Woolf?," (6) Fred Zinnemann for "A Man for All Seasons," (8) "A Man and a Woman," (France).

1967: (1) "In the Heat of the Night," (2) Rod Steiger in "In the Heat of the Night," (3) Katharine Hepburn in "Guess Who's Coming to Dinner," (4) George Kennedy in "Cool Hand Luke," (5) Estelle Parsons in "Bonnie and Clyde," (6) Mike Nichols for "The Graduate," (8) "Closely Watched Trains," (Czech).

1968: (1) "Oliver!" (2) Cliff Robertson in "Charly," (3) Katharine Hepburn in "The Lion in Winter," tied with Barbra Streisand in "Funny Girl," (4) Jack Albertson in "The Subject Was Roses," (5) Ruth Gordon in "Rosemary's Baby," (6) Carol Reed for "Oliver!," (7) Onna White for "Oliver!" choreography, John Chambers for "Planet of the Apes" makeup, (8) "War and Peace," (USSR).

1969: (1) "Midnight Cowboy," (2) John Wayne in "True Grit," (3) Maggie Smith in "The Prime of Miss Jean Brodie," (4) Gig Young in "They Shoot Horses, Don't They?," (5) Goldie Hawn in "Cactus Flower," (6) John Schlesinger for "Midnight Cowboy," (7) Cary Grant, (8) "Z," (Algeria).

Harold Russell   **Dorothy Malone**   **Billy Wilder**   **Shelley Winters**

1970: (1) "Patton," (2) George C. Scott in "Patton," (3) Glenda Jackson in "Women in Love," (4) John Mills in "Ryan's Daughter," (5) Helen Hayes in "Airport," (6) Franklin J. Schaffner for "Patton," (7) Lillian Gish, Orson Welles, (8) "Investigation of a Citizen Above Suspicion," (Italy).

1971: (1) "The French Connection," (2) Gene Hackman in "The French Connection," (3) Jane Fonda in "Klute," (4) Ben Johnson in "The Last Picture Show," (6) William Friedkin for "The French Connection," (7) Charles Chaplin, (8) "The Garden of the Finzi-Continis," (Italy).

1972: (1) "The Godfather," (2) Marlon Brando in "The Godfather," (3) Liza Minnelli in "Cabaret," (4) Joel Grey in "Cabaret," (5) Eileen Heckart in "Butterflies Are Free," (6) Bob Fosse for "Cabaret," (7) Edward G. Robinson, (8) "The Discreet Charm of the Bourgeoisie," (France).

1973: (1) "The Sting," (2) Jack Lemmon in "Save the Tiger," (3) Glenda Jackson in "A Touch of Class," (4) John Houseman in "The Paper Chase," (5) Tatum O'Neal in "Paper Moon," (6) George Roy Hill for "The Sting," (8) "Day for Night," (France).

1974: (1) "The Godfather Part II," (2) Art Carney in "Harry and Tonto," (3) Ellen Burstyn in "Alice Doesn't Live Here Anymore," (4) Robert DeNiro in "The Godfather Part II," (5) Ingrid Bergman in "Murder on the Orient Express," (6) Francis Ford Coppola for "The Godfather Part II," (7) Howard Hawks, Jean Renoir, (8) "Amarcord," (Italy).

1975: (1) "One Flew Over the Cuckoo's Nest," (2) Jack Nicholson in "One Flew Over the Cuckoo's Nest," (3) Louise Fletcher in "One Flew Over the Cuckoo's Nest," (4) George Burns in "The Sunshine Boys," (5) Lee Grant in "Shampoo," (6) Milos Forman for "One Flew Over the Cuckoo's Nest," (7) Mary Pickford, (8) "Dersu Uzala," (U.S.S.R.), (9) "The Man Who Skied Down Everest."

1976: (1) "Rocky," (2) Peter Finch in "Network," (3) Faye Dunaway in "Network," (4) Jason Robards in "All the President's Men," (5) Beatrice Straight in "Network," (6) John G. Avildsen for "Rocky," (8) "Black and White in Color," (Ivory Coast), (9) "Harlan County, U.S.A."

1977: (1) "Annie Hall," (2) Richard Dreyfuss in "The Goodbye Girl," (3) Diane Keaton in "Annie Hall," (4) Jason Robards in "Julia," (5) Vanessa Redgrave in "Julia," (6) Woody Allen for "Annie Hall," (7) Maggie Booth (film editor), (8) "Madame Rosa," (France), (9) "Who Are the DeBolts?"

1978: (1) "The Deer Hunter," (2) Jon Voight in "Coming Home," (3) Jane Fonda in "Coming Home," (4) Christopher Walken in "The Deer Hunter," (5) Maggie Smith in "California Suite," (6) Michael Cimino for "The Deer Hunter," (7) Laurence Olivier, King Vidor, (8) "Get Out Your Handkerchiefs," (France), (9) "Scared Straight."

1979: (1) "Kramer vs. Kramer," (2) Dustin Hoffman in "Kramer vs. Kramer," (3) Sally Field in "Norma Rae," (4) Melvyn Douglas in "Being There," (5) Meryl Streep in "Kramer vs. Kramer," (6) Robert Benton for "Kramer vs. Kramer," (7) Robert S. Benjamin, Hal Elias, Alec Guinness, (8) "The Tin Drum," (Germany), (9) "Best Boy."

1980: (1) "Ordinary People," (2) Robert DeNiro in "Raging Bull," (3) Sissy Spacek in "Coal Miner's Daughter," (4) Timothy Hutton in "Ordinary People," (5) Mary Steenburgen in "Melvin and Howard," (6) Robert Redford for "Ordinary People," (7) Henry Fonda, (8)

"Moscow Does Not Believe in Tears," (Russia), (9) "From Mao to Mozart: Isaac Stern in China."

1981: (1) "Chariots of Fire," (2) Henry Fonda in "On Golden Pond," (3) Katharine Hepburn in "On Golden Pond," (4) John Gielgud in "Arthur," (5) Maureen Stapleton in "Reds," (6) Warren Beatty for "Reds," (7) Fuji Photo Film Co., Barbara Stanwyck, (8) "Mephisto," (Hungary), (9) "Genocide."

1982: (1) "Gandhi," (2) Ben Kingsley in "Gandhi," (3) Meryl Streep in "Sophie's Choice," (4) Louis Gossett, Jr. in "An Officer and a Gentleman," (5) Jessica Lange in "Tootsie," (6) Richard Attenborough for "Gandhi," (7) Mickey Rooney, (8) "Volver a Empezar (To Begin Again)," (Spain), (9) "Just Another Missing Kid."

1983: (1) "Terms of Endearment," (2) Robert Duvall in "Tender Mercies," (3) Shirley MacLaine in "Terms of Endearment," (4) Jack Nicholson in "Terms of Endearment," (5) Linda Hunt in "The Year of Living Dangerously," (6) James L. Brooks for "Terms of Endearment," (7) Hal Roach, (8) "Fanny and Alexander," (Sweden), (9) "He Makes Me Feel Like Dancin'."

1984: (1) "Amadeus," (2) F. Murray Abraham in "Amadeus," (3) Sally Field in "Places in the Heart," (4) Haing S. Ngor in "The Killing Fields," (5) Peggy Ashcroft in "A Passage to India," (6) Milos Forman for "Amadeus," (7) James Stewart, (8) "Dangerous Moves," (Switzerland), (9) "The Times of Harvey Milk."

1985: (1) "Out of Africa," (2) William Hurt in "Kiss of the Spider Woman," (3) Geraldine Page in "The Trip to Bountiful," (4) Don Ameche in "Cocoon," (5) Anjelica Huston in "Prizzi's Honor," (6) Sydney Pollack for "Out of Africa," (7) Paul Newman, Alex North, (8) "The Official Story," (Argentina), (9) "Broken Rainbow."

1986: (1) "Platoon," (2) Paul Newman in "The Color of Money," (3) Marlee Matlin in "Children of a Lesser God," (4) Michael Caine in "Hannah and Her Sisters," (5) Dianne Wiest in "Hannah and Her Sisters," (6) Oliver Stone for "Platoon," (7) Ralph Bellamy, (8) "The Assault," (Netherlands), (9) "Artie Shaw: Time Is All You've Got" tied with "Down and Out in America."

1987: (1) "The Last Emperor," (2) Michael Douglas in "Wall Street," (3) Cher in "Moonstruck," (4) Sean Connery in "The Untouchables," (5) Olympia Dukakis in "Moonstruck," (6) Bernardo Bertolucci for "The Last Emperor," (8) "Babette's Feast," (Denmark), (9) "The Ten-Year Lunch: The Wit and Legend of the Algonquin Round Table."

1988: (1) "Rain Man," (2) Dustin Hoffman in "Rain Man," (3) Jodie Foster in "The Accused," (4) Kevin Kline in "A Fish Called Wanda," (5) Geena Davis in "The Accidental Tourist," (6) Barry Levinson for "Rain Man," (8) "Pelle the Conqueror," (Denmark), (9) "Hotel Terminus: The Life and Times of Klaus Barbie."

1989: (1) "Driving Miss Daisy," (2) Daniel Day-Lewis in "My Left Foot," (3) Jessica Tandy in "Driving Miss Daisy," (4) Denzel Washington in "Glory," (5) Brenda Fricker in "My Left Foot," (6) Oliver Stone for "Born on the Fourth of July," (7) Akira Kurosawa, (8) "Cinema Paradiso," (Italy), (9) "Common Threads."

1990: (1) "Dances With Wolves," (2) Jeremy Irons in "Reversal of Fortune," (3) Kathy Bates in "Misery," (4) Joe Pesci in "GoodFellas," (5) Whoopi Goldberg in "Ghost," (6) Kevin Costner for "Dances With Wolves," (7) Sophia Loren, Myrna Loy, (8) "Journey of Hope," (Switzerland), (9) "American Dream."

PROMISING NEW ACTORS OF 1991

TYRA FERRELL

CUBA GOODING, JR.

ANTHONY LaPAGLIA

ROBIN GIVENS

JULIETTE LEWIS

JOHN LEGUIZAMO

JOHN CAMERON MITCHELL

ADRIENNE SHELLY

185

BRAD PITT

JULIET STEVENSON

MARISA TOMEI

FRANK WHALEY

FOREIGN FILMS
RELEASED IN THE U.S. IN 1991

TAXI BLUES

(MK 2) Producer, Marin Karmitz; Director/Screenplay, Pavel Louguine; Photography, Denis Evstigneev; Music, Vladimir Chekassine; Art Director, Valery Yourkevitch; Editor, Elizabeth Guido; a Lenfilm/ASK Soviet American Films/MK 2 productions S.A./LA Sept co-production; Soviet-French; Color; Not rated; 110 minutes; January release

CAST

Lyosha	Piotr Mamonov
Chlykov	Piotr Zaitchenko
Old Netchiporenko	Vladimir Kachpour
Christina	Natalia Koliakanova
Himself	Hal Singer
Nina, Lyosha's Wife	Elena Safonova
Administrator	Serguei Gazarov
Bald Musician in taxi	Evgueni Gortchakov
Writer typing on train	Dimitri Prigov
Petiountchik	Igor Zolotovitsky
Fat Kolia	Valery Klevinsky
Smart Young Girl	Elena Stepanova
Long-haired Mechanic	Constantin Aphonsky
Passenger with newspaper	Alexandre Bouianov
The Guardian	Nicolai Ejevsky
Hippy	Sergei Galkine
Girl with black eye	Irina Gobratova
Mechanic at taxi depot	Viaceslav Gorbountchikov
Mercedes Owner	Alexandre Inchakov
Police Sergeant	Vladimir Lopatine
Blonde Ira	Natalia Markova
Man on sofa	Edouard Guimpel
His Wife	Galina Proxorova
Soldier	Youri Sokolov
Civil Servants	Your Yourtchenko, Gercubi Vassiliskov
The Producer	Pierre Rival
Japanese Man	Iassouo Hiougadsi

Top: Piotr Mamonov, Piotr Zaitchenko
Right: Mamonov, Elena Safonova
© *MK 2 Prods.*

Rentaro Mikuni, Tsutomu Yamazaki

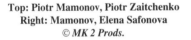

RIKYU

(CAPITOL ENTERTAINMENT) Executive Producers, Shizuo Yamanouchi, Hisao Minemura; Producers, Yoshisuke Mae, Hiroshi Morie; Director, Hiroshi Teshigahara; Screenplay, Genpei Akasegawa, Hiroshi Teshigahara; Based on the novel *Hideyoshi and Sen-no-Rikyu* by Yaeki Nogami; Photography, Fujio Morita; Art Directors, Yoshinobu Nishioka, Shigemori Shigeta; Costumes, Emi Wada; Music, Toru Takemitsu; Japanese; Color; Not rated; 116 minutes; January release

CAST

Sen-no Rikyu	Rentaro Mikuni
Hideyoshi Toyotomi	Tsutomu Yamazaki
Riki	Yoshiko Mita
Kita-no-mandokoro	Kyoko Kishida
Nobunaga Oda	Koshiro Matsumoto
Ieyasu Tokugawa	Kichiemon Nakamura
Hidenaga Toyotomi	Ryo Tamura
O-mandokoro	Tanie Kitabayashi
Chacha	Sayoko Yamaguchi
Ocho	Yoshiko Fujita
Mitsunari Ishida	Yasosuke Bando
Oribe Furuta	Keishi Arashi
Tadaoki Hosokawa	Hashinosuke Nakamura
Priest Kokei	Ichiro Zaitsu
Yahei Torigai	Hideo Kanze
Chika	Kyoko Enami
Soji Yamanoue	Hisashi Igawa

© *Capitol Entertainment*   **187**

MEMORIES OF A MARRIAGE
(Waltzing Regitze)

(NORDISK FILM/CITY CINEMAS) Producer, Lars Kolvig; Director/Screenplay, Kaspar Rostrup; Based on a novel by Martha Christensen; Photography, Claus Loof; Music, Fuzzy; Editor, Grete Moldrup; Set Designer, Henning Bahs; from Pathe-Nordisk Film Distribution, in cooperation with The Danish Film Institut; Danish; Color; Not rated; 90 minutes; January release

CAST

Karl Age	Frits Helmuth
Young Karl Age	Mikael Helmuth
Regitze	Ghita Norby
Young Regitze	Rikke Bendsen
Borge	Henning Moritzen
Young Borge	Michael Moritzen
Ilse	Anne Werner Thomsen
Young Ilse	Dorthe Simone Land
Rikard	Henning Ditlev
Young Rikard	Kim Romer
Annie	Birgit Sadolin
Young Annie	Nanna Moller
John - 40 yrs.	Hans Henrik Clemmensen
John - 19 yrs.	Peter Zhelder
John - 11-13 yrs.	Sylvester Zimsen
John - 3 yrs.	Troels Thers
John - 1 1/2 yrs.	Kasper Emil Storgaard
John - 1 month	Helmuth Jr.
Regitze's Mother	Kirsten Rolffes
Gloria	Birgit Zinn
Gloria's Husband	Torben Jensen
Jonas	Poul Clemmensen
Vera	Tove Maes
Vibeke	Lise Kamp Dahlerup
Boy Brian	Sune Kolster
Girl Susan	Jane Eggertsen
Freedom Fighter Leif	Thomas Mork
Young Nurse	Nonny Sand

Top Right: Mikael Helmuth, Rikke Bendsen Above Right: Sylvester Zimsen, Ghita Norby, Frits Helmuth
© Schecer Communications

HEAVEN AND EARTH

(TRITON PICTURES) Producer, Yutaka Okada; Director, Haruki Kadokawa; Screenplay, Toshio Kamata, Isao Yoshihara, Haruki Kadokawa; Based on the novel by Chogoro Kaionji; Photography, Yonezo Maeda; Designer, Hiroshi Tokuda; Costumes, Yoko Tashiro; Editors, Akira Suzuki, Robert C. Jones; Music, Tetsuya Komuro; Japanese; Alpha Cine color; Not rated; 105 minutes; February release

CAST

Kagetora	Takaaki Enoki
Takeda	Masahiko Tsugawa
Nami	Atsuko Asano
Usami	Tsunehiko Watase
Yae	Naomi Zaizen
Kakizaki	Binpachi Ito
Kansuke	Isao Natsuyagi
Naoe	Akira Hamada
Okuma	Masataka Naruse
Irobe	Osamu Yayama
Murakami	Takeshi Obayashi
Onikojima	Masayuki Sudo
Naya	Kaitaro Nozaki
Sone	Tatsuhiko Tomoi
Tokura	Takuya Goto
Akiyama	Satoshi Sadanaga
Taro	Hironobu Nomura
Obu	Hideo Murota
Tenkyu	Taro Ishida
Kosaka	Hiroyuki Okita
Hajikano	Akisato Yamada

and Morio Kazama (Imperial Messenger), Masuto Ibu (Shoda), Yuki Kazamatsuri (Shoda's Wife), Kyoko Kishida (Servant), Hideji Otaki (Rifle Merchant), Stuart Whitman (Narrator)

**Takaaki Enoki, Atsuko Asano
Above Left: Masahiko Tsugawa**

© Triton Pictures

AY, CARMELA!

(PRESTIGE) Producer, Andres Vicente Gomez; Director, Carlos Saura; Screenplay, Rafael Azcona; Photography, Jose Luis Alcaine; Art Director, Rafael Palermo; Assistant Director, Salvador Pons; Editor, Pablo G. Del Amo; a co-production by Iberoamericana Films, S.A. (Madrid) and ELLEPI (Rome) in collaboration with TVE, S.A.; Distributed by Miramax Films; Spanish-Italian; Color; Not rated; 95 minutes; February release

CAST

Carmela	Carmen Maura
Paulino	Andres Pajares
Gustavete	Gabino Diego
Lieutenant Ripamonte	Maurizio Di Razza
Interrogating Lieutenant	Miguel A. Rellan
Polish Officer	Edward Zentara
Bruno	Mario De Candia
Artillery Captain	Jose Sancho
Artillery Subaltern	Antonio Fuentes
Local Boss	Mario Martin
Mayor	Chema Mazo
Woman Prisoner	Silvia Casanova
Peasant Prisoner	Alfonso Guirao
Republican Doctor	Felipe Velez
Corporal Cardoso	Emilio Del Valle
Second Soldier CTV	Felix Pardo
Sentry	Rafael Diaz
Corporal	Manolo Millan
Officers	Victor Mendoza, Francisco Ferrer, Gabriel Moreno

Top Right: Carmen Maura, Andres Pajares
Right: Pajares, Maura
© *Prestige*

ROSENCRANTZ & GUILDENSTERN ARE DEAD

(CINECOM) Producers, Michael Brandman, Emanuel Azenberg; Executive Producers, Louise Stephens, Thomas J. Rizzo; Co-Producers, Iris Merlis, Patrick Whitley; Director/Screenplay, Tom Stoppard, based on his play; Photography, Peter Biziou; Music, Stanley Myers; Editor, Nicolas Gaster; Casting, Doreen Jones; Costumes, Andreane Neofitou; Designer, Vaughan Edwards; Assistant Director, Bill Westley; Presented in association with Thirteen WNET; British; Dolby Stereo; Color; Rated PG; 118 minutes; February release

CAST

Rosencrantz	Gary Oldman
Guildenstern	Tim Roth
The Player	Richard Dreyfuss
Ophelia	Joanna Roth
Hamlet	Iain Glen
Claudius	Donald Sumpter
Gertrude	Joanna Miles
Osric	Ljubo Zecevic
Polonius	Ian Richardson
Laertes	Sven Medvescek
Horatio	Vili Matula
Ambassador from England	John Burgess

and Livio Badurina, Tomislav Maretic, Mare Milacnik, Srdjan Soric, Mladen Vasary, Zeljko Vukmirica, Branko Zavrsan (Tragedians)

Above Left: Joanna Roth, Iain Glen
Below: Richard Dreyfuss, Tim Roth,
Gary Oldman © *Cinecom Entertainment*

THE SLEAZY UNCLE

(QUARTET FILMS/CASTLE HILL) Producers, Leo Pescarolo, Guido de Laurentiis; Director, Franco Brusati; Screenplay, Leo Benvenuti, Piero de Bernardi, Franco Brusati; Photography, Romano Albani; Music, Stefano Marcucci; Editor, Gianfranco Amicucci; an Ellepi Film production; Italian; Color; Not rated; 105 minutes; February release

CAST

Uncle Luca	Vittorio Gassman
Riccardo	Giancarlo Giannini
Teresa	Andréa Ferréol
Andrea	Kim Rossi Stuart
La Chanteuse	Beatrice Palme
Marina	Simona Cavallari
Isabella	Stefania Sandrelli

© *Quartet Films Inc.*

Vittorio Gassman, Giancarlo Giannini

LARKS ON A STRING

(INTERNATIONAL FILM EXCHANGE) Director, Jiri Menzel; Screenplay, Jiri Menzel, Bohumil Hrabal; Based on Hrabal's short story collection *Advertisement for a House I Do Not Want to Live in Anymore*; Photography, Jaromir Sofr; Art Director, Oldrich Bosak; Music, Jiri Sust; Editor, Jirina Lukesova; Produced by the Barrandov Film Studios; Czech, 1969; Color; Not rated; 96 minutes; February release

CAST

Pavel Hvezdar	Vaclav Neckar
The Government Agent	Rudolf Hrusinsky
Jitka	Jitka Zelenohorska
The Dairyman	Vladimir Ptacek
The Professor	Vlastimil Brodsky
Andel, the Guard	Jaroslav Satoransky
Lenka	Nad'a Urbankova
Kudla	Ferdinand Kruta
"Scrap"	Frantisek Rehak
The Prosecutor	Leos Sucharipa

Above Left: Vaclav Neckar, Jitka Zelenohorska
Left: Rudolf Hrusinsky
© *IFEX*

PRINCES IN EXILE

(FRIES ENTERTAINMENT) Producer, John Dunning; Executive Producers, Andre Link, Colin Neale; Producer for NFB, Marrin Canell; Director, Giles Walker; Screenplay, Joe Wiesenfeld; Based on the novel by Mark Schreiber; Supervising Producer, Irene Litinsky; Photography, Savas Kalogeras; Designer, Charles Dunlop; Music, Normand Corbeil; Editor, Richard Todd; Canadian; Color; Rated PG; 104 minutes; February release

CAST

Ryan Rafferty	Zachary Ansley
Holly	Stacie Mistysyn
Robert	Nicholas Shields
Dr. Merritt	Chuck Shamata
Gabriel	Alexander Chapman
Marlene Lancaster	Andrea Roth

Right: Zachary Ansley, Stacie Mistysyn
© *Fries Entertainment*

JU DOU

(MIRAMAX) Producers, Zhang Wenze, Yasuyoshi Tokuma, Hu Jian; Executive Producers, Zhao Hangao, Shigeru Moki, Hiro Yuki; Director, Zhang Yimou; Co-Director, Yang Fengliang; Screenplay, Liu Heng; Photography, Gu Changwei; Editor, Du Yuan; Music, Zhao Jipin; Art Directors, Cao Jiuping, Xia Rujin; Produced by China Film Co-production Corporation/China Film Export and Import Corp./Tokuma Shoten Publishing Co., Ltd./Tokuma Communications Co., Ltd., in cooperation with the Studio of Xi'an; Chinese; Color; Not rated; 95 minutes; March release

CAST

Ju Dou ....Gong Li
Yang Tianqing ....Li Bao-Tian
Yang Jinshan ....Li Wei
Yang Tianbai (Infant)..Zhang Yi
Yang Tianbai (Youth)......................................Zheng Jian

Top: Gong Li, Li Bao-Tian (also left and below right)
Below Left: Li
© Miramax Films

ARCHANGEL

(ZEITGEIST) Producer, Greg Klymkiw; Executive Producer, Andre Bennett; Director/Photography/Editor, Guy Maddin; Screenplay, Guy Maddin, George Toles; Art Directors, Guy Maddin, Jeff Solylo; Canadian; Black and white; Not rated; 90 minutes; March release

CAST

Lt. John Boles ....Kyle McCulloch
Veronkha ....Kathy Marykuca
Philbin..Ari Cohen
Danchuk..Sarah Neville
Jannings..Michael Gottli
Geza ....David Falkenberg
Doctor ....Michael O'Sullivan
Baba...Margaret Anne Macleod
Captain..Victor Cowie
Monk..Ihor Procak
Kaiser Wilhelm ....Professor Steve Snyder

© Zeitgeist Films

David Falkenberg, Sarah Neville,
Michael Gottli

Anne Parillaud, Jean-Hughes Anglade
Top Left: Parillaud Top Right: Tcheky Karyo
Below Right: Parillaud Right: Parillaud, Jeanne Moreau
© *Gaumont-Gaumont Production*

LA FEMME NIKITA

(SAMUEL GOLDWYN CO.) Director/Screenplay, Luc Besson; Photography, Thierry Arbogast; Designer, Dan Weil; Costumes, Anne Angelini; Music, Éric Serra; Editor, Olivier Mauffory; Casting, Nathalie Serfaty; a co-production of Gaumont Production and Cecchi Gori Group Tiger Cinematografica; French-Italian; Dolby Stereo; Technovision; Color; Rated R; 117 minutes; March release

CAST

Nikita	Anne Parillaud
Marco	Jean-Hughes Anglade
Bob	Tcheky Karyo
Amande	Jeanne Moreau
Nikita's Friend	Jean Reno
Chief of Intelligence	Jean Bouise
Ambassador	Philippe Du Anerand
Interrogating Officer	Roland Blanche
Chief Grossman	Philippe Leroy-Beaulieu
Rico	Marc Duret
Pharmacist	Jacques Boudet

Jean Reno, Anne Parillaud

Stian Smestad, Stamsö Munch, Louisa Haigh
Top: Smestad
© *Buena Vista Pictures*

SHIPWRECKED

(WALT DISNEY PICTURES) Producer, John M. Jacobsen; Director, Nils Gaup; Screenplay, Nils Gaup, Bob Foss, Greg Dinner, Nick Thiel; Based on the book *Haakon Haakonsen* by O.V. Falck-Ytter; Executive Producer, Nigel Wooll; Photography, Erling Thurmann-Andersen; Music, Patrick Doyle; Editor, Niels Pagh-Andersen; Special Effects, Richard Conway; Associate Producers, Erik Disch, Selwyn Remington; Designers, Harald Egede-Nissen, Roger Cain; Costumes, Lotte Dandanell, Bente Winther-Larsen; a co-production of Filmkameratene A/S and AB Svensk Filmindustri; Distributed by Buena Vista Pictures; Norwegian; Dolby Stereo; Panavision; Technicolor; Rated PG; 93 minutes; March release

CAST

Hakon Hakonsen	Stian Smestad
Merrick	Gabriel Byrne
Mary	Louisa Haigh
Jens	Trond Peter Stamsö Munch
Mr. Hakonsen	Björn Sundquist
Mrs. Hakonsen	Eva Von Hanno
Captain Madsen	Kjell Stormoen
Bosun	Karl Sundby
Berg	Knut Walle
Steine	Harald Brenna
Bakken	John Sigurd Kristensen
Old Salt	Geo Von Krogh
Wernes	Frank Krog
Ole	Joachim Rafaelson
Thatcher	Guy Fithen
Howell	Ian Mackenzie
Pirates	William Ilkley, Terry Duran
Sheriff	Rannov Nilsen
Rakel	Jannecke Öinæs
Sara	Mariken Bowles Sörhus
Friends	Thomas Fjeld Heltne, Benjamin Dootsen

THE COMFORT OF STRANGERS

(SKOURAS) Producer, Angelo Rizzoli; Executive Producer, Mario Cotone; Director, Paul Schrader; Screenplay, Harold Pinter; Based on the novel by Ian McEwan; Photography, Dante Spinotti; Designer, Gianni Quaranta; Editor, Bill Pankow; Music, Angelo Badalamenti; Casting, Mary Selway; an Erre Produzioni, Sovereign Pictures production in association with Reteitalia s.p.a.; Italian-U.S.; Color; Rated R; 105 minutes; March release

CAST

Robert	Christopher Walken
Mary	Natasha Richardson
Colin	Rupert Everett
Caroline	Helen Mirren
Concierge	Manfredi Aliquo
Waiters	David Ford, Daniel Franco
Hotel Maid	Rossana Caghiari
Bar Manager	Fabrizio Castellani
Policemen	Giancarlo Previati, Antonio Serrano
Detective	Mario Cotone

© *Skouras Pictures*

Natasha Richardson, Christopher Walken, **193**
Rupert Everett Above Right: Richardson, Everett

MISTER JOHNSON

(AVENUE PICTURES) Producer, Michael Fitzgerald; Executive Producer, Bill Benenson; Director, Bruce Beresford; Screenplay, William Boyd; Based on the novel by Joyce Cary; Photography, Peter James; Designer, Herbert Pinter; Costumes, Rosemary Burrows; Music, Georges Delerue; Editor, Humphrey Dixon; Assistant Director, Guy Travers; British; Technicolor; Rated PG; 101 minutes; March release

CAST

Mister Johnson	Maynard Eziashi
Harry Rudbeck	Pierce Brosnan
Sargy Gollup	Edward Woodward
Celia Rudbeck	Beatie Edney
Bulteen	Denis Quilley
Tring	Nick Reding
Bamu	Bella Enahoro
Waziri	Femi Fatoba
Benjamin	Kwabena Manso
Brimah	Chief Hubert Ogunde
Ajali	Sola Adeyemi
Saleh	Jerry Linus
Emir	George Menta
Aliu	Steve James
Jamesu	Tunde Kelani
Village Chief	Akinola Ayegbusi
Scribe	Albert Egbe
Police Sergeant	Sani Izang
Bamu's Mother	Ibidun Ogunde
Creditor Women	Hajia Nana Yahaya, Gladys Dadzie
Creditor Man	John Johnson

and Wali Umar (Suli), Lassisi Moshudu (Pagan Trader), Oladejo Adegboyega, Matt Dadzie (Guards), Laraba Ogomo (Bamu's Baby), Fred Ibrahim, Philip Elegonya (Policemen), Mary Kalu (Matumbi), Moses Okwe (Alhaji), Mallam Musa Udu (Trader), Charles Ani (Levi), Chris Erakptybor (Interpreter), Saidu Dahtru (Chair Boy)

Maynard Eziashi, Pierce Brosnan
© *Avenue Pictures*

OPEN DOORS

(ORION CLASSICS) Producer, Angelo Rizzoli; Director, Gianni Amelio; Screenplay, Gianni Amelio, Vincenzo Cerami, Alessandro Sermoneta; Based on the novel by Leonardo Sciascia; Photography, Tonino Nardi; Art Directors, Franco Velchi, Amedeo Fago; Costumes, Gianna Gissi; Music, Franco Piersanti; Editor, Simona Paggi; an Erre Produzioni - Instituto Luce - Urania Film production with the collaboration of RAIDUE; Italian; Color; Rated R; 108 minutes; March release

CAST

Vito Di Francesco	Gian Maria Volonte
Tommaso Scalia	Ennio Fantastichini
Judge Sanna	Renzo Giovampietro
Giovanni Consolo	Renato Carpentieri
Spadafora	Tuccio Musumeci
Public Prosecutor	Silverio Blasi
Rosa Scalia	Vitalba Andrea
The Prosecution	Giacomo Piperno
Marchioness Spadafora	Lydia Alfonsi
Chauffeur	Tony Palazzo
Independent Auditor	Roberto Nobile
Lo Prete	Antonio Appierto
Doctor Canillo	Nicola Badalucco
Don Michele	Paolo Volpicelli
Colao	Orazio Stracuzzi
Nora	Cinzia Insinga
Antonia	Maria Spadola
Vincenzo	Giancarlo Kory
Peppuccio	Francesco Sineri
Leonardo	Fabrizio Mendola
Carmelina	Eleonora Schinina
The Nun	Sara Micalizzi
Old Man at hospice	Nino Isaia
School Mistress	Gigliola Raja
Mrs. Sanna	Maria Lauretta

and Melita Poma (Young Girl at Sanna's), Turi Catanzaro, Francesco Gabriele, Pietro Bertone, Nicola Vigilante (Jurors), Vittorio Zarfati (Clerk of the Court), Luigi Stefanachi (Professor Sciuti), Domenico Gennaro (Man at cemetery), Egidio Termine (Fascist), Agostino Zumbo (Secretary to the President)

Eleonora Schinina, Gian Maria Volonte
Above: Ennio Fantastichini

© *Orion Classics*

CROSS MY HEART
(La Fracture du Myocarde)

(MK 2) Producers, Ludi Boeken, Jacques Fansten/Belbo Films; Executive Producers, Arlette Guibert/SFP; Director/Screenplay, Jacques Fansten; Photography, Jean-Claude Saillier; Editor, Colette Farruggia; Music, Jean-Marie Senia; Art Director, Gilbert Gagneux; Costumes, Helene Martel; Co-produced with Antenne 2 and Canal Plus and SFP; French; Color; Not rated; 105 minutes; April release

CAST

Martin	Sylvain Copans
Jerome	Nicolas Parodi
Marianne	Cecilia Rouaud
Helene	Delphine Gouttman
Antoine	Olivier Montiege
Claire	Lucie Blossier
Dede	Kaldi El Hadj
Nicolas	Mathieu Poussin
Mozart	Wilfried Flandrin
Pierrot	Romuald Jarny
Julien	Benoit Gautier
Olivier	Wilfrid Blin
Claire's Mother	Dominique Lavanant
Bicycle Clip	Jacques Bonnaffe
Titanic	Francois Dyrek
Mrs. Haudray	Christine Prieur
School Principal	Jacques Brunet
Neighbor	Maurice Benichou
Steps	Catherine Hubeau
Marianne's Mother	Renee Cousseau
Marianne's Father	Maurice Frydland
Nicolas' Father	Michel Pilorge
Nicolas' Mother	Laurence Imbert
Jerome's Mother	Huguette Hatier
Youth Home Director	Didier Lastere
The Judge	Gerard Croce
The Nurse	Cyrille Gaudin
Schoolyard Supervisor	Jean-Louis Boutevin

Sylvain Copans Top Right: Nicolas Parodi, Cecilia Rouaud, Olivier Montiege
© MK 2

DROWNING BY NUMBERS

(PRESTIGE) Producer, Kees Kasander, Denis Wigman; Director/Screenplay, Peter Greenaway; Photography, Sacha Vierny; Editor, John Wilson; Music, Michael Nyman; Costumes, Heather Williams; Distributed by Miramax Films; British; Dolby Stereo; Color; Not rated; 114 minutes; April release

CAST

Cissie Colpitts 1	Joan Plowright
Cissie Colpitts 2	Juliet Stevenson
Cissie Colpitts 3	Joely Richardson
Madgett	Bernard Hill
Smut	Jason Edwards
Jake	Bryan Pringle
Hardy	Trevor Cooper
Bellamy	David Morrissey
Gregory	John Rogan
Teigan	Paul Money
Nancy	Jane Gurnett
Jonah Bognor	Kenny Ireland
Moses Bognor	Michael Percival
Mrs. Hardy	Joanna Dickins
Marina Bellamy	Janine Duvitski
Mr. 70 Van Dyke	Michael Fitzgerald
Mr. 71 Van Dyke	Edward Tudor Pole
The Skipping Girl	Natalie Morse
Sid the Gravedigger	Arthur Spreckley
The Police Detective	Ian Talbot
The Policeman	Roderic Leigh
The Hare	Vanni Corbellini
Skipping Girl's Mother	Jose Berg

Bernard Hill, Joan Plowright, Juliet Stevenson, Jason Edwards Above: Joely Richardson, Stevenson, Plowright

© Prestige

KORCZAK

(NEW YORKER) Producers, Regina Ziegler, Janusz Morgenstern, Daniel Toscan Du Plantier; Director, Andrzej Wajda; Screenplay, Agnieszka Holland; Photography, Robby Muller; Designer, Allan Starski; Editor, Ewa Smal; Executive Producers, Wolfgang Hantke, Lew Rywin; Music, Wojciech Kilar; Costumes, Wieslawa Starska, Malgorzata Stefaniak; Polish; Color; Not rated; 120 minutes; April release

CAST

Korczak	Wojtek Pszoniak
Stefa	Ewa Dalkowska
Heniek	Piotr Kozlowski
Estera	Marzena Trybala
Szloma	Wojcieh Klata
Abramek	Adam Siemion
Natka	Karolina Czernicka
Ewka	Agnieszka Kruk

Top Right: Wojtek Pszoniak (c)
© New Yorker Films

REQUIEM FOR DOMINIC

(HEMDALE) Producer, Norbert Blecha; Director, Robert Dornhelm; Screenplay, Michael Kohlmeier, Felix Mitterer; Photography, Hans Selikovsky; Editors, Ingrid Koller, Barbara Heraut; Music, Harald Kloser; Costumes, Elisabeth Freiss; a John Daly & Derek Gibson presentation of a Terra Filmproduction; Austrian; Color; Rated R; 88 minutes; April release

CAST

Paul	Felix Mitterer
Clara	Viktoria Schubert
Dominic	August Schmolzer
Codruta	Angelica Schutz
Antonia	Antonia Rados
Nick	Nikolas Vogel
Mr. Ostenhof	Georg Hoffmann-Ostenhof
French Journalists	Alain Michel, Jean Marc Jouve
Viennese Doctor	Werner Prinz
Doctor	Regina Ahner
Nurse	Liselotte Weber
Factory Director	Oscar Schilz
Priest	Georg Metzenrad
Factory Workers	Adrian Ciuca, Tiberiu Kovacs, Michai Buzatu, Christian Cornea

Above Left: Viktoria Schubert, Felix Mitterer
Left: August Schmolzer
© Hemdale Film Corp.

FOREVER MARY

(CINEVISTA) Producer, Claudio Bonivento; Director, Marco Risi; Screenplay/Dialogue, Sandro Petraglia, Stefano Rulli; Based on the novel *Meri per sempre* by Aurelio Grimaldi; Story, Aurelio Grimaldi; Music, Giancarlo Bigazzi; Photography, Mauro Marchetti; Editor, Claudio Di Mauro; a Numero Uno International Sri Production; Italian; Color; Not rated; 100 minutes; April release

CAST

Marco Terzi	Michele Placido
Mary	Alessandro di Sanzo
Pietro	Claudio Amendola
Natale	Francesco Benigno

and Tony Sperandeo, Roberto Mariano, Maurizio Prollo, Filippo Genzardi, Giovanni Alamia, Alfredo Libassi, Salvatore Termini, Gianluca Favilla

© Cinevista

Allesandro di Sanzo, Michele Placido

THE OBJECT OF BEAUTY

John Malkovich, Andie MacDowell
© *Avenue Pictures*

(AVENUE PICTURES) Producer, Jon S. Denny; Director/Screenplay, Michael Lindsay-Hogg; Executive Producer, Cary Brokaw; Photography, David Watkin; Editor, Ruth Foster; Music, Tom Bahler; Designer, Derek Dodd; Costumes, Les Lansdown; Associate Producer, Richard Turner; Producer for BBC Films, Alex Gohar; Sculpture: "Head on a Bone Base" by Henry Moore; a co-presentation of BBC Films; British; Rank color; Rated R; 101 minutes; April release

CAST

Jake	John Malkovich
Tina	Andie MacDowell
Joan	Lolita Davidovich
Jenny	Rudi Davies
Mr. Mercer	Joss Ackland
Victor Swayle	Bill Paterson
Steve	Ricci Harnett
Larry	Peter Riegert
Mr. Slaughter	Jack Shepherd
Mrs. Doughty	Rosemary Martin
Frankie	Roger Lloyd Pack
Gordon	Andrew Hawkins
Art Evaluator	Pip Torrens
Mr. Mundy	Stephen Churchett
Housekeeper	Annie Hayes
Night Porter	Richard Ireson
Auctioneer	Barry J. Gordon
Jonathan	Jeremy Sinden
Melissa	Ginger Corbett
Waiter	John Crocker

and Victoria Willing, Lara De Almeida, Liz Daniels (Portuguese Maids), Andy Cavenash, Wayne Bailey, Colin Parker, Stewart Miller, Bryan Coyle, Dillon O'Mahoney (Steve's Friends), Massimo Burlini (Enrico), Mario Nocerino (Italian Father)

DADDY NOSTALGIA

(AVENUE PICTURES) Producer, Adolphe Viezzi; Director, Bertrand Tavernier; Screenplay, Colo Tavernier O'Hagan; Dialogue, Colo Tavernier O'Hagan, Bertrand Tavernier; Photography, Denis Lenoir; Art Director, Jean-Louis Poveda; Costumes, Christian Gasc; Editor, Ariane Boeglin; Music, Antoine Duhamel; Song: "These Foolish Things" by Eric Maschwitz, Jack Strachey-Lonk/performed by Jane Birkin, Jimmy Rowles; a Clea Productions - Little Bear - Solyfic -Eurisma Co-Production; French; Eastman color; Cinemascope; Dolby Stereo; Rated PG; 105 minutes; April release

CAST

Daddy	Dirk Bogarde
Caroline	Jane Birkin
Miche	Odette Laure
Juliette	Emmanuelle Bataille
Barbara	Charlotte Kady
Caroline as a child	Michele Minns
Nurses	Sophie Dalezio, Sylvie Segalas
Woman at hospital	Helen Lefumat
Yvonne	Andree Duranson
Jimmy	Raymond Defendente
The Fisherman	Fabrice Roux
Waiter at restaurant	Gilbert Guerrero
Old Gentleman in metro	Louis Ducreux

© *Avenue Pictures*

Jane Birkin, Odette Laure, Dirk Bogarde
Above Right: Bogarde, Birkin

TRULY, MADLY, DEEPLY

(SAMUEL GOLDWYN CO.) formerly *Cello*; Producer, Robert Cooper; Director/Screenplay, Anthony Minghella; Executive Producer, Mark Shivas; Photography, Remi Adefarasin; Designer, Barbara Gasnold; Editor, John Stothart; Music, Barrington Pheloung; Song: "The Sun Ain't Gonna Shine Anymore" by Crewe & Gaudio/performed by Juliet Stevenson and Alan Rickman; Casting, Michelle Guish; Assistant Director, Peter Markham; a BBC-TV production; British; Dolby Stereo; Eastman color; Not rated; 107 minutes; May release

CAST

Nina	Juliet Stevenson
Jamie	Alan Rickman
Sandy	Bill Paterson
Mark	Michael Maloney
Burge	Jenny Howe
Translator	Carolyn Choa
Titus	Christopher Rozycki
Plumber	Keith Bartlett
George	David Ryall
Maura	Stella Maris
Maura's Baby	Henry James
Claire	Deborah Findlay
Harry	Ian Hawkes
Frenchman	Vania Vilers
Roberto	Arturo Venegas
Symonds	Richard Syms
Isaac	Mark Long
Freddie	Teddy Kempner
Pierre	Graeme Du-Fresne
Bruno	Frank Baker
Anthony	Tony Bluto
Midwife	Heather Williams

and Members of the Reach Group, Swindom (Themselves), Awam Amkpa, Hamilton Baillie, Nick Burge, Steven Deproost, Nitin Ganatra, Leroy Joseph, Jonathan Lunn, Eddie Vincent, Tom Yang (Ghosts)

Michael Maloney, Juliet Stevenson
Top: Stevenson, Alan Rickman
© BBC

STRANGERS IN GOOD COMPANY

(FIRST RUN FEATURES/CASTLE HILL) Producer/Editor, David Wilson; Executive Producers, Colin Neale, Rina Fraticelli, Peter Katadotis; Associate Producer, Sally Bochner; Director, Cynthia Scott; Screenplay, Gloria Demers, Cynthia Scott, David Wilson, Sally Bochner; Photography, David de Volpi; Music, Marie Bernard; Costumes, Elaine Langlais; released in association with Bedford Entertainment; Canadian; Color; Rated PG; 101 minutes; May release

CAST

Alice	Alice Diabo
Constance	Constance Garneau
Winifred	Winifred Holden
Cissy	Cissy Meddings
Mary	Mary Meigs
Catherine	Catherine Roche
Michelle	Michelle Sweeney
Beth	Beth Webber

© First Run/Castle Hill

Mary Meigs, Alice Diabo, Winifred Holden
Above Right: Cissy Meddings, Alice Diabo

EVERYBODY'S FINE

(MIRAMAX) Producer, Angelo Rizzoli; Executive Producer, Mario Cotone; Director, Giuseppe Tornatore; Screenplay, Giuseppe Tornatore, Tonino Guerra; Photography, Blasco Giurato; Art Director, Andrea Crisanti; Costumes, Beatrice Bordoni; Editor, Mario Morra; Music, Ennio Morricone; Italian; Dolby Stereo; Color; Not rated; 112 minutes; May release

CAST

Matteo Scuro	Marcello Mastroianni
Woman on the train	Michele Morgan
Canio	Marino Cenna
Guglielmo	Roberto Nobile
Tosca	Valeria Cavali
Norma	Norma Martelli
Erina	Maria Concetta Vigilia
Canio's Wife	Cloris Brosca
Antonello	Fabio Iellini
Milo	Angelo Formica
Matteo's Mother	Antonella Attili
Lo Piparo	Giorgio Libassi
Station Master	Gioacchino Civiletti
Hotel Porter	Nicola Di Pinto
Angela Scuro	Suzanna Schemmari
Alvaro	Salvatore "Toto" Cascio

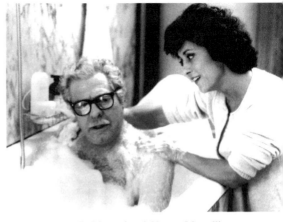

Marcello Mastroianni, Norma Martelli
© *Miramax Films*

Laurence Fevrier, Tsilla Chelton
Above Left: Chelton, Isabelle Nanty

TATIE DANIELLE

(PRESTIGE) Producer, Charles Gassot; Director, Etienne Chatiliez; Screenplay, Florence Quentin; Line Producer, Volker Lemke; Photography, Philippe Welt; Designer, Geoffroy Larcher; Music, Gabriel Yared; Song: "The Complaint of the Old Bitch" by Florence Quentin, Catherine Ringer (lyrics), and Gabriel Yared (music)/performed by Catherine Ringer; Editor, Catherine Renault; Costumes, Elisabeth Tavernier; Casting, Romain Bremond; Produced by TELEMA/FR3 Films Production/Champ Poirier Productions with the participation of Sofica Investimage, Sofica Creations, Sofimage and Images Investments; Distributed by Miramax Films; French; Color; Not rated; 110 minutes; May release

CAST

Tatie Danielle	Tsilla Chelton
Catherine Billard	Catherine Jacob
Sandrine	Isabelle Nanty
Odile	Neige Dolsky
Jean-Pierre Billard	Eric Prat
Jeanne Billard	Laurence Fevrier
Madame Lafosse	Virginie Pradal
Jean-Marie Billard	Mathieu Foulon
Totoff	Gary Ledoux
Doctor Wilms	Andre Wilms
Beggar	Patrick Bouchitey
Woman in taxi	Christine Pignet
Woman on bus	Evelyne Didi
Passerby	Isabelle Petit-Jacques
Agathe	Karine Viard
Madame Ladurie	Jacqueline Dufranne
Madame Lemoine	Dominique Mac Avoy
Monsieur Lemoine	Pierre Jean
Michael	Bradley Harryman
Madame Mauprivet	Madeleine Cheminat
Ginette Mauprivet	Nicole Chollet
Nurse (Camille)	Delphine Quentin
Nurse (Frederique)	Claire Marsden
Butcher	Olivier Saladin
Butcher's Wife	Lorella Cravotta

and Jean-Pierre Miquel (Doctor at hospital), Nadia-Marthe Barentin (Nurse - Suzanne), Brigitte Saint-Leon (Nurse - Sylvie), Patricia Eberhard (Nurse - Lydia), Anne-Marie Rateau (Nurse at hospital), Francoise Billet (Doctor's Assistant), Frederic Rossif (Man with the ducks), Josephine Sourdel (Mrs. Langman), Jean Chesnel (Mr. Burene), Catherine Jan (Mrs. Burene), Monique Pantel (Real Estate Woman), Francois-Regis Marchasson (Passerby), Marina Rodriguez-Tome (Concierge), Josette Guibert (Old Lady), Francis Boespflug, Gilles Loutfi (Journalists), Marie-France Cubadda, Jean-Jacques Dufour (TV Journalists), Denis Barbier (Attendant), Madeleine Antoine (Old Lady at Square), Christophe Malbranque (Friend of Jean-Marie)

© *Prestige*   **199**

AN ANGEL AT MY TABLE

(FINE LINE FEATURES) Producer, Bridget Ikin; Director, Jane Campion; Co-Producer, John Maynard; Screenplay, Laura Jones; Photography, Stuart Dryburgh; Designer, Grant Major; Costumes, Glenys Jackson; Editor, Veronika Haussler; Music, Don McGlashan; Casting, Diana Rowan; Australian; Color; Rated R; 154 minutes; May release

CAST

Janet	Kerry Fox
Young Janet	Alexia Keogh
Teenage Janet	Karen Fergusson
Mum	Iris Churn
Dad	K.J. Wilson
Myrtle	Melina Bernecker
Bruddie	Andrew Binns
Isabel	Glynis Angell
June	Sarah Smuts-Kennedy
Frank Sargeson	Martyn Sanderson
Patrick	David Letch
Bernard	William Brandt

Top Right: Kerry Fox Right: Karen Fergusson, Samantha Townsley, Sarah Llewellyn Below Left: William Brandt, Fox Below Right: Alexia Keogh
© *Fine Line Features*

A PAPER WEDDING

(CAPITOL ENTERTAINMENT) Producer, Aimee Danis; Director, Michel Brault; Screenplay, Jefferson Lewis, Andree Pelletier; Photography, Sylvain Brault; Associate Producer, Daniele Bussy; Editor, Jacques Gagne; Costumes, Mario Davignon; French Canadian; Color; Not rated; 90 minutes; June release

CAST

Claire	Genevieve Bujold
Pablo	Manuel Aranguiz
Annie	Dorothee Berryman
Gaby	Monique Lepage
Milosh	Teo Spychalski
Miguel	Jorge Fajardo
Bouchard	Gilbert Sicotte
Theriault	Jean Mathieu
Immigration Director	Robert Gravel

Genevieve Bujold, Manuel Aranguiz

© *Capitol Entertainment*

MY FATHER'S GLORY

(ORION CLASSICS) Producer, Alain Poiré; Director, Yves Robert; Screenplay, Jérôme Tonnere, Louis Nucera, Yves Robert; Based on Marcel Pagnol's *Memories of Childhood*; Photography, Robert Alazraki; Music, Vladimir Cosma; Casting, Gérard Moulevrier; Art Directors, Marc Goldstaub, Guy Azzi; Costumes, Agnès Negre; French; Color; Rated G; 110 minutes; June release

CAST

Joseph	Philippe Caubère
Augustine	Nathalie Roussel
Oncle Jules	Didier Pain
Tante Rose	Thérèse Liotard
Marcel (11 yrs.)	Julien Ciamaca
Paul (5 yrs.)	Victorien Delmare
Lili des Bellons	Joris Molinas
Mond des Parpaillouns	Paul Crauchet
François	Pierre Maguelon
Le facteur de la treille	Michel Modo
Le curè de la treille	Victor Garrivier
Le brocanteur	Jean Rougerie
M. Vincent	Raoul Curet
M. Besson	Renè Loyon
Mlle. Guimard	Michele Loubet
M. Arnaud	Maxime Lombard
Marcel (5 yrs.)	Benoit Martin
Paul (3 yrs.)	Benjamin Detriche
Voice of Marcel	Jean-Pierre Darras

Top Right: Julien Ciamaca, Paul Crauchet
Right: Philippe Caubère, Nathalie Roussel
© *Orion Classics*

EVERY OTHER WEEKEND

(MK 2) Producer, Alain Sarde; Director/Original Story, Nicole Garcia; Screenplay, Nicole Garcia, Jacques Fieschi, Anne-Marie Etienne, Philippe Le Guay; Photography, William Lubtchansky; Designer, Jean-Baptiste Poirot; Editor, Agnes Guillemot; Music, Oswald D'Andrea; Associate Producer, Christine Gozlan; Casting, Frederique Moidon; a Sara Films Production; French; Color; Not rated; 100 minutes; June release

CAST

Camille	Nathalie Baye
Vincent	Joachim Serreau
Gaelle	Felicie Pasotti
Adrian, the Father	Miki Manojlovic
Camille's Agent	Henri Garcin
Stephane	Gilles Treton
Graziella	Marie Daems
Marie-Ange	Michelle Goddet
Martha	Susan Carlson
Jacquet	Jacques Boudet
Lombard	Jacques Vincey
Hotel Manager	Sacha Briquet
Hertz Manager	Jean-Loup Wolff
Nurse	Frederique Ruchaud
Doctor	Jean-Marc Roulot
Maid	Sylvie Blotnikas
Bass Player	Yves Torchinsky
Swimmer	Nicolas Serreau
Magician	Jean Madd

and Martine Buffet (Hertz Employee), Hugues Avinens (Bus Driver), Lucette Filiu (Hotel Manager), Ghazi Younges (Hotel Receptionist), David Jalil (Fisherman), Zoubir Tligui (North African Son), Robert Perz (School Group Director), Paul Beauvais, Bruno Crovi (Customs Agents), Lise Norpel Mathieu (Box Office Woman)

Nathalie Baye, Miki Manojlovic
Above Left: Baye, Joachim Serreau

© *MK 2*

Marco Hofschneider, Andrzej Mastalerz Top Left:
Hofschneider, Left: Hofschneider, Delphine Forest
© *Orion Classics*

EUROPA, EUROPA

(ORION CLASSICS) Line Producers, Lew Rywin (Telmar International), Janusz Morgenstern (Perspektywa Film Unit); Executive Producers, Margaret Menegoz (Les Films du Losange), Arthur Brauner (CCC Filmkunst GMBH); Director/Screenplay, Agnieszka Holland, based on the autobiography of Solomon Perel; Photography, Jacek Petrycki; Art Director, Allan Starski; Editors, Ewa Smal, Isabelle Lorente; Music, Zbigniew Preisner; Costumes, Wieslawa Starska, Malgorzata Stefaniak; German-Russian-Polish; Color; Rated R; 115 minutes; June release

CAST

Solomon Perel (as a young man)	Marco Hofschneider
Isaak (Solomon's Brother)	Rene Hofschneider
David (Solomon's Brother)	Piotr Kozlowski
Solomon's Father	Klaus Abramowsky
Solomon's Mother	Michele Gleizer
Bertha (Solomon's Sister)	Marta Sandrowicz
Basia (The Cinema Cashier)	Nathalie Schmidt
Solomon Perel (today)	Solomon Perel

Komsomols:

Inna (The Teacher)	Delphine Forest
Zenek (The Young Pole)	Andrzej Mastalerz

In the Wehrmacht:

The Son of Stalin	Wlodzi Mierz Press
Ulmayer	Martin Maria Blau
Schulz	Klaus Kowatsch
Kramer	Holger Hunkel
Feidwebel	Bernhard Howe
Robert Kellerman	Andre Wilms
Captain von Lerenau	Hanns Zichler

At the Elite School for Hitler Youth:

Bannfuhrer	Jorg Schnass
Schwabe	Norbert Schwarz
Goethke	Eric Schwarz
Gerd	Ashley Wanninger
Leni	Julie Delpy
Leni's Mother	Halina Labonarska
Policeman	Wolfgang Bathke
The Soviet Major	Aleksy Awdiejew

Julie Delpy, Marco Hofschneider
Above: Delphine Forest

Halina Labonarska, Marco Hofschneider
Top Left: Hofschneider

Solomon Perel
Top Right: Julie Delpy, Marco Hofschneider

Rene Hofschneider, Marco Hofschneider

THE MIRACLE

(MIRAMAX) Producers, Stephen Woolley, Redmond Morris; Executive Producer, Nik Powell; Co-Executive Producers, Bob Weinstein, Harvey Weinstein; Director/Screenplay, Neil Jordan; Photography, Philippe Rousselot; Editor, Joke Van Wijk; Costumes, Sandy Powell; Designer, Gemma Jackson; Casting, Susie Figgis; Assistant Director, David Brown; Irish; Dolby Stereo; Color; Not rated; 97 minutes; July release

CAST

Renee	Beverly D'Angelo
Sam	Donal McCann
Jimmy	Niall Byrne
Rose	Lorraine Pilkington
Mr. Beausang	J.G. Devlin
Miss Strange	Cathleen Delaney
Tommy	Tom Hickey
Rose's Father	Shane Connaughton
Jonner	Mikkel Gaup
Muscular Lady	Sylvia Teron
Ballroom Singer	Anita Reeves
Barman	Ger O'Leary
Wardrobe Mistress	Ruth McCabe
Sam's Band	Earl Gill, Johnny Devlin, Chris Kenevey, Tommy Donaghue

and "Destry Rides Again": Patrick Mason (Director), Stephen Brennan (Johnny/Destry), Martin Dunne (Kent), Stanley Tonwsend (Washington), Dermod Moore (Brunowski), Mary Coughlan (Mrs. Brunowski), Mal Whyte (Mayor), Darragh Kelly, Alan Archbold (Cowboys), The Clane Musical Society (Chorus)

Top: Beverly D'Angelo, Niall Byrne Right: Byrne
© Miramax Films

Niall Byrne, Beverly D'Angelo Above: Mikkel Gaup, Byrne, Lorraine Pilkington

Niall Byrne, Lorraine Pilkington

MY MOTHER'S CASTLE

(ORION CLASSICS) Producer, Alain Poiré; Director, Yves Robert; Screenplay, Jérôme Tonnere, Louis Nucera, Yves Robert; Photography, Robert Alazraki; Art Directors, Marc Goldstaub, Guy Azzi; Music, Vladimir Cosma; Editor, Pierre Gillette; Costumes, Agnès Negre; Casting, Gérard Moulevrier; French; Color; Rated PG; 98 minutes; July release

CAST

Joseph	Philippe Caubère
Augustine	Nathalie Roussel
Uncle Jules	Didier Pain
Aunt Rose	Thérèse Liotard
Drunken Guard	Jean Carmet
Lois de Montmajour	Jean Rochefort
Bouzigue	Philippe Uchan
Mond des Parpaillouns	Paul Crauchet
Dominique	Patrick Prejean
Marcel	Julien Ciamaca
Paul	Victorien Delmare
Lili des Bellons	Joris Molinas
Isabelle	Julie Timmerman
Fenestrelle	Jean-Marie Juan
Binucci	Ticky Holgado
M. Besson	René Loyon
M. Arnaud	Maxime Lombard
Headmaster of the Chartreux School	André Chameau
François	Pierre Maguelon
Postman	Michel Modo
Marcel Pagnol, at 40 years old	Alain Ganas
Vladimir	Ivan Romeuf
Innkeeper at the Quatres Saisons	Jean Maurel
Baby	Elizabeth Macocco

and Michel Combale (Mr. Bonafe), Philippe Car (Mr. Mortier), Raoul Curet (Mr. Vincent), Paul Vilalte (Mr. Suzanne), Christina Karian (Rose and Jules' Maid), Josy Andreiu (Headmaster's Wife), Jean-Pierre Darras (Voice of Marcel)

Top Right: Nathalie Roussel, Julien Ciamaca
© *Orion Classics*

Chris Haywood
© *Cabriolet Films*

GOLDEN BRAID

(CABRIOLET) Producers, Paul Cox, Paul Ammitzboll, Santhana Naidu; Executive Producer, William T. Marshall; Director, Paul Cox; Screenplay, Paul Cox, Barry Dickins; Based on the short story "La Chevelure" by Guy de Maupassant; Photography, Nino G. Martinetti; Designer, Neil Angwin; Editor, Russell Hurley; Produced by the Australian Film Commission and Film Victoria, in association with Illumination Films; Australian; Eastmancolor; Not rated; 91 minutes; July release

CAST

Bernard	Chris Haywood
Terese	Gosia Dobrowolska
Joseph	Paul Chubb
Psychiatrist	Norman Kaye
Cleaning Woman	Marion Heathfield
Antique Shop Owner	Monica Maughan
Ernst	Robert Menzies
Paradise	Jo Kennedy
Cellist	Phillip Green
Lady with clock	Sheilah Florance
Bank Manager	George Fairfax
Clockmaker	Harold Baigent
Barber	Barry Dickins
Shop Assistant	Victoria Eagger
Female Clerk	Margaret Mills
Woman in dreams	Dawn Klingberg
Punk	Mark Little
Waitress	Terrie Waddell
Restaurant Owner	Dr. James Khong
Delivery Men	Francois Bernard, Manuel Bachet

DON JUAN, MY LOVE

(IFEX) Executive Producer, Jose Maria Calleja; Director, Antonio Mercero; Screenplay, Joaquin Oristrell, Antonio Mercero; Photography, Carlos Suarez; Designer, Rafael Palmero; Editor, Rosa Graceli-Salgado; Music, Bernardo Bonezzi; Choreographer, Paco Romero; a B.M.G. Films, S.A. production in collaboration with RTVE, S.A. and Productora Andaluza de Programas; Spanish; Color; Not rated; 96 minutes; July release

CAST

Don Juan/Juan Marquina	Juan Luis Galiardo
Dona Ines	Maria Barranco
Ana (Woman with castanets)	Loles Leon
Vuida Prodini (Acrobat)	Rossy de Palma
Senora Marquina	Veronica Forque
Police Commissioner Ulloa	Jose Sazatornil
Ciutti	Vicente Diez
Ruben (Theatre Director)	Pedro Reyes
Monreal	Luis Escobar
Mendez	Rafael Alvarez

Top Right: Maria Barranco, Juan Luis Galiardo
© IFEX

Beverly D'Angelo, Robbie Coltrane
© Miramax Films

THE POPE MUST DIE

(MIRAMAX) Producer, Stephen Woolley; Executive Producers, Michael White, Nik Powell; Director, Peter Richardson; Screenplay, Peter Richardson, Pete Richens; Photography, Frank Gell; Designer, John Ebden; Costumes, Sandy Powell; Editor, Katherine Wenning; Casting, Ross Hubbard, John Hubbard; Assistant Director, Glynn Purcell; a Palace and British Screen presentation in association with Film Four International; British; Dolby Stereo; Color; Rated R; 88 minutes; August release

CAST

Father Dave Albinizi (Pope David I)	Robbie Coltrane
Veronica Dante	Beverly D'Angelo
Vittorio Corelli	Herbert Lom
Cardinal Rocco	Alex Rocco
Monsignor Vitchie	Paul Bartel
Joe Don Dante	Balthazar Getty
Cardinal Verucci	William Hootkins
Carmelengo	Robert Stephens
Mother Superior	Annette Crosbie
Rico	Steve O'Donnell
Dino	John Sessions
Paulo	Salvatore Cascio
Bish	Peter Richardson
Luccia Corelli	Khedija Sassi
Rookie	Adrian Edmonson

Adrian Edmonson, Alex Rocco
Above Left: Herbert Lom

VOYEUR

(PRESTIGE) Producers, Laurens Geels, Dick Maas, Robert Swaab; Director/Screenplay, Alex Van Warmerdam; Adaptation, Otakar Votocek, Alex Van Warmerdam; Photography, Marc Felperlaan; Art Director, Harry Ammerlaan; Editor, Hans Van Dongen; Music, Vincent Van Warmerdam; Produced in cooperation with the Orkater Foundation and V.P.R.O. Television; Released through Miramax Films; Dutch, 1985; Color; Not rated; 100 minutes; August release

CAST

Abel	Alex Van Warmerdam
Victor	Henri Garcin
Dove	Olga Zuiderhoek
Sis	Annet Malherbe
Christine	Loes Luca
Psychiatrist	Arend Jan Heerma Van Voss
Magnetic Healer	Anton Kothuys
Director	Peer Mascini
Waitress	Elmar Schiphorst
Fishmonger	Marc Van Warmerdam
Old Cyclist	Jan-Willem Hees
Dying Cowboy	Jeroen Henneman
Couple with dog	Mieke Verdin, Josse De Pauw
Man with a cold	Otakar Votocek
Chairman of meeting	Aat Ceelen
Polishing Woman	Dorien De Jonge
De Beer (Man at meeting)	Rien Bogaart
Motorcyclist	Paul Höhner

Top Right: Alex Van Warmerdam
Right: Annet Malherbe
© Prestige

THE STORY OF BOYS AND GIRLS

(ARIES FILMS) Producer, Antonio Avati; Director/Screenplay/Story, Pupi Avati; Photography, Pasquale Rachini; Designers, Daria Ganassini, Giovanna Zighetti; Costumes, Graziella Virgili; Music, Riz Ortolani; Editor, Amedeo Salfa; Italian; Color; Not rated; 92 minutes; August release

CAST

Domenico	Felice Andreasi
Maria	Angiola Baggi
Angelo	Davide Bechini
Olimpia	Lina Bernardi
Amelia	Anna Bonaiuto
Baldo	Massimo Bonetti
Taddeo	Claudio Botosso
Valeria	Valeria Bruni Tadeschi
Donatella	Claudia Casaglia
Paola	Monica Cervini
Lele	Marcello Cesena
Dolores	Consuelo Ferrara
Antonia	Stefania Orsola Garello
Giulio	Alessandro Haber
Silvia	Lucrezia Lante Della Rovere
Renata	Susanna Marcomeni
Marco	Claudio Mazzanga
Linda	Enrico Maria Modungo
Nando	Ferdinando Orlandi
Loretta	Roberta Paladini
Gina	Claudia Pozzi
Don Luciano	Massimo Sarchielli
Augusto	Mattia Sbragia
Alberto	Ciro Scalera

Lucrezia Lante Della Rovere, Massimo Bonetti, Davide
Bechini Above: Della Rovere

© Aries Films

THE COMMITMENTS

(20th CENTURY FOX) Producers, Roger Randall-Cutler, Lynda Myles; Executive Producers, Armyan Bernstein, Tom Rosenberg, Souter Harris; Director, Alan Parker; Screenplay, Dick Clement, Ian La Frenais, Roddy Doyle; Based on the novel by Roddy Doyle; Line Producer, David Wimbury; Co-Producers, Dick Clement, Ian La Frenais, Marc Abraham; Photography, Gale Tattersall; Designer, Brian Morris; Editor, Gerry Hambling; Costumes, Penny Rose; Casting, John & Ros Hubbard; Music Supervisor, G. Mark Roswell; Assistant Director, Bill Westley; a Beacon presentation of a First Film Company/Dirty Hands production; British; Dolby Stereo; Deluxe color; Rated R; 118 minutes; August release

CAST

Jimmy Rabbitte	Robert Arkins
Steven Clifford	Michael Aherne
Imelda Quirke	Angeline Ball
Natalie Murphy	Maria Doyle
Mickah Wallace	Dave Finnegan
Bernie McGloughlin	Bronagh Gallagher
Dean Fay	Félim Gormley
Outspan Foster	Glen Hansard
Billy Mooney	Dick Massey
Joey "The Lips" Fagan	Johnny Murphy
Derek Scully	Kenneth McCluskey
Deco Cuffe	Andrew Strong
Mr. Rabbitte	Colm Meaney
Mrs. Rabbitte	Anne Kent
Sharon Rabbitte	Andrea Corr
Darren Rabbitte	Gerard Cassoni
Linda & Tracey Rabbitte	Ruth & Lindsay Fairclough
Greg	Michael O'Reilly
Duffy	Liam Carney
Pawnbroker	Ger Ryan
Father Molloy	Mark O'Regan

and Phelim Drew (Roddy the Reporter), Sean Hughes (Dave from Eejit Records), Philip Bredin (Ray), Aoife Lawless (Imelda's Sister), Lance Daly (Kid with harmonica), Conor Malone (Protest Song Singer), Jezz Bell (Heavy Metal Singer), Colm MacCon Iomaire (Fiddler Auditioner), Emily Dawson (Punk Girl Singer), Dave Kane, Kristel Harris, Maria Place (Coconuts Trio), Brian MacAodha (Uileann Pipe Player), Tricia Smith (Les Miserables Singer), Canice William (Smiths' Song Singer), Patrick Foy, Alan Murray, Jody Campbell (Cajun Trio), Eanna MacLiam (Failed Drug Buyer), Philomena Kavanagh (Rabbitte's Neighbor), Peter Rowen (Shy Skateboard Auditioner), Eamon O'Connor (Only De Lonely Singer), Maura O'Malley (Joey's Mother), Blaise Smith (Pool Hall Manager), Derek Herbert, Owen O'Gorman (Duffy's Sidekicks), Pat Leavy (Unemployment Official), John Cronin (Kid with horse), Rynagh O'Grady (Bernie's Mother), Sheila Flitton (Church Cleaner), Michael Bolger (Community Centre Kid), Mick Nolan (Imelda's Father), Eileen Reid (Imelda's Mother), Bob Navan (Regency Pub Barman), Derek Duggan (Photographer), Paddy O'Connor (Rock Salmon Man), Paul Bushnell, Jim Corr, Larry Hogan, Bernard Keelan (Avant-Garde-a-Clue Band), Ronan Hardiman (Dance Hall Manager), Mikel Murfi (Music Journalist), Josylen Lyons (Deco's Fan), Winston Dennis (Man in limousine), Alan Parker (Eejit Record Producer), Paul Bushnell (Eejit Engineer)

Top: Andrew Strong, Robert Arkins Right: Arkins
© *Beacon Communications*

Michael Aherne, Andrew Strong,
Robert Arkins, Kenneth McCluskey,
Glen Hansard

Andrew Strong (center)

Dick Massey, Felim Gormley, Maria Doyle, Robert Arkins, Glen Hansard Top Left: Gallagher, Doyle, Ball

Bronagh Gallagher, Angeline Ball, Maria Doyle, Andrew Strong Top Right: Dick Massey (left)

(Back Row) Félim Gormley, Johnny Murphy, Kenneth McCluskey, Michael Aherne, Dave Finnegan, (Front Row) Bronagh Gallagher, Glen Hansard, Andrew Strong, Maria Doyle, Angeline Ball

URANUS

(PRESTIGE) Executive Producer, Pierre Grunstein; Director, Claude Berri; Adaptation/Dialogue, Claude Berri, Arlette Langmann, based on the novel by Marcel Ayme; Photography, Renata Berta; Editor, Herve De Luze; Costumes, Caroline De Vivaise; Designer, Patrick Bordier; a Renn Productions - Films A2 - D.D. Productions co-production with the participation of Soficas Sofi-ARP - Sofica Investimage 2 and 3; French; Dolby Stereo; Color; Not rated; 100 minutes; August release

CAST

Watrin	Philippe Noiret
Leopold	Gerard Depardieu
Archambaud	Jean-Pierre Marielle
Gaigneux	Michel Blanc
Monglat	Michel Galabru
Maxime Loin	Gerard Desarthe
Jourdan	Fabrice Luchini
Rochard	Daniel Prevost
Marie-Anne	Florence Darel
Mme. Archambaud	Daniele Lebrun
Maria Gaigneux	Myriam Boyer
Andrea	Josiane Leveque
Michel Monglat	Dominique Bluzet
Brigadier	Yves Afonso
Megrin	Ticky Holgado
Pierre	Herve Rey
Ledieu	Vincent Grarls
Charles Watrin	Alain Stern
Policeman	Andre Chaumeau
Police Inspector	Bernard Ballet
Warden	Paul Doumer
Gallien	Gerard Bole De Chaumont
Montfort	Patrice Melennec
Alfred	Thierry Theoleyre
Mayor	Andre Charrondiere
Priest	Daniel Dedieu
Gaigneux's Children	Lydie Lorente, Sabine Lorente, Morgan Formes, Prune Semof

Top: Philippe Noiret, Gerard Depardieu Right: Depardieu, Daniel Prevost Below Left: Noiret, Jean-Pierre Marielle Below Right: Michel Blanc, Florence Darel © *Prestige*

BLACK LIZARD

(CINEVISTA) Director, Kinji Fukasaku; Screenplay, Masashige Narusawa; Based on the novel by Rampo Edogawa, and stage adaptation by Yukio Mishima; Photography, Hiroshi Dowaki; Music, Isao Tomita; Japanese, 1968; Color; Shochiku Grandscope; Not rated; 86 minutes; September release

CAST

Black Lizard	Akihiro Maruyama
Detective Akechi	Isao Kimura
Jeweler	Junya Usami
Sanaye	Kikko Matsuoka

and Yukio Mishima

© *Cinevista*

Yukio Mishima, Akihiro Maruyama

LIFE IS SWEET

(OCTOBER FILMS) Producer, Simon Channing-Williams; Director/Screenplay, Mike Leigh; Photography, Dick Pope; Editor, Jon Gregory; Designer, Alison Chitty; Costumes, Lindy Hemming; Assistant Director, Gus MacLean; Music, Rachel Portman; a Thin Man Films production; British; Color; Not rated; 102 minutes; October release

CAST

Wendy	Alison Steadman
Andy	Jim Broadbent
Natalie	Claire Skinner
Nicola	Jane Horrocks
Patsy	Stephen Rea
Aubrey	Timothy Spall
Nicola's Lover	David Thewlis
Paula	Moya Brady
Steve	David Neilson
Customer	Harriet Thorpe
Chef	Paul Trussel
Nigel	Jack Thorpe Baker

Top Right: Jane Horrocks, David Thewlis Below Left: Horrocks, Alison Steadman Below Right: Horrocks, Timothy Spall, Claire Skinner © *October Films*

**Bill Nighy, Saskia Reeves, Imelda Staunton
Above: Staunton**

ANTONIA & JANE

(MIRAMAX) Producer, George Faber; Director, Beeban Kidron; Screenplay, Marcy Kahan; Photography, Rex Maidment; Editor, Kate Evans; Designer, John Ashbridge; Music, Rachel Portman; Casting, Gail Stevens; a Malofilm presentation and a BBC Films production; British; Color; Not rated; 69 minutes; October release

CAST

Jane Hartman	Imelda Staunton
Rosa Gluberman	Patricia Leventon
Harry Rosenthal	Alfred Hoffman
Sylvia Pinker	Maria Charles
Irwin Carlinsky	John Bennett
Norman Beer	Richard Hope
Therapist	Brenda Bruce
Uncle Vladimir	Alfred Marks
Jane's Mother	Lila Kaye
Young Jane	Bonnie Parker
Antonia McGill	Saskia Reeves
Tutor	Sheila Allen
Howard Nash	Billy Nighy
Baby Daniel	Cato Sandford
Edgar	Iain Cuthbertson
Daniel Nash	Joe Absolom
Michael Ignatieff	Michael Ignatieff
Claire Rayner	Claire Rayner
Taxi Thief/A.D. Humphries	Trevor Peacock
Jeremy Woodward	Ian Redford
Stephen Carlinsky	Allan Corduner
Policewoman	Tania Rodrigues

© *Miramax Films*

TWENTY-ONE

(TRITON PICTURES) Producers, Morgan Mason, John Hardy; Executive Producers, Mike Curb, Lester Korn, Carole Curb; Director/Story, Don Boyd; Screenplay, Zoe Heller, Don Boyd; Photography, Keith Goddard; Costumes, Roger Murray-Leach; Editor, David Spiers; Music, Michael Berkeley; Electronic Music Composed and Performed by Phil Sawyer; Casting, Suzanne Crowley, Gilly Poole; from Curb Communications; British; Dolby Stereo; Rank color; Rated R; 101 minutes; October release

CAST

Katie	Patsy Kensit
Kenneth	Jack Shepherd
Jack	Patrick Ryecart
Baldie	Maynard Eziashi
Bobby	Rufus Sewell
Francesca	Sophie Thompson
Janet	Susan Wooldridge
Linda	Julia Goodman
Michael	Julian Firth
Marcus	Guy Oliver-Watts
Mr. Metcalfe	Robert Bathurst
Gerald Morris	Ben Murphy
Agency Woman	Shelley Borkum
Bobby's Aunt	Veronica Clifford
Bobby's Father	Donald Tandy
Bobby's Mother	Joan Campion
Pub Landlady	Maggie Norris
Pub Boys	Tip Tipping, Paul Heasman, Mark Newman
Fashion Editor	Tyger Kahn
Assistant Editor	Lolly Susi

and Anthony Gardner (Riverside Waiter), Rebecca Cardinale (Jack's Wife), Kim Kindersley (Best Man), Paul Arlington (Bride's Father), Anne Romyn (Melissa)

Top Left: Rufus Sewell, Patsy Kensit Left: Kensit, Maynard Eziashi © *Triton Pictures*

Emmanuelle Beart, Michel Piccoli © *MK 2*

LA BELLE NOISEUSE

(MK2) Producer, Pierre Grise; Director, Jacques Rivette; Screenplay, Pascal Bonitzer, Christine Laurent, Jacques Rivette; Photography, William Lubtchansky; Editor, Nicole Lubtchansky; Designer, Manu De Chauvigny; Costumes, Laurence Struz; Co-produced by FR3 Films Production and George Reinhart Productions with the participation of Centre National de la Cinematographie, Canal + and la Sofica Investimage 2 et 3 and with the help of Region Languedoc-Roussillon; French; Color; Not rated; 240 minutes; October release

CAST

Frenhofer	Michel Piccoli
Liz	Jane Birkin
Marianne	Emmanuelle Beart
Julienne	Marianne Denicourt
Nicolas	David Bursztein
Porbus	Gilles Arbona
The Painter's Hand	Bernard Dufour

**Jane Birkin, Emmanuelle Beart
Above Right: Beart, Michel Piccoli**

BLACK ROBE

(SAMUEL GOLDWYN CO.) Producers, Robert Lantos, Stephané Reichel, Sue Milliken; Executive Producers, Jake Eberts, Brian Moore, Denis Heroux; Director, Bruce Beresford; Screenplay, Brian Moore, based on his novel; Photography, Peter James; Designer, Herbert Pinter; Costumes, Renee April, John Hay; Editor, Tim Wellburn; Music, Georges Delerue; Casting, Clare Walker; an Alliance Communications and Samson Productions co-production, with the participation of Telefilm Canada & Australian Film Finances Corp.; Canadian-Australian; Dolby Stereo; Eastmancolor; Rated R; 100 minutes; October release

CAST

Father Laforgue	Lothaire Bluteau
Daniel	Aden Young
Annuka	Sandrine Holt
Chomina	August Schellenberg
Wife of Chomina	Tantoo Cardinal
Father Jerome	Frank Wilson
Ougebemat	Billy Two Rivers
Neehatin	Lawrence Bayne
Awandole	Harrison Liu
Mestigoit	Yvan Labelle

Top Left: August Schellenberg (c), Lothaire Bluteau
Left: Tantoo Cardinal Below Left: Schellenberg (r)
Below Right: Aden Young, Sandrine Holt
© *Samuel Goldwyn Co.*

PAUL McCARTNEY'S GET BACK

(7 ARTS/NEW LINE CINEMA) Producers, Henry Thomas, Philip Knatchbull; Executive Producer, Jake Eberts; Director, Richard Lester; Visual Consultant/Photography, Jordan Cronenweth; Photography, Robert Paynter; Theatrical Lighting Designer, Marc Brickman; Associate Producer, Dusty Symonds; Editor, John Victor Smith; 2nd Unit Directors, Aubrey Powell (35mm), Charles Stewart (16mm); an Allied Filmmakers presentation in association with MPL/a Front Page Films presentation; British; Dolby Stereo; Technicolor; Rated PG; 89 minutes; October release

CAST

The Band	Paul McCartney
	Linda McCartney
	Hamish Stuart
	Robbie McIntosh
	Paul "Wix" Wickens
	Chris Witten

© *7 Arts*

Paul McCartney

MY FATHER'S COMING

(TARA RELEASING) Producer/Director, Monika Treut; Screenplay, Monika Treut, Bruce Benderson; Photography, Elfi Mikesch; Editor, Steve Brown; Music, David Van Tieghem; from Hyena Films, Bluehorse Films, Inc.; Assistant Director, Christine LeGoff; Art Director, Robin Ford; German; Color; Not rated; 82 minutes; November release

CAST

Hans	Alfred Edel
Vicky	Shelley Kästner
Annie	Annie Sprinkle
Joe	Michael Massee
Lisa	Mary Lou Graulau
Ben	David Bronstein
Christa	Dominique Gaspar
Dora	Flora Gaspar
Fakir	Fakir Musafar
Tito	Israel Marti
Singer	Mario De Colombia
Allan	Bruce Benderson
Talk Show Hostess	Rebecca Lewin
Agent	Stephen Feld
Restaurant Manager	Charles-John Austen
Taxi Driver	Fidel Howden
Tito's Aunt	Mariana Diaz
Guest	Lynne Tillman
Streetcrazy	Susan McLeod
Lady on street	Ursule Molinaro

and Amanda Ma (Asian Actress), Kate Lane (Receptionist), Katarina Kaninchen (Assistant Director), Tracy Gale Norman (Drag Queen), Bobby Baden (Russian Bartender), Michael Waite (Bartender at Eileen's)

Top Right: Annie Sprinkle, Alfred Edel
© Tara Releasing

THE DOUBLE LIFE OF VERONIQUE

(MIRAMAX) Producer, Leonardo de la Fuente; Executive Producer, Bernard P. Guiremand; Director, Krzysztof Kieslowski; Screenplay, Krzysztof Kieslowski, Krzysztof Piesiewicz; Photography, Slawomir Idziak; Designer, Patrice Mercier; Music, Zbigniew Preisner; Editor, Jacques Witta; a Sideral Prods. (Paris) - Tor Prods. (Warsaw) - Le Studio Canal Plus (Paris) co-production in association with Norsk Film; French-Polish; Dolby Stereo; Color; Not rated; 90 minutes; November release

CAST

Veronique/Veronika	Irene Jacob
The Aunt	Halina Gryglaszewska
The Gaudy Woman	Kalina Jedrusik
Orchestra Conductor	Aleksander Bardini
Veronika's Father	Wladyslaw Kowalski
Antek	Jerzy Gudejko
The Lawyer	Jan Sterninski
Alexandre Fabbri	Philippe Volter
Catherine	Sandrine Dumas
The Professor	Louis Ducreux
Veronique's Father	Claude Duneton
Claude	Lorraine Evanoff
Serge	Guillaume de Tonquedec
Jean-Pierre	Gilles Gaston Dreyfus
The Mailman	Alain Frerot
The Railway Man	Youssef Hamid
The Professor	Thierry de Carbonnieres
The Receptionist	Chantal Neuwirth
Nicole	Nausicaa Rampony
The Woman with hat	Boguslawa Schubert
The Man with grey coat	Jacques Potin

and Philippe Campos (Nicole Pinaud), Dominika Szady (Beata Malczewska), Jacek Wojcicki (Barbara Szalapa), Wanda Kruszewska (Lucyna Zabawa), Pauline Monier (Bernadetta Kus)

214   Irene Jacob, Guillaume de Tonquedec
Above Left: Jacob

© Miramax Films

MEETING VENUS

(WARNER BROS.) Producer, David Puttnam; Director, István Szabó; Screenplay, István Szabó, Michael Hirst; Photography, Lajos Koltai; Associate Producers, Uberto Pasolini, Gabriella Prekop; Editor, Jim Clark; Casting, Patsy Pollock; Costumes, Catherine Leterrier; Designer, Attila Kovacs; Music, Richard Wagner; a Fujisankei Communications Group, British Sky Broadcasting and County Natwest Ventures presentation of an Enigma production; British; Dolby Stereo; Technicolor; Rated PG-13; 120 minutes; November release

CAST

Karin Anderson	Glenn Close
Zoltan Szanto	Niels Arestrup
von Schneider	Marian Labuda
Maria Krawiecki	Maite Nahyr
Stefano Del Sarto	Victor Poletti
Dancer	Johara Racz
Delfin van Delf	Rita Scholl
Cashier	Michael Kroecher
Etienne Tailleur	Andre Chaumeau
Stephen Taylor	Jay O. Sanders
von Binder	Dieter Laser
Monique Angelo	Johanna Ter Steege
Isaac Partnoi	Roberto Pollak
Thomas	Francois Delaive
Yvonne	Maria de Medeiros
Toushkau	Etienne Chicot
Jana	Ildiko Bánsági
Edith	Dorottya Udvaros
Jean Gabor	Moscu Alcalay
Miss Malikoff	Macha Meril
Jorge Picabia	Erland Josephson

and Maria Becker (Szanto's Mother), Eva Ebner (von Binder's Mother), Sándor Szabó (First Violinist M. Leuchter), András Márton (New First Violinist), Irén Bordán (Eurowood TV Crew Sound Organizer), Eszter Kárász (Malgrozeta), Erika Tóth (Eurowood TV Crew Director), András Vámosi (Eurowood TV Crew Sound Engineer), Zsuzsa Mányai (Fat Lady from the Chorus), Balázs Hantos, József Csör (French Singers), Lili Kepes, György Fenyves, Pat Schiffer (Journalists), Fruzsina Pregitzer (Marie France), Montieth Douglas (Computer Operator), Károly Ujlaky (Hotel Receptionist 1, Budapest), Zsuzsa Fazekas (Szanto's Daughter, Agnes), Brigitte Sy (French Customs Officer), Jenö Pataky (2nd Violinist), Györgyi Tarján, István Komlós (Orchestra Members), Manfred Andrae (Eurowood President), Buda Gulyás (Eurowood TV Crew Cameraman); Tannhäuser Highlights Performed by: Kiri Te Kanawa (Elisabeth), René Kollo (Tannhäuser), Hakan Hagegard (Wolfram von Eschenbach), Waltraud Meier (Venus), Renate Spingler (A Young Shepherd), Matthias Hölle (The Landgrave), Kim Begley (Walther von der Vogelweide), Robin Legatte (Heinrich der Schreiber), Rodney Macann (Biterolf), Roderick Earle (Reinmar von Zweter)

Top: Niels Arestrup, Glenn Close Below: Moscu Alcalay, Erland Josephson Left: Arestrup
© Warner Bros. Inc.

Maite Nahyr, Rita Scholl, Victor Poletti, Glenn Close

Maite Nahyr, Victor Poletti, Dieter Laser, Glenn Close, Niels Arestrup, Jay O. Sanders, Johanna Ter Steege, Marian Labuda, Maria De Medeiros (on floor)

YOUNG SOUL REBELS

(PRESTIGE) Producer, Nadine Marsh-Edwards; Executive Producers, Colin MacCabe, Ben Gibson; Director, Isaac Julien; Screenplay, Paul Hallam, Derrick Saldaan McClintock, Isaac Julien; Photography, Nina Kellgren; Costumes, Annie Curtis Jones; Music, Simon Boswell; Editor, John Wilson; Designer, Derek Brown; a presentation of The British Film Institute for Film Four International in association with Sankofa Film & Video, La Sept, Kinowelt & Iberoamericana; British; Dolby Stereo; Metrocolor; Not rated; 96 minutes; November release

CAST

Chris	Valentine Nonyela
Caz	Mo Sesay
Ken	Dorian Healy
Ann	Frances Barber
Tracy	Sophie Okonedo
Billibud	Jason Durr
Davis	Gary McDonald
Jill	Debra Gillett
Carlton	Eamon Walker
Sparky	James Bowyers
Kelly	Billy Braham
Bigsy	Wayne Norman
Trish	Danielle Scillitoe
Jeff Kane	Ray Shell
Cid Man	Nigel Harrison
Park Policeman	John Wilson
Policemen	Brian Conway, Mike Mungarvan
Asian Punk Girl	Sayan Akaddas
TJ	Shyro Chung
Bouncer	Adam Price

and Michael Mascoll, Freddie Brooks (Soul Boys), Rodriguez King-Dorset (Irvine), Lloyd Anderson (Barber), Adam Stuatt, Astley Harvey (Men in barber shop), Peter Harding (Radio Producer), Richard Jamieson (Football Supporter), Mark Brett (Stallkeeper), Joan Harsant (Blue Rinse Lady), Verona Marshall, Frankie Palma (Trish's Friend)

Top Right: Valentine Nonyela, Mo Sesay
Right: Sesay, Jason Durr
© Prestige

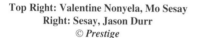

PROSPERO'S BOOKS

(MIRAMAX) Producer, Kees Kasander; Executive Producers, Kees Kasander, Denis Wigman; Co-Producers, Philippe Carcassonne, Michel Seydoux; Director/Adapted Screenplay, Peter Greenaway; Based on William Shakespeare's *The Tempest*; Associate Producers, Masato Hara, Roland Wigman; Photography, Sacha Vierny; Designers, Ben Van Os, Jan Roelfs; Music, Michael Nyman; Editor, Marina Bodbyl; an Allarts - Cinea/Camera One - Penta Co-Production in association with Elsevier Vendex Film, Film 4 International, VPRO Television, Canal Plus & NHK; British-French; Color; Rated R; 129 minutes; November release

CAST

Prospero	John Gielgud
Caliban	Michael Clark
Alonso	Michel Blanc
Gonzalo	Erland Josephson
Miranda	Isabelle Pasco
Antonio	Tom Bell
Sebastian	Kenneth Cranham
Ferdinand	Mark Rylance
Adrian	Gerard Thoolen
Francisco	Pierre Bokma
Trinculo	Jim Van Der Woude
Stephano	Michiel Romeyn
Ariel	Orpheo, Paul Russell, James Thierree, Emil Wolk
Iris	Marie Angel
Ceres	Ute Lemper
Juno	Deborah Conway

John Gielgud

© Miramax Films

OVERSEAS

(ARIES) Producer, Serge Cohen-Solal; Director/Story, Brigitte Rouan; Screenplay, Brigitte Rouan, Philippe Le Guay, Christian Rullier, Cédric Kahn; Photography, Dominique Chapuis; Costumes, Florence Emir; Music, Pierre and Mathieu Foldes; Editor, Yann Dedet; French; Color; Not rated; 98 minutes; November release

CAST

Zon	Nicole Garcia
Gritte	Marianne Basler
Malene	Brigitte Roüan
Paul	Philippe Galland
Gildas	Yann Dedet
Maxime	Bruno Todeschini
Uncle Alban	Pierre Doris

Top Right: Brigitte Roüan, Nicole Garcia, Marianne Basler © *Aries Films*

UNTIL THE END OF THE WORLD

(WARNER BROS.) Producer, Jonathan Taplin; Executive Producer, Anatole Dauman; Director, Wim Wenders; Screenplay, Peter Carey, Wim Wenders; Based on an original idea by Wim Wenders, Solveig Dommartin; Photography, Robby Müller; Designer, Thierry Flamand, Sally Campbell; Costumes, Montserrat Casanova; Music, Graeme Revell; Editor, Peter Przygodda; Co-Producer, Marc Monnet; Associate Producers, Masa Mikage, Julia Overton, Walter Donohue; a co-production of Village Roadshow Pictures Pty. Ltd., Road Movies Filmproduktion Gmbh and Argos Films SA; Australian-German-French; Dolby Stereo; Color; Rated R; 157 minutes; December release

CAST

Sam Farber (posing as Trevor McPhee)	William Hurt
Claire Tourneur	Solveig Dommartin
Eugene Fitzpatrick	Sam Neill
Dr. Henry Farber	Max von Sydow
Edith Farber	Jeanne Moreau
Philip Winter	Rüdiger Vogler
Burt	Ernie Dingo
Chico Remy	Chick Ortega
Raymond Monnet	Eddy Mitchell
Mario	Pietro Falcone
Doctor	Enzo Turrin
Makiko	Adelle Lutz
Mechanic	Jean Charles Dumay
Anton Farber	Ernest Berk
Irina Farber	Christine Osterlein
Receptionist	Diogo Doria
Woman in street car	Amalia Rodrigues
Krasikova	Elena Smirnova
Truck Driver	Zhang Jinzhan
Custodian	Naoto Takenaka
Hotel Guests	Hiroshi Kanbe, Yuji Ogata
Maid	Miwako Fujitani
Mrs. Mori	Kuniko Miyake
Mr. Mori	Ryu Chishu
Bernie, Used Car Dealer	Allen Garfield
Narcotics Agent	Alec Jason
Elsa Farber	Lois Chiles
Heidi	Lauren Graham
David	David Gulpilil
Policeman	Fred Welsh
Buzzer	Charlie McMahon
Old Man Alfred	Alfred Lynch
Maisie	Justine Saunders
Lydia	Kylie Belling
Ned	Bart Willoughby
Peter	Jimmy Little
Ronda	Rhoda Roberts
Karl	Paul Livingston
Nora Oliveira	Susan Leith
Astronaut	Detlef Winterberg

Max von Sydow, Jeanne Moreau

Above Left: Solveig Dommartin, William Hurt Below: Sam Neill © *Australian Film Finance Corp.*

217

LET HIM HAVE IT

(FINE LINE FEATURES) Producers, Luc Roeg, Robert Warr; Executive Producer, Jeremy Thomas; Director, Peter Medak; Screenplay, Neal Purvis, Robert Wade; Associate Producer, Jane Frazer; Photography, Oliver Stapleton; Designer, Michael Pickwoad; Editor, Ray Lovejoy; Costumes, Pam Tait; Casting, Lucy Boulting; a Le Studio Canal +, Film Trustees in association with British Screen presentation of a Vermillion Production (a Jennie and Co. Company), from New Line Cinema; British; Dolby Stereo; Color; Rated R; 114 minutes; December release

CAST

Derek Bentley	Chris Eccleston
Chris Craig	Paul Reynolds
William Bentley	Tom Courtenay
Fairfax	Tom Bell
Lilian Bentley	Eileen Atkins
Iris Bentley	Clare Holman
Niven Craig	Mark McGann
Lord Goddard	Michael Gough
Terry	Ian Deam
Vincent	Bert Tyler-Moore
Harrison	Steve Nicholson
McDonald	Niven Boyd
Stella	Serena Scott-Thomas
Niven's Judge	Ronald Fraser
Humphries	Peter Eyre
Cassels	James Villiers
Jack the Warder	Michael Elphick
Dennis Bentley	Ben Brazier
Secondary School Teacher	Murray Melvin
Small Boy in school	Tony Sands
School Boy in secondary school	Charlie Creed Miles
Boy, Fairview Road	Daniel Brazier
Reprieve Petition Woman	Linda Marlowe
Big Cecil	Francis Hope
Butcher	Peter Jonfield
West Indian Driver	Rudolph Walker
Posh TV Lady	Delia Lindsay
Mr. Craig	Denny Kirk
Mrs. Craig	Lottie Ward
9 Girl	Victoria Moore
Father	Glyn Grain
Mother	Karen Lewis
Police Desk Sergeant	William Waghorn
Miles	Robert Morgan

and Colin McCormack (Army Recruit Doctor), Joe Melia (Harry Proctor), Vernon Dobtcheff (Clerk of the Court), Jimmy Flint (Jones, the Prison Warder), Jeremy Sinden (Reporter), Terence Skelton (Conservative MP), Norman Rossington (Postman), Arthur Whybrow (Senior Prison Warder), Clive Revill (Pierrepoint), Peter Eccleston (Derek, Age 8), Rebecca Eccleston (Iris, Age 10), Geoffrey Drew (Prison Chaplain), Craig Turner (Derek, Age 14), Alan Starkey (Nightwatchman), Matthew De Vere, Micky Poppins (Boys in nightwatchman's hut), Joan Heal (Lady at butcher's), James Bowers (Police Officer), Iain Cuthbertson (Maxwell-Fyfe), James Snell (Man in suit), Linda Bassett (Mrs. Miles), Viv Warrentz (Woman with petition), Karl Johnson (Parris), Bill Dean (Foreman on the jury), Chris Darwin (Owner of the Milk Bar)

Top: Chris Eccleston, Paul Reynolds Below: Eccleston
© *New Line Cinema Corp.*

Paul Reynolds, Chris Eccleston Above:
Clare Holman, Tom Courtenay, Eileen Atkins

HIGH HEELS

(MIRAMAX) Executive Producer, Agustin Almodóvar; Director/Screenplay, Pedro Almodóvar; Associate Producer, Enrique Posner; Photography, Alberto Mayo; Music, Ryuichi Sakamoto; Assistant Director, Yousaf Bokhari; Editor, Jose Salcedo; Designer, Pierre-Louis Thevenet; Costumes, Jose Maria Cossio; an El Deseo and Ciby 2000 production; Spanish; Dolby Stereo; Eastmancolor; Not rated; 112 minutes; December release

CAST

Rebecca	Victoria Abril
Becky Del Paramo	Marisa Paredes
Femme Lethal	Miguel Bosé
Little Rebecca	Rocio Munoz
Luisa	Lupe Barrado
Hospital Priest	Juan Jose Otegui
Hospital Nurse	Paula Soldevilla
TV Floor Manager	Javier Bardem
TV News Director	Gabriel Garbisu
Nanny	Eva Siva
Makeup Girls	Montse G. Romeu, Lina Mira
Prison Doctor	Abraham Garcia
Prison Workers	Angelina Llongueras, Carmen Navarro
Dealer	Roxy Vaz
Photo Shop Attendant	Javier Benavente
Arresting Officer	Rodolfo Montero
Kleenex Cop	Luigi Martin
Priest	Jose M. Sacristan
Island Native	Placido Guimaraes
TV News Announcers	M. Pau Dominguez, Hilario Pino
Judicial Worker	Fernando Prados

and Bibi Andersen, Victoria Torres, Ana Garcia, Almudena De La Riva, Elia Camino, Raquel Sanchis, M. Dolores Ibanez, Yolanda Munoz (Dancers)

**Top Left: Victoria Abril, Miguel Bosé, Marisa Paredes
Left: Ana Lizaran, Paredes, Abril** © *Miramax Films*

RHAPSODY IN AUGUST

(ORION CLASSICS) Producer, Hisao Kurosawa; General Producer, Toru Okuyama; Director/Screenplay, Akira Kurosawa; Based on the novel *Nabe-No-Naka* by Kiyoko Murata; Photography, Takao Saito, Masaharu Ueda; Art Director, Yoshiro Muraki; Music, Shinichiro Ikebe; Associate Producers, Yoshio Inoue, Seikichi Iizumi; a Shochiku presentation of a Kurosawa production, from Feature Film Enterprise 2; Japanese; Color; Rated PG; 98 minutes; December release

CAST

Kane: Grandmother	Sachiko Murase
Tadao: Kane's Son	Hisashi Igawa
Machiko: Tadao's Wife	Narumi Kayashima
Tami: Tadao's Daughter	Tomoko Ohtakara
Shinjiro: Tadao's Daughter	Mitsunori Isaki
Yoshie: Kane's Daughter	Toshie Negishi
Noboru: Yoshie's Husband	Choichiro Kawarasaki
Tateo: Yoshie's Son	Hidetaka Yoshioka
Minako: Yoshie's Daughter	Mie Suzuki
Clark: Kane's Nephew	Richard Gere

© *Orion Classics*

**Hidetaka Yoshioka, Tomoko Ohtakara,
Sachiko Murase, Mitsunori Isaki, Mie Suzuki
Above: Murase, Richard Gere**

MADAME BOVARY

(SAMUEL GOLDWYN CO.) Producer, Marin Karmitz; Director/Screenplay, Claude Chabrol; Based on the novel by Gustave Flaubert; Photography, Jean Rabier; Music, Matthieu Chabrol; Editor, Monique Fardoulis; Set Designer, Michele Abbe; Costumes, Corinne Jorry; French; Color; Not rated; 130 minutes; December release

CAST

Emma Bovary ....Isabelle Huppert
Charles Bovary ....Jean-Francois Balmer
Rodolphe Boulanger ....Christophe Malavoy
Monsieur Homais, pharmacist ....Jean Yanne
Leon Dupuis ....Lucas Belvaux
Widow Lefrancois, owner of Lion D'Or ....Florent Gibassier
Monsieur Rouault.............................Jean-Claude Bouillaud
Felicite, the Bovary's Maid........................Sabeline Campo
Justin, pharmacy assistant...........................Yves Verhoeven
Mother Bovary..Marie Mergey
Lieuvain, advisor ....Francois Maistre
Madame Homais ....Dominique Clement
Master Guillaumin, notary ....Etienne Draber
Abbot Bournisien.....................................Jacques Dynam
Hivert, driver of "l'hirondelle" ....Pierre-Francois Dumeniaud
Mother Rolet, nurse ....Christine Paolini
The Viscount...Thomas Chabrol
Master Hareng, gentleman-usher ....Henri Attal
Doctor Canivet...Andre Thorent
Blind Man ....Dominique Zardi
Nastasie..Gilette Barbier
Narrator ....Francois Perier

Top: Jean-Francois Balmer, Isabelle Huppert
Left: Huppert, Christophe Malavoy
© *Samuel Goldwyn Co.*

Isabelle Huppert

Jean-Francois Balmer, Isabelle Huppert
Above: Huppert, Lucas Belvaux

Peter Weller, Robert A. Silverman Top Left: Ian Holm,
Weller Top Right: Judy Davis, Weller
Below Right: Weller, Joseph Scorsiani
© *Recorded Picture Co. Ltd.*

NAKED LUNCH

(**20th CENTURY FOX**) Producer, Jeremy Thomas; Co-Producer, Gabriella Martinelli; Director/Screenplay, David Cronenberg; Based on the book by William S. Burroughs; Photography, Peter Suschitzky; Designer, Carol Spier; Music, Howard Shore; Editor, Ronald Sanders; Costumes, Denise Cronenberg; Casting, Deirdre Bowen; Special Creatures and Effects Designer and Creator, Chris Walas; Assistant Director, John Board; Canadian-British; Dolby Stereo; Film House color; Rated R; 115 minutes; December release

CAST

Bill Lee	Peter Weller
Joan Frost/Joan Lee	Judy Davis
Tom Frost	Ian Holm
Yves Cloquet	Julian Sands
Dr. Benway	Roy Scheider
Fadela	Monique Mercure
Hank	Nicholas Campbell
Martin	Michael Zelniker
Hans	Robert A. Silverman
Kiki	Joseph Scorsiani
Creature Voices/Exterminator	Peter Boretski
Hafid	Yuval Daniel
Hauser	John Friesen
O'Brien	Sean McCann
A.J. Cohen	Howard Jerome
Pawnbroker	Michael Caruana
Exterminators	Kurt Reis, Justin Louis, Julian Richings
The Chink	Jim Yip
Forgeman	Claude Aflalo
Interzone Boys	Laurent Hazout, Joe Dimambro

Ian Holm, Judy Davis, Peter Weller   221
Above: Julian Sands, Weller

HEAR MY SONG

(MIRAMAX) Producer, Alison Owen; Executive Producers, Simon Fields, Russ Russell, John Paul Chapple; Director/Story, Peter Chelsom; Screenplay, Peter Chelsom, Adrian Dunbar; Photography, Sue Gibson; Designer, Caroline Hanania; Costumes, Lindy Hemming; Associate Producer, David Brown; Music, John Altman; Casting, Jane Frisby; Editor, Martin Walsh; a Film Four International, British Screen and Windmill Lane Productions presentation of a Limelight production; British-Irish; Dolby Stereo; Fujicolor; Rated R; 104 minutes; December release

CAST

Josef Locke	Ned Beatty
Micky O'Neill	Adrian Dunbar
Cathleen Doyle	Shirley Anne Field
Nancy Doyle	Tara Fitzgerald
Mr. X	William Hootkins
Benny Rose	Harold Berens
Jim Abbott	David McCallum
Derek	John Dair
Gordon	Stephen Marcus
Kitty Ryan	Britta Smith
Grandma Ryan	Gladys Sheehan
Brenda Ryan	Gina Moxley
Norman Vaughan	Norman Vaughan
Fintan O'Donnell	James Nesbitt
Young Micky O'Neill	Brian Flanagan
Nurse	Constance Cowley
Micky's Mum	Marie Mullen
Ronnie Lavelle	Phil Kelly
Ronnie's Mum	Jean Blanchflower
Oscar Harrison	John Neville Rufus Altman
Franc Cinatra	Joe Cuddy
Grandson Ryan	Ruaidhri Conroy
Barry Haden	Bill Maynard
Compere	Aiden Grennell
Young Cathleen	Donna McReady
Young Jo	Terry Mulligan
Dressmaker	Terry Adams
Receiver	Terence Orr
Brewery Man	Bal Moane
Molly	Laurie Morton
Barman	Brian McGrath
Drunk in pub	Jim Mooney
Mrs. McGlinchy	Anna Manahan
Old Musician	Tommy Lack
Receptionist	Agnes Bernelle
Librarian	Mary McLeod

and Jimmy Keogh, Liam O'Callaghan, Paddy Cole, Maurice Blake, Tony Morando (Jo's Boys), Pat Laffan, Frank Kelly, David Beggs (Taxi Drivers), Vernon Midgley (The Voice of Josef Locke)

Top: Tara Fitzgerald, Adrian Dunbar (also right)
Below: Ned Beatty, Shirley Anne Field
© Miramax Films

Tara Fitzgerald, Adrian Dunbar
Ned Beatty, Shirley Anne Field

Adrian Dunbar, James Nesbitt

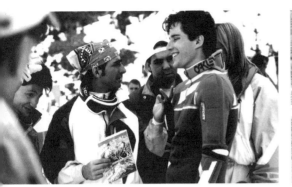

**Stuart Fratkin, Dean Cameron, Patrick Labyorteaux,
Tom Breznahan in *Ski School***
© *Moviestore Entertainment*

Ramiro Meneses in *Rodrigo D: No Future*
© *Kino Intl.*

SKI SCHOOL (Moviestore Entertainment) Producer/Director,
Damian Lee; Executive Producers, Ken Halloway, Jeff Sackman;
Screenplay, David Mitchell; Photography, Curtis Petersen; Editor,
Reid Dennison; a Rose & Ruby production; Canadian; Color; Rated
R; 88 minutes; January release. CAST: Dean Cameron (Dave), Tom
Breznahan (Johnny), Patrick Labyorteaux (Ed), Mark Thomas Miller
(Reid), Spencer Rochfort (Derek), Darlene Vogel (Lori), Stuart
Fratkin (Fitz), Charlie Spradling (Paulette), Ava Fabian (Victoria),
Gaetana Korbin (Bridget), Mark High (Bryce), John Pyper-Ferguson
(Erich), Johnny Askwith (Clint/Bart), Alison Dobie (Ooh Dave Girl),
Stacy Brink (Half-naked Woman), Kate Healey (Santa's Helper),
Karen Isaaks (Very Sweet Girl), Christina Marazzo (Young Woman)

SOLOVKI POWER (Mosfilm) Director/Photography, Marina
Goldovskaya; Screenplay, Viktor Listov, Dimitri Cukovsky; Music,
Nikolai Karetnikov, Marina Krutoyarskaya; Soviet; Color/black and
white; Not rated; 93 minutes; January release. Documentary

A TALE OF THE WIND (Capi Films) Directors, Joris Ivens,
Marceline Loridan; Executive Producer, Marceline Loridan;
Screenplay, Joris Ivens, Marceline Loridan, Elizabeth D.;
Photography, Thierry Arbogast, Jacques Loiseleux; Music, Michel
Portal; Editor, Genevieve Louveau; a La Sept co-production with the
participation of the Ministry of Culture; Dutch-French; Color; Not
rated; 80 minutes; January release. CAST: Joris Ivens, Han Zenxiang,
Wang Delong, Liu Zhuang, Wang Hong, Fu Dalin, Liu Guillian, Chen
Zhijian, Zou Qiaoyu, Paul Sergent

**CHILDREN OF BULLERBY VILLAGE (Minnesota Film
Center)** Producer, Waldemar Bergendahl; Director, Lasse Hallström;
Screenplay, Astrid Lindgren, based on her novel; Photography, Jens
Fischer; Music, George Riedel; Editor, Susanne Linnmann; a Svensk
Filmindustri production; Swedish, 1986; Fujicolor; Not rated; 90
minutes; January release. CAST: Linda Bergström (Lisa), Crispin
Dickson Wendenius (Lasse), Henrik Larsson (Bosse), Ellen Demerus
(Britta), Anna Sahlin (Anna), Harald Lonnbro (Olle), Tove Edfeldt
(Kerstin), Olof Sjögren (Shoemaker), Lasse Stahl (Country Store
Owner)

**MORE ABOUT THE CHILDREN OF BULLERBY VILLAGE
(Minnesota Film Center)** Producer, Waldemar Bergendahl; Director,

Lasse Hallstrom; Screenplay, Astrid Lindgren, based on her books;
Photography, Jens Fischer; Editor, Susanne Linnman; Music, George
Riedel; Swedish, 1987; Eastmancolor; Not rated; 86 minutes; January
release. CAST: Linda Bergström (Lisa), Crispin Dickson Wendenius
(Lasse), Henrik Larsson (Bosse), Ellen Demerus (Britta), Anna Sahlin
(Anna), Harald Lonnbro (Olle), Tove Edfeldt (Kerstin), Olof Sjörgen
(The Shoemaker)

RODRIGO D: NO FUTURE (Kino International) Director, Victor
Manuel Gaviria; Screenplay, Elsa Vasquez; Original Idea, Victor
Manuel Gaviria, Luis Fernando Calderon, Angela Perez;
Photography, Rodrigo Lalinde; Music, German Arrieta; Colombian-
Spanish; Color; Not rated; 92 minutes; January release. CAST:
Ramiro Meneses (Rodrigo), Carlos Mario Resrepo (Adolfo), Jackson
Idrian Gallego (Ramon), Vilma Dias (Rodrigo's Sister), Oscar
Hernandez (Rodrigo's Father), Alberto Cardona (Tavo), Irene de
Galvis (Adolfo's Mother), Wilson Blandon ("El Alacran"), Leonardo
Favio "Burrito" Sanchez (Francis), John Jairo Gomez (Little John),
Francisco Marin (Henry), Winston James Milan (Edgar)

THE RUNNER (International Home Cinema) Director, Amir
Naderi; Screenplay, Amir Naderi, Behruz Gharibpour; Photography,
Firouz Malekzadeh; Editor, Bahram Beyzai; Farsi; Color; Not rated;
94 minutes; January release. CAST: Madjid Niroumand (Amiro),
Musa Torkizadeh (Musa), A. Gholamzadeh (Uncle Gholam), Reza
Ramezani (Ramezan)

**THE NEVERENDING STORY II: THE NEXT CHAPTER
(Warner Bros.)** Producer, Dieter Geissler; Executive Producer, Tim
Hampton; Director, George Miller; Screenplay, Karin Howard; Based
on the novel *The Neverending Story* by Michael Ende; Photography,
Dave Connell; Music, Robert Folk; Editors, Peter Hollywood, Chris
Blunden; Designer, Bob Laing, Götz Weidner; Costumes Heidi
Weber; Special Effects, Derek Meddings; Creature Effects, Colin
Arthur; Casting, Hank McCann; German; Dolby Stereo; Panavision;
Eastman color; Rated PG; 89 minutes; February release. CAST:
Jonathan Brandis (Bastian Bux), Kenny Morrison (Atreyu), Clarissa
Burt (Xayide), Alexandra Johnes (Childlike Empress), Martin
Umbach (Nimbly), John Wesley Shipp (Barney Bux), Helena Michell
(Mrs. Bux), Chris Burton (Tri Face), Thomas Hill (Koreander)

Joris Ivens in *A Tale of the Wind*
© *Capi Films*

**Martin Umbach, Jonathan Brandis
in *The Neverending Story II***
© *Warner Bros. Inc.*

John Barrett, Brad Morris in *American Kickboxer 1*
© *Distant Horizon Corp.*

Robot Carnival
© *Streamline Pictures*

AMERICAN KICKBOXER 1 (Cannon) Producer, Anant Singh; Director, Frans Nel; Executive Producers, Sudhir Pragjee, Sanjeev Singh; Screenplay, Emil Kolbe; Photography, Paul Morkel; Music, Frank Becker; Editor, Renee Engelbrecht; a Global Pictures presentation of a Distant Horizon and Anant Singh production, a Cine-Clic Film; South African; Dolby Stereo; Agfa Color; Rated R; 95 minutes; February release. CAST: John Barrett (B.J. Quinn), Keith Vitali (Chad Hunter), Terry Norton (Carol), Brad Morris (Jacques Denard), Ted Le Plat (Willard), Michael Huff (Robert Bentley), Roger Yuan (Howard), Evan Klisser (Jason), Gavin Hood (Ken), Paddy Lyster (Prosecutor), Larry Martin (Judge), Garry Chalmers (Attorney), Frank Notaro (Doctor), Tootsie Lombard (Nurse), Jeff Fannel (Dick), Len Sparrowhawk (Bob Wiser), Alex Von Reumont (Jerry), Michael Megrian (Commentator), Alex Mathieson, Peter Ucko (Referees), Tom Agnew (Adrian Holligan Sr.), Judd Lasarow (Adrian Holligan Jr.), Zia Garfield (Daley Adams), Graham Clarke (Alex Bone), Caroline Smart (Doreen), Deon Stewardson (Sports Editor), Barbara Mathieson (Masseuse), Mark Mulder (Eugene)

EN TOUTE INNOCENCE (*No Harm Intended*) (Morris Project) Producer/Director, Alain Jessua; Screenplay, Dominique Roulet, Luc Bérard, Alain Jessua; Photography, Jean Rabier; Music, Michel Portal; Editor, Hélenè Plémiannikov; French, 1988; Color; Not rated; 95 minutes; February release. CAST: Michel Serrault (Paul Duchene), Nathalie Baye (Catherine), François Dunoyer (Thomas), Suzanne Flon (Clémence), Philippe Caroit (Didier), Sylvie Fennec (Genevieve), Bernard Fresson (Serge Cohen), André Valardi (Meunier), Anna Gaylor (Anna)

PERFECTLY NORMAL (Four Seasons Entertainment) Producer, Michael Burns; Director, Yves Simoneau; Screenplay, Eugene Lipinski, Paul Quarrington; Story, Rafe S. Engle; Photography, Alain Dostie; Designer, Anne Pritchard; Editor, Ronald Sanders; Music, Richard Gregoire; a production of Bialystock & Bloom Ltd. in association with Telefilm Canada/Ontario Film Development Corp./British Satellite Broadcasting/British Screen; Canadian; Dolby Stereo; Color; Rated R; 104 minutes; February release. CAST: Robbie Coltrane (Alonzo Turner), Michael Riley (Renzo Parachi), Deborah Duchene (Denise), Eugene Lipinski (Hopeless), Kenneth Welsh (Charlie Glesby), Patricia Gage (Mrs. Hathaway), Jack Nichols (Duane Bickle), Elizabeth Harpur (Gloria), Kristina Nicoll (Tiffany),

Peter Millard (Bunden), Bryan Foster (Gig Manyon), Andrew Miller (Pizza Guy), Warren Van Evera (Old Man), Douglas C. Frye (Boy in cab), Graham Harley (Middle-Aged Man), Ellen Ray Hennesey (Clairvoyant), Gene DiNovi (Priest), Gino Marrocco (Uncle Thomas), Roc Lafortune (St. John's Ambulance Man), Harry Ditson (Man in stand), Paul Rainville (Snack Bar Customer), Rina Polley (Restaurant Woman), Eric Keenleyside (Restaurant Man), Gina Vasic, Betty Orsatti (Women), Tom Melissis (Eastern Clay Player), Vivian Reis (Mrs. Parachi), Paul Smart (Practical Hockey Ref), Rummy Bishop (Willy Dunn), Paul Jolicoeur (Eddie Eggars)

ROBOT CARNIVAL (Streamline Pictures) Producers, Kazufumi Nomura, Carl Macek; Directors, Katsuhiro Otomo, Atsuko Fukushima, Kouji Morimoto, Hiroyuki Kitazume, Mao Lamdo, Hidetoshi Ohmori, Yasuomi Umetsu, Hiroyuki Kitakubo, Takashi Nakamura; Adaptation, Carl Macek; Music, Jo Hisaishi, Isaku Fujita, Yasunori Honda; an A.P.P. Co. Ltd. production; Japanese; Color; Not rated; 91 minutes; February release. Animated.

TERMINAL CITY RICOCHET (Festival Films) Producer, John Conti; Executive Producer, Dan Howard; Director, Zale Dalen; Screenplay, John Conti, Bill Mullan, Phil Savath, Al Thurgood, Ken Lester; Photography, Paul Sarossy; Editor, Haida Paul; an E. Motion Films production; Canadian; Color; Not rated; 100 minutes; February release. CAST: Peter Breck (Ross Glimore), Jello Biafra (Bruce Coddle), Germain Houde (Ace Tomlinson), Joe Keithley (Officer Friendly), Gene Kiniski (Officer Goodbuddy), Mark Bennett (Alex Stevens), Lisa Brown (Beatrice Tomlinson), Gabriel Khouth (Jim Glimore), Gerri Lee Smith (Tulip Glimore), Shawn Macdonald (Chip Ferguson)

TOUKI BOUKI (International Film Circuit) Director/Screenplay, Djibril Diop Mambety; Photography, Pap Samba Sow; Editors, Siro Asteni, Emma Mennenti; French-Senegalese, 1973; Color; Not rated; 95 minutes; February release. CAST: Magaye Niang (Mory), Marème Niang (Anta)

SHADOW OF CHINA (New Line Cinema) Producers, Elliott Lewitt, Don Guest; Executive Producer, Satoru Iseki; Director, Mitsuo Yanagimachi; Screenplay, Richard Maxwell, Mitsuo Yanagimachi; Based upon the novel *Snake Head* by Masaaki Nishiki; Music, Yasuaki Shimizu; Photography, Toyomichi Kurita; Designer,

224 Robbie Coltrane, Michael Riley
in *Perfectly Normal*
© *Four Seasons Ent.*

Magaye Niang, Marème Niang in *Touki Bouki*
© *Intl. Film Circuit*

Kenneth Tsang, John Lone in *Shadow of China*
© New Line Cinema

Samuel West, Christien Anholt in *Reunion*
© Castle Hill

Andrew McAlpine; Editor, Sachiko Yamagi; Costumes, Sandy Powell; Casting, Mali Finn, Patricia Pao; a Nippon Herald Films/Fuji Television Network/Marubeni/Nissh Iwai presentation; Japanese; Foto-Kem color; Not rated; 100 minutes; March release. CAST: John Lone (Wu Chang/Henry Wong), Koichi Sato (Akira), Sammi Davis (Katharine), Vivian Wu (Moo-Ling), Roland Harrah III (Xiao Niu), Roy Chiao (Lee Hok Chow), Constantine Gregory (Jameson), Colin George (Burke), Kenneth Tsang (Mr. Lau), Dennis Chan (Mr. Wu), Fredric Mao (Chi Fung), Yam Tat Wah (Po Kok), Ken Bennett (Watson), Yukio Yamato (Chen), Justina Vail (Helen), Teddy Chen (Bartender), Michael Mahony (Auctioneer), Ian Buruma, Michael Sandham (Reporters), John Dermot (T.V. Reporter), Diego Swing, Van Fat (Assassins), Danny Yip, Shinji Okido (Hoodlums), Colette Koo, Kae Nagaya (Hostesses), Richard Foo, Joe Wong (Businessmen), Simeon Jem Chiu (Young Henry), Liu Kwok Chi (Xiao Niu's Friend), Susumu Hirayanagi (Nightclub Manager), Junko Takasawa (Phantom Mother)

BECAUSE OF THAT WAR (Nurit Price) Producers, Shmuel Altman, David Schitz; Directors/Screenplay, Orna Ben Dor-Niv; Photography, Oren Schmukler; Music, Yehuda Poliker; Editor, Rachel Yagil; a Manor production; Israeli; Color; Not rated; 90 minutes; March release. Documentary

THE LOVES OF KAFKA (Morris Projects) Executive Producer, Karel Skop; Director/Screenplay, Beda Docampo Feijóo; Story, Beda Docampo Feijóo, Juan Bautista Stagnaro; Photography, Frantisek Uldrich; Art Director, Boris Moravec; Editor, César D'Angiolillo; Costumes, Dagmar Brezinova; Argentine, 1988; Color; Not rated; 103 minutes; March release. CAST: Susú Pecoraro (Milena Jesenska), Jorge Marrale (Franz Kafka), Villanueva Cosse (Kafka's Father), Cecilia Roth (Ottla), Salo Pasik (Federico-Max Brod), Sofía Viruboff (Julie), Jana Krausova-Pehrova (Interpreter), Ljuba Skorepova (Kafka's Mother), Jan Schanilec (Doctor at the Nazi camp), Karel Habl (Kafka's Doctor), Jiri Nemecek (Old Colonel), Oldrich Vlach (Austrian Officer), Lenka Termerova (Nurse), Jan Kuzelka (Officer at the border), Jiri Havel (Kafka's Boss), Karel Chromik (Sigmund Freud), Dana Moravkova (Young Girl in the clinic), Marta Richterova (Woman in the brothel)

REUNION (Castle Hill) Producer, Anne Francois; Director, Jerry Schatzberg; Executive Producer, Vincent Malle; Photography, Bruno De Keyzer; Designer, Alexandre Trauner; Screenplay, Harold Pinter; Based on the novel by Fred Uhlman; Music, Philippe Sarde; Editor, Martine Barraque; a Les Films Ariane and Tac Ltd. production, a Sovereign Pictures release; French-W. German-British; Panavision; Eastmancolor/Fujicolor; Not rated; 110 minutes; March release. CAST: Jason Robards (Henry), Christien Anholt (Hans Strauss), Samuel West (Konradin Von Lohenburg), Francoise Fabian (Grafin Von Lohenburg), Maureen Kerwin (Lisa), Dorothea Alexander (Grafin -Old), Frank Baker (The Zionist), Tim Barker (Herr Zimmerman), Gideon Boulting (Prince Hubertus), Alan Bowyer (Bollacher), Jacques Brunet (Herr Von Lohenburg), Rupert Degas (Muller), Gerhard Fries (Brossner), James Ind (Erhard), Barbara Jefford (Mrs. Strauss), Lee Lyford (Von Hankhofen), Nicholas Pandolfi (Reutter), Bert Parnaby (Herr Strauss), Steven Poynter (Frank), Luc-Antoine Diquero, Amelie Pick (Young Lovers), Struan Rodger (Pompetski), Roland Schaefer (Judge Freisler), Frederick Warder (Muscle Max), Shebah Ronay (Young Gertrude), Alexandre Trauner (Man at warehouse office)

SONG OF THE EXILE (Kino International) Producers, Deng-Fei Lin, Nai-Chung Chou; Executive Producer, Jessica Liu; Director, Ann Hui; Screenplay, Wu Nien-Jen; Photography, Chung Chi-Man; Music, Yang Chen; Editor, Yih-Shun Huang; Art Director, Yee Chung-Man; from COS Films Company Ltd./Central Motion Picture Co.; Cantonese; Color; Not rated; 100 minutes; March release. CAST: Shwu-Fen Chang (Aiko/Kwei Tzu), Maggie Cheung (Hueyin Cheung), Chi-Hung Lee (Hueyin's Father), Tien Feug (Hueyin's Grandfather)

BERLIN JERUSALEM (Jane Balfour Films) Director, Amos Gitai; Screenplay, Amos Gitai, Gudie Lawaetz; Photography, Henri Alekan, Nurith Aviv; Music, Markus Stockhausen; Editor, Luc Barnier; a Simon Mizrahi presentation of an AGAV Films production, co-produced with Channel 4, La Sept, Nova Films, RAI-2, Orthel Films, NOS, Transfax, La Maison de Culture du Havre, the Hubert Bals Fund, CNC; French-Israeli; Color; Not rated; 84 minutes; March release. CAST: Lisa Kreuzer (Elsa), Rivka Neuman (Mania), Markus Stockhausen, Benjamin Levy, Vernon Dobtcheff, Bernard Eisenschitz, Juliano Merr, Ohad Shachar, Keren Mor, Bilha Rosenfeld, Daniel Roth, Ori Levy, Yossi Graber

CITY ZERO (IFEX) Director, Karen Shakhnazarov; Screenplay, Karen Shakhnazarov, Alexander Borodyansky; Photography, Nikolai Nemolyayev; Art Director, Lyudmila Kusakova; Music, Eduard Artemiev; a Studio Mosfilm production; Soviet; Color; Not rated; 84 minutes; March release. CAST: Leonid Filatov (Alexei Varakin), Oleg Basilashvili, Vladimir Menshov, Armen Djigarkhanian, Vevgeny Yevstigenev, Elena Arjanik

THE FABLE OF THE BEAUTIFUL PIGEON FANCIER (Original Cinema/Fox Lorber) Producer, João Alfredo Viegas; Director, Ruy Guerra; Screenplay, Ruy Guerra, Gabriel García Márquez; Story, Gabriel García Márquez; Photography, Edgar Moura; Music, Egberto Gismonti; Editor, Mair Tavares; a co-production of Televisión Española, S.A. and International Network Group, S.A.; Portuguese; Color; Not rated; 75 minutes; March release. CAST: Ney Latorraca (Orestes), Claudia Ohana (Fulvia), Tonia Carrero (Orestes' Mother), Dina Sfat (Andrea), Chico Díaz (Fulvia's Husband), Cecil Thire (Patient), Ruy Rezende (Typographer), Julio Levy (Waiter), Ataíde (Barber)

Leonid Filatov in *City Zero*
© IFEX

225

Anne Archer, Donald Sutherland in *Eminent Domain*
© *Triumph Releasing*

Megan Follows, Colleen Dewhurst in *Termini Station*
© *Northern Arts*

ISLAND (Roxie Releasing) Producers, Paul Cox, Samantha K. Naidu; Executive Producers, William Marshall, Jeannine Seawell; Director/Screenplay, Paul Cox; Photography, Mike Edols; Editor, John Scott; Designer, Neil Angwin; an Illumination Films production; Australian; Color; Not rated; 93 minutes; March release. CAST: Eva Sitta (Eva), Irene Papas (Marquise), Anoja Weerasinghe (Sahana), Chris Haywood (Janis), Norman Kaye (Henry), François Bernard (Frenchman)

L'ANGE (First Run Features) Director/Image & Special Effects/Editor, Patrick Bokanowski; Photography, Philippe Lavalette; Music, Michele Bokanowski; Sets, Christian Daninos, Patrick Bokanowski; Masks, Christian Daninos; Costumes, Domenika; French; Color; Not rated; 70 minutes; March release. CAST: Maurice Baquet (The First Librarian), Jean-Marie Bon (The Man in a bath), Martine Couture (The Servant), Jacques Faure (The Swordsman/The Man without hands), Mario Gonzales (The Apprentice), Rene Patrignani (The Artist), Rita Renoir (The Woman)

EMINENT DOMAIN (Triumph Releasing) Producer, Shimon Arama; Director, John Irvin; Co-Producers, Claude Leger, Vera Belmont; Screenplay, Andrzej Krakowski, Richard Gregson; Story, Andrzej Krakowski; Editor, Peter Tanner; Photography, Witold Adamek; Line Producer, Rony Vacov; Music, Zbigniew Preisner; Designer, Allan Starski; Costumes, Dorota Roqueplo; an Alan Neuman, SVS Inc., Arama Entertainment Inc. and Harlech Films presentation; Canadian-Israeli-French; Eastmancolor; Rated PG-13; 107 minutes; April release. CAST: Donald Sutherland (Jozef Burski), Anne Archer (Mira Burski), Jodhi May (Ewa), Paul Freeman (Ben), Anthony Bate (Kowal), Pip Torrens (Anton), Bernard Hepton (Slowak), Françoise Michaud (Nicole), Yves Beneyton (Roger)

SWEET TALKER (7 Arts/New Line Cinema) Producer, Ben Gannon; Executive Producers, Taylor Hackford, Stuart Benjamin; Director, Michael Jenkins; Screenplay, Tony Morphett; Story, Bryan Brown, Tony Morphett; Photography, Russell Boyd; Designer, John Stoddart; Costumes, Terry Ryan; Casting, Liz Mullinar; Music/Songs, Richard Thompson, Peter Filleul; Editors, Sheldon Kahn, Neil Thumpston; a New Visions Pictures presentation released through New Line Cinema; Australian; Dolby Stereo; Eastmancolor; Rated PG; 88 minutes; May release. CAST: Bryan Brown (Harry Reynolds),

Karen Allen (Julie McGuire), Justin Rosniak (David), Chris Haywood (Bostock), Bill Kerr (Cec), Bruce Spence (Norman Foster), Bruce Myles (Scraper), Paul Chubb (Billy), Peter Hehir (Giles), Don Barker (Sgt. Watts), Bruno Lucia (Thomas), Benjamin Franklin (Larsen), Andrew S. Gilbert (Lewis), Gary Waddell (Bluey), Brian McDermott, Rob Steele (Officers), Werner Fritz Miersch (Coin Dealer), Edmund Pegge, Michael Kozuki (Businessman), Jim Morressey (Bus Driver), Michael Kitschke (Junkie), Melissa J. Hannan, Gabrielle Watkins, Imogen Annesley, Clare Chilton (Salespersons), Peter Nikolas (Taxi Driver)

TERMINI STATION (Northern Arts) Producer/Director, Allan King; Executive Producers, Don Haig, Douglas Leiterman; Associate Producers, John Board, Nicholas J. Gray; Screenplay, Colleen Murphy; Photography, Brian R.R. Hebb; Designer, Lillian Sarafinchan; Editor, Gordon McClellan; Music, Mychael Danna; Casting, Dorothy Gardner; a Saturday Plays presentation; Canadian; Color; Not rated; 105 minutes; May release. CAST: Colleen Dewhurst (Molly Dushane), Megan Follows (Micheline Dushane), Gordon Clapp (Harvey Dushane), Debra McGrath (Liz Dushane), Leon Pownall (Charles Marshall), Elliott Smith (Delaney), Norma Dell'Agnese (Valerie Dean), Hannah Lee (Nellie Wong), John Dolan (Libby), Judy Marshak (Betty Marshall), Francine Volker (Diane), Jo Ann McIntyre (Nurse Debbie), Paul Bettis (Dr. Lapinski), Steve Baker (Pock-marked Man), Heather Smith (Mona - Soap Opera), Lauri Waller-Benson (Vicky - Soap Opera), Robert Collins (Duke), Jean Daigle (Bucky), Wayne Taylor, Gary Menard (Hunters), Anna Starnino (Fat Lady), Brent Stait (Burt), Neil Foster (Mechanic), Lorna Wilson (Nurse #2), Isabelle Bridges (Carmel), Ron Tough (Policeman), Jay Pattison (Bus Driver), Eleanor Hutchinson (Receptionist), Joe Maille (Weenie), Marc Dassas (Alvin), Greg O'Hara (Taxi Driver)

LOVE WITHOUT PITY (Orion Classics) Producers, Alain Rocca, Les Productions Lazennec; Director/Screenplay, Eric Rochant; Photography, Pierre Novion; Editor, Michele Darmon; Music, Gerard Torikian; Costumes, Zelia Van Den Bulke; co-produced with Gerard Mital Productions/Christian Bourgois Productions/SGGC Jean Bernard Fetoux/FR3 Films Production; French; Color; Rated R; 94 minutes; May release. CAST: Hippolyte Girardot (Hippo), Mireille Perrier (Nathalie), Yvan Attal (Halpern), Jean Marie Rollin (Xavier), Cecile Mazan (Francine), Aline Still (The Mother), Paul Pavel (The

Karen Allen, Bryan Brown, Justin Rosniak, Bill Kerr in *Sweet Talker*
© *7 Arts*

Mireille Perrier, Hippolyte Girardot in *Love Without Pity*
© *Orion Classics*

Jeremy Cooper, Robert Koons in *The Reflecting Skin*
© *Prestige*

Amanda Donohoe, Gabriel Byrne in *Dark Obsession*
© *Circle Releasing*

Father), Anne Kessler (Adeline), Patrick Blondel (JF), Yves Boonen, Jean Luc Porraz, Vincent Vallier (The Students), Patrick Pineau, Pierre Trabut, Marc Behin (The Card Players), Biana (The University's Secretary), Herve Falloux (Denis), Bernard Mazzinghi (The Meter Man), Maryse Meryl (The Traffic Warden), Gerard Dauzat, Claude Segarel, Olivier Destrez (The Policemen), Paul Bisciglia (The News-Agent), Jean Clement (The District's Doorman), Marc Belini (The Brazilian Pal)

NOIR ET BLANC (Greycat Films) Director/Screenplay, Claire Devers; Photography, Daniel Desbois, Christopher Doyle, Alain Lasfargues, Jean Paul Da Costa; Editor, Fabienne Alvarez, Yves Sarda; a Films du Volcan production in association with the French Ministry of Culture; French; Black and white; Not rated; 80 minutes; May release. CAST: Francis Frappat (Antoine), Jacques Martial (Dominique), Josephine Fresson (Josy), Mark Berman (M. Roland), Claire Rigolleir (Edith), Catherine Belkodja (Cleaning Woman), Arnaud Carbonnier (Masseur), Benoit Regent (Night Watchman)

THE REFLECTING SKIN (Prestige) Producers, Dominic Anciano, Ray Burdis; Co-Producer, Di Roberts; Executive Producer, Jim Beach; Director/Screenplay, Philip Ridley; Photography, Dick Pope; Art Director, Rick Roberts; Editor, Scott Thomas; a Fugitive Films production; Distributed by Miramax Films; British; Color; Rated R; 93 minutes; June release. CAST: Viggo Mortensen (Cameron Dove), Lindsay Duncan (Dolphin Blue), Jeremy Cooper (Seth Dove), Sheila Moore (Ruth Dove), Duncan Fraser (Luke Dove), David Longworth (Joshua), Robert Koons (Sheriff Ticker), David Bloom (Deputy), Evan Hall (Kim), Codie Lucas Wilbee (Eben), Sherry Bie (Cassie), Jason Wolfe (Cadillac Driver), Jeff Walker (Adam Blue), Joyce Robbins, Jacqueline Robbins (Twins), Debi Greenawdt, Sandra Redmond (Women), Walt Healy (Old Man)

STRIP JACK NAKED (Frameline) Producer/Director, Ron Peck; Executive Producers, Kate Ogborn, Andy Powell; Screenplay, Ron Peck, Paul Hallam; Photography, Ron Peck, Christopher Hughes; Editors, Ron Peck, Adrian James Carbott; Music, Adrian James Carbott; a BFI production, in association with Channel 4 TV; British; Color; Not rated; 96 minutes; June release. A documentary on the making of Ron Peck's 1978 film *Nighthawks* featuring John Brown, John Daimon, Nick Bolton, and others

WHAT EVERY FRENCHWOMAN WANTS (Morris Project) formerly *The Exploits of a Young Don Juan*; Producer, Claire Duval; Executive Producer, Nicolas Duval; Director, Gianfranco Mingozzi; Screenplay, Jean-Claude Carriere, Peter Fleischman; Based on the novel by Guillaume Apollinaire; Photography, Luigi Verga; Music, Nicola Piovani; Editor, Alfredo Muschietti; an Orpheé Arts/Selena Audiovisual/Films Ariane/Lagonda Films/Antea co-production; French-Italian, 1987; Color; Not rated; 95 minutes; June release. CAST: Claudine Auger (The Mother), Serena Grandi (Ursule), Marina Vlady (Madam Muller), Fabrice Josso (Roger), François Perrot (The Father), Berangere Bonvoisin (Aunt Marguerite), Rufus (The Monk), Laurent Spielvogel (Mr. Frank), Rosette (Helene), Marion Peterson (Kate), Virginie Ledoyen (Berthe), Yves Lambrecht (Roland), Aurelien Recoing (Adolphe)

DARK OBSESSION (Circle Releasing) formerly *Diamond Skulls*; Producer, Tim Bevan; Director, Nick Broomfield; Screenplay, Tim Rose Price; Photography, Michael Coulter; Editor, Rodney Holland; Designer, Jocelyn James; Music, Hans Zimmer; Casting, Lucy Boulting; Costumes, Mary-Jane Reyner; Assistant Director, Waldo Roeg; a Film Four International and British Screen presentation of a Working Title production; British; Technicolor; Rated NC-17; 87 minutes; June release. CAST: Gabriel Byrne (Sir Hugo Buckton), Amanda Donohoe (Lady Virginia Buckton), Struan Rodger (Peter), Douglas Hodge (Jamie), Peter Sands (Colonel), David Delve (Alec), Ralph Brown (Jack), Alexander Clempson (Edward), Catherine Livesey (Nanny), Michael Hordern (Lord Crewne), Ian Carmichael (Exeter), Matthew Marsh (Raul), Judy Parfitt (Lady Crewne), Sadie Frost (Rebecca), Edward Burnham (John, the Gardner), Phyllida Hewat (Lady Castlemere), Patrick Field, Robin Summers (Detectives), Jay Benedict (Joe Dimandino), Eiji Kusuhara (Ewo Nagasaky), William Hoyland (Inspector Orchard)

EXTRAMUROS (Frameline) Producer, Antonio Martin; Director/Screenplay, Miguel Picazo; Based on a novel by Jesus Fernandez Santos; Music, Jose Nieto; Photography, Teo Escamilla; Editor, Jose Luis Matesanz; a Production of Blau Films S.A. -Miguel Picazo, P.C. in association with T.V.E., S.A.; Spanish, 1985; Color; Not rated; 119 minutes; June release. CAST: Carmen Maura (Sister Ana), Mercedes Sampietro (Sister Angela), Aurora Bautista (Prioress), Assumpta Serna (The Guest), Antonio Ferrandis (The Doctor)

Fabrice Josso (left) in *What Every Frenchwoman Wants*
© *Morris Project*

Mercedes Sampietro, Carmen Maura
in *Extramuros*
© *Frameline*

Terry O'Quinn, George Takei, Bryan Brown
in *Prisoners of the Sun*
© *Skouras Pictures*

Marquis
© *A.Y. Alligator Films*

FIRST DATE (Peter Wang Films) Producer, Xu Guo Liang; Director/ Screenplay, Peter Wang; Photography, Larry Banks; Editor, Li Shin Yu; Music, Zhang Hong Yi; Designer, Ren Shi Zheng; Taiwanese; Color; Not rated; 90 minutes; June release. CAST: Chang Shi (Yang Jia Luo), Li Xing Wen (Yo Fu Sheng), Shi Jun (Teacher Liu), Huang Jin Qing (Jade Cloud Lin), Zhang Zhi Hua (Mousie Guo), Xie Zu Wu (Birdie Gu), Peter Wang (Yang Huai Xun)

PRISONERS OF THE SUN (Skouras) formerly *Blood Oath*; Producers, Charles Waterstreet, Denis Whitburn, Brian A. Williams; Co-Producer, Annie Bleakley; Line Producer, Richard Brennan; Director, Stephen Wallace; Screenplay, Denis Whitburn, Brian A. Williams; Executive Producers, Graham Burke, Greg Coote, John Tarnoff; Photography, Russell Boyd; Designer, Bernard Hides; Music, David McHugh; Editor, Nicholas Beauman; Costumes, Roger Kirk; a Village Roadshow Pictures presentation; Australian; Color; Rated R; 109 minutes; July release. CAST: Bryan Brown (Capt. Robert Cooper), George Takei (Vice Adm. Baron Takahashi), Terry O'Quinn (Maj. Tom Beckett), John Bach (Maj. Frank Roberts), Toshi Shioya (Lt. Hideo Tanaka), John Clarke (Mike Sheedy), Deborah Unger (Sister Carol Littell), Jason Donovan (Pvt. Talbot), John Polson (Pvt. Jimmy Fenton), Russell Crowe (Lt. Jack Corbett), Nicholas Eadie (Sgt. Keenan), Tetsu Watanabe (Capt. Wadami Ikeuchi), Sokyu Fujita (Mr. Shinji Matsugae), Ray Barrett (Lt. Col. Johnson), Kazuhiro Muroyama (Lt. Noburo Kamura), David Argue (Flight Lt. Eddy Fenton), Yuichiro Senga (Lt. Shimada), Andrew Booth (Pvt. Bill Mitchell), Malcolm Cork (Australian Soldier), Donal Gibson (Corp. Patterson), Shane McNamara (Maj. Roberts' Aide), Peter Waterstreet (Flight Lt. O'Donnell), Tim Reuther (Flight Lt. Smith), Matthew Keyes (Flight Lt. Rogers), Christina Ongley (Nurse Pearson)

WEININGER'S LAST NIGHT (Cinepool/Wega-Film) Producer, Veit Heiduschka; Director/Screenplay, Paulus Manker; Based on the play by Joshua Sobol; Photography, Walter Kindler; Editors, Igrid Koller, Marie Homolkova; Austrian, 1989; Color; Not rated; 100 minutes; July release. CAST: Paulus Manker (Otto Weininger), Hilde Sochor (Adelaide Weininger/Adele/Janitor), Josefin Platt (Double), Seighardt Rupp (Leopold Weininger/Sigmund Freud), Andrea Eckert (Clara), Peter Faeber (Berger), Hermann Schmid (August Strindberg/Paul Julius Moebius)

THE FAMINE WITHIN (Direct Cinema Ltd.) Producer/Director/Screenplay, Katherine Gilday; Executive Producer, Paul Jay; Photography, Joan Hutton; Editor, Petra Valier; Canadian; Color; Not rated; 90 minutes; July release. Documentary

MARQUIS (A.Y. Alligator Films) Director, Henri Xhonneux; Screenplay, Roland Topor, Henri Xhonneux; Original Creature Design/Art Director, Roland Topor; Photography, Etienne Faudet; Music, Reinhardt Wagner; Creature Creators, Jacques and Frederic Gastineau; Costumes, Maryvonne Herzog; Editor, Chantal Hymans; Executive Producer, Eric Van Beuren; co-produced by Constellation Productions/Tchin Tchin Productions with assistance from the Ministry of the French Community in Belgium and the National Film Board in France; Belgian-French; Fujicolor; Not rated; 83 minutes; July release. CAST: Philippe Bizot, Bien de Moor, Gabrielle van Damme, Olivier Dechaveau, Bernard Cognaux, Pierre Decuypere

STREET OF NO RETURN (Thunder Films) Producer, Jacques Bral; Executive Producers, Jacques-Eric Strauss, Patrick Delaneux, Antonio Da Cunha Telles; Director, Samuel Fuller; Screenplay, Jacques Bral, Samuel Fuller; Based on the novel *Sans Espoir Deretour* by David Goodis; Photography, Pierre-William Glenn; Art Director, Geoffrey Larcher; Music, Karl-Hienz Schafer; a co-production of FR3 Films productions and Animatografo; French-Portuguese; Fuji color; Not rated; 90 minutes; August release. CAST: Keith Carradine (Michael), Valentina Vargas (Celia), Bill Duke (Borel), Andrea Ferreol (Rhoda), Bernard Fresson (Morin), Marc De Jonge (Eddie), Rebecca Potok (Bertha), Jacques Martial (Gérard), Sergio Godinho (Pernoy), Antonio Rosario (Meathead), Dominique Hulin (Dablin), Gordon Heath (Clochard Noir), Joe Abdo (Clochard Blanc), Trevor Stephens (Lambert), Filipe Ferrer (Gauvreau), Jeremy Boultbee (Doctor), Guilherme Filipe, Pedro Nunes (Patrolmen), Samuel Fuller (Police Commissioner), Joaquim Miranda, Luis Norton De Matos (Police), Christa Lang (Nurse), Samantha Fuller

CROSSING THE LINE (Miramax) a.k.a. *The Big Man*; Producer, Stephen Woolley; Director, David Leland; Screenplay, Don McPherson; Based on the novel *The Big Man* by William McIlvanney; Executive Producer, Nik Powell; Co-Executive Producers, Harvey Weinstein, Bob Weinstein; Photography, Ian Wilson; Designer, Caroline Amies; Music, Ennio Morricone; Editor,

Paulus Manker in *Weininger's Last Night*
© *Cinepool*

Keith Carradine in *Street of No Return*
© *Thunder Films*

Billy Connolly, Liam Neeson in *Crossing the Line*
© *Miramax Films*

Vincent D'Onofrio, Mathilda May in *Naked Tango*
© *Sugarloaf/Gotan Prods.*

George Akers; Costumes, Mary-Jane Reymer; Casting, Susie Figgis; British; Color; Rated R; 93 minutes; August release. CAST: Liam Neeson (Danny Scoular), Joanne Whalley-Kilmer (Beth Scoular), Ian Bannen (Matt Mason), Billy Connolly (Frankie), Hugh Grant (Gordon), Maurice Roeves (Cam Colvin), George Rossi (Eddie), Tom Watson (Tommy Brogan), Julie Graham (Melanie), Pat Roach (Billy), Rab Affleck (Cutty Dawson), Andrew Meadan (Wee Danny), Ashleigh Thomas (Young Kate), Joseph Greig (Willie), Sean Scanlan (Alan), Peter Mullan (Vince), James Copeland (Sam), Carla Cannon (Fiona Mason), Kenny Ireland (Tony), Ken Drury (Stalker), Ralph Riach (Laundry Manager), Michael Marra (Alex the Butcher), Phil McCall (Sandy the Chemist), Juliet Cadzow (Margaret Mason), Subash Singh Pal (Drinker), Jonathan Hackett (Roddy Stewart), Jack Shepard (Referee), Dougie Henshall (Davie Dawson)

THE YEN FAMILY (Fujisankei Communications Intl.) Director, Yojiri Takita; Screenplay, Nobuyuki Isshiki, based on a story by Toshihiko Tani; Photography, Yoichi Shiga; Japanese, 1988; Color; Not rated; 113 minutes; August release. CAST: Kaori Momoi (Noriko Kimura), Takeshi Kaga (Hajime Kimura), Mitsunori Isaki (Taro Kimura), Hiromi Iwasaki (Terumi Kimura)

NAKED TANGO (New Line Cinema) Producer, David Weisman; Co-Producers, Milena Canonero, Michael Maiello; Director/Screenplay, Leonard Schrader; Inspired by Manuel Puig; Photography, Juan Ruiz-Anchia; Designer, Anthony Pratt; Music, Thomas Newman; Editor, Debra McDermott Lee Percy; Costumes, Patricio Bisso; Choreographer, Carlos Rivarola; a Sugarloaf/Gotan production, in association with Towa Production Company Ltd. (Tokyo)/Praesens-Films AG (Zurich)/Grupo Baires Ltd. (Buenos Aires); Argentine-Swiss-Japanese-U.S.; Dolby Stereo; Color; Rated R; 90 minutes; August release. CAST: Vincent D'Onofrio (Cholo), Mathilda May (Alba/Stephanie), Esai Morales (Zico Borenstein), Fernando Rey (Judge Torres), Cipe Lincovski (Zico's Mama), Josh Mostel (Bertoni the Jeweler), Constance McCashin (Flora), Patricio Bisso (Bordello Hairdresser), Sergio Lerer (Fake Rabbi), Marcos Woinski (Big Italian Thug), Ruben Szuchmacher (Little Italian Thug), Jean-Pierre Reguerraz (Jewish Gang Boss), Ines Yujnovsky (Bébé), Javier Portales (Police Chief), Vando Villami, Nestor Zacco (Corrupt Cops), Harry Havilio (Doctor), Bill James (Butler)

FRIDA KAHLO: A RIBBON AROUND A BOMB (Roxie Releasing) Producers, Jeff Hurst, Cora Cardona, Ken Mandel; Director/Editor, Ken Mandel; Photography, Jeff Hurst; Music, John Bryant, Frank Hames; Excerpts from the play *The Diary of Frida Kahlo* by Abraham Oceransky; Color; Not rated; 71 minutes; August release. Performed by Cora Cardona, Quigley Provost, Costa Caglage

BEAUTIFUL DREAMERS (Hemdale) Producers, Michael Maclear, Martin Walters; Executive Producers, Stephen Roth, Colin Neale; Director/Screenplay, John Kent Harrison; Photography, François Protat; Music, Lawrence Shragge; Editor, Ron Wisman; a Cinexus/Famous Players and C/FP Distribution Inc. release; Canadian; Color; Rated PG-13; 105 minutes; September release. CAST: Colm Feore (Dr. Bucke), Rip Torn (Walt Whitman), Wendel Meldrum (Jessie Bucke), Sheila McCarthy (Mollie Jessop), Colin Fox (Rev. Haines), David Gardner (Dr. Lett), Barbara Gordon (Agatha Haines), Marsha Moreau (Birdie Bucke), Albert Schultz (Dr. John Burgess), Tom McCamus (Leonard)

SWAN LAKE - THE ZONE (Zeitgeist) Director/Photography, Yuri Illienko; Screenplay, Yuri Illienko, Sergei Paradjanov; Based on stories by Sergei Paradjanov; Music, Virko Baley; Ukrainian-Soviet-Swedish-U.S.-Canadian; Color; Not rated; 96 minutes; September release. CAST: Viktor Solovyov, Lyudmila Yefimenko

WHERE (Where Prods.) Producer/Director/Screenplay, Gabor Szabo; Photography, Nyika Jancso; Designer, Attila Kovacs; Associate Producer, Ann Bramhall; Hungarian-U.S.; Black and white; Not rated; 96 minutes; September release. CAST: Miklos Acs (H.), Renata Satler (E.), Dennis Cornel (Adolfo)

WHERE THE SPIRIT LIVES (L.W. Blair Films) Producers, Heather Goldin, Eric Jordan, Mary Young Leckie; Executive Producer, Paul Stephens; Director, Bruce Pittman; Screenplay, Keith Ross Leckie; Photography, Rene Ohashi; Music, Buffy Sainte Marie; Editor, Michael Todd; an Amazing Spirit production in association with the Canadian Broadcasting Corp., Mid-Canada TV and TV Ontario; Canadian; Color; Not rated; 97 minutes; September release. CAST: Michelle St. John (Komi/Amelia), Clayton Julian (Pita/Abraham), Heather Hess (Rachel), Ann-Marie Macdonald (Kathleen), Ron White (Taggert), Chapelle Jaffe (Miss Appleby), David Hemblen (Rev. Buckley), Patricia Collins (Mrs. Barrington)

The Yen Family
© *Fujisankei Communications*

Rip Torn, Colm Feore in *Beautiful Dreamers* 229
© *Hemdale Pictures*

Ian Bannen, Nathaniel Moreau in *George's Island*
© *New Line Cinema*

Klaus von Brucker in *No Skin Off My Ass*
© *Strand Releasing*

GEORGE'S ISLAND (New Line Cinema) Producer, Maura O'Connell; Co-Producer, Stefan Wodoslawsky; Director, Paul Donovan; Screenplay, Maura O'Connell, Paul Donovan; Executive Producers, Paul Donovan, Maura O'Connell, J. William Ritchie; Photography, Les Kriszan; Designer, Bill Fleming; Music, Marty Simon; a Salter Street Films production; Canadian; Color; Rated PG; 89 minutes; October release. CAST: Ian Bannen (Captain Waters), Sheila McCarthy (Miss Birdwood), Maury Chaykin (Mr. Droonfield), Nathaniel Moreau (George Waters), Vicki Ridler (Bonnie), Brian Downcy (Mr. Beane), Irene Hogan (Mrs. Beane)

THE RESTLESS CONSCIENCE (Beller) Producer/Director/ Screenplay, Hava Kohav Beller; Photography, Volker Rodde, Martin Schaer, Gabor Bagyoni; Editors, Tonicka Janek, Juliette Weber, David Rogow; Narrator, John Dildine; German; Color/Black and white; Not rated; 90 minutes; October release. Documentary on the German anti-Hitler resistance featuring Julius Leber, Count Helmuth James von Moltke, Adam von Trott zu Solz, Dr. Carl Goerdeler, Count Fritz-Dietlof von der Schulenberg, Maj. Gen. Henning von Tresckow, Dietrich Bonhoeffer, Alex von dem Bussche, Ewald-Heinrich von Kleist, Dr. Hans von Dohnanyi, Col. Hans Oster

SLOW BURN (World Screen Associates) Producer, Geoff Griffiths; Director, John E. Eyres; Screenplay, Steven Lister; Photography, Nathaniel Massey; Music, Alan Grey; an EGM Film Intl. production; Canadian; Color; Not rated; 100 minutes; October release. CAST: Anthony James, William Smith, Ivan Rogers, Scott Anderson, Mellisa Conroy

TWO EVIL EYES (Taurus) Producers, Achille Manzotti, Dario Argento; "The Truth about the Valdemar Case": Director/Screenplay, George Romero; "The Black Cat": Director, Dario Argento; Screenplay, Dario Argento, Franco Ferrini; Photography, Peter Reniers; Art Director, Cletus Anderson; Editor, Pat Buba; Music, Pino Donaggio; Makeup, Tom Savini; Italian; Color; Rated R; 122 minutes; October release. CAST: Adrienne Barbeau (Jessica Valdemar), E.G. Marshall (Steven Pike), Ramy Zada (Dr. Robert Hoffman), Bingo O'Malley (Ernest Valdemar), Harvey Keitel (Rod Usher), Madeleine Potter (Annabel), Martin Balsam (Mr. Bee), Kim Hunter (Mrs. Pee), Sally Kirkland (Eleanora), John Amos

NOTEBOOKS ON CITIES AND CLOTHES (Connoisseur) Producer, Ulrich Felsberg; Director/Screenplay, Wim Wenders; Photography, Robby Müller, Muriel Edelstein, Uli Kudicke, Wim Wenders; M. Nakajima, M. Chikamori; Music, Laurent Petitgand; Editors, Dominique Auvrey, Lenie Savietto, Anne Schnee; a Road Movies production; W. German; Color; Not rated; 80 minutes; October release. Documentary featuring Yohji Yamamoto

FIST OF THE NORTH STAR (Streamline) English Adaptation; Producer, Carl Macek; Director, Toyoo Ashida; Screenplay, Susumu Takahisa; English Dialogue Written and Directed by Tom Wyner; Based on the graphic novels by Buronson and Tetsuohara; Music, Katsuhisa Hattori; Art Director, Shiko Tanaka; Produced by Toei Animation Co. Ltd.; Japanese; Color; Not rated; 100 minutes; October release. VOICE CAST: John Vickery (Ken), Melodee Spivack (Julia), Wally Burr (Raoh), Michael McConnohie (Shin), Gregory Snegoff (Rei), Tony Oliver (Bat), Holly Sidell (Lynn), James Avery (Fang), Barbara Goodson (Ailie), Dan Woren (Jagi), Jeff Corey (Ryuken), Steve Bullen (Jackal), Dave Mallow (Hart)

THE ARCHITECTURE OF DOOM (First Run Features) Producer/ Director/Screenplay/Editor, Peter Cohen; Narrator, Bruno Ganz; Music, Richard Wagner, Hector Berlioz; co-produced by the Swedish Film Institute; German-Swedish; Color/Black and white; Not rated; 119 minutes; October release. Documentary

THE CRY OF THE OWL (R5/S8) Director, Claude Chabrol; Screenplay, Claude Chabrol, Odile Barski; Based on the novel by Patricia Highsmith; Photography, Jean Rabier; Music, Matthieu Chabrol; French; 1987; Color; Not rated; 102 minutes; October release. CAST: Christophe Malavoy (Robert), Mathilda May (Juliette), Jacques Penot (Patrick)

EXPOSURE (Miramax) formerly *High Art*; Producer, Alberto Flaksman; Director, Walter Salles, Jr.; Executive Producer, Paulo Carlos De Brito; Screenplay, Rubem Fonseca, based on his novel *High Art*; Photography, Jose Roberto Eliezer; Designers, Nico Faria, Beto Cavalcanti; Editor, Isabelle Rathery; Costumes, Mari Stockler; Music, Jurgen Kneiper, Todd Boekelheide; Casting, Graca Motta; Brazilian; Color; Rated R; 100 minutes; October release. CAST: Peter Coyote (Peter Mandrake), Tcheky Karyo (Hermes), Amanda Pays (Marie), Raul Cortez (Lima Prado), Giulia Gam (Gisela), Paulo Jose (Detective), Eduardo Conde (Roberto Mitry), Rene Ruiz (Jose Zakkai - "Iron Nose"), Tonico Pereira (Rafael), Miguel Angel (Camilo Fuentes), Cassia Kiss (Mercedes), Iza Do Eirado (Zelia), Tony Torndo (Iron Nose's Bodyguard), Eduardo Waddington (Knife Dealer), Alvaro Freire (Evilasio, Mitry's Butler), Maria Alves (Hotel Attendant), Peter Marchetti (Singer at Lesbos Nightclub), Katia Bronstein (Woman killed in hotel), Conny Renny (Lima Prado's Secretary), Sylvia De Carvalho, Don Marco Maguila (Couple Fighting), Maria Gladys (Woman under billboards), Roberto Lee (Man fighting with Hermes), Vanessa Franca (Girl at bar), Henrique Vasconcellos (Policeman), Mauro Mendonca, Beth Prado

NO SKIN OFF MY ASS (Strand Releasing) Producer, Jürgen Brüning, Bruce LaBruce; Director/Screenplay/Editor, Bruce LaBruce; Additional Dialogue, G.B. Jones; Based on the novel *That Cold Day in the Park* by Richard Miles; Photography, Bruce LaBruce, Candy Von Pauker, G.B. Jones, Su Rynard, Joe McLean; a co-presentation of the New Lavender Panthers of Gaytown production; Canadian; Black and white; Not rated; 73 minutes; November release. CAST:

Giulia Gam, Peter Coyote in *Exposure*
© *Miramax Films*

Amanda Donohoe, Paul McGann in *Paper Mask*
© *Castle Hill*

Yaiwaiak Chonchanakun in *Good Woman of Bangkok*
© *Roxie Releasing*

Bruce LaBruce (The Hairdresser), Klaus von Brücker (The Skinhead), G.B. Jones (Jonesy), Caroline Azar, Laurel Purvis, Kate Ashley, Beverly Breckinridge, Hannah Cooper-McLean, Jena Von Brücker

PAPER MASK (Castle Hill) Producer/Director, Christopher Morahan; Co-Producer, Sue Austen; Screenplay, John Collee; Photography, Nat Crosby; Designer, Caroline Hanania; Costumes, Amy Roberts; Editor, Peter Coulson; Music, Richard Harvey; British; Color; Not rated; 105 minutes; November release. CAST: Paul McGann (Matthew Harris), Amanda Donohoe (Christine Taylor), Frederick Treves (Dr. Mumford), Tom Wilkinson (Dr. Thorn), Barbara Leigh-Hunt (Celia Mumford), Jimmy Yuill (Alec Moran), Mark Lewis Jones (Dr. Lloyd), John Warnaby (Dr. Hammond), Alexandra Mathie (Beverley), Oliver Ford Davies (Coroner), Frank Baker (Happy), Clive Rowe (Ants), Robert Oates (Head Porter), Karen Ascoe (Alison), Dale Rapley (Dr. Simon Hennessey), Simon Adams (Laurence), Hetta Charnley (Medical Student), Dierdre Halligan (Old Patient), Freda Rogers (Dr. Thorn's Staff Nurse), Sally Thompson (Dr. Gemmel), Iain Locke (Dr. Sutherland), Dhirendra (Dr. Kassim), Michael Thomas (Teaching Doctor), Bridget Brammall (Girl in bed), Philip Fox (Anaesthetist), Harmage Singh Kalirai (Surgeon), Glyn Pritchard (Man with gashed thumb), Tank James (Biker), Charmain May (Radiographer), J-J Flynn (Child in casualty), Marilyn Finlay (Mother), Carmen Knight (Student Nurse), Harry Webster (Yellow Man), Nick Edmett (Ambulance Driver), Oliver Guilford (Schoolboy), Tam White (Blues Singer), Steve Waller (Pianist), Glen Le Fleur (Drummer), Ian Bairnson (Guitarist), Gary Twigg (Bass Guitarist), Juliette Grassby (Caitlin), Michael Bertenshaw (Coroner's Officer), Phillip Manikum (Maintenance Engineer), Lee Simpson (Reporter), Diana Payan (Salisbury Sister)

CLOSE MY EYES (Castle Hill) Producer, Thérèse Pickard; Director/Screenplay, Stephen Poliakoff; Photography, Witold Stok; Designer, Luciana Arrighi; Music, Michael Gibbs; Casting, Joyce Gallie; Editor, Michael Parkinson; Costumes, Amy Roberts; British; Dolby Stereo; Color; Not rated; 109 minutes; November release. CAST: Alan Rickman (Sinclair), Clive Owen (Richard), Saskia Reeves (Natalie), Karl Johnson (Colin), Lesley Sharp (Jessica), Kate Gartside (Paula), Karen Knight (Philippa), Niall Buggy (Geal), Campbell Morrison (Scotsman), Annie Hayes (Receptionist),

Maxwell Hutcheon (Interviewee), Geraldine Somerville (Natalie's Boss), Helen FitzGerald (Scottish Girl), Christopher Barr (Noley), Gordon Salkilld (Hotel Porter), Choy Ling Man (Maid), John Albasiny (Young Man), Marie Passarelli (Selina), Jan Winters (Doreen)

THE GOOD WOMAN OF BANGKOK (Roxie) Producer/Director/Screenplay/Photography, Dennis O'Rourke; Editor, Tim Litchfield; an O'Rourke and Associates Filmmakers production in association with The Australian Film Commission and Channel 4; Australian; Color; Not rated; 79 minutes; November release. Documentary with Yaiwaiak Chonchanakun

IMAGES OF THE WORLD AND THE INSCRIPTION OF WAR (Goethe House) Director/Screenplay, Harun Farocki; Narrator, Cynthia Beatt; German, 1988; Color; Not rated; 75 minutes; November release. Documentary

IRON MAZE (Castle Hill) Producers, Ilona Herzberg, Hidenori Ueki; Executive Producers, Edward R. Pressman, Oliver Stone; Co-Executive Producers, Hidenori Taga, Katsumi Kimura; Executive in Charge of Production, Caldecot Chubb; Director, Hiroaki Yoshida; Screenplay, Tim Metcalfe; Screenstory, Hiroaki Yoshida, Tim Metcalfe; Based on the short story "In a Grove" by Ryunosuke Akutagawa; Photography, Morio Saequsa; Designer, Toby Corbett; Editor, Bonnie Koehler; Music, Stanley Myers; Costumes, Susie DeSanto; Casting, Elisabeth Leustig; a Trans-Tokyo Corporation production; Japanese-U.S.; Dolby Stereo; CFI color; Rated R; 102 minutes; November release. CAST: Jeff Fahey (Barry Mikowski), Bridget Fonda (Chris), Hiroaki Murakami (Sugita), J.T. Walsh (Jack Ruhle), Gabriel Damon (Mikey), John Randolph (Mayor Peluso), Peter Allas (Eddie), Carmen Filpi (Charlie), Francis John Thornton (Womack), Jeffrey J. Stephan (Councilman), Mark Lowenthal (Dr. Rathman), Goh Misawa (Tanazaki), J. Michael Hunter (Louis), Lenora Nemetz (Margie), Steve Aronson (Jo Jo), Zachary Mott (Bud), Michael R. Aubele (Ray), John Hall, Dean E. Wells (Bar Players), Alice G. Eisner (Neddie), Don Wadsworth (Hotel Manager), Douglas Pona (Hotel Clerk), Maria Becoates-Bay (Dispatcher), Rohn Thomas (Doctor), Patricia Hicok, Lee Hayes, Saundra Mason (Nurses), David W. Butler (Steelworker), Lamont Arnold (Watkins), Lonzo Green (Norman), Laverne M. Yorkgitis (Waitress)

Saskia Reeves, Alan Rickman in *Close My Eyes*
© *Castle Hill*

Bridget Fonda, Jeff Fahey in *Iron Maze*
© *Castle Hill*

Todd Waring in *Love & Murder*
© Hemdale

Hsia Wen-Shi in *Rouge of the North*
© Filmcat Inc.

LOVE AND MURDER (Hemdale/Southpaw) Producer/Director/Screenplay, Steven Hilliard Stern; Executive Producer, Howard Deverett; Photography, David Herrington; Designer, Tony Hall; Editor, Ron Wisman; Music, Matthew MacCauley; a Sharmill Productions, Inc. production; Dolby Stereo; Color; Rated R; 88 minutes; November release. CAST: Todd Waring (Hal), Kathleen Lasky (Brenda), Ron White (Fred), Louis Negin (Ginger), Wayne Robson, Theresa Tova, Laurie Paton, Joyce Gordon, Keith Knight

UNCLE MOSES (National Center for Jewish Film) Directors, Sidney Godlin, Aubrey Scotto; Based on the novel by Sholem Asch; Yiddish, 1932; Black and white; Not rated; 87 minutes; November release. CAST: Maurice Schwartz (Uncle Moses), Judith Abarbanell (Masha), Zvee Scooler (Charlie), Rubin Goldberg (Moses' Father), Mark Schweid (Aaron)

DINGO (Greycat Films) Producers, Rolf de Heer, Marc Rosenberg; Executive Producers, Giorgio Draskovic, Marie Pascale Osterrieth; Director, Rolf de Heer; Screenplay, Marc Rosenberg; Photography, Denis Lenoir; Music, Michel Legrand, Miles Davis; Designer, Judi Russell; Editor, Surresh Ayyar; a Gevest Australia Prods. - AO Prods.-Dedra Films-Cine Cinq co-production with the participation of the Australian Film Finance Corp.; Australian-French; Panavision; Eastmancolor; Not rated; 109 minutes; December release. CAST: Colin Friels (John Anderson), Miles Davis (Billy Cross), Helen Buday (Jane Anderson), Joe Petruzzi (Peter), Bernadette Lafont (Angie Cross), Bernard Fresson, Brigitte Catillon, Steve Shaw, Helen Doig

INSPECTOR LAVARDIN (MK2) Producer, Martin Karmitz; Director, Claude Chabrol; Screenplay, Dominique Roulet; Based on an original idea and adaptation by Claude Chabrol, Dominique Roulet; Photography, Jean Rabier; Editors, Monique Fardoulis, Angela Braga-Mermet; Music, Matthieu Chabrol; French, 1986; Color; Not rated; 100 minutes; December release. CAST: Jean Poiret (Jean Lavardin), Jean-Claude Brialy (Claude Alvarez), Bernadette Lafont (Hélène Mons), Jean-Luc Bideau (Max Charnet), Jacques Dacqmine (Raoul Mons), Hermine Clair (Véronique Manguin), Pierre-François Dumeniaud (Marcel Vigouroux), Florent Gibassier (Francis), Guy Louret (Buci), Jean Depussé (Volga)

ROUGE OF THE NORTH (Greycat) Producers, Lin Tung-Fei, Chen Chun-Sung; Line Producer, Hsu Kuo-Liang; Producer in Charge, Chao Chi-Bin; Director/Screenplay, Fred Tan; Adapted from the novel by Eileen Chang; Executive Producer, James Y. Liu; Photography, Yang Wei-Han; Editor, Chen Po-Wen; Designer, Chow Chi-Liang; Costumes, Lu Chi-Liang; Music, Peter Chang; Chinese; Color; Not rated; 106 minutes; December release. CAST: Hsia Wen-Shi (Ying-Ti), Hsu Ming (Mr. Three), Kao-Chieh (Mr. Two), Hsiao-I (Mrs. 3), Lin Mei-Ling (Mrs. 1), Ma Shao-Chun (Yu-Shi), Hu Shian-Ping (Brother), Ting Yeh-Tieh (Sister-in-Law), Kwan-Yi (Old Mrs. Yao), Wu-Yien (Matchmaker), Li-Ying (Old Mr. Nine), Shirley Chen (Mrs. Pu), Emily Chang (Chi-Show, Daughter-in-Law), Chang Yu-Ling (Tung-Mei, 2nd Daughter-in-Law), Hang Tao-Kwong (Little Liu)

STRAND: UNDER THE DARK CLOTH (Kino International) Producer/ Photography/Director, John Walker; Screenplay, Seaton Findlay; Music, Jean Derome; Editors, Cathy Gulkin, John Kramer, Geoff Bowie; Canadian, 1989; Color; Not rated; 81 minutes; December release. Documentary with Georgia O'Keefe, Milton Brown, Fred Zinneman, Leo Hurwitz, Virginia Stevens, Hazel Strand, Cesare Zavattini, Blanche Brown, Walter Rosenblum

A WOMAN'S TALE (Orion Classics) Producers, Paul Cox, Santhana Naidu; Executive Producer, William Marshall; Director, Paul Cox; Screenplay, Paul Cox, Barry Dickins; Photography, Nino Martinetti; Designer, Neil Angwin; Editor, Russell Hurley; Music, Paul Grabowsky; an Illumination Films in association with Beyond Films Ltd. presentation; Australian; Color; Rated PG-13; 94 minutes; December release. CAST: Sheila Florance (Martha), Gosia Dobrowolska (Anna), Norman Kaye (Billy), Chris Haywood (Johnathan), Ernest Gray (Peter), Myrtle Woods (Miss Inchley), Bruce Myles, Alex Menglet (Cons), Francois Bernard, Manuel Bachet (Neighbors), Monica Maughan (Billy's Daughter), Max Gillies (Billy's Son-in-Law), Tony Llewellyn-Jones (Celebrant), David Reid (Don), Dawn Klingberg (Don's Wife), Marina Finlay (Prostitute), Victoria Eager, Marion Heathfield (Nurses), James Khong (Doctor), Kate Fewster (Young Martha), Carla Hoogeveen (Waitress), Nino Martinetti (Cafe Manager), Veronica Koca, Kyra Cox (Young Girls), Hal Todd (Hal Todd's Voice), Melita Juristic (Judy's Voice)

Maurice Schwartz, Judith Abarbanell
in *Uncle Moses*
© Natl. Center for Jewish Film

Myrtle Woods, Norman Kaye, Gosia Dobrowolska,
Sheila Florance in *A Woman's Tale*
© Orion Classics

| Ursula Andress | Lew Ayres | Carroll Baker | Robby Benson | Kathy Baker | Michael Biehn |

BIOGRAPHICAL DATA

(Name, real name, place and date of birth, school attended)

AAMES, WILLIE (William Upton): Los Angeles, CA, July 15, 1960.

AARON, CAROLINE: Richmond, VA, Aug. 7, 1954, CatholicU.

ABBOTT, DIAHNNE: NYC, 1945.

ABBOTT, JOHN: London, June 5, 1905.

ABRAHAM, F. MURRAY: Pittsburgh, PA, Oct. 24, 1939. UTx.

ADAMS, BROOKE: NYC, Feb. 8, 1949. Dalton.

ADAMS, DON: NYC, Apr. 13, 1926.

ADAMS, EDIE (Elizabeth Edith Enke): Kingston, PA, Apr. 16, 1927. Juilliard, Columbia.

ADAMS, JULIE (Betty May): Waterloo,Iowa, Oct. 17, 1926. Little Rock Jr. College.

ADAMS, MAUD (Maud Wikstrom): Lulea, Sweden, Feb. 12, 1945.

ADDY, WESLEY: Omaha, NE, Aug. 4, 1913. UCLA.

ADJANI, ISABELLE: Germany, June 27, 1955.

ADRIAN, IRIS (Iris Adrian Hostetter): Los Angeles, May 29, 1913.

AGAR, JOHN: Chicago. Jan. 31, 1921.

AGUTTER, JENNY: Taunton, Eng, Dec. 20, 1952.

AIELLO, DANNY: NYC. June 20, 1935.

AIMEE. ANOUK (Dreyfus): Paris, Apr. 27, 1934. Bauer-Therond.

AKERS, KAREN: NYC, Oct. 13, 1945, Hunter Col.

AKINS, CLAUDE: Nelson, GA, May 25, 1936. Northwestern U.

ALBERGHETTI, ANNA MARIA: Pesaro, Italy, May 15, 1936.

ALBERT, EDDIE (Eddie Albert Heimberger): Rock Island, IL, Apr. 22, 1908. U. of Minn.

ALBERT, EDWARD: Los Angeles, Feb. 20. 1951. UCLA.

ALBRIGHT, LOLA: Akron, OH, July 20, 1925.

ALDA, ALAN: NYC, Jan. 28, 1936. Fordham.

ALEJANDRO, MIGUEL: NYC, Feb. 21, 1958.

ALEXANDER, ERIKA: Philadelphia, PA, 1970.

ALEXANDER, JANE (Quigley): Boston, MA, Oct. 28, 1939. Sarah Lawrence.

ALEXANDER, JASON: Irvington, NJ, Sept. 23, 1959. Boston U.

ALICE, MARY: Indianola, MS, Dec. 3. 1941.

ALLEN, DEBBIE (Deborah): Houston, TX, Jan. 16, 1950, HowardU.

ALLEN, JOAN: Rochelle, IL, Aug. 20, 1956, EastIllU.

ALLEN, KAREN: Carrollton, IL, Oct. 5, 1951. UMd.

ALLEN, NANCY: NYC, June 24, 1950.

ALLEN, REX: Wilcox, AZ, Dec. 31, 1922.

ALLEN, STEVE: NYC, Dec. 26, 1921.

ALLEN, WOODY (Allen Stewart Konigsberg): Brooklyn, Dec. 1, 1935.

ALLEY, KIRSTIE: Wichita, KS, Jan. 12, 1955.

ALLYSON, JUNE (Ella Geisman): Westchester, NY, Oct. 7, 1917.

ALONSO, MARIA CONCHITA: Cuba, 1957.

ALT, CAROL: Queens, NY, Dec. 1, 1960.HofstraU.

ALVARADO, TRINI: NYC, 1967.

AMECHE, DON (Dominic Amichi): Kenosha, WI, May 31, 1908.

AMES, LEON (Leon Wycoff): Porlland, IN, Jan. 20, 1903.

AMIS, SUZY: Oklahoma City, OK, Jan. 5, 1958. Actors Studio.

AMOS, J0HN: Newark, NJ, Dec. 27, 1940. Colo. U.

ANDERSON, KEVIN: Illinois, Jan. 13, 1960.

ANDERSON, LONI: St. Paul, MN, Aug. 5, 1946.

ANDERSON, MELODY: Edmonton, Canada, 1955. Carlton U.

ANDERSON, MICHAEL, JR.: London, Eng., Aug. 6, 1943.

ANDERSON, RICHARD DEAN: Minneapolis, MN, Jan. 23, 1953.

ANDERSSON, BIBI: Stockholm, Nov. 11,1935. Royal Dramatic Sch.

ANDES, KEITH: Ocean City, NJ, July 12, 1920. Temple U., Oxford.

ANDRESS, URSULA: Berne, Switz., Mar. 19, 1936.

ANDREWS, ANTHONY: London, 1948.

ANDREWS, DANA: Collins, MS, Jan. 1, 1909. Sam Houston Col.

ANDREWS, JULIE (Julia Elizabeth Wells): Surrey, Eng., Oct. 1, 1935.

ANGLIM, PHILIP: San Francisco, CA, Feb. 11, 1953.

ANNABELLA (Suzanne Georgette Charpentier): Paris, France, July 14, 1912/1909.

ANN-MARGRET (Olsson): Valsjobyn, Sweden, Apr. 28, 1941. Northwestern U.

ANSARA, MICHAEL: Lowell, MA, Apr. 15, 1922. Pasadena Playhouse.

ANSPACH, SUSAN: NYC, Nov. 23, 1945.

ANTHONY, LYSETTE: London, 1963.

ANTHONY TONY: Clarksburg, WV, Oct.16, 1937. Carnegie Tech.

ANTON, SUSAN: Yucaipa, CA, Oct. 12, 1950. Bemardino Col.

ANTONELLI, LAURA: Pola, Italy, 1941.

ARANHA, RAY: Miami, FL, May 1, 1939. FlaA&M, AADA.

ARCHER, ANNE: Los Angeles, Aug. 25, 1947.

ARCHER, JOHN (Ralph Bowman): Osceola, NB, May 8, 1915. USC.

ARKIN, ADAM: Brooklyn, Aug. 19, 1956.

ARKIN, ALAN: NYC, Mar. 26, 1934. LACC.

ARMSTRONG, BESS: Baltimore, MD, Dec. 11, 1953.

ARNAZ, DESI, JR.: Los Angeles, Jan. 19, 1953.

ARNAZ, LUCIE: Hollywood, July 17,1951.

ARNESS, JAMES (Aurness): Minneapolis, MN, May 26, 1923. Beloit College.

ARNOLD, ROSEANNE (Barr): Salt Lake City, UT, Nov. 3, 1952.

ARQUETTE, ROSANNA: NYC, Aug. 10, 1959.

ARTHUR, BEATRICE (Frankel): NYC, May 13, 1924. New School.

ASHLEY, ELIZABETH (Elizabeth Ann Cole): Ocala, FL, Aug. 30, 1939.

ASNER, EDWARD: Kansas City, KS, Nov. 15, 1929.

ASSANTE, ARMAND: NYC, Oct. 4, 1949. AADA.

ASTIN, JOHN: Baltimore, MD, Mar. 30, 1930. U. Minn.

ASTIN, MacKENZIE: Los Angeles, 1973.

ASTIN, SEAN: Santa Monica, Feb. 25, 1971.

ATHERTON, WILLIAM: Orange, CT, July 30, 1947. Carnegie Tech.

ATKINS, CHRISTOPHER: Rye, NY, Feb. 21, 1961.

ATTENBOROUGH, RICHARD: Cambridge, Eng., Aug. 29, 1923. RADA.

AUBERJONOIS, RENE: NYC, June 1, 1940. Carnegie Tech.

AUDRAN, STEPHANE: Versailles, Fr., Nov. 8, 1933.

AUGER, CLAUDINE: Paris, Apr. 26,1942. Dramatic Cons.

AULIN, EWA: Stockholm, Sweden, Feb. 14, 1950.

AUMONT, JEAN PIERRE: Paris, Jan. 5, 1909. French Nat'l School of Drama.

AUTRY, GENE: Tioga, TX, Sept. 29, 1907.

AVALON, FRANKIE (Francis Thomas Avallone): Philadelphia, Sept. 18, 1940.

AYKROYD, DAN: Ottawa, Can., July 1, 1952.

AYRES, LEW: Minneapolis, MN, Dec. 28, 1908.

AZNAVOUR, CHARLES (Varenagh Aznourian): Paris, May 22, 1924.

AZZARA, CANDICE: Brooklyn, May 18, 1947.

BACALL, LAUREN (Betty Perske): NYC, Sept. 16, 1924. AADA.

BACH, BARBARA: Queens, NY, Aug. 27, 1946.

BACKER, BRIAN: NYC, Dec. 5, 1956. Neighborhood Playhouse.

BACON, KEVIN: Philadelphia, PA., July 8, 1958.

BAIN, BARBARA: Chicago, Sept. 13, 1934. U. ILL.

BAIO, SCOTT: Brooklyn, Sept. 22, 1961.

BAKER, BLANCHE: NYC, Dec. 20, 1956.

BAKER, CARROLL: Johnstown, PA, May 28, 1931. St. Petersburg Jr. College.

BAKER, DIANE: Hollywood, CA, Feb. 25, 1938. USC.

BAKER, JOE DON: Groesbeck, TX, Feb.12, 1936.

BAKER, KATHY: Midland, TX., June 8, 1950. UCBerkley.

BALABAN, BOB: Chicago, Aug. 16, 1945. Colgate.

BALDWIN, ADAM: Chicago, Feb. 27, 1962.

BALDWIN, ALEC: Massapequa, NY, Apr. 3, 1958. NYU.

BALE, CHRISTIAN: Pembrokeshire, West Wales, Jan. 30, 1974.

BALLARD, KAYE: Cleveland, OH, Nov. 20, 1926.

BALSAM, MARTIN: NYC, Nov. 4, 1919. Actors Studio.

BANCROFT, ANNE (Anna Maria Italiano): Bronx, Sept. 17, 1931. AADA.

BANERJEE, VICTOR: Calcutta, India, Oct. 15, 1946.

BANES, LISA: Chagrin Falls, OH, July 9, 1955. Juilliard.

BANNEN, IAN: Airdrie, Scot., June 29, 1928.

BARANSKI, CHRISTINE: Buffalo, NY, May 2, 1952. Juilliard.

BARBEAU, ADRIENNE: Sacramento, CA, June 11, 1945. Foothill Col.

BARDOT, BRIGITTE: Paris, Sept. 28, 1934.

BARKIN, ELLEN: Bronx, Apr. 16, 1954. Hunter Col.

BARNES, BINNIE (Gitelle Enoyce Barnes): London, Mar. 25, 1906

BARNES, C. B. (Christopher): Portland, ME, 1973.

BARR, JEAN-MARC: San Diego, CA, Sept. 1960.

BARRAULT, JEAN-LOUIS: Vesinet, France, Sept. 8, 1910.

BARRAULT, MARIE-CHRISTINE: Paris. Mar. 21, 1946.

BARREN, KEITH: Mexborough, Eng., Aug. 8, 1936. Sheffield Playhouse.

BARRETT, MAJEL (Hudec): Columbus, OH, Feb. 23. Western Reserve U.

BARRIE, BARBARA: Chicago, IL, May 23, 1931.

BARRY, GENE (Eugene Klass): NYC, June 14, 1921.

BARRY, NEILL: NYC, Nov. 29, 1965.

BARRYMORE, DREW: Los Angeles, Feb. 22, 1975.

BARRYMORE, JOHN DREW: Beverly Hills, CA, June 4, 1932. St. John's Military Academy.

BARTEL, PAUL: NYC, Aug. 6, 1938. UCLA.

BARTY, BILLY: Millsboro, PA, Oct. 25, 1924.

BARYSHNIKOV. MIKHAIL: Riga, Latvia, Jan. 27, 1948.

BASINGER, KIM: Athens, GA, Dec. 8, 1953. Neighborhood Playhouse.

BATEMAN, JASON: Rye, NY, Jan. 14, 1969.

BATEMAN, JUSTINE: Rye, NY, Feb. 19, 1966.

BATES, ALAN: Allestree, Derbyshire, Eng., Feb. 17, 1934. RADA.

BATES, JEANNE: San Francisco, CA, May 21. RADA.

BATES, KATHY: Memphis, TN, June 28, 1948. S. Methodist U.

BAUER, STEVEN: (Steven Rocky Echevarria): Havana, Cuba, Dec. 2, 1956. UMiami.

BAXTER, KEITH: South Wales,Eng., Apr. 29, 1933. RADA.

BAXTER, MEREDITH: Los Angeles, June 21, 1947. Intelochen Acad.

BEACHAM, STEPHANIE: England, 1946.

BEAL, JOHN (J. Alexander Bliedung): Joplin, MO, Aug. 13, 1909. PA. U.

BEALS, JENNIFER: Chicago, IL, Dec. 19, 1963.

BEART, EMMANUELLE: Gassin,France, 1965.

BEATTY, NED: Louisville, KY, July 6, 1937.

BEATTY, ROBERT: Hamilton, Ont., Can., Oct. 19, 1909. U. of Toronto.

BEATTY, WARREN: Richmond, VA, March 30, 1937.

BECK, JOHN: Chicago, IL, Jan. 28, 1943.

BECK, MICHAEL: Memphis, TN, Feb. 4, 1949. Millsap Col.

BEDELIA, BONNIE: NYC, Mar. 25, 1946. Hunter Col.

BEDI, KABIR: India, 1945.

BEERY, NOAH, JR.: NYC, Aug. 10, 1916. Harvard Military Academy.

BEGLEY, ED, JR.: NYC, Sept. 16, 1949.

BELAFONTE, HARRY: NYC, Mar. 1, 1927.

BEL GEDDES, BARBARA: NYC, Oct. 31, 1922.

BELL, TOM: Liverpool, Eng., 1932.

BELLER, KATHLEEN: NYC, Feb. 10, 1957.

BELLWOOD, PAMELA (King): Scarsdale, NY, June 26.

BELMONDO, JEAN PAUL: Paris, Apr. 9, 1933.

BELUSHI, JAMES: Chicago, May 15, 1954.

BENEDICT, DIRK (Niewoehner): White Sulphur Springs, MT, March 1, 1945. Whitman Col.

BENEDICT, PAUL: SilverCity, NM, Sept. 17, 1938.

BENING, ANNETTE: Topeka, KS, May 29, 1958. SFSt. U.

BENJAMIN, RICHARD: NYC, May 22, 1938. Northwestern U.

BENNENT, DAVID: Lausanne, Sept. 9, 1966.

BENNETT. BRUCE (Herman Brix): Tacoma, WA, May 19, 1909. U. Wash.

BENNETT, HYWEL: Garnant, So. Wales, Apr. 8, 1944.

BENSON, ROBBY: Dallas, TX, Jan 21, 1957.

BERENGER, TOM: Chicago, May 31, 1950, UMo.

BERENSON, MARISA: NYC, Feb. 15, 1947.

BERGEN, CANDICE: Los Angeles, May 9, 1946. U. PA.

BERGEN, POLLY: Knoxville, TN, July 14, 1930. Compton Jr. College.

BERGER, HELMUT: Salzburg, Aus., 1942.

BERGER, SENTA: Vienna, May 13, 1941. Vienna Sch. of Acting.

BERGER, WILLIAM: Austria, Jan. 20, 1928. Columbia.

| Susan | Matthew | Eileen | Timothy | Mia | Bill |
| Blakely | Broderick | Brennan | Busfield | Farrow | Cosby |

BERGERAC, JACQUES: Biarritz, France, May 26, 1927. Paris U.

BERLE, MILTON (Berlinger): NYC, July 12, 1908.

BERLIN, JEANNIE: Los Angeles, Nov. 1, 1949.

BERLINGER, WARREN: Brooklyn, Aug. 31, 1937. Columbia.

BERNHARD, SANDRA: Flint, MI, June 6, 1955.

BERNSEN, CORBIN: Los Angeles, Sept. 7, 1954. UCLA.

BERRI, CLAUDE (Langmann): Paris, July 1, 1934.

BERRIDGE, ELIZABETH: Westchester, NY, May 2, 1962. Strasberg Inst.

BERTINELLI, VALERIE: Wilmington, DE, Apr. 23, 1960.

BERTO, JULIET: Grenoble, France, Jan. 1947.

BEST, JAMES: Corydon, IN, July 26, 1926.

BETTGER, LYLE: Philadelphia, Feb. 13, 1915. AADA.

BEYMER, RICHARD: Avoca, IA, Feb. 21. 1939.

BIEHN, MICHAEL: Anniston, AL, 1957.

BIKEL, THEODORE: Vienna, May 2, 1924. RADA.

BILLINGSLEY, PETER: NYC, 1972.

BIRNEY, DAVID: Washington, DC, Apr. 23, 1939. Dartmouth, UCLA.

BIRNEY, REED: Alexandria, VA, Sept. 11, 1954. Boston U.

BISHOP, JOEY (Joseph Abraham Gotlieb): Bronx, NY, Feb. 3, 1918.

BISHOP, JULIE (formerly Jacqueline Wells): Denver, CO, Aug. 30, 1917. Westlake School.

BISSET, JACQUELINE: Waybridge, Eng., Sept. 13, 1944.

BIXBY, BILL: San Francisco, Jan. 22, 1934. U. CAL.

BLACK, KAREN (Ziegler): Park Ridge, IL, July 1, 1942. Northwestern.

BLADES, RUBEN: Panama, July 16, 1948. Harvard.

BLAINE, VIVIAN (Vivian Stapleton): Newark, NJ, Nov. 21, 1921.

BLAIR, BETSY (Betsy Boger): NYC, Dec. 11, 1923.

BLAIR, JANET (Martha Jane Lafferty): Blair, PA, Apr. 23, 1921.

BLAIR, LINDA: Westport, CT, Jan. 22, 1959.

BLAKE, ROBERT (Michael Gubitosi): Nutley, NJ, Sept. 18, 1933.

BLAKELY, SUSAN: Frankfurt, Germany, Sept. 7, 1950. U. TEX.

BLAKLEY, RONEE: Stanley, ID, 1946. Stanford U.

BLOOM, CLAIRE: London, Feb. 15, 1931. Badminton School.

BLOOM, VERNA: Lynn, MA, Aug. 7, 1939. Boston U.

BLUM, MARK: Newark, NJ, May 14, 1950. UMinn.

BLYTH, ANN: Mt. Kisco, NY, Aug. 16, 1928. New Waybum Dramatic School.

BOCHNER, HART: Toronto, Oct. 3, 1956. U. San Diego.

BOGARDE, DIRK: London, Mar. 28,1921. Glasgow & Univ. College.

BOGOSIAN, ERIC: Woburn, MA, Apr. 24, 1953. Oberlin Col.

BOHRINGER, RICHARD: Paris, 1942.

BOLKAN, FLORINDA (Florinda Soares Bulcao): Ceara, Brazil, Feb. 15, 1941.

BOLOGNA, JOSEPH: Brooklyn, Dec. 30, 1938. Brown U.

BOND, DEREK: Glasgow, Scot., Jan. 26,1920. Askes School.

BONET, LISA: San Francisco, Nov. 16, 1967.

BONHAM-CARTER, HELENA: London, Eng., May 26, 1966.

BONO, SONNY (Salvatore): Detroit, MI, Feb. 16, 1935.

BOONE, PAT: Jacksonville, FL, June 1, 1934. Columbia U.

BOOTHE, POWERS: Snyder, TX, 1949. So. Methodist U.

BORGNINE, ERNEST (Borgnino): Hamden, CT, Jan. 24, 1918. Randall School.

BOSCO, PHILIP: Jersey City, N J, Sept. 26, 1930. CatholicU.

BOSTWICK, BARRY: San Mateo, CA, Feb. 24, 1945. NYU.

BOTTOMS, JOSEPH: Santa Barbara, CA, Aug. 30, 1954.

BOTTOMS, SAM: Santa Barbara, CA, Oct.17, 1955.

BOTTOMS, TIMOTHY: Santa Barbara, CA, Aug. 30, 1951.

BOULTING, INGRID: Transvaal, So. Africa, 1947.

BOUTSIKARIS, DENNIS: Newark, NJ, Dec. 21, 1952. CatholicU.

BOVEE, LESLIE: Bend, OR, 1952.

BOWIE, DAVID: (David Robert Jones): Brixton, South London, Eng., Jan. 8, 1947.

BOWKER, JUDI: Shawford, Eng., Apr. 6, 1954.

BOXLEITNER, BRUCE: Elgin, IL, May 12, 1950.

BOYLE, LARA FLYNN: Davenport, IA, Mar. 24, 1970.

BOYLE, PETER: Philadelphia, PA, Oct. 18, 1933. LaSalle Col.

BRACCO, LORRAINE: Brooklyn, 1955.

BRACKEN, EDDIE: NYC, Feb. 7, 1920. Professional Children's School.

BRAEDEN, ERIC (Hans Gudegast): Kiel, Germany, Apr. 3.

BRAGA, SONIA: Maringa, Brazil, 1951.

BRANAGH, KENNETH: Belfast, No. Ire., Dec. 10, 1960.

BRANDAUER, KLAUS MARIA: Altaussee, Austria, June 22, 1944.

BRANDO, JOCELYN: San Francisco, Nov. 18, 1919. Lake Forest College, AADA.

BRANDO, MARLON: Omaha, NB, Apr. 3, 1924. New School.

BRANDON, CLARK: NYC, 1959.

BRANDON, MICHAEL (Feldman): Brooklyn.

BRANTLEY, BETSY: Rutherfordton, NC, 1955. London Central Sch. of Drama.

BRAZZI, ROSSANO: Bologna, Italy, Sept. 18, 1916. U. Florence.

BRENNAN, EILEEN: Los Angeles, CA, Sept. 3, 1935. AADA.

BRIALY, JEAN-CLAUDE: Aumale, Algeria, 1933. Strasbourg Cons.

BRIAN, DAVID: NYC, Aug. 5, 1914. CCNY.

BRIDGES, BEAU: Los Angeles, Dec. 9, 1941. UCLA.

BRIDGES, JEFF: Los Angeles, Dec. 4, 1949.

BRIDGES, LLOYD: San Leandro, CA, Jan. 15, 1913.

BRIMLEY, WILFORD: Salt Lake City, UT, Sept. 27, 1934.

BRINKLEY, CHRISTIE: Malibu, CA, Feb. 2, 1954.

BRISEBOIS, DANIELLE: Brooklyn, June 28, 1969.

BRITT, MAY (Maybritt Wilkins): Sweden, Mar. 22, 1936.

BRITTANY, MORGAN (Suzanne Caputo): Los Angeles, Dec. 5, 1950.

BRITTON, TONY: Birmingham, Eng., June 9, 1924.

BRODERICK, MATTHEW: NYC, Mar. 21, 1962.

BROLIN, JAMES: Los Angeles, July 18, 1940. UCLA.

BROMFIELD, JOHN (Farron Bromfield): South Bend, IN, June 11, 1922. St. Mary's College.

BRONSON, CHARLES (Buchinsky): Ehrenfield, PA, Nov. 3, 1920.

BROOKES, JACQUELINE: Montelair, NJ, July 24, 1930. RADA.

BROOKS, ALBERT (Einstein): Los Angeles, July 22, 1947.

BROOKS, MEL (Melvyn Kaminski): Brooklyn, June 28, 1926.

BROSNAN, PIERCE: County Meath, Ireland. May 16, 1952.

BROWN, BLAIR: Washington, DC, 1948. Pine Manor.

BROWN, BRYAN: Panania, Australia, June 23, 1947.

BROWN, GARY (Christian Brando): Hollywood, CA, 1958.

BROWN, GEORG STANFORD: Havana, Cuba, June 24, 1943. AMDA.

BROWN, JAMES: Desdemona, TX, Mar. 22, 1920. Baylor U.

BROWN, JIM: St. Simons Island, NY, Feb. 17, 1935. Syracuse U.

BROWNE, LESLIE: NYC, 1958.

BROWNE, ROSCOE LEE: Woodbury, NJ, May 2, 1925.

BUCHHOLZ, HORST: Berlin, Ger., Dec. 4, 1933. Ludwig Dramatic School.

BUCKLEY, BETTY: Big Spring, TX, July 3, 1947. TxCU.

BUJOLD, GENEVIEVE: Montreal, Can., July 1, 1942.

BURGHOFF, GARY: Bristol, Ct, May 24, 1943.

BURGI, RICHARD: Montclair, NJ, July 30, 1958.

BURKE, DELTA: Orlando, FL, July 30, 1956. LAMDA.

BURKE, PAUL: New Orleans, July 21, 1926. Pasadena Playhouse.

BURNETT, CAROL: San Antonio, TX, Apr. 26, 1933. UCLA.

BURNS, CATHERINE: NYC, Sept. 25, 1945. AADA.

BURNS, GEORGE (Nathan Birnbaum): NYC, Jan. 20, 1896.

BURR, RAYMOND: New Westminster, B.C., Can., May 21, 1917. Stanford, U. CAL., Columbia.

BURSTYN, ELLEN (Edna Rae Gillhooly): Detroit, MI, Dec. 7, 1932.

BURTON, LeVAR: Los Angeles, CA, Feb. 16, 1958. UCLA.

BUSEY, GARY: Goose Creek, TX, June 29, 1944.

BUSFIELD, TIMOTHY: Lansing, MI, June 12, 1957. E. Tenn. St. U.

BUSKER, RICKY: Rockford, IL, 1974

BUTTONS, RED (Aaron Chwatt): NYC, Feb. 5, 1919.

BUZZI, RUTH: Wequetequock, RI, July 24, 1936. Pasadena Playhouse.

BYGRAVES, MAX: London, Oct. 16, 1922. St. Joseph's School.

BYRNE, GABRIEL: Dublin, Ireland, 1950.

BYRNES, EDD: NYC, July 30, 1933. Haaren High.

CAAN, JAMES: Bronx, NY, Mar. 26,1939.

CAESAR, SID: Yonkers, NY, Sept. 8, 1922.

CAGE, NICOLAS: Long Beach, CA, Jan.7, 1964.

CAINE, MICHAEL (Maurice Micklewhite): London, Mar. 14, 1933.

CAINE, SHAKIRA (Baksh): Guyana, Feb. 23, 1947. Indian Trust Col.

CALHOUN, RORY (Francis Timothy Durgin): Los Angeles, Aug. 8, 1922.

CALLAN, MICHAEL (Martin Calinieff): Philadelphia, Nov. 22, 1935.

CALLOW, SIMON: London, June 15, 1949. Queens U.

CALVERT, PHYLLIS: London, Feb. 18, 1917. Margaret Morris School.

CALVET, CORRINE (Corinne Dibos): Paris, Apr. 30, 1925. U. Paris.

CAMERON, KIRK: Panorama City, CA, Oct. 12, 1970.

CAMP, COLLEEN: San Francisco, 1953.

CAMPBELL, BILL: Chicago, 1960.

CAMPBELL, GLEN: Delight, AR, Apr. 22, 1935.

CAMPBELL, TISHA: Newark, NJ, 1969.

CANALE, GIANNA MARIA: Reggio Calabria, Italy, Sept. 12.

CANDY, JOHN: Toronto, Can., Oct. 31, 1950.

CANNON, DYAN (Samille Diane Friesen): Tacoma, WA, Jan. 4, 1937.

CANTU, DOLORES: San Antonio, TX, 1957.

CAPERS, VIRGINIA: Sumter, SC, 1925. Juilliard.

CAPSHAW, KATE: Ft. Worth, TX, 1953. UMo.

CARA, IRENE: NYC, Mar. 18, 1958.

CARDINALE, CLAUDIA: Tunis, N. Africa. Apr. 15, 1939. College Paul Cambon.

CAREY, HARRY, JR.: Saugus, CA, May 16, 1921. Black Fox Military Academy.

CAREY, MACDONALD: Sioux City, IA, Mar. 15, 1913. U. of Wisc., U. Iowa.

CAREY, PHILIP: Hackensack, NJ, July 15, 1925. U. Miami.

CARIOU, LEN: Winnipeg, Can., Sept. 30, 1939.

CARLIN, GEORGE: NYC, May 12, 1938.

CARMEN, JULIE: Mt. Vernon, NY, Apr. 4, 1954.

CARMICHAEL, IAN: Hull, Eng., June 18, 1920. Scarborough Col.

CARNE, JUDY (Joyce Botterill): Northampton, Eng., 1939. Bush-Davis Theatre School.

CARNEY, ART: Mt. Vernon, NY, Nov. 4, 1918.

CARON, LESLIE: Paris, July 1, 1931. Nat'l Conservatory, Paris.

CARPENTER, CARLETON: Bennington, VT, July 10, 1926. Northwestern.

CARRADINE, DAVID: Hollywood, Dec. 8, 1936. San Francisco State.

CARRADINE, KEITH: San Mateo, CA, Aug. 8, 1950. Colo. State U.

CARRADINE, ROBERT: San Mateo, CA, Mar. 24, 1954.

CARREL, DANY: Tourane, Indochina, Sept. 20, 1936. Marseilles Cons.

CARRERA, BARBARA: Managua, Nicaragua, Dec. 31, 1945.

CARREY, JIM: Jacksons Point, Ontario, Can., Jan. 17, 1962.

CARRIERE, MATHIEU: West Germany, 1950.

CARROLL, DIAHANN (Johnson): NYC, July 17, 1935. NYU.

CARROLL, PAT: Shreveport, LA, May 5, 1927. Catholic U.

CARSON, JOHN DAVID: Calif.,1951. Valley Col.

CARSON, JOHNNY: Corning, IA, Oct. 23, 1925. U. of Neb.

CARSTEN, PETER (Ransenthaler): Weissenberg, Bavaria, Apr. 30, 1929. Munich Akademie.

CARTER, NELL: Birmingham, AL, Sept. 13, 1948.

CARTWRIGHT, VERONICA: Bristol, Eng., 1949.

CARVEY, DANA: Missoula, MT, Apr. 2, 1955. SFST.CoI.

CASEY, BERNIE: Wyco, WV, June 8, 1939.

CASH, ROSALIND: Atlantic City, NJ, Dec. 31, 1938. CCNY.

CASS, PEGGY (Mary Margaret): Boston, May 21, 1925.

CASSAVETES, NICK: NYC, 1959, Syracuse U, AADA.

CASSEL, JEAN-PIERRE: Paris, Oct. 27, 1932.

CASSIDY, DAVID: NYC, Apr. 12, 1950.

CASSIDY, JOANNA: Camden, NJ, Aug. 2, 1944. Syracuse U.

CASSIDY, PATRICK: Los Angeles, CA, Jan. 4, 1961.

CATES, PHOEBE: NYC, July 16, 1963.

CATTRALL, KIM: Liverpool, Eng., Aug. 21, 1956. AADA.

CAULFIELD, MAXWELL: Glasgow, Scot., Nov. 23, 1959.

CAVANI, LILIANA: Bologna, Italy, Jan. 12, 1937. U. Bologna.

CAVETT, DICK: Gibbon, NE, Nov. 19, 1936.

CHAKIRIS, GEORGE: Norwood, OH, Sept. 16, 1933.

CHAMBERLAIN, RICHARD: Beverly Hills, CA, March 31, 1935. Pomona.

CHAMPION, MARGE: Los Angeles, Sept. 2, 1923.

CHANNING, CAROL: Seattle, WA, Jan. 31, 1921. Bennington.

CHANNING, STOCKARD (Susan Stockard): NYC, Feb. 13, 1944. Radcliffe.

CHAPIN, MILES: NYC, Dec. 6, 1954. HB Studio.

CHAPLIN, GERALDINE: Santa Monica, CA, July 31, 1944. Royal Ballet.

CHAPLIN, SYDNEY: Los Angeles, Mar. 31, 1926. Lawrenceville.

CHARISSE, CYD (Tula Ellice Finklea): Amarillo, TX, Mar. 3, 1922. Hollywood Professional School.

CHARLES, WALTER: East Strousburg, PA, Apr. 4, 1945. Boston U.

CHASE, CHEVY (Cornelius Crane Chase): NYC, Oct. 8, 1943.

CHAVES, RICHARD: Jacksonville, FL, Oct. 9, 1951. Occidental Col.

CHEN, JOAN: Shanghai, 1961. CalState.

CHER (Cherilyn Sarkisian) El Centro, CA, May 20, 1946.

CHIARI, WALTER: Verona, Italy. 1930.

CHILES, LOIS: Alice, TX, 1950.

CHONG, RAE DAWN: Vancouver, Can., 1961.

CHONG, THOMAS: Edmonton, Alberta, Can., Ma.y 24, 1938.

CHRISTIAN, LINDA (Blanca Rosa Welter): Tampico, Mex., Nov. 13, 1923.

CHRISTIE, JULIE: Chukua, Assam, India, Apr. 14, 1941.

CHRISTOPHER, DENNIS (Carrelli): Philadelphia, PA, Dec. 2, 1955. Temple U.

CHRISTOPHER, JORDAN: Youngs-town, OH, Oct. 23, 1940. Kent Slate.

CILENTO, DIANE: Queensland, Australia, Oct. 5, 1933. AADA.

CLAPTON, ERIC: London. Mar. 30, 1945.

CLARK, CANDY: Norman, OK, June 20, 1947.

CLARK, DANE: NYC, Feb. 18, 1915. Cornell, Johns Hopkins U.

CLARK, DICK: Mt. Vernon, NY, Nov. 30, 1929. Syracuse U.

CLARK, MAE: Philadelphia, Aug. 16, 1910.

CLARK, MATT: Washington, DC, Nov. 25, 1936.

CLARK, PETULA: Epsom, England, Nov. 15, 1932.

CLARK, SUSAN: Sarnid, Ont., Can., Mar. 8, 1940. RADA.

CLAY, ANDREW DICE: Brooklyn, 1958, Kingsborough Col.

CLAYBURGH, JILL: NYC, Apr. 30, 1944. Sarah Lawrence.

CLEESE, JOHN: Weston-Super-Mare, Eng., Oct. 27, 1939, Cambridge.

CLERY, CORRINNE: Italy, 1950.

CLOONEY, ROSEMARY: Maysville, KY, May 23, 1928.

CLOSE, GLENN: Greenwich, CT, Mar. 19, 1947. William & Mary Col.

COBURN, JAMES: Laurel, NB, Aug. 31, 1928. LACC.

COCA, IMOGENE: Philadelphia, Nov. 18, 1908.

CODY, KATHLEEN: Bronx, NY, Oct. 30, 1953.

COFFEY, SCOTT: HI, 1967.

COLBERT, CLAUDETTE (Lily Chauchoin): Paris, Sept. 15, 1903. Art Students League.

COLE, GEORGE: London, Apr. 22, 1925.

COLEMAN, GARY: Zion, IL, Feb. 8, 1968.

COLEMAN, DABNEY: Austin, TX, Jan. 3, 1932.

COLIN, MARGARET: NYC, 1957.

COLEMAN, JACK: Easton, PA, 1958. Duke U.

COLLET, CHRISTOPHER: NYC, Mar. 13, 1968. Strasberg Inst.

COLLINS, JOAN: London, May 21, 1933. Francis Holland School.

COLLINS, PAULINE: Devon, Eng., Sept. 3, 1940.

COLLINS, STEPHEN: Des Moines, IA, Oct. 1, 1947. Amherst.

COLON, MIRIAM: Ponce, PR., 1945. UPR.

COLTRANE, ROBBIE: Ruthergien, Scot., 1950.

COMER, ANJANETTE: Dawson, TX, Aug. 7, 1942. Baylor, Tex. U.

CONANT, OLIVER: NYC, Nov. 15, 1955. Dalton.

CONAWAY, JEFF: NYC, Oct. 5, 1950. NYC.

CONNERY, SEAN: Edinburgh, Scot., Aug. 25, 1930.

CONNERY, JASON: London, 1962.

CONNICK, HARRY, JR.: New Orleans, LA, Sept. 11, 1967.

CONNORS, MIKE (Krekor Ohanian): Fresno, CA, Aug. 15, 1925. UCLA.

CONRAD, WILLIAM: Louisville, KY, Sept. 27, 1920.

CONROY, KEVIN: Westport, CT, 1956. Juilliard.

CONSTANTINE, MICHAEL: Reading, PA, May 22, 1927.

CONTI, TOM: Paisley, Scotland, Nov. 22, 1941.

CONVERSE, FRANK: St. Louis, MO, May 22, 1938. Carnegie Tech.

CONWAY, GARY: Boston, Feb. 4, 1936.

CONWAY, KEVIN: NYC, May 29, 1942.

CONWAY, TIM (Thomas Daniel): Willoughby, OH, Dec. 15, 1933. Bowling Green State.

COOGAN, KEITH (Keith Mitchell Franklin): Palm Springs, CA, Jan. 13, 1970.

COOK, ELISHA, JR.: San Francisco, Dec. 26, 1907. St. Albans.

COOK, PETER: Torqua, Eng., Nov. 17, 1937.

COOPER, BEN: Hartford, CT, Sept. 30, 1932. Columbia U.

COOPER, CHRIS: Kansas City, MO, July 9, 1951. UMo.

COOPER, JACKIE: Los Angeles, Sept. 15, 1921.

COPELAND, JOAN: NYC, June 1, 1922. Brooklyn Col., RADA.

CORBETT, GRETCHEN: Portland, OR, Aug. 13, 1947. Carnegie Tech.

CORBY, ELLEN (Hansen): Racine, WI, June 13, 1913.

CORCORAN, DONNA: Quincy, MA, Sept. 29, 1942.

CORD, ALEX (Viespi): Floral Park, NY, Aug. 3, 1931. NYU, Actors Studio.

CORDAY, MARA (Marilyn Watts): Santa Monica, CA, Jan. 3, 1932.

COREY, JEFF: NYC, Aug. 10, 1914. Fagin School.

CORLAN, ANTHONY: Cork City, Ire., May 9, 1947. Birmingham School of Dramatic Arts.

CORLEY, AL: Missouri, 1956. Actors Studio.

CORNTHWAITE, ROBERT: St. Helens, OR, Apr. 28, 1917. USC.

CORRI, ADRIENNE: Glasgow, Scot., Nov. 13, 1933. RADA.

CORT, BUD (Walter Edward Cox): New Rochelle, NY, Mar. 29, 1950. NYU.

CORTESA, VALENTINA: Milan, Italy, Jan. 1, 1925.

COSBY, BILL: Philadelphia, July 12, 1937. Temple U.

COSTER, NICOLAS: London, Dec. 3, 1934. Neighborhood Playhouse.

COSTNER, KEVIN: Lynwood, CA, Jan. 18, 1955. CalStaU.

COTTEN, JOSEPH: Petersburg, VA, May 13, 1905.

COURTENAY, TOM: Hull, Eng., Feb. 25, 1937. RADA.

COURTLAND, JEROME: Knoxville, TN, Dec. 27, 1926.

COYOTE, PETER (Cohon): NYC, 1942.

COX, COURTNEY: Birmingham, AL, June 15, 1964.

COX, RONNY: Cloudcroft, NM, Aug. 23, 1938.

CRAIG, MICHAEL: India, Jan. 27, 1929.

CRAIN, JEANNE: Barstow, CA, May 25, 1925.

CRAWFORD, MICHAEL (Dumbel-Smith): Salisbury, Eng., Jan. 19, 1942.

CREMER, BRUNO: Paris, 1929.

CRENNA, RICHARD: Los Angeles, Nov. 30, 1926. USC.

CRISTAL, LINDA (Victoria Moya): Buenos Aires, Feb. 25, 1934.

CRONYN, HUME (Blake): Ontario, Can, July 18, 1911.

CROSBY, DENISE: Hollywood, CA, 1958.

CROSBY, HARRY: Los Angeles, CA, Aug. 8, 1958.

CROSBY, MARY FRANCES: CA, Sept. 14, 1959.

CROSS, BEN: London, Dec. 16, 1948. RADA.

CROSS, MURPHY (Mary Jane): Laurelton, MD, June 22, 1950.

CROUSE, LINDSAY: NYC, May 12, 1948. Radcliffe.

CROWLEY, PAT: Olyphant, PA, Sept. 17, 1932.

CRUISE, TOM (T. C. Mapother IV): July 3, 1962, Syracuse, NY.

CRYER, JON: NYC, Apr. 16, 1965, RADA.

CRYSTAL, BILLY: Long Beach, NY, Mar. 14, 1947. Marshall U.

CULKIN, MACAULAY: NYC, Aug. 26, 1980.

CULLUM, JOHN: Knoxville, TN, Mar. 2, 1930. U. Tenn.

CULLUM, JOHN DAVID: NYC, Mar. 1, 1966.

CULP, ROBERT: Oakland, CA, Aug. 16, 1930. U. Wash.

CUMMINGS, CONSTANCE: Seattle, WA, May 15, 1910.

CUMMINGS, QUINN: Hollywood, Aug. 13, 1967.

CUMMINS, PEGGY: Prestatyn, N. Wales, Dec. 18, 1926. Alexandra School.

CURRY, TIM: Cheshire, Eng., Apr. 19, 1946.

CURTIN, JANE: Cambridge, MA, Sept. 6, 1947.

CURTIS, JAMIE LEE: Los Angeles, CA, Nov. 22, 1958.

CURTIS, KEENE: Salt Lake City, UT, Feb. 15, 1925. U. Utah.

CURTIS, TONY (Bernard Schwartz): NYC, June 3, 1924.

CUSACK, CYRIL: Durban, S. Africa, Nov. 26, 1910. Univ. Col.

CUSACK, JOAN: Evanston, IL, Oct. 11, 1962.

CUSACK, JOHN: Chicago, IL, June 28, 1966.

CUSHING, PETER: Kenley, Surrey, Eng., May 26, 1913.

DAFOE, WILLEM: Appleton, WI, July 22, 1955.

DAHL, ARLENE: Minneapolis, Aug. 11, 1928. U. Minn.

DALE, JIM: Rothwell, Eng., Aug. 15, 1935.

DALLESANDRO, JOE: Pensacola, FL, Dec. 31, 1948.

DALTON, TIMOTHY: Colwyn Bay, Wales, Mar. 21, 1946. RADA.

DALTREY, ROGER: London, Mar. 1, 1945.

DALY, TIMOTHY: NYC, Mar. 1, 1956. Bennington Col.

DALY, TYNE: Madison, WI, Feb. 21, 1947. AMDA.

DAMONE, VIC (Vito Farinola): Brooklyn, June 12, 1928.

DANCE, CHARLES: Plymouth, Eng., Oct. 10, 1946.

D'ANGELO, BEVERLY: Columbus, OH, Nov. 15, 1953.

DANGERFIELD, RODNEY (Jacob Cohen): Babylon, NY, Nov. 22, 1921.

DANIELS, JEFF: Georgia, Feb. 19, 1955. EastMichState.

DANIELS, WILLIAM: Brooklyn, Mar. 31, 1927. Northwestern.

DANNER, BLYTHE: Philadelphia, PA, Feb. 3, 1944. Bard Col.

DANO, ROYAL: NYC, Nov. 16, 1922. NYU.

DANSON, TED: San Diego, CA, Dec. 29, 1947. Stanford, Carnegie Tech.

DANTE, MICHAEL (Ralph Vitti): Stamford, CT, 1935. U. Miami.

DANZA, TONY: Brooklyn, Apr. 21, 1951. UDubuque.

DARBY, KIM: (Deborah Zerby): North Hollywood, CA, July 8, 1948.

DARCEL, DENISE (Denise Billecard): Paris, Sept. 8, 1925. U. Dijon.

DARREN, JAMES: Philadelphia, June 8, 1936. Stella Adler School.

DARRIEUX, DANIELLE: Bordeaux, France, May 1, 1917. Lycee LaTour.

DAVID, KEITH: NYC, May 8, 1954. Juilliard.

DAVIDSON, JOHN: Pittsburgh, Dec. 13, 1941. Denison U.

DAVIES, JOHN RHYS: Salisbury, Eng.,.May 5, 1944.

DAVIS, CLIFFON: Chicago, Oct. 4, 1945. Oakwood Col.

DAVIS, GEENA: Wareham, MA, Jan. 21, 1957.

DAVIS, JUDY: Perth, Australia, 1956.

DAVIS, MAC: Lubbock, TX, Jan. 21,1942.

DAVIS, NANCY (Anne Frances Robbins): NYC, July 6, 1921. Smith Col.

DAVIS, OSSIE: Cogdell, GA, Dec. 18, 1917. Howard U.

DAVIS, SKEETER (Mary Frances Penick): Dry Ridge, KY, Dec. 30, 1931.

DAVIS-VOSS, SAMMI: Kidderminster, Worcestershire, Eng., June 21, 1964.

DAVISON, BRUCE: Philadelphia, PA, June 28, 1946.

DAY, DORIS (Doris Kappelhoff): Cincinnati, Apr. 3, 1924.

DAY, LARAINE (Johnson): Roosevelt, UT, Oct. 13, 1917.

DAY LEWIS, DANIEL: London, Apr. 29, 1957. Bristol Old Vic.

DAYAN, ASSEF: Israel, 1945. U. Jerusalem.

DEAKINS, LUCY: NYC, 1971.

DEAN, JIMMY: Plainview, TX, Aug. 10, 1928.

DEAN, LOREN: Las Vegas, NV, July 31, 1969.

DECAMP, ROSEMARY: Prescott, AZ, Nov. 14, 1913.

DeCARLO, YVONNE (Peggy Yvonne Middleton): Vancouver, B.C., Can., Sept. 1, 1922. Vancouver School of Drama.

DEE, FRANCES: Los Angeles, Nov. 26, 1907. Chicago U.

DEE, JOEY (Joseph Di Nicola): Passaic, NJ, June 11, 1940. Patterson State College.

DEE, RUBY: Cleveland, OH, Oct. 27, 1924. Hunter Col.

DEE, SANDRA (Alexandra Zuck): Bayonne, NJ, Apr. 23, 1942.

DeFORE, DON: Cedar Rapids, IA, Aug. 25, 1917. U. Iowa.

DeHAVEN, GLORIA: Los Angeles, July 23, 1923.

DeHAVILLAND, OLIVIA: Tokyo, Japan, July 1, 1916. Notre Dame Convent School.

DELAIR, SUZY: Paris, Dec. 31, 1916.

DELANY, DANA: NYC, March 13, 1957. Wesleyan U.

DELPY, JULIE: Paris. 1970.

DELON, ALAIN: Sceaux, Fr., Nov. 8, 1935.

DELORME, DANIELE: Paris, Oct. 9, 1927. Sorbonne.

DeLUISE, DOM: Brooklyn, Aug. 1, 1933. Tufts Col.

DeLUISE, PETER: Hollywood, Ca., 1967.

DEMONGEOT, MYLENE: Nice, France, Sept. 29, 1938.

DeMORNAY, REBECCA: Los Angeles, Aug. 29, 1962. Strasberg Inst.

DEMPSEY, PATRICK: Turner, ME, Jan. 13, 1966.

DeMUNN, JEFFREY: Buffalo, NY, Apr. 25, 1947. Union Col.

DENEUVE, CATHERINE: Paris, Oct. 22, 1943.

DeNIRO, ROBERT: NYC, Aug. 17, 1943. Stella Adler.

DENISON, MICHAEL: Doncaster, York, Eng., Nov. 1, 1915. Oxford.

DENNEHY, BRIAN: Bridgeport, CT, Jul. 9, 1938. Columbia.

DENNER, CHARLES: Tarnow, Poland, May 29, 1926.

DENVER, BOB: New Rochelle, NY, Jan. 9, 1935.

DEPARDIEU, GERARD: Chateauroux, France, Dec. 27, 1948.

DEPP, JOHNNY: Owensboro, KY, June 9, 1963.

DEREK, BO (Mary Cathleen Collins): Long Beach, CA, Nov. 20, 1956.

DEREK, JOHN: Hollywood, Aug. 12, 1926.

DERN, BRUCE: Chicago, June 4, 1936. UPA.

DERN, LAURA: Los Angeles, Feb. 10, 1967.

DeSALVO, ANNE: Philadelphia, Apr. 3.

DEVANE, WILLIAM: Albany, NY, Sept. 5, 1939.

DEVINE, COLLEEN: San Gabriel, CA, June 22, 1960.

DeVITO, DANNY: Asbury Park, NJ, Nov. 17, 1944.

DEXTER, ANTHONY (Walter Reinhold Alfred Fleischmann): Talmadge, NB, Jan. 19, 1919. U. Iowa.

DEY, SUSAN: Pekin, IL, Dec. 10, 1953.

DeYOUNG, CLIFF: Los Angeles, CA, Feb. 12, 1945. Cal State.

DIAMOND, NEIL: NYC, Jan. 24, 1941. NYU.

DICKINSON, ANGIE: Kulm, ND, Sept. 30, 1932. Glendale College.

DIETRICH, MARLENE (Maria Magdalene von Losch): Berlin, Ger., Dec. 27, 1901. Berlin Music Academy.

DILLER, PHYLLIS (Driver): Lima, OH, July 17, 1917. Bluffton College.

DILLMAN, BRADFORD: San Francisco, Apr. 14, 1930. Yale.

DILLON, KEVIN: Mamaroneck, NY, Aug. 19, 1965.

| Rodney Dangerfield | Teri Garr | Stephen Geoffreys | Lillian Gish | David Marshall Grant | Veronica Hamel |

DILLON, MATT: Larchmont, NY, Feb. 18, 1964. AADA.

DILLON, MELINDA: Hope, AR, Oct. 13, 1939. Goodman Theatre School.

DIXON, DONNA: Alexandria, VA, July 20, 1957.

DOBSON, KEVIN: NYC, Mar. 18, 1944.

DOBSON, TAMARA: Baltimore, MD, 1947. MD Inst. of Art.

DOLAN, MICHAEL: Oklahoma City, OK, June 21, 1965.

DOMERGUE, FAITH: New Orleans, June 16, 1925.

DONAHUE, TROY (Merle Johnson): NYC, Jan. 27, 1937. Columbia U.

DONAT, PETER: Nova Scotia, Jan. 20, 1928. Yale.

DONNELLY, DONAL: Bradford, Eng., July 6, 1931.

D'ONOFRIO, VINCENT: Brooklyn, 1960.

DOOHAN, JAMES: Vancouver, BC, Mar. 3, 1920. Neighborhood Playhouse.

DOOLEY, PAUL: Parkersburg WV, Feb. 22, 1928. U. WV.

DOUGLAS, DONNA (Dorothy Bourgeois): Baywood, LA, Sept. 26, 1935.

DOUGLAS, KIRK (Issur Danielovitch): Amsterdam, NY, Dec. 9, 1916. St. Lawrence U.

DOUGLAS, MICHAEL: New Brunswick, NJ, Sept. 25, 1944. U. Cal.

DOUGLASS, ROBYN: Sendai, Japan, June 21, 1953. UCDavis.

DOURIF, BRAD: Huntington, WV, Mar. 18, 1950. Marshall U.

DOVE, BILLIE: NYC, May 14, 1904.

DOWN, LESLEY-ANN: London, Mar. 17, 1954.

DOWNEY, ROBERT, JR.: NYC, Apr. 4, 1965.

DRAKE, BETSY: Paris, Sept. 11, 1923.

DRAKE, CHARLES(Charles Rupert): NYC, Oct. 2, 1914. Nichols College.

DREW, ELLEN (formerly Terry Ray): Kansas City, MO, Nov. 23, 1915.

DREYFUSS, RICHARD: Brooklyn, Oct. 19, 1947.

DRILLINGER, BRIAN: Brooklyn, June 27, 1960. SUNY/Purchase.

DRU, JOANNE (Joanne LaCock): Logan, WV, Jan. 31, 1923. John Robert Powers School.

DRYER, JOHN: Hawthorne, CA, July 6, 1946.

DUDIKOFF, MICHAEL: Redondo Beach, CA, Oct. 8.

DUFFY, PATRICK: Townsend, MT, Mar. 17, 1949. U. Wash.

DUGAN, DENNIS: Wheaton, IL, Sept. 5, 1946.

DUKAKIS, OLYMPIA: Lowell, MA, June 20, 1931.

DUKE, PATTY (Anna Marie): NYC, Dec. 14, 1946.

DUKES, DAVID: San Francisco, June 6, 1945.

DULLEA, KEIR: Cleveland, NJ, May 30, 1936. SF State Col.

DUNAWAY, FAYE: Bascom, FL, Jan. 14, 1941, Fla. U.

DUNCAN, SANDY: Henderson, TX, Feb. 20, 1946. Len Morris Col.

DUNNE, GRIFFIN: NYC, June 8, 1955. Neighborhood Playhouse.

DUPEREY, ANNY: Paris, 1947.

DURBIN, DEANNA (Edna): Winnipeg, Can., Dec. 4, 1921.

DURNING, CHARLES: Highland Falls, NY, Feb. 28, 1933. NYU.

DUSSOLLIER, ANDRE: Annecy, France, Feb. 17, 1946.

DUTTON, CHARLES: Baltimore, MD, Jan. 30, 1951. Yale.

DUVALL, ROBERT: San Diego, CA, Jan. 5, 1931. Principia Col.

DUVALL, SHELLEY: Houston, TX, July 7, 1949.

DYSART, RICHARD: Brighton, ME, Mar. 30, 1929.

EASTON, ROBERT: Milwaukee, WI, Nov. 23, 1930. U. Texas.

EASTWOOD, CLINT: San Francisco, May 31, 1931. LACC.

EATON, SHIRLEY: London, 1937. Aida Foster School.

EBSEN, BUDDY (Christian, Jr.): Belleville, IL, Apr. 2, 1910. U. Fla.

ECKEMYR, AGNETA: Karlsborg, Swed., July 2. Actors Studio.

EDELMAN, GREGG: Chicago, IL, Sept. 12, 1958. Northwestern U.

EDEN, BARBARA (Moorhead): Tucson, AZ, Aug. 23, 1934.

EDWARDS, ANTHONY: Santa Barbara, CA, July 19, 1962. RADA.

EDWARDS, VINCE: NYC, July 9, 1928. AADA.

EGGAR, SAMANTHA: London, Mar. 5, 1939.

EICHHORN, LISA: Reading, PA, Feb. 4, 1952. Queens Ont. U. RADA.

EIKENBERRY, JILL: New Haven, CT, Jan. 21, 1947.

EILBER, JANET: Detroit, MI, July 27, 1951. Juilliard.

EKBERG, ANITA: Malmo, Sweden, Sept. 29, 1931.

EKLAND, BRITT: Stockholm, Swed., Oct. 6, 1942.

ELDARD, RON: NYC, 1964.

ELIZONDO, HECTOR: NYC, Dec. 22, 1936.

ELLIOTT, CHRIS: NYC, 1960.

ELLIOTT, PATRICIA: Gunnison, CO, July 21, 1942. UCol.

ELLIOTT, SAM: Sacramento, CA, Aug. 9, 1944. U. Ore.

ELWES, CARY: London, Oct. 26, 1962.

ELY, RON (Ronald Pierce): Hereford, TX, June 21, 1938.

ENGLISH, ALEX: USCar, 1954.

ENGLUND, ROBERT: Hollywood, CA, June 6, 1949.

ERDMAN, RICHARD: Enid, OK, June 1, 1925.

ERICSON, JOHN: Dusseldorf, Ger., Sept. 25, 1926. AADA.

ESMOND, CARL: Vienna, June 14, 1906. U. Vienna.

ESTEVEZ, EMILIO: NYC, May 12, 1962.

ESPOSITO, GIANCARLO: Copenhagen, Den., Apr. 26, 1958.

ESTRADA, ERIK: NYC, Mar. 16, 1949.

EVANS, DALE (Francis Smith): Uvalde, TX, Oct. 31, 1912.

EVANS, GENE: Holbrook, AZ, July 11, 1922.

EVANS, LINDA (Evanstad): Hartford, CT, Nov. 18, 1942.

EVERETT, CHAD (Ray Cramton): South Bend, IN, June 11, 1936.

EVERETT, RUPERT: Norfolk, Eng., 1959.

EVIGAN, GREG: South Amboy, NJ, 1954.

EWELL, TOM (Yewell Tompkins): Owensboro, KY, Apr. 29, 1909. U. Wisc.

FABARES, SHELLEY: Los Angeles, Jan. 19, 1944.

FABIAN (Fabian Forte): Philadelphia, Feb. 6, 1943.

FABRAY, NANETTE (Ruby Nanette Fabares): San Diego, Oct. 27, 1920.

FAIRBANKS, DOUGLAS, JR.: NYC, Dec. 9, 1907. Collegiate School.

FAIRCHILD, MORGAN (Patsy McClenny): Dallas, TX, Feb. 3, 1950. UCLA.

FALK, PETER: NYC, Sept. 16, 1927. New School.

FARENTINO, JAMES: Brooklyn, Feb. 24, 1938. AADA.

FARGAS, ANTONIO: Bronx, NY, Aug. 14, 1946.

FARINA, DENNIS: Chicago, IL, 1944.

FARINA, SANDY (Sandra Feldman): Newark, NJ, 1955.

FARR, FELICIA: Westchester, NY, Oct. 4, 1932. Penn State Col.

FARROW, MIA (Maria): Los Angeles, Feb. 9, 1945.

FAULKNER, GRAHAM: London, Sept. 26, 1947. Webber-Douglas.

FAWCETT, FARRAH: Corpus Christie, TX, Feb. 2, 1947. TexU.

FAYE, ALICE (Ann Leppert): NYC, May 5, 1912.

FEINSTEIN, ALAN: NYC, Sept. 8, 1941.

FELDMAN, COREY: Encino, CA, July 16, 1971.

FELDON, BARBARA (Hall): Pittsburgh, Mar. 12, 1941. Carnegie Tech.

FELDSHUH, TOVAH: NYC, Dec. 27, 1953, Sarah Lawrence Col.

FELLOWS, EDITH: Boston, May 20, 1923.

FERRELL, CONCHATA: Charleston, WV, Mar. 28, 1943. Marshall U.

FERRER, MEL: Elbeton, NJ, Aug. 25, 1912. Princeton U.

FERRER, MIGUEL: Santa Monica, CA, Feb. 7, 1954.

FERRIS, BARBARA: London, 1943.

FERZETTI, GABRIELE: Italy, 1927. Rome Acad. of Drama.

FIEDLER, JOHN: Plateville, WI, Feb. 3, 1925.

FIELD, SALLY: Pasadena, CA, Nov. 6, 1946.

FIERSTEIN, HARVEY: Brooklyn, June 6, 1954. Pratt Inst.

FIGUEROA, RUBEN: NYC, 1958.

FINNEY, ALBERT: Salford, Lancashire, Eng., May 9, 1936. RADA.

FIORENTINO, LINDA: Philadelphia, PA.

FIRESTONE, ROCHELLE: Kansas City, MO, June 14, 1949. NYU.

FIRTH, COLIN: Grayshott, Hampshire, Eng., Sept. 10, 1960.

FIRTH, PETER: Bradford, Eng., Oct. 27, 1953.

FISHBURNE, LARRY: Augusta, GA, July 30, 1961.

FISHER, CARRIE: Los Angeles, CA, Oct. 21, 1956. London Central School of Drama.

FISHER, EDDIE: Philadelphia, PA, Aug. 10, 1928.

FITZGERALD, BRIAN: Philadelphia, PA, 1960. West Chester U.

FITZGERALD, GERALDINE: Dublin, Ire., Nov. 24, 1914. Dublin Art School.

FLANNERY, SUSAN: Jersey City, NJ, July 31, 1943.

FLEMING, RHONDA (Marilyn Louis): Los Angeles, Aug. 10, 1922.

FLEMYNG, ROBERT: Liverpool, Eng., Jan. 3, 1912. Haileybury Col.

FLETCHER, LOUISE: Birmingham, AL, July 22 1934.

FOCH, NINA: Leyden, Holland, Apr. 20, 1924.

FOLDI, ERZSEBET: Queens, NY, 1967.

FOLLOWS, MEGAN: Toronto, Can., 1967.

FONDA, JANE: NYC, Dec. 21, 1937. Vassar.

FONDA, PETER: NYC, Feb. 23, 1939. U. Omaha.

FONTAINE, JOAN: Tokyo, Japan, Oct. 22, 1917.

FOOTE, HALLIE: NYC, 1953. UNH.

FORD, GLENN (Gwyllyn Samuel Newton Ford): Quebec, Can., May 1, 1916.

FORD, HARRISON: Chicago, IL, July 13, 1942. Ripon Col.

FOREST, MARK (Lou Degni): Brooklyn, Jan. 1933.

FORREST, FREDERIC: Waxahachie, TX, Dec. 23, 1936.

FORREST, STEVE: Huntsville, TX, Sept. 29, 1924. UCLA.

FORSLUND, CONNIE: San Diego, CA, June 19, 1950. NYU.

FORSTER, ROBERT (Foster, Jr.): Rochester, NY, July 13, 1941. Rochester U.

FORSYTHE, JOHN (Freund):Penn's Grove, NJ, Jan. 29, 1918.

FOSTER, JODIE (Ariane Munker): Bronx, NY, Nov. 19, 1962. Yale.

FOSTER, MEG: Reading, PA, May 14, 1948.

FOX, EDWARD: London, Apr. 13, 1937. RADA.

FOX, JAMES: London, May 19, 1939.

FOX, MICHAEL J.: Vancouver, BC, June 9, 1961.

FOXWORTH, ROBERT: Houston, TX, Nov. 1, 1941. Carnegie Tech.

FRAKES, JOHNATHAN: Bethlehem, PA, 1952. Harvard.

FRANCIOSA, ANTHONY (Papaleo): NYC, Oct. 25, 1928.

FRANCIS, ANNE: Ossining, NY, Sept. 16, 1932.

FRANCIS, ARLENE (Arlene Kazanjian): Boston, Oct. 20, 1908. Finch School.

FRANCIS, CONNIE (Constance Franconero): Newark, NJ, Dec. 12, 1938.

FRANCKS, DON: Vancouver, Can., Feb. 28, 1932.

FRANK, JEFFREY: Jackson Heights, NY, 1965.

FRANKLIN, PAMELA: Tokyo, Feb. 4, 1950.

FRANZ, ARTHUR: Perth Amboy, NJ, Feb. 29, 1920. Blue Ridge College.

FRANZ, DENNIS: Chicago, IL, Oct. 28, 1944.

FRAZIER, SHEILA: NYC, Nov. 13, 1948.

FRECHETTE, PETER: Warwick, RI, Oct. 1956. URI.

FREEMAN, AL, JR.: San Antonio, TX, Mar. 21, 1934. CCLA.

FREEMAN, MONA: Baltimore, MD, June 9, 1926.

FREEMAN, MORGAN: Memphis, TN, June 1, 1937. LACC.

FREWER, MATT: Washington, DC, Jan. 4, 1958, Old Vic.

FRICKER, BRENDA: Dublin, Ireland, Feb. 17, 1945.

FULLER, PENNY: Durham, NC, 1940. Northwestern U.

FURNEAUX, YVONNE: Lille, France, 1928. Oxford U.

FYODOROVA, VICTORIA: Russia, 1946.

GABLE, JOHN CLARK: Los Angeles, Mar. 20, 1961. Santa Monica Col.

GABOR, EVA: Budapest, Hungary, Feb. 11, 1920.

GABOR, ZSA ZSA (Sari Gabor): Budapest, Hungary, Feb. 6, 1918.

GAIL, MAX: Derfoil, MI, Apr. 5, 1943.

GAINES, BOYD: Atlanta, GA, May 11, 1953. Juilliard.

GALLAGHER, PETER: Armonk, NY, Aug. 19, 1955. Tufts U.

GALLIGAN, ZACH: NYC, Feb. 14, 1963. ColumbiaU.

GAM, RITA: Pittsburgh, PA, Apr. 2, 1928.

GAMBON, MICHAEL: Dublin, Ire., Oct. 19, 1940.

GARBER, VICTOR: Montreal, Can., Mar. 16, 1949.

GARCIA, ANDY: Havana, Cuba, Apr. 12, 1956. FlaInt 1U.

GARDENIA, VINCENT: Naples, Italy, Jan. 7, 1922.

GARFIELD, ALLEN (Allen Goorwitz): Newark, NJ, Nov. 22, 1939. Actors Studio.

GARFUNKEL, ART: NYC, Nov. 5, 1941.

GARLAND, BEVERLY: Santa Cruz, CA, Oct. 17, 1930. Glendale Col.

GARNER, JAMES (James Baumgarner): Norman, OK, Apr. 7, 1928. Okla. U.

GARR, TERI: Lakewood, OH, Dec. 11, 1949.

GARRETT, BETTY: St. Joseph, MO, May 23, 1919. Annie Wright Seminary.

GARRISON, SEAN: NYC, Oct. 19, 1937.

GARSON, GREER: Ireland, Sept. 29, 1908.

GARY, LORRAINE: NYC, Aug. 16, 1937.

GASSMAN, VITTORIO: Genoa, Italy, Sept. 1,1922. Rome Academy of Dramatic Art.

GAVIN, JOHN: Los Angeles, Apr. 8, 1935. Stanford U.

GAYLORD, MITCH: Van Nuys, CA, 1961. UCLA.

GAYNOR, MITZI (Francesca Marlene Von Gerber): Chicago, Sept. 4, 1930.

GAZZARA, BEN: NYC, Aug. 28, 1930. Actors Studio.

GEARY, ANTHONY: Coalsville, UT, May 29, 1947. UUt.

GEDRICK, JASON: Chicago, 1965. Drake U.

GEESON, JUDY: Arundel, Eng., Sept. 10, 1948. Corona.

GEOFFREYS, STEPHEN: Cincinnati, OH, Nov. 22, 1964. NYU.

GEORGE, SUSAN: West London, Eng., July 26, 1950.

GERARD, GIL: Little Rock, AR, Jan. 23, 1940.

GERE, RICHARD: Philadelphia, PA, Aug. 29, 1949. U. Mass.

GERROLL, DANIEL: London, Oct. 16, 1951. Central.

GERTZ, JAMI: Chicago, IL, Oct. 28, 1965.

GETTY, BALTHAZAR: Jan. 22, 1975.

GETTY, ESTELLE: NYC, July 25, 1923. New School.

GHOLSON, JULIE: Birmingham, AL, June 4, 1958.

GHOSTLEY, ALICE: Eve, MO, Aug. 14, 1926. Okla U.

GIAN, JOE: North Miami Beach, FL, 1962.

GIANNINI, CHERYL: Monessen, PA, June 15.

GIANNINI, GIANCARLO: Spezia, Italy, Aug. 1, 1942. Rome Acad. of Drama.

GIBB, CYNTHIA: Bennington, VT, Dec. 14, 1963.

GIBSON, HENRY: Germantown, PA, Sept. 21, 1935.

GIBSON, MEL: Peekskill, NY, Jan. 3, 1956. NIDA.

GIELGUD, JOHN: London, Apr. 14, 1904. RADA.

GILBERT-BRINKMAN, MELISSA: Los Angeles, CA, May 8, 1964.

GILES, NANCY: NYC, July 17, 1960, Oberlin Col.

GILLETTE, ANITA: Baltimore, MD, Aug. 16, 1938.

GILLIAM, TERRY: Minneapolis, MN, Nov. 22, 1940.

GILLIS, ANNE (Alma O'Connor): Little Rock, AR, Feb. 12, 1927.

GINTY, ROBERT: NYC, Nov. 14, 1948. Yale.

GIRARDOT, ANNIE: Paris, Oct. 25, 1931.

GIROLAMI, STEFANIA: Rome, 1963.

GISH, LILLIAN: Springfield, OH, Oct. 14, 1896.

GIVENS, ROBIN: NYC, Nov. 27, 1964.

GLASER, PAUL MICHAEL: Boston, MA, Mar. 25, 1943. Boston U.

GLASS, RON: Evansville, IN, July 10, 1945.

GLEASON, JOANNA: Winnipeg, Can., June 2, 1950. UCLA.

GLEASON, PAUL: Jersey City, NJ, May 4, 1944.

GLENN, SCOTT: Pittsburgh, PA, Jan. 26, 1942. William and Mary Col.

GLOVER, CRISPIN: NYC, 1964.

GLOVER, DANNY: San Francisco, CA, July 22, 1947. SFStateCol.

GLOVER, JOHN: Kingston, NY, Aug. 7, 1944.

GLYNN,CARLIN: Cleveland, Oh, Feb. 19, 1940. Actors Studio.

GODUNOV, ALEXANDER (Aleksandr): Sakhalin, USSR, Nov. 28, 1949.

GOLDBERG, WHOOPI (Caryn Johnson): NYC, Nov. 13, 1949.

GOLDBLUM, JEFF: Pittsburgh, PA, Oct. 22, 1952. Neighborhood Playhouse.

GOLDEN, ANNIE: Brooklyn, Oct. 19, 1951.

GOLDSTEIN, JENETTE: Beverly Hills, CA, 1960.

GOLDTHWAIT, BOB: Syracuse, NY, May 1962.

GOLDWYN, TONY: Los Angeles, May 20, 1960. LAMDA.

GONZALEZ, CORDELIA: Aug. 11, 1958, San Juan, PR. UPR.

GONZALES-GONZALEZ, PEDRO: Aguilares, TX, Dec. 21, 1926.

GOODMAN, DODY: Columbus, OH, Oct. 28, 1915.

GOODMAN, JOHN: St. Louis, MO, June 20, 1952.

GORDON, GALE (Aldrich): NYC, Feb. 2, 1906.

GORDON, KEITH: NYC, Feb. 3, 1961.

GORMAN, CLIFF: Jamaica, NY, Oct. 13, 1936. NYU.

GORSHIN, FRANK: Pittsburgh, PA, Apr. 5, 1933.

GORTNER, MARJOE: Long Beach, CA, Jan. 14, 1944.

GOSSETT, LOUIS, JR.: Brooklyn, May 27, 1936. NYU.

GOULD, ELLIOTT (Goldstein): Brooklyn, Aug. 29, 1938. Columbia U.

GOULD, HAROLD: Schenectady, NY, Dec. 10, 1923. Cornell.

GOULD, JASON: NYC, Dec. 29, 1966.

GOULET, ROBERT: Lawrence, MA, Nov. 26, 1933. Edmonton.

GRAF, DAVID: Lancaster, OH, Apr. 1950. OhStateU.

GRAFF, TODD: NYC, Oct. 22, 1959. SUNY/Purchase.

GRANGER, FARLEY: San Jose, CA, July 1, 1925.

GRANGER, STEWART (James Stewart): London, May 6, 1913. Webber-Douglas School of Acting.

GRANT, DAVID MARSHALL: Westport, CT, June 21, 1955. Yale.

GRANT, KATHRYN (Olive Grandstaff): Houston, TX, Nov. 25, 1933. UCLA.

GRANT, LEE: NYC, Oct. 31, 1930. Juilliard.

GRANT, RICHARD E: Mbabane, Swaziland, May 5, 1957. Cape Town U.

GRAVES, PETER (Aurness): Minneapolis, Mar. 18, 1926. U. Minn.

GRAVES, RUPERT: Weston-Super-Mare, Eng., June 30, 1963.

GRAY, CHARLES: Bournemouth, Eng., 1928.

GRAY, COLEEN (Doris Jensen): Staplehurst, NB, Oct. 23, 1922. Hamline.

GRAY, LINDA: Santa Monica, CA, Sept. 12, 1940.

GRAY, SPALDING: Barrington, RI, June 5, 1941.

GRAYSON, KATHRYN (Zelma Hedrick): Winston-Salem, NC, Feb. 9, 1922.

GREEN, KERRI: Fort Lee, NJ, 1967. Vassar.

GREENE, ELLEN: NYC, Feb. 22, 1950. Ryder Col.

GREER, JANE: Washington, DC, Sept. 9, 1924.

GREER, MICHAEL: Galesburg, IL, Apr. 20, 1943.

GREGORY, MARK: Rome, Italy, 1965.

GREIST, KIM: Stamford, CT, May 12, 1958.

GREY, JENNIFER: NYC, Mar. 26, 1960.

GREY, JOEL (Katz): Cleveland, OH, Apr. 11, 1932.

GREY, VIRGINIA: Los Angeles, Mar. 22, 1917.

GRIEM, HELMUT: Hamburg, Ger, 1940. U. Hamburg.

GRIFFITH, ANDY: Mt. Airy, NC, June 1, 1926. UNC.

GRIFFITH, MELANIE: NYC, Aug. 9, 1957. Pierce Col.

GRIMES, GARY: San Francisco, June 2, 1955.

GRIMES, SCOTT: Lowell, MA, July 9, 1971.

GRIMES, TAMMY: Lynn, MA, Jan. 30, 1934. Stephens Col.

GRIZZARD, GEORGE: Roanoke Rapids, NC, Apr. 1, 1928. UNC.

GRODIN, CHARLES: Pittsburgh, PA, Apr. 21, 1935.

GROH, DAVID: NYC, May 21, 1939. Brown U., LAMDA.

GROSS, MARY: Chicago, IL, Mar. 25, 1953.

GROSS, MICHAEL: Chicago, June 21, 1947.

GUARDINO, HARRY: Brooklyn, Dec. 23, 1925. Haaren High.

GUEST, CHRISTOPHER: NYC, Feb. 5, 1948.

GUEST, LANCE: Saratoga, CA, July 21, 1960. UCLA.

GUILLAUME, ROBERT (Williams): St. Louis, MO, Nov. 30, 1937.

GUINNESS, ALEC: London, Apr. 2, 1914. Pembroke Lodge School.

GUNN, MOSES: St. Louis, MO, Oct. 2, 1929. Tenn. State U.

GUTTENBERG, STEVE: Massapequa, NY, Aug. 24, 1958. UCLA.

GWILLIM, DAVID: Plymouth, Eng., Dec. 15, 1948. RADA.

GWYNNE, FRED: NYC, July 10, 1926.

HAAS, LUKAS: West Hollywood, CA, Apr. 16, 1976.

HACK, SHELLEY: Greenwich, CT, July 6, 1952.

HACKETT, BUDDY (Leonard Hacker): Brooklyn, Aug. 31, 1924.

HACKMAN, GENE: San Bernardino, CA, Jan. 30, 1931.

HADDON, DALE: Montreal, Can., May 26, 1949. Neighborhood Playhouse.

| Corey | Madeline | Page | Margot | Aron | Janet |
| Haim | Kahn | Johnson | Kidder | Kincaid | Leigh |

HAGERTY, JULIE: Cincinnati, OH, June 15, 1955. Juilliard.

HAGMAN, LARRY (Hageman): Weatherford, TX, Sept. 21, 1931. Bard.

HAIM, COREY: Toronto, Can., Dec. 23, 1972.

HALE, BARBARA: DeKalb, IL, Apr. 18, 1922. Chicago Academy of Fine Arts.

HALEY, JACKIE EARLE: Northridge, CA, July 14, 1961.

HALL, ALBERT: Boothton, AL, Nov. 10, 1937. Columbia.

HALL, ANTHONY MICHAEL: Boston, MA, Apr. 14, 1968.

HALL, ARSENIO: Cleveland, OH, Feb. 12, 1959.

HAMEL, VERONICA: Philadelphia, PA, Nov. 20, 1943.

HAMILL, MARK: Oakland, CA, Sept. 25, 1952. LACC.

HAMILTON, CARRIE: NYC, Dec. 5, 1963.

HAMILTON, GEORGE: Memphis, TN, Aug. 12, 1939. Hackley.

HAMILTON, LINDA: Salisbury, MD, Sept. 26, 1955.

HAMLIN, HARRY: Pasadena, CA, Oct. 30, 1951.

HAMPSHIRE, SUSAN: London, May 12, 1941.

HAN, MAGGIE: Providence, RI, 1959.

HANDLER, EVAN: NYC, Jan. 10, 1961. Juillard.

HANKS, TOM: Concord, CA, Jul. 9, 1956. CalStateU.

HANNAH, DARYL: Chicago, IL, 1960. UCLA.

HANNAH, PAGE: Chicago, IL, Apr. 13, 1964.

HARDIN, TY (Orison Whipple Hungerford II): NYC, June 1, 1930.

HAREWOOD, DORIAN: Dayton, OH, Aug. 6, 1950. U. Cinn.

HARMON, MARK: Los Angeles, CA, Sept. 2, 1951. UCLA.

HARPER, JESSICA: Chicago, IL, Oct. 10, 1949.

HARPER, TESS: Mammoth Spring, AK, 1952. SWMoState.

HARPER, VALERIE: Suffern, NY, Aug. 22, 1940.

HARRELSON, WOODY: Midland, TX, July 23, 1961. Hanover Col.

HARRINGTON, PAT: NYC, Aug. 13, 1929. Fordham U.

HARRIS, BARBARA (Sandra Markowitz): Evanston, IL, July 25, 1935.

HARRIS, ED: Tenafly, NJ, Nov. 28, 1950. Columbia.

HARRIS, JULIE: Grosse Point, MI, Dec. 2, 1925. Yale Drama School.

HARRIS, MEL (Mary Ellen): Bethlehem, PA, 1957. Columbia.

HARRIS, RICHARD: Limerick, Ire., Oct. 1, 1930. London Acad.

HARRIS, ROSEMARY: Ashby, Eng., Sept. 19, 1930. RADA.

HARRISON, GEORGE: Liverpool, Eng., Feb. 25, 1943.

HARRISON, GREGORY: Catalina Island,CA, May 31, 1950. Actors Studio.

HARRISON, NOEL: London, Jan. 29, 1936.

HARROLD, KATHRYN: Tazewell, VA, Aug. 2, 1950. Mills Col.

HARRY, DEBORAH: Miami, IL, July 1, 1945.

HART, ROXANNE: Trenton, NJ, 1952, Princeton.

HARTLEY, MARIETTE: NYC, June 21, 1941.

HARTMAN, DAVID: Pawtucket, RI, May 19, 1935. Duke U.

HASSETT, MARILYN: Los Angeles, CA, Dec. 17. 1947.

HAUER, RUTGER: Amsterdam, Hol., Jan. 23, 1944.

HAVER, JUNE: Rock Island, IL, June 10, 1926.

HAVOC, JUNE (Hovick): Seattle, WA, Nov. 8, 1916.

HAWKE, ETHAN: Austin, TX, Nov. 6, 1970.

HAWN, GOLDIE: Washington, DC, Nov. 21, 1945.

HAYES, HELEN (Helen Brown): Washington, DC, Oct. 10, 1900. Sacred Heart Convent.

HAYS, ROBERT: Bethesda, MD, July 24, 1947, SD State Col.

HEADLY, GLENNE: New London, CT, Mar. 13, 1955. AmCol.

HEALD, ANTHONY: New Rochelle, NY, Aug. 25, 1944. MIStateU.

HEARD, JOHN: Washington, DC, Mar. 7, 1946. Clark U.

HEATHERTON, JOEY: NYC, Sept. 14, 1944.

HECKART, EILEEN: Columbus, OH, Mar. 29, 1919. Ohio State U.

HEDISON, DAVID: Providence, RI, May 20, 1929. Brown U.

HEGYES, ROBERT: NJ, May 7, 1951.

HELMOND, KATHERINE: Galveston, TX, July 5, 1934.

HEMINGWAY, MARIEL: Ketchum, ID, Nov. 22, 1961.

HEMMINGS, DAVID: Guilford, Eng., Nov. 18, 1938.

HENDERSON, FLORENCE: Dale, IN, Feb. 14, 1934.

HENDERSON, MARCIA: Andover, MA, July 22, 1932. AADA.

HENDRY, GLORIA: Jacksonville, FL, 1949.

HENNER, MARILU: Chicago, IL, Apr. 6, 1952.

HENRY, BUCK (Henry Zuckerman): NYC, Dec. 9, 1930. Dartmouth.

HENRY, JUSTIN: Rye, NY, May 25, 1971.

HEPBURN, AUDREY: Brussels, Belgium, May 4, 1929.

HEPBURN, KATHARINE: Hartford, CT, May 12, 1907. Bryn Mawr.

HERMAN, PEE-WEE (Paul Reubenfeld): Peekskill, NY,Aug. 27, 1952.

HERRMANN, EDWARD: Washington, DC, July 21, 1943. Bucknell, LAMDA.

HERSHEY, BARBARA (Herzstein): Hollywood, CA, Feb. 5, 1948.

HESSEMAN. HOWARD: Lebanon, OR, Feb. 27, 1940.

HESTON, CHARLTON: Evanston, IL, Oct. 4, 1922. Northwestern U.

HEWITT, MARTIN: Claremont, CA, 1960. AADA.

HEYWOOD, ANNE (Violet Pretty): Birmingham, Eng., Dec. 11, 1932.

HICKEY, WILLLIAM: Brooklyn, 1928.

HICKMAN, DARRYL: Hollywood, CA, July 28, 1933. Loyola U.

HICKMAN, DWAYNE: Los Angeles, May 18, 1934. Loyola U.

HICKS, CATHERINE: NYC, Aug. 6, 1951. Notre Dame.

HIGGINS, MICHAEL: Brooklyn, Jan. 20, 1926. AmThWing.

HILL, ARTHUR: Saskatchewan, Can., Aug. 1, 1922. U. Brit. Col.

HILL, STEVEN: Seattle, WA, Feb. 24, 1922. U. Wash.

HILL, TERRENCE (Mario Girotti): Venice, Italy, Mar. 29, 1941. U. Rome.

HILLER, WENDY: Bramhall, Cheshire, Eng., Aug 15, 1912. Winceby House School.

HILLERMAN, JOHN: Denison, TX, Dec. 20, 1932.

HINGLE, PAT: Denver, CO, July 19, 1923. Tex. U.

HIRSCH, JUDD: NYC, Mar. 15, 1935. AADA.

HOBEL, MARA: NYC, June 18, 1971.

HODGE, PATRICIA: Lincolnshire, Eng., 1946. LAMDA.

HOFFMAN, DUSTIN: Los Angeles, Aug. 8, 1937. Pasadena Playhouse.

HOGAN, JONATHAN: Chicago, IL, June 13, 1951.

HOGAN, PAUL: Lightning Ridge, Australia, Oct. 8, 1939.

HOLBROOK, HAL (Harold): Cleveland, OH, Feb. 17, 1925. Denison.

HOLLIMAN, EARL: Tennesas Swamp, Delhi, LA, Sept. 11, 1928. UCLA.

HOLM, CELESTE: NYC, Apr. 29, 1919.

HOLM, IAN: Ilford, Essex, Eng., Sept. 12, 1931. RADA.

HOMEIER, SKIP (George Vincent Homeier): Chicago, Oct. 5, 1930. UCLA.

HOOKS, ROBERT: Washington, DC, Apr. 18, 1937. Temple.

HOPE, BOB (Leslie Townes Hope): London, May 26, 1903.

HOPKINS, ANTHONY: Port Talbot, So. Wales, Dec. 31, 1937. RADA.

HOPPER, DENNIS: Dodge City, KS, May 17, 1936.

HORNE, LENA: Brooklyn, June 30, 1917.

HORSLEY, LEE: Muleshoe, TX, May 15, 1955.

HORTON, ROBERT: Los Angeles, July 29, 1924. UCLA.

HOSKINS, BOB: Bury St. Edmunds, Eng., Oct. 26, 1942.

HOUGHTON, KATHARINE: Hartford, CT, Mar. 10, 1945. Sarah Lawrence.

HOUSER, JERRY: Los Angeles, July 14, 1952. Valley Jr. Col.

HOWARD, ARLISS: Independence, MO, 1955. Columbia Col.

HOWARD, KEN: El Centro, CA, Mar. 28, 1944. Yale.

HOWARD, RON: Duncan, OK, Mar. 1, 1954. USC.

HOWARD, RONALD: Norwood, Eng., Apr. 7, 1918. Jesus College.

HOWELL, C. THOMAS: Los Angeles, Dec. 7, 1966.

HOWELLS, URSULA: London, Sept. 17, 1922.

HOWES, SALLY ANN: London, July 20, 1930.

HOWLAND, BETH: Boston, MA, May 28, 1941.

HUBLEY, SEASON: NYC, May 14, 1951.

HUDDLESTON, DAVID: Vinton, VA, Sept. 17, 1930.

HUDDLESTON, MICHAEL: Roanoke, VA. AADA.

HUDSON, ERNIE: Benton Harbor, MI, Dec. 17, 1945.

HUGHES, BARNARD: Bedford Hills, NY, July 16, 1915. Manhattan Col.

HUGHES, KATHLEEN (Betty von Gerkan): Hollywood, CA, Nov. 14, 1928. UCLA.

HULCE, TOM: Plymouth, MI, Dec. 6, 1953. N.C. Sch. of Arts.

HUNNICUT, GAYLE: Ft. Worth, TX, Feb. 6, 1943. UCLA.

HUNT, HELEN: Los Angeles, June 15, 1963.

HUNT, LINDA: Morristown, NJ, Apr. 1945. Goodman Theatre.

HUNT, MARSHA: Chicago, Oct. 17, 1917.

HUNTER, HOLLY: Atlanta, GA, Mar. 20, 1958. Carnegie-Mellon.

HUNTER, KIM (Janet Cole): Detroit, Nov. 12, 1922.

HUNTER, TAB (Arthur Gelien): NYC, July 11, 1931.

HUPPERT, ISABELLE: Paris, Fr., Mar. 16, 1955.

HURT, JOHN: Lincolnshire, Eng., Jan. 22, 1940.

HURT, MARY BETH (Supinger): Marshalltown, IA, Sept. 26, 1948. NYU.

HURT, WILLIAM: Washington, DC, Mar. 20, 1950. Tufts, Juilliard.

HUSSEY, RUTH: Providence, RI, Oct. 30, 1917. U. Mich.

HUSTON, ANJELICA: Santa Monica, CA, July 9, 1951.

HUTTON, BETTY (Betty Thornberg): Battle Creek, MI, Feb. 26, 1921.

HUTTON, LAUREN (Mary): Charleston, SC, Nov. 17, 1943. Newcomb Col.

HUTTON, ROBERT (Winne): Kingston, NY, June 11, 1920. Blair Academy.

HUTTON, TIMOTHY: Malibu, CA, Aug. 16, 1960.

HYER, MARTHA: Fort Worth, TX, Aug. 10, 1924. Northwestern U.

IDLE, ERIC: South Shields, Durham, Eng,, Mar. 29, 1943. Cambridge.

INGELS, MARTY: Brooklyn, NY, Mar. 9, 1936.

IRONS, JEREMY: Cowes, Eng., Sept. 19, 1948. Old Vic.

IRVING, AMY: Palo Alto, CA, Sept. 10, 1953. LADA.

IRWIN, BILL: Santa Monica, CA, Apr. 11, 1950.

IVANEK, ZELJKO: Lujubljana, Yugo., Aug. 15, 1957. Yale, LAMDA.

IVES, BURL: Hunt Township, IL, June 14, 1909. Charleston IL Teachers College.

IVEY, JUDITH: El Paso, TX, Sept. 4, 1951.

JACKSON, ANNE: Alleghany, PA, Sept. 3, 1926. Neighborhood Playhouse.

JACKSON, GLENDA: Hoylake, Cheshire, Eng., May 9, 1936. RADA.

JACKSON, KATE: Birmingham, AL, Oct. 29, 1948. AADA.

JACKSON, MICHAEL: Gary, IN, Aug. 29, 1958.

JACKSON, VICTORIA: Miami, FL, Aug. 2, 1958.

JACOBI, DEREK: Leytonstone, London, Oct. 22, 1938. Cambridge.

JACOBI, LOU: Toronto, Can., Dec. 28, 1913.

JACOBS, LAWRENCE-HILTON: Virgin Islands, 1954.

JACOBY, SCOTT: Chicago, Nov. 19, 1956.

JAECKEL, RICHARD: Long Beach, NY, Oct. 10, 1926.

JAGGER, MICK: Dartford, Kent, Eng., July 26, 1943.

JAMES, CLIFTON: NYC, May 29, 1921. Ore. U.

JAMES, JOHN (Anderson): Apr. 18, 1956, New Canaan, CT. AADA.

JARMAN, CLAUDE, JR.: Nashville, TN, Sept. 27, 1934.

JASON, RICK: NYC, May 21, 1926. AADA.

JEAN, GLORIA (Gloria Jean Schoonover): Buffalo, NY, Apr. 14, 1927.

JEFFREYS, ANNE (Carmichael): Goldsboro, NC, Jan. 26, 1923. Anderson College.

JEFFRES, LIONEL: London, 1927. RADA.

JERGENS, ADELE: Brooklyn, Nov. 26, 1922.

JETER, MICHAEL: Lawrenceburg, TN, Aug. 26, 1952. Memphis St.U.

JETT, ROGER (Baker): Cumberland, MD, Oct. 2, 1946. AADA.

JILLIAN, ANN (Nauseda): Cambridge, MA, Jan. 29, 1951.

JOHANSEN, DAVID: Staten Island, NY, Jan. 9, 1950.

JOHN, ELTON (Reginald Dwight): Middlesex, Eng., Mar. 25, 1947. RAM.

JOHNS, GLYNIS: Durban, S. Africa, Oct. 5, 1923.

JOHNSON, BEN: Pawhuska, OK, June 13, 1918.

JOHNSON, DON: Galena, MO, Dec. 15, 1950. UKan.

JOHNSON, PAGE: Welch, WV, Aug. 25, 1930. Ithaca.

JOHNSON, RAFER: Hillsboro, TX, Aug. 18, 1935. UCLA.

JOHNSON, RICHARD: Essex, Eng., July 30, 1927. RADA.

JOHNSON, ROBIN: Brooklyn, May 29, 1964.

JOHNSON, VAN: Newport, RI, Aug. 28, 1916.

JONES, CHRISTOPHER: Jackson, TN, Aug. 18, 1941. Actors Studio.

JONES, DEAN: Decatur, AL, Jan. 25, 1931. Actors Studio.

JONES, GRACE: Spanishtown, Jamaica, May 19, 1952.

JONES, JACK: Bel-Air, CA, Jan. 14, 1938.

JONES, JAMES EARL: Arkabutla, MS, Jan. 17, 1931. U. Mich.

JONES, JEFFREY: Buffalo, NY, Sept. 28, 1947. LAMDA.

JONES, JENNIFER (Phyllis Isley): Tulsa, OK, Mar. 2, 1919. AADA.

JONES, SAM J.: Chicago, IL, Aug. 12, 1954.

JONES, SHIRLEY: Smithton, PA, March 31, 1934.

JONES, TERRY: Wales, Feb. 1, 1942.

JONES, TOMMY LEE: San Saba, TX, Sept. 15, 1946. Harvard.

JORDAN, RICHARD: NYC, July 19, 1938. Harvard.

JOURDAN, LOUIS: Marseilles, France, June 19, 1920.

JOY, ROBERT: Montreal, Can., Aug. 17, 1951. Oxford.

JULIA, RAUL: San Juan, PR, Mar. 9, 1943. U. PR.

JURADO, KATY (Maria Christina Jurado Garcia): Guadalajara, Mex., Jan. 16, 1927.

KACZMAREK, JANE: Milwaukee, WI, Dec. 21.

KAHN, MADELINE: Boston, MA, Sept. 29, 1942. Hofstra U.

KANE, CAROL: Cleveland, OH, June 18, 1952.

KAPLAN, MARVIN: Brooklyn, Jan. 24, 1924.

KAPOOR, SHASHI: Bombay, India, 1940.

KAPRISKY, VALERIE: Paris, 1963.

KARRAS, ALEX: Gary, IN, July 15, 1935.

KATT, WILLIAM: Los Angeles, CA, Feb. 16, 1955.

KAUFMANN, CHRISTINE: Lansdorf, Graz, Austria, Jan. 11, 1945.

KAVNER, JULIE: Burbank, CA, Sept. 7, 1951. UCLA.

KAYE, STUBBY: NYC, Nov. 11, 1918.

KAZAN, LAINIE (Levine): Brooklyn, May 15, 1942.

KEACH, STACY: Savannah, GA, June 2, 1941. U. Cal., Yale.

KEATON, DIANE (Hall): Los Angeles, CA, Jan. 5, 1946. Neighborhood Playhouse.

KEATON, MICHAEL: Coraopolis. PA, Sept. 9, 1951. KentStateU.

KEATS, STEVEN: Bronx, NY, 1945.

KEDROVA, LILA: Leningrad, 1918.

KEEL, HOWARD (Harold Leek): Gillespie, IL, Apr. 13, 1919.

KEELER, RUBY (Ethel): Halifax, N.S., Aug. 25, 1909.

KEITEL, HARVEY: Brooklyn, May 13, 1941.

KEITH, BRIAN: Bayonne, NJ, Nov. 15, 1921.

KEITH, DAVID: Knoxville, TN, May 8, 1954. UTN.

KELLER, MARTHE: Basel, Switz., 1945. Munich Stanislavsky Sch.

KELLERMAN, SALLY: Long Beach, CA, June 2, 1936. Actors Studio West.

KELLEY, DeFOREST: Atlanta, GA, Jan. 20, 1920.

KELLY, GENE: Pittsburgh, Aug. 23,1912. U. Pittsburgh.

KELLY, JACK: Astoria, NY, Sept. 16, 1927. UCLA.

KELLY, NANCY: Lowell, MA, Mar. 25, 1921. Bentley School.

KEMP, JEREMY (Wacker): Chesterfield, Eng., Feb. 3, 1935. Central Sch.

KENNEDY, GEORGE: NYC, Feb. 18, 1925.

KENNEDY, LEON ISAAC: Cleveland, OH, 1949.

KENSIT, PATSY: London, Mar. 4, 1968.

KERR, DEBORAH: Helensburg, Scot., Sept. 30, 1921. Smale Ballet School.

KERR, JOHN: NYC, Nov. 15, 1931. Harvard, Columbia.

KERWIN, BRIAN: Chicago, IL, Oct. 25, 1949.

KEYES, EVELYN: Port Arthur, TX, Nov. 20, 1919.

KHAMBATTA, PERSIS: Bombay, Oct. 2, 1950.

KIDDER, MARGOT: Yellow Knife, Can., Oct. 17, 1948. UBC.

KIEL, RICHARD: Detroit, MI, Sept. 13, 1939.

KIER, UDO: Germany, Oct. 14, 1944.

KILEY, RICHARD: Chicago, Mar. 31, 1922. Loyola.

KILMER, VAL: Los Angeles, Dec. 31, 1959. Juilliard.

KINCAID, ARON (Norman Neale Williams III: Los Angeles, June 15, 1943. UCLA.

KING, ALAN (Irwin Kniberg): Brooklyn, Dec. 26, 1927.

KING, PERRY: Alliance, OH, Apr. 30, 1948. Yale.

KINGSLEY, BEN (Krishna Bhanji): Snaiton, Yorkshire, Eng., Dec. 31, 1943.

KINSKI, NASTASSJA: Berlin, Ger., Jan. 24, 1960.

KIRKLAND, SALLY: NYC, Oct. 31, 1944. Actors Studio.

KITT, EARTHA: North, SC. Jan. 26, 1928.

KLEIN, ROBERT: NYC, Feb. 8, 1942. Alfred U.

KLEMPERER, WERNER: Cologne, Mar. 22, 1920.

KLINE, KEVIN: St. Louis, MO, Oct. 24, 1947. Juilliard.

KLUGMAN, JACK: Philadelphia, PA, Apr. 27, 1922. Carnegie Tech.

KNIGHT, MICHAEL: Princeton, NJ, 1959.

KNIGHT, SHIRLEY: Goessel, KS, July 5, 1937. Wichita U.

KNOWLES, PATRIC (Reginald Lawrence Knowles): Horsforth, Eng., Nov. 11, 1911.

KNOX, ALEXANDER: Strathroy, Ont., Can., Jan. 16, 1907.

KNOX, ELYSE: Hartford, CT, Dec. 14, 1917. Traphagen School.

KOENIG, WALTER: Chicago, IL, Sept. 14, 1936. UCLA.

KOHNER, SUSAN: Los Angeles, Nov. 11, 1936. U. Calif.

KORMAN, HARVEY: Chicago, IL, Feb. 15, 1927. Goodman.

KORSMO, CHARLIE: Minneapolis, MN, 1978.

KORVIN, CHARLES (Geza Korvin Karpathi): Czechoslovakia, Nov. 21, Sorbonne.

KOSLECK, MARTIN: Barkotzen, Ger., Mar. 24, 1907. Max Reinhardt School.

KOTEAS, ELIAS: Montreal, Quebec, Can., 1961. AADA.

KOTTO, YAPHET: NYC, Nov. 15, 1937.

KOZAK, HARLEY JANE: Wilkes-Barre, PA, Jan. 28, 1957. NYU.

KRABBE, JEROEN: Amsterdam, The Netherlands, Dec. 5, 1944.

KREUGER, KURT: St. Moritz, Switz., July 23, 1917. U. London.

KRIGE, ALICE: Upington, So. Africa, June 28, 1955.

KRISTEL, SYLVIA: Amsterdam, The Netherlands, Sept. 28, 1952.

KRISTOFFERSON, KRIS: Brownsville, TX, June 22, 1936, Pomona Col.

KRUGER, HARDY: Berlin, Ger., April 12, 1928.

KUNTSMANN, DORIS: Hamburg, Ger., 1944.

KURTZ, SWOOSIE: Omaha, NE, Sept. 6, 1944.

KWAN, NANCY: Hong Kong, May 19, 1939. Royal Ballet.

LaBELLE, PATTI: Philadelphia, PA, May 24, 1944.

LACY, JERRY: Sioux City, IA, Mar. 27, 1936. LACC.

LADD, CHERYL: (Stoppelmoor): Huron, SD. July 12, 1951.

LADD, DIANE: (Ladner): Meridian, MS, Nov. 29, 1932. Tulane U.

LaGRECA, PAUL: Bronx, NY, June 23, 1962. AADA.

LAHTI, CHRISTINE: Detroit, MI, Apr. 4, 1950. U. Mich.

LAKE, RICKI: NYC, Sept. 21, 1968.

LAMARR, HEDY (Hedwig Kiesler): Vienna, Sept. 11, 1913.

LAMAS, LORENZO: Los Angeles, Jan. 28, 1958.

LAMBERT, CHRISTOPHER: NYC, Mar. 29, 1958.

LAMOUR, DOROTHY (Mary Dorothy Slaton): New Orleans, LA, Dec. 10, 1914. Spence School.

LANCASTER, BURT: NYC, Nov. 2, 1913. NYU.

LANDAU, MARTIN: Brooklyn, June 20, 1931. Actors Studio.

LANDRUM, TERI: Enid, OK, 1960.

LANE, ABBE: Brooklyn, Dec. 14, 1935.

LANE, DIANE: NYC, Jan. 22, 1963.

LANE, NATHAN: Jersey City, NJ, Feb. 3, 1956.

LANG, STEPHEN: NYC, July 11, 1952. Swarthmore Col.

LANGE, HOPE: Redding Ridge, CT, Nov. 28, 1931. Reed Col.

LANGE, JESSICA: Cloquet, MN, Apr. 20, 1949. U. Minn.

LANGELLA, FRANK: Bayonne, NJ, Jan. 1, 1940. SyracuseU.

LANSBURY, ANGELA: London, Oct. 16, 1925. London Academy of Music.

LANSING, ROBERT (Brown): San Diego, CA, June 5, 1929.

LaPLANTE, LAURA: St. Louis, MO, Nov. 1,.1904.

LARROQUETTE, JOHN: New Orleans, LA, Nov. 25, 1947.

LASSER, LOUISE: NYC, Apr. 11, 1939. Brandeis U.

LAUGHLIN, JOHN: Memphis, TN, Apr. 3.

LAUGHLIN, TOM: Minneapolis, MN, 1938.

LAUPER, CYNDI: Astoria, Queens, NYC, June 20, 1953.

LAURE, CAROLE: Montreal, Can., 1951.

LAURIE, PIPER (Rosetta Jacobs): Detroit, MI, Jan. 22, 1932.

LAUTER, ED: Long Beach, NY, Oct. 30, 1940.

LAW, JOHN PHILLIP: Hollywood, CA, Sept. 7, 1937. Neighborhood Playhouse, U. Hawaii.

LAWRENCE, BARBARA: Carnegie, OK, Feb. 24, 1930. UCLA.

LAWRENCE, CAROL (Laraia): Melrose Park, IL, Sept. 5, 1935.

LAWRENCE, VICKI: Inglewood, CA, Mar. 26, 1949.

LAWSON, LEIGH: Atherston, Eng., July 21, 1945. RADA.

LEACHMAN, CLORIS: Des Moines, IA, Apr. 30, 1930. Northwestern U.

LEAUD, JEAN-PIERRE: Paris, 1944.

LEDERER, FRANCIS: Karlin, Prague, Czech., Nov. 6, 1906.

LEE, BRANDON: Feb. 1, 1965. Emerson Col.

LEE, CHRISTOPHER: London, May 27, 1922. Wellington College.

LEE, MARK: Australia, 1958

LEE, MICHELE (Dusiak): Los Angeles, June 24, 1942. LACC.

LEE, PEGGY (Norma Delores Egstrom): Jamestown, ND, May 26, 1920.

LEE, SPIKE (Shelton Lee): Atlanta, GA, Mar. 20, 1957.

LEGUIZAMO, JOHN: Columbia, July 22, 1965. NYU.

LEIBMAN, RON: NYC, Oct. 11, 1937. Ohio Wesleyan.

LEIGH, JANET (Jeanette Helen Morrison): Merced, CA, July 6, 1926. College of Pacific.

LEIGH, JENNIFER JASON: Los Angeles, Feb. 5, 1962.

LeMAT, PAUL: Rahway, NJ, Sept. 22, 1952.

LEMMON, CHRIS: Los Angeles, Jan. 22, 1954.

LEMMON, JACK: Boston, Feb. 8, 1925. Harvard.

LENO, JAY: New Rochelle, NY, Apr. 28, 1950. Emerson Col.

LENZ, KAY: Los Angeles, Mar. 4, 1953.

LENZ, RICK: Springfield, IL, Nov. 21, 1939. U. Mich.

LEONARD, ROBERT SEAN: Westwood, NJ, Feb. 28, 1969.

LEONARD, SHELDON (Bershad): NYC, Feb. 22, 1907, Syracuse U.

LERNER, MICHAEL: Brooklyn, NY, June 22, 1941.

LEROY, PHILIPPE: Paris, Oct. 15, 1930. U. Paris.

LESLIE, BETHEL: NYC, Aug. 3, 1929. Brearley School.

LESLIE, JOAN (Joan Brodell): Detroit, Jan. 26, 1925. St. Benedict's.

LESTER, MARK: Oxford, Eng., July 11, 1958.

LEVELS, CALVIN: Cleveland. OH, Sept. 30, 1954. CCC.

LEVIN, RACHEL: NYC, 1954. Goddard Col.

LEVINE, JERRY: New Brunswick, NJ, Mar. 12, 1957, Boston U.

LEVY, EUGENE: Hamilton, Can., Dec. 17, 1946. McMasterU.

LEWIS, CHARLOTTE: London, 1968.

LEWIS, JERRY (Joseph Levitch): Newark, NJ, Mar. 16, 1926.

LIGON, TOM: New Orleans, LA, Sept. 10, 1945.

LINCOLN, ABBEY (Anna Marie Wool-ridge): Chicago, Aug. 6. 1930.

LINDEN, HAL: Bronx, NY, Mar. 20, 1931. City Col. of NY.

LINDFORS, VIVECA: Uppsala, Sweden, Dec. 29, 1920. Stockholm Royal Dramatic School.

LINDSAY, ROBERT: Ilketson, Derby-shire, Eng., Dec. 13, 1951, RADA.

LINN-BAKER, MARK: St. Louis, MO, June 17, 1954, Yale.

LIOTTA, RAY: Newark, NJ, Dec. 18, 1955. UMiami.

LISI, VIRNA: Rome, Nov. 8, 1937.

LITHGOW, JOHN: Rochester, NY, Oct. 19, 1945. Harvard.

LLOYD, CHRISTOPHER: Stamford, CT, Oct. 22, 1938.

LLOYD, EMILY: London, Sept. 29, 1970.

LOCKE, SONDRA: Shelbyville, TN, May, 28, 1947.

LOCKHART, JUNE: NYC, June 25, 1925. Westlake School.

LOCKWOOD, GARY: Van Nuys, CA, Feb. 21, 1937.

LOGGIA, ROBERT: Staten Island, NY., Jan. 3, 1930. UMo.

LOLLOBRIGIDA, GINA: Subiaco, Italy, July 4, 1927. Rome Academy of Fine Arts.

LOM, HERBERT: Prague, Czechoslovakia, Jan 9, 1917. Prague U.

LOMEZ, CELINE: Montreal, Can., 1953.

LONDON, JULIE (Julie Peck): Santa Rosa, CA, Sept. 26, 1926.

LONE, JOHN: Hong Kong, 1952. AADA

LONG, SHELLEY: Ft. Wayne, IN, Aug. 23, 1949. Northwestern U.

LOPEZ, PERRY: NYC, July 22, 1931. NYU.

LORD, JACK (John Joseph Ryan): NYC, Dec. 30, 1928. NYU.

LOREN, SOPHIA (Sophia Scicolone): Rome, Italy, Sept. 20, 1934.

LOUISE, TINA (Blacker): NYC, Feb. 11, 1934, Miami U.

LOVITZ, JON: Tarzana, CA, July 21, 1957.

LOWE, CHAD: Dayton, OH, Jan. 15, 1968.

LOWE, ROB: Charlottesville, VA, Mar. 17, 1964.

LOWITSCH, KLAUS: Berlin, Apr. 8, 1936, Vienna Academy.

LOY, MYRNA (Myrna WIlliams): Helena, MT, Aug. 2, 1905. Westlake School.

LUCAS, LISA: Arizona, 1961.

LUCKINBILL, LAURENCE: Fort Smith, AK, Nov. 21, 1934.

LUFT, LORNA: Los Angeles, Nov. 21, 1952.

LULU: Glasgow, Scot., 1948.

LUNA, BARBARA: NYC, Mar. 2, 1939.

LUNDGREN, DOLPH: Stockolm, Sw., Nov. 3, 1959. Royal Inst.

LUPINO, IDA: London, Feb. 4, 1916. RADA

LuPONE, PATTI: Northport, NY Apr. 21, 1949, Juilliard.

LYDON, JAMES: Harrington Park, NJ, May 30, 1923.

LYNCH, KELLY: Minneapolis, MN, 1959.

LYNLEY, CAROL (Jones): NYC, Feb. 13, 1942.

LYNN, JEFFREY: Auburn, MA, Feb. 16, 1909. Bates College.

LYON, SUE: Davenport, IA, July 10, 1946.

MacARTHUR, JAMES: Los Angeles, Dec. 8, 1937. Harvard.

MACCHIO, RALPH: Huntington, NY, Nov. 4, 1961.

MacCORKINDALE, SIMON: Cambridge, Eng., Feb. 12, 1953.

MacDOWELL, ANDIE: Gaffney, SC, Apr. 21, 1958.

MacGINNIS, NIALL: Dublin, Ire., Mar. 29, 1913. Dublin U.

MacGRAW, ALI: NYC, Apr. 1, 1938. Wellesley.

MacLACHLAN, KYLE: Yakima, WA, Feb. 22, 1959. UWa.

MacLAINE, SHIRLEY (Beaty): Richmond, VA, Apr. 24, 1934.

MacLEOD, GAVIN: Mt. Kisco, NY, Feb. 28, 1931.

MacNAUGHTON, ROBERT: NYC, Dec. 19, 1966.

MACNEE, PATRICK: London, Feb. 1922.

MacNICOL, PETER: Dallas, TX, Apr. 10, 1954. UMN.

MACY, W.H.(William): Miami, FL, Mar. 13, 1950. Goddard College.

MADIGAN, AMY: Chicago, IL, Sept. 11, 1950. Marquette U.

MADISON, GUY (Robert Moseley): Bakersfield, CA, Jan. 19, 1922. Bakersfield Jr. College.

MADONNA (Madonna Louise Veronica Cicone): Bay City, MI, Aug. 16, 1958. UMi.

MADSEN, VIRGINIA: Winnetka, IL, Sept. 11, 1963.

MAGNUSON, ANN: Charleston, WV, Jan. 4, 1956.

MAHARIS, GEORGE: Astoria, NY, Sept. 1, 1928. Actors Studio.

MAHONEY, JOHN: Manchester, Eng., June 20, 1940, WUIll.

MAILER, KATE: NYC, 1962.

MAILER, STEPHEN: NYC, Mar. 10, 1966. NYU.

MAJORS, LEE: Wyandotte, MI, Apr. 23, 1940. E. Ky. State Col.

MAKEPEACE, CHRIS: Toronto, Can., Apr. 22, 1964.

MAKO: Kobe, Japan, Dec. 10, 1933. Pratt.

MALDEN, KARL (Mladen Sekulovich): Gary, IN, Mar. 22, 1914.

MALET, PIERRE: St. Tropez, Fr., 1955.

MALKOVICH, JOHN: Christopher, IL, Dec. 9, 1953, IllStateU.

MALONE, DOROTHY: Chicago, IL, Jan. 30, 1925.

MANN, KURT: Roslyn, NY, July 18, 1947.

MANN, TERRENCE: KY, 1945. NCSchl Arts.

MANOFF, DINAH: NYC, Jan. 25, 1958. CalArts.

MANTEGNA, JOE: Chicago, IL, Nov. 13, 1947. Goodman Theatre.

MANZ, LINDA: NYC, 1961.

MARAIS, JEAN: Cherbourg, France, Dec. 11, 1913, St. Germain.

MARCHAND, NANCY: Buffalo, NY, June 19, 1928.

MARCOVICCI, ANDREA: NYC, Nov. 18, 1948.

MARGOLIN, JANET: NYC, July 25, 1943. Walden School.

MARIN, CHEECH (Richard): Los Angeles, July 13, 1946.

MARIN, JACQUES: Paris, Sept. 9, 1919. Conservatoire National.

MARINARO, ED: NYC, 1951. Cornell.

MARS, KENNETH: Chicago, IL, 1936.

MARSH, JEAN: London, Eng., July 1, 1934.

MARSHALL, BRENDA (Ardis Anderson Gaines): Isle of Negros, P.I., Sept. 29, 1915. Texas State College.

MARSHALL, E.G.: Owatonna, MN, June 18, 1910. U. Minn.

MARSHALL, KEN: NYC, 1953. Juilliard.

MARSHALL, PENNY: Bronx, NY, Oct. 15, 1942. U.N. Mex.

MARSHALL, WILLIAM: Gary, IN, Aug. 19, 1924. NYU.

MARTIN, ANDREA: Portland, ME, Jan. 15, 1947.

MARTIN, DEAN (Dino Crocetti): Steubenville, OH, June 17, 1917.

MARTIN, GEORGE N.: NYC, Aug. 15, 1929.

MARTIN, MILLICENT: Romford, Eng., June 8, 1934.

MARTIN, PAMELA SUE: Westport, CT, Jan. 15, 1953.

MARTIN, STEVE: Waco, TX, Aug. 14, 1945. UCLA.

MARTIN, TONY (Alfred Norris): Oakland, CA, Dec. 25, 1913. St. Mary's College.

MASINA, GUILIETTA: Giorgio di Piano, Italy, Feb. 22, 1921.

MASON, MARSHA: St. Louis, MO, Apr. 3, 1942. Webster Col.

MASON, PAMELA (Pamela Kellino): Westgate, Eng., Mar. 10, 1918.

MASSEN, OSA: Copenhagen, Den., Jan. 13, 1916.

MASSEY, DANIEL: London, Oct. 10, 1933. Eton and King's Coll.

MASTERS, BEN: Corvallis, OR, May 6, 1947. UOr.

MASTERSON, MARY STUART: Los Angeles, June 28, 1966, NYU.

MASTERSON, PETER: Angleton, TX, June 1, 1934. Rice U.

MASTRANTONIO, MARY ELIZABETH: Chicago, IL, Nov. 17, 1958. UIll.

MASTROIANNI, MARCELLO: Fontana Liri, Italy, Sept. 28, 1924.

MASUR, RICHARD: NYC, Nov. 20, 1948.

MATHESON, TIM: Glendale, CA, Dec. 31, 1947. CalState.

MATLIN, MARLEE: Morton Grove, IL., Aug. 24, 1965.

MATTHAU, WALTER (Matuschanskayasky): NYC, Oct. 1, 1920.

MATTHEWS, BRIAN: Philadelphia, Jan. 24. 1953. St. Olaf.

MATURE, VICTOR: Louisville, KY, Jan. 29, 1915.

MAY, ELAINE (Berlin): Philadelphia, Apr. 21, 1932.

MAYEHOFF, EDDIE: Baltimore, July 7, 1914. Yale.

MAYO, VIRGINIA (Virginia Clara Jones): St. Louis, MO, Nov. 30, 1920.

MAYRON, MELANIE: Philadelphia, PA, Oct. 20, 1952. AADA.

MAZURSKY, PAUL: Brooklyn, NY, Apr. 25, 1930. Bklyn Col.

McCALLUM, DAVID: Scotland, Sept. 19, 1933. Chapman Col.

McCAMBRIDGE, MERCEDES: Joliet, IL, Mar. 17, 1918. Mundelein College.

McCARTHY, ANDREW: NYC, 1963, NYU.

McCARTHY, KEVIN: Seattle, WA, Feb. 15, 1914. Minn. U.

McCARTNEY, PAUL: Liverpool, England, June 18, 1942.

McCLANAHAN, RUE: Healdton, OK, Feb. 21, 1934.

McCLORY, SEAN: Dublin, Ire., Mar. 8, 1924. U. Galway.

McCLURE, DOUG: Glendale, CA, May 11, 1935. UCLA.

McCLURE, MARC: San Mateo, CA, Mar. 31, 1957.

McCLURG, EDIE: Kansas City, MO, July 23, 1950.

McCOWEN, ALEC: Tunbridge Wells, Eng., May 26, 1925. RADA.

McCRANE, PAUL: Philadelphia, PA, Jan. 19. 1961.

McCRARY, DARIUS: Walnut, CA, 1976.

McDERMOTT, DYLAN: Waterbury, CT, Oct. 26, 1962. Neighborhood Playhouse.

McDONNELL, MARY: Wilkes Barre, PA, 1952.

McDORMAND, FRANCES: Illinois, 1958.

McDOWALL, RODDY: London, Sept. 17, 1928. St. Joseph's.

McDOWELL, MALCOLM (Taylor): Leeds, Eng., June 19, 1943. LAMDA.

McENERY, PETER: Walsall, Eng., Feb. 21, 1940.

McFARLAND, SPANKY: Dallas, TX, Oct. 2, 1926.

McGAVIN, DARREN: Spokane, WA, May 7, 1922. College of Pacific.

McGILL, EVERETT: Miami Beach, FL, Oct. 21, 1945.

McGILLIS, KELLY: Newport Beach, CA, July 9, 1957. Juilliard.

McGOVERN, ELIZABETH: Evanston, IL. July 18, 1961. Juilliard.

McGOVERN, MAUREEN: Youngstown, OH, July 27, 1949.

McGREGOR. JEFF: Chicago, 1957. UMn.

McGUIRE, BIFF: New Haven, CT, Oct. 25. 1926. Mass. Stale Col.

McGUIRE, DOROTHY: Omaha, NE, June 14, 1918.

McHATTIE, STEPHEN: Antigonish, NS, Feb. 3. Acadia U. AADA.

McKAY, GARDNER: NYC, June 10, 1932. Cornell.

McKEAN, MICHAEL: NYC, Oct. 17, 1947.

McKEE, LONETTE: Detroit, MI, 1954.

McKELLEN, IAN: Burnley, Eng., May 25, 1939.

McKENNA, VIRGINIA: London, June 7, 1931.

McKEON, DOUG: Pompton Plains, NJ, June 10, 1966.

McKUEN, ROD: Oakland, CA, Apr. 29, 1933.

McLERIE, ALLYN ANN: Grand Mere, Can., Dec. 1, 1926.

McNAIR, BARBARA: Chicago, Mar. 4, 1939. UCLA.

McNALLY, STEPHEN (Horace McNally): NYC, July 29, 1913. Fordham U.

McNAMARA, WILLIAM: Dallas, TX, 1965.

McNICHOL, KRISTY: Los Angeles. CA, Sept. 11, 1962.

McQUEEN, ARMELIA: North Carolina, Jan. 6, 1952. Bklyn Consv.

McQUEEN, BUTTERFLY: Tampa, FL, Jan. 8, 1911. UCLA.

McQUEEN, CHAD: Los Angeles, CA, Dec. 28, 1960. Actors Studio.

McRANEY, GERALD: Collins, MS, Aug. 19, 1948.

McSHANE, IAN: Blackburn, Eng., Sept. 29, 1942. RADA.

MEADOWS, AUDREY: Wuchang, China, 1924. St. Margaret's.

MEADOWS, JAYNE (formerly, Jayne Cot ter): Wuchang, China, Sept. 27, 1920. St. Margaret's.

MEARA, ANNE: Brooklyn, NY, Sept. 20, 1929.

MEDWIN, MICHAEL: London, 1925. Instut Fischer.

MEISNER, GUNTER: Bremen, Ger., Apr. 18, 1926. Municipal Drama School.

MEKKA, EDDIE: Worcester, MA, 1932. Boston Cons.

Stephen Mailer	Amanda Pays	Trey Parker	Diana Ross	Donald Pleasence	Alexis Smith

MELATO, MARIANGELA: Milan, Italy, 1941. Milan Theatre Acad.

MELL, MARISA: Vienna, Austria, Feb. 25, 1939.

MERCADO, HECTOR JAIME: NYC, 1949. HB Studio.

MERCOURI, MELINA: Athens, Greece, Oct. 18, 1925.

MEREDITH, BURGESS: Cleveland, OH, Nov. 16, 1907. Amherst.

MEREDITH, LEE (Judi Lee Sauls): Oct. 22, 1947. AADA.

MERKERSON, S. EPATHA: Saganaw, MI, Nov. 28, 1952. Wayne St. Univ.

MERRILL, DINA (Nedinia Hutton): NYC, Dec. 29, 1925. AADA.

METCALF, LAURIE: Edwardsville, IL, June 16, 1955. IIIStU.

METZLER, JIM: Oneonda, NY, June 23. Dartmouth.

MICHELL, KEITH: Adelaide, Aus., Dec. 1, 1926.

MIDLER, BETTE: Honolulu, HI, Dec. 1, 1945.

MIFUNE, TOSHIRO: Tsingtao, China, Apr. 1, 1920.

MILANO, ALYSSA: Brooklyn, NY, 1975.

MILES, JOANNA: Nice, France, Mar. 6, 1940.

MILES, SARAH: Ingatestone, Eng. Dec. 31, 1941. RADA.

MILES, SYLVIA: NYC, Sept. 9, 1934. Actors Studio.

MILES, VERA (Ralston)**:** Boise City, OK, Aug. 23, 1929. UCLA.

MILLER, ANN (Lucille Ann Collier): Chireno, TX, Apr. 12, 1919. Lawler Professional School.

MILLER, PENELOPE ANN: Santa Monica, CA, Jan. 13, 1964.

MILLER, BARRY: Los Angeles, CA, Feb. 6, 1958.

MILLER, JASON: Long Island City, NY, Apr. 22, 1939. Catholic U.

MILLER, LINDA: NYC, Sept. 16, 1942. Catholic U.

MILLER, REBECCA: Roxbury, CT, 1962. Yale.

MILLS, HAYLEY: London, Apr. 18, 1946. Elmhurst School.

MILLS, JOHN: Suffolk, Eng., Feb. 22, 1908.

MILLS, JULIET: London, Nov. 21, 1941.

MILNER, MARTIN: Detroit, MI, Dec. 28, 1931.

MIMIEUX, YVETTE: Los Angeles, Jan. 8, 1941. Hollywood High.

MINNELLI, LIZA: Los Angeles, Mar. 19, 1946.

MIOU-MIOU: Paris, Feb. 22, 1950.

MIRREN, HELEN: London, 1946.

MITCHELL, CAMERON (MizeII): Dallastown, PA, Nov. 4, 1918. N.Y. Theatre School.

MITCHELL, JAMES: Sacramento, CA, Feb. 29, 1920. LACC

MITCHELL, JOHN CAMERON: El Paso, TX, Apr. 21, 1963. Northwestern Univ.

MITCHUM, JAMES: Los Angeles, CA, May 8, 1941.

MITCHUM, ROBERT: Bridgeport, CT, Aug. 6, 1917.

MODINE, MATTHEW: Loma Linda, CA, Mar. 22, 1959.

MOFFAT, DONALD: Plymouth, Eng., Dec. 26, 1930. RADA.

MOFFETT, D.W.: Highland Park, IL, Oct. 26, 1954. Stanford U.

MOKAE, ZAKES: Johannesburg, So. Africa, Aug. 5, 1935. RADA.

MOLINA, ALFRED: London, May 24, 1953. Guildhall.

MOLL, RICHARD: Pasadena, CA, Jan. 13, 1943.

MONTALBAN, RICARDO: Mexico City, Nov. 25, 1920.

MONTGOMERY, BELINDA: Winnipeg, Can., July 23, 1950.

MONTGOMERY, ELIZABETH: Los Angeles, Apr. 15, 1933. AADA.

MONTGOMERY, GEORGE (George Letz): Brady, MT, Aug. 29, 1916. U. Mont.

MOOR, BILL: Toledo, OH, July 13, 1931. Northwestern.

MOORE, CONSTANCE: Sioux City, IA, Jan. 18, 1919.

MOORE, DEMI (Guines): Roswell, NM, Nov. 11, 1962.

MOORE, DICK: Los Angeles, Sept. 12, 1925.

MOORE, DUDLEY: Dagenham, Essex, Eng., Apr. 19, 1935.

MOORE, FRANK: Bay-de-Verde, Newfoundland, 1946.

MOORE, KIERON: County Cork, Ire., 1925. St. Mary's College.

MOORE, MARY TYLER: Brooklyn, Dec. 29, 1936.

MOORE, ROGER: London, Oct. 14, 1927. RADA.

MOORE, TERRY (.Helen Koford): Los Angeles, Jan. 7, 1929.

MORALES, ESAI: Brooklyn, 1963.

MORANIS, RICK: Toronto, Can., Apr. 18, 1954.

MOREAU, JEANNE: Paris, Jan. 23, 1928.

MORENO, RITA (Rosita Alverio): Humacao, P.R., Dec. 11, 1931.

MORGAN, DENNIS (Stanley Momer): Prentice, WI, Dec. 10, 1910. Carroll College.

MORGAN, HARRY (HENRY) (Harry Bratsburg): Detroit, Apr. 10, 1915. U. Chicago.

MORGAN, MICHELE (Simone Roussel): Paris, Feb. 29, 1920. Paris Dramatic School.

MORIARTY, CATHY: Bronx, NY, Nov. 29, 1960.

MORIARTY, MICHAEL: Detroit, MI, Apr. 5, 1941. Dartmouth.

MORISON, PATRICIA: NYC, 1915.

MORITA, NORIYUKI "PAT": Isleton, CA, June 28, 1932.

MORRIS, ANITA: Durham, NC, 1943.

MORRIS, GREG: Cleveland, OH, Sept. 27, 1934. Ohio State.

MORRIS, HOWARD: NYC, Sept. 4, 1919. NYU.

MORSE, DAVID: Hamilton, MA, 1953.

MORSE, ROBERT: Newton, MA, May 18, 1931.

MORTON, JOE: NYC, Oct. 18, 1947. Hofstra U.

MOSES, WILLIAM: Los Angeles, Nov. 17, 1959.

MOSTEL, JOSH: NYC, Dec. 21, 1946. Brandeis U.

MOUCHET, CATHERINE: Paris, 1959. Ntl. Consv.

MOYA, EDDY: El Paso, TX, Apr. 11, 1963. LACC.

MULDAUR, DIANA: NYC, Aug. 19, 1938. Sweet Briar Col.

MULGREW, KATE: Dubuque, IA, Apr. 29, 1955. NYU.

MULHERN, MATT: Philadelphia, PA, July 21, 1960. Rutgers Univ.

MULL, MARTIN: N. Ridgefield, OH, Aug. 18, 1941. RISch. of Design.

MULLIGAN, RICHARD: NYC, Nov. 13, 1932.

MULRONEY, DERMOT: Alexandria, VA, Oct. 31, 1963. Northwestern.

MUMY, BILL (Charles William Mumy Jr.): San Gabriel, CA, Feb. 1, 1954.

MURPHY, EDDIE: Brooklyn, NY, Apr. 3, 1961.

MURPHY, MICHAEL: Los Angeles, CA, May 5, 1938. UAz.

MURRAY, BILL: Wilmette, IL, Sept. 21, 1950. Regis Col.

MUSANTE, TONY: Bridgeport, CT, June 30, 1936. Oberlin Col.

NABORS, JIM: Sylacauga, GA, June 12, 1932.

NADER, GEORGE: Pasadena, CA, Oct. 19, 1921. Occidental College.

NADER, MICHAEL: Los Angeles, CA, 1945.

NAMATH, JOE: Beaver Falls, PA, May 31, 1943. UAla.

NATWICK, MILDRED: Baltimore, June 19, 1908. Bryn Mawr.

NAUGHTON, DAVID: Hartford, CT, Feb. 13, 1951.

NAUGHTON, JAMES: Middletown, CT, Dec. 6, 1945.

NEAL, PATRICIA: Packard, KY, Jan. 20, 1926. Northwestern U.

NEESOM, LIAM: Ballymena, Northern Ireland, June 7, 1952.

NEFF, HILDEGARDE (Hildegard Knef): Ulm, Ger., Dec. 28, 1925. Berlin Art Academy.

NEILL, SAM: No. Ireland, 1948. U Canterbury.

NELL, NATHALIE: Paris, Oct. 1950.

NELLIGAN, KATE: London, Ont., Can., Mar. 16, 1951. U Toronto.

NELSON, BARRY (Robert Nielsen): Oakland, CA, Apr. 16, 1920.

NELSON, CRAIG T.: Spokane. WA, Apr. 4, 1946.

NELSON, GENE (Gene Berg): Seattle, WA, Mar. 24, 1920.

NELSON, HARRIET HILLIARD (Peggy Lou Snyder): Des Moines, IA, July 18, 1914.

NELSON, JUDD: Portland, ME, Nov. 28, 1959, Haverford Col.

NELSON, LORI (Dixie Kay Nelson): Santa Fe, NM, Aug. 15, 1933.

NELSON, TRACY: Santa Monica, CA, Oct. 25, 1963.

NELSON, WILLIE: Abbott, TX, Apr. 30, 1933.

NEMEC, CORIN: Little Rock, AK, Nov. 5, 1971.

NERO, FRANCO: Parma, Italy, 1941.

NETTLETON, LOIS: Oak Park, IL. Actors Studio.

NEWHART, BOB: Chicago, IL, Sept. 5, 1929. Loyola U.

NEWLEY, ANTHONY: Hackney, London, Sept. 24, 1931.

NEWMAN, BARRY: Boston, MA, Nov. 7, 1938. Brandeis U.

NEWMAN, NANETTE: Northampton, Eng., 1934.

NEWMAN, PAUL: Cleveland, OH. Jan. 26, 1925. Yale.

NEWMAR, JULIE (Newmeyer): Los Angeles, Aug. 16, 1933.

NEWTON-JOHN, OLIVIA: Cambridge, Eng., Sept. 26, 1948.

NGUYEN, DUSTIN: Saigon, 1962.

NICHOLAS, PAUL: London, 1945.

NICHOLSON, JACK: Neptune, NJ, Apr. 22, 1937.

NICKERSON, DENISE: NYC, 1959.

NICOL, ALEX: Ossining, NY, Jan. 20, 1919. Actors Studio.

NIELSEN, BRIGITTE: Denmark, July 15, 1963.

NIELSEN, LESLIE: Regina, Saskatchewan. Can., Feb. 11, 1926. Neighborhood Playhouse.

NIMOY, LEONARD: Boston, MA, Mar. 26, 1931. Boston Col., Antioch Col.

NIXON, CYNTHIA: NYC, Apr. 9, 1966. Columbia U.

NOBLE, JAMES: Dallas, TX, Mar. 5, 1922, SMU.

NOIRET, PHILIPPE: France, Oct. 1, 1930.

NOLAN, KATHLEEN: St. Louis, MO, Sept. 27, 1933. Neighborhood Playhouse.

NOLTE, NICK: Omaha, NE, Feb. 8, 1940. Pasadena City Col.

NORRIS, CHRISTOPHER: NYC, Oct. 7, 1943. Lincoln Square Acad.

NORRIS, CHUCK (Carlos Ray): Ryan,OK. Mar. 10, 1940.

NORTH, HEATHER: Pasadena, CA, Dec. 13, 1950. Actors Workshop.

NORTH, SHEREE (Dawn Bethel): Los Angeles. Jan. 17, 1933. Hollywood High

NORTON, KEN: Aug. 9, 1945.

NOURI, MICHAEL: Washington, DC, Dec. 9, 1945.

NOVAK, KIM (Marilyn Novak): Chicago, Feb. 13, 1933. LACC.

NUREYEV, RUDOLF: Russia, Mar. 17, 1938.

NUYEN, FRANCE (Vannga): Marseilles, France, July 31, 1939. Beaux Arts School.

O'BRIAN, HUGH (Hugh J. Krampe): Rochester, NY. Apr. 19, 1928. Cincinnati U.

O'BRIEN, CLAY: Ray, AZ, May 6, 1961.

O'BRIEN, MARGARET (Angela Maxine O'Brien): Los Angeles, Jan. 15, 1937.

O'CONNOR, CARROLL: Bronx, NY, Aug. 2, 1924. Dublin National Univ.

O'CONNOR, DONALD: Chicago, Aug. 28, 1925.

O'CONNOR, GLYNNIS: NYC, Nov. 19, 1955. NYSU.

O'HARA, CATHERINE: Toronto, Can., Mar. 4, 1954.

O'HARA, MAUREEN (Maureen Fitz-Simons): Dublin, Ire., Aug. 17, 1920. Abbey School.

O'HERLIHY, DAN: Wexford, Ire., May 1, 1919. National U.

O'KEEFE, MICHAEL: Paulland, NJ, Apr. 24, 1955. NYU, AADA.

OLDMAN, GARY: New Cross, South London, Eng., Mar. 21, 1958.

OLIN, LENA: Stockholm, Sweden, 1955.

OLMOS, EDWARD JAMES: Los Angeles, Feb. 24, 1947. CSLA.

O'LOUGHLIN, GERALD S.: NYC, Dec. 23, 1921. U. Rochester.

OLSON, JAMES: Evanston, IL, Oct. 8, 1930.

OLSON, NANCY: Milwaukee, WI, July 14, 1928. UCLA.

O'NEAL, GRIFFIN: Los Angeles, 1965.

O'NEAL, PATRICK: Ocala, FL, Sept. 26, 1927. U. Fla.

O'NEAL, RON: Utica, NY, Sept. 1, 1937. Ohio State.

O'NEAL, RYAN: Los Angeles, Apr. 20, 1941.

O'NEAL, TATUM: Los Angeles, Nov. 5, 1963.

O'NEIL, TRICIA: Shreveport, LA, Mar. 11, 1945. Baylor U.

O'NEILL, ED: Youngstown, OH, 1946.

O'NEILL, JENNIFER: Rio de Janeiro, Feb. 20, 1949. Neighborhood Playhouse.

ONTKEAN, MICHAEL: Vancouver, B.C., Can., Jan. 24, 1946.

ORBACH, JERRY: Bronx, NY, Oct. 20, 1935.

O'SHEA, MILO: Dublin, Ire., June 2, 1926.

O'SULLIVAN, MAUREEN: Byle, Ire., May 17, 1911. Sacred Heart Convent.

O'TOOLE, ANNETTE (Toole): Houston, TX, Apr. 1, 1953. UCLA.

O'TOOLE, PETER: Connemara, Ire., Aug. 2, 1932. RADA.

OVERALL, PARK: Nashville, TN, Mar. 15, 1957. Tusculum Col.

PACINO, AL: NYC, Apr. 25, 1940.

PACULA, JOANNA: Tamaszow Lubelski, Poland, Jan. 2, 1957. Polish Natl. Theatre Sch.

PAGE, TONY (Anthony Vitiello): Bronx, NY, 1940.

PAGET, DEBRA (Debralee Griffin): Denver, Aug. 19, 1933.

PAIGE, JANIS (Donna Mae Jaden): Tacoma. WA, Sept. 16, 1922.

PALANCE, JACK (Walter Palanuik): Lattimer, PA, Feb. 18, 1920. UNC.

PALIN, MICHAEL: Sheffield, Yorkshire, Eng., May 5, 1943, Oxford.

PALMER, BETSY: East Chicago, IN, Nov. 1, 1926. DePaul U.

PALMER, GREGG (Palmer Lee): San Francisco, Jan. 25, 1927. U. Utah.

PAMPANINI, SILVANA: Rome, Sept. 25, 1925.

PANEBIANCO, RICHARD: NYC, 1971.

PANKIN, STUART: Philadelphia, Apr. 8, 1946.

PANTALIANO, JOE: Jersey City, NJ, Sept. 12, 1954.

PAPAS, IRENE: Chiliomodion, Greece, Mar. 9, 1929.

PARE, MICHAEL: Brooklyn, NY, Oct. 9, 1959.

PARKER, COREY: NYC, July 8, 1965. NYU.

PARKER, ELEANOR: Cedarville, OH, June 26, 1922. Pasadena Playhouse.

PARKER, FESS: Fort Worth, TX, Aug. 16, 1925. USC.

PARKER, JAMESON: Baltimore, MD, Nov. 18, 1947. Beloit Col.

PARKER, JEAN (Mae Green): Deer Lodge, MT, Aug. 11, 1912.

PARKER, MARY-LOUISE: Ft. Jackson, SC, Aug. 2, 1964. Bard Col.

PARKER, NATHANIEL: London, 1963.

PARKER, SARAH JESSICA: Nelsonville, OH, Mar. 25, 1965.

PARKER, SUZY (Cecelia Parker): San Antonio, TX, Oct. 28, 1933.

PARKER, TREY: Auburn, AL, May 30, 1972.

PARKER, WILLARD (Worster Van Eps): NYC, Feb. 5, 1912.

PARKINS, BARBARA: Vancouver, Can., May 22, 1943.

PARKS, MICHAEL: Corona, CA, Apr. 4, 1938.

PARSONS, ESTELLE: Lynn, MA, Nov. 20, 1927. Boston U.

PARTON, DOLLY: Sevierville, TN, Jan. 19, 1946.

PATINKIN, MANDY: Chicago, IL, Nov. 30, 1952. Juilliard.

PATRIC, JASON: NYC, 1966.

PATRICK, DENNIS: Philadelphia, Mar. 14, 1918.

PATTERSON, LEE: Vancouver, Can., Mar. 31, 1929. Ontario Col.

PATTON, WILL: Charleston, SC, June 14, 1954.

PAVAN, MARISA (Marisa Pierangeli): Cagliari, Sardinia, June 19, 1932. Torquado Tasso College.

PAYS, AMANDA: Berkshire, Eng., June 6, 1959.

PEACH, MARY: Durbn, S. Africa, 1934.

PEARL, MINNIE (Sarah Cannon): Centerville, TN, Oct. 25, 1912.

PEARSON, BEATRICE: Dennison, TX, July 27, 1920.

PECK, GREGORY: La Jolla, CA, Apr. 5, 1916. U. Calif.

PELIKAN, LISA: Paris, July 12. Juilliard.

PEÑA, ELIZABETH: Cuba, Sept. 23, 1961.

PENDLETON, AUSTIN: Warren, OH, Mar. 27, 1940. Yale U.

PENHALL, BRUCE: Balboa, CA, Aug. 17, 1960.

PENN, SEAN: Burbank, CA, Aug. 17, 1960.

PEPPARD, GEORGE: Detroit, Oct. 1, 1928. Carnegie Tech.

PEREZ, JOSE: NYC, 1940.

PERKINS, ELIZABETH: Queens, NY, Nov. 18, 1960. Goodman School.

PERKINS, MILLIE: Passaic, NJ, May 12, 1938.

PERLMAN, RHEA: Brooklyn, NY, Mar. 31, 1948.

PERLMAN, RON: NYC, Apr. 13, 1950. UMn.

PERREAU, GIGI (Ghislaine): Los Angeles, Feb. 6, 1941.

PERRINE, VALERIE: Galveston, TX, Sept. 3, 1943. U. Ariz

PESCI, JOE: Newark, NJ. Feb. 9, 1943.

PESCOW, DONNA: Brooklyn, NY, Mar. 24, 1954.

PETERS, BERNADETTE (Lazzara): Jamaica, NY, Feb. 28, 1948.

PETERS, BROCK: NYC, July 2, 1927. CCNY.

PETERS, JEAN (Elizabeth): Caton, OH, Oct. 15, 1926. Ohio State U.

PETERS, MICHAEL: Brooklyn, NY, 1948.

PETERSEN, WILLIAM: Chicago, IL, 1953.

PETERSON, CASSANDRA: Colorado Springs, CO, Sept. 17, 1951.

PETTET, JOANNA: London, Nov. 16, 1944. Neighborhood Playhouse.

PFEIFFER, MICHELLE: Santa Ana, CA, Apr. 29, 1958.

PHILLIPS, LOU DIAMOND: Phillipines, Feb. 17, 1962, UTx.

PHILLIPS, MacKENZIE: Alexandria, VA, Nov. 10, 1959.

PHILLIPS, MICHELLE (Holly Gilliam): Long Beach, CA, June 4, 1944.

PHOENIX, RIVER: Madras, OR, Aug. 24, 1970.

PICARDO, ROBERT: Philadelphia, PA, Oct. 27, 1953. Yale.

PICERNI, PAUL: NYC, Dec. 1, 1922. Loyola U.

PINCHOT, BRONSON: NYC, May 20, 1959. Yale.

PINE, PHILLIP: Hanford, CA, July 16, 1925. Actors' Lab.

PISCOPO, JOE: Passaic. NJ, June 17, 1951.

PISIER, MARIE-FRANCE: Vietnam, May 10, 1944. U. Paris.

PITILLO, MARIA: Mahwah, NJ, 1965.

PITT, BRAD: Shawnee, OK, Dec. 18, 1963.

PLACE, MARY KAY: Tulsa OK, Sept. 23, 1947. U. Tulsa.

PLAYTEN, ALICE: NYC, Aug. 28, 1947. NYU.

PLEASENCE, DONALD: Workshop, Eng., Oct. 5, 1919. Sheffield School.

PLESHETTE, SUZANNE: NYC, Jan. 31, 1937. Syracuse U.

PLOWRIGHT, JOAN: Scunthorpe, Brigg, Lincolnshire, Eng., Oct. 28, 1929. Old Vic.

PLUMB, EVE: Burbank, CA, Apr. 29, 1958.

PLUMMER, AMANDA: NYC, Mar. 23, 1957. Middlebury Col.

PLUMMER, CHRISTOPHER: Toronto, Can., Dec. 13, 1927.

PODESTA, ROSSANA: Tripoli, June 20, 1934.

POITIER, SIDNEY: Miami, FL, Feb. 27, 1927.

POLITO, JON: Philadelphia, PA, Dec. 29, 1950. Villanova U.

POLITO, LINA: Naples, Italy, Aug. 11, 1954.

POLLAN, TRACY: NYC, 1962.

POLLARD, MICHAEL J.: Passaic, NJ, May 30, 1939.

PORTER, ERIC: London, Apr. 8, 1928. Wimbledon Col.

POTTS, ANNIE: Nashville, TN, Oct. 28, 1952. Stephens Col.

POWELL, JANE (Suzanne Burce): Portland, OR, Apr. 1, 1928.

POWELL, ROBERT: Salford, Eng., June 1, 1944. Manchester U.

POWER, TARYN: Los Angeles, CA, 1954.

POWER, TYRONE IV: Los Angeles, CA, Jan. 1959.

POWERS, MALA (Mary. Ellen): San Francisco, Dec. 29, 1921. UCLA.

POWERS, STEFANIE (Federkiewicz): Hollywood, CA, Oct. 12, 1942.

PRENTISS, PAULA (Paula Ragusa): San Antonio, TX, Mar. 4, 1939. Northwestern U.

PRESLE, MICHELINE (Micheline Chassagne): Paris, Aug. 22, 1922. Rouleau Drama School.

PRESLEY, PRISCILLA: Brooklyn, NY, May 24, 1945.

PRESNELL, HARVE: Modesto, CA, Sept. 14, 1933. USC.

PRESTON, KELLY: Honolulu, HI, Oct. 13, 1962. USC.

PRESTON, WILLIAM: Columbia, PA, Aug. 26, 1921. PaStateU.

PRICE, LONNY: NYC, Mar. 9, 1959. Juilliard.

PRICE, VINCENT: St. Louis, May 27, 1911. Yale.

PRIMUS, BARRY: NYC, Feb. 16, 1938. CCNY.

PRINCE (P. Rogers Nelson): Minneapolis, MN, June 7, 1958.

PRINCE, WILLIAM: Nicholas, NY, Jan. 26, 1913. Cornell U.

PRINCIPAL, VICTORIA: Fukuoka. Japan, Jan. 3, 1945. Dade Jr. Col.

PROCHNOW, JURGEN: Germany, 1941.

PROSKY, ROBERT: Philadelphia, PA, Dec. 13, 1930.

PROVAL, DAVID: Brooklyn, NY, 1943.

PROVINE, DOROTHY: Deadwood, SD, Jan. 20, 1937. U. Wash.

PROWSE, JULIET: Bombay, India, Sept. 25, 1936.

PRYCE, JONATHAN: Wales, UK, June 1, 1947, RADA.

PRYOR, RICHARD: Peoria, IL, Dec. 1, 1940.

PULLMAN, BILL: Delphi, NY, 1954, SUNY/Oneonta, UMass.

PURCELL, LEE: Cherry Point, NC, June 15, 1947. Stephens.

| Rick Rossovich | Kim Stanley | John Stockwell | Connie Stevens | James Tolkan | Victoria Tennant |

PURDOM, EDMUND: Welwyn Garden City, Eng., Dec. 19, 1924. St. Ignatius College.

PYLE, DENVER: Bethune, CO, May 11, 1920.

QUAID, DENNIS: Houston, TX, Apr. 9, 1954.

QUAID, RANDY: Houston, TX, Oct. 1, 1950. UHouston.

QUINLAN, KATHLEEN: Mill Valley, CA, Nov. 19, 1954.

QUINN, AIDAN: Chicago, IL, Mar. 8, 1959.

QUINN, ANTHONY: Chihuahua, Mex., Apr. 21, 1915.

RAFFERTY, FRANCES: Sioux City, IA, June 16, 1922. UCLA.

RAFFIN, DEBORAH: Los Angeles, Mar. 13, 1953. Valley Col.

RAGSDALE, WILLIAM: El Dorado, AK, Jan. 19, 1961. Hendrix Col.

RAINER, LUISE: Vienna, Aust., Jan. 12, 1910.

RALSTON, VERA: (Vera Helena Hruba): Prague, Czech., July 12, 1919.

RAMPLING, CHARLOTTE: Surmer, Eng., Feb. 5, 1946. U. Madrid.

RAMSEY, LOGAN: Long Beach, CA, Mar. 21, 1921. St. Joseph.

RANDALL, TONY (Leonard Rosenberg): Tulsa, OK, Feb. 26, 1920. Northwestern U.

RANDELL, RON: Sydney, Australia, Oct. 8, 1920. St. Mary's Col.

RASCHE, DAVID: St. Louis, MO, Aug. 7, 1944.

RAYE, MARTHA (Margie Yvonne Reed): Butte, MT, Aug. 27, 1916.

RAYMOND, GENE (Raymond Guion): NYC, Aug. 13, 1908.

REAGAN, RONALD: Tampico, IL, Feb. 6, 1911. Eureka College.

REASON, REX: Berlin, Ger., Nov. 30, 1928. Pasadena Playhouse.

REDDY, HELEN: Australia, Oct. 25, 1942.

REDFORD, ROBERT: Santa Monica, CA, Aug. 18, 1937. AADA.

REDGRAVE, CORIN: London, July 16, 1939.

REDGRAVE, LYNN: London, Mar. 8, 1943.

REDGRAVE, VANESSA: London, Jan. 30, 1937.

REDMAN, JOYCE: County Mayo, Ire., 1919. RADA.

REED, OLIVER: Wimbledon, Eng., Feb. 13, 1938.

REED, PAMELA: Tacoma, WA, Apr. 2, 1949.

REEMS, HARRY (Herbert Streicher): Bronx, NY, 1947. U. Pittsburgh.

REEVE, CHRISTOPHER: NYC, Sept. 25, 1952. Cornell, Juilliard.

REEVES, KEANU: Beiruit, Lebanon, Sept. 2, 1964.

REEVES, STEVE: Glasgow, MT, Jan. 21, 1926.

REGEHR, DUNCAN: Lethbridge, Can., 1954.

REID, ELLIOTT: NYC, Jan. 16, 1920.

REID, KATE: London, Nov. 4, 1930.

REINER, CARL: NYC, Mar. 20, 1922. Georgetown.

REINER, ROB: NYC, Mar. 6, 1945. UCLA.

REINHOLD, JUDGE (Edward Ernest, Jr.): Wilmington, DE, 1956. NCSchool of Arts.

REINKING, ANN: Seattle, WA, Nov. 10, 1949.

REISER, PAUL: NYC, Mar. 30, 1957.

REMAR, JAMES: Boston, MA, Dec. 31, 1953. Neighborhood Playhouse.

RETTIG, TOMMY: Jackson Heights, NY, Dec. 10, 1941.

REVILL, CLIVE: Wellington, NZ, Apr. 18, 1930.

REY, ANTONIA: Havana, Cuba, Oct. 12, 1927.

REY, FERNANDO: La Coruna, Spain, Sept. 20, 1917.

REYNOLDS, BURT: Waycross, GA, Feb. 11, 1935. Fla. State U.

REYNOLDS, DEBBIE (Mary Frances Reynolds): El Paso, TX, Apr. 1, 1932.

REYNOLDS, MARJORIE: Buhl, ID, Aug. 12, 1921.

RHOADES, BARBARA: Poughkeepsie, NY, 1947.

RICHARDS, JEFF (Richard Mansfield Taylor): Portland, OR, Nov. 1. USC.

RICHARDSON, LEE: Chicago, Sept. 11, 1926.

RICHARDSON, NATASHA: London, May 11, 1963.

RICKLES, DON: NYC, May 8, 1926. AADA.

RICKMAN, ALAN: Hammersmith, Eng., 1946.

RIEGERT, PETER: NYC, Apr. 11, 1947. U Buffalo.

RIGG, DIANA: Doncaster, Eng., July 20, 1938. RADA.

RINGWALD, MOLLY: Rosewood, CA. Feb. 16, 1968.

RITTER, JOHN: Burbank, CA, Sept. 17, 1948. U.S. Cal.

RIVERS, JOAN (Molinsky): Brooklyn, NY, June 8, 1933.

ROBARDS, JASON: Chicago, July 26, 1922. AADA.

ROBBINS, TIM: NYC, Oct. 16, 1958. UCLA.

ROBERTS, ERIC: Biloxi, MS, Apr. 18, 1956. RADA.

ROBERTS, JULIA: Atlanta, GA, Oct. 28, 1967.

ROBERTS, RALPH: Salisbury, NC, Aug. 17, 1922. UNC.

ROBERTS, TANYA (Leigh): NYC, 1955.

ROBERTS, TONY: NYC, Oct. 22, 1939. Northwestern U.

ROBERTSON, CLIFF: La Jolla, CA, Sept. 9, 1925. Antioch Col.

ROBERTSON, DALE: Oklahoma City, July 14, 1923.

ROBINSON, CHRIS: West Palm Beach, FL, Nov. 5, 1938. LACC.

ROBINSON, JAY: NYC, Apr. 14, 1930.

ROBINSON, ROGER: Seattle, WA, May 2, 1941. USC.

ROCHEFORT, JEAN: Paris, 1930.

ROCK-SAVAGE, STEVEN: Melville, LA, Dec. 14, 1958. LSU.

ROGERS, CHARLES "BUDDY": Olathe, KS, Aug. 13, 1904. U. Kan.

ROGERS, GINGER (Virginia Katherine McMath): Independence, MO, July 16, 1911.

ROGERS, MIMI: Coral Gables, FL, Jan. 27, 1956.

ROGERS, ROY (Leonard Slye): Cincinnati, Nov. 5, 1912.

ROGERS, WAYNE: Birmingham, AL, Apr. 7, 1933. Princeton.

ROLAND, GILBERT (Luis Antonio Damaso De Alonso): Juarez, Mex., Dec. 11, 1905.

ROLLE, ESTHER: Pompano Beach, FL, Nov. 8, 1922.

ROLLINS, HOWARD E., JR.: Baltimore, MD. Oct. 17, 1950.

ROMAN, RUTH: Boston, Dec. 23, 1922. Bishop Lee Dramatic School.

ROMANCE, VIVIANE (Pauline Ronacher Ortmanns): Vienna, Aust., 1912.

ROMERO, CESAR: NYC, Feb. 15, 1907. Collegiate School.

RONSTADT, LINDA: Tucson, AZ, July 15, 1946.

ROOKER, MICHAEL: Jasper, AL, 1955.

ROONEY, MICKEY (Joe Yule, Jr.): Brooklyn, Sept. 23, 1920.

ROSE, REVA: Chicago, IL, July 30, 1940. Goodman.

ROSS, DIANA: Detroit, MI, Mar. 26, 1944.

ROSS, JUSTIN: Brooklyn, NY, Dec. 15, 1954.

ROSS, KATHARINE: Hollywood, Jan. 29, 1943. Santa Rosa Col.

ROSSELLINI, ISABELLA: Rome, June 18, 1952.

ROSSOVICH, RICK: Palo Alto, CA, Aug. 28, 1957.

ROUNDTREE, RICHARD: New Rochelle, NY, Sept. 7, 1942. Southern Ill.

ROURKE, MICKEY: Schenectady, NY, 1956.

ROWE, NICHOLAS: London, Nov. 22, 1966, Eton.

ROWLANDS, GENA: Cambria, WI, June 19, 1934.

RUBIN, ANDREW: New Bedford, MA, June 22, 1946. AADA.

RUBINSTEIN, JOHN: Los Angeles, CA, Dec. 8, 1946. UCLA.

RUBINSTEIN, ZELDA: Pittsburgh, PA.

RUCKER, BO: Tampa, FL, Aug. 17, 1948.

RUDD, PAUL: Boston, MA, May 15, 1940.

RULE, JANICE: Cincinnati, OH, Aug. 15, 1931.

RUPERT, MICHAEL: Denver, CO, Oct. 23, 1951. Pasadena Playhouse.

RUSH, BARBARA: Denver, CO, Jan. 4, 1929. U. Calif.

RUSSELL, JANE: Bemidji, MI, June 21, 1921. Max Reinhardt School.

RUSSELL, KURT: Springfield, MA, Mar. 17, 1951.

RUSSELL, THERESA: San Diego, CA, Mar. 20, 1957.

RUSSO, JAMES: NYC, Apr. 23, 1953.

RUTHERFORD, ANN: Toronto, Can., Nov. 2, 1920.

RUYMEN, AYN: Brooklyn, July 18, 1947. HB Studio.

RYAN, MEG: Fairfield, CT, Nov. 19, 1961. NYU.

RYAN, TIM (Meineslschmidt): Staten Island, NY, 1958. Rutgers U.

RYDER, WINONA: Winona, MN, Oct. 29, 1971.

SACCHI, ROBERT: Bronx, NY, 1941. NYU.

SAGEBRECHT, MARIANNE: Starnberg, Bavaria, 1945.

SAINT, EVA MARIE: Newark, NJ, July 4, 1924. Bowling Green State U.

ST. JAMES, SUSAN (Suzie Jane Miller): Los Angeles, Aug. 14, 1946. Conn. Col.

ST. JOHN, BETTA: Hawthorne, CA, Nov. 26, 1929.

ST. JOHN, JILL (Jill Oppenheim): Los Angeles, Aug. 19, 1940.

SALA, JOHN: Los Angeles, CA, Oct. 5, 1962.

SALDANA, THERESA: Brooklyn, NY, 1955.

SALINGER, MATT: Windsor, VT, Feb. 13, 1960. Princeton, Columbia.

SALT, JENNIFER: Los Angeles, Sept. 4, 1944. Sarah Lawrence Col.

SAMMS, EMMA: London, Aug. 28, 1960.

SAN GIACOMO, LAURA: NJ, 1962.

SANDERS, JAY O.: Austin, TX, Apr. 16, 1953.

SANDS, JULIAN: Yorkshire, Eng., 1958.

SANDS, TOMMY: Chicago, Aug. 27, 1937.

SAN JUAN, OLGA: NYC, Mar. 16, 1927.

SARA, MIA: Brooklyn, NY, 1968.

SARANDON, CHRIS: Beckley, WV, July 24, 1942. U. WVa., Catholic U.

SARANDON, SUSAN (Tomalin): NYC, Oct. 4, 1946. Catholic U.

SARGENT, DICK (Richard Cox): Carmel, CA, 1933. Stanford.

SARRAZIN, MICHAEL: Quebec City, Can., May 22, 1940.

SAVAGE, FRED: Highland Park, IL, July 9, 1976.

SAVAGE, JOHN (Youngs): Long Island, NY, Aug. 25, 1949. AADA.

SAVALAS, TELLY (Aristotle): Garden City, NY, Jan. 21, 1925. Columbia.

SAVIOLA, CAMILLE: Bronx, NY, July 16, 1950.

SAVOY, TERESA ANN: London, July 18, 1955.

SAXON, JOHN (Carmen Orrico): Brooklyn, Aug. 5, 1935.

SBARGE, RAPHAEL: NYC, Feb. 12, 1964.

SCALIA, JACK: Brooklyn, NY, 1951.

SCARPELLI, GLEN: Staten Island, NY, July 1966.

SCARWID, DIANA: Savannah, GA. AADA. Pace U.

SCHEIDER, ROY: Orange, NJ, Nov. 10, 1932. Franklin-Marshall.

SCHEINE, RAYNOR: Emporia, VA, Nov. 10. VaCommonwealthU.

SCHELL, MARIA: Vienna, Jan. 15, 1926.

SCHELL, MAXIMILIAN: Vienna, Dec. 8, 1930.

SCHLATTER, CHARLIE: NYC, 1967. Ithaca Col.

SCHNEIDER, JOHN: Mt. Kisco, NY, Apr. 8, 1960.

SCHNEIDER, MARIA: Paris, Mar. 27, 1952.

SCHRODER, RICK: Staten Island, NY, Apr. 13, 1970.

SCHUCK, JOHN: Boston, MA, Feb. 4, 1940.

SCHWARZENEGGER, ARNOLD: Austria, July 30, 1947.

SCHYGULLA, HANNA: Katlowitz, Poland, 1943.

SCIORRA, ANNABELLA: NYC, 1964.

SCOFIELD, PAUL: Hurstpierpoint, Eng., Jan. 21,1922. London Mask Theatre School.

SCOLARI, PETER: Scarsdale, NY, Sept. 12, 1956. NYCC.

SCOTT, CAMPBELL: NYC, July 19, 1962. Lawrence.

SCOTT, DEBRALEE: Elizabeth, NJ, Apr. 2.

SCOTT, GEORGE C.: Wise, VA, Oct. 18, 1927. U. Mo.

SCOTT, GORDON (Gordon M. Werschkul): Portland, OR, Aug. 3, 1927. Oregon U.

SCOTT, LIZABETH (Emma Matso): Scranton, PA, Sept. 29, 1922.

SCOTT, MARTHA: Jamesport, MO, Sept. 22, 1914. U. Mich.

SCOTT-TAYLOR, JONATHAN: Brazil, 1962.

SEAGAL, STEVEN: Detroit, MI, Apr. 10, 1951.

SEARS, HEATHER: London, Sept. 28, 1935.

SECOMBE, HARRY: Swansea, Wales, Sept. 8, 1921.

SEGAL, GEORGE: NYC, Feb. 13, 1934. Columbia.

SELBY, DAVID: Morganstown, WV, Feb. 5, 1941. UWV.

SELLARS, ELIZABETH: Glasgow, Scot., May 6, 1923.

SELLECK, TOM: Detroit, MI, Jan. 29, 1945. USCal.

SELWART, TONIO: Watenberg, Ger., June 9, 1906. Munich U.

SERNAS, JACQUES: Lithuania, July 30, 1925.

SERRAULT, MICHEL: Brunoy, France. 1928. Paris Consv.

SETH, ROSHAN: New Delhi, India. 1942.

SEYMOUR, JANE (Joyce Frankenberg): Hillingdon, Eng., Feb. 15, 1952.

SHARIF, OMAR (Michel Shalhoub); Alexandria, Egypt, Apr. 10, 1932. Victoria Col.

SHARKEY, RAY: Brooklyn, Nov. 14, 1952. HB Studio.

SHATNER, WILLIAM: Montreal, Can., Mar. 22, 1931. McGill U.

SHAVER, HELEN: St. Thomas, Ontario, Can., Feb. 24, 1951.

SHAW, SEBASTIAN: Holt, Eng., May, 1905. Gresham School.

SHAW, STAN: Chicago, IL, 1952.

SHAWN, WALLACE: NYC, Nov. 12, 1943. Harvard.

SHEA, JOHN: North Conway, NH, Apr. 14, 1949. Bates, Yale.

SHEARER, HARRY: Los Angeles, Dec. 23, 1943. UCLA.

SHEARER, MOIRA: Dunfermline, Scot., Jan. 17, 1926. London Theatre School.

SHEEDY, ALLY: NYC, June 13, 1962. USC.

SHEEN, CHARLIE (Carlos Irwin Estevez): Santa Monica, CA, Sept. 3, 1965.

SHEEN, MARTIN (Ramon Estevez): Dayton, OH, Aug. 3, 1940.

SHEFFIELD, JOHN: Pasadena, CA, Apr.11, 1931. UCLA.

SHEPARD, SAM (Rogers): Ft. Sheridan, IL, Nov. 5, 1943.

SHEPHERD, CYBILL: Memphis, TN, Feb. 18, 1950. Hunter, NYU.

SHIELDS, BROOKE: NYC, May 31, 1965.

SHIRE, TALIA: Lake Success, NY, Apr. 25, 1946. Yale.

SHIRLEY, ANNE (Dawn Evelyn Paris): NYC, Apr. 17, 1918.

SHORE, DINAH (Frances Rose Shore): Winchester, TN, Mar. 1, 1917. Vanderbilt U.

SHORT, MARTIN: Toronto, Can., Mar. 26, 1950. McMasterU.

SHOWALTER, MAX (formerly Casey Adams): Caldwell, KS, June 2, 1917. Pasadena Playhouse.

SHULL, RICHARD B.: Evanston, IL, Feb. 24, 1929.

SIDNEY, SYLVIA: NYC, Aug. 8, 1910. Theatre Guild School.

SIEMASZKO, CASEY: Chicago, IL, March 17, 1961.

SIKKING, JAMES B.: Los Angeles, Mar. 5, 1934.

SILVER, RON: NYC, July 2, 1946. SUNY.

SILVERMAN, JONATHAN: Los Angeles, CA, Aug. 5, 1966. USCal.

SIMMONS, JEAN: London, Jan. 31, 1929. Aida Foster School.

SIMON, PAUL: Newark. NJ, Nov. 5, 1942.

SIMON, SIMONE: Marseilles, France, Apr. 23, 1910.

SIMPSON, O.J. (Orenthal James): San Francisco, CA, July 9, 1947. UCLA.

SINATRA, FRANK: Hoboken, NJ, Dec. 12, 1915.

SINCLAIR, JOHN (Gianluigi Loffredo): Rome, Italy, 1946.

SINDEN, DONALD: Plymouth, Eng., Oct. 9, 1923. Webber-Douglas.

SINGER, LORI: Corpus Christi, TX, May 6, 1962. Juilliard.

SKALA, LILIA: Vienna. U. Dresden.

SKELTON, RED (Richard): Vincennes, IN, July 18, 1910.

SKERRITT, TOM: Detroit, MI, Aug. 25, 1933. Wayne State U.

SKYE, IONE (Leitch): London, Eng., Sept. 4, 1971.

SLATER, CHRISTIAN: NYC, Aug. 18, 1969.

SLATER, HELEN: NYC, Dec. 15, 1965.

SMIRNOFF, YAKOV (Yakov Pokhis): Odessa, USSR, Jan. 24. 1951.

SMITH, ALEXIS: Penticton, Can., June 8, 1921. LACC.

SMITH, CHARLES MARTIN: Los Angeles, CA, Oct. 30, 1953. CalState U.

SMITH, JACLYN: Houston, TX, Oct. 26, 1947.

SMITH, JOHN (Robert E. Van Orden): Los Angeles, Mar. 6, 1931. UCLA.

SMITH, KURTWOOD: New Lisbon, WI, Jul. 3, 1942.

SMITH, LEWIS: Chattanooga, TN, 1958. Actors Studio.

SMITH, LOIS: Topeka, KS, Nov. 3, 1930. U. Wash.

SMITH, MAGGIE: Ilford, Eng., Dec. 28, 1934.

SMITH, ROGER: South Gate, CA, Dec. 18, 1932. U. Ariz.

SMITHERS, WILLIAM: Richmond, VA, July 10, 1927. Catholic U.

SMITS, JIMMY: Brooklyn, July 9, 1955. Cornell U.

SNIPES, WESLEY: NYC, July 31, 1963. SUNY/Purchase.

SNODGRESS, CARRIE: Chicago, Oct. 27, 1946. UNI.

SOLOMON, BRUCE: NYC, 1944. U. Miami, Wayne State U.

SOMERS, SUZANNE (Mahoney): San Bruno, CA, Oct. 16, 1946. Lone Mt. Col.

SOMMER, ELKE (Schletz): Berlin, Ger., Nov. 5, 1940.

SOMMER, JOSEF: Greifswald, Ger., June 26, 1934.

SORDI, ALBERTO: Rome, Italy, June 15, 1919.

SORVINO, PAUL: NYC, 1939. AMDA.

SOTHERN, ANN (Harriet Lake): Chicago, IL, Aug. 28, 1943.

SOTO, TALISA: Brooklyn, 1968.

SOUL, DAVID: Chicago, IL, Aug. 28, 1943.

SPACEK, SISSY: Quitman, TX, Dec. 25, 1949. Actors Studio.

SPACEY, KEVIN: So. Orange, NJ, July 26, 1959. Juilliard.

SPADER, JAMES: MA, Feb. 7, 1960.

SPANO, VINCENT: Brooklyn, NY, Oct. 18, 1962.

SPENSER, JEREMY: Ceylon, 1937.

SPRINGFIELD, RICK (Richard Spring Thorpe): Sydney, Aust., Aug. 23, 1949.

STACK, ROBERT: Los Angeles, Jan. 13, 1919. USC.

STADLEN, LEWIS J.: Brooklyn, Mar. 7, 1947. Neighborhood Playhouse.

STALLONE, FRANK: NYC, July 30, 1950.

STALLONE, SYLVESTER: NYC, July 6, 1946. U. Miami.

STAMP, TERENCE: London, July 23, 1939.

STANDER, LIONEL: NYC, Jan. 11, 1908. UNC.

STANG, ARNOLD: Chelsea, MA, Sept. 28, 1925.

STANLEY, KIM (Patricia Reid): Tularosa, NM, Feb. 11, 1925. U. Tex.

STANTON, HARRY DEAN: Lexington, KY, July 14, 1926.

STAPLETON, JEAN: NYC, Jan. 19, 1923.

STAPLETON, MAUREEN: Troy, NY, June 21, 1925.

STARR, RINGO (Richard Starkey): Liverpool, England, July 7, 1940.

STEEL, ANTHONY: London, May 21, 1920. Cambridge.

STEELE, TOMMY: London, Dec. 17, 1936.

STEENBURGEN, MARY: Newport, AR, 1953. Neighborhood Playhouse.

STEIGER, ROD: Westhampton, NY, Apr. 14, 1925.

STERLING, JAN (Jane Sterling Adriance): NYC, Apr. 3, 1923. Fay Compton School.

STERLING, ROBERT (William Sterling Hart): Newcastle, PA, Nov. 13, 1917. U.Pittsburgh.

STERN, DANIEL: Bethesda, MD, Aug. 28, 1957.

STERNHAGEN, FRANCES: Washington, DC, Jan. 13, 1932.

STEVENS, ANDREW: Memphis, TN, June 10, 1955.

STEVENS, CONNIE (Concetta Ann Ingolia): Brooklyn, Aug. 8, 1938. Hollywood Professional School.

STEVENS, FISHER: Chicago, IL, Nov. 27, 1963. NYU.

STEVENS, KAYE (Catherine): Pittsburgh, July 21, 1933.

STEVENS, MARK (Richard): Cleveland, OH, Dec. 13, 1920.

STEVENS, STELLA (Estelle Eggleston): Hot Coffee, MS, Oct. 1, 1936.

STEVENSON, PARKER: CT, June 4, 1953. Princeton.

STEWART, ALEXANDIA: Montreal, Can., June 10, 1939. Louvre.

STEWART, ELAINE: Montclair, NJ, May 31, 1929

STEWART, JAMES: Indiana, PA, May 20, 1908. Princeton.

STEWART, MARTHA (Martha Haworth): Bardwell, KY, Oct. 7, 1922.

STEWART, PATRICK: Mirfield, Eng., July 13, 1940.

STIERS, DAVID OGDEN: Peoria, IL, Oct. 31, 1942.

STILLER, JERRY: NYC, June 8, 1931.

STIMSON, SARA: Helotes, TX, 1973.

STING (Gordon Matthew Sumner): Wallsend, Eng., Oct. 2, 1951.

STOCKWELL, DEAN: Hollywood, Mar. 5, 1935.

STOCKWELL, JOHN (John Samuels IV): Galveston, Texas, March 25, 1961. Harvard.

STOLER, SHIRLEY: Brooklyn, NY, Mar. 30, 1929.

STOLTZ, ERIC: California, 1961. USC.

STONE, DEE WALLACE (Deanna Bowers): Kansas City, MO, Dec. 14, 1948. UKS.

STORM, GALE (Josephine Cottle): Bloomington, TX, Apr. 5, 1922.

STRAIGHT, BEATRICE: Old Westbury, NY, Aug. 2, 1916. Dartington Hall.

STRASBERG, SUSAN: NYC, May 22, 1938.

STRASSMAN, MARCIA: New Jersey, Apr. 28, 1948.

STRATHAIRN, DAVID: San Francisco, 1949.

STRAUSS, PETER: NYC, Feb. 20, 1947.

STREEP, MERYL (Mary Louise): Summit,.NJ, June 22, 1949. Vassar, Yale.

STREISAND, BARBRA: Brooklyn, Apr. 24, 1942.

STRITCH, ELAINE: Detroit, MI, Feb. 2, 1925. Drama Workshop.

STRODE, WOODY: Los Angeles, 1914.

STROUD, DON: Honolulu, HI, Sept. 1, 1937.

STRUTHERS, SALLY: Portland, OR, July 28, 1948. Pasadena Playhouse.

SULLIVAN, BARRY (Patrick Barry) NYC, Aug. 29, 1912. NYU.

SUMMER, DONNA (LaDonna Gaines): Boston, MA, Dec. 31, 1948.

SUTHERLAND, DONALD: St. John, New Brunswick, Can., July 17, 1935. U. Toronto.

SUTHERLAND, KIEFER: Los Angeles, CA, Dec. 18, 1966.

SVENSON, BO: Goreborg, Swed., Feb. 1941. UCLA.

SWAYZE, PATRICK: Houston, TX, Aug. 18, 1952.

SWEENEY, D. B. (Daniel Bernard): Shoreham, NY, 1961.

SWINBURNE, NORA: Bath, Eng., July 24, 1902. RADA.

SWIT, LORETTA: Passaic, NJ, Nov. 4, 1937, AADA.

SYLVESTER, WILLIAM: Oakland, CA, Jan. 31, 1922. RADA.

SYMONDS, ROBERT: Bistow, AK, Dec. 1, 1926. TexU.

SYMS, SYLVIA: London, June 1, 1934. Convent School.

SZARABAJKA, KEITH: Oak Park, IL, Dec. 2, 1952. UChicago.

T, MR. (Lawrence Tero): Chicago, May 21, 1952

TABORI, KRISTOFFER (Siegel): Los Angeles, Aug. 4, 1952.

TAKEI, GEORGE: Los Angeles, CA, Apr. 20, 1939. UCLA.

TALBOT, LYLE (Lysle Hollywood): Pittsburgh, Feb. 8, 1904.

TALBOT, NITA: NYC, Aug. 8, 1930. Irvine Studio School.

TAMBLYN, RUSS: Los Angeles, Dec. 30, 1934.

TANDY, JESSICA: London, June 7, 1909. Dame Owens' School.

TAYLOR, DON: Freeport, PA, Dec. 13, 1920. Penn State U.

TAYLOR, ELIZABETH: London, Feb. 27, 1932. Byron House School.

TAYLOR, RENEE: NYC, Mar. 19, 1935.

TAYLOR, ROD (Robert): Sydney, Aust., Jan. 11, 1929.

TAYLOR-YOUNG, LEIGH: Washington, DC, Jan. 25, 1945. Northwestern.

TEAGUE, ANTHONY SCOOTER: Jacksboro, TX, Jan. 4, 1940.

TEAGUE, MARSHALL: Newport, TN.

TEEFY, MAUREEN: Minneapolis, MN, 1954, Juilliard.

TEMPLE, SHIRLEY: Santa Monica, CA, Apr. 23, 1927.

TENNANT, VICTORIA: London, Eng., Sept. 30, 1950.

TERZIEFF, LAURENT: Paris, June 25, 1935.

TEWES, LAUREN: Pennsylvania, 1954.

THACKER, RUSS: Washington, DC, June 23, 1946. Montgomery Col.

THAXTER, PHYLLIS: Portland, ME, Nov. 20, 1921. St. Genevieve.

THELEN, JODI: St. Cloud, MN, 1963.

THOMAS, HENRY: San Antonio, TX, 1971.

THOMAS, MARLO (Margaret): Detroit, Nov. 21, 1938. USC.

THOMAS, PHILIP MICHAEL: Columbus, OH, May 26, 1949. Oakwood Col.

THOMAS, RICHARD: NYC, June 13, 1951. Columbia.

THOMPSON, JACK (John Payne): Sydney, Aus., 1940. U. Brisbane.

THOMPSON, LEA: Rochester, MN, May 31, 1961.

THOMPSON, REX: NYC, Dec. 14, 1942.

THOMPSON, SADA: Des Moines, IA, Sept. 27, 1929. Carnegie Tech.

THOMSON, GORDON: Ottawa, Can., 1945.

THORSON, LINDA: Toronto, Can., June 18, 1947. RADA

THULIN, INGRID: So11eftea, Sweden, Jan. 27, 1929. Royal Drama Theatre.

TICOTIN, RACHEL: Bronx, NY, Nov. 1, 1958.

TIERNEY, LAWRENCE: Brooklyn, Mar. 15, 1919. Manhattan College.

TIFFIN, PAMELA (Wonso): Oklahoma City, OK, Oct. 13, 1942.

TIGHE, KEVIN: Los Angeles, Aug. 13, 1944.

TILLY, MEG: Texada, Can., 1960.

TOBOLOWSKY, STEPHEN: Dallas, Tx, May 30, 1951. So. Methodist U.

TODD, ANN: Hartford, Eng., Jan. 24, 1909

TODD, BEVERLY: Chicago, IL, July 1, 1946.

TODD, RICHARD: Dublin, Ire., June 11, 1919. Shrewsbury School.

TOLKAN, JAMES: Calumet, MI, June 20, 1931.

TOLO, MARILU: Rome, Italy, 1944.

TOMEI, MARISA: Brooklyn, Dec. 4, 1964. NYU.

TOMLIN, LILY: Detroit, MI, Sept. 1, 1939. Wayne State U.

TOPOL (Chaim Topol): Tel-Aviv, Israel, Sept. 9, 1935.

TORN, RIP: Temple, TX, Feb. 6, 1931. U.Tex.

TORRES, LIZ: NYC, 1947. NYU.

TOTTER, AUDREY: Joliet, IL, Dec. 20, 1918.

TOWSEND, ROBERT: Chicago, Feb. 6, 1957.

TRAVANTI, DANIEL J.: Kenosha, WI, Mar. 7, 1940.

TRAVERS, BILL: Newcastle-on-Tyne, Eng., Jan. 3, 1922.

TRAVIS, RICHARD (William Justice): Carlsbad, NM, Apr. 17, 1913.

TRAVOLTA, JOEY: Englewood, NJ, 1952.

TRAVOLTA, JOHN: Englewood, NJ, Feb.18, 1954

TREMAYNE, LES: London, Apr. 16, 1913. Northwestern, Columbia, UCLA.

TREVOR, CLAIRE (Wemlinger): NYC, March 8, 1909.

TRINTIGNANT, JEAN-LOUIS: Pont-St. Esprit, France, Dec. 11, 1930. Dullin-Balachova Drama School.

TSOPEI, CORINNA: Athens, Greece, June 21, 1944.

TUBB, BARRY: Snyder, TX, 1963. AmConsv.Th.

TUCKER, MICHAEL: Baltimore, MD, Feb. 6, 1944.

TUNE, TOMMY: Wichita Falls, TX, Feb. 28, 1939.

TURNER, KATHLEEN: Springfield, MO, June 19, 1954. UMd.

TURNER, LANA (Julia Jean Mildred Frances Turner): Wallace, ID, Feb. 8, 1921.

TURNER, TINA: (Anna Mae Bullock) Nutbush, TN, Nov. 26, 1938.

TURTURRO, JOHN: Brooklyn, Feb. 28, 1957. Yale.

TUSHINGHAM, RITA: Liverpool, Eng., Mar. 14, 1940.

TUTIN, DOROTHY: London, Apr. 8, 1930.

TWIGGY (Lesley Hornby): London, Sept. 19, 1949.

TWOMEY, ANNE: Boston, MA, June 7, 1951. Temple U.

TYLER, BEVERLY (Beverly Jean Saul): Scranton, PA, July 5, 1928.

TYRRELL, SUSAN: San Francisco, 1946.

TYSON, CATHY: Liverpool, Eng., 1966. Royal Shake. Co.

TYSON, CICELY: NYC, Dec. 19, 1933. NYU.

UGGAMS, LESLIE: NYC, May 25, 1943. Juilliard.

ULLMAN, TRACEY: Slough, Eng., 1960.

ULLMANN, LIV: Tokyo, Dec. 10, 1938. Webber-Douglas Acad.

UMEKI, MIYOSHI: Otaru, Hokaido, Japan, 1929.

UNDERWOOD, BLAIR: Tacoma, WA, Aug. 25, 1964. Carnegie-Mellon U.

URICH, ROBERT: Toronto, Can., Dec. 19, 1946.

USTINOV, PETER: London, Apr. 16, 1921. Westminster School.

VACCARO, BRENDA: Brooklyn, Nov. 18, 1939. Neighborhood Playhouse.

VALANDREY, CHARLOTTE: (Anne-Charlone Pascal) Paris, 1968.

VALLI, ALIDA: Pola, Italy, May 31, 1921. Academy of Drama.

VALLONE, RAF: Riogio, Italy, Feb. 17, 1916. Turin U.

VAN ARK, JOAN: NYC, June 16, 1943. Yale.

VAN DE VEN, MONIQUE: Holland, 1957.

VAN DEVERE, TRISH (Patricia Dressel): Englewood Cliffs, NJ, Mar. 9, 1945. Ohio Wesleyan.

VAN DOREN, MAMIE (Joan Lucile Olander): Rowena SD, Feb. 6, 1933.

VAN DYKE, DICK: West Plains, MO, Dec. 13, 1925.

Marlo Thomas	Jean-Louis Trintignant	Lea Thompson	Barry Tubb	Rachel Ticotin	James Victor

VAN FLEET, JO: Oakland, CA, Dec. 30, 1919.

VAN DAMME, JEAN CLAUDE: Brussels, Belgium, 1961.

VANITY (Denise Mathews): Niagara, Ont., Can, 1963.

VAN PALLANDT, NINA: Copenhagen, Denmark, July 15, 1932.

VAN PATTEN, DICK: NYC, Dec. 9, 1928.

VAN PATTEN, JOYCE: NYC, Mar. 9, 1934.

VAN PEEBLES, MARIO: NYC, Jan. 15, 1958. Columbia U.

VANCE, COURTNEY B.: Detroit, MI, Mar. 12, 1960.

VARNEY, JIM: Lexington, KY, June 15, 1949.

VAUGHN, ROBERT: NYC, Nov. 22, 1932. USC.

VEGA, ISELA: Mexico, 1940.

VENNERA, CHICK: Herkimer, NY, Mar. 27, 1952. Pasadena Playhouse.

VENORA, DIANE: Hartford, CT, 1952. Juilliard.

VENUTA, BENAY: San Francisco, Jan. 27, 1911.

VERDON, GWEN: Culver City, CA, Jan.13, 1925.

VERNON, JOHN: Montreal, Can., Feb. 24, 1932.

VEREEN, BEN: Miami, FL, Oct. 10, 1946.

VICTOR, JAMES (Lincoln Rafael Peralta Diaz): Santiago, D.R., July 27, 1939. Haaren HS/NYC.

VILLECHAIZE, HERVE: Paris, Apr 23, 1943.

VINCENT, JAN-MICHAEL: Denver, CO, July 15, 1944. Ventura.

VIOLET, ULTRA (Isabelle Collin-Dufresne): Grenoble, France.

VITALE, MILLY: Rome, Italy, July 16, 1938. Lycee Chateaubriand.

VOHS, JOAN: St. Albans, NY, July 30, 1931.

VOIGHT, JON: Yonkers, NY, Dec. 29, 1938. Catholic U.

VOLONTE, GIAN MARIA: Milan, Italy, Apr. 9, 1933.

VON DOHLEN, LENNY: Augusta, GA, Dec. 22, 1958. UTex.

VON SYDOW, MAX: Lund, Swed., July 10, 1929. Royal Drama Theatre.

WAGNER, LINDSAY: Los Angeles, June 22. 1949.

WAGNER, ROBERT: Detroit, Feb. 10, 1930.

WAHL, KEN: Chicago, IL, Feb. 14, 1953.

WAITE, GENEVIEVE: South Africa,1949.

WAITS, TOM: Pomona, CA, Dec. 7, 1949.

WALKEN, CHRISTOPHER: Astoria, NY, Mar. 31, 1943. Hofstra.

WALKER, CLINT: Hartfold, IL, May 30, 1927. USC.

WALLACH, ELI: Brooklyn, Dec. 7, 1915. CCNY, U. Tex.

WALLACH, ROBERTA: NYC, Aug. 2, 1955.

WALLIS, SHANI: London, Apr. 5, 1941.

WALSH, M. EMMET: Ogdensburg, NY, Mar. 22, 1935. Clarkson Col., AADA.

WALSTON, RAY: New Orleans, Nov. 22, 1917. Cleveland Playhouse.

WALTER, JESSICA: Brooklyn, Jan. 31, 1940. Neighborhood Playhouse.

WALTER, TRACEY: Jersey City, NJ, Nov. 25.

WALTERS, JULIE: London, Feb. 22, 1950.

WALTON, EMMA: London, Nov. 1962. Brown U.

WANAMAKER, SAM: Chicago, June 14, 1919. Drake.

WARD, BURT (Gervis): Los Angeles, July 6, 1945.

WARD, FRED: San Diego, CA, 1943.

WARD, RACHEL: London, 1957.

WARD, SIMON: London, Oct. 19, 1941.

WARDEN, JACK: Newark, NJ, Sept. 18, 1920.

WARNER, DAVID: Manchester, Eng., July 29, 1941. RADA.

WARREN, JENNIFER: NYC, Aug. 12, 1941. U. Wisc.

WARREN, LESLEY ANN: NYC, Aug. 16, 1946.

WARREN, MICHAEL: South Bend, IN, Mar. 5, 1946. UCLA.

WARRICK, RUTH: St. Joseph, MO, June 29, 1915. U. Mo.

WASHINGTON, DENZEL: Mt. Vernon, NY, Dec. 28, 1954. Fordham.

WASSON, CRAIG: Ontario, OR, Mar. 15, 1954. UOre.

WATERSTON, SAM: Cambridge, MA, Nov. 15, 1940. Yale.

WATLING,JACK: London, Jan. 13, 1923. Italia Conti School.

WAYANS, DAMON: NYC, 1960.

WAYANS, KEENEN IVORY: NYC, June 8, 1958. Tuskegee Inst.

WAYNE, DAVID (Wayne McKeehan): Travers City, MI, Jan. 30, 1914. Western Michigan State U.

WAYNE, PATRICK: Los Angeles, July 15, 1939. Loyola.

WEATHERS, CARL: New Orleans, LA, Jan. 14, 1948. Long Beach CC.

WEAVER, DENNIS: Joplin, MO, June 4, 1924. U. Okla.

WEAVER, FRITZ: Pittsburgh, PA, Jan. 19, 1926.

WEAVER, MARJORIE: Crossville, TN, Mar. 2, 1913. Indiana U.

WEAVER, SIGOURNEY (Susan): NYC, Oct. 8, 1949. Stanford, Yale.

WEDGEWORTH, ANN: Abilene, TX, Jan. 21, 1935. U. Tex.

WELCH, RAQUEL (Tejada): Chicago, IL, Sept. 5, 1940.

WELD, TUESDAY (Susan): NYC, Aug. 27, 1943. Hollywood Professional School.

WELDON, JOAN: San Francisco, Aug. 5, 1933. San Francisco Conservatory.

WELLER, PETER: Stevens Point, WI, June 24, 1947. AmThWing.

WELLES, GWEN: NYC, Mar. 4.

WENDT, GEORGE: Chicago, IL, Oct. 17, 1948.

WESLEY, BILLY: NYC, July 1966.

WEST, ADAM (William Anderson): Walla Walla, WA, Sept. 19, 1929.

WESTON, JACK (Morris Weinstein): Cleveland, OH, Aug. 21, 1924.

WHALEY, FRANK: Syracuse, NY, 1963. SUNY/Albany.

WHALLEY-KILMER, JOANNE: Manchester, Eng., Aug. 25, 1964.

WHEATON, WIL: Burbank, CA, July 29, 1972.

WHITAKER, FOREST: Longview, TX, July 15, 1961.

WHITAKER, JOHNNY: Van Nuys, CA, Dec. 13, 1959.

WHITE, BETTY: Oak Park, IL, Jan. 17, 1922.

| Tracey Walter | Meg Tilly | Fred Ward | Cicely Tyson | David Warner | Rachel Ward |

WHITE, CAROL: London, Apr. 1, 1944.

WHITE, CHARLES: Perth Amboy, NJ, Aug. 29, 1920. Rutgers U.

WHITE, JESSE: Buffalo, NY, Jan. 3, 1919.

WHITMAN, STUART: San Francisco, Feb. 1, 1929. CCLA.

WHITMORE, JAMES: White Plains, NY, Oct. 1, 1921. Yale.

WHITNEY, GRACE LEE: Detroit, MI, Apr. 1, 1930.

WHITTON, MARGARET: Philadelphia, PA, Nov, 30, 1950.

WIDDOES, KATHLEEN: Wilmington, DE, Mar. 21, 1939.

WIDMARK, RICHARD: Sunrise, MN, Dec. 26, 1914. Lake Forest.

WIEST, DIANNE: Kansas City, MO, Mar. 28, 1948. UMd.

WILBY. JAMES: Burma, Feb. 20, 1958.

WILCOX, COLIN: Highlands, NC, Feb. 4, 1937. U. Tenn.

WILDER, GENE (Jerome Silberman): Milwaukee, WI, June 11, 1935. UIowa.

WILLIAMS, BILLY DEE: NYC, Apr. 6, 1937.

WILLIAMS, CINDY: Van Nuys, CA, Aug. 22, 1947. KACC.

WILLIAMS, CLARENCE III: NYC, Aug. 21, 1939.

WILLIAMS, DICK A.: Chicago, IL, Aug. 9, 1938.

WILLIAMS, ESTHER: Los Angeles, Aug. 8, 1921.

WILLIAMS, JOBETH: Houston, TX, 1953. BrownU.

WILLIAMS, PAUL: Omaha, NE, Sept. 19, 1940.

WILLIAMS, ROBIN: Chicago, IL, July 21, 1951. Juilliard.

WILLIAMS, TREAT (Richard): Rowayton, CT, Dec. 1, 1951.

WILLIAMSON, FRED: Gary, IN, Mar. 5, 1938. Northwestern.

WILLIAMSON, NICOL: Hamilton, Scot., Sept. 14, 1938.

WILLIS, BRUCE: Penns Grove, NJ, Mar. 19, 1955.

WILLISON, WALTER: Monterey Park, CA, June 24, 1947.

WILSON, DEMOND: NYC, Oct. 13, 1946. Hunter Col.

WILSON, ELIZABETH: Grand Rapids, MI, Apr. 4, 1925.

WILSON, FLIP (Clerow Wilson): Jersey City, NJ, Dec. 8, 1933.

WILSON, LAMBERT: Paris, 1959.

WILSON, NANCY: Chillicothe, OH, Feb. 20, 1937.

WILSON, SCOTT: Atlanta, GA, 1942.

WINCOTT, JEFF: Toronto, Can., 1957.

WINDE, BEATRICE: Chicago, Jan. 6.

WINDOM, WILLIAM: NYC, Sept. 28, 1923. Williams Col.

WINDSOR, MARIE (Emily Marie Bertelson): Marysvale, UT, Dec. 11, 1924. Brigham Young U.

WINFIELD, PAUL: Los Angeles, May 22, 1940. UCLA.

WINFREY, OPRAH: Kosciusko, MS, Jan. 29, 1954. TnStateU.

WINGER, DEBRA: Cleveland, OH, May 17, 1955. Cal State.

WINKLER, HENRY: NYC, Oct. 30, 1945. Yale.

WINN, KITTY: Washingtohn, D.C., 1944. Boston U.

WINNINGHAM, MARE: Phoenix, AZ, May 6, 1959.

WINSLOW, MICHAEL: Spokane, WA, Sept. 6, 1960.

WINTER, ALEX: London, July 17, 1965. NYU.

WINTERS, JONATHAN: Dayton, OH, Nov. 11, 1925. Kenyon Col.

WINTERS, SHELLEY (Shirley Schrift): St. Louis, Aug. 18, 1922. Wayne U.

WITHERS, GOOGIE: Karachi, India, Mar. 12, 1917. Italia Conti.

WITHERS, JANE: Atlanta, GA, Apr. 12, 1926.

WONG, B.D.: San Francisco, Oct. 24,1962.

WONG, RUSSELL: Troy, NY, 1963. SantaMonica Col.

WOODARD, ALFRE: Tulsa, OK, Nov. 2, 1953. Boston U.

WOODLAWN, HOLLY (Harold Ajzenberg): Juana Diaz, PR, 1947.

WOODS, JAMES: Vernal, UT, Apr. 18, 1947. MIT.

WOODWARD, EDWARD: Croyden, Surrey, Eng., June 1, 1930.

WOODWARD, JOANNE: Thomasville, GA, Feb. 27, 1930. Neighborhood Playhouse.

WORONOV, MARY: Brooklyn, Dec. 8, 1946. Cornell.

WORTH, IRENE (Hattie Abrams): Nebraska, June 23, 1916. UCLA.

WRAY, FAY: Alberta, Can., Sept. 15, 1907.

WRIGHT, AMY: Chicago, Apr. 15, 1950.

WRIGHT, MAX: Detroit, MI, Aug. 2, 1943. WayneStateU.

WRIGHT, ROBIN: Texas, 1966.

WRIGHT, TERESA: NYC, Oct. 27, 1918.

WUHL, ROBERT: Union City, NJ, Oct. 9, 1951. UHouston.

WYATT, JANE: NYC, Aug. 10, 1910. Barnard College.

WYMAN, JANE (Sarah Jane Fulks): St. Joseph, MO, Jan. 4, 1914.

WYMORE, PATRICE: Miltonvale, KS, Dec. 17, 1926.

WYNN, MAY (Donna Lee Hickey): NYC, Jan. 8, 1930.

WYNTER, DANA (Dagmar): London, June 8. 1927. Rhodes U.

YORK, DICK: Fort Wayne, IN, Sept. 4, 1928. De Paul U.

YORK, MICHAEL: Fulmer, Eng., Mar. 27, 1942. Oxford.

YORK, SUSANNAH: London, Jan. 9, 1941. RADA.

YOUNG, ALAN (Angus): North Shield, Eng., Nov. 19, 1919.

YOUNG, BURT: Queens, NY, Apr. 30, 1940.

YOUNG, LORETTA (Gretchen): Salt Lake City, UT, Jan. 6, 1912. Immaculate Heart College.

YOUNG, ROBERT: Chicago, Feb. 22, 1907.

YOUNG, SEAN: Louisville, KY, Nov. 20, 1959. Interlochen.

ZACHARIAS, ANN: Stockholm, Swed., 1956.

ZADORA, PIA: Hoboken, NJ, 1954.

ZAPPA, DWEEZIL: Hollywood, CA, 1970.

ZETTERLING, MAI: Sweden, May 27, 1925. Ordtuery Theatre School.

ZIMBALIST, EFREM, JR.: NYC, Nov.30, 1918. Yale.

ZUNIGA, DAPHNE: Berkeley, CA, 1963. UCLA.

Irwin
Allen

Jean
Arthur

Peggy
Ashcroft

OBITUARIES

IRWIN ALLEN, 75, New York City-born producer-director-writer, best known for his 1970's "disaster" epics, *The Poseidon Adventure* and *The Towering Inferno*, died on Nov. 11, 1991 at Santa Monica Hospital Medical Center of a heart attack. He won an Academy Award for producing the 1952 documentary *The Sea Around Us*. His other credits as producer and/or director include the films *The Story of Mankind*, *The Big Circus*, *The Lost World*, *Voyage to the Bottom of the Sea* (and the subsequent TV series), *Five Weeks in a Balloon*, *The Swarm*, *When Time Ran Out*, and the TV series *Lost in Space*, *The Time Tunnel*, and *Land of the Giants*. He is survived by his wife, former actress Sheila Matthews.

JEAN ARTHUR (Gladys Georgianna Greene), 90, New York City-born screen, stage and TV actress, one of the great stars of the 1930's and 40's, died on June 19, 1991 in Carmel, CA, of heart failure. She was perhaps best known for a trio of films she starred in for director Frank Capra: *Mr. Deeds Goes to Town*, *You Can't Take It With You*, and *Mr. Smith Goes to Washington*. Following her 1923 debut in *Cameo Kirby* she appeared in such films as *Easy Come Easy Go*, *The Canary Murder Case*, *The Saturday Night Kid*, *Halfway to Heaven*, *Paramount on Parade*, *The Whole Town's Talking*, *Diamond Jim*, *If You Could Only Cook*, *The Ex-Mrs. Bradford*, *The Plainsman* (as Calamity Jane), *History Is Made at Night*, *Easy Living*, *Only Angels Have Wings*, *Too Many Husbands*, *Arizona*, *The Devil and Miss Jones*, *The Talk of the Town*, *The More the Merrier* (for which she received an Academy Award nomination), *A Lady Takes a Chance*, *The Impatient Years*, *A Foreign Affair*, and her last, *Shane*, in 1953. No survivors.

DAME PEGGY ASHCROFT, 83, British screen, stage and TV actress, who won the 1984 Academy Award for her role as Mrs. Moore in *A Passage to India*, died on June 14, 1991 in London following a stroke. Known primarily for her theatre work her film credits include *The Wandering Jew* (debut, 1933), *The 39 Steps* (1935), *Quiet Wedding*, *The Nun's Story*, *Secret Ceremony*, *Sunday Bloody Sunday*, *Joseph Andrews*, and *Madame Sousatzka*. She is survived by two children.

HOWARD ASHMAN, 40, Baltimore-born lyricist, who, with his partner, composer Alan Menken, won an Academy Award for the song "Under the Sea" from the 1989 Disney animated feature *The Little Mermaid*, died on Mar. 14, 1991 in New York of AIDS. They also wrote the scores for *Little Shop of Horrors* (from their Off-Broadway hit), *Beauty and the Beast* (for which Ashman received a posthumous Oscar), and *Aladdin*. He is survived by his companion, and his mother and sister.

RALPH BELLAMY, 87, Chicago-born screen, stage and TV actor, whose more than 100 film roles included an Academy Award nomination for the 1937 screwball comedy classic *The Awful Truth*, died on Nov. 29, 1991 in Santa Monica, CA, after a long illness. Following his 1931 debut in *The Secret Six* his movies over the next 59 years included *Woman in Room 13*, *Parole Girl*, *Spitfire*, *Wedding Night*, *Hands Across the Table*, *The Man Who Lived Twice*, *Let's Get*

Married, *Boy Meets Girl*, *Carefree*, *Let Us Live*, *His Girl Friday*, *Brother Orchid*, *Dance Girl Dance*, *Footsteps in the Dark*, *Dive Bomber*, *The Wolf Man*, *The Ghost of Frankenstein*, *Stage Door Canteen*, *Lady on a Train*, *The Court-Martial of Billy Mitchell*, *Sunrise at Campobello* (in his most famous role, as Franklin Roosevelt), *The Professionals*, *Rosemary's Baby*, *Cancel My Reservation*, *Oh God!*, *Trading Places*, *The Good Mother*, and his last, *Pretty Woman*, in 1990. He is survived by his fourth wife, an adopted son, a daughter, and a sister.

MAURICE BINDER, 72, British title designer, best known for his work on the James Bond films, died on Apr. 9, 1991 in London of lung cancer. His other credits include *Damn Yankees*, *The Mouse That Roared*, *Charade*, *Repulsion*, *Arabesque*, *Two for the Road*, *The Private Life of Sherlock Holmes*, *The Last Emperor*, *The Sheltering Sky*, and *Mister Johnson*. Survived by a brother.

LILLIAN BOND, 83, British screen and stage actress, died on Jan. 18, 1991 in Reseda, CA. of unspecified causes. Her films include *The Squaw Man* (1931), *The Old Dark House*, *Affairs of a Gentleman*, *Hot Saturday*, *China Seas*, *The Westerner* (as Lilly Langtry), *The Picture of Dorian Gray*, and *Pirates of Tripoli*. She is survived by her stepson.

EDWINA BOOTH, 86, screen actress, died on May 18, 1991 in Los Angeles of heart failure. Her films include *Manhattan Cocktail*, *Our Modern Maidens*, and *Trader Horn*, after which she retired following that much publicized illness. She is survived by a brother, sister, and two stepdaughters.

JULIE BOVASSO, 61, screen, stage, and TV actress, died on Sept. 14, 1991 in New York of cancer. Her movies include *Saturday Night Fever* (as John Travolta's mother), *Willie and Phil*, *The Verdict*, *Staying Alive*, *Moonstruck*, and *Betsy's Wedding*. Survived by her mother and brother.

LINO BROCKA, 51, Philippine filmmaker, died on May 22, 1991 in Manila in an automobile accident. He directed such films as *Wanted: Perfect Mother*, *Insiang*, *Bayan Ko*, *Macho Dancer*, and *Fight for Us*. No reported survivors.

CORAL BROWNE, 77, Australia-born screen, stage, and TV actress, died on May 29, 1991 in Los Angeles of breast cancer. Her films include *The Amateur Gentleman*, *Auntie Mame* (as Vera Charles), *The Roman Spring of Mrs. Stone*, *Dr. Crippen*, *The Killing of Sister George*, *Theatre of Blood*, *The Drowning Pool*, *American Dreamer*, and *Dream Child*. She is survived by her husband, actor Vincent Price.

NIVEN BUSCH, 88, New York-born screenwriter and novelist, died on Aug. 25, 1991 in San Francisco of heart failure. His scripts include *The Crowd Roars*, *In Old Chicago* (for which he received an Oscar nomination), *The Westerner*, *The Postman Always Rings Twice*

Ralph
Bellamy

Coral
Browne

Frank
Capra

(1946), *Pursued, The Furies,* and *The Man from the Alamo.* His most famous novel was *Duel in the Sun.* He is survived by his wife, five sons, two daughters, two stepsons, a stepdaughter, and a sister.

FRANK CAPRA, 94, one of Hollywood's great directors, whose films often celebrated the common man, died on Sept. 3, 1991 at his home in La Quinta, CA. One of the few directors whose name could attract audiences, he won Academy Awards for directing *It Happened One Night, Mr. Deeds Goes to Town,* and *You Can't Take It With You.* His other films include *Ladies of Leisure, Dirigible, The Miracle Woman, Platinum Blonde, American Madness, The Bitter Tea of General Yen, Lady for a Day, Broadway Bill, Lost Horizon* (1937), *Mr. Smith Goes to Washington, Meet John Doe, Arsenic and Old Lace, It's a Wonderful Life, State of the Union, Riding High, Here Comes the Groom, A Hole in the Head,* and *Pocketful of Miracles.* His many other honors include the American Film Institute Life Achievement Award. He is survived by two sons, a daughter, and 10 grandchildren.

JOAN CAULFIELD, 69, New Jersey-born screen and TV actress, died on June 18, 1991 in Los Angeles following cancer surgery. Her films include *Miss Susie Slagle's, Monsieur Beaucaire, Blue Skies, Dear Ruth, Welcome Stranger, The Unsuspected, The Sainted Sisters, Larceny, Dear Wife, The Lady Says No, The Rains of Ranchipur,* and *Buckskin.* No reported survivors.

BERT CONVY, 57, St. Louis-born screen, stage, and TV actor, died on July 15, 1991 of a brain tumor. In addition to acting he became well known on TV as a game show host of such programs as *Tattletales, Win Lose or Draw,* and *Super Password.* His films include *Gunman's Walk, A Bucket of Blood, Susan Slade, Act One, Semi-Tough, Jennifer, Hero at Large,* and *The Cannonball Run.* He is survived by his second wife, and three children from his first marriage.

KEN CURTIS (Curtis Gates), 74, Colorado-born screen and TV actor best known for playing Festus on the long-running western television series, *Gunsmoke,* died on Apr. 28, 1991 at his home in Fresno, CA. Following a career as a singer, during which he introduced the hit song "Tumbling Tumbleweeds," he acted in such movies as *The Quiet Man, Mister Roberts, Wings of Eagles, The Last Hurrah, The Killer Shrews* (which he also produced), *The Alamo,* and *Cheyenne Autumn.* He is survived by his wife, two children, and eight grandchildren.

BRAD DAVIS, 41, Florida-born screen, stage, and TV actor, best known for his role as Billy Hayes in the 1978 film *Midnight Express,* died on Sept. 8, 1991 in Los Angeles of AIDS. His other movies include *A Small Circle of Friends, Chariots of Fire, Querelle,* and *Rosalie Goes Shopping.* He is survived by his wife, daughter, parents, and brother.

CAROL DEMPSTER, 89, Minnesota-born silent movie actress, died on Feb. 1, 1991, in La Jolla, CA, after a long illness. Her films include *Scarlet Days, True Heart Susie, The White Rose, America, Isn't Life Wonderful, Sally of the Sawdust, That Royle Girl,* and *Sherlock Holmes.* She retired from the screen in 1926. No reported survivors.

COLLEEN DEWHURST, 67, Montreal-born screen, stage, and TV actress, died of cancer on August 22, 1991 at her home in South Salem, NY. She was best known for her outstanding work in the New York theatre where she won Tony awards for her roles in *All the Way Home* and *A Moon for the Misbegotten.* Her films include *The Nun's Story, A Fine Madness, The Last Run, The Cowboys, Annie Hall, Ice Castles, When a Stranger Calls, Tribute, The Dead Zone, The Boy Who Could Fly, Termini Station,* and *Dying Young,* in which she appeared with her son from her marriage to George C. Scott, actor Campbell Scott. She is survived by her two sons and two grandchildren.

DIXIE DUNBAR (Christine King), 72, screen and stage actress, died on Aug. 29, 1991 in Miami Beach, FL, following a series of heart attacks. Her films include *George White's Scandals, Girls' Dormitory, King of Burlesque, One in a Million, Sing Baby Sing, Life Begins in College,* and *Alexander's Ragtime Band.* No survivors.

MILDRED DUNNOCK, 90, Baltimore-born screen, stage, and TV actress died on July 5, 1991 at Martha's Vineyard Hospital in Oak Bluffs, MA, of old age. She was perhaps best known for playing the role of Linda Loman in *Death of a Salesman* in the original Broadway production, the 1951 film (for which she received an Academy Award nomination), and on television. Her other movies include *The Corn is Green* (debut, 1945), *Kiss of Death, Viva Zapata!, The Jazz Singer* (1953), *The Trouble with Harry, Love Me Tender, Baby Doll* (Academy Award nomination), *Peyton Place, The Nun's Story, The Story on Page One, Butterfield 8, Sweet Bird of Youth, Behold a Pale Horse, Youngblood Hawke, Seven Women, Whatever Happened to Aunt Alice?,* and *The Pick-Up Artist.* She is survived by her husband, a daughter, and three grandchildren.

REDD FOXX (John Elroy Sanford), 68, St. Louis-born comedian-actor died on Oct. 11, 1991 in Los Angeles after suffering a heart attack on the set of his TV series *The Royal Family.* Noted for his risqué stand-up routines and "party records," he found his greatest fame in the 1970's on the hit sit-com *Sanford and Son.* He appeared in three films: *Cotton Comes to Harlem, Norman Is That You?,* and *Harlem Nights.* Survivors include his fourth wife, his mother, and an adopted daughter.

JAMES FRANCISCUS, 57, Missouri-born screen, stage, and TV actor, died on July 8, 1991 of emphysema at the Medical Center of North Hollywood. He was best known for his roles on such TV shows as *The Naked City, Mr. Novak, Longstreet,* and *Doc Elliot.* His films include *Four Boys and a Gun, I Passed for White, The Outsider, Youngblood Hawke, Valley of Gwangi, Marooned, Beneath the Planet of the Apes, Cat O'Nine Tails, The Amazing Dobermans, The Greek Tycoon, Good Guys Wear Black, When Time Ran Out,* and *Butterfly.* He is survived by his second wife, and four daughters.

ANTON FURST (Anthony Francis Furst), 47, art director and special effects designer who won an Oscar for his set creations for *Batman,* died on Nov. 24, 1991 in Los Angeles after jumping from the eighth floor of a parking deck. His laser effects appeared in such films as *Star Wars, Superman,* and *Alien,* while his credits as production designer include *The Company of Wolves, Full Metal Jacket,* and *Awakenings.* He is survived by his son, daughter, mother, and sister.

| Joan Caulfield | Bert Convy | Brad Davis | Colleen Dewhurst | Mildred Dunnock | Redd Foxx |

GEORGE GOBEL, 71, Chicago-born screen, TV, stage, and radio actor-comedian, died on Feb. 24, 1991, in Encino, CA, of complications following bypass surgery on a major artery in his leg. His greatest fame came with the 1950's television series *The George Gobel Show*. He appeared in the movies *The Birds and the Bees, I Married a Woman, Rabbit Test,* and *Ellie*. He is survived by his wife, a son, two daughters, and three grandchildren.

BILL GRAHAM (Wolfgang Grajonca), 60, Berlin-born rock promoter died in a helicopter crash near San Francisco on Oct. 26, 1991. He appeared in the movies *Apocalypse Now* and *Bugsy* (as "Lucky" Luciano). Survived by two sons, a stepson, and three sisters.

KEVIN PETER HALL, 35, Pittsburgh-born screen and TV actor, who played Harry in the 1987 movie *Harry and the Hendersons* and its TV spin-off, died on Apr. 10, 1991 in Los Angeles of AIDS. He also played the title role in *Predator* and its sequel. He is survived by his wife, actress Alaina Reed Hall, and two children.

GLORIA HOLDEN, 82, British screen and TV actress, who played the title role in the 1936 horror film *Dracula's Daughter*, died on Mar. 22, 1991 in Redlands, CA, of a heart attack. Her other films include *The Life of Emile Zola, Wife vs. Secretary, Test Pilot, The Corsican Brothers* (1941), *Miss Annie Rooney, The Hucksters, Killer McCoy, A Kiss for Corliss, Dream Wife,* and *The Eddy Duchin Story*. She is survived by her husband and a brother.

DONALD HOUSTON, 67, British screen, stage, and TV actor, died on Oct. 13, 1991 at Coimbra, Portugal, of undisclosed causes. His movies include *The Blue Lagoon* (1949), *The Red Beret, Doctor in the House, The Man Upstairs, Room at the Top, The Mark, 300 Spartans, Doctor in Distress, 633 Squadron, A Study in Terror, Where Eagles Dare, Tales That Witness Madness, Voyage of the Damned, Clash of the Titans,* and *The Sea Wolves*. He is survived by a daughter, and a brother, actor Glyn Houston.

JOHN HOYT (John Hoysradt), 87, New York-born screen, stage, and TV character actor, died on Sept. 15, 1991 in Santa Cruz, CA, of lung cancer. Among the 80 features he appeared in were *Brute Force, My Favorite Brunette, The Desert Fox, When Worlds Collide, Androcles and the Lion, Julius Caesar, Blackboard Jungle, Trial, The Big Combo, Attack of the Puppet People, The Conqueror, Never So Few, Cleopatra* (1963), *X - The Man with the X-Ray Eyes,* and *Flesh Gordon*. He is survived by his wife and son.

IAN McCLELLAN HUNTER, 75, screen and TV writer, who won an Oscar for his original story for *Roman Holiday*, died on Mar. 5, 1991 in New York of an apparent heart attack. His other film credits include *Second Chorus, Mr. District Attorney, Up in Central Park,* and *A Dream of Kings*. He is survived by his wife, his son, director Tim Hunter, a sister, and four grandchildren.

WILFRID HYDE-WHITE, 87, British screen, stage, and television actor, died on May 6, 1991 of congestive heart failure at the Motion Picture and Television Hospital in Woodland Hills, CA. His film career spanned some sixty years and included appearances in *Rembrandt, The Winslow Boy, The Third Man, The Browning Version, The Story and Gilbert and Sullivan, See How They Run, Quentin Durwood, North West Frontier, Two-Way Stretch, Ada, John Goldfarb Please Come Home, My Fair Lady* (as Col. Pickering), *Ten Little Indians* (1965), *Chamber of Horrors, Gaily Gaily, Oh God Book II,* and *The Toy*. He is survived by his second wife, actress Ethel Drew, two sons, one of whom, Alex, is an actor, a daughter, and four

grandsons.

HERB JAFFE, 70, film producer and former United Artists executive, died on Dec. 7, 1991 in Beverly Hills of cancer. His movie credits include *The Wind and the Lion, Who'll Stop the Rain, Time After Time, Those Lips Those Eyes, Motel Hell, Jinxed, The Lords of Discipline, Fright Night,* and *Maid to Order*. He is surivived by his wife and two sons.

DEAN JAGGER, 87, Ohio-born screen, stage, and TV actor, died on Feb. 5, 1991 at his home in Santa Monica, CA. He had suffered from heart disease. One of the movies' most reliable supporting players, he won an Academy Award for his role in the 1949 war drama *Twelve O'Clock High*. His many films include *Woman from Hell* (debut in 1929), *College Rhythm, Wings in the Dark, Behold My Wife, Brigham Young - Frontiersman, Western Union, The North Star, Sister Kenny, Dark City, My Son John, It Grows on Trees, The Robe, Executive Suite, White Christmas, Bad Day at Black Rock, The Great Man, X the Unknown, Bernardine, The Proud Rebel, King Creole, The Nun's Story, Cash McCall, Elmer Gantry, Parrish, The Honeymoon Machine, Firecreek, The Kremlin Letter,* and *Alligator*. He is survived by his third wife, a daughter, two stepsons, a sister, and six grandchildren.

SYLVIA FINE KAYE, 78, Brooklyn-born lyricist-composer, who wrote many of the best known musical routines and songs for her late husband, Danny Kaye, died on Oct. 28, 1991 in New York of emphysema. Her work was featured in such Kaye films as *Up in Arms, Wonder Man, The Secret Life of Walter Mitty, The Inspector General, Knock on Wood, The Court Jester,* and *The Five Pennies*. She is survived by her daughter, a sister, and a brother.

KLAUS KINSKI (Nikolaus Nakzynski), 65, Poland-born screen, stage, and TV actor, perhaps best known for his starring roles in the Werner Herzog movies *Aguirre: The Wrath of God, Nosferatu,* and *Fitzcarraldo*, was found dead on Nov. 23, 1991 at his home in Lagunitas, CA, apparently of natural causes due to a heart problem. His other films include *For a Few Dollars More, Dr. Zhivago, Circus of Fear, Schizoid, Count Dracula, Love and Money, Buddy Buddy, Android,* and *The Little Drummer Girl*. Survived by his second wife, his daughter, actress Nastassja Kinski, and a son.

JERZY KOSINSKI, 57, acclaimed Poland-born novelist was found dead on May 3, 1991 in the bathtub of his New York apartment, an apparent suicide. He adapted his own novel, *Being There*, for the screen in 1979 and acted in *Reds*. He is survived by his wife and a stepbrother.

NANCY KULP, 69, Pennsylvania-born screen, stage, and TV character actress, best remembered for her role as Jane Hathaway on the hit television series *The Beverly Hillbillies*, died on February 3, 1991 in Palm Desert, CA, of cancer. Her movies include *The Model and the Marriage Broker, Shane, Sabrina, You're Never Too Young, Count Three and Pray, Forever Darling, Three Faces of Eve, Five Gates to Hell, The Parent Trap, Who's Minding the Store?, The Patsy,* and *The Night of the Grizzly*. There are no survivors.

EVA LA GALLIENNE, 92, British screen and stage actress, died on June 3, 1991 in Weston, CT, of heart failure. Best known for her theatre performances she appeared in only a few films including *Prince of Players, The Devil's Disciple,* and *Resurrection*, for which she received an Academy Award nomination. No immediate survivors.

| James Franciscus | George Gobel | Wilfrid Hyde-White | Dean Jagger | Klaus Kinski | Eva LaGallienne |

NALD LACEY, 55, British screen, stage and TV actor, perhaps known for playing the black-garbed villain Toht in *Raiders of the Ark*, died on May 15, 1991 in London of cancer. His other ies include *Nijinsky, Zulu Dawn, Firefox, Trenchcoat, Sahara, king the Grade, The Adventures of Buckaroo Banzai, Sword of the iant*, and *Valmont*. He is survived by a daughter and two sons.

CHAEL LANDON (Eugene Maurice Orowitz), 54, New York-n screen and TV actor-director-producer-writer, who starred in e successive hit TV series, *Bonanza, Little House on the Prairie, Highway to Heaven*, died of liver and pancreatic cancer on July 1, 1 at his home in Malibu, CA. His film credits are *I Was a Teenage rewolf, God's Little Acre, The Legend of Tom Dooley, Maracaibo, h School Confidential, The Errand Boy*, and *Sam's Son* (which he directed and wrote). He is survived by his third wife, and nine dren.

ENN LANGAN, 73, Denver-born screen, stage, and TV actor, d on Jan. 26, 1991 in Camarillo, CA, of lymphoma. His films ude *Four Jills in a Jeep, Wing and a Prayer, A Bell for Adano, agover Square, Margie, Dragonwyck, Forever Amber, The Snake Treasure of Monte Cristo, Hangman's Knot, 99 River Street, The azing Colossal Man, Mutiny in Outer Space*, and *Chisum*. He is vived by his wife, actress Adele Jergens, and a son.

R DAVID LEAN, 83, British motion picture director, writer, ducer, and editor, one of cinema's master filmmakers, died on ril 16, 1991 at his home in London of undisclosed causes. He won ademy Awards for directing *The Bridge on the River Kwai* (1957) Lawrence of Arabia* (1962). As an editor, he worked on such ns as *Pygmalion, Major Barbara*, and *The 49th Parallel*, before king his directorial debut on *In Which We Serve* (sharing credit h Noel Coward). His other credits as director are *This Happy eed, Blithe Spirit, Brief Encounter, Great Expectations, The ssionate Friends (One Woman's Story), Oliver Twist, Madeleine, aking the Sound Barrier, Hobson's Choice, Summertime (Summer dness), Dr. Zhivago, Ryan's Daughter*, and *A Passage to India*. In 90 he received the American Film Institute's Life Achievement ard. Survivors include his sixth wife, and a son from a previous rriage.

BERT Q. LEWIS, 71, TV and radio game show host and film or, died on Dec. 11, 1991 in Los Angeles of emphysema. His films lude *An Affair to Remember, Good Neighbor Sam, How to Succeed Business Without Really Trying*, and *Everything You Always nted to Know About Sex*. He is survived by a brother.

YE LUKE, 86, China-born screen and TV actor, one of the siest and most notable Asian-American performers in films, died on . 12, 1991 in Whittier, CA, following a stroke. In addition to eral appearances as Charlie Chan's Number One Son his movies lude *The Painted Veil* (debut, 1934), *Mad Love, Anything Goes 36), King of Burlesque, The Good Earth, Disputed Passage, No nds on the Clock, Mr. & Mrs. North, Journey for Margaret, isible Agent, Across the Pacific, Somewhere I'll Find You, Dragon ed, Three Men in White, Andy Hardy's Blonde Trouble, Tokyo se, Sleep My Love, Young Man With a Horn, Fair Wind in Java, uth Sea Woman, Love Is a Many-Splendored Thing, Around the rld in 80 Days, The Chairman, The Hawaiians, Won Ton the g Who Saved Hollywood, Gremlins*, and his last, *Alice*, in 1990. On he co-starred in the series *Kung Fu*. No reported survivors.

INE MacMAHON, 92, Pennsylvania-born screen, stage, and TV ress, who contributed solid support to more than 40 films, died on

Oct. 12, 1991 at her New York home from pneumonia. She was nominated for an Academy Award for her performance in the 1944 film *Dragon Seed*. Her other films include *Five Star Final* (her debut in 1931), *One Way Passage, Gold Diggers of 1933, Life of Jimmy Dolan, Babbitt, Ah Wilderness, Back Door to Heaven, Out of the Fog, The Lady is Willing, Stage Door Canteen, The Mighty McGurk, The Search, Roseanna McCoy, The Flame and the Arrow, The Eddie Cantor Story, Man from Laramie, The Young Doctors, I Could Go on Singing, Diamond Head*, and *All the Way Home*. No suvivors.

FRED MacMURRAY, 83, Illinois-born screen, stage, and TV actor, an adept light comedian during the 1930's and 40's, who also played effective heavies in the films *Double Indemnity, The Caine Mutiny*, and *The Apartment*, died on Nov. 5, 1991 in Santa Monica, CA, of pneumonia. His many other films include *The Gilded Lily, Alice Adams, Hands Across the Table, The Bride Comes Home, Trail of the Lonesome Pine, The Princess Comes Across, The Texas Rangers, Maid of Salem, Swing High Swing Lowe, Sing You Sinners, Men With Wings, Cafe Society, Remember the Night, Dive Bomber, Forest Rangers, Above Suspicion, No Time for Love, And the Angels Sing, Murder He Says, Where Do We Go from Here?, Smoky, The Egg and I, Family Honeymoon, Pushover, The Far Horizons, Day of the Badman, The Shaggy Dog, The Absent-Minded Professor, Bon Voyage, Son of Flubber, Follow Me Boys, The Happiest Millionaire*, and *The Swarm*. From 1960 to 1972 he starred in the phenomenally successful TV sitcom *My Three Sons*. He is survived by his wife, former actress June Haver, three daughters, a son, seven grandchildren, and one great-grandchild.

DANIEL MANN (Daniel Chugerman), 79, Brooklyn-born screen, stage,and TV director, died on Nov. 21, 1991 in Los Angeles of heart failure. He directed three actresses in their Oscar-winning roles: Shirley Booth in *Come Back Little Sheba*, Anna Magnani in *The Rose Tattoo*, and Elizabeth Taylor in *Butterfield 8*. Among his other movies are *About Mrs. Leslie, I'll Cry Tomorrow, Teahouse of the August Moon, The Last Angry Man, Five Finger Exercise, Who's Been Sleeping in My Bed?, Our Man Flint, For Love of Ivy*, and *Willard*. Survived by three children.

JOHN McINTIRE, 83, Spokane-born screen, radio, and TV character actor, died on Jan. 30, 1991 in Pasadena, CA, of emphysema and cancer. His films include *The Asphalt Jungle, Winchester '73, A Lion is in the Streets, Apache, The Far Country, The Phenix City Story, The Tin Star, Flaming Star, Psycho, Summer and Smoke, Rough Night in Jericho, Herbie Rides Again, Rooster Cogburn, Honky Tonk Man, Cloak and Dagger*, and *Turner and Hooch*. He also appeared in the TV series *Wagon Train*. He is survived by his wife, actress Jeanette Nolan, a daughter and a grandson. His son Tim, also an actor, passed away in 1986.

BERNARD MILES, 83, British screen and stage actor and founder of London's Mermaid Theatre, died on June 14, 1991 in Knaresborough, Yorkshire, England, of undisclosed causes. Following his 1933 debut in *Channel Crossing*, he appeared in such films as *The Lion Has Wings, Quiet Wedding, A Voice in the Night, One of Our Aircraft is Missing, The Avengers, In Which We Serve, Spitfire, Tawny Pipit* (which he also co-wrote, co-directed, and produced), *Great Expectations, Nicholas Nickleby, The Guinea Pig* (which he also co-wrote), *Chance of a Lifetime* (also co-writer, co-director, and producer), *The Magic Box, Never Let Me Go, The Man Who Knew Too Much* (1956), *Moby Dick, Saint Joan, The Smallest Show on Earth, tom thumb, Heavens Above*, and *Run Wild Run Free*. He is survived by his son and daughter.

| Michael Landon | Glenn Langan | David Lean | Aline MacMahon | Fred MacMurray | Yves Montand |

CARLOS MONTALBAN, 87, Mexico-born screen, stage, and TV actor, died on Mar. 28, 1991 in New York of heart failure. Although he acted in such films as *The Harder They Fall, The Out-of-Towners,* and *Bananas,* he was best known for playing El Exigente in TV commercials for Savarin coffee. He is survived by his wife, his brother, actor Ricardo Montalban, and his sister.

YVES MONTAND (Ivo Livi), 70, Italy-born screen, stage, and TV actor and music hall singer, who became one of France's most notable stars, died on Nov. 9, 1991 of a heart attack in Senlis, France, after becoming ill on the set of his latest movie. His films include *Gates of the Night, The Idol, The Wages of Fear, Heroes and Sinners, The Crucible, The Wide Blue Road, Where the Hot Wind Blows, Let's Make Love, Sanctuary, Goodbye Again, My Geisha, The Sleeping Car Murder, La Guerre est finie, Grand Prix, Is Paris Burning?, Live for Life, Z, On a Clear Day You Can See Forever, The Confession, Tout va bien, Cesar and Rosalie, State of Siege, Vincent Francois Paul and the Others, Lovers Like Us, Clair de Femme, Le Choix des armes, Jean de Florette,* and *Manon of the Spring.* He had been married for 35 years to actress Simone Signoret, who died in 1985. A son by his companion, actress Carole Amiel, survives.

REGGIE NALDER (Alfred Reginald Natzler), 80, Austrian screen, stage, and TV actor, died on Nov. 19, 1991 in Santa Monica, CA, of bone cancer. He was perhaps best known for playing the assassin who fell from the balcony at Albert Hall in Alfred Hitchcock's 1956 version of *The Man Who Knew Too Much.* His other films include *The Manchurian Candidate, Convicts 4, The Spiral Road, The Day and the Hour, The Bird with the Crystal Plumage,* and *Fellini's Casanova.* Survived by two cousins.

ALEX NORTH, 81, film, TV, and theatre composer, whose motion picture scores garnered him 15 Academy Award nominations, died on Sept. 8, 1991 in Pacific Palisades, CA, of pancreatic cancer. His movie credits include *A Streetcar Named Desire, Death of a Salesman, Viva Zapata!, The Rose Tattoo, Unchained* (which featured the hit song "Unchained Melody"), *The Rainmaker, Spartacus, The Misfits, Cleopatra, The Agony and the Ecstasy, Who's Afraid of Virginia Woolf?, The Shoes of the Fisherman, The Devil's Brigade, Shanks, Bite the Bullet, Carny, Under the Volcano,* and *The Dead.* In 1986 he was awarded an honorary Oscar. He is survived by his wife, two sons, a daughter, and two brothers.

JOE PASTERNAK, 89, Hungarian-born Hollywood producer, best known for his musicals at Universal and MGM, died on Sept. 13, 1991 in Beverly Hills, CA. He had suffered from Parkinson's disease. His main credits include *Three Smart Girls, One Hundred Men and a Girl, That Certain Age, Destry Rides Again, It Started With Eve, Presenting Lily Mars, Two Girls and a Sailor, Anchors Aweigh, Two Sisters from Boston, Holiday in Mexico, On an Island With You, A Date With Judy, In the Good Old Summertime, That Midnight Kiss, The Great Caruso, Summer Stock, Small Town Girl (1953), Easy to Love, Hit the Deck, Love Me or Leave Me, Please Don't Eat the Daisies, Where the Boys Are (1960), Billy Rose's Jumbo,* and *The Courtship of Eddie's Father.* He is survived by his second wife, former actress Dorothy Darrel, 3 sons, and a sister.

BEN PIAZZA, 58, screen, stage, and TV actor, died on Sept. 7, 1991 in Sherman Oaks, CA, of cancer. His films include *A Dangerous Age, The Hanging Tree, No Exit, Tell Me That You Love Me Junie Moon, The Bad News Bears, I Never Promised You a Rose Garden, Apocalypse Now, Mask, Clean and Sober,* and *Guilty by Suspicion.*

He is survived by his companion, two sisters and six brothers.

THALMUS RASULALA (Jack Crowder), 55, Miami-born screen, stage, and TV actor, died on Oct. 9, 1991, in Albuquerque, NM, of a heart attack. He had suffered from leukemia. His movie credits include *Fun With Dick and Jane, Above the Law, Bulletproof, The Package, Lambada,* and *New Jack City.* Survived by his wife and four children.

ALDO RAY (Aldo Da Re), 64, Pennsylvania-born screen actor who specialized in tough guy roles, died on Mar. 27, 1991 in Martinez, CA, of throat cancer and complications from pneumonia. His films include *The Marrying Kind, Pat and Mike, Let's Do It Again, Miss Sadie Thompson, Battle Cry, We're No Angels* (1955), *Men in War, God's Little Acre, The Naked and the Dead, The Day They Robbed the Bank of England, Sylvia, What Did You Do in the War Daddy?, Dead Heat on a Merry-Go-Round, Welcome to Hard Times, Riot on Sunset Strip, The Green Berets, And Hope to Die,* and *The Sicilian.* He is survived by two sons, one of whom, Eric DaRe, is an actor, a daughter, his mother, three brothers, a sister, and a granddaughter.

LEE REMICK, 55, Boston-born screen, stage, and TV actress, who received an Academy Award nomination for her performance in *Days of Wine and Roses* (1962), died on July 2, 1991 of cancer at her home in Brentwood, CA. Following her screen debut in 1957 in *A Face in the Crowd* she appeared in such films as *The Long Hot Summer, These Thousand Hills, Anatomy of a Murder, Wild River, Sanctuary, Experiment in Terror, The Running Man* (1963), *The Wheeler Dealers, The Hallelujah Trail, Baby the Rain Must Fall, No Way to Treat a Lady, The Detective, A Severed Head, Loot, Sometimes a Great Notion, A Delicate Balance, Hennessey, The Omen, Telefon, The Europeans, The Competition,* and *Tribute.* She is survived by her husband, producer William "Kip" Gowans, two children, two stepdaughters, and her mother.

TONY RICHARDSON, 63, British screen, stage, and TV director, who received an Academy Award for the 1963 film *Tom Jones,* died on Nov. 14, 1991 in Los Angeles of AIDS. His other credits include *Look Back in Anger, The Entertainer, Saturday Night and Sunday Morning, A Taste of Honey, The Loneliness of the Long Distance Runner, The Loved One, The Sailor from Gibraltar, The Charge of the Light Brigade* (1968), *Hamlet* (1969), *Ned Kelly, A Delicate Balance, Joseph Andrews, The Border, The Hotel New Hampshire,* and his last, *Blue Skies,* released posthumously. He is survived by two daughters from his marriage to Vanessa Redgrave, actresses Natasha and Joely Richardson, and a third daughter from another marriage.

JEAN ROGERS (Eleanor Lovegren), 74, Massachusetts-born screen actress who played Dale Arden in the Flash Gordon serials, died on Feb. 24, 1991 in Sherman Oaks, CA, following surgery. Her films include *Night Key, Heaven With a Barbed Wire Fence, My Man Godfrey, Yesterday's Heroes, Whistling in Brooklyn,* and *Speed to Spare.* No reported survivors.

GENE RODDENBERRY, 70, Texas-born writer-producer, who created the 1960's sci-fi series *Star Trek,* died on Oct. 24, 1991 of a massive blood clot. He later produced the 1979 *Star Trek* feature and served as creative consultant for subsequent films in the series. He was producer and writer of the 1971 feature *Pretty Maids in a Row* and executive producer for the TV spin-off *Star Trek - The Next Generation.* He is survived by his wife, actress Majel Barrett, a son, two daughters, his mother, a brother, and a sister.

Thalmus Rasulala	Aldo Ray	Lee Remick	Danny Thomas	Gene Tierney	Tom Tryon

ANGELO ROSSITTO, 83, screen and TV actor died on Sept. 21, 1991 in Los Angeles, from complications from surgery. Following his 1926 debut as Beppo the Dwarf in *The Beloved Rogue* he appeared in such films as *Laugh Clown Laugh, Mysterious Island* (1929), *The Wizard of Oz, Dementia, Doctor Doolittle, The Trip, Brain of Blood,* and *Mad Max Beyond Thunderdome.* He is survived by a brother, and two children.

NATALIE SCHAFER, 90, New Jersey-born screen, stage, and TV actress, best known for her role as Mrs. Howell on the 1960's sit-com *Gilligan's Island,* died on Apr. 10, 1991 in Los Angeles of cancer. Her film appearances include *Marriage is a Private Affair, Wonder Man, Dishonored Lady, The Snake Pit, Anastasia, Oh Men Oh Women, Forever Darling, Susan Slade, 40 Carats,* and *The Day of the Locust.* She is survived by her companion.

DR. SEUSS (Theodor Seuss Geisel), 87, Massachusetts-born writer and illustrator who created such classic children's books as *The Cat in the Hat, Horton Hears a Who,* and *How the Grinch Stole Christmas,* died on Sept. 25, 1991 in La Jolla, CA, after suffering from respiratory and kidney problems for several months. He co-wrote the screenplay for the 1953 fantasy feature *The 5,000 Fingers of Dr. T,* and the Oscar-winning shorts *Hitler Lives* and *Design for Death.* He is survived by his wife, and two stepdaughters.

DON SIEGEL, 78, Chicago-born director, perhaps best known for the films *Invasion of the Body Snatchers* (1956) and *Dirty Harry,* died on Apr. 20, 1991 in Nipoma, CA, of cancer. His other credits include *Night Unto Night, Riot in Cell Block 11, Crime in the Streets, Baby Face Nelson, The Lineup, Hound Dog Man, Edge of Eternity, Flaming Star, Hell is for Heroes, Madigan, Coogan's Bluff, Two Mules for Sister Sara, The Beguiled, Charlie Varrick, The Shootist, Telefon, Escape from Alcatraz, Rough Cut,* and *Jinxed.* Survived by his third wife, and five children, one of whom is actor Kristoffer Tabori.

DANNY THOMAS (Amos Jacobs), 79, Michigan-born screen, radio, and TV actor-performer, died on Feb. 6, 1991 at Cedars-Sinai Medical Center in Los Angeles, following a heart attack at his home in Beverly Hills. He had his greatest fame in the long-running television sit-com *Make Room for Daddy* (later known as *The Danny Thomas Show*). Although principally a night club and TV performer he appeared in a handful of films: *The Unfinished Dance, The Big City, Call Me Mister, I'll See You in My Dreams,* the 1953 remake of *The Jazz Singer, Looking for Love,* and *Don't Worry We'll Think of a Title.* He is survived by his wife, three children (including actress Marlo Thomas and producer Tony Thomas), and five grandchildren.

RICHARD THORPE (Rollo Thorpe), 95, Kansas-born film director, died on May 1, 1991 in Palm Springs, CA. Starting in the silent era his credits include *The Feminine Touch, Night Must Fall* (1937), *The Earl of Chicago, The Thin Man Goes Home, Tarzan's New York Adventure, Two Girls and a Sailor, Her Highness and the Bellboy, A Date with Judy, Malaya, The Sun Comes Up, Three Little Words, The Black Hand, The Great Caruso, Knights of the Round Table, Carbine Williams, The Iron Petticoat, The Honeymoon Machine,* and *The Horizontal Lieutenant.* He is survived by his son, producer-director Jerry Thorpe, and four grandchildren.

GENE TIERNEY, 70, Brooklyn-born screen, stage, and TV actress,

perhaps best remembered for her leading roles in the 1940's dramas *Laura* and *Leave Her to Heaven* (for which she received an Oscar nomination), died on Nov. 6, 1991 in Houston, TX of emphysema. Following her 1940 debut in *The Return of Frank James* she appeared in such movies as *Hudson's Bay, Tobacco Road, Belle Starr, Shanghai Gesture, Son of Fury, Heaven Can Wait* (1943), *A Bell for Adano, Dragonwyck, The Razor's Edge* (1946), *The Ghost and Mrs. Muir, That Wonderful Urge, Whirlpool, Where the Sidewalk Ends, Night and the City, The Mating Season, On the Riviera, Plymouth Adventure, Never Let Me Go, The Egyptian, Left Hand of God, Advise and Consent, Toys in the Attic,* and *The Pleasure Seekers.* She is survived by two daughters from her first marriage to designer Oleg Cassini, four grandchildren, and a sister.

REGIS TOOMEY, 93, Pittsburgh-born screen, stage, and TV character actor, died on Oct. 12, 1991 in Woodland Hills, CA. His many films include *Union Pacific, Meet John Doe, His Girl Friday, Northwest Passage, They Died with Their Boots On, You're in the Army Now, The Bishop's Wife, The Boy with the Green Hair, Show Boat* (1951), *The Tall Target, The People Against O'Hara, The High and the Mighty, Guys and Dolls, Warlock, The Last Sunset, Voyage to the Bottom of the Sea, Gunn, Change of Habit,* and *The Carey Treatment.* He is survived by a brother.

THOMAS TRYON, 65, Connecticut-born screen, stage, and TV actor-turned-author, died on Sept. 4, 1991 of cancer at his home in Los Angeles. He was perhaps best known for playing the title role in Otto Preminger's 1963 film *The Cardinal.* His other movies include *The Scarlet Hour, Three Violent People, I Married a Monster from Outer Space, Moon Pilot, Marines Let's Go, In Harm's Way,* and *The Glory Guys.* As a best-selling novelist his works include *The Other* (which he adapted into a film in 1972), *Harvest Home,* and *Crowned Heads.* He is survived by two brothers.

THORLEY WALTERS, 78, British screen, stage, and TV actor, died on July 6, 1991 in London of undisclosed causes. He appeared in such movies as *They Were Sisters, Private's Progress, Man in a Cocked Hat (Carlton Browne of the F.O.), Dracula: Prince of Darkness, The Earth Dies Screaming, Two-Way Stretch, Murder She Said, The Pure Hell of St. Trinian's, Rotten to the Core, A Study in Terror, Trog, There's a Girl in My Soup, Mr. Forbush and the Penguins, The Adventures of Sherlock Holmes' Smarter Brother,* and *The Little Drummer Girl.* No reported survivors.

BYRON WEBSTER, 58, London-born screen, stage, and TV actor, died of AIDS on Dec. 1, 1991 in Sherman Oaks, CA. He appeared in such films as *The Killing of Sister George, On a Clear Day You Can See Forever, The Poseidon Adventure, That Man Bolt, Time After Time,* and *Only When I Laugh.* He is survived by his companion and two sisters.

THEODORE WILSON, 47, screen, stage, and TV actor, died on July 21, 1991 in Los Angeles of a stroke. His film appearances include *The River Niger, Carny, The Hunter, A Fine Mess, That's Life,* and *Life Stinks.* No reported survivors.

LUIGI ZAMPA, 86, Italian film director, died on Aug. 15, 1991 in Rome following a long illness. His works include *To Live in Peace, Angelina, Difficult Years, City on Trial, A Question of Honor,* and *A Girl in Australia.* He is survived by two children.

INDEX

262

Bernardi, Adam, 162-163
Bernardi, Lina, 207
Bernecker, Melina, 200
Bernelle, Agnes, 222
Bernhard, Jusak, 75
Bernhard, Sandra, 47, 54, 235
Berniker, Flora, 111
Bernsen, Collin, 151
Bernsen, Corbin, 110, 235
Bernstein, Armyan, 208
Bernstein, Elmer, 42, 45, 95, 120
Bernstein, Sheryl, 77
Bernuth, Nico, 153
Beroza, Janet, 94
Berri, Claude, 210, 235
Berridge, Elizabeth, 235
Berrios, Sandra, 51
Berry, Halle, 62, 119, 138
Berry, Stan, 78
Berry, Tom, 160
Berryman, Dorothee, 160, 200
Berta, Renata, 210
Bertenshaw, Michael, 231
Berthy, Claude, 38
Bertinelli, Valerie, 235
Berto, Juliet, 235
Bertok, Semka Sokolovic, 156
Bertolucci, Bernardo, 183
Bertone, Pietro, 194
Besser, Stuart M., 118
Besson, Luc, 192
Best, James, 235
Betancourt, Anne, 77
Betancourt, Carlos, 68
Bethea, Melvin, 62
Bethke, Tom, 156
Bethune, Ivy, 153
Bettger, Lyle, 235
Bettis, John, 114, 138
Bettis, Paul, 226
Betts, Jack, 166
Betzer, Just, 172
Bevan, Tim, 156, 227
Bevis, Leslie, 41
Beyda, Kent, 89
Beyer, Troy, 35
Beymer, Richard, 235
Beyzai, Bahram, 223
Bharadwaj, Radha, 153
Biafra, Jello, 224
Bialor, Alan, 39
Bialy, Sharon, 160
Biana, 227
Biddle, Adrian, 56
Bideau, Jean-Luc, 232
Bie, Sherry, 227
Bieber, Arnold, 171
Biechler, Merri, 23
Biehn, Michael, 167, 233, 235
Biesk, Adam, 11, 15
Big Daddy, 14
Bigagli, Claudio, 180
Bigazzi, Giancarlo, 180, 196
Bigelow, Kathryn, 71
Biggerstaff, Caroline, 149, 171
Biggs, Jason, 169
Biggs, Jerry, 132
Biggs, Roxann, 30
Bigham, Lexie, 72
Bigwood, James, 28
Bikel, Theodore, 110, 235
Bikini Island, 163
Bilbrey, James, 89
Bilgore, Andrew, 125
Bill & Ted's Bogus Journey, 74
Bill, Francesca, 152
Billet, Francoise, 199
Billings, Joshua, 31
Billinsley, Peter, 235
Billups, Eddie, 168
Billy Bathgate, 116
Bilson, Danny, 66
Bilzerian, Laurence, 153
Binder, Maurice, 256
Bing, Steve, 163
Bingo, 164
Bingo, 164
Binion, Crawford, 171
Binion, Reid, 34, 148
Binns, Andrew, 200
Binns, James, 95
Birch, Thora, 92, 124
Birch, Yan, 118
Birchfield, Rick L., 49
Bird, Bonnie, 173
Birdine, Sabrina, 171
Birk, Raye, 80
Birke, David, 162
Birkin, David, 38
Birkin, Jane, 197, 212
Birman, Matt, 157
Birney, David, 235
Birney, Reed, 235
Birt, Christopher, 77
Bisciglia, Paul, 227
Bisgeier, Mark, 93
Bishop, Andrew, 37
Bishop, Dan, 41, 112, 132
Bishop, Ed, 156
Bishop, Joey, 235
Bishop, John, 168
Bishop, Julie, 235
Bishop, Kelly, 16
Bishop, Rummy, 224
Bishop, Stephen, 124
Bisio, Claudio, 180
Bissell, Jim, 66
Bisset, Jacqueline, 235
Bissett, Josie, 14, 24
Bisso, Patricio, 229
Bivins, Carol, 32
Bixby, Bill, 235
Bixby, Emerson, 163
Biziou, Peter, 189
Bizot, Philippe, 228
Bjorkland, Janis, 80
Black Lizard, 210
Black Robe, 213
Black, Allen, 51
Black, Beth, 32
Black, Dorise, 51
Black, Ian, 83
Black, Karen, 83, 235
Black, Larry, 171
Black, Lewis, 27
Black, Louis, 162
Black, Robert, 51, 89
Black, Shane, 138
Blackburn, Ticia, 169
Blackledge, Cynthia, 89
Blackmam, Sean, 78
Blackstone, Wendy, 166, 168-169
Blackwell, Douglas, 64
Blackwell, Robert A., 21
Blades, Lisa, 96
Blades, Ruben, 107, 235
Blain, Brian, 165
Blaine, Vivian, 235
Blair, Betsy, 235
Blair, Janet, 235
Blair, Linda, 235
Blaisdell, Brad, 150, 154-155
Blake, Andre, 174
Blake, Grace, 174
Blake, Maurice, 222
Blake, Robert, 235
Blake, Stephanie, 106
Blake, Yvonne, 90
Blakely, Cameron, 21
Blakely, Don, 117
Blakely, Susan, 235
Blakley, Ronee, 235
Blanc, Michel, 210, 216
Blanchard, Clayton, 164
Blanchard, Greg, 149
Blanchard, Terence, 62
Blanche, Roland, 192
Blanchflower, Jean, 222
Blanding, Lorie, 90
Blandon, Wilson, 223
Blank, Kenny, 107
Blankfein, Fredric B., 92
Blanks, Billy, 9, 138, 167
Blanton, Arell, 32
Blasi, Silverio, 194
Blasman, Chris, 106
Blau, Martin Maria, 202
Blayne, Curtis, 152
Bleakley, Annie, 228
Blecha, Norbert, 196
Blessed, Brian, 64
Blevins, Daniel W., 169
Blicker, Jason, 170
Bliese, Joachim, 90
Blin, Wilfrid, 195
Block, Billy, 14
Block, Bruce A., 139
Block, J.S., 108
Block, Mitchell, 77
Blodgett, Michael, 152
Blomquist, Alan C., 30
Blondel, Patrick, 227
Blood & Concrete, 152, 166
Blood in the Face, 152
Blood Massacre, 166
Bloom, Claire, 235
Bloom, Claudia, 14
Bloom, David, 227
Bloom, Jim, 133, 161
Bloom, John, 133
Bloom, Verna, 235
Bloomfield, John, 64
Blossier, Lucie, 195
Blossom, Roberts, 80
Blotnikas, Sylvie, 201
Blount, Lisa, 166
Blowback, 166
Bludsworth, Charles, 166
Blue, Alexander Fehr, 117
Blum, Mark, 235
Blumenfeld, Alan, 161
Blumenthal, Brad, 134
Blunden, Chris, 223
Bluteau, Lothaire, 213
Bluto, Tony, 198
Bluzet, Dominique, 210
Blyth, Anne, 235
Boalo, Tammy, 161
Board, John, 221, 226
Bobbitt, Russell, 30, 50
Boccanfuso, Vito "Baldie," 117
Boccelli, Dick, 168
Bocchicchio, Albina, 136
Bochner, Hart, 235
Bochner, Lloyd, 68
Bochner, Sally, 198
Bock, Larry, 160
Bocquet, Gavin, 130
Bodbyl, Marina, 216
Bode, Ralf, 46
Bodibe, Bhubhesi, 107
Bodie, W. Paul, 120
Body Parts, 163
Boeglin, Ariane, 197
Boeke, Jim, 133
Boekelheide, Todd, 128, 230
Boeken, Ludi, 195
Boen, Earl, 69
Boespflug, Francis, 199
Bofshever, Michael, 133
Bogaart, Rien, 207
Bogarde, Dirk, 197, 235
Bogart, Humphrey, 182
Bogart, Peter, 165
Boggs, Gail, 114
Bogni, Gerald, 170
Bogosian, Eric, 94, 235
Bogren, Erika, 166
Bohlen, Anne, 152
Bohn, Tim, 67
Bohringer, Richard, 235
Boileau-Narcejac, 163
Bokanowski, Michele, 226
Bokanowski, Patrick, 226
Bokhari, Yousaf, 219
Bokma, Pierre, 216
Bolden, Gigi, 35
Boldroff, Keith, 165
Bolender, Bill, 140
Bolger, John Michael, 82
Bolger, Michael, 82, 208
Bolinski, James W., 114
Bolkan, Florinda, 235
Bollinger, Andre, 134
Bollow, Jeff, 160
Bologna, Gabe, 125
Bologna, Joseph, 235
Bolton, Gregory Wm., 170
Bolton, Michael, 10
Bolton, Nick, 227
Bombyk, David, 88
Bon, Jean-Marie, 226
Bonaca, Gianpaolo, 33
Bonaiuto, Anna, 207
Bonaiuto, David, 173
Bonanno, Louie, 171
Bonanno, Salvatore, 39
Bonato, Don, 168
Bond, Derek, 235
Bond, Lillian, 256
Bond, Steve, 169
Bonet, Lisa, 235
Bonetti, Massimo, 207
Bonezzi, Bernardo, 206
Bonfanti, James, 44
Bongiorno, Benedetto, 39
Bonham-Carter, Helena, 235
Bonhoeffer, Dietrich, 230
Bonifant, D. Adam, 43
Bonifant, Tod, 43
Bonitzer, Pascal, 212
Bonivento, Claudio, 143, 196
Bonnaffe, Jacques, 195
Bonnano, Vivian, 150
Bonnefil, Carol, 117
Bonner, Frank, 164
Bonney, Lawrence A., 174
Bono, Sonny, 235
Bonta, Vanna, 128
Bontempo, Pietro, 118
Bonvoisin, Berangere, 227
Book of Love, 14
Booker, Harry, 157
Booker, Jonathan, Ph.D., 45
Boone, Pat, 235
Boone, Walker, 157
Boonen, Yves, 227
Booth, Andrew, 228
Booth, Edwina, 256
Booth, James, 154
Booth, Maggie, 183
Booth, Shirley, 182
Boothe, Powers, 235
Bordán, Irén, 215
Borden, Bill, 105
Borden, Ross, 162
Borden, Roy, 43
Bordier, Patrick, 210
Bordoni, Beatrice, 199
Boretski, Peter, 157, 221
Borghese, Julian Paul, 155
Borgnine, Ernest, 182, 235
Borkan, Gene, 138, 174
Borkum, Shelley, 212
Born to Ski, 169
Borodyansky, Alexander, 225
Borowitz, Katherine, 151
Borrower, The, 164
Bortman, Michael, 156
Borzage, Frank, 181
Borzunova, Elena, 143
Bosak, Oldrich, 190
Bosco, Mario, 27
Bosco, Philip, 31, 157, 235
Bosé, Miguel, 219
Bosley, Roz, 9
Boss, Mary R., 18
Bostwick, Barry, 235
Boswell, Charles, 154
Boswell, Robert, 156
Boswell, Simon, 216
Bosworth, Brian, 49
Botosso, Claudio, 207
Bottoms, Joseph, 235
Bottoms, Sam, 128, 235
Bottoms, Timothy, 235
Boucher, Savannah Smith, 15
Bouchitey, Patrick, 199
Bouchner, Vitezsalv, 130
Boudet, Jacques, 192, 201
Bouianov, Alexandre, 187
Bouillaud, Jean-Claude, 220
Bouise, Jean, 192
Boultbee, Jeremy, 228
Boulting, Gideon, 225
Boulting, Ingrid, 235
Boulting, Lucy, 218, 227
Bounds, Lataunya, 170
Bourland, Kevin, 138
Bourne, Mel, 96
Boutevin, Jean-Louis, 195
Boutsikaris, Dennis, 41, 169, 235
Bovasso, Julie, 256
Bovee, Leslie, 235
Bowden, Mark, 96
Bowe, David, 125
Bowe, Tyler, 155
Bowen, Deirdre, 221
Bowen, Jay, 99
Bowen, Michael, 170
Bowen, Peter, 161
Bowen, Roger, 50
Bower, Tom, 41
Bowers, George, 17
Bowers, James, 218
Bowers, P. Randall, 54
Bowie, David, 235
Bowie, Geoff, 232
Bowker, Judi, 235
Bowman, Melodee, 140
Bowman, Teresa, 157
Bowyer, Alan, 225
Bowyers, James, 216
Boxleitner, Bruce, 155, 235
Boy Who Cried Bitch, The, 169
Boyce, Rodger, 100
Boyd, Blake, 149
Boyd, Bob, 162
Boyd, Don, 212
Boyd, Guy, 154
Boyd, Lee, 117
Boyd, Niven, 218
Boyd, Russell, 226, 228
Boyd, Sue, 31
Boyd, Susan, 165
Boyd, William, 194
Boyer, Charles, 181
Boyer, Myriam, 210
Boyett, William, 66
Boyle, Chris, 24
Boyle, Kerry, 45
Boyle, Lara Flynn, 78, 163, 235
Boyle, Peter, 64, 151, 160, 235
Boyle, Sharon, 16
Boys from Baltimore, The, 23
Boyz N The Hood, 72
Bozman, Ron, 174
Bracco, Lorraine, 41, 48, 235
Bracken, Eddie, 42, 235
Brackett, Charles, 182
Bradfield, Marilyn Raye, 88
Bradford, Jesse, 169
Bradford, Richard, 157
Bradford, Sidney Karlos, 100
Bradley, Alfred Bruce, 37
Bradley, Brian, 35
Bradley, Christopher, 35
Bradley, Dan, 15, 165
Bradley, David, 154
Bradley, Joanne, 158
Bradley, Paul, 44
Bradley, Terry, 170
Bradsell, Michael, 44
Bradshaw, Joan, 46
Brady, Alice, 181
Brady, John, 33
Brady, Moya, 211
Braeden, Eric, 235
Brafstein, Irene, 46
Braga, Sonia, 235
Braga-Mermet, Angela, 232
Braggs, Christina, 168
Braham, Billy, 216
Brainard, Wendy, 160
Bral, Jacques, 228
Bramhall, Ann, 229
Bramlett, Bonnie, 24
Brammall, Bridget, 231
Bramon, Risa, 24, 46, 140, 159
Branagh, Kenneth, 86, 235
Branaman, Rustam, 103
Brancato, John D., 166
Brand, Gibby, 139
Brand, Tony, 101
Brandauer, Klaus Maria, 10, 235
Brandis, Jonathan, 223
Brandman, Michael, 189
Brando, Jocelyn, 235
Brando, Marlon, 181-183, 235
Brandon, Clark, 235
Brandon, Maryann, 164
Brandon, Michael, 235
Brandsen, Jill, 156
Brandt, Alicia, 46
Brandt, Janet, 16
Brandt, Walker, 60
Brandt, William, 200
Bransfield, Marjorie, 104
Brantley, Betsy, 235
Bratt, Benjamin, 46, 159
Brattlestreet, Caliope, 165
Brault, Michel, 200
Brault, Sylvain, 200
Braun, Bob, 32
Braun, Harold, 88
Brauner, Arthur, 202
Braunstein, Alan, 162
Braverman, Marvin, 77, 111
Bravo, Oscar, 149
Bravos, Eugenia, 111
Bravos, Gena, 111
Brayboy, Gary, 79
Brazeau, Jay, 12
Brazelton, Conni Marie, 118
Brazier, Ben, 218
Brazier, Daniel, 218
Brazzi, Rossano, 235
Breakstone, Bambi, 114
Breaux, Walter, Jr., 132
Breaux, Walter, 140
Brecht, Susan, 172
Breck, Peter, 224
Breckinridge, Beverly, 231
Breckman, Andy, 89
Bredin, Philip, 208
Breen, Joseph, 182
Breen, Kristi, 102
Breeze, Robert, 151
Breitmayer, Peter, 156
Bremond, Romain, 199
Brenn, Janni, 36
Brenna, Harald, 193
Brennan, Eileen, 161, 235
Brennan, John H., 82
Brennan, Meg, 162
Brennan, Richard, 228
Brennan, Stephen, 204, 228
Brennan, Walter, 181
Brenner, Albert, 52, 111
Brenner, David, 24
Brenner, Dori, 125
Brenner, Todd, 116
Breslau, Susan, 68
Bresnick, Adam, 161
Brestoff, Richard, 170
Breton, Brooke, 133
Brett, Mark, 216
Brevig, Eric, 134
Brezinova, Dagmar, 225
Breznahan, Tom, 155, 223
Brialy, Jean-Claude, 232, 235
Brian, David, 235
Brick, Richard, 51
Brickman, I.D., 140
Brickman, Marc, 213
Brickman, Marshall, 125
Brickner, Howard M., 89
Bricmont, Wendy Greene, 129
Bricusse, Leslie, 134
Bride of Re-Animator, 151
Bridges, Beau, 235
Bridges, Isabelle, 226
Bridges, Jeff, 96-97, 235
Bridges, Lloyd, 79, 235
Bridgewater, Paul, 171
Bridgewater, Stephen, 96
Briggs, Brad, 164
Bright Angel, 159
Bright, Jeff, 79
Bright, John, 10
Brightman, Lucy, 23
Brill, Charlie, 167
Brill, Fran, 50
Brimble, Nick, 64
Brimhall, Cynthia, 159
Brimley, Wilford, 235
Brinegar, Lisa, 69
Bringelson, Mark, 15, 88, 96
Brink, Stacy, 223
Brinkley, Christie, 236
Brinkley, Ritch, 14
Brinkmann, Robert, 106
Briquet, Sacha, 201
Brisbin, David, 101, 156
Brisebois, Danielle, 236
Brisendine, Yvonne, 146
Bristow, Patrick, 82
Britt, Bill, 23
Britt, May, 236
Brittain, Ross, 48
Brittany, Morgan, 236
Britton, Tony, 236
Britton, Tracy, 157
Briz, Rosa Maria, 75
Broadbent, Jim, 211
Broadman, Richard, 168
Brocco, Peter, 113
Brochu, Donald, 39
Brock, Adam, 161
Brock, Phil, 172
Brock, Sarah, 58
Brock, Stanley, 77
Brocka, Lino, 256
Brockett, Don, 78, 174
Brocksmith, Roy, 74
Broder, Josh, 174
Broderick, Beth, 41
Broderick, John, 165
Broderick, Matthew, 235-236
Broderick, Suzanne, 28, 171
Brodie, Bill, 163
Brodsky, Jack, 21-22
Brodsky, Vlastimil, 190
Brody, Adrien, 169
Brokaw, Cary, 94, 197
Broker, Lee, 157
Brolin, Don, 169
Brolin, James, 236
Brolin, Jim, 173
Brolly, Clark Heathcliffe, 78
Bromfield, John, 236

265

269

273

274

275

276

277

281

283

286

288